MANAGING ACROSS LEVELS OF GOVERNMENT

ORGANISATION FOR ECONOMIC CO-OPERATION AND DEVELOPMENT

ORGANISATION FOR ECONOMIC CO-OPERATION AND DEVELOPMENT

Pursuant to Article 1 of the Convention signed in Paris on 14th December 1960, and which came into force on 30th September 1961, the Organisation for Economic Co-operation and Development (OECD) shall promote policies designed:

- to achieve the highest sustainable economic growth and employment and a rising standard of living in Member countries, while maintaining financial stability, and thus to contribute to the development of the world economy;
- to contribute to sound economic expansion in Member as well as non-member countries in the process of economic development; and
- to contribute to the expansion of world trade on a multilateral, non-discriminatory basis in accordance with international obligations.

The original Member countries of the OECD are Austria, Belgium, Canada, Denmark, France, Germany, Greece, Iceland, Ireland, Italy, Luxembourg, the Netherlands, Norway, Portugal, Spain, Sweden, Switzerland, Turkey, the United Kingdom and the United States. The following countries became Members subsequently through accession at the dates indicated hereafter: Japan (28th April 1964), Finland (28th January 1969), Australia (7th June 1971), New Zealand (29th May 1973), Mexico (18th May 1994), the Czech Republic (21st December 1995), Hungary (7th May 1996), Poland (22nd November 1996) and the Republic of Korea (12th December 1996). The Commission of the European Communities takes part in the work of the OECD (Article 13 of the OECD Convention).

Publié en français sous le titre :
LA GESTION PUBLIQUE À TRAVERS LES DIFFÉRENTS NIVEAUX D'ADMINISTRATION

© OECD 1997
Permission to reproduce a portion of this work for non-commercial purposes or classroom use should be obtained through the Centre français d'exploitation du droit de copie (CFC), 20, rue des Grands-Augustins, 75006 Paris, France, Tel. (33-1) 44 07 47 70, Fax (33-1) 46 34 67 19, for every country except the United States. In the United States permission should be obtained through the Copyright Clearance Center, Customer Service, (508)750-8400, 222 Rosewood Drive, Danvers, MA 01923 USA, or CCC Online: http://www.copyright.com/. All other applications for permission to reproduce or translate all or part of this book should be made to OECD Publications, 2, rue André-Pascal, 75775 Paris Cedex 16, France.

FOREWORD

This set of national reports is the end product of more than two years of work which started with a pilot study of nine countries to test the proposed approach and key concerns. After modification the full study was launched in 1995.

Individual chapters for 26 OECD countries were drafted according to a standard structure, either by experts in the field, national officials or the Secretariat. The draft chapters were then submitted to the member of the Public Management Committee concerned who was asked to co-ordinate comments on the chapter and responses to an enquiry on implications of (de)centralisation for central management and its effects on the system of governance as a whole.

Responses received to the enquiry were used by the Secretariat, together with the country chapters themselves, to draft the analysis which forms the Overview to this report and which was submitted for comment to the Public Management Committee.

The study was managed by David Rushforth, assisted by Frédéric Bouder and Elisabeth Lacey. The report is published on the responsibility of the Secretary-General of the OECD.

ACKNOWLEDGEMENTS

The Secretariat would like to thank all those involved in the preparation of the country chapters, and in particular the contributions made by the following: John Halligan (Australia); M. Mabille (Belgium); Albert Breton (Canada); Gerard Marcou (Czech Republic); Jan Olsen (Denmark); Sirpa Kekkonen (Finland); Jacques Ziller (France); Louis Wassenhoven (Greece); Arnar Jonsson (Iceland); Denis Conlan (Ireland); George France (Italy); Akira Nakamura (Japan); Corina Cadena Migueres (Mexico); Fritz van der Meer (Netherlands); Tom Fookes and Bruce Hucker (New Zealand); Jorge Castanyer (Spain); Richard Murray (Sweden); Ferzan Yildirim (Turkey); and Michael Clarke (United Kingdom). The chapter on the United States is based on material drafted by DeWitt John (National Academy of Public Administration) and Alexis Halley (Meridian International Institute) and does not necessarily represent the views of the United States government.

TABLE OF CONTENTS

Foreword 3
Acknowledgements 3
Executive summary 7

Part one
OVERVIEW

A. INTRODUCTION 15
B. SOME EMERGING TRENDS 19
    I. Structural development 20
    II. Financial and fiscal relations 32
    III. Regulatory reform 45
    IV. Human resource management 46
C. ISSUES 46
    I. Tensions and challenges 46
    II. Implications for managers at the centre 52
D. CONCLUDING COMMENTS 63

Part two
COUNTRY REPORTS

Australia 67
Austria 83
Belgium 95
Canada 107
Czech republic 127
Denmark 141
Finland 151
France 165
Germany 179
Greece 191
Iceland 203
Ireland 215
Italy 235
Japan 245
Luxembourg 257

Mexico 265
Netherlands 281
New zealand 295
Norway 307
Portugal 317
Spain 327
Sweden 341
Switzerland 355
Turkey 373
United kingdom 389
United states 405

STRUCTURE OF COUNTRY REPORTS

1. INSTITUTIONS AND AUTHORITY
    1.1 Structures
    1.2 Powers
    1.3 Responsibilities
2. MANAGEMENT FUNCTIONS
    2.1 Policy-making and co-ordination
    2.2 Financial management
    2.3 Performance management
    2.4 Human resource management
    2.5 Regulatory management and reform
3. TRENDS IN REDISTRIBUTING AUTHORITY ACROSS LEVELS OF GOVERNMENT
    3.1 Evolving tendencies
    3.2 The current debate
    3.3 Driving forces

EXECUTIVE SUMMARY

This report presents a synthesis of work so far on "Managing across Levels of Government". It is the first time that the OECD's Public Management Committee has directly addressed issues of inter-governmental management, although its annual **Survey of Public Management Developments** has shown that improving management across levels of government has been an important item on the agenda of many Member countries for some time.

The publication is in two main parts. **First**, an overview of the main emerging trends in inter-governmental management, some of the resulting tensions and challenges for inter-governmental relations, and the implications for managers in central government; and **second**, a set of 26 country chapters which map out the current and evolving distribution of functions, powers, and resources between levels of government -- and the debate and pressures behind the changes occurring

A mix of economic, political and cultural factors is driving the growing interest in governance, of which inter-governmental management is an integral part. New approaches by central governments towards public management are also at play in response to pressures for budgetary discipline and improved democracy. In this context the main objectives underpinning the changes are to:

- facilitate the achievement of national objectives, e.g. fiscal strategy;
- remove unnecessary duplication and overlap;
- obtain better value for taxpayers' money;
- make services more responsive to local needs; and
- empower citizens to participate more in decision-making.

These objectives give rise to several problem areas specific to inter-governmental management. In summary, Member governments need to decide on how to:

- adjust government structures to achieve a more coherent approach to governance;
- allocate responsibilities and degrees of autonomy to each level of government;
- strengthen mechanisms of inter-governmental co-ordination;
- apply performance management techniques to improving inter-governmental relations;
- adapt inter-governmental financing to facilitate accountability and fiscal restraint.

SOME EMERGING TRENDS

Structural changes: "regionalisation" and rationalisation

Over recent decades inter-governmental structural changes have primarily taken the form of creating new intermediary levels and of local "rationalisation". Few countries have eliminated a level of sub-national government. Local level rationalisation has taken place in most Member countries, usually in the form of aggregation aimed at creating larger units capable of providing a wider range of local services more efficiently. These changes have, in all cases, resulted in a more decentralised hierarchical structure for making and implementing decisions. At the same time, central governments have tended to deconcentrate their services. These changes have modified roles and the relations between, central and sub-national governments; as well as blurring lines of accountability.

More complex patterns of responsibility

It is difficult to identify a clear sectoral emphasis in changes in the division of responsibilities across levels of government in recent decades, but most interest appears to have been shown in the education, health and welfare sectors. Numerous redistributions of responsibility have been made -- some big and some small -- and usually downwards to sub-national government. Change has often taken the form of greater sharing of tasks and a greater mix of financing and implementing responsibilities, leading to more interdependence. Exactly how responsibilities are distributed across levels of government, the degree and nature of autonomy, and the reasons for the changes that are taking place all vary according to different types of inter-governmental systems. Inter-governmental relations may tend more towards negotiation, collaboration, paternalism or confrontation depending on the country. It is difficult to generalise about trends in these relationships, but the growing interest in result-oriented management and inter-governmental partnerships is encouraging more consultation to agree on objectives, standards and cost-sharing arrangements.

Central government sub-nationally: the accent on co-ordination

Central government's presence sub-nationally takes two main forms:- a) networks of deconcentrated central administrations (in all Member countries); and b) an official (prefect) appointed by, and representing, central government sub-nationally (in most Member countries). Both of these systems have evolved significantly over the past 20 years. Deconcentrated administrations have become more aware of the need to be efficient and responsive, and to adopt methods of management which emphasise flexibility and co-ordination. In a similar way, the role of the prefectural system has moved away from being directive and hierarchical, towards fostering co-operation and partnership between all actors.

Financial constraints, fiscal interdependence, and discretion coupled with results

Countries are using a wide range of policies and instruments to address public sector budgetary problems, many of which have a direct impact on inter-governmental relations. Financial pressures at the sub-national level are the result of an expansion of activities and increased demand for services, heightened by dependence on income-inelastic revenues such as property taxes. Any shortfall has to be met largely by increased transfers from central government. As national budgetary situations have deteriorated, many sub-national governments have been required to share in cutbacks. Some national governments are downsizing by off-loading tasks to sub-national governments while at the same time seeking more control over aggregate public sector expenditures. However, unfunded mandates only transfer problems and add to existing mistrust across levels of government. The emergence of a sub-national "fiscal crisis" and concern with levels of sub-national debt in some countries suggests that more attention needs to be directed to the intersection of fiscal federalism and performance management.

Changing distributions of responsibilities is resulting in more inter-governmental partnership through shared financing and service delivery arrangements, and/or agreed objectives. This can help to promote a more comprehensive view of public sector finances and the broad goals of governance with national fiscal strategies which encompass all levels of government. The importance of improving the overall transparency of the management of public funds is increasingly recognised across all Member countries. However, inter-governmental systems are, and always will be, in a state of change and budgetary strategies must take account of this.

The need to restrain total public expenditure and to reduce public deficits is prompting many central governments to re-examine the amount and nature of transfers to sub-national governments. Specific grants may enable central governments to set standards for locally provided services. On the other hand, the increased use of general grants in many countries, gives the recipients more discretion and encourages negotiation between central and sub-national governments on national guidelines within which minimum standards may be set. The shift to general grants also changes central government's role to one of "more steering and less rowing".

Regulation: less vertical duplication, more cost-efficiency

Regulation must be a major component of any comprehensive inter-governmental reform process. Although there is much rhetoric about rationalising and streamlining government regulation, most OECD countries have reformed exclusively at the national level. Only during the last few years have countries started to make progress towards greater regulatory co-ordination and the elimination of regulatory duplication between levels of government. Comprehensive attempts at reform are rare, but it appears that significant gains can be made through better communication and co-ordination between levels of government, resulting in more effective and cost-efficient regulatory action.

The regulatory regimes in Member countries are diverse. Some countries share responsibility for regulation across different levels of government, often involving multiple bodies at each level, while others are very centralised, with almost all authority vested in national ministries. However, there appears to be a general convergence as decentralised countries attempt to reduce duplication and regulatory costs by creating national standards, and centralised countries move towards power-sharing arrangements and a shift of responsibility away from central government.

TENSIONS AND CHALLENGES

As a result of the above trends some broad shifts are occurring in systems of governance. They are becoming more fragmented as the number and variety of actors increases. There is more inter-dependence between levels of government as the problems to be addressed become more complex and difficult to resolve unilaterally. Divisions of responsibility for the design, implementation and evaluation of programmes are changing; and the distinction between who finances, delivers, and administers is increasingly unclear in many programmes. The search for greater flexibility in managing public programmes can blur lines of accountability. The overall effect is to make inter-governmental relations more complex; and sub-national government a more important partner in the broad patterns of governance.

Aligning central and sub-national government policies (on matters such as fiscal strategy) is critical to the successful implementation of reform programmes which are aimed at improving public sector efficiency, effectiveness and responsiveness. This requires coherence in the goals and values at **all** levels of government, but is often exacerbated by political differences between levels.

But diversity through decentralisation can also lead to tensions and may present serious challenges to coherent inter-governmental relations. The centre seeks enough overall control to protect the national interest -- both economic and democratic -- while sub-national governments want sufficient autonomy to be responsive to local preferences and needs. These objectives may be in conflict. Inter-governmental management can help to identify the sources of tension and their implications for central management. These may be seen as a set of dichotomies, or trade-offs, between:

- encouraging more *autonomy* at lower levels of government, while providing overall *direction*;

- allowing for *differentiation* through flexibility, yet ensuring some minimum degree of *uniformity*; and

- catering for more responsiveness to local needs, but not to the detriment of *efficiency* and *economy*.

IMPLICATIONS FOR MANAGERS AT THE CENTRE:

The ongoing challenge to effective inter-governmental relations is to monitor and manage the balance between the above tensions. For central governments, this requires judicious use and regular adjustment of the instruments of control, co-ordination, consultation and accountability, which are the key tools determining the shape of inter-governmental relations.

Control

Decentralisation is not only about transferring tasks and resources from one level of government to another. It is also about reducing and changing the nature of central government involvement in the tasks performed by sub-national authorities. The type and number of controls operating across levels of government are key factors. In those countries with long traditions of local self-government there tends to be more diversity in the methods of control used, with ex post review and the role of courts becoming more important. At the same time, countries with a tradition of detailed controls over sub-national governments are becoming less interventionist due to the increasing complexity of the tasks undertaken.

The move towards performance management based on targets and results, and away from detailed regulation and control of inputs, is encouraging the shift from specific grants in favour of general grants. This shift provides the incentive and opportunity for central and sub-national governments to consult on developing guidelines and standards. It also helps to achieve agreement on which functions require a high degree of national uniformity or supervision and those where more account should be taken of local or regional priorities. In particular, the opportunities for performance benchmarking and better ex post review facilitate co-operative inter-governmental relations, provided there are clear lines of accountability and appropriate consultation.

Co-ordination and consultation

There is concern in all Member countries to improve both horizontal and vertical co-ordination and to introduce more effective methods of collaboration between levels of government. This reflects growing awareness of the extent and costs of duplication and overlap, whether the culture of inter-governmental relations is relatively co-operative or more adversarial in style. Fiscal arrangements involving the use of shared taxes, joint-financing of projects and equalisation formulae to distribute funds among sub-national units of government all oblige different levels to consult and negotiate. As the use of performance management tools becomes more widespread, formal consultation will be enhanced, although a role will remain for less formal arrangements.

Accountability

Accountability may be defined as the management of responsibility. It is important to distinguish between the public accountability of elected officials and that of managers who are hierarchically accountable for results. The former may take two forms: "democratic" accountability which seeks to involve citizens more as taxpayers through greater transparency; or "client" accountability which is directed more to citizens' rights as consumers of public services. For managerial accountability, the shift away from accountability for compliance with procedures towards accountability for performance or results, is putting more emphasis on evaluating the efficiency with which resources are used and the extent to which targets have been achieved. This implies defining common goals and setting performance standards. By "trading" specific levels of performance (which can be monitored) for greater administrative discretion, a bridge can be built between accountability and flexibility.

There is clearly no single "best" model for how power and responsibility should be distributed vertically across governments. Each country has its own cultural, economic and political contexts which largely determine what is desirable and possible. Equally, while budgetary pressures and new public management developments encourage more devolution, it is for each country to ascertain its own strategic mix of decentralisation and deconcentration -- and how, where, and at what speed it will be realised. While broad goals such as improving responsiveness and subsidiarity are generally shared, other objectives such as actively "enabling" lower levels of government to take on additional responsibilities require further efforts in collaborative governance which will differ between countries.

> **Definitions used in this work:**
> ***Decentralisation***: - the transfer of responsibility to democratically independent lower levels of government, thereby giving them more managerial discretion but not necessarily more financial independence.
> ***Deconcentration***: - the transfer of responsibility from central ministries to field offices or more autonomous agencies, thereby becoming closer to citizens while remaining part of central government.
> **NOTE**: - Given the differences of meaning attached to these and related terms across countries, ***devolution*** has also been used in other PUMA work as an umbrella term covering all transfers of responsibility. And in the regulatory area, **delegation** is used for the formal relationship in which competence for an aspect of the regulatory process is given by one level of government to a second level of government.

Part one

OVERVIEW

OVERVIEW

A. INTRODUCTION

This introduction provides the context for the discussion of emerging trends in "managing across levels of government" which follows. It looks at the concept of governance and relates it to recent public management reforms and changes in inter-governmental relations in OECD Member countries. In Part B several critical aspects of managing across levels of government are "examined: firstly evolving patterns in the structures, responsibilities and powers of sub-national governments; then the shifting financial and fiscal relations between the centre and other levels of government; and finally trends in regulatory reform and human resource management. Part C presents some implicit tensions in inter-governmental relations; and resulting challenges for systems of governance which are increasingly complex and diverse. Some implications of these observations for central managers are then elaborated in terms of the changes needed in the mechanisms of inter-governmental management.

At the **Ministerial Symposium on the Future of Public Services** -- the first OECD meeting at the Ministerial level on public management -- held in Paris in March 1996, the Statement by the Chair (Alice Rivlin) noted that:

> Developments are forcing, as well as enabling, changes in the structure and boundaries of government. There has long been a debate about the size of government, as well as whether to centralise or decentralise. ... We must now be willing to move in both directions -- decentralising some functions while centralising other critical policy-making responsibilities. Such changes are under way in all countries.

The arrival of "managing across levels of government" (MALG) on the agenda of the OECD's Public Management Committee reflects some new attitudes by central governments towards public management and governance. This comes in response to the twin pressures of budgetary deficits and calls for better quality democracy. In this context, the main concerns underpinning this work are to:

- facilitate the achievement of national objectives, e.g. fiscal strategy;
- remove unnecessary duplication and overlap;
- obtain better value for taxpayers' money;
- make services more responsive to local needs; and
- empower citizens to participate more in decision-making.

The box which follows confirms that despite their complexity and political sensitivity, issues of inter-governmental management, are high on the current agenda of many OECD Member countries.

First, a few words about the notion of governance -- what it means, why it is important, and how it affects inter-governmental management.

Governance reflects a pluralisation of the important actors in governing and in providing public services. The configuration of public institutions is changing; the roles of supra- and sub-national bodies

> **Some recent developments in inter-governmental management in OECD countries**
>
> - **Australia**: a Steering Committee for Review of Commonwealth/State Service Provision published its first annual report in 1995 after much collaboration between all levels of government. It contains much performance data (on both efficiency and effectiveness) for key social services;
> - **Belgium**: progressive transformation from a unitary to a federal state culminated in the 1993 Constitution changes and debate on the distribution of responsibilities between levels continues;
> - **Canada**: since 1994, a "Program Review" has put focus on effective and cost-efficient services; redefined the role of the federal government; and proposed stronger partnerships with the provinces in efforts to "get government right". The 1995 referendum on Quebec has brought the Constitution and all other devices for devolution to the top of the national agenda;
> - **Finland**: Regional Councils were established through legislation in 1994;
> - **France**: the 1982 decentralisation reforms created the region as a new territorial authority and the 1992 "Deconcentration Charter" significantly changed the responsibilities of the prefects;
> - **Greece**: much discussion continues around the new regional tier of government created in 1994;
> - **Ireland**: Regional authorities were created in 1994 mainly for co-ordination but not directly elected, a Strategic Management Initiative is encouraging central/local consultation, a Devolution Commission was set up in 1995, in 1996 a Local Government Reorganisation Commission made recommendations;
> - **Japan**: the Decentralisation Promotion Law of 1995 set up a Commission with the same name in the Prime Minister's Office charged with recommending a decentralisation package;
> - **Netherlands**: in the past 15 years some 10 bill. guilders have been "structurally decentralised";
> - **Mexico**: since 1995 "New Federalism" has been a key objective; the National Development Plan 1994-2000 puts decentralisation and new instruments for fiscal co-ordination high on agenda;
> - **Portugal**: regional institutions have been at the centre of political debate for several years;
> - **Spain**: Autonomous Communities cover the country since 1983 and enjoy large degree of regional self-government. A framework to extend and standardise their powers was agreed in 1992 and a reform of the Senate is now planned to strengthen regional constituencies for the election of senators;
> - **Sweden**: in 1995 a Parliamentary commission proposed a new type of directly elected regional government with regional development functions in addition to those of existing county councils.
> - **Switzerland**: the Federal Council started reforms in 1994 including a working party with canton representatives to strengthen their financial capacities and guarantee the subsidiarity principle;
> - **United Kingdom**: in July 1996 the House of Lords Select Committee on Relations Between Central and Local Government published a report on the current state of those relations and the factors leading to them, and made recommendations for improvement. In response the Government published a White Paper in November 1996 with a programme of action to strengthen local democracy, promote the local leadership role of local authorities and improve further the relations between central and local government Over 40 "Citizens Charters" now spell out the standards of service which can be expected;
> - **United States**: the 1995 Unfunded Mandate legislation restricts the ability of Congress to impose costly mandates on sub-national governments; and the National Performance Review and "Reinventing Government" initiatives have put much emphasis on empowering state and local governments -- particularly through partnership agreements with federal agencies.

are becoming more important; and semi-public and private sector actors are becoming more widely and deeply involved. At the same time, interaction is becoming less authoritative and more co-operative. New policy challenges (such as the environment and regional development) are undermining long-established habits of compartmentalisation. As a result, inter-governmental relations are more complex and need to be considered more comprehensively as a system -- hence governance.

The implication of all this for managing across levels of government are far-reaching. New skills are needed to manage multi-tiered systems with diverse, fragmented and inter-dependent components. In addition, moves to improve the quality of local democracy (such as more directly elected posts and wider use of consultative councils) are increasing the tensions between local authority and central steering. Fiscal squeeze is exacerbating those tensions. The overall effect has been to make inter-governmental relations much more complex and sub-national governments a more important partner in patterns of governance as a whole.

The public sector management reform strategies being designed and implemented in OECD countries to address these challenges have many points in common, and taken together they may be seen to represent a paradigm shift. The elements of this change have been spelt out in the Committee's 1995 publication, *Governance in Transition*. They place the focus on:

- results and increased value for money;
- devolution of authority and enhanced flexibility;
- strengthened accountability and control;
- a client and service orientation;
- strengthened capacity for developing strategy and policy;
- introducing competition and other market elements; and
- changed relationships with other levels of government.

The changes reported in this present publication need to be considered in the context of these developments. The bottom line, especially when times are financially difficult, is that the centre is seeking to retain some overall control of expenditures and revenues, while local resistance mounts and calls for greater freedom of action grow stronger. Fiscal issues are, therefore, at the heart of many of these tensions, and in many countries fiscal and financial pressures have been the major factor in seeking more decentralised modes of governance. In **Mexico**, for example, fiscal federalism is a key concern -- but political factors are also crucial. In other countries, the push to decentralisation has been driven primarily by a call for greater democracy, not a quest for greater efficiency. Such is clearly the case in **Spain**, for example, and in **Belgium**, also, it is political and cultural concerns which have been dominant.

There is growing recognition that any public management reform strategy must be an astute combination of overall steering and enhanced flexibility. Aligning central and sub-national government policies is critical to the successful implementation of reform programmes which are aimed at improving the overall efficiency, effectiveness and economy of the public sector. All countries seek to perform better when competing in the international arena; addressing national social and economic problems; and providing quality public services to individual citizens. This requires a coherent merging of the goals and the values present at *all* levels of government.

The approach and the constraints

The publication attempts to map out the current and evolving distribution of responsibilities and authority across levels of government in 26 OECD Member countries. (Since preparation Hungary, Korea and Poland have also become Member countries). It also presents the current debate and driving forces behind the changes currently taking place. Each country chapter has a standard structure which was established after a pilot study involving a representative group of OECD countries.

All Member governments have assisted in the preparation of their respective country chapters. They were also asked to respond to a questionnaire dealing with some of the implications for central managers of a more (de)centralised environment. Their responses have been used, along with the material in the country chapters, for drafting this Overview. Members of the Public Management Committee -- who were the addressees (and are the prime clients) of this study -- were also asked to circulate the questionnaire to representatives of sub-national governments in their country. This was intended to give another perspective to some of the issues under discussion, but such material was provided by only a small number of countries.

The size and complexity of the subject requires an approach which is selective and where value may be added by dealing with the issues in a broad comparative way. There is, therefore, a focus on inter-governmental aspects of policy co-ordination and financial and performance management. By the same token, human resource management and regulatory management are not dealt with in any detail.

The wide variety of country-specific local and regional government structures, practices and political and administrative cultures means that there is no single best model for (de)centralisation. Countries are moving in different directions, at different speeds, in different sectors, from different starting points, and with different objectives and priorities. Different political parties holding office at different levels of government further complicates matters. A focus on inter-governmental management transcends the uniqueness of each national situation. It can help to identify and explain evolving inter-governmental relations and may lead to practical conclusions on ways of making existing systems of governance -- in all their diversity -- more efficient, effective and responsive.

Some definitions

Moves along the centralisation-decentralisation spectrum may take any of several guises. They may involve decentralisation, deconcentration, devolution and/or delegation -- and these may be alternative strategies to achieve the same results. Different shades of meaning may, however, be attached to these options across countries, so it is useful at the outset to establish what these alternatives are and how they are understood in this publication. The following definitions have been adopted throughout this study. They reflect distinctions between the transfer of responsibilities and discretion out and down organisations, and the implications for accountability:

- **Decentralisation:** the transfer of responsibility to democratically independent lower levels of government, thereby giving them more managerial discretion, but not necessarily more financial independence.

- **Deconcentration:** the transfer of responsibility from central ministries to field offices or more autonomous agencies, thereby becoming closer to citizens while remaining part of central government.

Given the differences of meaning attached to these and related terms such as delegation in different countries, **devolution** has also been used in other PUMA work as an umbrella term covering all forms of transfers of responsibility. And, in the regulatory area, **delegation** is used for the formal relationship in which competence for an aspect of the regulatory process is given by one level of government to a second level of government.

In this report "**central**" (or "**state**") government refers to national governments in federal and unitary countries; "**state**" government is used only for the intermediary order in federal countries (provinces, *Länder*); and "**local**" government is either the third tier in federal countries or the second and third tiers in unitary countries (regions, counties, municipalities, communities, etc.). "**Sub-national**" includes all governments other than that at the centre. In the System of National Accounts (SNA), "**general government**" is broken down into four sub-sectors or levels i.e. central government, state government, local government, and social security funds. The graphs in this report merge the state and local levels of government into one category -- "sub-national".

Finally, it is tempting to try to devise statistical measures according to which countries may be placed on a scale of decentralisation. A large range of parameters can indicate different facets of decentralisation in quantitative terms. They are all, however, only partial measures of what is a very complex phenomenon. And even taken together, they remain simplistic and unable to reflect adequately the essential political and administrative components which make up the real "quality of decentralisation" in any country. Finance, but also administration, control, regulation, reporting and accountability are all key factors in decentralisation and have implications for the efficiency of resource allocation; effectiveness of governance; and degree of equity. The quantitative data included here to illustrate specific financial and fiscal aspects of managing across levels of government should, therefore, be read with due caution.

The statistical charts in this chapter are for countries for which OECD data are available on the variable and in the year required. If a country is not represented in a chart, it is because suitable data were not available at the time of preparation. Similarly, for time series, certain countries do not have the complete set of data, in which case the time series has been shortened accordingly. Differences of this nature have been footnoted. The figures in the charts are drawn from the OECD public sector data base which assembles data found in other relevant OECD data bases (National Accounts, the analytical database, and revenue statistics). The table on public employment by level of government has been taken from the Public Management Service's database on public sector pay and employment.

Statistical tables in the individual country chapters are from various national and international sources, as noted in each case. Because of differences in definitions, figures in the country chapters may not always match figures taken from National Accounts and the OECD public sector database. Country-specific statistics quoted in this Overview have been taken from the country chapters, unless noted otherwise.

B. SOME EMERGING TRENDS

The following box indicates some recent shifts in responsibilities across levels of government in those OECD countries reporting significant change. Such shifts -- between existing levels of government and to newly-created regional tiers -- have increasingly become a subject of interest. While the general trend has been one of decentralisation, there have been exceptions to this tendency.

Recent changes in responsibilities across levels of government

Austria	Functions such as housing are shifting from the central to the *Länder* level; local governments are playing a larger role in economic expansion and social change; and there is a growing federal and *Länder* concern with macro-economic management and reduction of regional and social disparities.
Canada	The federal government has delegated to the provinces activities such as administration and enforcement of the Criminal Code and regulation of interprovincial and international highway traffic. The federal government has withdrawn from labour market training, forestry, mining, and recreation, and has proposed a much strengthened partnership with the provinces on such items as food inspection, environmental management, social housing, and tourism. Many municipalities have transferred responsibility for health, social services and education to the provinces because of the high costs involved.
Denmark	During the 1970s and 1980s, responsibility for social security was shifted to municipalities, and responsibility for regional planning, primary health services, care for the handicapped and disabled, secondary schools, environmental quality, and public transport moved to the counties.
Finland	There has been a transfer of power from central government's deconcentrated administration to new regional joint authorities controlled by municipalities since 1994 in areas such as regional planning and development and environmental policy.
France	The 1982 decentralisation plan gave full independence to the regions and the *départements* in a range of areas such as education, economic support measures, and local transport. It also gave responsibility for the construction and maintenance of primary schools to the municipalities, while retaining responsibility for most other education policy at the central level.
Greece	Responsibilities delegated to the new level of regional administration created in 1994 include land use planning, public land disposal, licensing of industrial development, and the administration of primary and secondary school staff.
Iceland	All responsibility for primary education was transferred from central to local government in August 1996. An experiment with "pilot authorities" seeks to transfer some central government responsibilities to selected local authorities.
Ireland	The responsibilities of the local government have been greatly increased, and a wide range of central controls removed from matters such as land disposals, staffing, personnel, and housing construction. Local authorities have acquired additional functions such as urban renewal, housing, physical planning, road traffic, amenity provision, and building control. Environmental functions have been transferred to a national agency.
Italy	The period since 1970 has seen the transfer from the State to the regions of manpower training, health care, agriculture, transport, environmental protection, and economic development. In 1990, a law was passed that sets the stage for a major reorganisation of the provinces and municipalities, which should lead to a major reallocation of functions between levels of government.

Recent changes in responsibilities across levels of government, *cont.*

Mexico	In 1983, the Constitution gave municipalities more regulatory power and exclusive authority over the real estate tax. Municipalities' functions were enlarged from 1989-1994 to include the approval and administration of urban development plans, the legalisation of land holdings, and the provision of water, electricity, sewer and policing. In 1992, the federal government transferred the operation of educational services to the states, including responsibility for schools, budgets, and human resources. Decentralisation is still high on the agenda and extended to health, agriculture, social development, transport and communications by transferring resources, authority and powers to the states.
Portugal	The new Government (October 1995) has put the transfer of responsibilities to local governments high on the political agenda in areas such as pre-school care, social housing, public security, tax collection, and environmental matters.
Spain	The creation of the Autonomous Communities has brought significant transfers of responsibility. This has included the decentralisation of the health and educational systems, as well as public works, agriculture, environmental protection, regional development, and social assistance. The process is continuing as new sets of functions continue to devolve.
Sweden	Since the 1960s there has been a transfer of responsibility to local government of services such as schools, old-age and child care, and health care. There has also been some centralisation of functions and tasks, such as the social security administration, the administration of student aid and grants, the national tax administration, employment of disabled and handicapped persons, and the administration of housing subsidies. In 1992, local governments took over responsibility for long-term medical care of the elderly and handicapped, and county councils took responsibility for public transportation.
Switzerland	Simplification of the currently very complex distribution of responsibilities between the federal and cantonal levels is presently the subject of possible Constitutional reform.
Turkey	Many government functions were transferred to the municipal level after World War II: the construction and provision of public housing and some urban planning and development (1950s), the regulation of urban economic activity and consumption (1960s), and certain duties in the area of environmental protection (1970s). The transition to civilian government in 1984 led to the devolution of development planning to the municipalities.
United Kingdom	In the past 15 years there has been some centralisation of power so as to set national direction, standards and policy frameworks; but there have been parallel moves downwards, particularly to service users themselves, using Citizen's Charters to define specific service standards and rights of redress. Recently, the role of local government has put more emphasis on securing services rather than providing them directly.
United States	A shift in responsibilities has come about as a result of the increased tendency of the federal government to approve waivers that allow the states to experiment in important policy areas such as welfare and health care. The number of waivers granted in the 1990s has increased, and the states have taken the lead in formulating innovative approaches. Congress has also passed a welfare reform bill that converts current federal spending into block grants, ends the federal entitlement to welfare benefits, and shifts many responsibilities to the states.

I. Structural development

Structural development, as used here, mainly concerns territorial changes that have occurred sub-nationally in recent decades and shifts in the distribution of authority or the performance of tasks. National administration has also undergone changes, especially in terms of the presence of the "centre" at sub-national level. In some countries, the creation of a new level has altered the functions of the centre's representative when, for example, some tasks are decentralised. More often, however, they are related to developments in the mode of public management which affect the role played by the centre and its representative. The changes connected with deconcentrated national government and its relations with local authorities form another important subject, but one which lies outside the scope of this analysis and which is mentioned here only briefly. Another equally important aspect, also outside the scope of the present study, is the growing involvement of private and para-public actors in sub-national public affairs, and the effect on management.

1. *Structural changes*

Over the past quarter of a century, most OECD countries have witnessed structural changes sub-nationally. The scale of these changes and the reasons for them vary according to the country. They can, however, be broadly summed up in two types of change: territorial re-organisation, and "rationalisation" at the local level. Whatever the nature of these changes, they have altered and blurred the traditional typology which in the past distinguished federal and unitary systems.

Territorial re-organisation has taken different forms. The countries in which it has been extensive have in the main been strongly centralised unitary States. The creation of new levels has led to a modification of the national structure, as in **Belgium** which recently became a federal State, or **Spain** and **Italy** which have become regional countries and have thus introduced a new type of institutional organisation. The bodies so created often arise from a division of territory reflecting cultural, linguistic or historical contexts. These bodies often have legislative powers which can vary across regions. Other countries have instituted a regional or intermediate level with its own political "force". Thus **France**, by virtue of its policy of decentralisation, has created a regional level, and **Greece** has also instituted a regional level with an elected prefect. **Finland** has created a new level formed by the voluntary association of municipalities at the regional level, which is now calling into question the role of the Finnish provincial administration; while in the **Czech Republic** there is continuing debate on the nature and responsibilities of any new regional tier of government -- and on how many regions there should be. In some European countries, accession to the European Union has given more importance to the regional level, particularly due to the process of allocating European funds. The elimination of a tier, on the other hand, is more rare and few countries have attempted it. In **Germany**, some *Länder* have decided to eliminate districts, and in the **United Kingdom** the number of levels in the local government system throughout Scotland and Wales and in some parts of England has been reduced from two to one.

Rationalisation at the local level is something which has occurred in the vast majority of OECD countries. It has taken the form of municipal amalgamations (even of *Kreise* in **Germany**), being seen by central government as a way of establishing economically viable units better able to provide local services. Such mergers are usually carried out with the consent of the communities involved and within a legal framework. In most cases they involve simple amalgamations and the disappearance of the old authorities. The ability of the municipalities concerned to resist mergers depends on the extent of their autonomy. In **Australia** and **Canada**, for example, each state or province issues its own rules on the matter. In some countries the amalgamation process is very protracted, in others it does not exist at all. Where, for example, there is a strong tradition of municipal independence, it has bred opposition to any kind of imposed merger -- as in **Iceland**, where mergers can take place only at the instigation of the municipalities concerned, or **Finland** where, despite government efforts, large numbers of small municipalities survive as they view amalgamations as an attempt to reduce their independence. Other factors such as the status of the municipal executive can also slow down the merger process. It is of interest to note that in **Sweden**, following a period of imposed mergers, despite strong opposition from the municipalities, a reverse trend now appears to be occurring, explained by the distance between inhabitants and their elected representatives once a municipality grows beyond a certain size.

In addition to simple amalgamations, mergers of associated municipalities also take place and give a degree of administrative freedom to the authorities involved. This is the case for example in **France** -- another country where there remains a large number of municipalities and which prefer to form inter-municipal associations for carrying out works in their common interest. Such groupings of municipalities occur in most countries. Inter-municipal co-operation of this nature is often voluntary, done within a legal framework, based on shared interests, and allows each municipality to retain its own institutions. The type and degree of autonomy of these associations or inter-community organisations varies across countries, such that in **Switzerland**, and equally in **Italy**, they may constitute an additional administrative tier between the local and cantonal levels. In most countries, metropolitan areas have emerged which can give rise to new local levels (as in **Canada**) and which may herald new administrative levels. In the case of both amalgamations and associations, the bodies are usually headed by a council -- elected directly or indirectly.

Another structural development in many countries, but notably the **United States** and **Canada**, and which is not strictly speaking territorial, is the impressive number of specific purpose bodies set up at all levels -- not only by central or federal governments (see section 3) but also by local authorities. Their freedom of action varies, but is often limited to a particular field. These organisations may be part of the local authority system and governed by an elected council, as in the **United States**, or not be part of that system and have at their head a council, the members of which are nominated by the local authorities, as in **Ireland**. These organisations or associations may be mandatory or formed on a contractual basis, as in **Finland**. There are also bodies which have been created as a result of local government reforms, as in the **United Kingdom**, which have inherited the functions previously entrusted to local authorities, and which have a specific task and members appointed by central government or from the local community. Another possible category is government "agencies" whose competence extends across state and provincial borders in federal countries, as well as trade associations, and interest groups working across levels in the same field and associated among themselves. All these bodies — whether certain countries call them "districts", "councils", "agencies" or "associations" and regardless of their status and attachment (to central government, local government, or other) — play a part in the decision-making and co-ordination system and have a definite influence on the complexity of the chain of responsibility, particularly where the provision of services is concerned.

The stratification observed in most countries can sometimes spark debate. The exact role of the new levels can take a long time to define (as in **Finland**), since this entails redefining the role and functions of the levels already in existence. Some countries (**Denmark, Ireland, Belgium, Spain, Sweden**) are reviewing the role or the number of existing sub-national levels. Others again are experiencing the development of entwined or superimposed levels. The question arises of whether the creation of new intermediate levels such as in the Nordic countries where there is a strong tradition of municipal independence, impinges on the freedom of action of local authorities. This vertical multiplication, combined with a horizontal expansion of bodies (specific or general-purpose, public or private, or deconcentrated parts of central government ministries) also raises the question of how all these bodies inter-relate.

2. *Distribution of responsibilities*

There are two aspects to the distribution of responsibilities: the principles and machinery of distribution, and the mode of application. Each aspect in turn has two angles: formal features and operational reality. The gap between the two can stem from a formal structure which is ill-adjusted to real situations (e.g. environmental protection, which was less important thirty or forty years ago), from economic developments (especially social protection policies), or more simply from the fact that the competent sub-national level does not have, or no longer has, the means to cope with the financial costs attached to its responsibilities.

a)   Distribution principles and machinery

This subject requires at least a passing reference to the constitutional arrangements in force: the status of the sub-national levels and the amount of autonomy officially attributed to them, the official distribution of responsibilities, and the way this distribution has developed in practice and now operates. The task is not an easy one, for the subject has become increasingly complex —owing in part to the large number of systems and traditions in operation, and in part to the growth in shared functions.

The classical analytical criteria by which "degrees of autonomy" could be determined, like the theoretical distinction between intrinsic and delegated fields of authority, are no longer fully valid. There are some systems in which the centre intervenes increasingly in the management of the "intrinsic" competences of sub-national governments. In the **Netherlands**, this kind of intervention operates via co-administration. In many countries, on the other hand, delegated authority is being exercised with increased independence in certain fields.

Countries may nonetheless be classified by type of structure: federal countries, unitary countries, and countries tending towards regionalism. Countries in each category share common features as regards the status of sub-national levels and the formal distribution of tasks.

Within the federal category, certain sub-groups may be distinguished:

North American federal countries and Australia: The **United States**, **Canada**, **Australia** and, to some extent, **Mexico**, may be characterised as having only their two upper levels (federal level, and state or provincial level) mentioned in the federal constitution. Local administrations are "creatures" of the intermediate level. This intermediate level has its own constitution. Authority is distributed between the federal and intermediate levels, generally "by default". The constitution either mentions the broad principles and general areas, or defines the prerogatives of a single level, the remainder being assumed by the other level. The history of this distribution is reflected in an extremely complex state of affairs in which the growth of federal funding and regulation has created a great tangle of overlapping roles and responsibilities. The sovereignty/autonomy conferred under the constitution on the intermediate levels is very much affected by this situation. In the **United States**, the proliferation and interpenetration of the different local bodies (whether general or single purpose) has produced much dispersion in the provision of services (and has certainly weakened the chain of authority).

Germanic federal countries: These are **Germany** and **Austria**. Also, especially in its German-speaking cantons, **Switzerland**, shows features similar to the Germanic systems, but for the rest remains atypical. In **Germany** and **Austria**, the constitution guarantees the existence of the *Länder* and municipalities, the latter being considered independent and autonomous; and in practice they are quite powerful. The constitution provides for a distribution of responsibilities (in detail in **Germany**, "by default" in **Austria**). The *Länder* and the municipalities perform both their intrinsic tasks and devolved tasks (either compulsory or optional). In **Germany**, the concept of "co-operative federalism", while favouring the development of tasks and, especially, resources that are shared among the three levels, has resulted in difficulties regarding clear priority assignment. It has also resulted in a need (felt by each level) to guard against too much interference from the level above and in growing task distribution problems. In **Austria**, the independence of the *Länder* is curtailed from the outset by the constitution. The increased complexity of relations among the different levels (particularly as regards the sharing of tax revenues, and joint decision-making on co-financing) is a source of friction among them. The freedom of action of the municipalities has been restricted by the devolution of federal powers to the *Länder*.

Atypical federal systems: In **Switzerland**, the confederation is an emanation of the cantons, as befits the Germanic principle of "self-administration" (*Selbstverwaltung*). **Switzerland** differs considerably from **Germany** and **Austria** in that the principle of self-administration is interpreted in a much broader sense. Under the federal constitution, the cantons are sovereign entities which exercise all the powers and responsibilities not delegated by them to the federal authority. Each federal responsibility must be identified in the constitution. The cantons have authority over the status of their municipalities, whose tasks they determine. The Swiss system is in this sense not unlike those of North America and Australia. The end result is wide diversity, although two groups may be distinguished: municipalities in the Germanic-type cantons, which are often larger and wealthier; and those in the French-type cantons, which are often smaller and less wealthy. The autonomy of the municipalities is not guaranteed by the constitution; it varies markedly from one local authority to another. In practice, the cantons' sovereignty is limited by the extension of federal power and greater federal intervention in all fields. There seems to be a tendency towards the centralisation of powers at the federal level. The distribution of responsibilities among the three levels is extremely complex: a large number of tasks are shared (of 160 responsibilities counted, two-thirds are exercised jointly by the Confederation and the cantons). This executive federalism is responsible for the very complex distribution of activities, which becomes more complicated as the degree of service to be provided increases.

Belgium has a singular federal system resulting from a long process of federalisation. The autonomy of the language-based communities and of the regions is far-reaching, since in principle the rules which they promulgate have the same legal weight as federal ones. As in **Switzerland**, the constitution confers only "residual competence" on the federal state. The detailed distribution of responsibilities among sub-national levels is set out in the constitution and legislation on institutional reform. Another result of federalisation has been to transfer supervisory authority to local government (provinces and municipalities) without, however, transforming them into "creatures" of the regions. More particularly, the notion of "exclusively provincial and local interests" has been recognised, making the overlapping of responsibilities more likely.

The unitary countries may be divided into the "classic" unitary states and the Nordic countries, which form a fairly homogeneous group.

Classic unitary states: These countries, although highly disparate, may be divided into two broad groups -- on the one hand, "Westminster-style" countries, influenced by the British tradition, such as the **United Kingdom, Ireland** and **New Zealand**; and, on the other hand, "Napoleonic-style" countries, influenced by structures inherited from the French model based on the unity and indivisibility of the State, namely **France, Greece, Luxemburg,** the **Netherlands, Portugal** and **Turkey.** Some of these latter countries, especially in southern Europe, have retained a largely centralised mode of government. In others, a devolution of competences has developed over the years, as in the **Netherlands** and, since 1982, in **France**.

Japan is a case apart, difficult to classify in either group, owing to its roots in another sphere of culture (despite Western, mostly Prussian and Anglo-Saxon, influences).

The degree of centralisation in these unitary countries varies enormously according to the country and fields of responsibility, but State sovereignty remains at the centre. It is this aspect which unites these countries which are very different concerning the autonomy they accord to their sub-national levels. Legislative authority, for instance, is never shared; it remains exclusively the responsibility of the national parliament. Matters are less simple where regulatory authority is concerned, owing to the need for taking decisions which will ensure good local governance. While sub-national governments have decision-making authority in their fields of responsibility, they may not exercise general regulatory power, as in **France**, or such power is at best limited, as in the **United Kingdom** and **Ireland**. The only exception is the **Netherlands**, where the constitution gives autonomous and general decision-making authority to sub-national governments in respect of their own affairs (authority admittedly eaten into by the growth of "co-administration").

Legal protection of sub-national responsibility is also less extensive than in federal systems. In unitary countries, only the State has "responsibility for its own responsibilities"; in other words, sub-national governments cannot alone determine their fields of action. Furthermore, the responsibilities of sub-national governments are not normally mentioned in the constitution. Even where an intermediate (regional) level exists between the national and the local level, its responsibilities are generally set out in specific legislation but not in the constitution. It is thus easier to contest the powers and responsibilities of sub-national governments in unitary than in federal or regional systems. Occasionally, as in **Greece** or **Turkey**, the executive branch holds substantial prerogatives regarding the distribution of tasks. In **Greece**, for example, the amount of autonomy and freedom enjoyed by regional governments in conducting their own policies depends, according to the legislation of 1994, on the power conferred on them by Presidential decree.

However, in some cases, the courts have extended their control over such law. A general principle of 'free administration" sometimes provides sub-national governments with constitutional protection -- as in **France**. This does not guarantee them the right to any specific responsibilities -- that power remains in the hands of the legislator -- but it does guarantee them freedom in how those responsibilities are carried out. French jurisprudence also recognises the competence of each level of government concerning its "local affairs".

The Nordic countries: **Sweden, Denmark, Norway, Iceland** and **Finland** (though the creation of a regional level, and rather less freedom of action at local level, distinguish it from the others) undoubtedly belong with the unitary countries. They have a number of common features which set them apart, however: the principle of local self government (enshrined in the constitution, except in **Norway**), and the extent of local freedom of action. Local government may have several levels, each with its attributes, but without any order of rank. This is a feature common to other kinds of unitary system, such as in **France**. Local levels are regulated by a framework law and their responsibilities are defined by legislation. The principle for determining where to locate responsibilities is that they should be at the level most suited for supplying a particular service. Local levels are generally responsible for the tasks entrusted to them, and thus differ radically from those in Napoleonic systems. Some of the tasks are compulsory; others are optional and undertaken at the discretion of municipalities according to need or available financial resources. Municipalities can, in most cases, levy their own taxes, within limits which are (except in **Denmark**) determined by Parliament. They enjoy considerable freedom of action in the performance of their tasks. In **Iceland**, the situation is slightly different: the smallness of local units and of the population obliges central government to be involved in many activities customarily reserved for the local level. The distribution of responsibility is far from clear due to the complex pattern of decision-making and roles. In **Finland**, the creation of a regional level (composed of regional councils formed by the voluntary association of town councils) marks a transfer of authority and responsibility from, in particular, the provinces to the regional level. Seeing that these regional councils do not have constitutional status, it is unlikely that the municipalities will lose their role as main actors in the municipal sector or their general responsibility concerning their territory.

Regional countries: A new category has emerged, that of regional systems. There are two "regional" countries, which grant degrees of autonomy to their regions, i.e. **Spain** and **Italy**. These countries have evolved from centralism to regionalism quite recently. The regions are inscribed in the constitution, which defines their status and responsibilities, both of which vary according to the region, but the similarity stops there. In **Spain**, the constitution lists the functions of the regions and those that remain the prerogative of the State. Functions not in the list remain with the State unless they are claimed by the regions. The distribution of responsibilities may be modified by a ruling of the constitutional court. The municipalities have, in theory, numerous functions. In practice, they are few and may be related to decisions taken by central and regional governments. The sum of these arrangements is reflected in the growing number of fields governed by different legislation in different parts of the country. In **Italy**, the legislative authority of the region is concomitant or shared with the State, so that their autonomy is limited. The regions are independent with regard to administrative matters. The municipalities and provinces have their own statutes and are entitled to choose their own form of internal organisation and administrative machinery. The constitution lays down the responsibilities of the regions (a large part of them transferred from the State), which have delegated executive authority to the provinces, municipalities and other administrative agencies. This decentralisation of responsibilities has been accompanied by budgetary centralisation, mostly at the expense of the municipalities. There is a possibility that the provinces and municipalities will be re-organised and that the present distribution of functions among administrative levels will be reviewed.

Despite guarantees and a distribution of responsibilities that varies from country to country, sub-national authorities in the OECD countries are often required to perform rather similar tasks. This is particularly true at municipal level. While it is impossible to list all the responsibilities exercised in all OECD countries, a summary distinction may be drawn among three types of responsibility.

- First, responsibilities which by their nature belong only to the centre, whether the system be federal, regional or unitary (e.g. diplomacy, defence, and monetary policy). The centre also conserves a regulatory role through the setting of objectives.

- Second, tasks which are, practically everywhere, the exclusive domain of the local level, commonly called "classic local public services". These include town planning, local transport, sewage systems, refuse collection, and water supply. Most related reforms aim at giving local authorities full use of their prerogatives in these matters, as is the case in **Portugal**, for example.

- Third, shared tasks and responsibilities. These are of two types: those shared between different tiers of central government, and those shared between central and sub-national governments. In most countries, they are connected with the implementation of social (health, education, social assistance) or environmental policies. The sharing may be intended, that is, each level is granted part of the responsibility in a given field. In **France**, for example, responsibilities in education are shared among the three levels: university education is attributed to central government; secondary schooling to the intermediate levels; and primary education to the local level. Teachers and education policy are the responsibility of the centre, whereas each level of deconcentrated administration has responsibility for the buildings used for their own education cycle. The sharing may also result from changing economic circumstances. Formal responsibility may be attributed to one level but, owing to subsidies or other factors, its clarity may become clouded. In **Canada**, for example, health, which is nominally the responsibility of the provinces, has gradually become an area in which the federal level plays an important part.

In short, the grey area induced by overlapping or complexity of responsibilities is not peculiar to any one system (although federal countries provide more favourable conditions than others for the development of such situations), and a review of task distribution across levels of government forms part of the reform agenda of many OECD Member countries.

b)   Exercise of responsibilities

An overview of how responsibilities are carried out and of the means available to sub-national levels requires a different approach. The influence of each national tradition and culture is very important and leads to another type of classification. On the assumption that all countries do their best to provide high-quality service equitably, other criteria apply which vary by group according to whether a country's culture is primarily directed towards efficiency, effectiveness, value for money, satisfaction of citizens' needs or strict enforcement of the law. The means available to sub-national levels also vary depending on whether the tradition of relations among levels of administration is mainly one of negotiation, of consultation, or of confrontation.

It is possible to distinguish between two main categories: those countries where the exercise of responsibility is based on a legal tradition, as in the "Napoleonic" or "Germanic" countries, and where the local level is largely regulated by the centre; and those countries where a "managerial" culture is more predominant, as in the Anglo-Saxon countries, for example, where the search for efficiency is an important objective and in the Nordic countries with their traditions of negotiation and consultation. Clearly, in each category, cultural factors influence how policies are implemented.

The continental European countries, heirs to a legalistic culture, have many points in common. Even so, a distinction must be made between the Napoleonic and the Germanic countries.

In the Napoleonic countries (**France, Italy, Spain, Belgium, Luxemburg, the Netherlands** and, to a certain extent, the southern countries, **Portugal, Greece** and **Turkey**), detailed legislation determines the sphere of action of each protagonist and tries to avoid any overlapping of responsibilities. Since there is a tradition of distrust between levels of government (in all countries), separation of the blocks of tasks assigned to each level is felt to be necessary. This separation is also seen as a guarantee of efficiency. Priority is given to the coherence of the institutional framework, and good governance should flow from that coherence. Even in systems which are now regional, central government tries to maintain a certain degree of involvement. The citizen is traditionally looked upon as a "subject", although this view is changing. Market-type mechanisms have gained ground for services which are traditionally provided by public enterprises rather than by private institutions. Changes are also taking place in this area. The **Netherlands** differs from these countries through a tradition which is strongly attached to compromise and by the development of the co-administration of responsibilities.

The Germanic countries, **Germany, Austria** and **Switzerland** (at least in its German-speaking cantons) are also heirs to a legalistic culture. Grounded in respect for the law, which determines many things, they also rely on co-operative mechanisms to ensure that responsibilities are carried out as they should be at each level. The intermediate levels play an important part in the federal legislative process. This is not to say that efficiency is neglected. Local authorities are entitled by statute to use market mechanisms in the provision of services for which they are responsible and may be flexible in adjusting to circumstances. Tasks which exceed the capacity of the municipalities are entrusted to intermediate levels. Health care is divided between the regional level and the municipalities, as is education (although secondary education is usually handled at regional level).

The situation in **Switzerland** is somewhat unusual. Local (direct) democracy is strong, and the cantons wield a large amount of power (financially and administratively). The cantons determine their own administrative structure, so may decide on the appropriateness of introducing market mechanisms in carrying out their responsibilities and on the type of services they will provide. Taxpayers have a wide right to oversee the operation of their institutions.

Japan, because of its cultural specificity, cannot be easily classified in either system. What is striking is that the central government is perceived as a leader with a mission to regulate society and local actors should help it in that mission.

The Anglo-Saxon countries (**United States, Canada, Australia, United Kingdom, New Zealand, Ireland**) put particular emphasis on efficiency, effectiveness, and value for money. They are more likely to introduce market mechanisms and notions of competitiveness carrying out their responsibilities, both of which disadvantage bodies with few resources. The citizen is viewed primarily as a consumer of services, as a client. In **Canada** and **Australia**, where most major responsibilities such as health, education or agriculture are entrusted to intermediate levels (albeit with growing federal intervention), classic local public services are left to the local levels. However, in some provinces and states, a centralisation of these tasks may be observed since they overstrain the resources of the local communities. In the **United States**, local governments play a bigger role in regard to their allotted responsibilities, but they depend financially on subsidies and the way they carry out their responsibilities is significantly affected by the rules and terms imposed by the federal administration.

The Nordic countries (**Denmark, Finland, Iceland, Norway, Sweden**) belong to another "cultural category", more concerned with meeting citizens' needs. They also have a tradition of negotiation and consultation. Central government regulation has on the whole been eased with the aim of giving local levels the possibility of better adjusting to local conditions and using their finances in accordance with local priorities. An important part of this approach is the ability of local authorities to organise their funds according to their needs. While local levels enjoy considerable power, citizens themselves play an important part in local government decision-making. The search for efficiency and effectiveness involves satisfying citizens' wishes; it is they who should remain in charge of the process.

3. *Representation of the centre*

In all countries (the federal countries being no exception), some form of central representation exists at the sub-national level. Its nature is closely related to deconcentration and decentralisation policies. The centre's presence takes two main forms. One consists of a network of central government offices at the sub-national level (a system of agencies for example) -- often called "deconcentrated administrations" to reflect the certain amount of independence which characterises them. The other type comprises, a "prefect system" in which an official is charged with representing the centre at the sub-national level. Both of these forms exist together in about half of the OECD countries -- an indication of the desire to devolve and decentralise the administration. Relations between these forms of central representation and sub-national government may give rise to problems, especially in fields where the sub-national and deconcentrated authorities have competing responsibilities.

a)   Deconcentrated administration

Deconcentrated administrations exist in all countries (even **Switzerland** has deconcentrated services -- the civil servants working for the post office [PTT], for example, are subject to federal statute even though working in administrative units throughout the country).

While this ensures the presence of the centre at the local level, the field of action, local presence and degree of autonomy of deconcentrated administrations vary widely. In **France** public establishments, sometimes likened to the "agencies" of the Anglo-Saxon countries, in fact enjoy greater legal autonomy (they have legal personality, for example). **Ireland**'s system of "boards" is extremely independent. Agencies in the Nordic countries have both considerable freedom over financial management and broad decision-making powers.

In **Sweden**, where the centre's representative is by tradition less present than in countries with a "Jacobin" tradition, the county administration helps in co-ordinating State action at the local level, along with the local agencies of the central government. Its system is sometimes described as "functional" rather than "prefectoral". In unitary countries without a central representative at the local level (in particular, the **United Kingdom** and **New Zealand**), the agency system is also highly developed.

In the federal countries, the federal presence at the local level can be strong, whereas in unitary countries, even the decentralised ones, the regional level is not represented at the lower levels. In **Germany**, for example, both federal and *Länder* administrations are present at the local level.

In some countries, it is difficult to make the distinction, in certain areas, between deconcentrated departments and sub-national authorities, particularly where a non-elected local administration is endowed with general responsibilities (while at the same time particular central ministries are represented locally, irrespective of the form taken by this representation). This is the case in **Finland**, where regional administrations holding general powers exist without necessarily being separated from the central State apparatus. This is a country where, in accordance with a highly developed process of deconcentration, each ministry is represented at the local level. In the **United Kingdom**, Scotland and Wales have their own structures in a certain number of fields (agriculture, fisheries, health, education) and Scotland has special legislation, as its legal system is different from that of the rest of the United Kingdom. This does not, however, make it a sub-national administration. The Scottish Office and the Welsh Office, in which a large number of secondary administrations are grouped, are directed by a member of the Cabinet.

In the interests of efficient territorial development and infrastructure policies, many countries (including **Australia**, **Canada**, the **United States** and **Ireland**) have set up "regional structures" which help in organising the central government's territorial action. The political influence of these regions varies but is always restricted to their particular sphere of action. They are involved (in ways and to degrees that vary across countries) in the integration of the centre at the sub-national level. In **Ireland**, the regional and local authorities, whose degree of autonomy varies, are entrusted with performing a certain number of tasks in specific fields such as fisheries, health, tourism, and local development

It should be noted that, depending on the country, different local authorities have boundaries which do not always coincide with the traditional administrative units. This may reflect flexibility and adaptation to needs, but may also add to fragmentation. In the **United States**, regional structures usually extend beyond state borders and have no constitutional status at either the federal or state level. In **Canada**, regional development policy needs have led to the creation of four large territorial regions, each including several provinces. These regional bodies may take part in the provision of services.

The conclusion to be drawn from these examples is that the degree of integration by the centre in the country as a whole is very much a function of how the deconcentrated administration is organised and operates. Factors which help to understand the centre's position include the role of general purpose or specific administrations, the type of links with the centre, and the extent of co-ordination between local services. This is usually offset by other mechanisms. Given the growing interdependence in central and sub-national responsibilities in most OECD countries, a better understanding of the relations between the regional bodies of central government and sub-national authorities seems indispensable.

Like the prefect system, deconcentrated government is an essential part of the provision of public services. It is often firmly implanted in the institutional landscape, and the intricate networks that have been developed are likely to ensure its continued survival.

This structural stability can, in some countries, be a hindrance to modernisation -- in contrast to the changing role of the prefect in response to new challenges. Regarding **France**, Robert Herzog, in *Entre l'Europe et la Décentralisation*, writes, "When one sees how difficult it is to redivide the departmental directorates of the [Ministry for] Infrastructure, and the near-impossibility of even touching those of [the Ministry of] Agriculture, it is hard to be optimistic."

Structural stability need not be a hindrance to innovation in management. In such countries as the **United Kingdom, Canada, New Zealand**, the **Netherlands** as well as in the Nordic countries, administrative modernisation reforms have been successfully undertaken within government agencies.

The place of agencies in administrative modernisation: the Nordic example

State territorial administration takes many different forms in OECD countries. These include the external services of central ministries, regional organisations emanating from the centre, and boards. One of the approaches most widely developed in recent years is the "agency" system. While the legal status of these "agencies" varies according to country, they have usually been important players in the territorial administration modernisation policies of central government.

In the Nordic countries, central government ministries are now much reduced in size, and the agencies have been granted extensive freedom to decide and manage.

- In **Sweden**, where the agency model has a long tradition, the power of independent decision-making of agencies was strengthened in 1986-1989 and again in 1991. With their greater flexibility, they have been given the task of improving access to public services. They must report to the government on the measures taken and the results achieved at regular intervals. They are also now in charge of their own staff management and training.
- In **Norway**, after a period of budget reform aimed at putting more emphasis on performance, certain agencies have become public enterprises operating under market rules.
- In **Denmark**, where the bond between ministries and agencies is traditionally strong, greater managerial freedom was granted in 1991-1992 to a number of agencies in exchange for tighter control of performance.
- The basic development in **Finland** focuses on performance management and the progressive transformation of the agencies into public enterprises.
- In **Iceland**, contract management, which provides agencies with greater managerial freedom and introduces performance-based control, is being developed.

These examples show the key role of agencies in government modernisation efforts in the Nordic countries. It may be surmised that in future, on account of the services they provide and their involvement in the supervision of sub-national governments, they will become increasingly important links in the relations between central and sub-national governments.

---

b)   Prefect system

Under one form or another, a prefectoral system exists in most OECD countries. It is the result of an evolution specific to some countries and can be found in almost all the unitary systems which are not of the "Westminster" kind. As to the federal countries, where a representative of the centre at sub-national level is the exception rather than the rule, the federated States have sometimes instituted a similar system at the local level.

The representative of the centre is traditionally vested with two main duties. Apart from his role in maintaining order, he is involved in the supervision of the sub-national governments and acts as an intermediary between the central administration and its external offshoots. It may be noted that where there is such a representative, his or her presence is rarely contested, even in the event of a move towards decentralisation. In some countries, decentralisation has even been followed by a widening of the prefectoral system; in other countries, such as **Spain**, the existing system prevailed as the Communities came into being.

In brief, the prefect system is alive and well. The centre has managed, especially since the early 1980s, to develop the institution, even taking account of the introduction of new methods of oversight. The centre's representative occupies a key position, since he has shown himself to be a valuable link between national and sub-national government. He is thus involved in public management at both these levels.

The action of prefects in sub-national public management has often taken the form of administrative supervision of local governments which can involve overseeing legality and advisability. In some systems, the State's representative also acts as local executive. Although these functions have often evolved, as under decentralisation policies, the institution of prefect is rarely completely absent from sub-national public management, if only via participation in joint projects, especially those involving areas of shared competence. The State's representative, insofar as he often has the job of co-ordinating central government action at the sub-national level, is also associated with central public management. He acts as the channel of communication, helping to centralise the information flowing from the centre and arising from the sub-national levels.

The "prefect system", where it exists, varies significantly according to the traditions and history of each country. Without any attempt at strict typology, certain systems may be grouped together on the basis of common features.

- The "Napoleonic" prefect model first influenced the traditions of the unitary states of continental Europe. It is a legacy of the Jacobins (the centralist movement born out of the 1789 French Revolution). The different systems have changed but the institution has remained, whether it be in states that are still centralised such as **Turkey**, **Greece** (where decentralisation is currently under way) or **Luxemburg**, those that are decentralised such as **France** or the **Netherlands**, those that are "autonomic" and regional such as **Spain** or **Italy** or those that are now federal such as **Belgium**. In **Belgium** and the **Netherlands**, mayors also are designated by the centre; there are other countries where, although elected, they exercise part of their competences on behalf of the State.

- The Nordic countries, with the exception of **Iceland**, all have a system not far removed from this tradition. A representative of the centre is in charge of the counties. The relations among the different administrative levels are, however, by tradition less "hierarchical" or "vertical" than in the Napoleonic model countries. In **Denmark**, for example, the representative heads a council which oversees the local authorities; the local authorities association takes part in the nomination of members to this council.

- The systems derived from the British tradition, whether unitary (**United Kingdom**, **Ireland** and **New Zealand**) or federal (**Canada** and **Australia**), are foreign to this institution, long considered as being contrary to "self-administration". This lack of a central representative at sub-national level, along with a network of local State agencies, is one of the distinguishing features of these systems. It does not prevent them today from being centralised in certain respects, including their finances.

- There is not often a prefect system in countries with other traditions, the **United States** and **Mexico**, for example, although institutions of a related kind may sometimes be found, mainly at local level. In **Switzerland**, with its sovereign-state cantons, a prefect system would appear to serve no purpose; yet the cantons have on occasion created sub-districts directed by a prefect who may be elected or appointed depending on the situation. **Austria** has its "Chief District Administrative Authorities" who direct the indirect (deconcentrated) federal administration but do not exercise authority over the *Länder* or the municipalities. It may be noted that watchdog institutions have sometimes been set up by the governments of federal countries to supervise the action of local bodies. In **Germany**, district administrations depend on a district commissioner whose function is similar to that of French prefects before the decentralisation laws were passed, although this system does not operate in all *Länder*. In **Japan**, the intermediate administrative level (Prefectorates) is presided over by governors who used to be appointed by the central government before the Second World War and are now elected. This change has not brought about any strengthening of local authority, however, the governor generally ensuring correct local implementation of central government directives.

All these examples go to show that a direct relation between the prefect system and the amount of centralisation or central direction cannot nowadays be established. They also imply that the old typologies (e.g. distinction between federal and unitary systems) are inadequate where this subject is concerned.

In most OECD countries, big changes have taken place, leading to extremely varied situations as regards the authority and role of the centre's representative. These changes are linked to the development of public management priorities: trend towards a less vertical supervisory system; need for better co-ordination of State action in the field; search for forms of partnership or collaboration with sub-national authorities, on the one hand, and with other public and para-public actors on the other. This evolution takes the form of a shift towards more comprehensive governance. The structural transformations made in many countries over the past twenty years have often affected the central representative's role. His position often gives a clear picture of the kind of relations, vertical or co-operative, which the centre tries to maintain with local government.

Carrying out tasks on behalf of central government is increasingly being shared with other bodies, especially local governments. In some countries, the mayor traditionally performs some responsibilities on behalf of the centre. The constitutional reforms which have taken place in **Greece** concerning the new regional administration also follow this trend. This form of evolution may call for additional efforts at co-ordination.

It is clear that, in many systems, the prefect has lost his powers of coercion. (In **France**, in favour of the courts; in **Belgium**, in favour of other administrative levels; in **Spain** and **Italy**, his main function is the maintenance of public order; in the **Netherlands**, the municipalities and provinces are involved in his designation.) This trend can be traced to a desire to conduct a coherent policy of decentralisation, as in **Spain**. The loss of authority may in some cases but not all (**Belgium**) be offset by additional functions, or the restoration of functions attributed in former times (see box below).

Development of the prefectoral function in France

The effect of the 1982-1983 decentralisation policy was to replace the prefect by an elected Departmental and regional authority. The tutelage which he exercised over the acts of sub-national governments was changed into a post factum control via the courts. The prefect's power in this respect is now limited to taking the case to the appropriate court. He retains in essence his position as the sole representative of the centre at the sub-national level.

The prefect's position has, on the other hand, been strengthened vis-à-vis the State's territorial administration. Regional prefects have been introduced. The prefect has become the linchpin of deconcentration policy, especially since the "Deconcentration Charter" of 1 July 1992, which reinforces the prefect's powers of co-ordination over all the central government's deconcentrated services. He also has a budget for local development. The loss of his local executive role was in the early stages accompanied by a decrease in the funds which he could distribute. Since 1992, this situation has been reversed and he now once again has "envelopes" to be spent on particular policies. Under the three-year State reform plan, prefects are due to receive even greater resources (2 billion FF and 2 000 extra jobs for the 95 *départements*).

An effort has also been made to dissipate the authoritarian and hierarchical image associated with prefects and instead to promote their role as partners and experts interested in the social and economic development of the country. Inter-service "missions" have been created to permit a better flow of information. These have sometimes been left out of the picture by department heads who prefer to go directly to the prefect, who is their equal in terms of rank (a good indication of the prefect's influence on the local scene in terms of status). Another function which could be developed is conciliation, a role which could be aided by the deep roots and longevity of the prefect as an institution.

One of the basic problems of the prefect's function today stems from the perception that this local co-ordinator of State services lacks many of the elements needed to give unity to a widely dispersed system of action. The policies of specific ministries and direct communication between central and deconcentrated government administrations also tend to short-circuit the prefect's action.

In the Napoleonic countries, with their Jacobin and centralist tradition, the function of the prefect has been preserved in formal terms but has also often evolved along with the decentralisation of national institutions. Many of these countries are now very decentralised. Where this is so, the prefect, whose office may be said to be suffering from an identity crisis, has an important role to play in fostering co-operation among levels of government. On the other hand, the absence of a prefect system has not prevented certain countries in the Anglo-Saxon tradition, the **United Kingdom** first among them, from becoming more centralised, especially on questions of finance. The agency system, with its broad managerial freedoms combined with linkage to the central government (as in the Nordic model), has in such cases served as a platform for introducing reform. Clearly, the absence of a prefectural institution does not imply a reduced central presence at sub-national levels.

II. Financial and fiscal relations

> Designing government programmes so that activities are performed at the appropriate level of government is one of the most difficult challenges associated with the task of making government more efficient and effective....Devising policies that ensure accountability and that protect the national interest, while also allowing for flexibility, adaptability, and innovation at the state, local and individual levels is a great challenge.
>
> *Economic Report of the President to Congress*, Washington DC, February 1996.

Adjusting institutional frameworks and patterns of responsibility and authority is part of the larger issue of how to improve inter-governmental financial and fiscal arrangements. The latter hold the key to understanding the nature and extent of the real autonomy of each level and shifting patterns of dependence. Views on how best to achieve gains in efficiency and economy of service delivery, be more responsive, bring greater equity, and marry these economic objectives with democratic ones, can vary significantly depending on whether there is a central or sub-national perspective. That is why inter-governmental financial and fiscal relations have become so complex -- and why the control of public expenditures and revenues are at the heart of inter-governmental management. It is also why issues of fiscal federalism such as the nature and amount of inter-governmental transfers, equalisation policy and unfunded mandates are currently at the forefront of political debate in many countries. These matters are dealt with in turn below.

1. *Public expenditure across levels of government*:

The dramatic increases in overall public expenditure in OECD countries over the last 40 years reflect, in particular, the very significant expansion of the role of government as the "welfare state" has evolved. Associated with this have been increases in the level of demand for services from the public -- in the form of both higher standards for established public services and calls for new types of services. More recently, expenditure has been subject to pressure from slower economic growth and big increases in unemployment benefit payments. As a result government spending in the OECD area has risen by about 50 per cent relative to GDP since 1960 and real government final consumption expenditure per capita roughly doubled in the 1980s.

Charts 1 and 2 illustrate how the public sector has expanded since 1970, measured by the ratio of government expenditures and receipts to GDP. Although the total level and overall growth of *expenditures* differs across countries, expenditures as a percentage of GDP have grown in all the 21 countries depicted (five OECD Member countries are not included because of incomplete data). Large increases can be found in both federal and unitary countries. Government *receipts* have followed a similar path, with receipts as a percentage of GDP rising since 1970 in most countries for which data is available.

OVERVIEW

◆ Chart 1. *Total government expenditures as a percentage of GDP 1970-1994*[1]

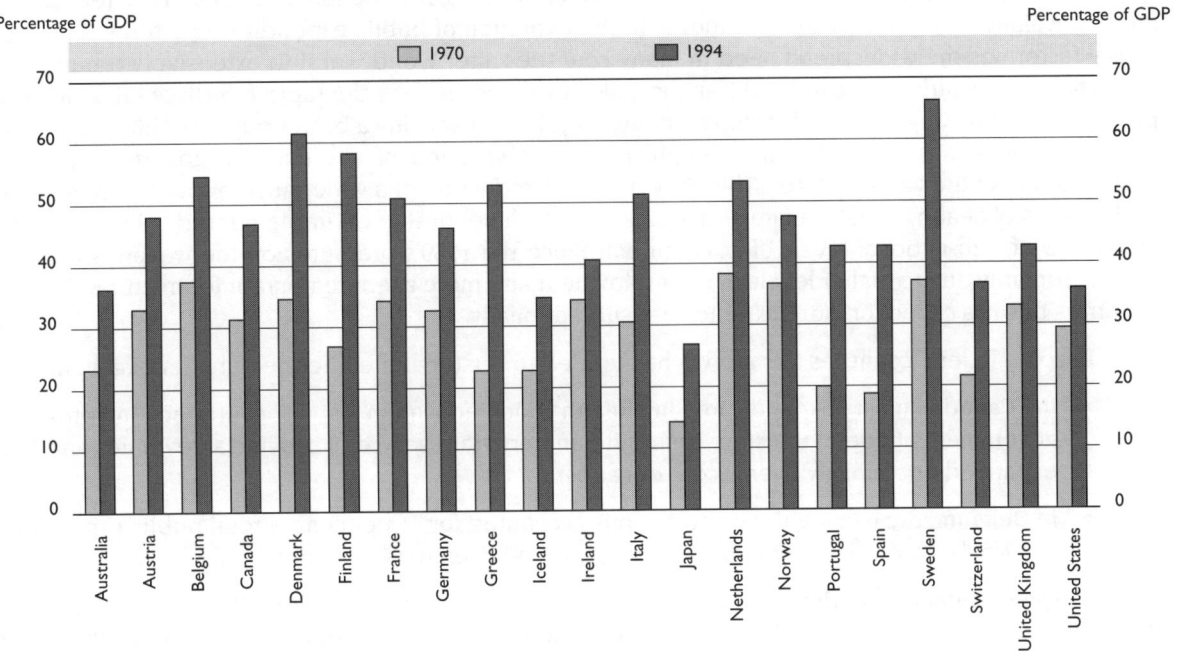

◆ Chart 2. *Total government receipts as a percentage of GDP 1970-1994*[1]

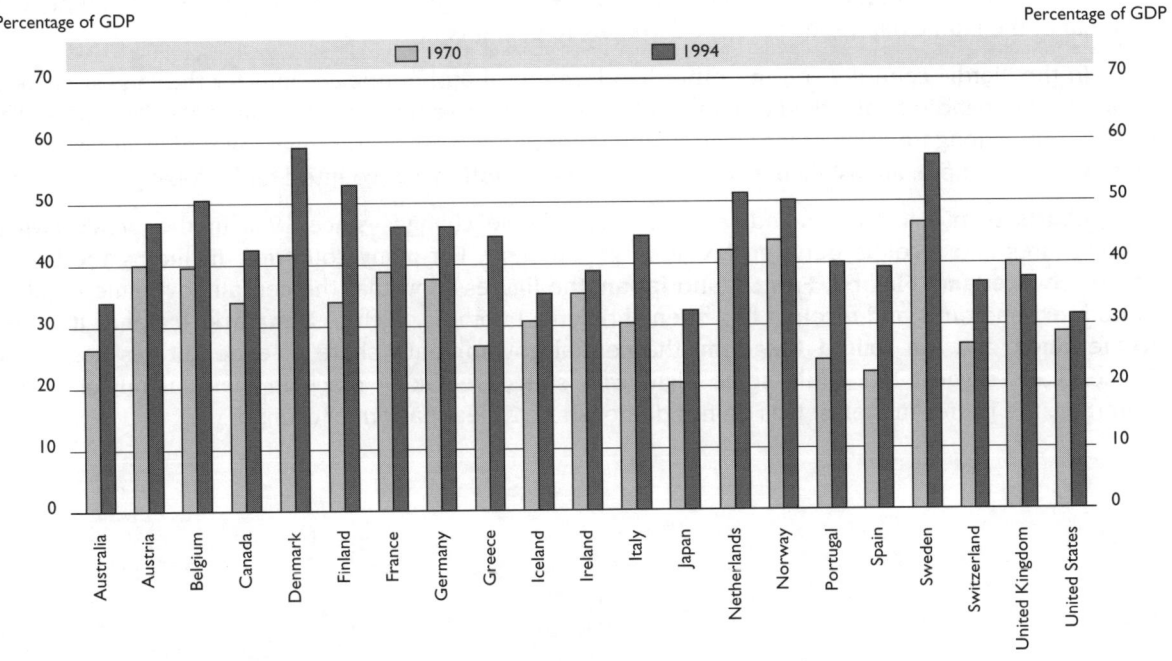

1. For Ireland, Portugal and United States, the chart uses 1970/1993 figures.
Total government expenditures = the sum of total current government disbursements (also called current public expenditure), gross fixed capital formation, increase in stocks, net purchases of land and intangible assets, and net capital transfers.
Total government receipts = the sum of current government receipts (also called current public receipts), provisions for consumption of fixed capital, and capital transfers received.
Note: Because of differences in definitions, figures in country chapters may not always match those from National Accounts.
Source: OECD National Accounts.

Today, despite downsizing in many countries, levels of aggregate public expenditure remain high. Countries are using a range of policies to address the deterioration in financial balances including numerous measures which have a direct impact on inter-governmental relations. This reflects the growing weight of sub-national governments in the evolution of public expenditure patterns. One early causal factor was the widespread need in many countries after World War II to extensively rebuild local infra-structure including housing and transport facilities. Another was the rapid growth of urban areas as people migrated away from rural regions looking for jobs and seeking a better quality of life. But the key prevailing factor has been the increasingly important vocation of sub-national government as the "handmaiden of the welfare state". This reflects the introduction of a wide range of public programmes in the fields of health, social welfare and education which needed to be implemented -- by, or with the assistance of, sub-national levels of government. Since the 1980's pressures on the welfare state have grown, primarily due to higher levels of unemployment and more aged demographic structures. In many countries this has called for more expenditure sub-nationally.

In some federal countries this growth has tended to cluster at the intermediary tier of government

- in **Canada** most expenditure in health and education is concentrated in provincial governments (federal transfers constitute an important source of provincial revenues and have expanded enormously over recent decades) ;
- in **Belgium**, the communities and regions accounted for 31 per cent of total public expenditure in 1985, but by 1994, after federalisation, this had risen to 66 per cent.

In some unitary countries new tiers of government have been created thereby adding to the importance of the regional level. The share of consolidated public expenditure of the **Spanish** regions, for example, rose from 15.2 per cent in 1985 to 25.3 per cent in 1994 and in the ten years from 1982 to 1993 the number of people employed in the civil service rose by over 40 per cent, with much of the increase being at the regional level. Similarly in **France**, the level of revenues in the regions has more than tripled since 1985 while their share of all sub-national revenues has increased from 4 to 9 per cent and that of the municipalities has dropped from 64 to 60 per cent.

In the Nordic countries, on the other hand, the local authorities account for the largest share of total public expenditure and deal with most of the redistributive functions typical of a welfare state. This reflects their strong tradition of local self-government and the associated high level of local taxation. In **Sweden**, for example, almost 80 per cent of public consumption is accounted for by local governments.

Charts 3 and 4 give an indication of the relative changes since 1970 in the breakdown of expenditures and receipts between levels of government. For many countries, including the **United States, Switzerland, Finland, France**, and **Japan**, the figures show that the central government's share of both expenditures and receipts has been shrinking. In others, such as **Denmark, Iceland, Italy, the Netherlands**, and the **United Kingdom**, the central government's share of expenditures has grown. These charts suggest that while some significant shifts are taking place in many, if not all, OECD countries, the figures in themselves do not demonstrate a clear pattern of change.

OVERVIEW

◆ Chart 3. **Share of total government expenditures**
(by level of government) 1970-1980-1994[1]

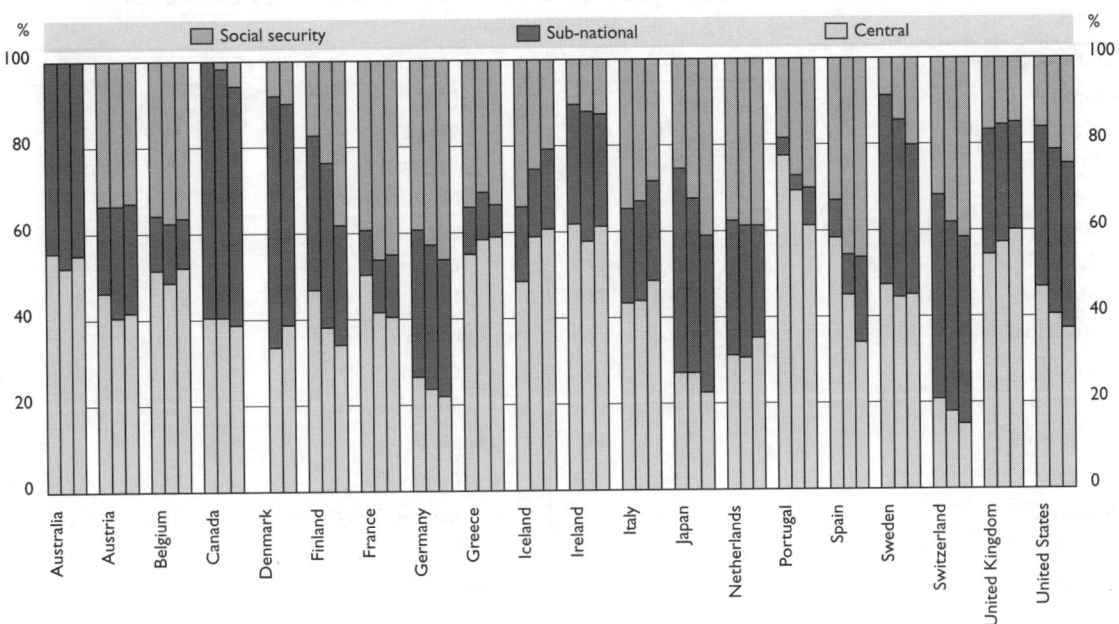

◆ Chart 4. **Share of total government receipts**
(by level of government) 1970-1980-1994[1]

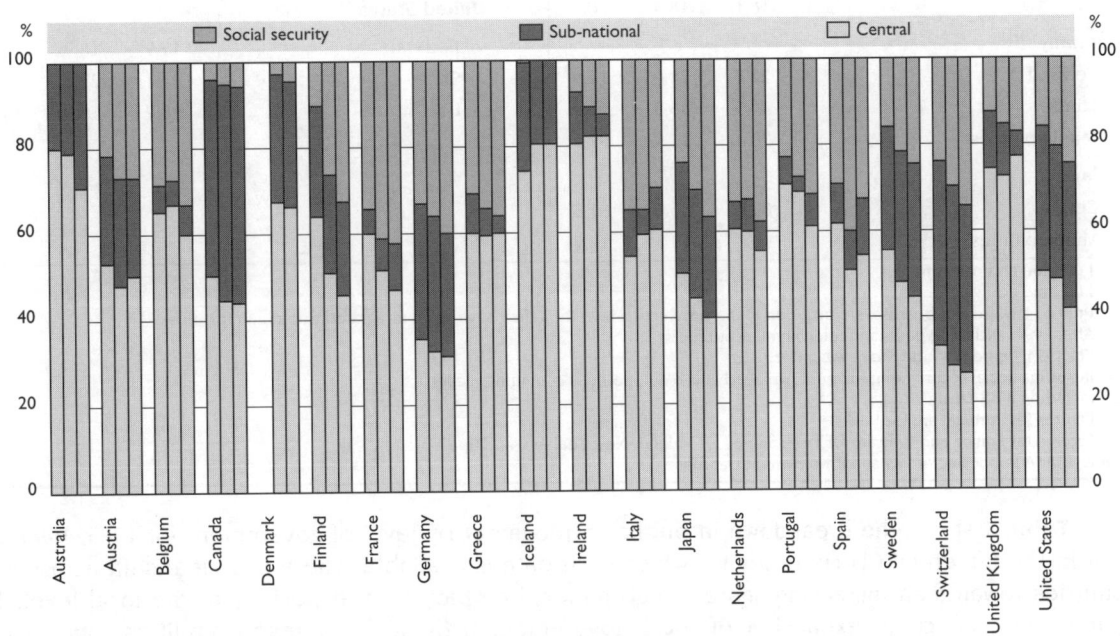

1. For Ireland, The Netherlands, Portugal, Spain, and United States, the chart uses 1970/1980/1993 figures.
Note: The term "sub-national" refers to all levels of government -- regional, state, or local -- below the national level. Because of differences in definitions, figures in country chapters may not always match those from National Accounts.
Source: OECD National Accounts.

Other indicators of the relative weight of sub-national governments include numbers of staff employed at each level of government.

Table 1. **Share of public employment by level of government in some OECD countries**
(percentages)

Level of Government	1985	1990*	1994**	Level of Government	1985	1990*	1994**
Australia[1]				**Italy**[2]			
Commonwealth	..	15.0	14.6	Central	62.9	63.0	63.0
State	..	74.2	73.3	Regional	21.7	20.9	23.0
Local	..	10.7	12.1	Municipalities	15.4	16.1	14.0
Austria[2]				**New Zealand**			
Federal	..	51.0	44.5	Central	..	..	89.7
Länder	..	26.2	28.1	Local	..	..	10.3
Municipalities	..	22.8	27.4	**Portugal**[1]			
Canada[1]				Central	82.8	83.8	86.0
Federal	..	17.9	17.1	Municipalities	17.2	16.2	14.0
Provinces [3]	..	63.5	44.1	**Spain**[1]			
Local [3]	..	18.6	38.9	Central [6]	58.8	50.7	47.1
Denmark[2]				Autonomous comm.[6]	23.2	29.7	31.4
Central	31.3	29.2	27.1	Local	18.1	19.6	21.5
Local	68.7	70.8	72.9	**Sweden**[2]			
Finland[2]				Central	27.2	26.7	17.3
Central	33.3	24.3	25.2	Regional	26.9	27.8	24.6
Municipalities	66.7	75.7	74.8	Municipalities	45.9	45.5	58.1
France[2]				**United Kingdom**[2]			
Central [4]	56.3	55.0	48.7	Central [7]	48.0	47.7	47.7
Sub-national	25.6	26.6	30.7	Local	52.0	52.3	52.3
Health	18.1	18.4	20.6	**United States**[1]			
Germany[5][1]				Federal	17.9	16.9	15.2
Federal	22.1	21.6	11.9	State	22.1	22.4	22.6
Länder	47.5	46.5	51.0	Local	58.7	59.5	61.1
Municipalities	30.4	31.9	37.1				
Ireland[1]							
Central	85.0	86.5	87.3				
Municipalities	15.0	13.5	12.7				

1. Full time and part time.
2. Full time equivalent.
3. Prior to 1992 school boards were included in the provinces; since then they have been integrated with municipalities.
4. After 1991, excluding posts and telecommunications.
5. For 1994, figures include the new Länder.
6. Including social security employment managed at the autonomous community level.
7. Including NHS Trusts.
* Figures for Portugal are for 1989.
** Figures for France and Italy are for 1993; figures for Ireland, New Zealand, and Spain are for 1995.
Source: PUMA Public Sector Pay and Employment Database.

Table 1 shows the breakdown in public employment by level of government for 1985, 1990, and 1994 in the fifteen OECD countries for which such data is available. There is a clear shift across most countries towards an increasing share of sub-national employment, especially at the local level. The figures may reflect an expansion of local government activities and responsibilities, bureaucratic inflation, changes in the status of some central or sub-national bodies, and/or an effort by central government at downsizing. In **Finland**, for example, the significant shift in central and municipal public employment is largely explained by a change in the status of some State enterprises. **Spain** saw its share of public employment at the central level drop from 58.8 per cent to 47.1 per cent. Even in the three countries that showed increases in central government employment, the gains were either small (**Portugal** and **Ireland**) or negligible (**Italy**).

2. *Evolving patterns of sub-national revenues*:

There are five basic sources of funding available to sub-national levels of government:

- transfers from other levels (in particular as specific or general grants);

- shared taxes;

- local (own) taxes;

- user charges, fees, and other sources of income (e.g. property); and

- loans.

The relative weight of each of the above sources varies significantly across countries. Sub-national governments in federal countries, for example, tend to rely more on several sources of revenue, with states generally having more spending and taxing powers than do local authorities in many unitary countries. And within countries there can be much variation across different jurisdictions. In **Norway**, for example, the proportion of total income coming from local taxes varies between municipalities across the country from 15 to 85 per cent. In a number of countries there have also been considerable shifts in the relative importance of the five sources across time. In the **United States**, for example, only 15 per cent of all state and local expenditures came from federal grants in 1960. That proportion rose to 28 per cent in 1980 and stood at 23 per cent in 1995. There is some direct federal assistance to local governments, but it declined sharply in the 1980s and as a result local governments now rely more heavily on state grants.

Broadly speaking, the expansion of sub-national tasks has not been matched by increases in the independent local revenue base. Furthermore, the financial problems created by an increased service demand are heightened by dependence on income-inelastic revenues such as property taxes. (Although the latter have the advantage of being relatively stable irrespective of the economic cycle.) Any shortfall has had to be met largely by increased transfers from central government, but as national financial situations have deteriorated, many sub-national governments have been required to share in cutbacks. Hence the emergence of the sub-national "fiscal crisis" with concerns about the levels of sub-national debt and underfunded mandates.

- In **the Netherlands**, the financial position of municipalities and provinces is seen as one of the key challenges to local government in the 1990s. The choices of raising property taxes and fees or making cutbacks are difficult options and not very palatable to either local elected officials or local citizens and taxpayers. But they must be faced given that funds from higher levels of government can no longer be guaranteed to continue at the same levels as in the past.

One indicator of the relative "autonomy" of each level of government is the percentage of "own receipts" received by that level of government, defined as total current receipts minus current transfers from other levels of government. In other words, "own receipts" at the sub-national level represents the amount of all sources of revenue received directly at the sub-national level, *except* revenue from inter-governmental transfers.

The data presented in **Chart 5** shows the level of own receipts as a percentage of total receipts at the sub-national level for 1980 and 1994. The trend across OECD countries has been mixed over the period, with just under two-thirds of the 19 countries depicted showing an increase in the percentage of own receipts and the rest showing moderate to steep decreases.

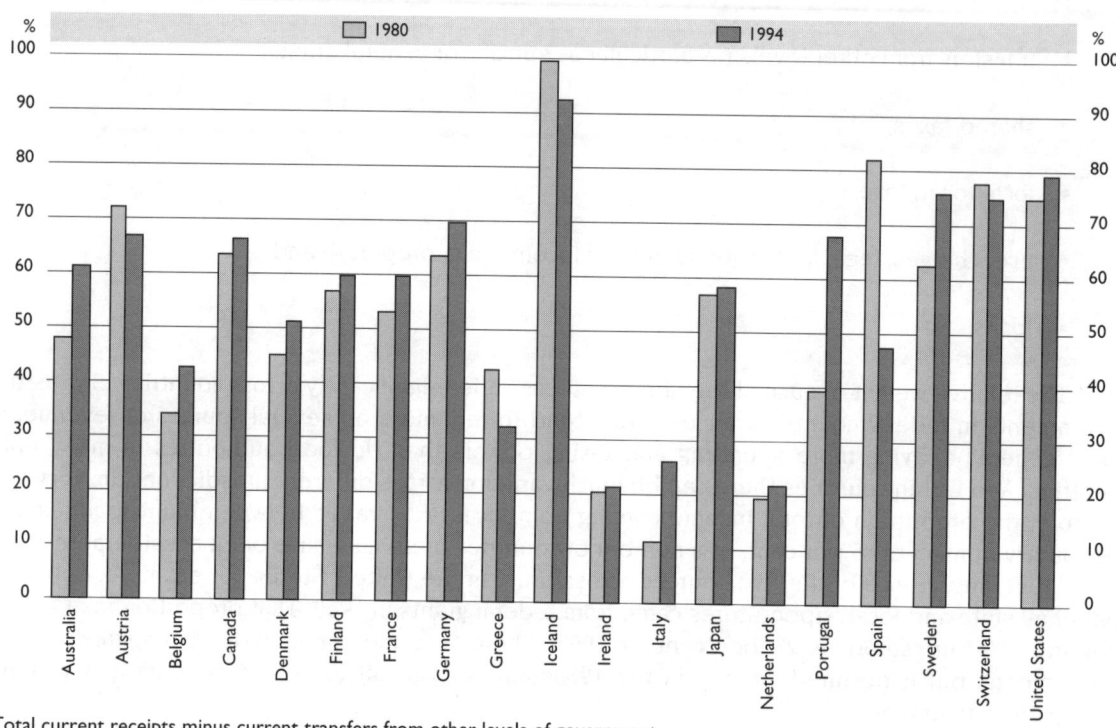

◆ Chart 5. *"Own receipts[1] at the sub-national level[2] as a percentage of total sub-national receipts (1980/1994)[3]*

1. Total current receipts minus current transfers from other levels of government.
2. Sub-national includes *all* levels of government below the central level, except in the cases of Switzerland, Austria, Germany, and Canada, where data for the state/ provincial level are *not* included.
3. For Ireland, Portugal, Spain and the United States, the chart uses 1980/1993 figures.

Source: OECD National Accounts.

Fiscal federalism is concerned with the inter-governmental coincidence of abilities and responsibilities, i.e. the relative taxation and spending powers of each level of government. Its focus is on fiscal relationships among decision-makers at those different levels and it demonstrates the extent to which central and sub-national government budgets are interdependent. Fiscal federalism is not limited to federal countries. Some federal countries have very centralised fiscal systems and in some unitary countries local governments can largely finance their own needs from their own receipts, but there is much variety.

- In **Australia** fiscal patterns are typified by large flows of funds from the federal level (which collects about three-quarters of all tax revenue) to the states (which ceased to impose separate income taxes in 1942).

- In **Canada**, both federal and provincial governments transfer very large sums of money to other levels of government. The collection of revenues is far more centralised than is the delivery of services. There are, therefore, perceived problems of political visibility for the levels of government responsible for collecting taxes, while more local levels of government are seen as providing the services.

In unitary countries, sub-national levels are often largely dependent on one main source of local tax revenue -- which is frequently a property tax. This can be a problem for local governments if there is too much dependence on it as it lacks buoyancy and may become a source of strain during periods

> In the **United States**, "project grants" give federal officials a lot of discretion in shaping state and local activities, but a much larger volume of funds are "formula grants" where the amount going to each state is established by a formula. This gives little discretion in the **amount** of the grant, but allows the federal government to require plans for how the funds will be used. Almost 90 per cent of these formula grants are for narrow, "categorical" purposes and there is active negotiation between levels of government on the terms of the grants. Total federal aid to states has recently reached historically high levels -- with recent increases coming primarily from grants passed on to individuals, especially for medical care for the poor. In 1980, aid to individuals comprised 40 per cent of all federal grants, and this figure had risen to over 60 per cent by 1995. (Medicaid is now the largest grant programme, jointly financed by federal and state government, but administered at the state level.) The effect of the shift from programme grants to aid for individuals is that state and local governments have less discretion over how federal funds are spent, although there has been a big increase in the number of waivers allowed by the federal government to allow states more flexibility in the design of social programmes -- although this can be a costly and complex process.

when the economy is less strong. In the Nordic countries, however, local income taxes are predominant and local governments' tax-raising powers are considerably greater than those of the states in many federal countries:

- In **Denmark**, in 1994, counties and municipalities received 62 per cent and 54 per cent respectively of their total financing from local taxes. There are no formal limits on local income tax rates but they are negotiated between the national association of local authorities and the central government in the interests of overall economic control.

- In **Sweden**, less than 20 per cent of local governments' revenues stem from national government grants, the balance coming from local taxes and user fees.

- In **Greece**, the freedom of local authorities to finance their own activities has increased in the last decade (by increasing local rates, borrowing in the private market, or entering into partnerships with other public or private bodies), and the range of activities in which they can engage has also expanded so that the main limitation on them now is local taxpayer resistance to higher rates.

- In **Japan**, local taxation is the most important single source of local revenue, although it has declined (from 44 per cent in 1988 to 35 per cent in 1993).

a) Transfers

> The role of the federal government in transferring resources to states and localities is more complicated, both in theory and in practice, than is often recognised.
> *Economic Report of the President to Congress*, Washington DC, February 1996.

Government revenues, broadly speaking, are characterised by the centre's prime position as tax recipient and hence its key responsibility for transfers to sub-national levels of government. Central governments have, however, recently been obliged to carefully review the nature and size of transfers -- because of the huge amounts involved and because of overall fiscal pressures. This is partly due to the resources currently needed for servicing debts -- in **Canada**, for example, the federal government currently spends 36 per cent of its revenues on debt-servicing charges, and the provinces an average of 14 per cent.

Reducing transfers, as opposed to "own purpose" expenditures, can be a less painful way for central government to balance the national budget. But transfers are often the largest of the various sources of revenue available to sub-national governments, so any such moves can have some very significant consequences for overall patterns of sub-national revenues:

- transfer payments may be reduced;
- expenditure functions may be added without an equivalent transfer of revenues.

Both of these phenomena have been observed in a number of Member countries in recent years. Both bring the risk of relocating financial problems from one level of government to another without, necessarily, any improvement to the basic fiscal malaise of the public sector as a whole. But both may also be justified by central government to the extent that efficiency gains can be expected when functions are decentralised -- if service levels remain the same.

Transfers are used to varying degrees in all countries to fill the gap between the revenue-raising capacities and the expenditure requirements of the lower levels. In this sense they provide a crude measure of the degree of dependence of sub-national governments, although the nature of the transfers between levels (their degree of specificity and the type and number of conditions attached) are equally important in determining the degree of local autonomy. Following are some examples:

- **Italy** is rather centralised in financial terms: transfers represented around 90 per cent of regional funding, 75 per cent of that of the provinces, and 55 per cent for the municipalities in 1991.

- **Spain**, despite the growing importance of regional taxation, has Autonomous Communities (regions) which depend on the centre for a very substantial part of their revenue (65 per cent in 1994) -- half of which is in the form of general rather than specific transfers. The municipalities enjoy greater autonomy in that they control more of their own income (50 to 60 per cent from own sources). In order to balance the autonomy and taxation capacity of the Communities, a reform of the financial system has started (September 1996) with agreements between the State and Autonomous Communities on "fiscal accountability".

- **Turkey** took measures in 1984 to significantly increase municipal revenues in both absolute terms and as a share of the national budget. This broadened their tax-base, but real local decision-making authority still remains rather limited.

There are many types of transfer arrangements. They form a continuum in terms of the degree of discretion available to sub-national governments. Some are relatively simple, others involve complex conditions and formulae for determining the amounts to be transferred. The type of grant used can be a critical factor affecting accountability by making vertical lines of responsibility more transparent.

Specific grants are associated with mandatory tasks. They must be spent by the receiving authority for the use identified -- which may be very precise or rather broad. General grants, on the other hand, may be used for any service provided by the authority to which they are granted. Specific grants may be justified when they are for services provided locally on behalf of central government, and where it is seen to be desirable that central government sets minimum standards on locally provided services so as to influence outcomes (e.g. to address equity issues). In some countries their use has grown:

- In **the Netherlands**, specific grants have gradually become the most important source of sub-national government income (from 30 per cent in 1950 to 59 per cent in 1994) although their total number has reduced significantly (from 537 in 1983 to 143 in 1995). At the same time, financial cutbacks at the centre have encouraged attempts to reduce local financial dependence on the centre, and as a result local financing from own sources increased from 4 per cent in 1975 to 11 per cent in 1994.

- In **Australia**, specific purpose grants now account for over 50 per cent of the transfers from the federal to the state level -- a much higher proportion than in the 1980s. At the same time there have been substantial cuts in payments from the federal government, while general revenue sharing has increased.

General grants, understandably, are preferred by sub-national governments. They enhance the freedom of local authorities to exercise discretion with regard to expenditure priorities, although at the same time it is easier to reduce a general grant than to cut individual specific grants. General grants can be either at the discretion of central government or mandatory.

The Council of Europe's Charter of Local Self-Government, recommends that general grants be used wherever possible and a shift in the balance between specific and general grants in favour of the latter is evident in numerous countries including **Finland**, **France** and **Japan**. (In the latter country, 63 per cent of municipal income came from central government grants in 1993 -- but most were "general purpose" allowing for a considerable degree of local discretion). **Norway** also reports a shift from specific to general grants in the last decade in that the number of specific grants has reduced, but at the same time their volume has increased. And in **Sweden**, since 1992 specific grants have been heavily reduced in number and replaced by a single general block grant. The specific grants were often created when local governments took over a specific task from the centre, while the general grants have the sole aim of equalising the financial demands on sub-national governments.

b) *Shared taxes*

Tax sharing is an approach which gives sub-national authorities the right to a share of the yield of certain national taxes. It is an attractive source of revenue to sub-national governments as it is relatively low on administrative costs, and tax sharing agreements have the advantage for sub-national governments of usually reflecting some long-term agreement or constitutional arrangement. At the same time, tax sharing carries the risk that central government will seek to impose some conditions or controls. When there are several shared taxes, each may have a different share going to each level of government. This gives rise to much political debate and negotiation -- in both the vertical sense (re the respective shares of central and sub-national government); and horizontal sense (re the basis of allocation between sub-national units). The following examples come from federal countries, although it is also common in some unitary countries such as the **Netherlands**. **Australia**, **Canada** and **Germany** all share "federal" revenues; many taxes are shared in **Austria** (with rather complex rules for determining the sub-national shares); and in **Mexico**, the states are heavily dependent on revenue-sharing with the centre and must pass on a minimum of 20 per cent of those funds to the municipalities. In the **United States**, there is much sharing of funding between the federal and state levels for certain programmes.

> In **Germany** there are three main shared or "joint" taxes: income tax, corporation tax and value-added tax. Together they account for about 75 per cent of all tax revenues. 15% of income tax goes to local authorities, and the balance is divided equally between the federal and *Land* governments; while the other two taxes are both split equally between the federation and *Länder*. However, there is much variation across the Länder. The Basic Law provides, therefore, that there must be "reasonable" equalisation between the financially weaker and stronger *Länder*. At the local level, 28 per cent of total tax revenue comes from financial equalisation within the *Land*, based on local needs and capacities and aimed at creating equal living standards while also enforcing the political objectives of the *Länder*. In addition some transfers are specific purpose and are passed from the federal to the *Land* level before reaching the municipalities. These provide an element of central influence through co-operative federalism, but this is measured to retain local self-government. Since 1995 the eastern *Länder* have been fully tied into the general federal equalisation system and the structure of revenues will become similar to that in the western *Länder*.

c) *Local (own) taxes*

The extent and nature of exclusive local taxes and the authority to set the rates of those taxes are key factors in the autonomy and accountability of sub-national governments. This is dealt with in the following section, but it is worthy of note here that this is another form of trade-off as more local discretion in this field can hamper the centre's interests in controlling overall tax burdens and aggregate public expenditure. Thus in **Italy**, for example, public expenditure control has been the driving force behind the centralisation of tax powers, especially concerning the regions. And in **Norway**, the proportion of total sub-national revenue from local taxation has been decreasing steadily since 1945, mainly because sub-national government has been given new and costly new responsibilities by the centre -- and this calls for more central transfers to satisfy the goal of providing services of similar scope and quality to all citizens.

d) User charges, fees, and other sources of income

The more widespread adoption of market-type mechanisms, especially in the form of *user charges and fees*, is another factor of growing importance in the autonomy of sub-national governments. Charges for locally provided services are relatively efficient and low on administrative costs, and able to produce quite significant revenues. They can also reduce excess demand for services and improve service quality as customers tend to demand better and more tailored services when they pay for them directly. In the **United States**, user charges accounted for about 14 per cent of total state and local government revenues in 1992.

e) Loans

The discretion afforded sub-national governments to *borrow* (on what markets and for what purposes) is an increasingly significant facet of their need and their ability to manage their own affairs as loans are likely to substitute for government grants. Generally, a case can be made for borrowing to finance capital projects -- especially if they are revenue-earning -- as they usually have a long life, making it reasonable that they be paid for as they are used. In many countries, however, local governments require the authorisation of central government to raise loans. **Iceland**, is one exception to this practice. In **France**, sub-national governments have been free to borrow money wherever they please, including abroad and in foreign currencies, since 1990. In **Ireland**, there are no legal limits on the revenue raising capacities of local authorities, but borrowing must be approved by the relevant minister. The purposes for which long-term borrowing can be incurred are now very limited. In some countries, notably **the United States**, sub-national governments have credit ratings which act as an incentive to perform better.

3. Issues of horizontal and vertical distribution

Strategies relating to the overall public sector budget deficit (and in some cases also level of public sector debt), covering all levels of government, have been developed in a number of countries. Such strategies reflect a perceived need for the public sector to both limit and co-ordinate its borrowings on capital markets both to prevent the public sector from "crowding out" private sector investment and to avoid upward pressure on interest rates. In a number of European Union countries such strategies are reinforced by the criteria set for membership of the European Monetary Union by the Maastricht Treaty. These criteria relate to the level of total public sector deficits and debt.

Such national fiscal strategies clearly have a major impact on the financial relations between national and sub-national governments. In a situation where national governments control or dominate the fiscal position of sub-national governments it is clearly easier to obtain adherence to the strategies. National governments may directly control the budgets of sub-national governments e.g. have power to determine their size, or control directly or indirectly their major revenues. Consultation mechanisms nevertheless exist in most countries but in situations where the national government has less direct control more complex consultation mechanisms may be required.

> In **Germany** a Financial Planning Council, chaired by the Federal Minister of Finance, makes recommendations on the co-ordination of budgets and financial plans of the federal, *Länder* and local governments, although it cannot make any binding decisions. The Council comprises the ministers of finance of the federation and the *Länder*, the Federal Minister of Economics, and representatives of the municipalities. The Bundesbank also participates.

Central grants can be used for equalisation purposes (either openly or implicitly), but many countries have, in addition, established equalisation systems. These may deal with imbalances across governments either vertically between levels or horizontally between different local authorities or states, and may take several forms:

- by having sub-national authorities pay into a fund from which amounts are then transferred to different authorities according to their needs and resources;
- by providing central (or state) government grants to the most needy local authorities;
- by weighting the distribution of tax sharing to allow for differences in costs or fiscal capacities.

The first approach is generally confined to countries where imbalances are not large, but still provides for considerable debate because of its very transparent nature; the second is particularly important in federal countries where there may be wide disparities across federal states.

The following examples illustrate the diversity and complexity associated with equalisation systems:

- **Iceland** has a Municipal Equalisation Fund which provides both block and special grants from central government to municipalities, with the special grants being directed to those with a lower potential for raising revenues.
- **Norway** introduced a system of block grants (General Purpose Grants Scheme) in the 1980s to replace about 50 earmarked grants and become the main instrument for redistributing income. In the 1990s sectoral grants have been amalgamated into a single expenditure equalisation grant (covering health, transport and secondary schools for counties; and primary schools, culture, health and social services for municipalities).
- In **Sweden**, in 1996 a new equalisation system for municipalities and county councils was introduced. Its main components are income equalisation, equalisation of structurally related cost differences, a general block grant and certain transitional rules. The income equalisation system implies a far-reaching equalisation of both municipal and county council taxation revenue. After equalisation, all municipalities and county councils should have incomes corresponding to the national average.
- In the **Netherlands**, general grants come from a Municipal and Provincial Fund which is administered and fed by central government -- in part from national tax revenues, the exact percentage being decided each year.
- **Ireland** is considering moving towards a formula-based method of grant distribution to local authorities but this has not yet been agreed. This is in the context of demands to increase the overall level of local funding and to give more discretion in local revenue raising.
- In **Portugal**, while the central government's Financial Equalisation Fund is the principal single source of local government revenue (a block grant), it now represents only one third of total revenues compared with over one half in 1986 as funds from the European Union have increasingly been used.
- In **Austria**, the Financial Equalisation Act provides for relative stability in fiscal transfers, although this does not prevent ongoing discussion between the Länder and the federal government about the distribution of revenues in the context of a possible restructuring of competences across levels.
- **Australia**'s Commonwealth Grants Commission makes annual recommendations which embody the principle of horizontal equalisation to ensure that each state has the capacity to provide the average standard of state type public services, if it makes the same effort to raise revenue as the states on average and it operates at an average level of efficiency. In each state,

a Local Government Grants Commission allocates federal funds to local governments using an equalisation formula.

- A system of federal transfer payments was introduced in **Canada** in 1957 to ensure equity in public services across the provinces, and in 1982 equalisation transfers were enshrined in the Constitution. These have increased enormously over recent decades, the largest by far being the Canada Health and Social Transfer which relies mostly on federal spending power.

- **Mexico**, which has particularly difficult problems of imbalance across the country and its inhabitants, has recently created a "Municipal Promotion Fund" to help local bodies with the lowest levels of development to receive support directly from the federal government.

- In **Switzerland** the entire equalisation system between the Confederation and the cantons is currently being examined with a view to guaranteeing the principle of subsidiarity and strengthening the financial capacity of the cantons.

The issue of unfunded mandates seems to have become most pronounced in, but not exclusive to, federal or regionalised countries. It has led, for example, to the passing of the Unfunded Mandates Reform legislation in the **United States** in 1995 due to the very significant costs, especially to local governments, of inadequately compensated federal and state mandates. The new legislation restricts, to some extent, the ability of Congress to impose costly mandates on sub-national governments and requires assessment of what those costs are. In **New Zealand**, some unfunded mandating has led to calls for more revenue sharing, but the central government currently prefers to give priority to efficiency improvements in sub-national government as a means of improving their financial position. In **Norway**, municipalities complain of doing more tasks on behalf of central government without a proportional increase in resources. A Committee was, however, set up in 1994 to examine the cost implications of Parliamentary reforms which have to be implemented by local government. It has representatives of all levels of government and aims to test feasibility and to improve consultation. And in **Sweden** the municipalities see the restructuring of public finances, which has given them more tasks and costs, as an acute problem. However, the principle has been established that all transfers of responsibility between the central and municipal levels should be subject to comprehensive financial scrutiny and arrangements.

Finally, the nature and extent of cost-sharing, especially for capital projects, can be an additional significant factor in inter-governmental financial relations. In some countries (e.g. **France, Iceland**), this practice is rather extensive and provides an important opportunity for negotiation.

4. Implications for management

The need to cut back total public expenditure and to reduce public deficits is encouraging many central governments to seriously re-examine the amounts, nature and conditions attached to the often enormous transfers which they make to lower levels of government. Greater inter-dependence and shared responsibilities can promote a more comprehensive view of public sector finances and the broad issues and goals of governance. But downsizing which involves off-loading tasks to sub-national governments and seeking more control over aggregate expenditures may run counter to some of the key objectives of the new public management paradigm aiming to increase flexibility, discretion and responsiveness. Underfunded mandates only displace problems and add to existing mistrust across levels of government. Restructuring responsibilities brings an opportunity for inter-governmental partnership through shared financing and/or agreed goals. This is generally desirable, provided that such arrangements are designed so as to avoid perverse incentives. More attention should, therefore, be directed at the critical intersection of fiscal federalism and performance management. Two examples from the Nordic countries serve to illustrate this point:

- In **Denmark**, the greater use of block grants is reported to have increased the freedom of local authorities to set their own priorities, but within national frameworks and standards. In **Sweden**, specific grants have been largely replaced by general grants and the centre's control of municipalities reduced accordingly. Instructions in the use of grants have been replaced by goal-setting.

Central (or state) governments may *impose* minimum standards on certain local services when they are financed by specific grants -- in the interests of equity and influencing outcomes. But the more widespread use of general rather than specific grants, in many countries, provides opportunities for "more steering and less rowing" by central government. This also, is an incentive for negotiating *agreements* between central and sub-national governments on acceptable national guidelines within which minimum standards may be set. In this context, improvements may also be achieved in the quality of regulation; performance management may be strengthened by comparing targets against results; and encouragement may be given to more rigorous quantitative approaches such as accrual accounting.

The importance of improving the overall transparency of the management of public funds is increasingly recognised across all Member countries. This is also true of national *fiscal strategies*, which encompass all levels of government. This said, inter-governmental systems are, and always will be, in a state of change -- and budgetary strategies must take account of this. The most original attempt, so far, to put the formulation and conduct of fiscal policy in a *legal* framework has been in **New Zealand**. There the 1994 "Fiscal Responsibility Act" introduced a significant strengthening of the reporting requirements on central government and incorporated a long-term orientation to the budget process. Its principles are now being extended to local government.

III. Regulatory reform

Regulation is widely used at all levels of government to carry out public policy, and must therefore be a major component of any comprehensive inter-governmental reform process. Although there is much rhetoric about attempts to rationalise and streamline government regulation, most OECD countries have reformed exclusively at the national level, and started to make progress only during the last few years towards greater regulatory co-ordination and the elimination of regulatory duplication between levels of government.

The regulatory regimes in Member countries are diverse. Some countries share responsibility for regulation across different levels of government, often involving multiple bodies at each level, while others are very centralised, with almost all authority vested in national ministries. However, there appears to be a general movement towards a common middle ground as decentralised countries attempt to reduce duplication and regulatory costs by creating national standards, and centralised countries move towards power-sharing arrangements and a shift of responsibility away from central government.

For instance, in the federal countries: **Australia**'s complex and multi-layered regulatory system has long been a subject of concern with respect to the efficiency of the national economy and the effectiveness of government action. However, considerable efforts have been made to improve co-ordination in rule-making between state and federal levels, including: the adoption of a set of national regulatory principles and guidelines that specify a nationally-consistent assessment process and require the preparation of regulatory impact statements; the emergence of regulatory reform "competition" between the states as each tries to reduce red-tape; and the creation of new institutional structures.

Canada also has a great deal of inter-governmental inter-dependence and collaboration in regulatory affairs. The decentralised regulatory system has led to concern about inter-provincial trade barriers, duplication between provincial and federal regulations, and rising regulatory costs. To tackle these problems, Canada has undergone both a harmonisation and a rationalisation of regulation. In 1995, the Agreement on Internal Trade went into effect, establishing a broad framework for rules of internal trade and reducing barriers and distortions. Both the central government and the provinces have been examining existing regulations and re-justifying their regulatory programmes.

Over the past several decades, **Germany** and the **United States** have experienced a steady centralisation of regulatory authority at the federal level. As the problems confronting *Länder* and states grew in size and complexity, the federal authorities have tended to take responsibility for regulation, a trend supported, in the case of Germany, by membership of the European Union and implementation of European Single Market. Recently, however, both countries have attempted to reverse this trend by decentralising regulatory authority, but it is too early to know how successful these reforms will be.

Although inter-governmental regulatory reform is more visible in federal systems, unitary States have also been addressing the design and implementation of regulations across levels of government. In the **United Kingdom**, local governments play a major regulatory role -- both directly and as an enforcer of national regulations. During the past few years, emphasis has been on improving co-ordination, communication, consultation, and understanding of regulatory impacts at the local level. This has led to the creation of Local Business Partnerships; the adoption by national enforcement agencies of a code based on openness, transparency, and fairness; and the granting of new rights to businesses subjected to enforcement action. In **Japan**, which has a highly centralised regulatory system, there has been a slow transfer of regulatory authority from the national to local level in areas such as agricultural land usage and municipal planning. Pilot programmes have also been developed to test the transfer of responsibility for welfare, public health, and education. In **Finland**, there has been a general movement to reduce the number of regulations by the central government on municipalities and to improve the quality of those regulations that remain.

Regulatory reform has become a high priority in a number of Member countries, but comprehensive attempts at reform that cut across levels of government are rare. It is in this area of inter-governmental relations, however, that significant gains can be made through better communication and co-ordination between levels of government, resulting in more effective and cost-efficient regulatory action.

IV. Human resource management

In most countries (**Australia**, **Norway**, **Sweden**, and the **United Kingdom**, are particular examples) there is no formal civil service bridging all levels of government, but a different system at each level of government. Other countries, such as **France**, **Germany, and Iceland**, have established civil service structures which grant civil servants at all levels a number of protections and subject them to certain laws. National labour legislation may also be applicable to sub-national public services, although this may be an area of dispute where sub-national governments also have powers in this.

An area of human resource policy that has generally received little attention is that of public service mobility between levels of government. Few countries seem to encourage or even allow civil servants to move easily between central and sub-national levels of government, or vice-versa.

C. ISSUES

The issues which need to be addressed by central governments in improving the management of inter-governmental relations are as multi-faceted, complex and inter-dependent as the relationships themselves. For the purposes of this report, the issues are dealt with in two ways. Firstly, as a set of *tensions and challenges* which reflect the fact that there is both a top-down and a bottom-up perspective on all of these matters; and secondly as some specific *implications*, for managers in central government, of the evolution which is taking place, since they are the prime clients of this work.

I. Tensions and challenges

A trait noted by several countries, is that sub-national orders of government may be better disposed than national governments to adopt features of the "new public management" such as service quality initiatives, the use of market-type mechanisms and performance management. Reasons for this, other than the very nature of many of the tasks involved, include the fact that numerous relatively small units encourage competition and choice; and that the shorter distance between those holding office and citizens is generally good for responsiveness, accountability and performance. There are, therefore, significant incentives and opportunities for sub-national governments to practice the rhetoric of "working better, costing less".

In fact, in both federal and unitary countries, the sub-national (and especially local) level is serving as a valuable "laboratory" for innovation with public management methods. In **Japan**, for example, nationwide improvements in health and social security programmes have been based on lessons drawn from local government experiences. Local authority innovations have also provided the basis for subsequent national legislation (e.g. in the **United States**); and have been used to develop similar exercises in other local authorities (as in the **Nordic** countries and **Switzerland**). In **Canada**, such innovation is encouraged by central government (especially in the health sector) -- but they can also be the fruit of purely local effort (as, for example, in **Germany**).

This disposition for innovation and entrepreneurship, is not, however, present to the same degree everywhere in sub-national government. The same factors which promote efficiency, effectiveness and responsiveness locally can also, therefore, reinforce inequalities. This presents some serious challenges to both the vertical and horizontal dimensions of inter-governmental management. The centre seeks to ensure an adequate measure of overall control so as to protect a coherent approach to policies; while sub-national governments seek autonomy so as to be fully responsive to local preferences and needs.

These objectives may be in conflict. However, inter-governmental management may be able to identify the sources of tension and their implications for central management. These may be seen as a set of dichotomies between:

- autonomy and direction;
- variety and uniformity; and
- responsiveness and efficiency.

Taken together, these reflect the polarisation of inter-governmental issues between the centre and other levels of government.

1. Discretion or direction?

> In the comparative study of inter-governmental relations, the degree of autonomy and discretion of sub-national governments, in particular local governments, *vis-à-vis* national authorities has traditionally been regarded as the most important characteristic distinguishing different national systems.
>
> Goetz and Margetts in *Responsive Government*, OECD, 1996.

Granting more discretion to lower hierarchical levels is an integral part of the public management currently in vogue. In the context of this report, it is the granting of authority to sub-national levels of government to make decisions on matters which affect them, and the implications of that decentralisation for central management bodies, which is of principal interest. This embraces both the transfer of responsibility for a new task to a lower level and the freeing-up of higher level control over how existing tasks are carried out.

A key issue is how to adjust inter-governmental relations so that national objectives for the public sector as a whole are not compromised. There are *trade-offs* between allowing more discretion to a lower level of government and maintaining a steering capacity at the higher level. The benefits of more autonomy for sub-national government have to be weighed with care against the risks to national goals, and the potential costs to the system of governance as a whole through loss of coherence. Growing inter-dependence adds to the complexity of inter-governmental relations.

These concerns raise basic questions about the most appropriate roles for each level of government; which mechanisms perform best; and which are most needed in the interests of good governance. For the purposes of this discussion, three aspects of the discretion enjoyed by sub-national levels of government *vis-à-vis* the centre are dealt with:

   a) the types of autonomy;

   b) the nature of the responsibility (i.e. mandatory, shared, optional);

   c) the amount of financial discretion available.

a)   Types of autonomy

There is enormous variety and complexity in how power relations may operate between different levels of government. Some systems put emphasis on the "division" of powers, and others rely more on "joint exercises" in which all levels involved are restricted in their scope of action. Three basic "typologies" of autonomy may be constructed. All three may be present in a country at the same time, but operating in different sectors. They are as follows:

- considerable sub-national discretion within a broadly defined *framework* of powers and duties;

- emphasis on *interaction* based on discussion and mutual influence;

- an *agency* relationship wherein sub-national governments help to implement national policies by adapting them to local circumstances.

The Nordic countries, and those federal countries where local self-government is guaranteed in the Constitution, belong most closely to the first category. In **Germany** about 75 per cent of all federal statutes are directly addressed to and implemented by the *Länder* and municipalities and the Basic Law includes the principle of *Länder* sovereignty which implies that laws passed by the *Land* parliaments should not contravene federal legislation. If it does, the federal law takes precedent. In the Nordic countries the municipalities implement national policies but are largely autonomous in doing so. This is the case in **Finland** and **Norway** (where central government cannot instruct local government) and in **Sweden**, where the two main sub-national levels (municipalities and counties) are both vested by the Constitution with great freedom.

France belongs more to the second configuration. There is no hierarchy between the three levels of sub-national government (which have no legislatory powers), and where many responsibilities and much financing is shared across different levels; and in **Austria**, the amount of local government autonomy allowed varies across the *Länder*, but generally the system is less decentralised than in most other federal countries (giving a higher degree of homogeneity). There is also, however, a high degree of constitutional protection, particularly through the Constitutional Court, to safeguard the rather complex divisions of competence between federal and provincial lawmakers.

Japan and the **United Kingdom** may be considered to follow more the third approach.

b)   Nature of responsibility

The challenge here is to design mechanisms which allow for the effective distribution of responsibilities and funds between levels of government, while at the same time providing flexibility and financial accountability. This is a factor of many things including the extent to which responsibilities are mandatory or optional, clearly defined or indistinct, exclusive or shared with another level, and how many levels exist.

The extent to which any given level of government is obliged to carry out certain tasks might be expected to reflect the extent to which its operations are financially dependent upon a higher tier of government. In **Sweden** however (where the level of local "own receipts" is rather high) about 80 per cent of total local government expenditure is for mandatory assignments of government and parliamentary policies -- the number of which has significantly increased since 1977. And in **Ireland**, where many non-local government bodies have mandatory rather than optional functions (e.g. health, environment), debate on more devolution of responsibilities from central to local government is made more complex as the big need now is for local authorities to become a focus for partnership and co-ordination.

Another consideration is the prevalence of tasks which are shared by different levels rather than exclusive to one level. In **Germany**, the concept of co-operative federalism provides for tasks to be undertaken jointly by the federal and *Länder* levels. But the joint decision-making which this calls for brings problems of fixing clear priorities -- and avoiding excessive federal interference. During the 1980s there was an increase in distributional conflicts among levels of government and between local governments and local government is seen to have become more politicised due to co-operative federalism.

In **France**, there is a large number of very small communities which have less capacity to fulfil tasks and hence have less autonomy. The degree of autonomy in spending depends on whether services are mandatory or not and this is a factor of the size of the community.

Another consideration is the extent to which there is clear definition of the responsibilities of each level in the constitution or whether that is left indistinct. The latter can encourage healthy debate and consultation processes but also carries the risk of conflict and tension resulting from an adversarial rather than a collaborative approach. In **Norway**, for example, there is no stipulation in the Constitution nor any general legislation on how government functions are to be divided between levels. The distribution which results is a mix of parliamentary decisions and local initiatives and a recurrent theme of debate. And in **Canada**, the 1867 Constitution sets out a separation of powers between the federal and provincial tiers of government, but it is silent, or does not clearly define which level should intervene, on some important current issues such as job training. A 1991 study argued that there is almost no duplication, but the First Ministers agreed, in 1994, to address the issues of overlap and duplication in their "Efficiency of the Federation Initiative".

The number of *tiers* of government, is another factor in the extent to which problems of duplication and overlap of functions between levels are likely to occur. While frequently mentioned by federal countries, they do not have a monopoly on this malaise. In **Belgium**, given that there are five levels of administration in such a relatively small country, some overlapping of competences seems to be inevitable but there is awareness of this problem and a rather clear division of responsibilities -- partly attributable to the desire of each Community to have a guarantee of autonomy in specific spheres.

The principle of *subsidiarity* has been developed in the context of the European Union to deal with issues about which is the most appropriate level of government at which tasks should be carried out. While its meaning is not entirely clear, it basically holds that functions should be placed at the lowest level able to perform them. In other words, it reflects a political philosophy which seeks to locate decision-making as close as possible to the citizen. Some countries report that this principle is increasingly cited as grounds for a review of the division of functions - between both the local and regional levels and the regional and national levels.

c)   Degree of financial discretion

The main determinants of autonomy are in the financial realm. The parameters involved here include the:

- proportion of revenue which is locally generated;

- limits to, and conditions on, the resources received from other levels of government (especially the balance between specific and general grants); and

- powers of sub-national governments to raise taxes, set tax rates, apply user charges, and borrow money.

As discussed in the section dealing with financial and fiscal relations, there is a significant tendency for central government to give sub-national governments more discretion by switching from specific grants to general ones, and there is a growing interest in the ability of sub-national governments to raise money on the capital markets. The focus here is on the powers accorded to sub-national governments to define their own tax levels.

The difficult challenges involved in this may be illustrated by the case of **Canada**. Reductions in the growth of federal transfers have squeezed the provinces which have often responded by putting fiscal pressure on the municipalities. Provinces exert some control over local borrowing and all aspects of the property tax base, including its rates, but costs and demands for municipal services have increased a lot. Municipalities are expected to deliver services mandated by other levels, control their costs, and also finance them. This pressure is exacerbated by differentials in staff pay between the federal, provincial and local levels.

In the Nordic countries the situation varies as follows:

- In **Denmark**, municipalities are free to determine their own level of taxation as well as the level of services to be provided, but they must comply with legislative regulation on minimum standards. There are no formal mechanisms through which central government can influence the levels of taxation or expenditure sub-nationally. The main means by which the centre "controls" local governments are through negotiation and agreements with associations of county and municipal councils.

- In **Finland,** municipalities raise income taxes and are free to define levels of taxation; they may issue local regulations but do not have full regulatory powers; and may decide on their own staffing levels.

- In **Iceland**, the level of local income and property tax and of other public levies must be within limits prescribed by central government but these give local authorities some latitude as to maximum and minimum levels.

- In **Norway**, the right of counties and municipalities to levy taxes is limited to maximum and minimum rates determined by Parliament each year. In practice all local authorities levy the maximum rate and this lack of differentiation has been perceived as diluting local financial accountability. There is some municipal dissatisfaction as although they have considerable discretion over fund allocation within the total amount transferred, they have no control over what the total amount is. But there is a trend to more municipal independence over how money is spent locally.

- In **Sweden**, all four levels of government have the right to tax their citizens. The municipal and county levels have the right to set the local tax rate in the form of a percentage of personal income. All other tax related decisions and administration are handled by the central government.

In **France,** sub-national governments enjoy considerable autonomy. They have some latitude in setting tax rates which leads to substantial disparities in local tax rates from one area to another. Since 1979 State grants have gradually shifted from being specific to general. In **the Netherlands**, changes to municipal taxes require the approval of central government; and in **Ireland**, local tax powers are limited to levying a property tax (but not on residential property).

In the **United Kingdom** a system of "capping" operates. Where the central government considers that a local authority's budget for a year is excessive, or represents an excessive increase over the previous year, a maximum or "cap" can be set. It must be either agreed by the authority concerned or approved by the House of Commons. It requires that the local authority reduces its budget to conform with the maximum and makes commensurate reductions in its council tax.

2. Variety or uniformity?

Decentralisation presumes that a degree of variety is healthy. Marketisation introduces competition and choice to public services in the interests of efficiency and responsiveness, irrespective of which level of government is involved. In many Member countries both decentralisation and marketisation are taking place to some degree at the same time. This may result in widening disparities between areas and between individuals in the quality and quantity of services provided. Decentralisation and marketisation have, therefore, encouraged governments to move away from seeking *uniform and stable* national standards, and towards desirable *minimum* levels of service.

If central government is to monitor performance effectively and retain control over aggregate public expenditures across levels of government, it must develop new steering and reporting systems -- at the same as it marketises and decentralises. Without such tools it cannot ensure policy co-ordination and coherence. This challenge to redesign the information and accountability systems is the key factor in contemporary inter-governmental management and is dealt with further in the next section of this report. Harnessing computer technology and revising management processes and instruments are essential if this challenge is to be met effectively. If not, administrative costs may rise, transparency decline, and unethical behaviour be encouraged.

Few countries have as yet faced up squarely to the management challenges of seeking a happier marriage between differentiation (responsiveness and flexibility) and uniformity. Moves to more use of targets, standards and guidelines go in the right direction but their design and application must be accompanied by adequate consultation processes.

3. *Responsiveness or efficiency?*

Improving responsiveness and efficiency are two cornerstones of decentralisation. But, at least in the context of local level "rationalisation", there is an inherent incompatibility between increasing the size of units of government to achieve economies of scale, and reducing their size to shorten distances between citizens and elected representatives. There is no optimum size, but over recent decades many countries have encouraged significant amalgamation of small local authorities with a view to providing more and better services at the lowest level of government. Such restructuring has often been related to the growing range of responsibilities at the local level and the need for units of a sufficiently large size to employ suitably specialised staff. In this context, there has been a reaction in some countries to improve the quality of local democracy by facilitating citizen participation in finding good local solutions (for example, "district committees" in **Sweden**).

The challenge, therefore, is to find the size of unit and number of levels which can at the same time meet economic criteria and satisfy the need for responding to specific local demands. Thus, for example:

- In **Denmark**, the move to restructure and reduce the number of local authorities was driven by the principle of having municipalities with sufficient population for an efficient primary school system, and counties the right size for the efficient running of hospitals.

- In **Norway**, there is debate about amalgamation in the context of a wider range of municipal responsibilities, need for economies of scale, and a grant distribution system that favours the smallest municipalities. (There was a wave of amalgamations from the late 1950s which reduced the number of municipalities by about 40 per cent.)

- In **Sweden**, the sharp increase in the range of tasks carried out by municipalities resulted in many municipalities being too small to bear the costs. As a result amalgamations (some imposed) took place in the 1950s-60s.

- In **New Zealand**, the number of territorial local authorities was reduced from over 200 to 74 in 1989 by a Local Government Commission using a set of demographic, social, cultural, administrative and efficiency criteria.

- In **Germany**, extensive administrative and territorial reform in the western *Länder* between 1965 and 1977 aimed at creating bigger units with more administrative capacity and more capable of a wide range of services. Municipalities reduced in number from 24 000 to 8 500.

- In the **United Kingdom**, a major process of reorganisation has removed a tier of government in Scotland and Wales and in some parts of England. This has changed the size of some local authorities and reduced their number, with the aim of improving local government administration, providing better value for money, and improving authorities' responsiveness to their citizens.

In **Iceland**, amalgamation is seen as part of the process of decentralisation in that both the Union of Local Authorities and the central government see it as a prerequisite to any further modifications in the division of responsibility between central and local government. In this context, territorial fragmentation may be said to support centralisation The number of local authorities has been reduced from 229 in 1950, to 171 in 1994, but attempts to impose amalgamation have not met with great success. As a result there are many co-operative bodies which enhance efficiency, but may also blur lines of accountability.

This solution is also favoured in **France**, where the very large number of local units is detrimental to achieving economies of scale. Co-operation is encouraged between local authorities, particularly for the provision of basic services such as water supply and sewerage. This is also the case in **Finland**, where there has been little success in merging municipalities, so joint municipal boards are used for functions which are too extensive or expensive for a single municipality; and in the **Netherlands**, where inter-municipal co-operation has been the preferred option for dealing with regional problems and there has been much debate about the minimum population size for municipalities with respect to the quality of local services.

In both approaches, information technology can play a key role in bridging the gap between responsiveness and efficiency by enhancing transparency and communication.

Recent Developments in Norway

Norway is a relatively small, consensus-oriented country where much emphasis is now being placed on informal mechanisms and more negotiation is taking place. This is in part due to the **1992 Local Government Act**, which seeks to balance effective local democracy and regard for national control. The Act reflects considerable debate over the *raison d'être* of local government, and is in part based on the experiences of a "Free Municipalities" experiment. The view of the centre tends to be that the local level is primarily a service delivery system, therefore the key task is to make it as efficient as possible. The other view is that, while service provision is important, local government is legitimate in its own right as an essential part of the democratic system.

The main objectives of the Act are to strengthen sub-national autonomy while establishing conditions that enable local authorities to become efficient suppliers of services. This is being achieved by giving them more freedom to organise their activities based on local needs and by reducing the centre's supervision and control. This has involved, for example, abolishing the requirement for central approval of local budgets.

II. Implications for managers at the centre

The ongoing challenge to effective inter-governmental relations is to monitor and manage the balance between the above tensions. For central governments to rise to this challenge, requires judicious use and regular adjustment of the instruments of control, co-ordination, consultation and accountability. These, the key tools determining the shape of inter-governmental relations, are dealt with in turn below.

Improving the efficiency of public services requires those in charge at each level to have clearly defined objectives, adequate freedom of action in management, and for results to be regularly assessed.

Marcel Pochard, Public Management Committee, March 1996.

1. *Control*

Decentralisation is not only about transferring tasks and resources from one level of government to another. It is also about reducing and changing the nature of involvement by central government in the tasks performed by sub-national authorities. The nature and number of controls operating across levels of government are key factors in the autonomy debate. But control is not an easy term to define. It has many interpretations across administrative and political cultures; particularly according to whether one is in control or being controlled.

There are two basic types of control: performance-based and administration- or rule-based. Both have their role in the present climate which favours managerial flexibility tempered with financial constraint. On the one hand controls become less strict, on the other limits must be set and adhered to.

a) Performance-based control

There is growing recognition that it is desirable to move away from detailed rigid regulation and financial control and towards managing for results. Performance-based controls focus on output and process. This involves merging the objectives and techniques of financial and performance management. And, perhaps even more than within central government, this is particularly pertinent to the management of inter-governmental relations. At the same time sub-national governments themselves have, in a number of countries, started to develop performance indicators and regular reporting practices on quality management which could serve as useful examples at all levels of government.

Specific earmarked grants are becoming less common in favour of general grants. This shift provides the incentive and opportunity for central and sub-national governments to consult more on appropriate guidelines and minimum standards. It also helps to achieve agreement on for which functions a high degree of national uniformity or supervision is necessary; and those where more account should be taken of local or regional priorities.

In particular, the opportunities for benchmarking and better review of implementation facilitate smoother inter-governmental relations provided that there are clear lines of accountability and appropriate consultation. The following examples illustrate some of the developments in this field:

- In **Australia**, a Steering Committee for the Review of Commonwealth/State Service Provision has published its first two reports (1995 and 1997) containing much performance data (on both efficiency and effectiveness) for key social services. The new focus is on monitoring outcomes rather than inputs or outputs.

- In **Canada**, national standards exist, or are being developed, in a number of sectors and the standards are being reviewed for their relevance. Provincial and other stakeholders are increasingly being involved when these are formulated. At the provincial/local level, although there are already often detailed performance standards for municipalities to obtain provincial grants, an issue is how to focus provincial controls more on quality and performance mechanisms.

- In **Ireland**, a framework of performance indicators has been suggested to local authorities and their role in setting objectives underlined. It is felt that less central involvement in detailed approvals gives more time for maintaining an overview and monitoring standards throughout the local government system.

- In **Denmark**, there is much concern with quality standards and the Ministry of Local Government publishes a yearly set of national statistics on service standards, productivity and output levels which are used as a benchmark for local decisions. Service and quality objectives are set involving citizens. Performance initiatives have been developed at the local level, without central monitoring or control. There is some concern over disparities in service levels from one part of the country to another.

- In the **Netherlands**, new methods of performance monitoring are being examined with less focus on details and more on self-regulation. Some local authorities use performance measures and budgeting is increasingly being based on results using comparisons of costs and benefits between municipalities.

- In **Norway**, the performance monitoring system is still being developed and service standard objectives are seen as an integral part of performance management reform. Local governments are required to supply much information to central ministries but, as yet, there is little systematic analysis of data designed for comparing performance or productivity -- either across time or local authorities. There is debate on whether or not to introduce national minimum standards. (Some sectors have minimum legal standards, others have recommended standards.) A recent tendency (especially in health and education) is to use charters and guarantees which clarify the legal rights of individuals to specific services.

- In **Finland**, minimum standards for services are usually specified, and recent reforms have opened the door to the possibility of some variation in services between municipalities.

- In **Iceland** contract management is being developed to give more freedom from government rules and regulations in return for more managerial responsibility using performance indicators.

- In **Italy**, the crisis in public finances has created more interest in performance. Sector-specific agreements are now being signed between central and regional governments which establish priorities, quantify funding levels, set completion times, and assign tasks to each level of government.

- In **Sweden**, detailed rules on how to carry out activities have been replaced by sectoral goals set by the centre as broad guidelines and supplemented by specific targets able to be monitored for results. Municipalities can decide what means to use to achieve the objectives. The new central government funding system combines numerous special grants for specific purposes into a general grant, thereby reducing the restrictions imposed by central government and allowing local priorities to determine how the money will be spent. But at the same time the switch has been linked to a general reduction in central grants to municipalities.

- In the **United Kingdom**, the independent Audit Commission has developed a set of indicators for measuring the performance of local government service provision. Councils must publish details of how they perform in terms of these indicators and the Commission publishes comparative data annually.

- In the **United States**, "performance partnerships" between the federal and state/local governments are increasingly being used to promote inter-governmental agreement on goals, performance measures, and the means to achieve them. In Oregon, for example, a memorandum of understanding has been signed between federal, state and local officials aimed at identifying benchmarks to improve service delivery -- and many critical indicators are now measuring performance against agreed targets and standards. At the same time, federal agencies are giving their state counterparts more freedom in how to spend federal money in exchange for commitment to be accountable for achieving measurable results.

The important relationship between performance management and accountability is discussed later under the heading of "accountability".

b)   Administrative control

At the same time as the above managerial changes are taking place, there remain, to varying degrees across countries, more traditional forms of institutional oversight of sub-national governments, which put the emphasis on legality and regularity -- but also the appropriateness of actions. The institutions involved comprise: Parliaments, which set frameworks for action and have the authority to make investigations; central management bodies, in particular Ministries of Finance and of the Interior (or their equivalents) which exercise considerable supervision over the activities of sub-national governments; and various forms of more or less independent bodies charged with jurisdictional control. The latter is primarily in the hands of independent courts exercising *ex ante* rather than *a priori* control.

There are many modes of administrative control in OECD countries. The nature of vertical monitoring is evolving -- generally away from detailed interference in local affairs and towards broader policy orientation. In the **United Kingdom**, for example, the Audit Commission appoints to each local authority an independent auditor who has responsibilities in relation to financial regularity and value-for-money. The existence of a form of guardianship (*tutelle*) between central and sub-national governments, where it remains, is being challenged, as for example with the evolution of prefect-type institutions. In countries, such as **Belgium** and **Spain** where there has been major structural reform of the public sector, the process has been accompanied by a move away from the traditional techniques of control set up in a more centralised framework. Jurisdictional controls are also changing in that, along with checking the "regularity" of actions, increasingly there is also a concern for results and performance. Such control reinforces proportionality and cost/benefit assessment.

The notion of "subsidiarity" is relevant in federal countries such as **Switzerland** where the increase of shared responsibilities has, over time, blurred the division of tasks, and **Canada**, where the appropriate role of the federal government is being reconsidered in the context of providing services at the level best able to respond to the needs of the public.

The place of deconcentrated administration in the control of sub-national governments

Relationships between prefectural-type institutions, deconcentrated and decentralised administrations vary depending on the country. The prime function of deconcentrated administrations has never, however, been to exert guardianship (*tutelle*) over sub-national governments. In **France**, there is a strict separation between the two. Prior to the 1982-3 reforms, the prefect had *tutelle* over sub-national governments. Since then the only type of control exercised over sub-national governments has been jurisdictional -- but they do not have the right to contest local actions by the central government.

In other countries, control relationships between sub-national governments and deconcentrated administration may be more complex in that their respective areas of responsibility are not always clear. This seems to be particularly the case in countries where the prefectural tradition is not strong. In **Ireland**, for example, while Boards are part of the central government administration, some members are nominated by local authorities, and this local presence gives the Boards a certain influence in local policy-making. In **Finland**, the district administrations of the central government participate in the monitoring of local governments and there is a wide range of shared responsibilities, which favours inter-action. Similarly, in **Sweden**, sectoral agencies are responsible for monitoring and evaluating municipal activities.

These differences raise the question of the extent to which deconcentrated administrations might, in the future, be more involved in some form of supervision of local government. Given the methods of performance management and use of general grants often applied by agencies, greater coherence between central and sub-national policies may be built upon the experience of the deconcentrated administrations. But any such roles should take account of the extent to which the authority is directly exercised by a democratically elected body.

Less hierarchical forms of monitoring, which are often informal and sometimes encouraged by joint financing, also exist in many countries. In **Denmark** and **Sweden** for example, vertical controls are traditionally weak and local government associations have a partnership type of relationship with the centre which encourages forms of "self-monitoring". In **Japan**, while governors are elected, they act as agents of central government in implementing mandated functions. And in **Switzerland** the principle of "confederal courtesy" imposes considerable constraint on the federal level in its relations with the cantons, but without excluding an influence by the centre over cantonal decisions, for example in the parliamentary consultation procedures between the Confederation and the cantons. And sometimes controls are externalised, as in **Canada** with joint financing for example, where control functions are increasingly given to a third party rather than the administration.

One of the new challenges in this area is how to control the "privatised" and private actors which are playing an increasing role in local governance. The rights of the traditional controlling institutions in these cases remain unclear.

2. *Co-ordination and consultation*:

a)   The need for more co-ordination and consultation:

The more complex distribution of tasks between levels of government demands better policy co-ordination. Relations based on collaboration between levels rather than on direct vertical controls also call for improved co-ordination mechanisms. Traditional control mechanisms (themselves being significantly modified) are often no longer sufficient to guarantee the coherence of the whole system. Thus, co-ordination is directly related to both the "style" of the relationship between levels, which is often evolving towards more collaboration and the systems of "control" which operate.

The less directive nature of current modes of management in most Member countries, suggests that the sub-national perspective should be taken more into account to make public sector activities more coherent and policy more relevant to real needs. The proliferation of more-or-less independent actors involved in implementing public policies also produces a greater need for co-ordination.

The creation of new levels of government may reflect efforts to enhance governance through responsiveness, but can also add to already complex inter-governmental relations. The founding of the European Union, for example, calls for considerable co-ordination at both the infra- and supra-national levels, particularly for managing regional funds. And in the federal countries, where there is a particular risk of excessive fragmentation and overlap, co-ordination remains a key challenge.

More effective co-ordination mechanisms may thus be justified on several grounds:

- to help clarify broad national goals;
- to bring diverse actors together around compatible goals and programmes;
- to benefit from the local experiences which abound when responsibilities are decentralised.

It is difficult to establish a direct correlation between the degree of (de)centralisation and the need for co-ordination. The dilemma is how to allow sub-national authorities to freely exercise their rights and avoid divergent actions harmful to existing coherence. No countries escape this problem. The co-ordination mechanisms which result vary according to the type of inter-governmental relationships.

b)   Duplication

Different levels of government are liable to have policies which overlap, duplicate or even compete. Although the problem occurs to different degrees across Member countries, as it is closely related to the way in which responsibilities are divided. Duplication appears more frequently in sectors such as education, health and environment where responsibilities tend to be spread more across different levels of government. In **France**, for example, sub-national governments are responsible for the construction and maintenance of schools, while education policy remains a central government responsibility. In **Spain**, there are numerous "grey zones" where the State and the Autonomous Communities are both involved, although there has been recent progress towards resolving some of these overlaps. In the **Netherlands**, duplication problems are reported to have been largely avoided by regular communication between levels of government -- although it is admitted that the information flows are complicated as there are many participants.

There are a number of current efforts to address these problems. In **Australia**, for example, an Audit Commission has recently examined the extent of duplication across levels of government; **Finland** is currently making efforts to clarify responsibilities at all levels; and in **Canada**, there is a public perception that there is wasteful overlap and duplication between federal and provincial governments.

In 1994 First Ministers agreed on an "Efficiency of the Federation Initiative" in which areas for increased administrative efficiencies were identified, objectives agreed, and a timetable to address the issues of overlap and duplication negotiated.

The problem of duplication is not present to the same extent in all countries, but is a particular issue in the federal context. And even there, it has been suggested that the phenomenon of overlap can be beneficial by creating a dual accountability -- i.e. to both federal and state levels of government -- in the same programme area.

c) *Need for consultation*

Formal and informal mechanisms of consultation stimulate information flows between levels of government. Measures have been taken in a number of countries to improve and make such exchanges more systematic. The centre may want the policies it defines to have an impact on sub-national management without necessarily strengthening directive mechanisms. This calls for better information flows to convey the message. At the same time, it is also desirable that the centre is kept informed of sub-national policies so as to clarify its own priorities and to draw conclusions for its own activities. This is particularly relevant to collecting statistics which allow local policies to be reliably evaluated.

There are also some disadvantages in setting up consultation mechanisms. Too many requirements may slow down the decision-making process; and the involvement of too many "pressure groups" can detract from the general interest. This is a problem in **Japan,** for example, given the many modes of informal consultation and the networks of influence which result. But, as their name suggests, the mechanisms are consultative, and the centre is rarely bound by sub-national decisions. Moreover the centre often remains the master of whatever consultation procedures are created, even when they are not discretionary -- which is often the case.

d) *Different co-operative cultures*

In the context of more inter-dependence, most OECD countries are seeking new forms of collaboration between levels of government rather than strengthening formal controls. This requires the cultural specificities of each system to be taken into account -- in particular the traditional distinction between countries primarily seeking consensus and those where an adversarial approach is more common. Two distinct cultural attitudes, which may be caricatured as being "co-operative" or "conflictual", have a major impact on how the political system operates and on relations between levels of government.

A *co-operative* approach tends to seek consensus, which fosters collaboration. In political terms, this is reflected in coalition governments based on political compromise, as in the Nordic countries, for example. Consensus building promotes understanding between those in power as, for example, in **Japan** where open conflicts between levels of government are uncommon. It may, on the other hand, sometimes encourage a degree of decision-making "paralysis" due to the large number of consultations, meetings and committees which consensus building calls for.

A more *adversarial* approach is often associated with bipartisan political systems. This tends to favour clear decision-making, but often with little consultation, and it can involve costly legal procedures. Collaboration is less well catered for, although important co-ordination mechanisms may exist. In this context there is frequently a degree of mistrust between levels of government -- the centre, for example, claiming that sub-national governments don't have enough know-how to participate in central government decision-making processes. As a consequence the relationship between central and sub-national government can be very hierarchical.

In the Nordic and German-speaking countries, there is a strong tradition of both vertical and horizontal collaboration. In **Sweden**, for example, this has permitted the regrouping as "one-stop-shops" of both central and sub-national bodies involved in service provision.

Strong associations of local authorities are a factor in promoting horizontal collaboration, but they may also encourage vertical collaboration based on "partnerships" between different levels of government. Thus, in **Denmark**, where a negotiation culture has developed with a focus on co-operation, a key role is played by the national association of local governments. In the **Netherlands**, "partnership" is manifest as a growing number of agreements in the form of conventions (*convenanten*). This is also happening in **Mexico** between the federal and state levels. And in **Australia** the current Government intends to conclude a "Memorandum of Understanding" between federal and local governments. (An "Accord" between the two levels had already been signed by the previous Government at the end of 1995.)

In countries traditionally having a strong prefect-type institution, if control by that body is weakened, it may well be replaced by a more collaborative approach. Thus, in **France**, for example, the prefect is increasingly a key player in the centre's initiatives to co-operate with sub-national governments. And in **Norway**, the role of the county governor (who represents central government in the counties) is moving towards one based more on advising and encouraging dialogue between central and local government.

The growing complexity of tasks and overlapping of policies at different levels raises the dilemma of whether to seek rationalisation or inexpensive but effective mechanisms for collaboration between levels. In countries such as **Canada** the search for cost efficiency is the driving force behind the desire to improve collaboration. In all cases, the result is a growing need for co-ordination mechanisms which are at the same time sufficiently formal to be stable, and sufficiently supple to avoid further bureaucratisation.

e)   Forms of co-ordination and consultation

Co-ordination may be:

- horizontal and/or vertical;

- more or less formal (based on informal practices or more formal "understandings" or conventions);

- structural or procedural (using special co-ordinating bodies or achieved through procedural means);

- institutionalised versus ad hoc (in principle either open-ended or limited in duration);

- mandatory (legal requirements) or voluntary;

- binding or non-binding;

- primary or subsidiary (inter-institutional co-operation may be the primary mode of policy-making or only come into play under certain conditions).

Particularly effective vertical co-ordination is needed when the centre is engaged on an ambitious programme which calls for implementation by local actors. There are even greater coherence problems when the political majority at the centre differs from that at the sub-national level(s). This may give rise to significant divergence of policy priorities. Generally, what is considered necessary at the local level may not be desirable at the national level for reasons of national priorities or overall expenditure control.

In **Japan**, although guidance is generally provided by the centre and followed locally, there is relatively little need for vertical co-ordination -- there are enough informal consultation mechanisms to ensure sufficient policy co-ordination. There is however, a need for better horizontal co-ordination at the centre as is the case generally in all Member countries.

The involvement of several levels of government in joint programmes encourages mixed financing and action, and this also requires effective co-ordination. Such arrangements are desirable as they promote a clear division of responsibilities between all participants and avoid the emergence of "hidden tutelles" based on the financial and other influences of each actor. The centre may in this case, as in **France** for example, impose some horizontal co-ordination on sub-national bodies.

In a growing number of countries co-ordination is now being encouraged by new management methods based on performance and result-oriented control, standards and incentives for providing more uniform services. In **Ireland**, for example, the Department of the Environment's Strategic Management Statement puts the focus on, inter alia, developing co-operation and partnership with the local level.

Some mechanisms for vertical and horizontal co-ordination in OECD countries

Vertical co-ordination seeks mainly to assure top-down policy coherence. There is usually some broad co-ordination by the legislative authority, but of variable intensity. In **Australia**, the COAG (Council of Australian Governments) gathers together Commonwealth and state and territory ministers as well as the President of the Australian Local Government Association. Its role is to increase co-operation among governments on reform of the economy and ongoing structural reform of government, and to provide a forum for consultation on major issues of governance. In the **United Kingdom**, financial centralisation and an emphasis on effective vertical co-ordination go hand in hand. Central ministries also play an important co-ordinating role.

Some form of "jurisdictional co-ordination" based on court decisions exists in most countries. In countries with prefectural systems, the representative of the centre generally has significant co-ordination functions; although that role can be reduced by direct relationships between central ministries and their field agencies. In most federal countries, but also increasingly in unitary countries (especially those with regional systems) co-ordination mechanisms have been created at more than one level. In **Germany**, for example, there are "high-level councils" between the federal and the Länder level as well as inter-ministerial co-ordination meetings.

Horizontal co-ordination is a particularly big challenge in federal countries. In **Australia**, the Conference of State Premiers and meetings of state ministers are very important for co-ordination at the state level; and **Canada**, has an annual meeting of its provincial/territorial First Ministers. Some initiatives promote both vertical and horizontal coherence (for example the sectoral "Strategic Result Areas" in **New Zealand** and the "Strategic Management Initiative" in **Ireland**).

---

f)   Consultation

The extent to which consultation is formalised and extensive varies across countries. In **Iceland**, for example, no political or management decision which affects local interests can be taken without prior consultation. In **France**, on the other hand, there are requirements for the centre and sub-national levels to consult in specific legislation, but there is no general obligation for consultation. While in **Norway**, since 1995, new control processes have been set up in the form of instructions asking the main ministries involved with sub-national governments to consult with them concerning the implementation of any new measures. The Ministry of Finance should consult on costs, the Ministry of Public Administration on administrative effects, and the Ministry of Local Government and Labour on local impacts.

There are several means whereby sub-national representation can play a consultative role at the central level. Associations of local authorities, for example, may play major formal and informal roles in consultation processes with the central level of government. But, particularly in federal countries, second chambers in Parliament constitute the most important consultation mechanism and a way to guarantee sub-national interests at the centre. In **Germany**, for example, the Bundesrat comprises members of the *Länder* governments or their delegates.

Informal modes of consultation also abound, but practices remain a function of the culture of each country. In **Greece**, for example, the administrative system generally prefers conflicts to be resolved in an informal way; and in **Australia**, contact and informal negotiation have developed in specific policy areas. The role of staff is often important in informal networking -- as in **France,** where such networks of central and sub-national elected officials are an important element in co-ordination, along with multiple mandates, which are particulary well developed in Napoleonic countries.

Existing institutional relations and co-ordination mechanisms, and the cultural context all influence the modes of consultation employed between levels of government:

- In **Canada** there is an increased willingness on the part of the federal government to enter into partnership arrangements with the provinces and to develop frameworks with them. Co-ordination between the provinces and the local level, on the other hand, tends to take the form of directives and mandates which leave a minimum of place for consultation with local authorities.

- In **France**, the principle of equality amongst sub-national authorities results in fewer obligations for consultation between sub-national levels compared with those with the centre. And while the prefect may be the advocate of the centre, the role played *vis-à-vis* sub-national affairs is increasingly consultative.

- In **Italy**, regional statutes require that the region consults the provinces and local communities when annual and multi-year budgets and sectoral plans are established. Consultation also extends to unions and chambers.

- In **Spain** important Bills are normally presented to the Autonomous Communities before being submitted to the legislative authority, even if they clearly refer to central government responsibility.

- In **Japan**, despite strong centralisation of most powers, the place given to seeking consensus involves important participation by sub-national authorities in decision-making. Local and national networks, based on permanent informal consultation, permits influence to be exerted in both directions.

- In **Ireland**, the regional authorities, whose role is to promote co-ordination between levels of government, have also become a forum for consultation.

The role of local authority associations in consultation

In many countries local government associations are the main interlocutor with the centre when it consults with sub-national governments. But the role they play varies considerably.

In the **Nordic** countries the local authority associations are relatively strong and are consulted on all Bills which concern them. In these countries such consultation is an integral part of the policy-making process between levels of government. In **Denmark**, in particular, there is an annual negotiation ending in an agreement on general grants and other financial matters affecting local authorities. Key actors in this process are the Ministry of Finance and the National Association of Local Authorities.

In **Luxemburg**, in addition to the association of towns and communities, another body (SYVICOL) participates in the legislative and regulatory process. Bills are sent to it for comment, it is recognised by the central government as an interlocutor, and it participates in a number of committees and groups. Local authority associations often play a strong role as a pressure group. This is the case in **Italy** and **Portugal** (where the National Association of Communities will be involved in the next debate on transferring responsibilities).

---

3. *Accountability*

Accountability may be defined as the "management of responsibility". However, to make lines of accountability as clear as possible, it is important to distinguish between the public accountability of elected officials and that of managers who are hierarchically accountable for results. The definition of accountability used for the OECD's ministerial symposium on "The Future of Public Services", organised in March 1996 by the Public Management Committee, was as follows:

> Accountability: Exists where there is a hierarchical relationship within which one party accounts to another for the performance of tasks or functions conferred. It goes hand in hand with devolution and flexibility: managers are held accountable for results once they are given the authority to make decisions that are part of producing those results. Another important aspect of accountability is the public accountability of those who govern to elected bodies and thence to the public at large.
>
> (OECD, *Issues and Developments in Public Management, Survey 1996-1997*, 1997)

The two facets of accountability are dealt with here in turn, firstly in terms of the relationship between accountability and performance management, and secondly from a more political and client perspective.

a) Accountability and performance management

All levels of government are obliged to perform the tasks and manage the resources allocated to them as efficiently and effectively as possible, and there are institutions in all countries charged with ensuring that this is the case, although their mandate does not always range across all levels of government. **Australian** states, for example, have their own auditors; and in **France**, the 1982-3 decentralisation reform was accompanied by the creation of regional chambers of accounts (*Chambres Regionales des Comptes*) responsible for monitoring local finances by preparing reports which are in turn submitted for comment to the national Court of Accounts (*Cour des Comptes*). This type of financial accountability is primarily concerned with checking compliance with legal procedures and rules, but managerial and qualitative functions are also being developed. It is still to be found, legitimately, in the inter-governmental relations of all countries. The present economic climate is, however, generating strong pressures for improving the mechanisms of accountability in its managerial dimensions.

> If the sense of accountability for federal funds is different from that for funds raised through state or local taxes, federal grants may be spent unwisely.....One approach is to ensure accountability through results-oriented measures, rather than conventional rules and regulations. This allows states more flexibility ... subjecting government expenditure to this discipline is likely to be the best way to improve government efficiency....but this enhanced flexibility must be provided in a way that protects the national interest and advances the objectives of the programmes.
>
> *Economic Report of the President*, Washington DC, February 1996

Managerial accountability is particularly pertinent in the context of inter-governmental management given that "true accountability requires autonomy and flexibility" [Governance in Transition]. The shift away from accountability for compliance with procedures towards accountability for performance or results, is putting more emphasis on evaluating the efficiency with which resources are used and the extent to which targets have been achieved. This implies defining common goals and setting performance standards as discussed in the earlier section on performance-based control. Problems are likely to arise if funding is reduced at the same time as sensitive trade-offs between accountability and flexibility are agreed. But by "trading" specific levels of performance (which can be monitored) for greater administrative discretion, a bridge can be built between accountability and flexibility.

- In **Australia**, the state governments have subjected local governments to greater accountability requirements and performance management relying on various indicators.
- In **Canada**, the reduction and capping of federal funding requires lower orders of government to do more with less, and makes them solely accountable for any cost over-runs. On the other hand, they benefit from flexibility to innovate and to retain efficiencies realised through their own policy and administrative initiatives.

- In the **United States**, a problem perceived with revenue-sharing arrangements or pure block grants is that they introduce a separation of functions -- for example, when the federal government finances a programme but policy decisions are made at the state level. This may increase the likelihood that taxpayers' money is not well spent. The 1996 Economic Report of the President notes that state taxpayers are content to give state government officials more discretion over funds coming from Washington than over funds contributed by their own state tax dollars. This means that, while the federal government can influence the pattern of state spending more easily (and it is the federal desire to do so that justifies a federal role), if the substitution of federal for local funding leads to less diligent monitoring by taxpayers, the money may not be spent as well as it could and should be.

- Questions being asked in the **United Kingdom** on this subject include whether the relationship between central and local governments should be based on publicly accountable contracts, or whether there should be some formal mechanism for mediating disputes arising within the relationship; and if accountability at the local level can be an effective alternative to regulation from the centre.

b)   Improving public accountability

The shorter distance between citizens and elected representatives sub-nationally, and the scope for greater transparency about how and where money is spent locally, together make accountability generally a more tangible issue at the sub-national level. And, while election processes and terms of office vary considerably across countries, one factor which all countries have in common is that sub-nationally it is possible to "vote with one's feet" by moving to another area to live, work, study or receive treatment. Debate about the accountability of sub-national governments should not, therefore, be limited only to considerations of economy, efficiency and effectiveness. It should also be recognised that in many countries new structures have evolved in response to more political than financial preoccupations.

- In **Spain**, for example, the creation of the Autonomous Communities was mainly motivated by political concerns: economic factors were secondary. But the new administrations were set up according to the traditional central management pattern resulting in the creation of new local bureaucracies. Initiatives have now been taken to break with this tendency, for example in the health sector, where steps have been taken to improve transparency.

There are, in fact, two aspects of public accountability sub-nationally. One relates to concerns for more participatory democracy, the other is more focused on serving the citizen better as a client. In both cases diverse national traditions and political cultures give rise to a wide variety of approaches.

Democratic accountability has at least three dimensions:

- representation (e.g. the weight of elected councils or directly elected heads of administrations);

- participation (e.g. referenda and consultative neighbourhood fora);

- transparency.

Some traditions give much importance to democratic processes which are participative. This is especially the case in **Switzerland**, for example, where citizens are consulted directly on some cantonal bills and cantonal expenditures are subject to a referendum. In other countries (e.g. **Belgium, Italy, the United States**) direct democracy involves representative bodies such as unions and lobby groups participate in some decision-making. There is a strong tradition of local democracy in the **Nordic countries**; and the new ""Political Reform of the State" initiative in **Mexico** aims to improve local democracy and in particular to improve the participation of the Indian communities. In countries such as **France**, electoral accountability is guaranteed by the Constitution and/or a "constitutional judge". And in many countries, public consultation processes have increased in recent years, particularly in fields such as land-use planning.

The focus on client satisfaction is another facet of improving public accountability, but client-oriented mechanisms and feed-back information must be distinguished from democratic mechanisms. In the **United Kingdom**, for example, one of the first initiatives inspired by the Citizen's Charter was to give the Audit Commission a legal duty to draw up each year a list of indicators measuring the performance of local government services. Councils are obliged to measure and report their own performance against these indicators. The more client-oriented approach is also illustrated in **Australia** by attempts to make sub-national authorities more accountable to financial markets. In **Canada**, as the order of government "closest to the people", municipalities are directly accountable to the public for the programmes and services they provide themselves or on behalf of other levels of government. The proliferation of special purpose bodies funded by a mix of revenue and often with a high degree of autonomy presents some problems of accountability. For example, primary and secondary schools claim a large part of local tax revenues but local government cannot interfere with the policy decisions of school boards so are denied effective means of exercising budgetary control. Similarly, the extent to which local hospital boards should be more accountable to the public (provincial and local government) is being debated.

Both approaches may be present at the same time but to different degrees: **Denmark**, where there is a high level of accountability to the electorate, is also studying client satisfaction; and **Finland**, where recent reforms have strengthened the political accountability of the municipal manager, municipal audits are carried jointly by the elected council and professional accountants who are closer to market-type mechanisms.

And when amalgamation of local units in the interests of economies of scale takes place, it results in a distancing of citizens. This needs to compensated for by, for example, more scope for representation of neighbourhood and lobby groups.

Finally, shifting responsibility down to lower levels of government does not necessarily improve performance. In the **United States**, for example, a Job Training Partnership Act was designed in 1982 to reduce the role of the federal government, enhance that of the states, and retain a strong role for local policy-making and initiative. But it became overly bureaucratised and new legislation in 1992 reasserted federal accountability. A new Bill is now being proposed based on a different model. It seeks to replace bureaucratic accountability with market-driven accountability based on individual empowerment, informed customer choice, and competition; and to establish appropriate and complementary roles for all three levels of government in the design, implementation and oversight of the programme.

D. CONCLUDING COMMENTS

The emerging trends described in Part B of this Overview underline evolving patterns in the structures and division of responsibilities across levels of government; and changing fiscal/financial relations. Structural reorganisation often takes the form of "regionalisation" (adding or strengthening the intermediary tier of government) and/or "rationalisation". The latter may involve reductions in the number of local units through aggregation in the interests of economies of scales; and/or associations of existing units to create larger bodies better able to provide infra-structure efficiently and to deal with economic development policy. One of the main challenges for central managers in this area, is to deal with the fragmentation which results from the creation of new tiers of government, the growing importance of deconcentrated agencies, and the emergence of new non-governmental local actors.

The distribution of responsibilities across levels shows that central and local levels generally have basically similar "core" functions, but there are many grey areas where (to differing degrees) an intermediate tier is involved. While it is difficult to identify a clear trend in the redistribution of responsibilities across levels, most interest has been shown in the education, health and welfare sectors. There is also an increasing number of shared responsibilities. Central managers must, therefore, face the challenge of managing a more complex distribution of responsibilities. The cultural context is particularly important in how tasks are distributed and, together with financial and political considerations, is at the heart of the debate on autonomy. The degree and nature of sub-national autonomy may vary a lot from one sector of responsibility to another. This diversity is a richness, but can make it difficult to determine the appropriate trade-off between autonomy and ensuring that national objectives for the governance of the public sector as a whole are not compromised.

Evolving fiscal and financial relations across levels of government reflect a more pronounced interdependence between levels, given the limitations of local authorities to generate their own revenues and, in most countries, the growing number of tasks being performed sub-nationally. This situation is leading to new forms of partnership between levels of government; and revisions of tax sharing schemes and of equalisation policies. In parallel, transfers to lower levels are generally shifting away from specific-purpose grants, thereby providing opportunities for broad goals and targets to be agreed and in particular underlining the importance of setting national objectives and achieving fiscal strategies.

The issues identified from the country chapters highlight a number of basic tensions in intergovernmental relations which are evident, to some degree, in all OECD Member countries in the mid 1990s. These challenges may be summarised as finding the right balance between:

- encouraging more *autonomy* at lower levels of government, while providing overall *direction*;

- allowing for *differentiation* through flexibility, yet ensuring some minimum degree of *uniformity*;

- catering for more *responsiveness* to local needs, but not to the detriment *of efficiency and economy*.

These inherent tensions have important implications for central governmental management *vis-à-vis* sub-national levels:

- adjusting financial and administrative *controls* away from detailed, top-down requirements and towards broadly-agreed frameworks and *ex post*, result-oriented instruments;

- developing *co-ordination and consultation* mechanisms for a more comprehensive and coherent approach to target-based governance and which fit the cultural context and the "style of relationship" in each country and sector;

- promoting *accountability* procedures which combine managerial responsibility for financial results with political accountability to the public which are in accordance with the shift towards greater participation by citizens.

These conflicting pressures are often exacerbated by a basic lack of confidence between levels of government in all countries. The problem of mistrust across levels of government, although not directly addressed in this report, is mutual in that it operates in both directions. Such suspicion does not augur well for improving synergies in governance -- but the problem can be reduced if transparency and communication is improved.

Judging which level of government is best placed to be responsible for a particular activity or decision involves a complex mix of factors, and demands effective consultation and negotiation. It is central government which ultimately decides on many financial matters and which must take the initiative to build the partnerships needed. The bottom-line challenge to public managers in central government is, therefore, to incorporate appropriate and clear lines of accountability into its decision-making processes.

To sum up, there is clearly no single "best" model for how power and responsibility should be distributed vertically across governments. Each country has its own cultural, economic and political contexts which largely determine what is desirable and possible. Equally, while economic imperatives and new public management philosophy encourage more devolution, it is for each country to ascertain its own strategic mix of decentralisation and deconcentration -- and how, where, and at what speed it will be realised. Only broad goals such as improving responsiveness and subsidiarity are generally shared. Other objectives such as actively "enabling" lower levels of government to take on additional responsibilities require further efforts in collaborative governance.

Part Two

COUNTRY CHAPTERS

AUSTRALIA

1. INSTITUTIONS AND AUTHORITY

1.1 Structures

Description of levels

The Australian Constitution brought into being the federal government in 1901 by fusing into one nation six states, each with its own parliament, executive government and judiciary. In addition, there are two "territories" – the Northern Territory (which was granted self-government in 1978) and the Australian Capital Territory (the site of Canberra, the federal capital, which achieved self government in 1989) – and which, along with the states, are represented in the Senate and the House of Representatives. Each state has its own constitution but which must be read subject to the Australian Constitution. Local government is established by state (or territory) legislation and may be recognised in state constitutions.

There are three levels of sub-national administration in Australia: state, regional and local. But they are not consistent across the country. A distinction can be made between administration at the three levels and governments' operational activities at these levels.

The Commonwealth (or federal) government primarily operates at the national level, but its departments and agencies also have state, regional and local offices. State governments operate at the state level, but have regional and local offices. Local government comes in a range of forms and in addition to operating locally has sought to perform roles at the regional level (e.g. joint arrangements; multifunctional associations of municipalities).

At the **state** level there are six states and two "territories" as shown in . Most of the country is covered by the states. Of the two territories, one is large in area and it is possible that it may be granted statehood in the future; the other, the Australian Capital Territory, is a state/local hybrid.

Table 1: **Area and population of sub-national governments**

	Population	Area (sq. km)
States:		
New South Wales	6 115 100	801 600
Queensland	3 277 000	1 727 200
South Australia	1 474 000	984 000
Tasmania	473 022	67 800
Victoria	4 502 200	227 600
Western Australia	1 731 700	2 525 500
Territories:		
Australian Capital Territory	304 100	2 400
Northern Territory	173 878	1 346 200
TOTAL	18 051 600	7 682 300

Source: Australian Bureau of Statistics, 1995.

The broad structure of local government is in . It includes 92 community governments that have been established to reflect the needs of Aboriginal and Torres Strait Islander communities. They are mostly small and remote community councils. Table 3 illustrates some of the key characteristics of selected councils.

Table 2. **Rural/urban structure of local government by state**

State/Territory	Urban	Rural	Total
New South Wales	82	96	178
Victoria	57	21	78
Queensland	30	126 [1]	156
South Australia	45	79 [1]	124
Western Australia	38	104	142
Tasmania	10	19	29
Northern Territory	5	62 [1]	67
TOTAL	267	507	774

1. Includes Northern Territory 51, Queensland 31, and South Australia 5, Aboriginal and Torres Strait Islander community governments.
Source: National Office of Local Government.

Table 3. **Characteristics of selected councils**

Council	Description	Area (sq km)	Population	Total expenditure ($'000)	General Purpose grant ($/capital)	Expenditure
Stephen Island	Remote community	0.4	45	66.0	432	1 467
Peppermint Grove	Small Urban	1.5	1 547	1 575.1	21	1 018
Brisbane City Council	Large Urban	1 218	786 442	401 183.7[1]	20	510
East Pilbara	Remote	378 533	9 436	8 535.2	122	905
Windouran	Small Rural	5 065	430	1 295.0	462	3 012
Gosford	Fringe Urban	1 028	142 150	142 072.0	37	999
Marngarr	Remote Community	2.7	206	45.5	43	221
Wanneroo	Urban Fringe	786	197 134	62 760.3	14	318

1. Excludes expenditure related to water and sewerage and public transportation.
Source: State Grants Commission data.

Creation, elimination and restructuring

The Commonwealth Government is established by, and state governments recognised under, the Australian Constitution. Local government is established by state (or territory) legislation, and this may include recognition in state constitutions. The creation of administrative units, and their field operations at different levels, is a question for government decision making, and occurs at the departmental level. Departments can be established without legislation although it is common for specialised authorities to be so enacted.

A recent development has been the emergence of the "service agency" within the federal sphere. In the 1996-97 Budget the Government announced its decision to form a new Commonwealth Services Delivery Agency. The Agency, which is based on the "one stop shop" concept, will bring together services from different Commonwealth Departments, so that people can get the help they need in one place. Once the necessary legislation is passed, the Agency will delivery the full range of income support and related services. From September 1997 the Agency will progressively delivery student assistance services, some employment services and, from January 1998, child care payments.

Local government: Extensive reform of local government has been occurring in recent years. This has involved the legislation governing councils, relations between levels and boundary review. A complete reorganisation of the external boundaries of local government has occurred in Tasmania and Victoria, and South Australia is implementing a widespread reform of boundaries. Several amalgamations have occurred in Queensland and some interest exists in other states.

An effect of the reorganisation in Victoria has been to resolve the tensions between the residential and business interests of the council for the central business district of the state capital, Melbourne. This has involved minimising the residential areas served by the council while extending the council area to include nearby commercial areas, including the port of Melbourne. Similarly, in Western Australia, the former council responsible for the central part of the state capital, Perth, was subdivided such that there remained one council responsible for the central business district and new councils were created for the surrounding residential areas.

Additional informal bodies located in remote areas continue to be recognised as local governments for purposes such as to receive Commonwealth financial assistance. These bodies are usually outside of areas serviced by councils, populated by indigenous peoples and provide essential services. Provision of Commonwealth assistance to these bodies commenced in 1985-86 with grants totalling $290 000. In 1996-97, a total of 92 bodies received grants of $13.4m and served 50 000 people.

In addition to boundary reform, state governments have introduced a number of other reforms of local government through legislation. These vary between states but include subjecting minimum specified proportions of expenditure to market testing (compulsory competitive tendering); prescribing increasing reporting and accountability provisions and rate capping. State governments are also requiring local government to conform with undertakings made to the Commonwealth government concerning competition policy. In short, this policy requires that significant government owned businesses should not enjoy any competitive advantage as a result of their ownership, unless shown to be in the public interest.

A long term trend has favoured centralising sub-national responsibilities at the state level (i.e. vertical movement of responsibilities from local to state government). At the same time new legislation controlling local government has been more empowering and less prescriptive of functions performed, and councils are increasingly diversifying their functions into local community needs not met by other levels.

State government: State governments have been comprehensively reforming their public sectors for a decade or more. This has received renewed impetus with the election of new style conservative governments (i.e. managerialist) in recent years (in comparison with the 1980s when new style Labor governments, also managerialist, were dominant at this level). For example, traditional core functions may now be subject to market testing and contracting out through competitive tendering; and the non-budget sector has experienced significant privatisation.

Control bodies

Several different types of institution are involved in the control of the legality and/or efficiency of actions of sub-national bodies. They are both internal and external to the administration and include both central agencies (responsible for co-ordinating finance, personnel and policy) and external review bodies. There are, for example, central agencies of the Commonwealth government such as the Local Government Division of the Department of Environment, Sport and Territories, and the Department of Finance. There are also the central agencies of the state governments, which go under different names, but include a finance/treasury department and some form of public management office. Externally, parliaments have a role with the ministers being accountable for their departments. Audit offices in the states report to parliament, and maintain oversight of financial management and efficiency. The local government department/office of each state is responsible for many local government activities; other financial or policy related activities would involve the relevant state (and possibly Commonwealth) government department or ministry. There is also a Commonwealth Ombudsman and an ombudsman in each state and in the Northern and Australian Capital Territories.

1.2 Powers

Nature of sub-national institutions

Sub-nationally, there are two levels of directly elected government: state and local. The sub-national legislature is bicameral-cameral for five states. One state (Queensland) and the two territories have unicameral parliaments. The authority of some state governments is affected by the composition of upper houses (and the single chamber in the case of the Australian Capital Territory) where independents hold the balance of power. State representatives are directly elected by single-member (sometimes multi-member electorates). There is also extensive use of appointments to administrative positions (boards of agencies etc.) at regional and state levels.

The cabinet, based on portfolio ministers, is the main decision making body at the state level. Under this system responsibility is normally delegated to the minister for his/her portfolio, with the expectation that matters of political and strategic importance or with cross-portfolio implications will be raised with cabinet.

State governments rely on the ministerial department for the core public sector (i.e. the public service) and on the government business enterprise for commercial activities. Various forms of statutory authority are also widely used.

Local government authorities have elected councils of between 9 and 21 members (for the most part). Councils are directly elected by a variety of systems depending on the state. These vary from the single-member electorate system in the largest City (Brisbane) to multi-member electorates with staggered elections.

Administration in local government is usually divided into several departments, responsible to a chief executive officer (traditional statutory positions such as the shire or town clerk now becoming uncommon) who is increasingly likely to be employed on a contract. Two significant trends are changing the nature of local administration: one is curtailing the role of elected representatives by explicitly limiting their roles to policy not administration, the other has been the introduction of modern management methods to improve the effectiveness and efficiency of councils.

Type and degree of autonomy

The states are among the most powerful intermediate governments in the world because of the breadth of their functions and their substantial role in service delivery (in large part a function of the centralisation at the sub-national level, which occurs at the expense of local government). The states enjoy considerable autonomy based on constitutionally prescribed rights. However, overlapping roles and responsibilities between state and federal levels reduces this in practice. Nevertheless, the states (and territories) have the capacity to initiate policy and a range of mechanisms for pursuing it. The degree of autonomy varies according to the policy field.

Local government has often been described as a 'creature of the states'. It has always been confined to a relatively narrow range of functions (on a world scale). This plus the fragmentation of the system – small in population and often in area (where urban) – has worked against high autonomy.

Tax powers: The states ceased imposing separate income taxes in 1942 when the Commonwealth imposed uniform income tax arrangements as a wartime measure. The states were compensated by grants from the Commonwealth and have not imposed income taxes since then. Broad-based taxes on the production and sale of goods are not available to the states. Consequently about three-quarters of all tax revenue is collected by the Commonwealth.

Local government is able to strike a rate based on property valuations, but is otherwise limited in its right to tax. Councils have the right to make policy within parameters determined by state government, and this certainly extends to organisational design. (A general competence power was given to councils in Queensland but this was eroded over time by state legislation.)

The powers of the Commonwealth are defined by the constitution. The states can undertake the residual. Only a small number of functions can be regarded as exclusive to a level. In practice most functions are shared to some degree.

1.3 Responsibilities

Distribution of responsibilities

The 1990s have been unusual for the level of debate and exchanges among the larger units of the federal system (Commonwealth and the states/territories) about the distribution of responsibilities and the need to achieve rationalisation and efficiencies in accordance with the national micro-economic reform agenda.

All levels of government have competencies related to policy implementation. Service delivery is not automatically moved among the levels of government but is often retained by the two upper tiers (i.e. the Commonwealth and the states) which implement policy through their own forms of deconcentration. This may become less common in the future. The relationships are increasingly being conceptualised in purchaser/provider terms.

As a creation of state legislation, local government is not directly controlled by the Commonwealth government. The Commonwealth does however share some responsibilities with local government by providing it with specific purpose grants. The Commonwealth also shares general revenue with local government by providing general purpose funding.

Mandatory, optional and shared responsibilities

At the federal level the Commonwealth is entirely responsible for external affairs, defence and air transport, and plays a major role in social security and welfare payments. However, shared responsibilities have been highly prevalent. Major fields of overlap are education, health and transport, as although they are state responsibilities, they are mostly financed by Commonwealth funds.

Overlapping competences are dealt with in several ways. State governments have been inclined to seek rationalisation of the overlaps with local governments by legislating for their centralisation at the state level. Ministerial councils have existed as part of co-operative federalism for handling broad-based overlaps between the Commonwealth and the states. Otherwise these may be negotiated on a bicameral-lateral basis. A standard practice has been for each of the two or three levels to assume specific roles (planning, financing, co-ordinating, monitoring and delivery), although the mix varies between policy fields.

Responsibilities may be redistributed by constitutional amendment, but this approach has rarely been successful. There has been a Council of Australian Governments (COAG) since 1992 (described below), which has had among its briefs the question of reviewing responsibilities. Current examples of responsibilities being reviewed include regulation in the areas of environment and food standards.

COAG has recognised that an explicit allocation of a functional responsibility to one level may be desirable and that where shared responsibilities are maintained roles should be delineated in order to avoid duplication, improve accountability and minimise inefficiencies.

States currently have *exclusive* powers for most areas of service delivery and education, energy, agriculture, health, transport, housing and development, police and justice systems, and local government. Local governments, on the other hand, are mostly responsible for service delivery in the areas of community services, recreation and culture, and road transport. Most also exercise an array of planning and approval responsibilities.

2. MANAGEMENT FUNCTIONS

2.1 Policy-making and co-ordination

The Australian Constitution was originally written to create two sets of authorities – federal and state – that would act independently of each other in their respective spheres. That is, relations between federal and state governments are constitutionally based on a "co-ordinate federalism". Referenda have rejected constitutional amendments proposing more co-operative structures.

Coherence, consultation and conflict resolution

Various devices are used for conflict resolution and consultation between levels and with citizens/groups. The concept of co-operative federalism, which involves joint action between levels of government, covers a range of mechanisms designed to handle intergovernmental relations. The key ones have been mentioned above. Nationally, the ministerial councils have been a prime means for providing a consultative policy forum, with over 40 at their peak. Informal contact and negotiation between officials in specific policy sectors from different levels is also a constant feature.

With the advent of 'client focus' in the 1990s, and the move away from the 'top-down' approach of the 1980s, linkages with customers and citizens have been developed. Customer councils and other types of consultative mechanisms are increasingly used by state departments. Precinct committees exist in some council areas. Overall, however, consultative mechanisms are still not well developed.

Formal and informal mechanisms

The following mechanisms have been used for vertical co-ordination:

- Formal bodies with defined financial powers: Commonwealth Grants Commission (which advises on the allocation of Commonwealth general purpose funding among the states); Loan Council; and the Premiers' Conference. Through the Commonwealth Grants Commission there has been a long tradition of fiscal equalisation between the states.

- Premiers' Conference: the annual meeting of the Commonwealth and State and Territory Ministers evolved out of meetings confined to state premiers. Its main focus has been co-ordination of economic policy and financial matters (Treasurers usually meet at the same time).

- Ministerial councils: conferences of Commonwealth and State and Territory Ministers for specific policy sectors (and associated meetings of officials).

- Intergovernmental agreements of many kinds (which range from formal written agreements and contracts to informal arrangements).

- Intergovernmental programmes which specify conditions (and which may be the subject of intergovernmental agreements), and include programme monitoring and evaluation.

In 1990, the heads of the Commonwealth, states, and territorial governments began to meet in regular Special Premiers' Conferences (SPC) to pursue a common micro-economic reform agenda including deregulation, harmonisation, mutual recognition, and regulatory co-ordination between federal and state governments. The ad hoc SPCs were replaced in 1992 by the permanent Council of Australian Governments (COAG). It co-exists with the Premiers' Conference (having generally the same membership except COAG also includes the President of the Australian Local Government Association). They may meet separately or on consecutive days. COAG's role is to increase co-operation among governments on reform of the economy and ongoing structural reform of government. It also provides a forum for consultation of major whole-of-government issues. COAG therefore provides a formal mechanism during a period of public sector change which specialises in the reform agenda. It is served by a number of working groups (see below).

Horizontal co-ordination within the state level is pursued through central and independent performance monitoring and review of policy outcomes. At the local level it has been sought through state government monitoring of programme implementation. There has often been insufficient co-ordination of funding programmes involving state and local governments (including the various aspects of the funding system: policy development, programme planning, programme administration and resource allocation).

There have also been various experiments at the regional level (the aspirations extending to regional budgeting) including attempts at standardising regional boundaries in order to achieve greater consistency.

At the federal level, the Department of the Prime Minister and Cabinet has the prime responsibility for policy co-ordination across the Commonwealth departments and for relations with the states. Horizontal co-ordination within the Commonwealth has also been pursued through the Regional Advisory Management Committee, consisting of key Commonwealth Departments and agencies. Amongst its purposes is the encouragement of policies and programme design and delivery which is capable of responding to the particular economic development needs of individual regions. It is also a forum through which RDOs have been able to present and promote their regional development strategies and priorities to the Commonwealth Government.

At the state level, the Premier's department (known usually as Department of Premier and Cabinet) is responsible for policy co-ordination. Finance/Treasury is also important. Two other types of body are the state co-ordination council which has been used for bringing together CEOs, and the management council composed of senior officials from the central agencies. The local government department (or its equivalent office) is responsible for co-ordinating local government matters. For specific policies (e.g. health) the line department will be responsible for vertical linkages (either with the federal or local levels). Cabinet committees have also played active roles (possibly with the assistance of officials groups).

2.2 Financial management

Federal fiscal arrangements in Australia are characterised by a significant difference between the relative revenue and expenditure responsibilities of the Commonwealth and state and local governments. The amount of own-source revenue raised by the Commonwealth is considerably larger than its own-purpose outlays. In contrast, state and local government own-purpose outlays outweigh the amount which they fund from their own-source revenue. Table 4 shows the composition of general government own-source revenue and own purpose outlays in 1995-96.

Table 4. **Composition of General Government Revenue and Outlays, 1995-96**
(percent shares)

	Own-Source Revenue	Own-Purpose Outlays
Commonwealth	72	58
State	24	38
Local	4	4

The distribution of relative revenue and expenditure responsibilities necessitates a substantial flow of funds from the Commonwealth to the sub-national levels of government. In 1996-97, payments to state and local government (excluding very large one-off items) are expected to account for around 26 per cent of total Commonwealth outlays, with these grants from the Commonwealth expected to account for 42 per cent of state and local government revenue.

Commonwealth payments to state and local government are in the form of either general purpose payments (GPPs) or specific purpose payments (SPPs).

General purpose payments to the states

GPPs are funds that are provided free of any conditions attached to their use by the states. In 1996-97, GPPs are expected to account for around 48 per cent of Commonwealth funds provided to the states. The growth and distribution of GPPs are considered annually at the Premiers' Conference and are expected to total A$16.4 billion in 1996-97. The main components of GPPs are detailed below:

- Financial assistance grants represent the bulk of GPPs and are expected to total A$15.4 billion in 1996-97.

- Special revenue assistance is provided to some states to address specific circumstances and is expected to total A$480 million in 1996-97.

- National competition payments will commence in 1997-98 under a Commonwealth/State agreement (Agreement to Implement the National Competition Policy [NCP] and Related Reforms) to implement microeconomic reform. Under the Agreement, the Commonwealth will provide the states with a payment of around A$215 million in 1997-98 which will be distributed among the states on an equal per capita basis.

- A state must meet its obligations under the NCP Agreement before receiving its payment.

Financial Assistance Grants (FAGs)

Since 1994-95, FAGs have been indexed for population growth as well as for inflation. A rolling three year real per capita guarantee for FAGs was extended to 1999-2000 at the 1997 Premiers' Conference. The per capita component of the guarantee is conditional on the states complying with their obligations under the NCP Agreement.

FAGs are distributed among the states on the basis of horizontal fiscal equalisation (HFE) principles which are reflected in the per capita relativities recommended by an independent body called the Commonwealth Grants Commission (CGC). The CGC seeks to ensure that each state has the capacity to provide the average standard of state type services, if it makes the same effort to raise revenue as the states on average and it operates at an average level of efficiency. The CGC takes into account the differences in the capacities of the states to raise their own revenue and also takes into account factors which affect the relative cost of providing the average level of state-type public services (such as population dispersion and isolation). The estimated 1996-97 distribution of FAGs between the eight jurisdictions which are included in the HFE arrangements is shown below in Table 5. The Table indicates that in 1996-97 five jurisdictions will receive a greater amount of FAGs under the HFE arrangements than if FAGs were allocated solely on the basis of population.

Table 5. **Impact of Horizontal Fiscal Equalisation on Estimated Distribution of Financial Assistance Grants, 1996-97 ($ million)**

	HFE Distribution	Equal Per Capita Distribution	Difference
New South Wales	4 371	5 200	-829
Victoria	3 211	3 814	-602
Queensland	3 004	2 860	144
Western Australia	1 537	1 513	24
South Australia	1 512	1 221	291
Tasmania	665	394	271
Australian Capital Territory	233	269	-36
Northern Territory	902	164	738
Total	15 436	15 436	0

In light of the Commonwealth's fiscal position, the states have agreed to make payments to the Commonwealth of A$619 million in 1996-97, A$627 million in 1997-98 and A$313 million in 1998-99 to contribute to the Commonwealth's deficit reduction programme. The method of payment varies among the states and has been by way of direct payments to the Commonwealth, deductions from FAGs or reductions in the Commonwealth's contribution to an SPP.

Specific purpose payments to the states

Most SPPs are paid to the states on the basis that policy objectives set by the Commonwealth, or national policy objectives agreed between the Commonwealth and the states, are met. It is because of the conditions attached to SPPs that they are sometimes called 'tied grants'.

In 1996-97, SPPs (excluding very large one-off items) are expected to total A$18.0 billion and account for around 52 per cent of Commonwealth payments to the states. SPPs paid 'to' the states (these are made direct to state governments for funding expenditures by the states) are expected to be A$10.2 billion, and SPPs paid 'through' the states (payments to state governments to be passed on to other bodies or individuals such as higher education and local governments) are expected to be A$7.8 billion.

The conditions imposed on individual SPPs vary considerably in both degree and form. They may involve a requirement that the payment be expended for a specified activity, with varying degrees of budgetary discretion available to the states according to conditions placed on payments; or general policy requirements on states (for example, that the states provide free public hospital treatment to Medicare patients as a condition of receiving hospital funding grants).

SPPs that are paid 'through' the states have a minimal impact on state budgets as they are essentially Commonwealth own-purpose outlays, with the states acting as the Commonwealth's agent.

Commonwealth payments to local government

Local government receives financial assistance from the Commonwealth in the form of untied general purpose assistance and some SPPs which are paid direct to local government. In 1996-97, general purpose assistance is expected to account for almost 83 per cent of total Commonwealth payments to local government.

General purpose assistance to local government is increased each year on the basis of an escalation factor which is determined by the Commonwealth Treasurer in light of the underlying movements in FAGs and special revenue assistance provided to the states. In 1996-97, these payments are expected to amount to A$1 216 million, comprising A$843 million of local government FAGs and A$374 million of identified road funding.

Local government FAGs are distributed among the states on an equal per capita basis, while identified road funding is distributed on the basis of historical shares. The distribution of local government funding within each state is on the basis of recommendations of independent State Grants Commissions which are determined on the basis of fiscal equalisation.

The SPPs which the Commonwealth makes direct to local government are expected to be A$260 million in 1996-97. These tied grants are utilised in certain areas of interest to both Commonwealth and local governments, such as home and community care and environmental management.

Sources of revenue and expenditure responsibilities

The main sources of revenue and expenditure responsibilities of each sub-national level of government are set out in Table 6 and Table 7 respectively.

2.3 Performance management

Mechanisms

A range of audit and accountability mechanisms operate within and across levels. Government bodies are subject to external audit. State audit offices carry out financial and performance audits and may take on special reviews and investigations. They independently assess and report on the operations of the public sector organisations and seek to improve accountability. The Australian National Audit Office has also conducted audits of financial programmes (e.g. specific purpose payments) and commented on Commonwealth-state agreements.

Table 6. **Main revenue sources of state and local governments 1995-1996** [1]
(percentage)

State Government		Local Government	
Taxes, fees and fines:	39	Municipal rates	55
– Payroll tax (9%)		Fees and fines	5
– Taxes on financial and capital transactions (8%)		Other own source	18
		Grants from Commonwealth [3]	15
– Motor vehicle taxes (4%)		Grants from states [4]	7
– Franchise taxes (6%)			
– Other (11%)			
Other own sources	26		
Grants from Commonwealth [2]	35		
TOTAL	100	TOTAL	100

1. On a non financial public sector basis. Some data are preliminary.
2. Grants from Commonwealth for own use.
3. Direct payments and general purpose assistance.
4. Data abstracts from the financial effects of the transfer of roads from the state government sector to the local government sector in NSW in 1995-96. This transfer resulted in a temporary increase in grants to the local government sector of A$8.0 billion.

Source: ABS, Government Financial Estimates, Australia (5501), ABS, Taxation Revenue, Australia (5506) and unpublished ABS data.

Table 7. **Main expenditure patterns of state and local governments 1995-1996** [1]
(percentage)

State Government		Local Government	
Education	31	Transport and communication [2]	27
Health	21	Housing and community amenities	21
Transport and communication	12	Recreation and culture	20
Public order and safety	9	General public services	18
General public services	5	Social security and welfare	6
Other expenditure	22	Other expenditure	8
TOTAL	100	TOTAL	100

1. On a non financial public sector basis. Some data are preliminary.
2. Abstracts from the temporary increase in expenditure of $8 billion as a result of the transfer of roads from the state government sector to the local government sector in NSW.

Source: ABS, Government Financial Statistics, Australia (5501) and unpublished ABS data.

State governments have for some time been reforming their management systems in accordance with accountability for results principles and have been moving towards improved public reporting of performance. Accrual accounting and output budgeting have become widely accepted. Attention has also been given to improving internal auditing.

Local councils use annual plans and performance-based controls for senior staff, and reporting to enhance accountability for performance. State governments conduct management reviews. Annual reports to voters is a new device which is being used in some local government jurisdictions.

Benchmarking has become accepted as a standard means for comparing performance and determining best practice. A benchmarking project, sponsored by the Local Government Ministers' Conference, has recently reported on the potentiality for extending benchmarking systematically, and the constraints on covering up to 800 councils and 100 services. A system for assessing the efficiency of councils in delivering selected services is being implemented which will allow comparisons of performances nationally and over time.

A Review of State and Commonwealth Service Provision was commissioned by the Premiers' Conference at its July 1993 meeting. Its purpose is to develop and publish performance indicators to allow governments to assess relative efficiency and effectiveness in service provision. Its focus is on results benchmarking in the areas of education, public housing, community services, hospitals and justice. It has provided two reports in 1995 and 1997.

In 1994 the Local Government Ministers Conference funded a national Benchmarking Project to be undertaken by the Victoria Office of Local Government. The first phase was a pilot study to develop and test benchmarking methods. The second phase was the production of aids for benchmarking and a Practical Guide was published in September 1995. As a follow-up, Commonwealth and State Local Government Ministers and the President of the Australian Local Government Association have now decided to implement a major benchmarking and efficiency programme.

In its May 1995 Budget, the Commonwealth Government allocated up to A$ 2 million per year for the next five years for benchmarking and efficiency projects as part of its new Local Government Development Programme, starting in 1995/1996.

Service quality standards

Service quality standards have become common. Performance indicators are widely used although their effectiveness is variable. The Review of Commonwealth and State Service Provision (for the Council of Australian Governments) is collecting and publishing quantitative performance indicators in order to permit comparisons of efficiency and evaluation of service provision reforms.

Citizen's Charter-like arrangements have been increasingly adopted at the state/territory level: e.g. Guarantee of Service, Community Contracts and Service Commitment program. In the Commonwealth sphere, from July 1997 all government bodies which provide services to the public will be required to develop individual Government Service Charters. Where relevant, charters will guarantee specific standards for service delivery.

Service quality standards are established in a variety of ways but usually through a review process which involves customers and staff (although the extent and quality of consultation varies). The standards are generally more concerned with service delivery (i.e. process matters such as timeliness and accuracy) than outcomes, although aspirations are in the latter direction. The changes taking place in this field include the recognition of the limitations of existing procedures, the need for greater attention to performance indicators and the use of standards, the importance of involving customers more effectively in these processes and a range of performance improvement tools.

Studies have reported problems with accountability in service provision stemming from lack of clarity in objectives and roles. Inter-governmental agreements may not be subject to proper public scrutiny, and this affects performance.

State governments have been moving towards demanding more explicit performance requirements of local government. For example, councils are being required to employ the Australian Accountancy Standard requirements, a move which is designed to permit benchmarking and comparisons of performance.

2.4 Human resource management

Statutory distinctions

Statutory and status distinctions are specific to personnel at each level. Most states have established a Senior Executive Service. Complicated classification systems have generally been revised, and the trend is to reducing classifications further. There is a move towards broadbanding which means a reduction in levels (perhaps to five or less), and which may be linked to pay increases by performance rather than routine increments.

Local government has normally made a distinction between officers and outdoor staff. There is a trend towards abolishing statutory positions. For example, most town or shire clerks have been replaced by officials called chief executive officers or city managers; and statutory positions such as "city engineer" have been abolished.

Managerial autonomy: The sub-national levels of government have managerial autonomy with regard to employment, pay, recruitment, promotion and dismissal. Negotiation is organised sub-nationally.

The Public Service Board/Commissioner (or equivalent) has traditionally been the employer at the state level. This function has been increasingly devolved from state central agencies with the emergence of enterprise bargaining which envisages the development of agency-based roles and the application of the principle that the department or agency should be the employer for bargaining purposes. The chief executive officer is responsible for the negotiation of enterprise agreements. In some states, however, there continues to be a significant role for the agency responsible for employment or industrial relations.

Staffing decisions about levels once were the preserve of a state's central agency, the Public Service Board, but since its demise they are generally made at agency level. Standard practice is for staffing to be handled through the Budget process: the chief executive determining the number of designations of employees subject to available funds.

The Australian Public Service accounts for 9.1% of employed wage and salary earners in the public sector, and 2.4% of employed wage and salary earners in the whole labour force.

Mobility: Programmes have existed for facilitating mobility between levels of government, but the transfer of benefits has continued to be problematic. A working group of COAG has considered obstacles to mobility of public employees between jurisdictions. There were no significant constraints on short term secondments, but new employees have experienced a significant impediment with the transfer of superannuation. COAG policy is to support mobility, and bilateral arrangements are seeking to overcome the superannuation problem.

2.5 Regulatory management and reform

Regulatory relations between national and sub-national governments

The development of an institutional basis for inter-governmental co-ordination in the early 1990s through "co-operative federalism" has provided substantial scope for regulatory reform.. The impetus for reform has been based on the realisation of the benefits in moving further away from fragmented state-based markets to a single national market, thereby improving the efficiency of the national economy. The core of the new federalism is a set of creative administrative power-sharing arrangements between federal, state, and even local governments.

With the creation of the permanent Council of Australian Governments (COAG) in 1992, new frameworks were created in which federal, state, and territorial governments can adopt common policies, co-ordinate programmes, and draw up common legislation. Among the key outputs of these co-operative frameworks have been a series of intergovernmental agreements that create new regulatory processes and institutions in which powers are shared, responsibilities are delegated, and single bodies are left to develop regulations without interference from multiple levels of government.

Many Commonwealth-State Ministerial Councils and National Standards Setting Bodies (NSSB) have a regulatory role and produce standardised national regulations and, to a lesser extent, strategies for enforcing these standards. By 1995-96, over 40 Councils and eleven NSSBs were operational. These processes have produced a mix of national regulatory institutions carrying out a variety of tasks.

The regulatory proposals of these bodies are adopted into law via a range of processes. For example, the Australia New Zealand Food Authority (ANZFA) and National Road Transport Commission (NRTC) recommendations are considered by the relevant ministerial councils and then implemented by the states and Commonwealth via two different forms of parallel legislation. ANZFA recommendations are adopted by the Australia New Zealand Food Standards Council into the Food Standards Code, which is adopted "by reference" in state and territory laws. The NRTC operates on a 'template legislation' model, in which an act containing the regulation is passed in one jurisdiction, and other jurisdictions adopt its provisions in their own law. Ministerial Councils set binding national standards, the enforcement of which typically is retained at the state and local level.

Given concerns about the quality of the regulations and standards in April 1995, heads of federal and state governments adopted a set of *Principles and Guidelines for National Standard Setting and Regulatory Action* that specified that all national standards made by such bodies must be subject to a nationally-consistent assessment process and that regulatory impact statements would be prepared. The federal Office of Regulatory Review advises agencies on the quality of their impact statements and suggests ways they could be improved. These guidelines are currently under review.

Under the Competition Principles Agreement, an intergovernmental agreement signed in April 1996, all jurisdictions will review by the year 2000 all of their respective legislation that restricts competition. The guiding principle for the review process is that legislation should not restrict competition unless it can be demonstrated that the benefits of the restriction outweigh the cost and that the objective of the legislation can only be achieved by restricting competition.

Regulatory relations between states

A major concern about state regulation has been its effect on interstate trade and mobility of persons in registered occupations. Inconsistent regulatory controls and laws between the states in areas such as transport, food and packaging standards, and occupational qualifications have created trade barriers and major inefficiencies in the Australian economy.

In May 1992, a Mutual Recognition Agreement (MRA) was signed, establishing two principles:

- if goods comply with the regulations of the state or territory in which they are manufactured or to which they are imported, then they can be sold in any other participating state or territory without further need to comply with that jurisdiction's regulations; and

- a person registered to practise an occupation in one state or territory can obtain registration to practice an equivalent occupation in all other participating states or territories.

Exemptions and exceptions (including occupational health and safety, regulations for the use of goods etc.) to the MRA are allowed, and jurisdictions can trigger a temporary twelve month exemption, pending a review. The MRA also provides for harmonised national standards where significant social and environmental externalises exist and where uniformity would improve national economic efficiency. As a vehicle for harmonisation, the Australian governments relied on an increasing number of joint regulatory bodies - such as the Commonwealth/State Ministerial Councils or the national commissions - with the authority to develop national regulations and standards.

A recent evaluation indicates that the MRA is having the desired impact:

- for goods, mutual recognition appears to have enhanced interstate trade in some sectors of the economy by removing regulatory impediments to such trade. It has contributed to the development of national standards in some sectors, and has not resulted in the sale of goods with unacceptably low standards;

- for occupations, mutual recognition seems to be achieving its primary goal of overcoming many regulatory barriers to the movement of people in registered occupations. It does not appear to have had any significant unintended consequences.

Further impetus for regulatory reform at a state/territory level is the desire to reduce regulatory barriers to new investment within each state's boundaries

3. TRENDS IN REDISTRIBUTING AUTHORITY ACROSS LEVELS OF GOVERNMENT

All levels of government have been experiencing reform for at least twenty years, although the pace and magnitude of change accelerated in the 1980s and early 1990s, and the reform agenda has shifted over time.

Australian government is distinguished by four relevant features in this context:

- a federal system which mixes the devolution between the levels of government with extensive decentralisation within levels;

- sub-national centralisation at the state level (which means a weak and limited local government level);

- fiscal imbalance with regard to revenue, which entails a major transfer role for the federal revenue collector;

- limited capacity or inclination to engage in significant redistribution of authority across levels, particularly downwards.

3.1 Evolving tendencies

The most significant recent changes to the distribution of powers are not readily summarised. There has been a long term centralisation of powers at the federal and state levels, usually at the expense of the level immediately below. There have been experiments with general grants based on personal income tax as well as general revenue. The reviews of Commonwealth-state relations and responsibilities is producing some rationalisation, but progress has been relatively slow. Local government's discretion has been affected over time, with the clearest trend being reductions in its capacity to act. But the pattern is variable and the potential of local government is meant to be enhanced by recent reforms.

Public sector reforms at the *state* level started in the 1980s and have been rather comprehensive. They have covered financial management of the budget sector, workplace reforms, structural reorganisation, new management practices, service delivery (customer/consumer focus), restructuring (corporatisation) of government business enterprises, new asset management and information systems.

The main trends in redistributing authority across levels are as follows:

- continuing pressure for review and rationalisation as Australia moves towards the centenary of the federal system and the micro-economic agenda continues to dominate;

- specific exercises designed to produce clarification of roles and responsibilities (under the Council of Australian Governments);

- greater emphasis on performance management within and between levels;

- the increasing interest in applying the purchase/provider principle to traditional inter-governmental arrangements;

While there has been some support for overlapping jurisdictions (particularly from some advocates of state rights), in the 1990s the desire for rationalisation has acquired great prominence. The duplication of services and management between levels has become a focus for intergovernmental reform. The problems have included substantial bureaucracies at more than one level and the resultant complexities and inefficiencies of the system. One argument is that responsibilities relevant to running the national economy should reside with the Commonwealth and that therefore, for example, industrial relations (which was originally regarded a state matter, except for issues spanning states) should form one system. The states' position has been that the Commonwealth is duplicating their services in areas such as environment, education, health and housing.

National standards have been developed and inconsistencies in the regulations of different jurisdictions have been reduced. A more national (rather than a state-based) approach is increasingly being adopted for judging performance and reforms. There has been some rationalisation of shared responsibilities (e.g. road funding), and integration of aspects of national infrastructure networks (electricity and gas).

Work is being undertaken by governments on the relationship between inputs, outputs and outcomes, but there is certainly scope for greater progress. The quality of services and their delivery, which has attracted much recent attention, also offers potential for further development.

Reform has been extensive within levels. National reform – that is reform of sectors – has made some progress. With regard to inter-level reform, it is arguably more advanced for the local-state relationship than the state-Commonwealth. The general view is that progress with the latter has been slow but that the foundations have been laid and that the inter-governmental reform agenda will continue to be important for the rest of this decade as it was for the corresponding decade last century which culminated in the Australian federation in 1901.

3.2 The current debate

The current debates are not clearly about centralising or decentralising, although participants will variously view them as one or the other. The nature of the discussion depends on whether it is intra or inter level.

The federal debate involving the Commonwealth and the states recognises the need for some decentralisation. The most explicit agenda on this has been the one mounted by the state governments. This has envisaged both a reduced role for the Commonwealth in some functional areas and a shift from tied grants to general revenue payments.

Within the Commonwealth and state government levels, deconcentration has been proceeding for some time. The Commonwealth, for example, adopted 'devolution' (which included deconcentration) as a central element of its reform agenda in the 1980s.

The local government reforms encompassed in the new Act and in separate state initiatives (especially those in Victoria and South Australia), concentrate specifically on the local government sphere, and will achieve improved efficiency and effectiveness in that level of government. While state/territory statutory responsibility will remain in the foreseeable future, the national principles and national reporting required by the Act and the national system of benchmarking and performance indicators will provide a national focus on the reform process.

3.3 Driving forces and influences

The micro-economic agenda which has been running now since the mid-1980s, continues to provide a major impetus for change. Following the agreement by the Council of Australian Governments (COAG) in April 1995 to implement the national competition policy regime, recent emphasis has been placed on reducing the regulatory burden on small business. Working groups, established under the auspices of COAG, are to report on a range of matters including the development of nationally consistent occupational health and safety and workers' compensation arrangements, the development of a national framework for building regulation, reviews of regulation in the food industry and in agricultural and veterinary chemicals, and developing mechanisms for streamlining information exchange.

The need to address the respective roles and responsibilities of the different levels of government remains a live issue and is being addressed on a case by case basis through issue specific forums, for example, health ministers looking at the health system and the Intergovernmental Committee on Ecologically Sustainable Development undertaking a review of roles and responsibilities in relation to the environment.

AUSTRIA

1. INSTITUTIONS AND AUTHORITY

1.1 Structures

Description of levels

Austria is a federal republic consisting of 9 states (*Länder*) and 2 355 municipalities (*Gemeinde*) at the local level. Both the federal and *Länder* levels have law-making authority. The Federal Constitution (*Bundesverfassung*) provides that the municipalities have an area of jurisdiction of their own as well as one delegated from the federation or the *Länder*. The city of Vienna is both a municipality and a *Land*. *Länder* administrations are divided into districts (*Bezirke*), and some municipalities which do not have a charter fall under the administration of a district. If special *Land* authorities do not exist, the *Land* government devolves most of its administrative tasks to the districts.

Table 1: **Area and population of sub-national governments (1995)**

Number	Länder 9		Municipalities 2 301	
	Area (km²)	Population	Area (km²)	Population
Largest	19 173 [1]	1 539 849 [2]	46.688 [3]	1 539 848 [2]
Smallest	2 004 [4]	270 880 [5]	0.011 [6]	50 [7]

Number of municipalities and population distribution	
Population size	Number of municipalities
up to 1 000	623
1 000-5 000	1 528
5 000-10 000	130
10 000-50 000	62
50 000-100 000	17
over 100 000	7

1. Lower Austria.   2. Vienna.   3. Sölden.   4. Vorarlberg.
5. Burgenland.   6. Rattenberg.   7. Gramais.
Source: Austrian Central Statistical Office (*österreichisches Statistisches Zentralamt*, öSTAT).

The total area of Austria is 83 000 square kilometres and the total population in 1994 was 8 031 000. The eight *Länder*, excluding the city of Vienna, are very unequal in terms of both area and population (see). The average number of inhabitants per local authority is about 3 215.

Central government at sub-national levels

At the district level administrative affairs are carried out by a specially-appointed federal government official, the district commissioner (*Bezirkshauptmann*) and his office. For all matters to be executed by the district authorities (*Bezirkshauptmannschaften*), the district commissioner is responsible to the *Land* Governor (*Landeshauptmann*). Appeals against the district authorities are also dealt with at the *Land* level.

In sectors where the federal government retains some administrative responsibility (e.g. labour, taxation), these tasks are carried out by field offices of the ministries concerned.

Creation, elimination and restructuring

The *Länder* are laid down in the Federal Constitution. Any creation, restructuring or suppression of *Länder* is, therefore, impossible without a change to the Constitution.

The legal position of the municipalities has also been laid down in the Federal Constitution. The Länder are responsible for restructuring local authorities within their boundaries. Territorial reform took place at the local level in the 1970s – when some smaller municipalities were merged, reducing their number by 1 200 from around 3 500. Nevertheless the number of municipalities has continued to evolve; and in a few of the municipalities where unification took place, there has been re-separation.

The Federal Constitution provides for the creation of local and municipal government associations for co-operation in providing basic infrastructure.

Control bodies

Several means of judicial control exist in Austria:

- Control of the administration lies with the Constitutional Court where constitutional matters are concerned. To safeguard the complex lines of competence between federal and *Länder* lawmakers, the respective governments were authorised to challenge the laws of competing territorial bodies before the Constitutional Court. Otherwise responsibility for control lies with the Administrative High Court, in the field of administrative law; and with the Independent Administrative Boards (*Unabhängige Verwaltungssenate*) established in 1991 in each Land. The latter deal with administrative criminal matters, petitions against acts of immediate command and compulsion, and some civil law cases.

- The Court of Audit (*Rechnungshof*) controls the entire federal administration, the *Länder* administration, municipalities with more than 20 000 inhabitants, and other public bodies and public enterprises on behalf of the Federal Parliament. Recently the *Länder* have created *Länder* audit courts, and their findings are presented to the *Länder* parliaments annually.

1.2 Powers

Nature of sub-national institutions

Each *Land* has its own constitution, parliament and government.

Legislative bodies: *Länder* parliaments (*Landtag*) are the legislative bodies of every *Land* except Vienna. In Vienna, the city council (*Gemeinderat*) also fulfils the functions of a *Land* parliament. These parliaments elect, by proportional representation, a collegial governing body (*Landesregierung*) with two to nine members (nine to fifteen in Vienna) and its head – the Governor (*Landeshauptmann*).

Each municipality has a council which acts as a deliberating body, and has supreme decision-making power as well as supervisory functions. The members of the council (varying from 11 to 60 according to the number of inhabitants) are elected, usually for a period of five years, on the basis of proportional representation. Citizens are entitled to vote if their main residence is within the municipality. Decisions to be made are prepared by committees (e.g. finance, and social and cultural affairs), formed by members of the council.

Executive bodies: The *Land* government exercises executive power in fields of specific *Land* responsibilities, and on behalf of the Federation when no relevant federal authorities exist at the *Land* level. Unless there are separate federal authorities, the *Landeshauptmann* and the *Land* authorities subordinate to him are the executive bodies of the Federation within the area of the *Länder* (indirect federal administration). The *Landeshauptmann* is the sole recipient of directives from the Federal Government or from individual federal ministries concerning matters of indirect federal administration.

An executive committee (*Gemeindevorstand*) is elected from the local council or, in bigger municipalities, from the *Stadtsenat*. This committee makes decisions on various minor matters. The mayor is also elected by the council. He represents the local authority (as the ceremonial head), has decision-making power on all minor current affairs, and is the formal head of the local administration. The direct election of the mayor by the citizens in the municipality is currently being discussed at the political level. In three *Länder* the mayor is already directly elected.

Type and degree of autonomy

Legislative and administrative responsibilities are divided between the Federation (*Bund*) and the *Länder* according to provisions of the Federal Constitution. The Federal Constitution leaves legislative and executive powers to the *Länder* in all matters which are not expressly attributed to the federal level. Under the system of "indirect federal administration" mandatory instructions ("directives") can be issued by the Federal Minister in charge. These directives have to be followed and significantly affect the opportunities of the lower-level authority to act independently. A list of areas in which the Federal Parliament may legislate is specified in the Constitution. Areas not mentioned are considered to be the responsibility of *Länder* parliaments. These latter exercise their power of legislation in areas such as social welfare, nature conservation, building regulations and regional planning.

Länder are active in legislative procedures at the federal level through the *Land* Assembly (*Bundesrat*), which represents the federal principle in the legislative system. The members of the *Bundesrat* are elected by the *Land* parliaments, their numbers being in proportion to the population of the individual *Länder*. The *Bundesrat* may object to any legislation approved by the national parliament (*Nationalrat*), but this has only a delaying effect.

Municipalities have a right to self-administration. Their function is administrative and they have no power to pass legislation, but they can regulate local affairs (their "own domain") within the legal framework established by the higher levels of government and the Federal Constitution. The Federal Constitution grants local authorities the right to undertake commercial activities. They may own assets of any kind, operate enterprises or participate in them. The question of whether they may undertake commercial activities to the same extent as private legal entities is disputed. Some *Länder* restrict such activities to areas which cannot be operated equally well by private business enterprises, but the constitutionality of such limitations is disputed.

Each level of government is entitled to raise its own taxes. Joint taxes (which accrue jointly to the Federation, *Länder* and municipalities) have also been provided for by the Constitution.

The organisational authority of the *Länder* is considerably weakened by some special provisions in the Federal Constitution. *Land* laws amending or revising the organisation of general public administrative authorities in the *Länder* may be promulgated only with the consent of the federal government. This restriction affects the most important *Land* authorities, i.e. the *Land* governments and the chief district administrative authorities (*Bezirkshauptmannschaften*) and is mainly due to Austria's transition from a decentralised unitary State, the Austro-Hungarian monarchy, to a federal State. Limitations such as these are unusual in federal systems. The existence of an indirect federal administration in the *Länder* contributes to the considerable influence of the federal government on the administrative organisation of the *Länder*. From a federal point of view, it is difficult to justify that the chief executive of the *Land* is paid by the federal government, is subject to directives by the highest federal executive bodies and may be held responsible at *Land* level by the federal government with the possibility of losing his official functions. Indirect federal administration nevertheless enables the *Länder* to exert administrative influence in some areas of federal administration and thus to increase their political weight.

Municipal administration is organised homogeneously (except that local authorities with very few staff have no formally structured administration). It is headed by a chief administrative officer and is usually divided into five departments: the chief administrative officer's department; the Treasurer's department; and those for legal matters; building, planning, and civil engineering; and for social and cultural services. Internally, these departments tend to be organised hierarchically.

1.3 Responsibilities

Distribution of responsibilities

Länder have general competence for all fields not covered by the Federal Constitution. Most federal administrative tasks are delegated to the *Länder*. Exceptions, where the federal government retains some administrative responsibility, are labour affairs, taxation, security and military matters. In these areas field offices of ministries fulfil the administrative tasks.

The Federal Constitution allows for administrative execution of federal tasks by the *Länder* through the *Landeshauptmann* (indirect federal administration). The Federal Constitution also provides for mandatory administration by the *Landeshauptmann* of specific federal economic affairs such as the planning, construction and administration of highways, and official buildings.

Local authorities perform traditional public tasks such as health inspection, local planning, policing and various infrastructure provision functions such as water, sewerage, waste disposal, electric power generation, and roads. In addition, most local authorities run various social and health care services, primary education, culture and leisure activities. These basic public tasks must be provided by every local authority. The infrastructure provision tasks and other services become more specialised and more developed when the size of the municipality increases and/or when there is a more diversified economic structure.

The following functions have been guaranteed to the local authority by the Federal Constitution: local security, traffic and market police; administration of municipal parking areas; local sanitary, building and fire inspection; and regional planning. Local authorities also run a great variety of commercial enterprises ranging from gasworks, and power stations, to swimming pools, gravel pits, cinemas, poster companies, brickworks and abattoirs. In addition municipalities execute some tasks on behalf of the federation (e.g. elections), or of the *Länder* (e.g. citizenship procedures).

Mandatory, optional and shared responsibilities

The municipalities, as self-governing bodies, have responsibility for dealing with all matters "within their own domain" falling under the exclusive or overriding interest of the local community. As an administrative district of the *Land* administration, subordinate to the Federal and *Land* administrative authorities, they must also attend to functions "within the delegated domain" which are allocated to them by Federal legislation or the laws of the respective *Land*. Towns with more than 20 000 inhabitants may also be given those functions of the Federal and *Land* administration which are otherwise allocated to the chief district administrative authority.

Within the general description of "own domain" the Federal Constitution stipulates the principle of the "uniform community". This means that all matters which are generally in the interest of, and can be dealt with by, the local community itself must be qualified as falling within its "own domain". The Federal Constitution stipulates that Federal and *Länder* laws must expressly describe matters complying with the preconditions for being dealt with in the community's "own domain" as being of that domain. This does not apply to local authority's activities in the private sector of the economy and is guaranteed by the constitution directly.

This assignment of functions according to the principle of the "uniform community" may cause excessive demands to be made on individual local authorities in terms of the functions they are expected to fulfil. The Federal Constitution therefore allows that, if requested by a local authority, individual matters within their "own domain" may be assigned to a *Land* authority.

Although functions within the local authority's "own domain" predominate in both a qualitative and quantitative sense, functions in the delegated domain are also very numerous. These include keeping the registers of births, deaths, marriages and citizenship; participating in the implementation of elections; dealing with water control and water protection, meat and livestock inspection; helping with population, civil status and industrial censuses and with statistical surveys; participating in the implementation of laws promoting livestock breeding, and laws on real estate transactions.

2. MANAGEMENT FUNCTIONS

2.1 Policy-making and co-ordination

Coherence, consultation and conflict resolution

The primary role of the Federation is to legislate. The *Länder* have the right to protest to the Constitutional Court if any federal legislation appears to encroach on their authority. As far as legislation by the *Bund* and the *Länder* is concerned, the Federal Constitution of 1920 makes provision for a balanced mutual participation of bodies which represent the interest of the *Bund* and the *Länder*. All enactments of the *Land* parliaments (*Landtage*) should, immediately after they have been passed, be notified to the Federal Chancellery prior to their publication. The Federal Government can, within eight weeks from the day of an enactment's receipt at the Federal Chancellery, object to a *Land* parliament enactment on the grounds that it jeopardises Federal interests.

The *Bund* and the *Länder* may conclude agreements on matters within their respective spheres of competence. Agreements between the *Länder* can only be made on matters pertaining to their autonomous sphere of competence and must, without delay, be made known to the federal government. This instrument has proven effective in, for instance, the field of hospital financing.

Each *Land* is independently responsible for its own administrative tasks, but for delegated federal administrative tasks the *Land* authorities are bound by the federal government and are accountable to it. The Governor is bound by the minister in charge and accountable to him. Matters pertaining to both the *Land* administration and the indirect federal administration are shared among the members of the *Land* government. For matters of indirect federal administration, members of the *Land* government are as much bound by the instructions of the Governor as is the latter by instructions from the federal level. The Governor cannot give directives to the members of the *Land* government concerning the conduct of business in other areas. To assist with their administrative functions, *Land* governments are supported by the Office of the *Landesregierung*, which is staffed by civil servants.

Many of the smaller local authorities co-operate for the provision of basic infrastructure services such as sewerage and water purification plants, and to do so they form joint authorities. This form of inter-municipal co-operation is generally subsidised by federal and *Länder* governments.

Local authorities are responsible for safeguarding the interests of the local community and for this purpose they have the right to participate in the administrative legal process and to be heard in the relevant proceedings. Other laws grant municipalities the right to send members to certain committees.

Formal and informal mechanisms

In 1974 a provision was introduced to the Federal Constitution concerning agreements between the Federation and the *Länder* or among the *Länder*. This has become important in formal co-ordination (both multilateral and bilateral), particularly in the field of economic development and in establishing joint bodies.

As all territorial authorities are under obligation to maintain a balanced budget, there is a need to co-ordinate budgetary plans and decisions. Some informal institutions meet regularly with federal officials, e.g. the Conference of the *Länder* Governors and the Conference of the *Länder* Financial Heads.

For co-ordination and the common interest of the *Länder* a "Liaison Office of the *Länder*" was set up in 1951, now with a subsidiary in Brussels. The tasks of the Liaison Office include to:

- ensure a permanent link among *Länder* and between the *Länder* and the federal government;

- co-ordinate the views of the *Länder* in matters relating to their responsibilities;
- act as "post office", i.e. to distribute federal government comments, Bills, etc., among the *Länder*;
- act as a secretariat to the *Land* Governors' Conference, the Conference of Directors-General of the *Land* Governments, and the Conferences of Experts.

The *Land* Governors' Conference aims at harmonizing the interests of the *Länder* vis-à-vis the *Bund*. This co-ordination is reflected in the decisions taken by the Conference, which in turn are based on the unanimous decisions of the individual *Land* governments. In this manner, catalogues of demands by the *Länder* were developed, in which the *Länder* requested the improvement and strengthening of their position. The meetings of the Conference are prepared by the conference of Directors-General of the *Land* Governments. Items for the agenda are suggested by individual participants. The Conference of Directors-General draws up the recommendations for the decisions of the *Land* Governors' Conference. There are also various "Conferences of Experts" at both the political and administrative level.

In addition to these instruments there is the Austrian Conference of Regional Planning (öROK) which helps to co-ordinate regionally-relevant planning projects and policies among the corporate territorial authorities according to the "transcompetence" character of Austrian regional planning law.

The Austrian Association of Towns also plays a crucial role in developing the constitutional foundations for municipalities and in the financial protection of their economies. Currently some 215 municipalities are affiliated, accounting for more than half of the inhabitants of Austria.

2.2 Financial management

Sources of revenue

In 1995 the income of the federal government totalled about 576.9 million schillings, the income of the *Länder* about 167.2 million schillings and that of the municipalities about 157.7 million schillings. Overall, 74 per cent of gross revenues (including social security contributions) go to the federal government. Conversely the *Länder* and municipalities can rely to only a small extent on "own" revenue sources of finance. Consequently, most of the *Länder* revenues and 30 per cent of municipal revenues are received from the federal level (see Table 3). These consist either of fixed shares of the major revenues collected centrally (see Table 2), or of transfers – some of which are earmarked for specific responsibilities (e.g. compulsory education, housing) carried out by the *Länder*. The revenue-sharing process is rather complex – the percentage of tax revenues passed onto the *Länder* and municipalities is negotiated for each tax separately and laid down in a federal law. As a result, the proportion of their gross revenue which the *Länder* can spend at their own discretion rises to about 40 per cent – a degree of "self-financing" which is quite low compared with other federal countries. The municipalities, on the other hand, have a relatively high ratio of their revenues coming from "own" taxes and central revenue shares. Transfers from other levels of government constitute less than 10 per cent of their revenues (see Table 3). The transfer procedure is guided by two principles: productivity, based on regional/local tax revenues; and demography, based on the number of inhabitants.

The Austrian system of "linked" taxation between the Federal Government, *Länder* and municipalities is designed to enable each community – irrespective of which tax sources it is able to use itself – to have a certain minimum available.

The municipalities have various sources of revenue including payroll (*Kommunalsteuer*), commercial, real estate, beverage and entertainment taxes. Other sources are dog licenses; fees and charges for local infrastructure and other services; participation in "fiscal liaison". Through the latter local authorities receive a share of the most important federal taxes [wage and income tax: tax on investment income turnover (VAT), beer, wine, real property acquisition and mineral oil; and levies on gambling establishments]. Apart from this revenue from taxation, there are special grants or subsidies (incentives) for special functions, e.g. to cover expenditure for hospitals. About 20 per cent of the income share of municipalities is reserved for compensation arrangements in favour of financially weaker municipalities. Given the rather clear constitutional regulations and the consensus policy pursued between the Federal, *Land* and municipality levels, local autonomy is relatively well protected.

Table 2. **The sharing of joint federal revenues (1985, 1995)**
(Per cent shares of total revenue by tax)

Tax	Sch billion Revenue 1985	Sch billion Revenue 1995 [1]	Federal government 1985	Federal government 1995	Länder 1985	Länder 1995	Municipalities 1985	Municipalities 1995
Taxes on income and property	87.4	182.3	54.7	59.2	24.8	22.2	20.5	18.6
of which:								
Income tax	19.2	20.6	42.2	46.1	30.8	29.1	27.0	24.8
Wage tax	66.6	135.1	58.6	63.2	23.2	20.6	18.2	16.2
Capital gains tax	0.7	3.8	10.0	19.9	15.0	13.3	75.0	66.8
Interest income tax	–	21.5	–	53.0	–	27.0	–	20.0
Inheritance and gift tax	0.9	1.3	70.0	70.0	30.0	30.0	–	0.0
Other taxes	152.3	233.8	69.2	69.2	18.4	18.4	12.4	12.4
of which:								
Value-added tax	125.7	186.7	69.4	69.4	18.8	18.8	11.8	11.8
Mineral oil tax	15.9	29.3	88.6	88.6	8.6	8.6	2.8	2.8
Real estate tax	2.6	5.5	4.0	4.0	–	–	96.0	96.0
Motor car taxes	4.8	9.3	50.0	53.8	50.0	46.2	–	–
Beverage taxes	3.3	3.0	36.4	38.6	36.4	33.9	27.2	27.5
Other revenues	0.6	1.3	–	–	–	–	–	–
TOTAL tax revenues	240.3	417.4	63.8	64.8	21.0	20.1	15.2	15.1

1. Estimated revenue.
Source: Austrian Ministry of Finance (1986, 1995).

Table 3. **Revenue structure of *Länder* and municipalities (1985, 1993)**
(Percentage of total revenue)

	1985 Länder	1985 Municipalities[1]	1993 Länder	1993 Municipalities[1]
Own taxes	1.9	15.7	1.8	14.4
Federal revenue shares	44.3	28.9	44.9	27.9
Transfers from other public authorities	48.3 [2]	10.9	48.4 [2]	10.0
Debt raised	3.6	3.8	2.5	4.8
Public charges	–	5.3	–	6.0
Other revenues	1.9	35.5	2.5	36.9
TOTAL	100.0	100.0	100.0	100.0

1. Including Vienna.
2. Earmarked transfers for housing subsidies, cost defrayal for teachers' salaries, community contribution to *Länder*.
Source: Austrian Central Statistical Office (*österreichisches Statistisches Zentralamt*, öSTAT), 1995.

Expenditure responsibilities

In 1995 federal expenditures comprised about 692.9 million schillings, the expenditure of the *Länder* about 169.7 million schillings and those of the municipalities about 169.5 million schillings.

Gross public expenditure is concentrated in the hands of the central government to a much higher degree than in other OECD federal countries (almost half – see table 4). This is only partly explained by the relatively substantial transfers from the *Bund* to lower levels of government. This central dominance is mostly at the expense of the *Länder* – the expenditure share of municipalities being similar to that of other federal countries.

The most important categories of expenditure, representing approximately two thirds of the total, are salaries and wages and investments (mainly in infrastructure).

Table 4. **Gross public expenditure by level of government (1980, 90, 93)**
(Percentage of total)

	1980	1990	1993	1993 (Sch. bill.)
Federal government [1]	46.5	48.7	47.7	822.2
Länder [2]	12.8	11.8	11.6	220.5
Municipalities [3]	17.4	15.5	16.6	285.4
Chambers	1.5	1.7	1.5	25.0
Social security	21.8	22.3	22.6	389.0
TOTAL	100.0	100.0	100.0	1 722.1

1. Including federal government funds.
2. Excluding Vienna.
3. Including Vienna.
Source: OECD Economic Surveys: Austria, OECD, 1994.

Balance between discretion and control

The Federal Constitution obliges all territorial authorities to strive for equilibrium in the overall economy in operating their budgets.

Municipal services are generally financed from local resources (47.2 per cent), transfers from the federal government (45.7 per cent) and the Land (7.1 per cent). In principle, Land governments are financially self-supporting, but there is no constitutional provision which specifies the distribution of tax powers. Instead, a special federal law, the Finance Equalisation Act, is negotiated between the Federation and the Länder for a period of several years, although it can be modified unilaterally by the federal legislator. A system of inter-governmental transfers has also been established for covering the costs of special Land and municipal projects.

The distribution of financial resources to the local authorities through "fiscal liaison" is carried out in two stages, starting with a distribution to the individual local authorities within a Land. This follows various criteria, the most important being the number of inhabitants. Even if consultation between different levels of government under the Financial Equalisation Act is considered a weak form of co-operation in a federal state, the outcome is relative stability in fiscal transfers. Nevertheless there is a trend towards centralisation and the share of local taxes in the total tax receipts of local authorities has reduced since the 1970s.

The fiscal potential of local authorities is quite considerable. The share of local government expenditure (including the city of Vienna) in total public expenditure was about 22 per cent in 1986, whereas the federal share was approximately 60 per cent. With regard to investment expenditure, however, the share of local authorities (including the city of Vienna) was about 60 per cent; that of the federal level was only 29 per cent.

2.3 Performance management

The reports of the Court of Audit are published following their presentation to the Lower House of Parliament (Nationalrat) or the Land parliament (Landtag) and the local council (Gemeinderat). The Länder parliaments are entitled to initiate an audit. The focus is now shifting from regularity audits to performance audits. In March 1991 there was a call for a "more effective means of monitoring the regularity and efficiency of the public budgets and public enterprises" to develop, in particular, the idea that the audit procedure should be structured in the same way on all territorial levels.

For the moment quality standards are not used within the public administration. But this is becoming a main issue of the Austrian administrative reform programme at the federal level, with the intention of building up a system of performance measurement data.

2.4 Human resource management

Statutory distinctions: An important element of the Austrian administration is the distinction between public employees who are civil servants (*Beamte*), linked with their employer for life by their "appointment"; and contracted staff employed on the basis of a bilateral contract of private law. This distinction is made at every level of government. Teachers in *Länder* schools are federally-paid *Land* employees.

Table 5: **Public employees by level of government (1990-94)**

	1990 [1]	1991 [1]	1992 [1]	1993 [2]	1994 [2]
Federal	308 789	308 270	301 630	245 794	247 239
Länder	159 200	145 649	146 183	148 416	143 880
Municipalities	71 269	74 218	76 252	78 222	79 193
Vienna	67 490	62 539	66 797	66 291	67 623
TOTAL	606 748	590 676	590 862	538 723	537 935

1. Posts.
2. Full-time equivalents.
Source: Federal Chancellery, 1995.

Application of the principle of homogeneity results in a certain unity of legislation regarding conditions of service and staff representation for all territorial bodies, although today this homogeneity relates only to the basic structures. Large parts of the federal legislation have been taken over practically intact by various *Land* legislators. In some cases it may be said that the employees of other territorial bodies enjoy better conditions than those of federal employees.

The structure of *Land* legislation, essentially follows the federal example. A standard of legality requires that public service rules should be determined, as a matter of principle, on the Federal or *Land* level. However, legislation through "simple" decisions of the *Land* parliament plays an important role in salary legislation. Austrian legislation links rules concerning public employees in such a way that reform is difficult in Federal and *Land* authorities.

Pay bargaining is an annual process of negotiation between the *Land* secretary in charge of the civil service and contracted staff. Monitoring of staffing levels, pay, recruitment, and dismissal is shared with the Federal Chancellery (co-ordinating pay and, for example, approval of special personnel decisions and support in recruitment) and individual ministries (recruitment, dismissal).

There is almost no mobility between levels of government in Austria.

2.5 Regulatory management and reform

European Union (EU) membership has had a significant impact on *Länder* responsibilities, notably as regards land purchase and the building sector, and as a result regulations are being, or will need to be, reviewed.

The EU membership has also led to constitutional amendments concerning the participation of the *Länder* in matters of European integration. The *Bund* must inform the *Länder* without delay about all projects within the framework of the European Union which affect the *Länder*'s autonomous sphere of competence or could otherwise be of interest to them. It must also allow them the opportunity to present their views via the Federal Chancellery within a reasonable interval to be fixed by the *Bund*. The same holds good for the municipalities concerning their own sphere of competence or when other important municipal interests are affected. Representation of the municipalities is in these matters incumbent upon the Austrian Municipal Federation and the Austrian Federation of Towns.

3. TRENDS IN REDISTRIBUTING AUTHORITY ACROSS LEVELS OF GOVERNMENT

3.1 Evolving tendencies

1918 saw the evolution of Austria from the constitutional monarchy of the Austro-Hungarian empire to a republic. After a transitional period lasting until October 1920 a Federal Constitution was introduced which established the Republic of Austria as a federal State. After the restoration of the Austrian Republic in 1945, it was decided to re-adopt the parliamentary democracy provided for in the Constitution of 1920. Although details of the Federal Constitution have been adjusted since then, (e.g. the division of responsibilities between federal and Land authorities), its fundamental character remains unchanged.

The legal and institutional organisation of local government has remained relatively unchanged for many years. There are few signs of any alteration to the legal and financial foundations of local government activities in the near future. This institutional stability over several decades is remarkable given the social and economic changes which have taken place during this time and is mostly seen as a consequence of the broad and flexible concept of local self-government which leaves considerable scope for adaptation and change.

Nevertheless the relationships between the federal level, the Länder and local governments have changed during recent years. This has been due to the growing importance of local government in dealing with the consequences of economic expansion and social change as well as federal and Länder concerns with macro-economic management and reduction of social and regional disparities. The pressure for inter-governmental co-ordination has grown as improvements in service delivery, management of the business cycle, supervision over local authorities (e.g. in the field of debt-contracting), and in land-use planning have been demanded. In addition, central-local relations have become more complicated as regards the allocation of tax revenues.

The possibility of joining the European Union generated a debate which revolved around how Länder and municipal interests will be affected and what their role will be vis-à-vis the federal level. One concrete result was the agreement between the Federation and the Länder of 1992 on the rights of participation in matters of European integration. This provides obligations to inform the Länder and municipalities and to be bound by common decisions of the Länder. The main provisions were adopted in the 1994 amendment of the Federal Constitution.

3.2 The current debate

There is presently a general feeling that joint decision-making within the administrative and political spheres of the three levels of government has become insufficiently productive in several respects including the co-financing of services and infrastructure installations.

The present process of decentralisation is shifting certain functions (e.g. the promotion of housing) from the federal to the Länder level, and has caused some distrust on the part of the local authorities. There are demands for further decentralisation at the local level, in order to respond better to needs.

However, there is a contradiction in the present situation. On the one hand, there is concern about unemployment and the need for economic and urban restructuring; hence the mounting pressure from many sides to revive policies at the local level; while, on the other hand, the scope for local government has recently been considerably reduced.

The reform of the federal state has also been the subject of an ongoing discussion since 1987. A commission of experts made several proposals concerning the redistribution of federal responsibilities. These proposals aimed at a more balanced distribution of tasks between the Federation and the Länder, with more consideration being given to the principle of subsidiarity and to administrative simplification. Further negotiations between the Länder and the Federation led to recommendations for an amendment to the constitution to reorganise the federal structure. These included: distributing responsibilities among levels of government according to the subsidiarity principle; elimination of the system of "indirect federal administration"; restriction of decisions by federal ministers to general topics in the case of mandatory administration; inclusion in the Constitution of "direct federal administrative" competences; delegation of legislative power to the *Länder*; development of the administrative courts in the *Länder*; strengthening of co-operation among the regions; adjustment to mechanisms for distributing revenues; and strengthening the power of the B*undesrat*.

This proposed amendment could not be adopted because agreement was not reached on changes in the tax distribution scheme and no acceptable mechanism could be found for compensating the *Länder*. The whole discussion about the reform of the federal State and redistributing responsibilities between the federation and the *Länder* originates in problems concerning the distribution of revenues between the levels of government. Serious budgetary problems, partially in connection with entry into European Union at the beginning of 1995, fuelled this debate.

Further negotiations concerning a reform of the fiscal system are planned for 1996, but it is unlikely that fundamental changes will be made to the federal structure. Several reasons suggest this: the distributional importance of the existing fiscal system (the western part of the country finances the eastern part); severe structural problems prevent the *Länder* from exploring tax revenues; "elimination of the indirect administration" is no longer discussed. As the *Länder* act outside their own budgets when fulfilling tasks under indirect administration, the elimination of this system would result (despite a gain in autonomy) in higher costs for the *Länder*. In spite of the fact that municipalities have to accept the elimination in principle, there remain many unsettled questions.

3.3 Driving forces

During the years when the system of public finances provided increasing tax receipts and when debt payments by local authorities were low, joint decision-making and central-local relations were harmonious because there was sufficient scope for new initiatives. The situation changed at the end of the 1970s, when economic conditions deteriorated. This was in part manifest by an increasing polarisation between prosperous and peripheral regions. As a result, debate on structural reform and tighter public finances placed stress on the relations between Federal, *Land* and local authorities. The range of activities carried out by local authorities has been markedly reduced and financial conflicts between levels of government have increased.

There appears to be a persistent prejudice that local politics represents only a training ground for politics at a higher level of government. Most local authorities seem not to be ready, or able, to take more responsibility for "reviving politics from below".

In October 1996 the Federal minister of finance and the Federal minister responsible for co-ordination with the *Länder* decided to introduce a mechanism for consultation on regulations which generate costs at more than one level of government. A consultation group will monitor estimates of the likely costs of all such proposed regulations.

BELGIUM

1. INSTITUTIONS AND AUTHORITY

1.1 Structures

Description of levels

Under its Constitution, as revised in 1993 and co-ordinated in 1994, "Belgium is a federal State made up of Communities and Regions" (Article 1). Belgium has a total area of 30 500 square kilometres, and its population in 1994 was 10 116 000.

Belgium "is made up of three Communities: the French Community, the Flemish Community and the German-speaking Community" (Art. 2), as well as "three Regions: the Walloon Region, the Flemish Region and the Brussels Region".

The territory of the Walloon and Flemish regions is determined in Article 5 of the Constitution. The Flemish Region is made up of five provinces: Antwerp, Flemish Brabant, East Flanders, West Flanders and Limburg. The Walloon Region is also made up of five provinces: Walloon Brabant, Hainaut, Liege, Luxembourg and Namur. The Brussels Region comprises 19 municipalities.

Regions divide the country along strictly geographical lines, whereas Communities are based on geographical and linguistic criteria alike. In practice, this dual structure means that people living in the Brussels-Capital Region, which has the status of a "bilingual region", may opt into either the French-speaking or the Flemish Community; similarly, inhabitants of the German-speaking region belong to the Walloon Region yet constitute the German-speaking Community which exerts its competencies in the municipalities of Ambleve, Bullange, Burg-Reuland, Butgenbach, Eupen, La Calamine, Lontzen, Raeren, and Saint-Vith. At the same time, residents of the Flemish Region automatically belong to the Flemish Community, while people living in the Walloon Region, except for the German-speaking region, automatically belong to the French-speaking Community.

Belgium currently has 589 municipalities, located as follows:

- 262 in the Walloon Region;
- 308 in the Flemish Region;
- 19 in the Brussels-Capital Region.

Central government at sub-national levels

Governors of provinces and mayors of municipalities are appointed by the Crown and represent central authority. Both are characterised by a dual functionality. Thus, on the one hand, they are agents of the federal government exercising general interest tasks in the provinces and municipalities respectively; and on the other hand they chair the executive bodies of the provinces and the municipalities (the municipal council in the case of the mayor). Thus they act as bodies of decentralised authority, exercising either provincial or municipal responsibilities, depending on the case.

As representatives of central authority at the municipal level, mayors are appointed by the Crown from among the elected members of municipal councils or, in exceptional cases and with the approval of

Table 1. **Area and population of sub-national governments (1990)**[1]

	Regions	Provinces	Municipalities [2]
Number	3	10	589
Area (sq. km.)			
Maximum	16 844.3	4 439.7	213.75 [3]
Minimum	161.4	1 090.5	1.14 [4]
Population			
Maximum	5 768 925	1 605 187	459 072 [5]
Minimum	954 045	232 813	92 [6]

Breakdown of the number of municipalities by population	
Population	Number of municipalities
0-1 000	1
1 000-4 999	101
5 000-9 999	171
10 000-49 999	289
50 000-99 999	19
over 100 000	8

1. This table does not take the three Communities into account.
2. Data are for 1995.
3. Tournai.
4. Saint-Josse-ten-Noode.
5. Antwerp.
6. Herstappe.

Sources: *Structure and Operation of Local and Regional Democracy: Belgium*, Council of Europe, 1993.
Ministry for the Public Service, 1995.

the provincial executive (*députation permanente*), from among non-councillors who are registered voters of the municipality and aged 25 years or more (Section 13 of the new Municipalities Act). It is also in that capacity that mayors are invested by Section 133, paragraph 1 of the same act with the power to carry out laws, decrees, orders, regulations and directives of the State, unless such authority is formally assigned to the municipal executive, consisting of the mayor and aldermen (*échevins*), or to the municipal council. Notwithstanding, mayors are at the same time the supreme magistrates of their municipalities.

At the provincial level, the duties of government commissioner are carried out by a Crown-appointed governor (Section 4, paragraphs 1 and 2 of the Provinces Act of 30 April 1836). Under Section 104, paragraph 1 of that same act, the governor presides over the provincial executive, in which he possesses a vote. It is in his capacity as representative of the State in the province that the governor, under Section 124, paragraph 1 of that same act, carries out laws, decrees and general administrative directives, along with directives of the executives (currently the governments) of the Communities or Regions, unless the law, the decree, the Crown or the executives provide otherwise.

Creation, elimination and restructuring

Under the Constitution, "It lies with the law to divide the territory into a greater number of provinces, if need be" (Art. 5). In addition, "The limits of the State, the provinces and the municipalities can only be changed or modified by law" (Art. 7). The most recent mergers of municipalities entered into force on 1 January 1977 and, in respect of Antwerp, on 1 January 1983.

Municipalities may band together for the joint delivery of certain services, such as supplying water, gas or electricity.

Control bodies

Ever since Belgium became a federation, the Regions have exercised supervisory authority over the provinces and municipalities, except for the appointment of governors of provinces and mayors, and for the establishment of operational guidelines for municipal police forces, which are powers vested in the federal authority. Section 7, paragraph 1 of the special institutional reform Act of 8 August 1980 gives Regions the power to assign and exercise administrative control over provinces, municipalities, urban areas and federations of municipalities. Nonetheless, the same provision excludes from the jurisdiction of Regions certain powers that are conferred at the national or Community levels and for which the Act or decree specifically assigns jurisdiction.

Under paragraph 2 of that same provision, as amended by the special Act of 16 July 1993, the federal authority nevertheless reserves the power to assign and exercise ordinary administrative jurisdiction over municipalities in the German-speaking Region and to assign such jurisdiction over the municipalities on the outskirts of Brussels where residents are afforded linguistic "facilities" (*communes à facilités*), and over the municipalities of Comines-Warneton and Fourons.

Under Article 162, paragraph 2 of the Constitution, the higher authority is invested with power of approval only in cases and in the manner determined by law. Supervisory powers are exercised over both the legality and the suitability (i.e. compatibility with the general interest) of the actions of local authorities (on this point, see the stipulation in Article 162, paragraph 2 of the Constitution). Regional governments, provincial executives and provincial governors, as the case may be, also act as control bodies. Furthermore, at each level, financial inspectors oversee the advisability of expenditure. The Court of Auditors oversees the accounts of the State, the Autonomous Communities, the Regions and the provinces -- but not those of the municipalities.

1.2 Powers

Nature of sub-national institutions

Federal level

Federal legislative authority is exercised collectively by the Crown, the House of Representatives, and the Senate. Federal executive authority is exercised by the Crown and his ministers, i.e. the federal government.

The House of Representatives is made up of 150 directly elected members. The Senate is made up of 71 regular members, including: 40 directly elected senators, of whom 25 are elected by the Dutch-speaking electoral college (all registered voters in the Flemish Region and those in the Brussels-Capital Region who opt to vote for Flemish lists) and 15 by the French-speaking electoral college (all registered voters in the Walloon Region and those in the Brussels-Capital Region who opt to vote for lists of French-speaking candidates); Community senators, of whom 10 are appointed by and from within the Flemish Council, 10 by and from within the Council of the French-speaking Community and one by and from within the Council of the German-speaking Community; 10 senators co-opted by the other 61. There is also another category of senators -- those who are senators by right (the King's children or descendants of the heir apparent).

By law, federal ministers and Secretaries of State are appointed by the Crown. In practice, the composition of the government is the result of a negotiated agreement among the parties that form a majority in the House.

Community and regional levels

In the Walloon Region: the Walloon Council, made up of 75 directly elected members; the Walloon regional government, whose members are elected by the Council.

In the Brussels-Capital Region: the Brussels-Capital Regional Council, made up of 75 members elected directly from lists of French-speaking or Flemish candidates; the regional government, whose members are elected by the Council and which must have the support of a majority of each linguistic group.

In the Flemish Community: the Flemish Council, made up of 118 directly elected members from the Flemish Region and six Flemish members of the Brussels-Capital Regional Council; the Flemish government, whose members are elected by the Council.

In the French-speaking Community: the Council of the French-speaking Community, (theoretically) made up of the 75 members of the Walloon Council and 19 French-speaking members of the Brussels-

Capital Regional Council; the government of the French-speaking Community, made up of two members of the Walloon government, a French-speaking member of the Brussels-Capital regional government and a member elected by the Council of the French-speaking Community.

In the German-speaking Community: the Council of the German-speaking Community, made up of 25 directly elected members; the government of the German-speaking Community, whose members are elected by the Council.

In the provinces: the provincial council, made up of directly elected members; the provincial executive, whose members are elected by the provincial council; the governor; and the clerk of the provincial court.

In the municipalities:the municipal council, made up of directly elected members; the municipal executive, made up of the mayor and aldermen; the mayor.

Aldermen are elected by the municipal council except in the municipalities adjacent to Brussels and the municipalities of Comines-Warneton and Fourons where they are directly elected by the local voters. The mayor is appointed by the Crown. In addition, the provincial executive is presided over by the governor, who is not elected, but appointed by the Crown. The municipal executive comprises the aldermen and the mayor and is presided over by the mayor, who is appointed by the Crown, on the recommendation of the municipal council, and is generally an elected member of that council.

Institutions of the Flemish Community exercise regional powers in the Flemish Region, which therefore has no institutions of its own.

Type and degree of autonomy

Except as provided otherwise, measures enacted by political institutions of the Communities and Regions have the same force of law as those enacted by federal political institutions. Communities and Regions enjoy vast autonomy for the exercise of their own specific powers.

In addition, the Constitution gives the Council of the French-speaking Community, the Walloon Council and the Flemish Council constitutive autonomy. Accordingly, each of the three assemblies may adopt decrees, if approved by at least two-thirds of its members, to amend key features of its own composition, election and internal procedures, as well as decrees concerning the operation of its government. The Brussels-Capital Regional Council and the Council of the German-speaking Community do not have constitutive autonomy.

The Constitution, as it stands today, stipulates that "The federal authority only has power in the matters that are formally attributed to it by the Constitution and the laws carried in pursuance of the Constitution itself" and that "The Communities and the Regions, each in its own field of concern, have power for the other matters, under the conditions and in the terms stipulated by law" (Art. 35). The federal authority has jurisdiction over provincial and municipal law.

Notwithstanding, in the absence of an article of the Constitution enumerating exclusive powers of the federal authority, it is the jurisdiction of the Communities and the Regions that is delimited by the Constitution and by law, and the federal authority has jurisdiction over all other matters.

Since 1989, Community and regional finances have been governed by law. A system of taxation specific to the Communities and Regions is planned. The French-speaking and Flemish Communities both have jurisdiction within the territory of the Brussels-Capital Region -- a situation that in certain ways makes it difficult for the Communities to exercise their powers of taxation.

The Provinces and Municipalities Acts stipulate the respective jurisdictions and autonomy of provinces and municipalities. Municipalities have a power to tax.

The Regions are responsible for the organisation of, and have general administrative supervision over, the Provinces, the municipalities, municipal groupings, and urban agglomerations.

1.3 Responsibilities

Distribution of responsibilities

The distribution of responsibilities among the federal authority, the Communities and the Regions is established by the Constitution and institutional reform acts. The following lists for each level of government are intended only as examples.

Federal level: The powers of the federal authority lie essentially in the following areas: economic union; monetary unity; taxation; foreign affairs; justice; national defence; the gendarmerie; social security; federal cultural and scientific institutions; pensions; public health; public debt; law and order; the public service; scientific policy; foreign trade.

The federal authority retains some jurisdiction over matters attributed to the Regions, such as economic expansion, environmental policy, energy policy, public works and transport.

The Provincial Governors have retained only limited supervisory responsibilities, based on a decree of the Walloon Regional Council in July 1989 which specifies the supervision over the municipalities, provinces, and municipal groupings in the Walloon Region; the decree of the Flemish Council in April 1993 regulating the administrative supervision of the municipalities in the Flemish Region; and a Royal Order of July 1985 (modified in January 1989) concerning the administrative supervision of the Brussels agglomeration and the municipalities making up the Brussels-Capital Region.

Community level: The powers of the Communities lie essentially in the following areas:

- cultural matters, i.e.: safeguarding and promoting the language; promoting the training of researchers; fine arts; cultural heritage, museums; libraries and record collections; radio and television; support for the press; youth policies; ongoing education and cultural events; physical education and sport; recreation and tourism; pre-school training, adult education, and extra-curricular, artistic, intellectual, civic and social training; social promotion;

- occupational training and redeployment;

- education, except for setting the upper and lower age limits for compulsory schooling, minimum requirements for degrees, and the education pension scheme, which continue to fall under federal jurisdiction;

- certain major aspects of the health care and social welfare policies;

- the use of languages, with exceptions concerning special-status municipalities, services whose activities extend beyond the linguistic region in which they are established, and federal and international institutions whose activities are common to more than one Community.

Regional level: The powers of the Regions lie essentially in the following areas: land-use planning; the environment and water policy; rural renewal and conservation of nature; city planning and housing; agricultural policy; energy policy; subsidiary powers and administrative jurisdiction; employment policy; public works and transport.

Federalisation has also shifted supervision of local authorities from the federal to the regional level.

Local level: The general principle of the assignment of jurisdiction to local authorities is set out in Article 41 of the Constitution, under which "Interests which are exclusively of a municipal or provincial nature are ruled on by municipal or provincial councils, according to the principles established by the Constitution." Moreover, Article 162, paragraph 2 of the Constitution requires that certain powers be decentralised to provincial or municipal institutions.

The vagueness of the concept of "interests which are exclusively of a municipal or provincial nature" has allowed local authorities to expand the number and scope of their powers imperceptibly over the years. Even so, a great many municipal and provincial powers are still conferred powers (i.e. bestowed by the Constitution or by laws enacted by virtue thereof) arising out of the process of decentralisation.

The powers of the Regions lie essentially in the following areas: municipal police (urban or rural); land-use planning (special land allocation plans, city planning permits, municipal development plans, etc.); the granting of social assistance (and, in particular, the *"minimex"* guaranteed minimum income benefit) via public social welfare centres, which provide help for the needy; archiving; public libraries; supervision of the unemployed (compulsory checking-in); recording domicile and changes thereof; issuing identity cards, driving licences and various records, copies (official or not) of certificates relating to nationality, domicile, household members, criminal records, etc.; population registers; municipal schools; street lights; municipal roads, parks and gardens; facilities that are hazardous, or insanitary or cause nuisance; funerals and burials (including cemeteries); insanitary housing; fitting out sporting and cultural facilities, etc.

Among the responsibilities of provinces are to certify the results of municipal elections, recommend appellate court counsellors and presiding and associate justices of courts of first instance, and adjust certain territorial boundaries. Moreover, provinces traditionally enjoy relatively broad autonomy with respect to education, social and cultural facilities (training centres, rest homes, etc.), preventive medicine, assistance to individuals (housing subsidies, disability pensions, entrepreneurial assistance, etc.), the environment, roads, and rivers and streams. Local authorities can thus deploy instruments of economic, cultural and sporting policy.

Governors and mayors bear responsibilities in the areas of law and order and civil defence; to that end, they may call upon the gendarmerie and the civil defence force.

Mandatory, optional and shared responsibilities

The principle of "federal loyalty" was enshrined during the most recent phase of institutional reform. What this means is that the federal authority, Communities and Regions not only adhere to their respective areas of responsibility but also act in such a way as to avoid all conflict of interest among themselves, the objective being to ensure that the various institutions function as a balanced whole.

Defining responsibilities through reference to notions of municipal or provincial interests can lead to overlapping areas of authority. Furthermore, separate authorities may have jurisdiction over different aspects of the same issue at the same time (as is the case with education and land-use planning). For example, alongside networks of private schools are municipal, provincial and Community school systems. There have been calls for rationalisation of supply, even though, in practice, there can be genuine complementarity in the field.

2. MANAGEMENT FUNCTIONS

2.1 Policy-making and co-ordination

Coherence, consultation and conflict-resolution

The coherence function essentially belongs to the government in Cabinet. Its main source of assistance in this task is the Finance Inspectorate, which is required to give advice on the budgetary impact of proposals and hence their feasibility. The Budget Division may also be consulted on budget matters and the General Administration Service on personnel matters.

Non-financial aspects of policy implementation are more often than not neglected. However, greater attention is starting to be paid to practical results and the method of implementation, including information and training, as the relatively new concern of improving the functioning of the administrative machinery develops.

Mechanisms had been introduced from the very earliest stages in the reform process to ensure that there were forms of association, consultation, co-operation and co-ordination and to prevent, and if necessary resolve, any conflicts of responsibility or interest.

Formal and informal mechanisms

Whilst the various authorities are autonomous, and their respective legislation equipollent (except in the case of the local authorities, which come under the federal government and the regions), numerous mechanisms are available to ensure coherence.

The Co-ordination Committee: the purpose of this Committee, which comprises political representatives from the various authorities and to which each can refer matters of dispute, is to find political responses to these disputes by consensus.

Interministerial Conferences: the purpose of these conferences, which comprise ministers from different authorities exercising powers in the same or related areas, is to harmonise action and co-ordinate them at field level. Its initiatives may include co-operation agreements setting out the practicalities of co-operation.

The Court of Arbitration has had some jurisdictional tasks, but is not part of the judiciary. Its work includes ruling on conflicts of responsibility between authorities.

The Council of State is an administrative jurisdiction exercising over all authorities, so there is uniform interpretation of the law. Its legislation review section, which gives opinions on bills and draft decrees, is responsible for ensuring that no authority exceeds its own powers.

The High Finance Board, made up of representatives from the various authorities and financial and monetary experts, is responsible for monitoring the economic and monetary union of the country. It recommends the maximum financial requirements authorised for each authority and tracks developments.

A Royal Decree covering the general principles of staff employment lays down the regulations (administration, rights of association, remuneration) that each authority is required to apply. The Act on minimum entitlements also sets out the minimum entitlements that each authority has to offer its staff in terms of leave, allowances, health cover and accident insurance. Staff pensions remain a federal responsibility.

The diplomatic representation of the country abroad is the task of the federal government, even though the responsibility of each authority extends to international relations on matters within its sphere of competence. The machinery of diplomacy is thus at the service of all authorities. They can send special representatives abroad, although they are subject to the authority of the head of the diplomatic mission. A co-operation agreement lays down the procedures for representation in international negotiations, depending on whether the matters being addressed are the sole responsibility of an authority or not. Co-ordination meetings are held regularly on European Union matters.

The Finance Inspectorate exercises budgetary control over the different authorities on behalf of each authority's Minister for the Budget. A management committee made up of the budget ministers handles the assignment of inspectors to authorities. Similarly, the Court of Auditors acts on behalf of the elected assemblies responsible for exercising budgetary control over their respective executives. The uniformity of budgetary control by a single body, in these two cases, ensures a consistent approach.

Finally, at political level the parties may also serve as an informal mechanism to ensure coherent action by elected representatives and government members.

"Horizontal" coherence within the same statutory authority is achieved via the executive which meets in council to address any matters which, under existing regulations, can only be decided at that level (bills and draft decrees and orders which require formal discussion, public contracts above certain amounts, etc.) or which are of sufficient political importance to warrant the agreement of the whole executive.

At civil servant level, there are also standing interdepartmental committees (for international relations and in particular policy on the European Union, foreign trade, science policy, and economic forecasting) or co-operation protocols (recently, for instance, on clamping down on fraudulent social security claims).

At federal level, the College of Secretaries-General, which normally meets weekly, is made up of the senior officials in the ministries (fifteen in all), together with the secretary of the Council of Ministers. It ensures coherence in management of the government service. The College of administrators of social security bodies performs a similar role in that sector.

However, spontaneous collaboration between government departments to tackle common problems is still uncommon. It is mainly restricted to ministers' offices, though civil servants have become increasingly involved in the work of the offices over the last few years.

Informal consultations naturally take place between elected representatives and bodies representing particular groups or interests (trade unions, mutual insurance associations, employers). Alongside these informal contacts, sometimes reinforced by the presence of a delegate from an association in a minister's office, formal consultations are held in fora such as the National Labour Board (employment legislation) or the Central Economics Board (economic policy, including incomes policy). The bodies responsible for social security are jointly managed (the management committees of these bodies comprise representatives of employers' organisations and trade unions). Consultation on economic and industrial matters is also a tradition, with government representatives, employers' organisations and trade unions coming together to reach broad intersectoral agreements. The population is also formally consulted in some cases, for instance when formulating national development schemes.

2.2 Financial management

The Constitution gives both the communities and the regions their own tax system, but because the jurisdiction of both the French-speaking and Flemish communities extends to the Brussels-Capital region there are difficulties in exercising the communities' power of taxation.

Sources of revenue

The 1989 Funding Act, amended in 1993, specified the following sources of revenue for the regions: regional taxes (tax on gaming and betting, tax on slot machines, trading tax on bars selling fermented drinks, inheritance tax and succession duty, property tax, registration duty on property sales, motor vehicle tax, environmental taxes); supplementary proportional taxes, collected by the federal government and remitted to the regions; allocation of a share of personal income tax; a federal solidarity contribution; non-tax revenue (proceeds from forestry, shooting and fishing permits, tolls, etc.); loans.

The same Act specified the following sources of revenue for the communities: allocation of radio and television licence fees (which became a community tax in 1993); allocation of a share of value added tax and personal income tax; non-tax revenue; loans.

The tax revenue is either assessed wholly by the communities and regions (though it may actually be collected by the federal government, as with the property tax, the gaming, betting and slot machine taxes, bar trading tax, environmental taxes, registration duty on property sales, inheritance tax, and the radio and television licence fee), or is an allocated share of revenue from personal income tax and value added tax.

The revenue of the provinces and municipalities comes from transfers from the supervisory authorities, from non-tax receipts, and from supplementary proportional levies (*centimes additionnels*) on personal income tax and property tax. These supplementary levies are assessed by the local authorities, subject to ceilings set by the supervisory authorities, and add an additional percentage to the income on property tax payable. Thus, a taxpayer liable to pay BF 600 000 in income tax who lives in a municipality where the supplementary levy is 6 per cent has to pay an extra BF 36 000 in tax for the municipality. This tax is collected by the federal government and handed back to the provinces and municipalities.

Table 3 below shows the distribution of revenue collected by the communities and regions. The lion's share of revenue can be seen to come from personal income tax and VAT.

Table 2. **Main revenue sources of different levels of government (1985, 1990, 1994)**
(in BF billions)

	1985	1990	1994
Federal government	1 391.3	1 122.2	1 373.3
Communities and regions	130.5	673.5	889.4
Local authorities (provinces and municipalities)	350.5	379.1	482.9
of which:			
income and property tax	91.9	97.7	137.1
business tax	18.5	26.5	36.6
public sector transfers	214.1	217.0	263.3

Source: *Note de conjoncture*, Ministry of Finance.

Table 3. **Breakdown of revenue sources of communities and regions (1995)**
(in BF billions)

Property tax	4.5
Gaming and betting	2.4
Slot machines	1.3
Bar trading tax	0.6
Environmental tax	--
Registration duty	17.8
Inheritance tax	25.6
Allocated share of personal income tax	410.4
Allocated share of VAT	345.8

Source: *Note de conjoncture*, Ministry of Finance.

Expenditure responsibilities

Table 4 shows the patterns of expenditure of sub-national governments over the last ten years. The evolution of both revenues and expenditures is essentially the result of transfers of responsibility and the associated funding between the federal authorities on the one hand, and the Communities and Regions on the other.

Table 4. **Main expenditure patterns by level of government (1985, 1990, 1994)**

	1985	1990	1994
Federal Government	1 882.2	1 483.8	1 670.3
Communities and regions	149.6	701.3	938.2
Local authorities (provinces and municipalities)	343.4	382.5	484.9

Source: *Note de conjoncture*, Ministry of Finance.

Balance between discretion and control

The Constitution and the Funding Act for the communities and regions have given these entities wide financial discretion, while at the same time safeguarding federal economic and monetary union.

Funding is based on two principles: these entities have financial responsibility, meaning that they are free to manage their own resources, a principle referred to as "financial discretion", and "federal solidarity", which only concerns the regions, is designed to help the region with the lowest average per capita income tax revenue.

Within the above framework, the political institutions (assemblies and executives) at the different policy-making levels (federal government, communities, regions) are fully responsible for setting their own expenditure budgets.

The funding rules for the communities and regions were enacted in special legislation requiring approval by a two-thirds majority and by an absolute majority of members of each community.

2.3 Performance management

These audit mechanisms are still in their infancy (at least at federal level). Education and health are subject to specific inspections by the competent authorities.

Local authorities clearly have a high degree of political accountability and the ultimate sanction is the six-yearly elections. People can also "vote with their feet" and move to municipalities that offer better value for money in terms of services and rates of tax.

The transfer techniques used by the supervisory authorities are such as to encourage the formulation of high-quality policy as they are partly based on the principle of additionality (grants).

2.4 Human resource management

Statutory distinctions: The local authorities have discretion to draw up their own rules of staff employment, within the applicable statutory framework. Thus, under the terms of Article 145, paragraph 1, of the new Municipalities Act, the municipal council sets the framework and conditions for the recruitment and promotion of municipality staff. This paragraph also lays down the financial terms of employment and the salary scales for most municipality staff. Further, Article 149 of the Municipalities Act gives the municipal council the power to appoint staff whose appointments are not regulated by law. This power can be delegated to the municipal executive, except in the cases of medical doctors, surgeons and obstetricians, and veterinary surgeons, to whom special duties are assigned in the interest of the municipality, and of the teaching profession.

There is also a federal body responsible for social security for local authority staff. The local authorities must, among other things, contribute a percentage of their wage bill to a pension scheme. The percentage is so calculated as to balance revenues and expenditures. This system does not exist at federal level, where the government includes its staff's pension costs in its annual budget. The federal government is also responsible for the pensions of staff in the communities and regions. However, the latter are required to top up the government's contribution if their wage bill grows faster, proportionately, than it did in a reference year (to encourage responsible pay settlements).

Table 5. **Public sector employment by level of government (1985, 1991, 1994)**

	June 1985	December 1991	January 1994
National level	622 291	301 113	293 763
Communities and regions of which:	12 567	344 140	353 187
Ministries	--	23 301	24 244
Scientific establishments	--	193	198
Public interest bodies	--	43 214	48 737
Teaching personnel [1]	--	277 432	280 008
Provincial and local administrations [2]	181 058	239 924	237 368
TOTAL PUBLIC SECTOR	815 916	885 177	884 318

-- Data not available.
1. including those of the provinces and municipalities.
2. In 1985, local authorities (including municipalities, public social assistance centres, and provinces).

Source: *Public Management Developments: Update 1995*, OECD, 1995.

Each level of government has responsibility for negotiations with employees' organisations. However, some negotiations involve all the authorities, in cases where subjects are of common interest as defined in the general rules of staff employment.

Each authority has autonomy to decide on its level of recruitment, but actual recruitment must be carried out by the Permanent Secretariat for Public Service Recruitment when the posts are for established officials. The rules are the same as at central level, with one difference: the authority is free to recruit any of the candidates who passed the exam, while at central government level (federal, community and regional) the posts must be filled according to exam result rankings.

Each authority also has autonomy to decide on pay levels, subject to respecting the minimum and maximum entitlements laid down by the federal government after consulting the other authorities. There is a solidarity mechanism by which authorities have to contribute to the federal government's pensions budget to offset the impact of pay settlements on the pension bill.

As part of the decentralisation of services to the communities and regions, formal procedures have been introduced so that staff from these services can ask to swap posts with staff employed in the services that have remained federal who would like to be transferred to the decentralised services.

Mobility: Mobility between levels of government is not common in practice, though the principle appears in the Order laying down the general rules of staff employment.

2.5 Regulatory management and reform

As stated above, the Constitution was amended in 1970, 1980 and 1989, radically altering the division of responsibility between the levels of decision-making: State, communities, regions.

Decisions with force of law are drafted and passed by the federal assembly (acts), community assemblies (decrees) and regional assemblies (decrees or statutory orders). Likewise, the federal government and the governments of the communities and regions draft and pass regulations in their respective fields of responsibility. Decisions taken by the provincial and municipal authorities are subject, in various forms, to supervision by the regions.

Whilst there are some concerns as to the quality and consistency of regulatory decisions, it should be said that the philosophy underpinning the various stages in institutional reform has served to strengthen the autonomy of the communities and regions.

The autonomy of the communities and regions, and the rule that prevents municipal and provincial bodies as such from acting together, mean that there are scarcely any mechanisms for co-operation in drafting or applying regulations. Forms of co-operation between municipalities do exist, but they are confined to the management of activities. None concern the drafting or enforcement of regulations.

The autonomy which today characterises the Communities and Regions takes account of the differences which may be observed in the contents and the quality of regulations, as well as their eventual impact in terms of efficiency and competitivity. Given the very wide discretion of the Communities and the Regions, some competition may sometimes result.

3. TRENDS IN REDISTRIBUTING AUTHORITY ACROSS LEVELS OF GOVERNMENT

3.1 Evolving tendencies

In the last twenty-five years, Belgium has undergone a process of institutional reform. At the end of this process, the unitary State created in 1830-1831, and which had survived in that form until 1970, had been transformed into a federal State. Whilst there had always been several policy-making levels (State, province, municipality), under the unitary system that had prevailed up until 1970 it was at State level that legal rules with force of law were drafted, passed, given royal assent and promulgated. Whilst the provinces and municipalities did have real discretion, both entities were conceived as subordinate authorities subject to supervision by central government.

Not only did the transformation of the unitary State into a federal State lead to a proliferation of policy-making levels and the setting up or restructuring of institutions at each level, it also had an important impact on the organisation of government services.

The four major stages in the institutional reform process were:

- in 1970, recognition of the existence of cultural communities and regions; definition of fields of responsibility and creation of political institutions in the cultural communities;

- in 1980, extension of the field of responsibility of the communities; definition of the field of responsibility of the regions; creation of political institutions in the communities and regions (except Brussels);

- in 1988-1989, extension of the fields of responsibility of the communities and regions; creation of political institutions in the Brussels-Capital Region;

- in 1993, enshrinement of the federal nature of the State; introduction of direct elections to all community and regional assemblies.

The reforms were introduced to settle the disputes that stemmed from linguistic and cultural diversity and the complexity of the regional situation which had called into question the State's unitary and centralised nature.

The trends in the redistribution of authority mirrored those in the political institutions. In 1979 new authorities were created through the decisions or plans for the autonomy of communities and regions: Ministry of the Flemish Community, Ministry of the French-speaking Community, Ministry of the Walloon Region, Ministry of the Brussels Region. Their structures then evolved as a result of the subsequent changes that occurred at each stage in the institutional reform process (in 1980, 1988-1989 and 1993). The most complex structures are those in the Brussels Region.

In addition, among the decisions which have affected the trends at federal level, particular mention should be made of the decision, introduced by the Royal Decree of 19 September 1994, to create a Ministry of Public Service totally separate from the Ministry of the Interior, bringing under its umbrella a number of services such as the General Administration Service, the Permanent Secretariat for Public Service Recruitment and the General Directorate for Selection and Training.

3.2 The current debate

The government agreement of June 1995 contained no major new decisions on this subject. However, the parliamentary elections on 21 May 1995 were called following a new declaration of intent to amend the Constitution which was passed and published. The federal assemblies that were then elected therefore have a mandate to revise the Constitution.

Some parties, groups or sections of opinion are nevertheless lobbying for further institutional reform in order either to extend the field of responsibility of the communities and regions, or to bring some areas of responsibility more clearcut. Now that certain provincial responsibilities are likely to be centralised in the communities and regions, some people are openly questioning the need for the provincial tier.

3.3 Driving forces

In the recent past, some parties have acted as a driving force in the institutional reform process, particularly the Dutch-speaking Christian Socialists and the French-speaking Socialists. The gradual transformation of the unitary State into a federal State has affected a large number of sectors. To assign any real value as examples to any of these cases would be arbitrary.

CANADA

1. INSTITUTIONS AND AUTHORITY

1.1 Structures

Description of levels

Canada is a federal state of ten provinces and two territories (the Yukon Territory and the Northwest Territories). The Northwest Territories will be divided to form two separate territories in 1999. The eastern territory will be called Nunavut and the western territory will continue to carry the name of Northwest Territories. The provinces and territories vary considerably in size and population, as Table 1 indicates.

Table 1. **Area and population of provinces (1995)**

	Area (thousands of km^2)	Population (thousands)	Population density (per km^2)
Newfoundland	372	574.2	1.5
Prince Edward Island	6	136.1	24.0
Nova Scotia	53	937.8	17.7
New Brunswick	72	760.1	10.6
Quebec	1 358	7 334.2	5.4
Ontario	917	11 100.3	12.1
Manitoba	548	1 137.5	2.1
Saskatchewan	570	1 015.6	1.8
Alberta	638	2 747.0	4.3
British Columbia	893	3 766.0	4.2
Yukon	532	30.1	0.06
North-West Territories	3 246	65.8	0.02
CANADA	9 203	29 606.1	3.2

Source: Demography Division, Statistics Canada.

The *Constitution Act*, 1867 set up a system of government which establishes a separation of powers between two levels of government, the federal and the provincial. The two territories enjoy some of the powers of the provinces while being under the jurisdiction of the federal government.

Municipal institutions come under the jurisdiction of the provinces. Municipal governments are set up by the provincial legislatures, and have the powers that the legislatures assign to them. However, owing to the demographic, economic and political development of municipalities, the municipal political and administrative structures are now widely regarded as another level of government. Some of the larger municipalities have much larger populations than do the smaller provinces. The municipalities, even though do not have a defined constitutional status, pursue their interests with provincial governments and to a certain extent with the federal government, both individually and through the Federation of Canadian Municipalities.

Table 2. **Number of municipalities by province and territory (1968, 1978, 1988, 1995)**

Province or Territory	1968	1978	1988	1995
Newfoundland	159	307	313	290
Prince Edward Island	30	37	86	75
Nova Scotia	66	65	66	81
New Brunswick	114	112	114	112
Quebec	1 726	1 577	1 598	1 531
Ontario	964	837	839	816
Manitoba	214	202	201	202
Saskatchewan	803	791	835	849
Alberta	366	351	364	372
British Columbia	65	437	172	179
SUBTOTAL	4 507	4 716	4 588	4 507
Yukon	N/A	N/A	N/A	10
Northwest Territories	N/A	N/A	N/A	48
TOTAL	N/A	N/A	N/A	4 565

Sources: For 1968 and 1978, Harry M. Kitchen, *Local Government Finance in Canada*, (Toronto: Canadian Tax Foundation, 1984), Table 1.2, p. 11; for 1988, Statistics Canada, *Canada Year Book*, (Ottawa: Queen's Printer, 1989), Table 19.7, pp. 19-27 and 28; for 1995, Public Institutions Division, Statistics Canada.

This constitutional situation means that Canada has ten different municipal systems, although they have a number of points in common. The local administrative unit is the municipality which is incorporated as a city, town, village, township or other designation. The type of structure generally depends on the number of citizens in the unit. If one aggregates the local governments over the whole country, there are (1991) approximately 5 000 "unitary" municipalities in Canada. These are made up of nearly 120 cities, about 800 towns, over 1 000 villages, and almost 3 000 rural municipalities.

As the size of urban populations has grown, most of the major urban centres have a "two-tier" municipal structure, with an "upper-tier" regional government responsible for financing and implementing infrastructure projects for the territory of the upper-tier structure. Other areas are structured as county or regional districts. In some other cases, the local governments are placed under the supervision of a county or of a regional administration. Large sparsely populated areas, known as "quasi-municipalities", are usually administered by provincial governments. Depending on the province, there are also a variety of special-purpose organisations or bodies at the local level, each with a specific-purpose responsibility. The most important of these special purpose bodies are school boards.

The Aboriginal Peoples of Canada have rights and freedoms that are included in the Constitution. The Constitution Act, 1982 recognises and affirms the existing "aboriginal and treaty rights" of the Aboriginal peoples. Aboriginal peoples have maintained that they have an inherent right of Aboriginal self-government, which should be recognised by all Canadians. The federal government is ready to enter into negotiations with Aboriginal people based on the premise that there is an inherent right, and has recently developed a policy to guide the implementation of Aboriginal self-government through agreements with provinces and Aboriginal groups.

Central government at sub-national levels

The lieutenant-governor of the province (see section on provincial powers below) is appointed by the federal cabinet, but this position is now almost entirely symbolic. The federal cabinet also appoints judges to all the courts from the county courts up, but the judges are independent of the federal cabinet once appointed.

Creation, elimination and restructuring

The *Constitution Act*, 1867, gave the federal Parliament power to create new provinces out of the territories, and also the power to change provincial boundaries with the consent of the provinces concerned. It is doubtful that the federal government would choose to exercise these powers in a unilateral fashion at the present time.

Municipal governments – cities, towns, villages, counties, districts, metropolitan regions – are set up by the provincial legislatures, and have such powers as the legislatures see fit to give them. Provincial governments have encouraged – with varying degrees of success – the amalgamation of municipalities in order to reduce their number and streamline their administration. Provincial government determination to reduce the numbers of municipalities has varied across time. At the present time this question is being pursued vigorously by a number of the provincial governments.

Control bodies

Most provincial governments have bodies that regulate various municipal aspects of provincial public policy (e.g. public health, building standards), control the fiscal decisions of municipalities and in some cases also control local planning decisions. In the case of some provinces, these powers are exercised directly by provincial ministers, in others by boards or commissions set up specifically to exercise these powers of control.

1.2 Powers

Nature of sub-national institutions

The separation of powers is mainly set out in the *Constitution Act*, 1867. Generally speaking, the federal government was given greater powers in the economic area (particularly as envisaged in 1867) and for matters involving interprovincial dimensions, while the provinces have greater responsibilities in social policy areas (education and health) and local matters.

In theory, each level of government is sovereign within its area of jurisdiction. The development of the federal system, however, has often transformed this concept of sovereignty into inter-dependence between the two levels. In the twentieth century, the federal government has used its spending power to act in social policy areas. Many of Canada's major policies since 1960 have been implemented in the context of joint federal/provincial activity.

The federal government has delegated some activities to the provinces. Parliament can delegate the administration of a federal act to provincial agencies. Administration and enforcement of the Criminal Code, a federal statute, for example, are delegated to the provinces. Parliament has also delegated responsibility for the regulation of interprovincial and international highway traffic to the provinces. Such devolution is known as "administrative delegation" and it is an important aspect of the flexibility of the Canadian federal system.

Provinces: Section 92 of the *Constitution Act*, 1867 empowers the provinces to make laws concerning direct taxation within a province, the management and sale of public lands and timber and wood belonging to the province, municipal institutions, property and civil rights, and all matters of a merely local or private nature, including education, health, natural resources and social services.

Section 95 defines certain concurrent or joint powers: for example, agriculture, fisheries and immigration come under the jurisdiction of both levels of government. Such areas require extensive parliamentary or judicial review and federal/provincial negotiation to achieve consensus. In the event of a conflict, however, federal law prevails. In the Speech from the Throne in February 1996, the federal government indicated its willingness to pursue clarification of roles between the federal government and the provinces in areas including labour markets, manpower training, the environment, freshwater fisheries, forestry and mining. Concurrent powers also exist for old age pensions and other similar benefits, although in this case the provinces have the final say. The level of activity of the sub-national units in these areas of concurrent jurisdiction varies greatly. In the area of immigration, for example, Quebec is particularly active, in terms of the agreements between the federal government and Quebec in the area.

The Federal, the provincial and the territorial governments of Canada are all parliamentary governments, though no two are exactly alike. Only the federal Parliament is bicameral. In all the provinces and the Yukon territory, there are legislative bodies in which the majority party forms an executive, the Cabinet of elected members. (Candidates for the legislature of Northwest Territories have chosen not to align with political parties.) Only the Cabinet can introduce money legislation (private members bills can also be introduced but are rarely proceeded with) and is responsible to the assembly. Cabinet, and individual ministers, as the Executive arm of government, are, therefore, responsible for the public bureaucracy.

Each province has a comparable political structure. A lieutenant-governor, appointed by the Governor General-in-Council (in practice, the federal Cabinet), represents the Queen in the province and acts on the advice and with the assistance of his executive council (provincial Cabinet), which is responsible for the legislature. The lieutenant-governor's powers, like the Governor General's, are now largely symbolic.

The legislatures of the provinces consist of a single house, as legislative assembly. This assembly is elected by universal suffrage for a statutory term of five years. Provincial elections are often held before the end of the period (generally after four years). All provinces have Cabinet forms of government. The size of Cabinet varies, consisting of about 30 members in the most populous provinces and a smaller number in the others.

Subject to the limitations imposed by the Constitution Act, 1982, the provinces can amend their own constitutions by an ordinary act of the legislature, restricted to changes in the internal machinery of the provincial government. They cannot, however, change the provisions relating to the office of the lieutenant-governor. Provincial legislatures are limited to those powers explicitly given to them by the written Constitution or as decided through judicial interpretation to be within their explicit designation of powers.

Local government: The governments of local authorities are not parliamentary governments, though in almost all instances those who govern are popularly elected. The council-manager form of government has been adopted generally by municipalities across Canada. A municipality establishes policy and administers responsibility through an elected council. Mayors, reeves, and councillors are elected on such basis as the provincial legislature prescribes. In most cases relatively small councils made up of elected officials exist. Elected councillors usually represent a sub-area of the municipality (although in some cases the elected representatives are elected on the base of the whole municipality) whereas mayors and reeves are typically elected from the whole municipality. The council sets strategic priorities and adopts a budget. Within the framework agreed by council, the executive function of local government is performed by a chief administrative officer, who manages specific programs and services, and in turn delegates operational implementation to specific department heads. Municipal governments are often complemented by a variety of local agencies, boards and commissions such a school boards, police commissions, conservation authorities, parks boards, health units, public utilities commissions and voluntary associations.

Municipal councils have the authority to authorise expenditures on municipal services and to raise money through taxes to finance these services. Municipalities have a wide range of regulatory powers to ensure public safety. Protective services include police, fire and ambulance services. Health services are directed to the prevention and control of communicable disease, the availability of potable water, the maintenance of sanitary standards in the handling of food and the management of waste. Municipalities may inspect construction sites to ensure the application of safety standards, conduct health inspections of locally licensed establishments (e.g. restaurants), and license everything from animals to street vendors. A variety of forms of executive structures exist and the degree of formalisation of these structures generally is directly related to the size of the municipality. In the larger municipalities, there is an evolution towards more formalised and more centralised executive structures.

Type and degree of autonomy

Provincial taxing powers are constitutionally more restricted than those of the federal government. In practice, however, as a consequence of judicial interpretation the taxing powers of the provinces have been considerably broadened, to the point that there are presently few tax bases that provincial governments cannot exploit – the exceptions are taxes on imports (customs duties) and taxes that would interfere with intra-Canada trade. Nor are there any real restrictions on the borrowing powers and decisions of the federal and provincial governments, except those imposed by the market.

The spending and revenue-raising powers of local governments are not only derived from the provincial governments, but they are, in addition, circumscribed by many rules and regulations which emanate from these same provincial governments. The major local source of revenue comes from property taxes, although revenue from sales and services is an increasingly important local source. Local governments also receive very considerable amounts in grants from the provincial governments. In most of the provinces, the vast majority of these grants are conditional grants, designated for particular areas of activity. The federal government has no role to play in this matter. In addition, the provincial governments regulate borrowing by local governments although the particulars vary from province to province.

Local governments prepare land-use plans which are heavily circumscribed by provincial guidelines and controls. In some cases the initial plans are formulated by the provincial governments with local governments being required to plan within the framework of the provincial plans, whereas in other cases the provincial control comes after the formulation of the local plans, in the form of provincial approval of the local plans.

1.3 Responsibilities

Distribution of responsibilities

Provinces: Section 92 of the *Constitution Act*, 1867 assigns to the provinces such tasks as the administration of justice, municipal institutions, public lands, and the establishment and maintenance of hospitals. The provinces are also assigned exclusive authority over "Property and Civil Rights" and "generally all matters of a merely local or private nature in the province". In the twentieth century, the expansion of government activity in social areas has led to the considerable growth of the provincial governments. In budgetary terms the major areas of provincial expenditures are health and education.

Local government: There are close to 5 000 municipal governments which provide a range of services: Municipalities provide roads, sidewalks, street lights and bridges. They provide and regulate transportation systems, including urban transit, airports, harbours, taxi industries, and generally the movement of traffic and parking. Physical services include the provision of water and sewage treatment systems, garbage collection and waste disposal. Urban planning, the regulation of land use and economic development also fall within the municipal mandate. Schools are generally looked after by school boards or commissions elected under provincial education acts. Some services, such as in health, social services and education which were previously the responsibility of municipalities have been gradually transferred to provincial governments because of the costs involved. In some provinces, important residual responsibilities remain at the local level whereas in other provinces all responsibility has been transferred to the provincial level.

Mandatory, optional and shared responsibilities

Section 95 of the 1867 Constitution gives concurrent authority over agriculture and immigration to both federal and provincial levels of government. Since the 1960s the area of regional development has been a major area of shared responsibility as has been job training. The question of the appropriate roles for the federal and provincial governments in these areas is a major subject of discussion at the present time.

2. MANAGEMENT FUNCTIONS

2.1 Policy-making and co-ordination

To understand inter-governmental relations in the Canadian governmental system, it is imperative to distinguish between the relations of federal and provincial governments and those of provincial and local governments. The two sets of relations are as different as they are for one very simple reason: the federal and provincial orders of government are entrenched in the Constitution as 'sovereign' or independent orders, while the Constitution makes the local governments 'creatures' of the provinces. However, the influence of federal-provincial relations plays itself out in provincial-municipal relations and makes somewhat more complex the relation of local governments to provincial governments.

Federal/provincial relations: The structure of federal/provincial relations in Canada reflects the fact that the country's governmental system is a **parliamentary** system in which the Cabinet plays a central role. Because of this, federal/provincial relations tend to be relations between federal and provincial Cabinet Ministers and their officials; and this has been at the origin of the expression 'Executive Federalism'. To understand the evolution of federal/provincial relations, it is useful to appreciate the dynamic between the individual or departmental responsibilities of Ministers and the collective responsibility of Cabinet. With the new federal government of 1993, there has been some shift away from the previous evolution toward "institutionalised cabinets which, in recognition of the greater complexity and interdependence of areas of government involvement became more "collegial" and where the role of central agencies, such as the Prime Minister's Office, the Privy Council Office, Finance and Treasury Board was very strong. The new federal government has returned to a system of a Cabinet organisation, which may be described as "departmentalised", in which ministers are assigned responsibility for a particular portfolio. The number of portfolios has been reduced and portfolios are administered with less formal co-ordination with others.

The Executive Federalism in the Canadian context has two organisational facets:

- "Functional federalism", in which ministers and officials, usually from corresponding federal and provincial departments, meet to share views on specific undertakings negotiate. These meetings are sometimes multilateral, involving the federal government and all the provinces, at other times they are multilateral-regional, bringing a number of provinces with the federal government, and at other times still, they are bilateral – the federal government and one provincial government. There are more than 500 intergovernmental meetings a year involving federal provincial councils of ministers and committees of officials. Almost all of the meetings are "departmental", focusing on particular issues where co-ordination of policy positions or program delivery mechanisms is necessary. The meetings deal with diverse subjects ranging from law enforcement, through tourism, to budgetary policy.

- "Summit federalism". This refers to the meetings of First Ministers (the term used to refer to the Prime Minister of Canada and to the ten Provincial Premiers and two territorial leaders together). These summit meetings are always given a lot of publicity – they are sometimes televised – and they have at times been successful forums for negotiations of difficult 'horizontal' problems, namely problems that extend to more than one department of government. There have been more than 60 First Ministers' Conferences since Confederation.

"Executive inter-provincialism" refers to meetings of all or some of the Provincial and Territorial First Ministers and their officials, but without the participation of the federal government. There is an annual meeting of the Provincial/Territorial First Ministers and this meeting has established sub-committees that deal with particular policy areas. In some cases, provincial ministers meet together before meeting in a federal-provincial format (as for instance with the Forum of Labour Market Ministers – the FLMM). In the case of education (a field of exclusive provincial jurisdiction), a Council of Ministers of Education has been formed including the Ministers of Education from all the provinces. The Council provides a mechanism for consultation in educational matters of mutual interest and concern to the provinces. It facilitates co-operation among the provinces and serves as a focal point for interprovincial co-operation on education-related matters involving the federal government. The Council is supported by a permanent secretariat. There is also a Canadian Council of Ministers of the Environment, in an area of joint jurisdiction, which brings together the federal and the provincial ministers and serves as a forum for co-ordination of policy decisions and activities. The provincial Ministers responsible for social policy have met and prepared a Ministerial Council on Social Policy Reform report which they put forward to the federal government for discussion.

The structure of federal regional development programming is based on a decentralisation of administration and authority from Ottawa to federal agencies, the Atlantic Canada Opportunities Agency (ACOA), the Federal Office for Regional Development – Quebec (FORD-Q), and Western Economic Diversification (WED), which have primary responsibility for regional development within their local areas. In January 1996, the government decided to consolidate responsibility for the three regional development agencies in the industry portfolio. The transfer of responsibility to the Minister of Industry was intended to improve service and support the government's agenda for jobs and growth. Regional development is seen as a shared responsibility with federal and provincial governments having complementary roles in addressing regional problems.

Federal agencies operate alongside (often in partnership with) provincial government organisations which also have economic development responsibilities and sometimes a separate hierarchy of offices at sub-regional level. In both Quebec and Atlantic Canada for example, provincial governments have their own structures of economic development organisations at regional and local levels.

An important area where management across the levels of government can be seen in action is that of standards-settings. National standards have been jointly set in the Canada Health Act and the National Building Code. In food inspection a major effort is being made, alongside the federal announcement to consolidate food inspection activities, to develop national codes, as well as to implement a co-operative national food inspection system.

Provincial/local relations: These relations reflect extensive involvement by provincial government in local affairs – to the extent that local government autonomy has been eroded. Provincial governments intervene in local affairs through directives and mandates which may be issued with a minimum of consultation. The intervention takes many forms, from complete provincial control over certain functions, to the specification of standards for the local provision of many goods and services. Provincial-local relations involve both relations between provincial governments (usually through a Minister of Municipal Affairs) and organisations representing local governments and relations between one individual local government and the provincial government. The strength of these organisations and their influence at the provincial level varies considerably across the provinces.

2.2 Financial management

Provincial and territorial governments are independent of the federal government with regard to their revenue and expenditure policies (i.e. there are no federal restrictions on provincial and territorial decisions in this domain). There are periodic meetings of the federal Minister of Finance and his provincial counterparts to exchange views on fiscal and economic policy and for negotiations regarding the large block transfer payments. Local governments are incorporated by each province to perform certain functions falling within provincial jurisdiction. Generally local government taxation revenues are limited to property taxes, but there is a growing trend at the present time to increase local government revenues from sales and services.

Sources of revenue

Provinces: As a general principle, the provincial and federal levels have equal powers in raising taxes (apart from customs taxes which remain with the federal level).

The federal government has since Confederation made transfer payments to provinces to allow them to carry out their responsibilities. Federal transfers to provinces and territories constitute an important source of their revenue and have expanded enormously over the last decades, amounting to some C$ 38.8 billion in 1995-96. They can be categorised in several ways. Some have a specific constitutional basis, such as Equalisation – the commitment to which was enshrined in the Constitution in 1982. Other transfers rely largely upon the federal spending power, such as the Canada Health and Social Transfer (CHST) (see below). Among the host of other transfer programmes are those which provide general support to territorial governments, and support joint initiatives with provinces in areas of concurrent jurisdiction such as agriculture.

Federal transfer programmes can also be classified according to whether the assistance is conditional or unconditional. Among the former are programmes where assistance is conditional upon provincial expenditures in a given sector or upon adherence to specific programme principles. A related distinction is between specific-purpose programmes (such as the Vocational Rehabilitation Of Disabled Persons program) and those (such as Equalisation) whose purpose is more general in nature. The impact of federal transfers varies considerably across the provinces, as can be seen in Table 3.

Federal financial support is provided in two ways: through cash and tax transfers. The major transfer programme is the Canada Health and Social Transfer which replaced earlier programmes as of 1996-97. The CHST is a block fund provided for health, post-secondary education and social services and it is spent in accordance with provincial priorities. The CHST will total an estimated C$ 26.9 billion in 1996-97 and C$ 25.1 billion for 1997-98. The cash payment portion is equal to C$ 15 billion in 1996-97 and C$ 12.5 billion in 1997-98. The CHST allows provinces greater flexibility to design programmes, based on mutual consent in important areas. The CHST safeguards national standards or principles regarding health and social services. The CHST maintains the principles of the Canada Health Act and requires provinces to provide social assistance without imposing minimum residency requirements. The government will continue to work with the provinces to develop by mutual consent the values, principles and objectives that underlie the CHST.

The Equalisation Programme (around C$ 8.8 billion in 1996-97 – 24.4 per cent of total transfers) is the main mechanism for redistributing revenues. It provides transfers to the lower-income provinces to ensure that provincial governments have sufficient revenues to provide reasonably comparable levels of public services at reasonably comparable levels of taxation Equalisation payments are calculated on the basis of a formula that compares the revenue-raising capacities of the provinces. Any province which has a per capita yield below the programme standard receives an Equalisation payment for the amount of the shortfall. The Equalisation Programme was renewed in 1994 for a five-year period.

The Canada Pension Plan (CPP): The CPP is administered jointly by the federal and provincial governments. The federal and provincial governments are required to review the CPP every five years. Public consultations are being held across Canada as part of the current review.

Local government: Municipalities have been historically limited to one source of revenue the taxation of real property. Other sources of revenue include grants from provinces and the federal government, and miscellaneous revenues from user fees, licenses, permits, fines, etc.. Although all forms of municipal revenue must have provincial/territorial authorisation, municipalities have discretion in terms of the level of taxation and to the quality of services provided. They also derive revenue from the taxation of businesses and amusements, and from licences, permits, rents, fines, etc. As this revenue proved insufficient, provincial governments have greatly increased their grants to local governments (municipalities and school boards) in the past forty years. In 1956 provincial transfers represented 19 per cent of local expenditures. This figure grew to 33.8 per cent in 1966 and to 42.6 per cent in 1976. The rate of increase has slowed considerably since this time and reductions to provincial

Table 3. **Provincial revenues from federal transfers and own sources (%), 1984/1985, 1989/1990, 1994/1995**

	Federal transfers						Other governmental & enterprise transfers			From own sources		
	General purpose			Specific purpose								
	1984/5	1989/90	1994/5	1984/5	1989/90	1994/5	1984/5	1989/90	1994/5	1984/5	1989/90	1994/5
Newfoundland	28.2	31.8	27.5	19.1	13.9	18.0	0.0	0.0	0.0	52.7	54.3	54.5
Prince Edward Island	30.8	29.9	25.1	17.0	14.7	15.7	0.0	0.0	0.0	52.2	55.5	59.1
Nova Scotia	22.7	22.6	22.9	19.0	15.7	17.6	0.0	0.1	0.0	58.2	61.6	59.5
New Brunswick	22.5	23.9	21.8	20.1	14.7	13.7	0.1	0.0	0.0	57.3	61.4	64.5
Quebec	12.2	10.2	8.7	13.1	9.0	10.0	0.4	0.5	0.5	74.2	80.4	80.7
Ontario	0.5	0.5	0.5	16.4	11.4	14.7	0.3	0.1	0.1	82.9	88.0	84.7
Manitoba	13.3	15.6	15.8	16.4	12.9	12.8	0.3	0.3	0.1	70.0	71.3	71.3
Saskatchewan	2.0	10.6	8.9	17.3	13.0	14.5	0.2	0.1	0.0	80.5	76.3	76.6
Alberta	2.9	1.1	1.1	8.6	13.1	11.3	0.1	0.0	0.0	88.5	85.7	87.6
British Columbia	0.7	0.2	0.0	16.6	13.1	11.1	0.0	0.0	0.0	82.7	86.7	88.9
North-West Territories	47.6	68.3	68.3	22.2	10.0	9.7	2.2	0.0	0.2	28.0	21.6	21.7
Yukon	41.3	60.5	59.3	30.5	11.9	16.0	0.0	0.1	0.0	28.1	27.5	24.6

Source: Public Institutions Division, Financial Management System, Statistics Canada.

transfers are being pursued at the present time in a number of provinces. As Table 4 indicates, the vast majority of provincial transfers take the form of conditional grants, although the extent to which this is true varies across the provinces. Local governments, operate with more autonomy in some provinces than others. Typically, provinces exercise more control over municipal operations where transfer, particularly conditional grants constitute a large part of municipal revenues. Unconditional grants provide for much greater autonomy. In those provinces where there is a greater reliance on own source revenues, municipalities tend to operate with significant independence. Table 5 gives the main sources of local government revenues (property and related taxes; sales and services; conditional and unconditional grants) by provinces/territories and shows some sometimes significant differences in trends over the three years for which data are supplied.

Table 4. **Provincial Governments: General purpose and specific purpose grants to municipalities**
(1967, 1970, 1975, 1980, 1985, 1990, 1994)

Year [1]	General purpose grants	Specific purpose grants	Total grants	Total grants as a percent of Provincial expenditure	Local revenue
	C$ million	C$ million	C$ million	%	%
1967	259	1 980	2 239	23.8	40.3
1970	341	3 158	3 499	23.0	44.3
1975	893	6 256	7 149	20.8	48.1
1980	1 231	11 136	12 367	19.9	45.4
1985	1 854	17 136	18 990	17.6	46.3
1990	2 297	23 586	25 883	17.1	42.6
1994	2 034	28 607	30 641	17.5	43.5

1. Fiscal year nearest to December 31 of year named.
Source: Public Institutions Division, Financial Management System, Statistics Canada.

Expenditure responsibilities

As Table 6 indicates, both the federal government and provincial governments are responsible for transferring very large sums of money to other levels of government. Collection of revenue is far more centralised than is the delivery of services. This has created problems of political visibility for levels of government responsible for collecting taxes while other, more localised, levels of government are seen as providing services Table 7, which gives local government expenditures by function and provinces/territories in 1985 and 1994, shows some significant differences across areas.

Balance between discretion and control

All provinces have the right to impose their own income tax. In general, they top-up federal taxes on a percentage basis. Provinces also have the right to raise taxes through social insurance charges, and through indirect taxation (sales taxes). Three of the provinces have their own collection system for corporate taxes. All other provinces raise corporate income taxes using the federal corporate income tax structure and administration. No legal limit is imposed on the provinces in raising taxes. To ensure that the combination of federal and provincial tax rates are kept within reasonable limits, thorough discussion is needed prior to agreement – the final decision remaining entirely with each province. The Canadian tax system has been described in the past as relatively co-ordinated at the level of income tax but unco-ordinated and overlapping in the area of indirect taxes, particularly sales taxes. The two orders of government have taken steps to improve their co-ordination of sales taxes. Three Atlantic provinces agreed in April 1996 to harmonize their provincial sales taxes with the federal government's sales tax, and Quebec's sales tax is already harmonized with the federal tax. A single collector for both provincial and federal sales taxes therefore exists in these four provinces. There is still room for further rationalisation between the two levels. In the March 1996 budget, the federal government proposed the creation of a Canada Revenue Commission as a vehicle to deliver federal and provincial programmes in the area, to be called the Canada Border and Revenue Service.

CANADA

Table 5. **Sources of local government revenues by provinces/territories (for fiscal years 1985, 1990, 1994**[1]
[percentage]

	Property and related taxes			Sales and services			Unconditional grants			Conditional grants			Other			Total
	1985	1980	1994	1985	1980	1994	1985	1980	1994	1985	1980	1994	1985	1980	1994	
NFLD	40.2	39.6	45.4	11.5	11.4	13.3	15.8	16.4	12.8	20.0	16.9	20.0	12.5	15.7	8.5	100.0
PEI	11.0	12.2	13.1	7.2	7.0	8.1	3.2	2.9	2.8	76.5	75.9	73.9	2.2	2.0	2.1	100.0
NS	23.2	26.5	27.4	7.9	8.3	8.9	2.5	2.2	2.1	58.2	55.0	54.7	8.1	7.9	6.9	100.0
NB	28.1	35.9	39.4	16.6	18.3	18.6	28.5	23.0	18.9	15.2	10.3	11.0	11.6	12.4	12.2	100.0
QUE	33.0	35.7	39.4	8.1	10.1	10.0	0.2	0.5	0.7	51.1	45.9	43.1	7.7	7.8	6.9	100.0
ONT	41.3	42.9	44.9	11.3	12.2	10.8	4.6	3.3	2.0	36.1	33.9	35.9	6.6	7.7	6.4	100.0
MAN	32.1	33.7	35.2	9.0	9.1	9.8	3.1	3.4	2.9	44.6	44.1	42.8	11.2	9.7	9.2	100.0
SASK	35.8	37.5	40.8	9.1	10.2	11.0	4.8	3.9	2.7	40.1	38.5	36.2	10.3	9.8	9.2	100.0
ALTA	25.8	27.8	24.2	13.8	15.7	16.4	1.8	3.0	2.2	46.4	40.3	46.2	12.2	13.2	11.1	100.0
BC	36.7	28.9	23.2	12.3	14.0	13.8	2.6	2.4	1.9	39.0	43.9	53.0	9.4	10.9	8.1	100.0
YUK	29.2	23.2	26.0	16.5	12.9	13.6	11.0	8.7	4.5	28.8	35.0	40.8	14.6	20.1	15.1	100.0
NWT	10.8	12.1	12.8	21.0	29.8	26.2	11.0	6.5	6.0	49.4	44.1	49.2	7.8	7.5	5.8	100.0
CAN	35.3	36.9	37.9	10.8	12.1	11.6	3.1	2.8	2.0	42.4	39.3	41.0	8.4	8.9	7.5	100.0

Notes: Fiscal year-end closest to 31 December.
Data as of release date 15 January 1996.
1. for 1994, figures are not actual but estimates.
Source: Financial Mangement System, Statistics Canada.

Table 6. **Revenue and expenditure of all levels of governments (1985, 1995)**

	Federal	Provincial	Local	Hospitals	CPP and QPP [1]	TOTAL
1985			millions of Canadian dollars			
Revenue from own sources	83 237	77 297	19 724	881	9 892	191 031
Plus grants from:						
Federal government		21 240	506			21 746
Provincial governments			17 033	14 352		31 385
Local governments		89		20		109
Total revenue	83 237	98 626	37 263	15 253	9 892	244 271
Expenditure for own purposes	86 546	66 640	38 040	14 645	6 717	212 588
Plus grants to						
Provincial governments	21 240		89			21 329
Local governments	506	17 033				17 539
Hospitals		14 352	20			14 372
Total expenditure	108 292	98 025	38 149	14 645	6 717	265 828
Surplus or deficit (-)	-25 055	601	-886	608	3 175	-21 557
1995						
Revenue from own sources	148 312	133 001	37 044	1 557	19 830	339 744
Plus grants from:						
Federal government		30 735	1 390			32 125
Provincial governments			28 971	22 658		51 629
Local governments		96		20		116
Total revenue	148 312	118 554	65 194	24 188	20 948	371 637
Expenditure for own purposes	142 753	118 554	65 194	24 188	20 948	371 637
Plus grants to						
Provincial governments	30 735		96			30 831
Local governments	1 390	28 971				30 361
Hospitals		22 658	20			22 678
Total expenditure	174 878	170 183	65 130	24 188	20 948	445 507
Surplus or deficit (-)	-26 566	-6 351	2 095	47	1 118	-31 893

1. CPP = Canadian Pension Plan – QPP = Quebec Pension Plan
Source: National Accounts and Environment Division, Statistics Canada.

Table 7. **Local government expenditures by function and provinces/territories (1985, 1994 [1])**

	Nfld	PEI	NS	NB	Que.	Ont.	Man.	Sask.	Alta	BC	Yuk.	NWT	Can.
1985													
General services	11.6	2.9	3.7	6.4	7.4	4.2	5.6	4.5	4.1	4.3	15.2	17.6	5.1
Protection	7.2	4.2	7.4	20.7	7.9	8.6	7.9	6.4	5.8	10.8	9.2	4.0	8.1
Transportation	22.4	4.0	5.2	22.3	10.1	9.7	10.6	12.4	12.2	8.5	17.2	19.9	10.2
Health	0.0	0.0	7.9	0.8	0.1	5.5	7.4	13.9	16.7	2.1	0.2	0.7	5.8
Social services	0.0	0.0	12.3	0.0	0.3	7.4	2.8	0.9	0.9	0.2	0.0	1.8	3.6
Education	8.5	74.0	46.4	0.0	44.0	42.2	43.0	43.0	31.2	41.9	0.0	14.8	40.7
Environment	20.1	4.2	5.5	19.5	8.0	6.8	5.8	6.5	5.7	7.4	16.0	21.7	7.1
Rec. & culture	8.9	4.6	4.2	12.4	5.4	6.2	5.6	6.2	6.5	8.5	31.9	14.3	6.3
Debt charges	17.3	5.5	4.3	11.9	11.0	3.6	7.5	3.6	11.7	13.3	5.9	2.9	7.8
Other	4.0	0.5	3.1	6.0	5.8	6.0	3.8	2.8	5.3	3.0	4.4	2.2	5.2
TOTAL	100	100	100	100	100	100	100	100	100	100	100	100	100
1994													
General services	13.8	2.9	3.3	7.9	6.7	4.5	5.3	5.8	4.5	4.6	19.0	14.4	5.1
Protection	7.7	5.1	6.2	23.0	8.7	7.5	8.2	6.7	6.5	9.9	7.2	3.8	8.0
Transportation	26.6	4.4	4.1	22.0	11.5	7.4	9.3	10.3	12.2	7.4	16.7	10.8	9.2
Health	0.0	0.0	8.6	1.1	0.0	4.7	7.7	15.1	15.1	2.6	0.3	0.3	5.0
Social services	0.0	0.0	19.8	0.0	0.4	15.4	5.6	0.3	1.0	0.1	0.0	2.7	7.7
Education	0.0	71.5	39.1	0.0	39.6	40.5	42.9	41.3	32.1	44.5	0.0	31.7	39.4
Environment	17.4	3.2	10.3	19.7	10.4	7.3	7.7	8.6	7.4	9.4	34.9	21.9	8.6
Rec. & culture	10.0	3.6	4.3	15.1	6.3	5.4	4.6	6.6	6.9	8.8	17.0	9.9	6.2
Debt charges	19.3	8.9	2.1	6.6	9.7	2.5	6.5	2.2	8.7	9.5	1.8	2.6	5.9
Other	5.1	0.3	2.4	4.5	6.6	4.9	2.3	3.1	5.6	3.3	3.2	2.0	4.9
TOTAL	100	100	100	100	100	100	100	100	100	100	100	100	100

Notes: Fiscal year-end closest to 31 December.
Data as of release date – 15 January 1996.
1. for 1994, figures are not actual but estimates.
Source: Financial Management System, Statistics Canada.

In general, with variation from province to province, provincial governments maintain some control over local borrowing, often through the mediation of appointed municipal boards, over all aspects of the property tax base, as well as over property tax rates. The provinces also oversee local governments' planning decisions and monitor local expenditures. In addition to the use of directives and mandates, their control is exercised through conditional grants.

2.3 Performance management

Mechanisms

In some cases, both federal grants to provinces and provincial grants to local governments are given conditional to certain performance standards. In the case of federal grants to provincial governments, since the 1960s grants are increasingly less tied to specific conditions. However, in some areas, such as health, there are some conditions relating to performance. In the case of provincial-local grants, there are very often highly detailed performance standards to be met by local governments in order to obtain the provincial grants.

Quality standards

All levels of government in Canada are increasingly concerned to evaluate performance in terms of output measurements and measurements of quality. Traditionally, intergovernmental controls, both federal-provincial and provincial-local, focused on whether the funds were being spent according to the regulatory framework rather than whether the desired outcomes were achieved. There is now considerable discussion in the provincial-local area as to how provincial controls could better focus on quality and performance mechanisms. The general trend in municipal financial management is a combination of ensuring money is spent legally and wisely. Value-for-money auditing has contributed significantly to a process under which priorities are predetermined and results are evaluated relative to these priorities. As the order of government "closest to the people" municipalities are directly accountable to the public for the programs and services they provide themselves or on behalf of other levels of government. Municipalities have argued that they lack the flexibility to adjust federal and provincial programs and services to meet local conditions and circumstances.

An important area where management across the levels of government can be seen in action is that of standards-setting. National standards have been jointly set in the Canada Health Act and the National Building Code. In food inspection a major effort is being made, alongside the federal announcement to consolidate food inspection activities, to develop and implement national codes.

2.4 Human resource management

Statutory distinctions and managerial autonomy: The guiding principle is that each province is sovereign in its own affairs, including managing its human resources. Each province, therefore, designs its own legal framework and organises its own civil service. A common feature to all provinces is that they all have a professional civil service.

Since the late 1960s provincial governments have extended bargaining rights to their public sector employees. The extent to which collective bargaining takes place at the provincial or local levels varies across provinces. Each provincial government sets its own pay rates.

As a rule each province has its own dismissal system. In some provinces, changes of government have seen changes of some senior officials. All municipal employees are employees of the municipal government concerned.

Table 8. **Government employment by level (1990, 1993)**

	1990	1993
Federal government [1] *of which*:	408 770	405 822
administration	289 991	292 645
military [2]	118 779	113 177
Provincial/territorial government *of which*:	1 039 997	1 039 502
administration [3]	487 447	486 925
public hospitals [4]	552 550	552 577
Local government *of which*:	857 192	904 246
administration	358 853	373 824
local school boards	498 340	530 423
TOTAL GOVERNMENT *of which*:	2 305 959	2 349 571
administration	1 136 290	1 153 394
public hospitals	552 550	552 577
local school boards	498 340	530 423
military	118 779	113 177

Note: Figures may not add to totals due to rounding.
1. Includes military, government-owned hospitals and education.
2. Includes regular and reserve forces.
3. Includes government-owned hospitals and community colleges.
4. Includes provincial, territorial, municipal and lay and religious hospitals.

Source: Public Institutions Division, Statistics Canada, 1996.

Mobility: There is some pension mobility but no job mobility between the different provincial and municipal civil services. There are some exchange programmes (between federal and provincial levels) but these are very limited in size.

2.5 Regulatory management and reform

The courts have given wide interpretation to provincial powers, especially "property and civil rights" (which have been interpreted to include most labour law and social security) and somewhat narrower interpretations to federal powers (federal powers over "trade and commerce," for example, have been reduced to inter-provincial and international trade and commerce). In addition, a wide variety of working relationships between federal and provincial powers have evolved, including delegation of programme administration from federal to provincial and vice versa. Such flexible relationships have, in many areas, transformed the notion of "sovereignty" into one of federal/provincial interdependence and collaboration.

As a result of these actions, the evolution of federal/provincial regulatory relations has been one of increasing decision-making in the provinces, and today, Canada is one of the most decentralised states in the OECD.

Regulation by the various levels of government in the Canadian federal system has given rise to three kinds of inter-governmental" regulatory challenges): inter-provincial trade barriers established by regulations, duplication between provincial and federal regulations, and rising aggregate regulatory costs.

Inter-provincial barriers to trade have for many years been recognised as a serious problem. Many non-tariff trade barriers have been erected. Restrictions against commerce and advertising across provincial borders and varying produce standards have splintered the Canadian market and kept businesses small, hindering investment and competitiveness. Professional accreditations are often not recognised across province lines, restricting labour mobility. The Canadian Manufacturers' Association has estimated that such barriers impose direct costs of about C$ 6.5 billion annually, or 1 to 1.5 per cent of GDP. A number of steps, outlined below, are being taken to deal with this.

By 1991, the Free Trade Agreement with the United States, the example of the EU Single Market Programme, and proposals for a common-market clause in the Canadian constitution brought the issue into focus. In March 1993, governments began negotiations to reduce and eliminate barriers to trade within Canada. On 18 July 1994, First Ministers signed the policy text of the Agreement on Internal Trade. The date of entry into force was set as 1 July 1995 to give governments time to make appropriate legislative changes.

The Internal Trade Agreement establishes a broad framework of rules for internal trade, with specific chapters dealing with the particular circumstances in ten different economic sectors or areas to ensure the free flow of people, goods, services and capital across Canada. The Agreement includes commitments to reconcile standards-related regulations and, in particular, to place increased reliance on the National Standards System (NSS) which is overseen by the Standards Council of Canada. The Agreement also provides a framework for co-operation among governments in respect of other regulatory measures and regulatory regimes. These have been important first steps in dealing with internal market barriers and distortions, but it remains in the national interest to improve and expand the disciplines, to resolve outstanding issues, to strengthen dispute resolution mechanisms and to foster greater practical co-operation in and co-ordination of economic activities.

Duplication and undesirable interactions between federal and provincial regulation have for years been an irritant between governments and business. For example, the combined effect of regulations on working hours of truck drivers (provincial road safety regulations) and regulations limiting the time that animals could remain in trucks (federal animal health regulations) made it difficult to transport some animals over long distances. To deal with these problems, governments are now actively harmonizing regulations in a broad range of sectors.

In 1992, the federal government launched departmental and parliamentary reviews of regulations. In these reviews, departments examined their existing regulations and re-justified their regulatory programs. Work was also done to determine the effect that federal regulations had on Canadian competitiveness and to identify ways of improving regulatory programs, processes, and intergovernmental collaboration.

The Federal Regulatory Policy (revised in 1995) requires, among other things, that regulatory authorities show that they have respected intergovernmental agreements and have taken full advantage of opportunities for co-ordination with other governments and agencies.

Most provinces are now also engaged in extensive regulatory reviews, ranging from the practical (reviewing internal regulatory processes to improve efficiency) to the strategic (examining the very essence and need for regulations).

The closer "regulatory" collaboration between governments in Canada aims at building a more rational, responsive and reliable regulatory system. This reflects the objectives of the OECD resolution passed in March 1995, that recommends, "Member countries take effective measures to ensure the quality and transparency of government regulations". In most regulatory areas there is intergovernmental machinery in place to address regulatory issues. These can be as formal as the Canadian Council of Ministers of the Environment, established in 1989 with its own secretariat, to less formal but frequent meetings of ministers and officials (e.g. the Federal-Provincial Committee on Environmental and Occupational Health).

The direct cost of federal, provincial and municipal regulation is another concern. Although there is no reliable benchmark of the cumulative regulatory compliance and administrative costs to the economy, it has been estimated that federal regulation alone may entail costs of between C$ 30 and C$ 50 billion annually. Costs of provincial and municipal regulation are likely to be equally large. Despite the roughness of these estimates, and even if fully offset by benefits, the magnitude of these costs demonstrates the importance of ensuring regulatory program designs are as cost-effective as possible – and that governments work together to reduce costs to the extent possible.

3. TRENDS IN REDISTRIBUTING AUTHORITY ACROSS LEVELS OF GOVERNMENT

3.1 Evolving tendencies

The situation in Canada in this field is particularly complex and dynamic – if only because of the great diversity and high degree of decentralisation to the ten provinces and significant variations across different sectoral areas.

From the late 1950s to the early 1970s, largely due to strong productivity growth, there was a significant increase in government programme expenditure and the introduction of major new programmes (federal or federal-provincial). The use of federal spending power to support provincial programmes of health, post-secondary education and welfare and generally to "equalise" provincial fiscal capacity; and revenue growth helped bring Canada into the era of the modern welfare state. 1974 marked the beginning of a period of deficit combined with inflation and recession. Indexation of personal income tax and of a number of expenditure programmes (including federal finance for health) reduced revenue growth and increased spending. In the late 1970s some federal transfers were reformed, then growth was gradually capped in the 1980/90s.

The health sector provides a good example of how federal/provincial relations have evolved over recent decades – especially in terms of the interaction between funding and delivery responsibilities. The provinces generally have "formal" responsibility for health care. In 1945, the Federal Government used its "spending power" and made grants available to provinces for particular health functions. This development cannot be disassociated from the 1941 federal-provincial Tax Rental Agreement (and ensuing agreements) whereby the provincial governments agreed to refrain from collecting personal and corporation income taxes until the end of the War and received in exchange a partial compensation ("rent").

From 1957 onwards the federal government increased its presence in the health sector through an increasing role in the financing of provincial government expenditures on health services, subject to concomitant criteria for funding. These helped shape the current public health system (by setting broad national principles for the health care system as conditions of eligibility for grants).

In 1977, federal funding of provincial health and post-secondary education expenditures was converted into "block" funding, instead of "cost-sharing" tied to specific expenditures. When it appeared that the national health principles were in danger of being undermined, the 1984 Canada Health Act restored the original principles as conditions for eligibility for federal funding (with provision for withholding funds in certain cases). This Act also opposed practices such as "extra billing" and user fees which some provinces might have used to deal with escalating medical expenditures – although provinces remained free to introduce such measures (but at the risk of losing some federal funding). The responsibility of the provinces in respect of the delivery of health services and in respect of the operation of their own health insurance programmes was not altered by this new Act. As from April 1, 1996 federal health transfer payments are part of a general "block" transfer payment supporting provincial health, social, and post-secondary education expenditures (the Canada Health and Social Transfer – CHST). The 1984 Act funding criteria will continue to be applied by the federal government.

The evolving tendencies have been towards reductions in transfers from federal to provincial governments and from provincial to local governments. At the same time there are also tendencies to decentralise responsibilities, from federal to provincial governments and from provincial to local. Transfers from federal to provincial governments are, however, stabilising. In the current five-year Equalisation arrangement, transfers are projected to grow from C$ 8.5 billion to C$ 9.6 billion from 1994-95 to 1998-99 CHST transfers decline in 1996-97 and 1997-98 to C$ 26.9 billion and C$ 25.1 billion respectively. Thereafter, under the new CHST arrangement covering the five-year period from fiscal year 1998-99 through to 2002-03, provinces will see federal financial support stabilising and then increasing to C$ 27.4 billion by 2002-03.

Related to moves to decentralise responsibilities to local governments are moves, on the part of several provincial governments, to amalgamate or otherwise regionalise local governments. This involves the restructuring of school boards and of local governments. In the case of Toronto and Montreal, recent studies have suggested significant structural reorganisation at the level of the overall urbanised area.

3.2 The current debate

Recent developments

Most governments are undertaking fundamental reviews of their roles in various aspects of the economy and society and are examining alternatives such as the privatisation, commercialisation or elimination of certain functions. The current federal Government was elected on an understanding that it would emphasize non-constitutional solutions focusing primarily on social and economic policy reforms and the sorting out more generally of overlapping roles and responsibilities.

In the last two years, the Government has made significant changes in a number of areas. The Government is committed to working with the provinces and individual Canadians to ensure that the Canadian federation is modernised to meet the needs of the 21st century. The government considers that any such changes must respect Canada's diversity and be based on partnership and dialogue with the provinces. Accordingly, the federal government has proposed to the provinces a much strengthened process to work in partnership, focusing on such priorities as food inspection, environmental management, social housing, tourism and freshwater fish habitat. The Federal government has also made it clear that it will not use its spending power to create new shared-cost programs in areas of exclusive provincial jurisdiction without the consent of a majority of the provinces. Any new program will be designed so that non-participating provinces will be compensated provided they establish equivalent or comparable initiatives. The Federal government has announced its withdrawal from functions in such areas as labour market training, forestry, mining, and recreation, that are more appropriately the responsibility of others, including provincial governments, local authorities or the private sector.

An important issue is the public perception that there is a lot of wasteful overlap and duplication between federal and provincial governments. The federal government understands that it should continue to work with the provinces to address this issue appropriately and as required. Accordingly, First Ministers agreed in 1994 on the Efficiency of the Federation Initiative in which government identified areas for increased administrative efficiencies and negotiated toward agreed-upon objectives and timetable to address the issue of overlap and duplication.

A factor here is that the Constitution is silent on some important current issues or does not define clearly which level (Federal or Provincial) should intervene, where, and how. The area currently under most discussion is that of job training where the federal government has made an offer to terminate its activity in this area, while delegating much of the responsibility related to active labour market measures under agreed conditions tailored to the specific needs of each province. This policy area is currently under intense discussion, with provincial government reaction to the federal proposal varying greatly. A pattern of "jurisdictional specialisation" has, nevertheless, developed between tiers of government. Exogenous events may change this pattern and adjustments are made primarily through the political process: financing arrangements (fiscal federalism); inter-governmental agreements or understandings; and policy designs which take other government programmes into account. And occasionally, over time, also by formal constitutional amendments or judicial interpretation of constitutional documents. This has all had an impact on the practical balance of powers (and therefore on the degree of devolution). This balance varies, naturally, across different policy fields. Thus, the notion that the level of government which can give the best service should occupy a particular field, based on efficiency criteria for service delivery and in co-operation with other government's relevant programmes, has recently been discussed.

Budget deficits and the control of overall fiscal/expenditure pressures

Federal government reduction in the growth of transfers had the effect of squeezing the provinces; which often responded in turn, by putting fiscal pressure on local governments. The latter not only saw (and are seeing) a sharp increase in the costs of their own services but are also faced with new demands (environment, social initiatives) resulting either from provincial regulations or from growing demands for social services. Local governments are expected to deliver services mandated by other levels of government, to control their costs more stringently, and increasingly, to finance them as well.

Local governments are faced with serious problems of how to meet these additional demands – including the issue of pay differentials between staff at the federal, provincial and local levels. Municipalities are demanding more autonomy and recognition, arguing that they are required by other orders of government to do more with less. They have limited capacity to fund programs on their own, because their capacity to raise revenue is basically limited to property taxes. There are public pressures to hold property taxes at current levels, or reduce them. The basic trade-off at the local level is tax reductions versus service improvements. Funding reductions are forcing some municipalities and school boards to amalgamate or look at alternative structures. Municipalities also fear that health system reforms of the type being discussed in the current Health Forum (although not all of the provinces currently participate in it) could place additional demands on local authorities.

Fragmentation of local service provision

A further development is the proliferation of special purpose bodies (Commissions, boards, agencies) which provide a wide range of government services, in particular at the community or "regional" (sub-provincial) level. A majority of these bodies are funded by mixes of revenue from the sale of their output, grants from provincial governments (which in turn, are supported by federal funding) and local property taxes. These bodies generally have a high level of autonomy (policy direction as well as spending); are chartered by provincial legislation; may be governed by individually elected boards; and determine their financial needs independently. At the local level, some of these bodies lay claim to substantial portions of local tax revenues (e.g. primary and secondary education). But because in many cases local councils cannot interfere with the policy decisions of separate bodies – although provincial governments may do so, at community behest, they are denied an effective means of exercising proper budgetary control.

Another issue is the extent to which boards (e.g. those for local hospitals) are, or should, be made more accountable – to the public; the provinces; and to local government.

3.3 Driving forces

The forces driving the current trends and current debates in the redistribution of activities across levels of government in Canada can be divided into economic forces, political forces and demographic forces.

Economic: (*i*) the current trends towards the globalisation of the economy are one of the forces behind the moves to redistribute activities and have drawn attention to the existence of internal barriers to trade and efficiency within the Canadian union; (*ii*) recent unfavourable economic conditions have affected government budgets and accelerated debates about fiscal constraints.

Political: (*i*) fiscal pressures on governments have been major factors in moves towards decentralisation; (*ii*) the question of Quebec and its status vis-à-vis Canada is clearly one of the major driving forces in all discussions about the distribution of activities; (*iii*) the recognition of aboriginal rights also raises a number of questions that bear on the intergovernmental distribution of activities such as the working out of governmental autonomy for the aboriginal peoples, and the question of the provincial government role in health, education and social services to aboriginal peoples living off the reserves.

Demographic: (*i*) the continued move of the population into the urban, and particularly the metropolitan, areas affects current trends. This raises the question of how should the metropolitan areas be structured politically and what responsibilities can they most effectively carry out? (*ii*) the fact that recent immigration is so highly localised in the larger metropolitan areas may well have an increasing impact on the distribution of governmental activities. Given the extent to which recent immigration is focused on Toronto, Montreal and Vancouver, a question is: how does this affect the need for particular public services and how should these be financed and implemented?

CZECH REPUBLIC

1. INSTITUTIONS AND AUTHORITY

The Czech Republic has been an independent unitary State since 1 January 1993. It was a member State of the Socialist Republic of Czechoslovakia, from 1969, and then for a short time a member State of the Czech and Slovak Federal Republic from 1990 until the end of 1992. Its present constitution is the Constitutional Act of 16 December 1992, adopted by the former Czech National Council.

These two political changes have created a complicated situation for both legal issues and for statistical data in the Czech Republic. Institutions and legal rules still exist from the former socialist regime or from the short-lived Czech and Slovak Federal Republic, and the continuity of statistical data is not always assured.

Until 1990 local government in the Czech Republic was based on elected national committees established at three levels: the municipality, the district, and the region. National committees, as local authorities of the soviet type, were removed by the Constitutional Act of the Czech and Slovak Federal Republic in 1990. In the Czech Republic, as in other former communist countries, priority has been given to restoring municipal self-government. The intermediate tier of government has been held in distrust because of its key role in the former centralised planning system.

1.1 Structures

Description of levels

The Czech Republic today has two layers of government vested with general responsibility for local affairs: the municipalities and the districts (*okres*) which are deconcentrated State administrations. Only municipalities are at present local self-governing territorial communities, but the creation of a second level of local self-government is being discussed.

The Czech Republic has an area of 78 864 km^2 and a total population of 10.4 million. . The country is divided into 6 233 municipalities and 76 districts (as of 1 January 1996). At that time, 4 971 of the municipalities had less than 1 000 inhabitants. The three largest cities (Brno, Ostrava and Plzen) carry out district responsibilities in their territory (which is called a district). Thirteen "statutory cities" may divide their territory into urban districts (*mèstsk*), but few have so far done so. Prague has more than 1.2 million inhabitants and has a special status defined by the 1990 Act on the Capital City of Prague (and its amendments). It is divided into 57 urban neighbourhoods (*mèstská cást*), which are not self-governing communities, although each has an elected council, an elected mayor, and an office for discharging administrative tasks delegated by the city council. The ten former city districts remain as constituencies for the State administration.

There are legal provisions aimed at promoting co-operation between municipalities and the large number of small communities as the smallest are unable to carry out the tasks allocated to them, especially those transferred from the State administration. The Government has, therefore, defined 383 communities with the "designated local authority" to exercise additional competences which have been transferred from the State administration.

Table 1. **Municipalities according to population (1 January 1994)**

Population range	Number of municipalities	Number of inhabitants Total	%
Less than 1 000	4 972	1 726 625	16.6
1 000 to 4 999	991	1 942 320	18.9
5 000 to 9 999	135	934 377	9.0
10 000 to 49 999	108	2 148 324	20.8
50 000 and over	24	3 582 367	34.7
TOTAL	6 230	10 334 013	100.0

Source: O. Vidláková, "La réforme des structures locales dans la République tchèque", *Revue française d'administration publique*, n°74, April-June 1995.

At the regional level, there are no longer any regional/provincial offices with general competence. Administrative responsibilities previously exercised at this level have been transferred to the district offices (108 items), the central State administration (63 items), or communities with designated local authority (19 items). A further 60 items have been cancelled. Regions were abolished in 1990, as one of the first reforms after the collapse of the communist regime. However, the regional level still exists as an administrative division special to some ministries, but is not the same for all ministries concerned. The creation of regions or provinces as a second level of local self-government has been discussed for several years, but no decision has been taken yet (see section 3.2).

Central government at sub-national levels

Districts are territorial divisions for deconcentrated State authorities having, on average, about 120 000 inhabitants. The least populated district (Jesenik) has about 43 000 inhabitants; the most populated district outside Prague (Brno City) has about 388 000 inhabitants.

In each district, there is a district office representing central government. They have general competence and are responsible for a number of government departments. In the cities of Brno, Ostrava and Plzen there is no district office; and the relevant tasks are performed by the municipal office.

District offices were established by Act in 1990 by the Czech National Council, after the removal of national committees. They inherited most of the former responsibilities of national committees at the district and regional levels. The district office is headed by a chief district officer appointed and dismissed by the Government of the Czech Republic, on the proposal of the Minister of the Interior.

District offices may issue by-laws, in accordance with the law (including secondary legislation) and can take decisions within their competence which affect individuals. They also have a key role in the oversight of municipalities. District offices have a deconcentrated budget which, together with the budget for the municipalities, is under the heading of "local budgets" -- a mix of State administration and self-government. District offices are subordinate to the Ministry of the Interior, which controls their activity.

The performance of State functions by district offices is controlled by central government bodies. The Minister of the Interior is entitled to quash any by-law issued by a district office which deviates from the law. Any other illegal or inappropriate measure taken by a district office may be overruled by the competent State authority. In particular, administrative decisions taken by district offices under the Administrative Procedure Code are subject to a review by the minister in terms of legality and merit. Decisions can also be referred to courts. Each area having a district office also has a district assembly (see also section 1.2).

There are various other field services of central government ministries which may follow district or different boundaries. The most significant field services of central government include those of the Ministry of Finance (eight financial directorates at the regional level, 233 financial offices, and 21 customs offices); the Ministry of Labour and Social Affairs (76 offices of labour and 76 offices of social security); and the Ministry of Education (85 school offices).

Creation, elimination and restructuring

The Czech countries (and also the former Czechoslovakia, and the Slovak Republic) have always been characterised by a very fragmented municipal structure, and a huge number of small communities. The number of municipalities decreased regularly from the fifties due to urbanisation and administrative reforms aiming at the amalgamation of very small municipalities during the sixties and the seventies. However, the collapse of the communist regime gave rise to a revival of numerous small municipalities which were able to recover their former autonomy (see Table 2).

Districts, a traditional constituency of State field administration, were also amalgamated: their number decreased from 179 in 1950 down to 72 in 1993. New districts may be created by the central government and one (Jesenik) had been created as at 1 January 1996.

Table 2. **Number of municipalities in the Czech countries (1851-1995)**

Year	Number of municipalities
1851	11 925
1857	12 636
1881	10 245
1921	11 435
1931	11 793
1951	10 870
1961	7 557
1971	7 308
1981	4 571
1990	5 749
1993	6 196
1995	6 232

Source: D. Hendrych, R. Pomahac, O. Vidláková, P. Zárecky (1993), *Toward a decentralised government: the case of the Czech Republic*.

Splitting up municipalities was facilitated by the Czech Local Government Act of 1990 and its amendments of 1992. According to this legislation, the amalgamation and division of existing municipalities is part of their new self-governing rights.

Amalgamation may be decided by an agreement between the municipalities concerned, after consultations with the district office, or with central government if municipalities belong to different districts. The agreement may be signed after being decided by municipal councils, if there is no referendum initiative within 30 days after the publication of the decision. If such an initiative claims successfully for a referendum in one municipality, it has to take place in this municipality; the amalgamation may be take place only if the majority of voters in this municipality is in favour of the amalgamation.

Conversely, a municipality may be split into two or more new municipalities. This must be proposed by the existing municipality to the Ministry of the Interior, following the results of a referendum organised in any part of the municipality wanting to secede. The division has to be approved by the minister. It was thus almost impossible to oppose the will directly expressed by the voters, especially in a period when the pressure for more democracy was very strong. However, the law now requires a minimum size of 300 inhabitants for new municipalities.

According to the Local Government Act of 1990, municipalities may establish associations on the basis of a voluntary agreement to perform tasks within their competence such as: education, social relief, health care, cultural activities, environment protection, refuse collection, water supply, creation, maintenance and operation of local public services. These associations of municipalities are not legal persons of public law. Their creation, management and dissolution are subject to provisions of the Civil Code on associations of legal bodies for common purposes. Corresponding financial means and properties may be transferred by municipalities to these associations. The association has its own budget and should adopt its own statute. There is, however, very little co-operation between Czech municipalities.

The three statutory cities may be divided into urban districts with an elected body and tasks delegated to them by the city -- but they are not territorial self-governing communities.

Control bodies

Municipal activities (both those delegated/transferred from the State administration and those associated with self-government) are subject to several control bodies: the district office, the Ministry of the Interior, the Parliament (Chamber of Deputies), the Constitutional Court, and civil law courts.

- The district office is responsible for day-to-day oversight of municipal by-laws or decisions. The powers of the district office vary depending on whether the municipal body is acting in its own competence or is performing delegated State functions.

- The Ministry of the Interior supervises self-government by-laws and also decisions by the municipal councils in the three statutory cities.

- The Chamber of Deputies may be referred to by the district office concerning a municipal by-law considered by the district office as unlawful. This is a remnant of the former national committee system, and now inconsistent with the new local government system.

- The Constitutional Court may decide that a municipal by-law (in own competence or in delegated matters) is unlawful.

Individuals may also lodge an appeal against decisions taken by municipal bodies, subject to the Administrative Procedure Code (1967), and have those decisions reviewed by a higher authority. The 1993 Act provides that administrative decision is subject to judicial review, but the Supreme Administrative Court provided for by the Constitution has not yet been established.

The financial review of local government is exercised by the Ministry of Finance. It is applied to expenses funded by the State budget. The district office checks economic activities performed by municipalities; and the results of this inspection have to be submitted to the municipal council.

The supervision of legal acts by municipal bodies depends on whether they are specific municipal responsibilities or delegated State administration functions; and whether they are by-laws or administrative decisions. By-laws must comply with the Constitution and national (primary and secondary) legislation, and are normally enforceable 15 days after their publication. Their purpose must be to carry out tasks related to local municipal affairs. The supervision of by-laws is restricted to their legality and is exercised by the district office and the Constitutional Court.

1.2 Powers

Nature of sub-national institutions

The right of territorial communities of the Czech Republic to self-government is one of the basic provisions of the Czech Constitution. Local self-governing communities may be municipalities or regions (or provinces), but at present only municipalities have that status.

Self-government rights are based on legal capacity (territorial self-governing communities are legal persons of public law), on ownership rights, on election of municipal bodies and on budgetary autonomy. The right of municipalities to own public property exists only since the 1991 Act of the Czech National Council which transferred properties of the Czech Republic to municipalities. The properties transferred were: immovable properties belonging to municipalities before 1949, those managed previously by the national committees, newly created municipal goods, dwelling houses and premises. Municipalities could also claim for the transfer of other properties managed by district offices or ministries (such as museums, schools, or other cultural premises).

Territorial communities are managed by a directly elected council and an elected executive. Councils are elected for four years by a system of proportional representation. The municipal council is an elected representative body comprising from 5 to 55 members depending on the number of inhabitants and the area. Voters (who must be Czech citizens) may choose between voting for lists or voting for individuals on the lists. The last municipal elections took place in November 1994, with a participation rate of 62.3 per cent.

In municipalities with more than 3 000 inhabitants and at least 15 councillors, the municipal council elects an executive committee from among its members. It also elects the mayor and deputy mayors. In smaller municipalities, the mayor, rather than the municipal committee, exercises the executive functions.

The municipal committee comprises between 5 and 11 members, but should not exceed one-third of the council membership. It is the executive organ of the municipal council in matters which are the specific responsibility of municipalities and for which it is responsible to the municipal council. It also has regulatory powers concerning delegated State functions, and for these it is accountable to the upper State body. The municipal committee may establish commissions as advisory or supervisory bodies, for functions for which it is directly responsible (e.g. finance, health, environment); others such as that on administrative offences are required by law. Commissions may be vested by the mayor, in agreement with the district office, with executive tasks in matters belonging to delegated State functions. Where such commissions do not exist, decisions are made by the mayor or department head.

The mayor is the chairman of the municipal committee, convenes its meetings, and prepares and executes its resolutions or by-laws. The mayor reports to the municipal council. He is in charge of the organisation of the municipal office. The municipal committee may decide that designated functions of the mayor will be taken over by his deputies.

The municipal office comprises the mayor, deputy mayors, other members such as a secretary (where the municipal council has decided to create at least two departments), and all public employees of the municipality. It is in charge of executing all administrative tasks of the municipality, delegated State functions, and tasks which are specific municipal responsibilities. The mayor is also the head of the municipal office.

A local referendum may be organised by the municipal council on any issue within the municipal competence, but not on the following matters: *i)* the local budget and charges; *ii)* the election or revocation of the mayor, his deputies and other elected bodies; *iii)* questions conflicting with binding legal provisions; *iv)* matters subject to the Administrative Procedure Code; *v)* subjects dealt with by referendum during the preceding 24 months; *vi)* matters decided by the municipal council after a referendum. No referendum may be held within six months of the next municipal election.

A district assembly is formed in each area with a district office. The district assembly is composed of representatives from the municipal councils in the district, elected by each municipal council. The number of assembly members depends on the number of municipalities and the number of inhabitants of the district. Decisions for approval by the district assembly are the allocation to municipalities of the global State grant received by the district, approval of the district budget (a deconcentrated budget), supervision of the execution of the budget, and other tasks resulting from special laws. If a decision of the district assembly is in conflict with the law, the chief district officer shall suspend its execution and refer it to the Government for decision.

Type and degree of autonomy

Self-government is a right for territorial communities which is recognised by the Constitution at two levels: the municipality and the region or province. This means that a territorial self-governed community could not be created at the district level.

The Constitution also limits the intervention of the State in local government affairs. The State may intervene in local government activities only to enforce the law and by the means provided by the law. Functions of the State administration may be delegated to self-government authorities only in cases provided for by the law. This aims at protecting municipalities (in the first place) against any attempt of central government to shift the burden of certain tasks upon municipalities.

Local representative councils (at present only municipal councils) may refer to the Constitutional Court against any unlawful interference of the State in local government affairs and in the case of disputes between the State and local self-government bodies, on the limits of their competence.

Municipal councils may issue by-laws within the limits of municipal competences, and within their territory. This is the purpose of local self-government. But a municipality is not entitled to issue regulations where it feels that national regulations are missing -- filling the holes of national legislation is *ultra vires* for municipal councils. According to the Constitutional Court, the list of matters of municipal competence which is laid down by the Local Government Act of 1990 is exclusive, in the case of by-laws which are binding for legal subjects.

As an executive body of the municipal council, the municipal committee may inflict penalties for offences as provided by the law. These are the breach of duty to remove consequences of a disaster, breach of duty in keeping premises clean and in good order, offence to amenities or the environment of the municipality, pollution offence, and breach of a by-law in exercising an industrial or commercial activity.

In matters of delegated State functions, local self-government bodies may issue regulations on the basis of, and within the limits of, the law, just as ministers and other central government bodies. These regulations are secondary legislation, since they always have to be based on a legal provision. They are issued by the municipal committee, and not by the municipal council (or by the mayor in smaller municipalities where there is no municipal committee).

Municipalities have wide discretion to borrow, since there is at present no regulation on local debt. They can get bank credits, loans, or issue bonds. Prague, for example, was successful in issuing bonds, and five Czech cities were able to borrow on foreign capital markets. Municipalities, however, have only limited powers to raise taxes (see section 2.2).

1.3 Responsibilities

Municipal responsibilities are divided into those "proper" to the municipalities, and matters delegated to them from the State administration. This distinction is traditional in the Czech territories, dating back to the law of 1864 on municipal government for the province of Bohemia.

   a) *Competences specific to municipalities*: Municipalities have a general competence of principle concerning all local affairs. (If, therefore, regions or provinces are created, their competence would be limited to those matters listed by the law). As territorial self-governing communities, the municipalities are legal entities of public law. They have property rights, and are entitled to manage their own budgets. According to the Local Government Act of 1990, municipalities rule their own affairs autonomously and assure economic, social and cultural development, and the protection and creation of a healthy environment on their territory.

   Included in these municipal responsibilities are the following matters: managing municipal assets; adopting and managing the annual municipal budget; adopting and implementing a development programme; organising local referendums (e.g. on any proposals for splitting up the municipality); agreeing modifications to municipal boundaries; maintaining public order locally and establishing a municipal police corps; establishing optional local fees, and setting their rates; local responsibilities in the fields of culture, social relief, health care, and education (maintenance of school buildings -- teachers are employed and paid by the State); the creation, maintenance and operation of local public services; public hygiene, refuse collection and disposal, and street cleaning; water supply and treatment; sewerage.

Czech municipalities are also responsible for fire protection and public transport. On the other hand, according to the 1992 Planning and Building Act, only the city of Prague and listed cities are empowered to issue spatial planning regulations which are binding on owners. Elsewhere, municipalities have only advisory powers. Planning rules are issued by district offices and building permits are granted by district offices unless this authority is delegated to municipalities. Municipalities are also responsible for housing in that State housing was transferred to municipalities by the 1991 Act on Municipal Property; and flats are now being privatised.

b) *Delegated responsibilities*: Municipalities do not all exercise the same delegated responsibilities. There are two main divisions in this context: between ordinary municipalities and cities, and between cities and statutory cities.

All municipalities have to exercise State responsibilities in basic delegated matters, according to the Local Government Act. These include police regulations concerning selling alcohol or tobacco, and environment protection. District offices may delegate the power to grant building permits to municipalities and currently about 700 of them exercise this delegated power. The 383 communities with "designated local authority", as defined by a 1995 Government Order, also perform State responsibilities for smaller surrounding municipalities.

2. MANAGEMENT FUNCTIONS

2.1 Policy-making and co-ordination

Coherence, consultation and conflict resolution

The division of "proper" municipal competences and of responsibilities transferred to municipalities by the State is legally determined, and Parliament is entitled to revise the boundary between these two traditional kinds of responsibilities. Most municipal responsibilities (of both kinds) result from the former national committees, the local soviet-type State bodies which were removed in 1990, although in them there was no place for a distinction between State and local self-government competences.

At present deconcentration and the sharing between municipalities and State authorities of some functions of the State administration might help overcome the present fragmentation of the local government system. The district assembly seems to be currently the only forum where municipalities can discuss issues of common interest.

The tendency regarding conflict resolution seems to be towards an increasing role for the courts, and especially the Constitutional Court on the initiative of the chief district officer.

Formal and informal mechanisms

A lobby of cities has existed since very soon after the collapse of the communist regime. The Union of Cities and Municipalities was created in early 1990 and played a significant role in the preparation of the Local Government Act. It pushed strongly in favour of radical decentralisation, for deconcentrated State administration to be put under the control of local government, and for State administration to implement its decisions through local government. The mayor of Prague and the leader of the Union were invited to a cabinet meeting, and then involved at the committee stage in the parliamentary debates on the Bill. As a result, the Union contributed significantly to the final text of the new law on local government.

This evidence suggests that the Union of Cities and Municipalities has quickly reached the status of an influential lobby for the institutional interests of local government. However, not all municipalities are members of the Union. Smaller ones are reluctant to pay a fee from their very small budget. Consequently, members tend to be cities and larger municipalities, and as evident in the first years of its existence, bigger cities, including the capital city, took the lead in the Union.

2.2 Financial management

Sources of revenue

In 1995 local budgets (an aggregate of municipal and district budgets) represented 22.2 per cent of total consolidated general government expenditure and over 62 per cent of the gross fixed capital formation of governments. In the same year municipal revenues totalled 106 479 million Korunya and accounted for 82.5 per cent of the total local budget, the remaining 17.5 per cent being the district budget. Table 3 presents the composition of municipal revenues in 1995.

Table 3. **Main revenue sources of municipalities (1995)**
(in million Koruny)

Revenue sources	
Income tax on legal bodies	3 145
Personal income tax	47 935
Real property tax	3 799
Miscellaneous taxes	340
Total tax revenues	55 219
Revenues from budgetary organisations	12 072
Transfers from non-budgetary organisations	77
Administrative fees	1 940
Local fees	1 196
Interests received	840
Miscellaneous non tax revenues	4 154
Total non tax revenues	20 278
Total tax and non tax revenues	75 496
Capital incomes from selling properties	4 420
Transfers from the State budget *of which*:	21 013
-- grants	11 242
-- State social relief	208
-- subsidies for current expenses	4 954
-- subsidies for capital expenses	4 609
Transfers from state funds and various non budgetary sources of central bodies	2 607
Gifts and affected contributions	1 110
Miscellaneous (non-budgetary grants and cross-subsidies between municipalities)	1 831
TOTAL REVENUES	**106 479**
Other non budgetary resources: *of which*:	17 597
-- withdrawals from reserves	13 132
-- loans and credits	4 465

Source: Ministry of Finance.

The main sources of municipal revenues are the personal income tax (45 per cent of municipal budgets), transfers from the State budget (19.7 per cent), and own non tax revenues (19 per cent).

Most tax revenues are tax shares. Up to 1995 the yield of the income tax on salaries was shared between the district budgets and municipal budgets within each district, but from 1996 only 60 per cent of this amount will be shared. The yield of income tax on revenues from unincorporated activities is allocated in total to the budget of the municipality where it has been collected.

The income tax on legal persons (corporate income tax) is basically a tax revenue of the State budget. It amounted to Kc 70.9 billion in 1993 but from 1994 a small share of this tax has been released to municipalities where the tax yield was generated (Kc 128 million in 1994 and Kc 3 145 million in 1995).

Own tax revenues in the proper sense are very limited: the real property tax, and a small amount from a number of low yield taxes. Non tax revenues, on the other hand, are a significant resource, but also a heterogeneous one. Local fees include dog licenses, entrance tickets, fees for the use of public areas, permits to sell tobacco or alcoholic drinks, municipal motor vehicle permits, advertisement permits, hotel bed taxes, and recreation facility user fees.

During recent years, there has been a sharp increase in the yield of income taxes and of the real property tax, and municipalities have benefited from this tendency. The yield of the income tax on salaries was Kc 25.5 billion in 1993, Kc 48.7 billion in 1994 and Kc 60 billion in 1995. This resource represented 27.1 per cent of local budgets in 1993, and 35 per cent in 1995. The increase of the property tax yield has been less significant -- from Kc 3 billion in 1993 up to Kc 3.8 billion in both 1994 and 1995.

Transfers from the state budget are the fourth main source of revenues for local budgets. About half of these budgetary transfers are grants which serve different purposes and which municipalities may use freely. The general grant is divided into different shares:

- A share calculated to cover State administration tasks, such as delivering building permits. It is calculated on the basis of several criteria reflecting the size of the municipality and the burden of the administrative tasks carried out for the State.

- Shares for secondary schools and kindergartens (a fixed amount per pupil), for social care facilities, such as homes for elderly people, and mentally or physically disabled persons (a fixed amount per bed).

- A share for social benefits paid by municipalities (to be spent only for this purpose).

- A share for fire protection.

- A share for equalisation, which is allocated by the district assembly to municipalities of the district, in order to offset the difference between the average and the tax base per capita of poorer municipalities. Its amount decreased sharply, from Kc 9.9 billion in 1993 to Kc 2.9 billion in 1994.

Specific subsidies are granted to finance capital expenditures, including building elderly care facilities, housing development projects, schools or hospitals, or to restore the historical areas in cities, or to repair environmental damage.

During recent years there has been a sharp decrease of non-budgeted subsidies (from about Kc 11 billion in 1993 down to Kc 2.6 billion in 1995). On the other hand, there was an even more important increase in transfers from the State budget to local government budgets (from Kc 17 billion in 1993 up to Kc 28.4 billion in 1994 and Kc 32.3 billion in 1995).

Debt remains at a rather low level in local government resources. The amount of credit involved in 1995 was just in excess of 13 per cent of the total amount of capital expenditures, and at about Kc 6.7 billion, much lower than in 1994 (Kc 11.5 billion). But the ratio of the debt load is still low at 3 per cent of the total of current tax and non tax revenues.

Prague, Brno, Plzen and Ostrava enjoy more financial autonomy not only because of their size, but because they act as both municipalities and district offices. As a whole, the city of Prague represents probably nearly one-fifth of the total local budgets of the Czech Republic.

Expenditure responsibilities

No detailed functional breakdown of municipal budgets is available except for the city of Prague. It is only possible, therefore, to analyse the distribution of local expenditures according to their nature. These are summarised in Table 4 by comparing the budgets of municipalities and district offices.

In 1993, local public expenditure represented 9.8 per cent of the GDP. About 87 per cent of the local government capital expenditure was carried out by municipalities in 1995, the balance by the

Table 4. **Municipal and district office expenditures by type (1995)**
(in million Koruny)

Class of expenditure	municipalities	district offices
Current expenditures	**65 309**	**16 144**
of which:		
-- purchases of goods and services	32 696	3 791
-- personnel expenditure	9 685	3 305
-- grants and other current transfer expenditures:	9 954	1 940
• to municipal enterprises	6 036	1
• to budgetary organisations	3 918	1 939
-- other transfers (to institutions)	11 725	7 103
Capital expenditures	**45 171**	**6 691**
of which:		
-- investment expenditures	39 044	2 674
Total expenditure	110 480	21 835

Source: Ministry of Finance.

district offices. In the city of Prague, one third of its total budget is spent on transportation, but less than 7 per cent on education and only 2 per cent on health care.

Balance between discretion and control

It is generally acknowledged that municipalities have far more discretion in spending than in obtaining resources. In fact, municipalities may spend freely the tax shares and grants they receive from the State budget. However, in 1995 grants represented only 45 per cent of all State budget transfers. The State social relief grant, subsidies for current expenses and subsidies for capital expenses, on the other hand, are affected to specific purposes. Nevertheless of a total expenditure of Kc 106.5 billion only Kc 13.4 billion are resources for specific purposes.

On the revenue side municipalities have very little autonomy. The main source of municipal revenue is income tax. Tax bases are set and evaluated by the State administration, and tax rates are set by Parliament. Municipalities exercise no tax power on incomes; they only benefit from the revenues allocated to them. The yield of the income tax on unincorporated activities is allocated totally to the municipalities where it is collected. The yield of the income tax on salaries and wages was, until the end of 1995, shared within each district between the district office and municipalities of the district on an even (50/50) basis. Starting in 1996 this formula was changed with the aim of linking tax revenues of municipalities to the economic activities of entrepreneurs operating within the municipality, for 10 per cent of the tax yield.

The income tax on legal persons (corporate income tax) is a national tax and the tax bases and tax rates, as well as taxation conditions are determined nationwide by law. Since 1994, municipalities where the tax yield is generated get a small tax share, but they exercise no tax power. To a certain extent, they can influence the location of companies, but geographical factors are likely to prevail.

Real property tax, it is based on physical parameters (surface, location, and type of land use), and municipalities are divided into six groups according to their population, with different rates for each group. Each municipal council may choose between two rates and, to that extent, municipalities have a limited tax power. Revenues from the real property tax are significant only for small municipalities. But the development of the real property market, especially in cities, should make it possible to increase the yield of this tax by a reform of the criteria and by giving municipalities wider discretion for rate setting.

The amount of local fees and charges is set by municipalities within limits fixed by law; and several non tax revenues can be influenced by municipalities.

Thus tax shares cannot be considered as own tax revenues, since municipalities exert no influence on the corresponding taxes. They are rather to be considered as transfers with allocation criteria based on the location of tax bases. However, it is possible to consider the income tax on unincorporated activities as a very local tax, since municipalities are able to influence directly the amount of the tax bases located in their jurisdiction with appropriate policy. The same can be said for the income tax on legal persons, for the share which is granted to municipalities. But the only way for municipalities to get more from these two sources is to support unincorporated independent activities and to attract businesses to their territory. In total, therefore, municipalities enjoy a relatively high level of resources independent of central government (38 per cent), but the volume upon which tax power may be exercised, within narrow limits, is not higher than 4.7 per cent of the total budgetary revenues of municipalities.

2.3 Performance management

There is little to say on this subject at present. Structural reforms in the public administration are not yet completed, and the issues of management are heavily dependent on policy choices which are still to be made concerning the fragmentation of municipalities, a second level of local government, the organisation of the public service and the personnel policy within it.

However, in September 1994 the Czech Government approved a document submitted to the Parliament under the title: *Intentions of the Government of the Czech Republic in the field of public administration*. This policy document emphasises effectiveness, rationalisation and cost-minimisation, and it assumes that the reform will be a long-term process, with several steps to be implemented successively. Decentralisation and public service reform are parts of this process. The new situation of municipalities in the political and administrative system involves a major learning process for local government and local government employees. They have to ensure better satisfaction of public needs, seek more efficiency in the use of limited resources, and find new sources of finance without deviating from their basic duties as agents of territorial communities. The difficulty of this transition resides in the fact that basic principles of public administration such as accountability, loyalty, ethics, and compliance which must be implemented at the same time as the new requirements of a market-type economy put public administration under pressure to introduce new management methods based on market-type behaviour.

In October 1995, another Cabinet decision sought to develop more consumer-oriented attitudes among local government public officials in their relations with citizens, and to make institutions and procedures more transparent.

2.4 Human resource management

Statutory distinctions

Civil service reform is still on the agenda of the Government in the Czech Republic. According to the Constitution of 1992, the legal status of public officials in ministries and in other government bodies is ruled by law. A general law on the public service has, therefore, been proposed in government programmes since 1992, and again after the general elections of June 1996. According to the draft Public Service Reform Bill the new public service would be based on a career system. The Bill includes provisions on recruitment, examinations and other obligations for performance assessment, pay, health and social insurance provisions, and the protection the political neutrality of the public service up to the level of deputy ministers.

Such a law would apply both to State and local government public officials. To that extent the uniformity of the legal situation of State and local government employees will remain, as it is now, but with a major shift in the legal conception of the public service.

Until the new Public Service Act is adopted, all public employees are employed under the Labour Code. This has been the case from the early times of the socialist regime in Czechoslovakia. Nevertheless, the Labour Code has been modified to require State employees to respect the following obligations: i) impartiality in decision-making; ii) confidentiality; iii) integrity and honesty; and iv) disinterestedness (not to take advantage or information from one's position for personal benefit or the benefit of another person). All employees including those in local government have a labour contract with the government body which employs them, subject to collective contracts which are established nation-wide. Only judges, the police and the army are subject to special laws.

There was no career system in the management of government employees in the past. However, this did not rule out competitions organised to recruit employees in positions where special expertise was needed. On this basis, government employees were organised in branch trade unions along with workers and employees of enterprises (for example light industry, health care, and agriculture). Staff were thus managed not only as government employees, but also as part of the general work force. Only personnel employed in "horizontal" government administrations were managed purely as government employees, and counted as government employees in the statistics. These included local government employees as well as those of "horizontal" ministries such as the Ministry of Finance and the Ministry of Justice.

Table 5. Municipal employees (1993)

Class of personnel	Number of employees
Executive	1 870
Administrative	15 870
Clerk	1 090
TOTAL	18 830

Source: Council of Europe, 1993.

Managerial autonomy

Municipalities presently have considerable managerial autonomy regarding their personnel, although this largely results from the absence of adequate regulation. Any municipality may hire the employees it needs, at any level of qualification – the only limit is the budget of the municipality. There is no obligatory or recommended structure for local government staff in municipalities issued by central government. There is nevertheless a central government regulation on salaries. The discretion of municipalities in their personnel policy is therefore limited by a national wage policy.

Mobility

Mobility between local and central government is not at present much of an issue. More problematic is the drift between the public and the private sector. In a situation characterised by a relatively low level of unemployment, a gap in wages between the public and the private sector such that young graduates can hope for much higher salaries and more rapid promotion in the latter, it is difficult for municipalities to attract or even to keep the best people. As a result, municipalities, and in particular smaller municipalities, lack qualified staff. In general, the number of skilled officials is decreasing, in spite of an increase of the personnel as a whole. The mobility of staff members is considerable, and the declared intention of the Government to reduce the number of public employees has also had a negative impact.

3. TRENDS IN REDISTRIBUTING AUTHORITY ACROSS LEVELS OF GOVERNMENT

3.1 Evolving tendencies

The Czech Republic has experienced a decentralisation process encouraged by the rapid revitalisation of municipalities and the transfer of numerous administrative responsibilities from the regional level to the district and municipal levels. This shift has been facilitated by new legislation. However, this evolution is limited by the excessive fragmentation of local government, which is not compensated for by co-operation between municipalities. Many small municipalities cannot attract qualified staff members and their limited budgets give them no room for initiative. The deconcentrated district administration also suffers from too much fragmentation. The district offices regroup only some ministerial departments whereas many others have their own field services – a situation making co-ordination more difficult.

The present system might generate the risk of increasing territorial inequalities. Local autonomy and the present trends in tax revenues favour bigger cities. Income tax has become the main source of revenues for municipalities, supplemented in bigger cities by the tax share from the income tax on companies. These resources are heavily conditioned by economic development which tends to concentrate in a small number of sites and largely beyond municipal influence. This will result in increasing inequalities in the resources of municipalities, as bigger cities receive more revenues, and smaller municipalities will have more and more difficulty in maintaining the levels of service expected by their citizens. At the same time, as the equalisation grant, allocated at the district level, has declined, it can be expected that local finance reform will soon come onto the agenda, and equalisation will probably become a big issue.

Another tendency is the development of the deconcentrated administration. The Czech Republic was prepared for such a development through its Administrative Procedure Code, which is inherited from the former Austrian Empire. After the abolition of the national committee system and restoration of municipal self-government, the deconcentration of State functions at the district level was seen as a temporary solution prior to regional reforms. Deconcentration is now likely to stay, making it possible for central government to keep under its control some functions which have to be performed locally. If this evolution is confirmed, it would imply the separation of State and local government at least at the intermediary level, rather than them being fused into a single office reporting to an elected council, as is the case at present in cities performing State functions for surrounding municipalities.

A further tendency is the reduction of public property as a whole, and in particular that of municipalities. One of the major changes with the restoration of municipal local government was to transfer in full to municipalities the property that they previously managed as State bodies. While this tendency is in general quite natural, it could present problems in the longer term in some cases. Cities have been inclined to sell land properties in order to collect resources they needed for other purposes. If this was done without sufficient care for future developments needs , they might face difficulties if obliged to buy land at higher prices or to give up some projects which would otherwise be desirable.

3.2 The current debate

The current debate on government levels in the Czech Republic is dominated by the issue of the "second level" of local self-government, i.e. "provinces or regions" as provided for in the Constitution as "upper level local self-governed communities" (art. 99). This formulation reflects the uncertainty about the kind of upper tier of local government which should be established.

Discussions on the nature, number, and responsibilities of regions or provinces are continuing. A Bill on the creation of 17 regions, adopted by the Cabinet with a small majority against another project in favour of only 13 regions, was submitted to Parliament but it was rejected in June 1994 and again in June 1995. In December 1995, Parliament voted that a Bill on the upper tier had to be prepared and that 9 regions should be created. Nevertheless, the Government still favours a division into 17 regions. Many other proposals have been formulated, from a minimum of 3 regions (Bohemia, Moravia and Silesia – at the time of the discussion on the Czech Constitution), to a division of the territory into 25 or 30 smaller "regions". (The Czech territory was divided into 14 regions in 1950; this number was reduced to 8, including Prague, in 1962.)

According to the Government Bill, the following responsibilities would be transferred to the regions: water management, public works for flood protection, secondary schools (management but not of the teaching personnel), health care (hospitals), culture, support for municipalities, and regional planning. Resources would be granted basically through tax-sharing. At present there is no certainty about which choices will be made.

Some other issues still to be decided are whether district offices are maintained or suppressed; and whether State functions at the regional level will be performed by a regional office accountable to an elected regional council or by a separate regional office of the State administration -- a solution which would be more consistent with the trend in favour of deconcentration.

Another issue, although less discussed, is the future pattern of municipalities. Some territorial reform may be necessary if the alternative of voluntary co-operation between municipalities is not sufficient.

3.3 Driving forces

It is not easy to identify the main driving forces behind current local government reforms in the Czech Republic. The present pattern of economic development favours big cities and economic concentration. There is no clear political expression by small municipalities, and cities are dominant in the national Union of Cities and Municipalities. However, territorial inequalities and trade unions representing interests of those suffering from the decline of obsolete industries -- a process which is only just beginning in the Czech Republic -- will probably push for a better balance. This could facilitate a vote in favour of regional reform and bring about adjustments in the local finance system, particularly the introduction of more equalisation policies.

DENMARK

1. INSTITUTIONS AND AUTHORITY

1.1 Structures

Description of levels

The Danish administrative system is a unitary one. The Danish Constitution establishes local self-government. The structure of sub-national government is based on a two-tier system: counties and municipalities, the municipalities belonging to one of the counties. However, the general rule is that the counties are not superior to the municipalities. They each have their own tasks. Regulations governing local government are laid down in the 1991 Local Government Act and are the same for all municipalities and counties apart from the municipality of Copenhagen.

The total area of Denmark is 43 100 square kilometres and the total population in 1994 was 5 206 000. There are currently a total of 14 counties and 275 municipalities. The municipalities of Copenhagen and Frederiksberg each have the dual status of municipality and county. Table 1 summarises the size distribution of these authorities in 1995.

Table 1. **Area and population of sub-national governments (1995)**

Number	Counties 14		Municipalities 275	
	Area (km²)	Population	Area (km²)	Population
Largest	6 173	605 868	564	471 300
Smallest	526	44 936	9	2 388

Number of municipalities and population distribution

Population size	Number of municipalities
0-1 000	0
1 000-5 000	18
5 000-10 000	119
10 000-50 000	122
50 000-100 000	12
over 100 000	4

Source: Statistics Denmark, 1995.

Central government at sub-national levels

There are 14 offices of county prefects (*Statsamter*) which have the same geographical area as the counties. The prefect (*Statsamtmand*) is nominated by central government. The main tasks of the county prefect office are to make decisions concerning family law. It also acts as the secretariat for the county board of appeal which examines decisions made by local authorities on social questions. The board is chaired by the prefect, its two other members being appointed by the minister of social affairs after nomination by the local authority association.

Creation, elimination and restructuring

The ultimate authority for defining the boundaries of local authorities lies with the Parliament. Structural reform which took place in 1970 laid the basis of the present Danish local government system. The point of departure of that restructuring was to establish municipalities with a sufficient population base to handle a number of service tasks and to make them responsible for the financing of expenses through local taxation and central government subsidies.

A first guiding principle was that the municipalities should be responsible for primary school education and it was estimated that a population basis of 4 000-5 000 inhabitants was necessary to ensure a viable economic base for the running of a primary school. Similarly for counties, the guiding principle was the efficient running of hospitals.

Before the 1970 reform, Denmark was divided into 1 391 municipalities and 25 counties. After the reform, the number was reduced to the present 275 municipalities and 14 counties. The reform thus provided the necessary population in each municipality for bearing the costs of an administration based on a comprehensive transfer of tasks from the State to municipalities and counties.

Control bodies

According to the Danish Constitution, central government supervises the self-government of local authorities but today in practise general supervision is of a limited nature. Broad supervision of local authorities lies with the County Supervisory Committees which control the legality of acts of local authorities. There is such a corporate body in each county, the chairman being the county prefect and the other four members being elected by the county council from amongst its members. The Ministry of the Interior is the highest authority of supervision, and exercises controls over the County Supervisory Committees.

Professional auditing of all municipal and county authority accounts is a statutory requirement, carried out in most cases by an inter-municipal institution set up by the Local Government Association, the Local Government Auditing Department. The counties and municipalities are, however, allowed to use any authorised auditor.

1.2 Powers

Nature of sub-national institutions

County councils are directly elected for a four-year period. Anyone aged 18 including non-naturalised Danish citizens with a permanent residence in Denmark can vote. The county council must have a minimum of 13 members and a maximum of 31. It is chaired by the county mayor elected for four years by the council from among its members. Municipal councils and their chairman are elected in the same way as the county councils.

Each county and municipal council must appoint a Finance Committee of which the Mayor is the chairman. The Mayor is also head of the administration. Each council also appoints standing committees which usually have five or seven members, who must also be members of the council. The seats of a committee are distributed among political parties in proportion to the number of councillors represented. All the committees except the financial committee appoint their own chairman and are responsible within their area for direct administration, running activities and institutions and supervising planning.

The number of committees can vary among counties but generally speaking, there are committees of finance; education and culture; technical and environmental matters; social security and health; and for hospitals. They are responsible for the preparation and implementation of council decisions. They also make decisions on behalf of the council. The finance committee has extensive powers, its most important responsibility being the preparation of the draft budget. The finance committee is also responsible for the administration of staff. It also functions as a planning committee and as such co-ordinates local economic and physical planning.

The structure of the administration usually corresponds to the committee structure: a central administration under the direction of a county director and four sectoral administrations.

Municipal councils appoint standing committees. Although their structure may differ, most councils appoint such committees for social services, education, cultural affairs, and in the technical and environmental areas. Each committee is directly responsible for matters in its area.

The mayor is the leader of the administration and has ultimate responsibility for day-to-day management of the municipal authority. The chief executive officer acts as advisor to the finance committee and the council and is often also the chief personnel officer. The head of the other sectors of the administration are subordinate to the chief executive in matters of management but report to a committee and its chairman on substantive matters.

The biggest municipalities run a different system with five to seven aldermen proportionally elected by the council. The administration is managed by a corporate body, the Executive, comprising the mayor and the aldermen. It performs the functions which in smaller municipalities are the responsibility of the finance committee and each member of the executive carries out functions which in smaller municipalities are carried out by standing committees.

Type and degree of autonomy

County and municipal administration must be in accordance with legislation published by the Parliament (*Folketing*). According to the Constitution, municipalities have the right to manage their own affairs, under State supervision. Today general supervision is of a limited nature. Those affairs delegated by the *Folketing* are executed by county and municipal councils without interference from central government.

In practice, the distribution of public tasks between the State, counties and municipalities implies that decision-making responsibility is usually left to municipal and county councils. This makes it easier for citizens to participate in – or influence – the decisions made in their own area.

The municipal or county council may make decisions on any local matter, but in practice only decisions on important issues are made in the council. Some matters, however, must be decided by the council, especially the annual budget (including taxation), the annual accounts, the organisation and powers of the committees, the election of members of committees, the election of auditors, physical planning and agreements between local authorities for joint action.

The powers of the finance committee are expressly stated in the Local Government Act. The powers of the standing committees are set out in standing orders, although only in terms of areas of responsibility. In all municipal matters power under the Act rests with the council, but under Danish law there is no general limit to the delegation of powers. Any member of a committee may request that any matter dealt with by the committee should be put before the council.

In general, the Danish system of local government is very comprehensive, both as to the share of the overall public tasks carried out by municipalities, and the right of municipalities and counties to impose taxes and to determine their own levels of taxation and service. A very large share of Danish municipal expenditure is financed by municipal income. This limits the formal possibilities of central government to influence the overall level of taxation and of public expenditure.

The Local Government Act contains provisions governing the internal structure of local authorities and provisions regulating the activities and duties of the council, the committees (finance, standing and advisory) and the Mayor. It contains no provision regarding local government administration, as the council must be free to adapt its administration as circumstances may require. Special legislation contains some provisions which require the local authorities to set up specific bodies. The trend, however, is towards their abolition. The counties and municipalities themselves determine how their administration functions and their approach to tasks. Parliament can, however, regulate areas of expenditure and thus the way in which tasks are handled.

1.3 Responsibilities

Distribution of responsibilities

The principle of decentralisation which formed the basis of the redistribution of tasks in the 1970s was that tasks should be accomplished as close to the citizens as possible. As a result the distribution of tasks between the State, the counties and the municipalities implies that most functions which directly concern local citizens have been transferred to municipalities and counties. The two levels of local government are co-ordinated – each solving their own tasks. The division of tasks is defined through legislation.

County tasks include public transport across municipal boundaries, hospitals, secondary education and regional physical planning. They also decide some environmental issues.

Municipalities are responsible for a large number of public service tasks in the social, education, technical, environmental and cultural sectors. These include day care for children and services for the elderly such as special housing and old people's homes, meals-on-wheels, nurses and helpers in private homes. The municipalities administer various social benefits. They are also responsible for primary schools (7-16 years), cultural activities such as libraries and subsidies to sport clubs, as well as local roads, environmental protection, town planning, water supply, sewage, local industry and employment policy. They also administer the system of local income taxes.

Where functions are nation-wide in scope, and where the nature of the duty so requires, these stay with the State. These include foreign affairs, defence, police and overall communication. The central level also prepares new Bills, and develops regulations within the framework laid down by the Danish Parliament.

Mandatory, optional and shared responsibilities

The principle governing the distribution of tasks between Danish counties and municipalities is that the counties deal with tasks concerning a bigger population than present in most municipalities. Counties therefore have tasks delegated to them which require an administrative machinery which is not available in the average municipality. The general rule is that the counties are not superior to the municipalities, rather each has its own tasks.

2. MANAGEMENT FUNCTIONS

2.1 Policy-making and co-ordination

Coherence, consultation and conflict resolution

Central government (the Ministry of the Environment) is responsible for national planning, which includes the framework for regional planning. Regional plans are drawn up by county councils on the basis of proposals submitted by the individual municipal councils. Local governments, on the other hand, play an important role as co-ordinating links between the central authorities and the citizens.

The 1970 local government reform addressed ways of ensuring co-ordination between the State, the counties and the municipalities in line with the transfer of tasks from the State to lower levels. A system of sector plans was established whereby plans prepared for primary education, social tasks, the environment etc. should be sent to each Ministry concerned, which was then made responsible for ensuring co-ordination. The main objective of the plans was to give the central authorities information about decisions at the local level and thereby make it possible for the State to take its own initiatives if the general objectives were not fulfilled. This system was fully developed during the 1970s. It became apparent, however, that this planning system had its weaknesses. Much of the information transmitted to the State by the municipalities was not relevant to current political questions, the process was perceived as too bureaucratic and focusing on an extension of public services when questions of restructuring and cost effectiveness were more relevant. This planning system was, therefore, abolished at the beginning of the 1980s. Instead, exchanges of information took take place only when justified by a political interest.

The Association of County Councils in Denmark, and the National Association of Local Authorities in Denmark (the corresponding organisation for municipalities) are important bodies for co-operation with central government. All county and local authorities except the municipalities of Copenhagen and Frederiksberg are members. Legislation and other initiatives of importance to local government are not prepared without negotiations with these organisations. Central government policy control over matters of sub-national government (especially expenditure limits) are usually settled through agreement so that formal legislation is not needed.

Both of these organisations are governed by private law and are very important for co-operation with central government, particularly for matters concerning legislation and other initiatives of importance to sub-national government. Wages is the only area in which these organisations can conclude agreements which are legally binding on the local authorities. The Association of County Councils in Denmark can and does, however, conclude legally binding agreements with the Danish doctors organisation and also the Danish dentists organisation.

Inter-municipal activities and institutions are a fairly common feature. There are various structures: self-governing institutions, partnerships, limited companies and other private organisation forms. In principle, the formation of inter-municipal activities is voluntary, but in a few cases such co-operation may be compulsory, for example public transport, refuse collection and disposal.

Nation-wide inter-municipal activities are run by associations of local and county authorities. There is, for example, a local and regional authorities EDP-organisation, which co-ordinates matters concerning information technology.

Formal and informal mechanisms

Apart from the legislative regulation on minimum standards etc., there are no formal methods by which the State can control local authorities. The most important informal instrument is the annual agreements between the State and the local authorities, where agreements on the general grants are established.

2.2 Financial management

Sources of revenue

Danish local authorities are primarily financed through local taxes and general block grants. More than half of local government expenditure is financed by local taxes as shown in Table 2. Only a small fraction of the total local tax revenue is in the form of shared taxes, i.e. taxes raised by the central government of which the local authority receives a share.

Income tax covers more than 90 per cent of the total local tax revenue. There are no formal limits to the local income tax rate. Counties raised on average 10.54 per cent on taxable (assessed) income and the municipalities raised on average 19.88 per cent in 1996. The range, in 1994, was from 13 per cent to more than 22 per cent.

Current revenue comprises many different items. All expenses for sewers and waste disposal is fully met by the users through specific payments. Several local authorities also supply water, district heating and electricity. In these instances costs are also covered by the users according to consumption. Parents pay partly for the costs for children attending nursery schools.

Danish municipalities finance a very large share of their expenditure by means of their own income. In 1994, 77.6 per cent of their gross expenditure was financed by revenue from taxation and other local sources. The State's share – i.e. block grants and refundings – constituted the other 22.4 per cent.

Table 2. **Local government financing structure (1994)**
(percentage)

	Counties	Copenhagen/ Frederiksberg	Municipalities	Overall	Overall (Dkr millions)
Taxes	62.2	50.3	53.5	55.2	147 709
Refunding	0.6	8.9	10.4	7.8	20 732
Operating revenues	17.1	25.5	22.1	21.3	56 995
General grants	18.6	12.2	11.8	13.6	36 259
Other means of financing	1.5	3.1	2.2	2.2	5 760
TOTAL: (percentage)	100.0	100.0	100.0	100.1	
(Dkr millions)	67 154	162 573	37 726		267 455

Source: Ministry of Finance: *Kommunal budgetoversigt* December 1995 (Overview of local government budgets).

Expenditure responsibilities

In 1993, after the redistribution of tasks and financial reforms, municipalities and counties dealt with approximately 50 per cent of total public expenditure in Denmark. The liberty to establish expenditure priorities is closely connected with responsibility for financing.

Tasks which are delegated by the State can be roughly grouped as follows: provision of services to the individual citizens; planning and running of schools, hospitals and social institutions; planning and running of public utilities and roads; controlling land-use and environmental monitoring; public transport. As shown in Table 3, the largest single expenditure item for municipalities is primary schools and the most significant change in the period 1990-94 has been the increase in social cash payments. In the counties, on the other hand, hospitals account for almost half of net current expenditure (see Table 4).

Table 3. **Distribution of municipal net current expenditure (1990, 1994)**
(percentage)

	1990 [1]	1994 [2]
Primary schools	23.0	21.2
Services to the elderly	20.3	19.5
Administration	15.8	14.7
Day institutions for children and young people	11.4	13.7
Social cash payments	8.8	13.4
Libraries, leisure-time education, etc.	5.0	5.2
Roads, environment, etc.	3.8	3.4
Other social expenditure	11.9	8.9
TOTAL	100.0	100.0

Sources: 1. *Local Government in the Nordic Countries: Facts and Figures*, Kommuneforlaget, 1991.
2. Statistics Denmark: *De kommunale regnskaber for* 1994 (Balance sheets for the local authorities).

Table 4. **Distribution of county net current expenditure (1994)**
(percentage)

Hospitals	48.1
Health care	16.0
Education (high schools)	13.1
24-hour institutions for children and young people	4.3
Administration	5.1
Services for the handicapped	3.4
Public transportation	2.2
Roads, environment, etc.	2.1
Other social expenditure	5.7
TOTAL	100.0

Source: Statistics Denmark: *De kommunale regnskaber for* 1994 (Balance sheets for the local authorities).

A substantial part of the legislation passed by Parliament, and many decisions made by the central administration, impact on local government activities, in particular on local government finance and spending. To protect the local authorities from additional spending obligations without accompanying financial support, an agreement has been reached between the National Association of Local Authorities (NALA) and the Government on a principle that the general grant should be adjusted annually to balance the calculated effects on local government spending. This applies when the local government spending effects are due to parliamentary decisions. Thus, in principle, there is no justification for raising local taxes because of pressure from central government requirements. This "Principle of Compensation", which has been endorsed by Parliament, excludes external effects such as changes in demographic pressures on expenditure.

The ministries are obliged to negotiate with NALA on the expenditure effects of each legislative proposal and an agreement must be sought before the proposal is presented to Parliament or before administrative guidelines are implemented. A ministry placing additional spending requirements on local government is generally obliged to finance the resulting increase in the general grant by cutting its own expenditure. The adjustments are summed annually and the general grant adjusted according to this net sum.

Balance between discretion and control

A predominant feature of public finances in Denmark over the last 25 years has been the switch from earmarked, selective, matching grants to non-matching general grants. There has been a successful effort to abolish all central government refunds (reimbursements) as a certain percentage of local government expenditure in connection with services and to maintain only those central government refunds on local government expenditure in connection with transfers to individual persons.

Financial reform has included a revision of how municipal and county tasks are financed. Before the reform, most municipal functions were financed by State refund of part of the municipal expenditure. After the reform, some of the refunding schemes concerning municipal services were replaced by general (block) grants. The reason for this change was to create a better interaction between municipal tasks and financial responsibility, as refunds tend to weaken this interaction. The transition to general grants meant that financially municipalities had more freedom to decide task priorities, and at the same time had more opportunity to plan municipal services according to local needs.

Together with the transformation of the grant system to non-matching grants the local authorities have achieved a high degree of freedom to set their own level of standard in the various fields of public service. Legislation contains only very few, if any, minimum requirements as to the content of local government service. Primary education is an example. There are variations in the number of weekly lessons each pupil receives although the legislation contains minimum requirements. Some local authorities favour comparatively small classes and a relatively low number of weekly lessons while other local authorities prefer larger classes, as this enables them to offer more lessons each week.

Tools to control spending and revenue-raising capacities

The Danish system of annual negotiations and agreements between the central government and local government associations has allowed the emergence of a broad consensus on the level of expenditure and taxes at the local level. Economic control is exercised through agreement between central government and the national associations of municipalities and counties concerning the rate of taxation and the level of expenditure by municipalities and counties.

The annual negotiations begin with a joint assessment of local government finances for the coming year, assuming no change in tax rates and a level of local activity similar to the previous year. This is the basic equation for the negotiations. Central government is expected to make finances available if there is a gap. Local governments have to accept cuts in the grants if there is a surplus in the local accounts.

When agreement is reached, the local government authorities are expected to support a joint recommendation to their members not to increase taxes or expenditure, depending on how the agreement is framed. The local government authorities can only accept the text of an agreement if they are reasonably sure that their members can, and will, follow the recommendation. Central government has, therefore, to make the offer sufficiently attractive to ensure that that is the case.

Negotiations offer an effective control over local expenditure as they are not only about grants and recommendations on taxes or expenditure ceilings but also include issues in the existing legislation, which local authorities find difficult to administer, or which prevent them from holding back on expenditure increases. The negotiations are conducted by the Ministry of Finance and Ministry of Interior and result in many changes to rules and regulations which were constraining local authorities from using the most efficient means of providing services.

2.3 Performance management

Mechanisms

Many of the initiatives to promote performance are being developed at the local level and are not centrally monitored or controlled. In Denmark, as in other Nordic countries, local government have a high degree of electoral and financial accountability. For example the Danish legislation requires local authorities to publicise information concerning their budget. There is also a publication by the Ministry of the Interior of "Local Authority Key Data" which contains key figures on population, housing, labour market conditions, taxation, economy, child care, education and culture, care for the elderly, other social expenditure and the environment. The figures for each municipality are compared with the average figures for the municipalities in their county and for all municipalities. For the counties, the publication also includes health care.

Differences in the extent and quality of individual benefits inevitably occur between individual municipalities and counties – within the standards and framework fixed by law. These differences reflect the varied needs and wishes in the local communities, and consequently the ability of the municipal and county councils to decide priorities on the basis of local conditions and demands.

Quality standards

Local authorities have been active in raising service standards through customer enquiry centres aimed at providing speedy, convenient and accurate information. Timeliness, accessibility and accuracy have been emphasised along with measuring customer satisfaction.

The Danish approach to performance measurement is based on evaluation of service quality as well as on efficiency and effectiveness. Decentralised government may be part of the explanation: the service providers are close to the clients and the quality of service becomes a more central issue in the provider-client relationship.

The initiatives taken involving service quality are diverse. They include service standards, service statements, client surveys, quality management and one stop shops. The initiatives are occurring at both central and local levels. Local governments make extensive use of goals and standards, emphasising client opinion surveys rather than formal performance indicators. National statistics on service standards, productivity and output levels are published by the Ministry of Local Government each year, and compare individual local authorities across a range of measures. These serve as a benchmark and a starting point for local decisions, rather than a judgement on relative levels of performance.

2.4 Human resource management

Statutory distinctions and managerial autonomy

Local councils have full responsibility for the government and administration of their municipalities and counties. This includes the freedom to determine their own administrative structures. No State regulations apply to local authority personnel. Local authorities are, therefore, independent of central government and make their own decisions concerning their staff. Municipal and county councils and their finance committees in particular are responsible for the staffing of the authorities. Local employees (like national employees) are not appointed politically and they are not replaced after an election.

All local authorities have authorised their respective organisations to conclude binding agreements with their staff organisation concerning wages. Wages follow standards fixed centrally by the Local Government Salary Board, which consists of councillors appointed by the Minister of the Interior on the recommendation of the local government associations.

Table 5. **Public sector employment by level of government (1990-1994)**
(full-time equivalents)

	1990	1991	1992	1993	1994 [1]
State	188 605	182 375	180 095	178 854	182 422
Counties	127 308	126 188	123 975	123 799	123 932
Municipalities	305 974	306 596	315 928	320 663	311 529
Copenhagen and Frederiksberg	67 547	66 577	65 506	66 606	57 359
TOTAL	689 434	681 736	685 504	689 922	675 242

1. Due to changes in the guidelines for reporting employment figures to Statistics Denmark, figures for 1994 are not directly comparable to figures for 1993 and earlier.
Sources: Ministry of the Interior, Det kommunale budget, 1996 (The local government budget) and Ministry of Finance, Budgetredegorelse 1995 (Budget review).

Mobility: Staff mobility between levels of government is quite low in Denmark, and there is no formal co-operation on staff exchanges between levels of government.

3. TRENDS IN REDISTRIBUTING AUTHORITY ACROSS LEVELS OF GOVERNMENT

3.1 Evolving tendencies

The Danish system of local government is laid down in the Danish Constitution which stipulates that "the right of local authorities to govern independently under the supervision of the State must be laid down by law". The Constitution thus gives local authorities an important influence on affairs of local interest.

During the last 30 years, Denmark has gone through a period of very comprehensive reform of the entire local government system. This process included three reforms which are connected but which were undertaken in series as follows:

- restructuring;
- redistribution of tasks;
- financial reforms.

The restructuring reform was implemented, beginning in the 1960s, with voluntary amalgamations of very small municipalities into larger units. This prepared the ground for the important reforms of the 1970s. These aimed at a redistribution and an administrative decentralisation of tasks from the central level to the municipal and county levels. One of its basic principles is that of subsidiarity – i.e. the decentralisation of powers towards the lowest acceptable level of administration.

Functions have been gradually transferred from the State to sub-national governments. This transfer has continued since the 1970 reforms, and includes other important reforms, such as those of social security in 1976-77 which transferred responsibility for the social security system to local authorities.

The 1970 reform provided the management and financial conditions for the transfer of tasks and responsibilities from State to municipalities and counties during the 1970s. Since then the decentralisation process has continued locally with the delegation of competencies to municipal institutions. This originally took place for financial reasons, especially the wish to pursue a tight expenditure policy by framework management of the institutional economy. It also established a connection between professional and financial responsibility. During the 1980s, it became common for municipalities to fix the financial framework, including freedom to decide priorities for municipal institutions.

The decentralisation efforts of the 1980s formed the basis for further devolution during the 1990s, when possibilities for improving municipal services by means of increased user influence and the preparation of service and quality objects were included.

Up to 1989 local governments were subject to formal regulation imposed by central government, but the efficiency and funding of the system was questionable. In 1989 a number of laws deregulated local government and since then the municipalities have used their new freedom to set up administrative reforms in different ways. Trends which can be distinguished include that about 100 municipalities have reduced the number of their council committees by at least one; and in many municipalities the work of the council has become more focused, so that politicians spend less time at committee meetings and more time establishing direct contacts with citizens. The need to concentrate more on formulating programmes in order to articulate objectives and standards for performance control rather than intervene in each individual case has also been recognised.

3.2   The current debate

During the last 10 years there has been a general debate on the modernisation of the public sector. Objectives concerning economic effectiveness and user's influence on public services have been accepted by the Danish Parliament. The law governing the municipalities was changed in 1995 in order to make all municipalities obliged to inform citizens about their services. There is general agreement, firstly that citizens should have more choice of public services and secondly that public procurement practices affect efficient management – but less agreement on how these should be achieved.

There has also been a debate on the number of tiers of local government. In the late 80s the former conservative Prime Minister suggested abolishing the counties and strengthening the municipalities. This proposition has, however, not met with support in Parliament.

In April 1994 the Ministry of the Interior published a White Paper suggesting ways of improving innovation and effectiveness in local government. It included proposals on how to strengthen the exchange of information between the State and municipalities in specific fields and, through a dialogue, to formulate common general objectives.

3.3   Driving forces

Until 1970, a number of local State agencies were established, as deconcentrated administrations, partly due to the increasing difficulties of municipalities in handling major administrative problems. A still larger combination of hierarchical State agencies and local government agencies came into existence, resulting in a centralisation of the whole system. Due to the increasing number of social service functions to be provided during the 1950s and 1960s, demands for comprehensive local reform grew stronger. Many of these demands were due to an "overburdening" of the central bureaucracy with individual cases.

In the mid-60s the general objectives of decentralisation, which formed the basis of the 1970 reform, were widely accepted by the Danish Parliament (*Folketing*).

During the last 30 years changing governments – both social democratic and conservative – have respected the general objective to strengthen local authorities in order to ensure that public tasks are solved through a democratic process at the local level and as close to the citizens as possible.

Different governments have of course pursued different policies in different sectors. This is, for instance, the case with the amount of public services and the issue of diversity in service levels from one part of the country to another. In recent years there have also been different political attitudes to the question of public procurement. However, divergent policies of different governments are not seen in Denmark as a disagreement on the basic idea of decentralisation, but rather as a debate on concrete solutions in the public sector.

FINLAND

1. INSTITUTIONS AND AUTHORITY

In recent years in Finland public services in many fields that were traditionally part of the State administration have been converted into public enterprises or companies which are no longer considered part of the State administration. Public enterprises and companies operate outside the State budgetary system, are economically self-supporting and thus are free to organise their regional activities in the most cost-effective way. The regional organisations of these new types of public enterprises are not dealt with in this chapter. The district courts and the district organisation of the military service are also excluded from this chapter.

1.1 Structures

Description of levels

Sub-national administration in Finland comprises two systems, one being part of the State administration and the other having its basis in self-governing municipalities. Both the State and municipal sectors have organisations at the regional and local levels.

The legal basis for regional and local administration lies in the Constitution Act (article 50) which, for the purposes of general administration, divides Finland into provinces, districts and municipalities. According to the Finnish Constitution the Åland Islands have a special autonomous status in the Finnish administrative system. Thus the country is currently divided into 12 provinces (including the Åland Islands) and 455 municipalities of which 104 are towns or cities. In December 1996 Parliament decided, based on a proposal by the government, that the number of provinces on the mainland be reduced from 11 to 5. The number of districts (the regional bodies of the sectoral ministries) varies according to the ministry from 4 to 19 – such that their boundaries do not always coincide with those of the provinces. The total area of Finland is 338 000 square kilometres and the total population in 1994 was 5 088 000.

At the beginning of 1994, a new type of regional institution (the Regional Council) with specific regional development functions, was created by the Regional Development Act.

Table 1. **Number of municipalities and population distribution (1994)**

Population size	Number of municipalities
up to 1 000	22
1 000-5 000	203
5 000-10 000	119
10 000-50 000	97
50 000-100 000	8
over 100 000	6

Source: Ministry of Finance.

Central government at sub-national levels

The regional administration of the State consists of a) **provincial governments**, with general authority in their areas and b) **State district administration**, entrusted with the sectoral tasks of ministries and agencies, such as the environment, labour protection, and roading. In total, 20 sectors have some 200 district units. The number of district units varies depending on the sector (in the environment administration there are 13 districts while the customs administration has 7). In December 1996 Parliament decided to adopt new legislation on the State's regional administration based on a proposal by the government. This will bring together under one roof the present district offices of the Ministry of Trade and Industry's Business Service; the offices in Finland of TEKES (Technology Research Centre of Finland); the regional units of the Finnish Guarantee Board; the regional units of the Finnish Foreign Trade Association; the labour district offices and the rural business district offices. For this purpose it is planned to set up Employment and Economic Development Centres by the autumn of 1997.

In addition the State has local representatives in many fields including the police, taxation, and labour administration. Due to the great variation of the regional divisions, the number of local units varies from sector to sector making the present State local administrative system rather complicated.. As examples, the police has some 250 local units; the number of local labour offices is 200; and in the tax administration there are some 120 local offices. The total personnel of the State local-level administration in 1993 was some 40 000.

Creation, elimination and restructuring

The decision-making authority for dividing the country into municipalities as well as its State regional divisions lies with the Council of State. And, after the agreement of the municipalities involved, the Council of State also has the authority to determine the areas of the Regional Councils. The division of the country into provinces has been decided through a parliamentary law. The breakdown was revised in a decision made by the Finnish Parliament in December 1996 which reduced the number of mainland provinces from 11 to 5.

The self-governing status of municipalities is defined in the Finnish Constitution. There are a considerable number of small municipalities despite the long-standing policy aimed at encouraging the merger of small municipalities into bigger administrative units

The Municipal Act includes general legal provisions defining the organisation of joint municipal boards and how they relate to the parent municipalities. The new legislation has given freedom to the municipalities to agree on arrangements between themselves. Joint municipal authorities are based on an agreement signed by two or more municipalities which have agreed to establish a separate body for a specific function. There are in total about 300 joint municipal boards. All municipalities are members of several of such organisations. Compulsory joint boards look after hospital care, and homes for elderly people are often run by voluntarily formed joint boards.

The Municipal Act also includes regulations concerning how municipalities can operate jointly for certain functions for which there is no legal obligation on a contractual basis. Contractual agreements are signed between municipalities, and can, for example, make one municipality responsible for certain services in the name of several municipalities.

The Regional Councils are based on the voluntary association of municipalities through unanimous agreement of all the municipalities in the region. The incentive for the municipalities to join a Regional Council is that by doing so they will become responsible for the regional development functions of the provincial governments. With this voluntary principle, the Regional Councils were gradually established throughout 1994. Legally the Regional Councils are in the same position as the other statutory joint municipal boards. Their administrative structure is thus defined in the Municipal Act. In this sense Regional Councils are part of municipal sector. By the beginning of 1995 all Finnish municipalities belonged to one of the 19 Regional Councils.

Control bodies

Employees throughout the public sector are bound by the principle of administrative legality. This principle has its expression in the Finnish Constitution. Control of the legality as well as the efficiency of the administration is largely based on internal control mechanisms through hierarchical supervision built into the administrative system – from the head of an administrative unit to the Council of State and the President of the Republic.

The institutions, external to the administration, that have been given responsibility for supervising and controlling the compliance of government officials with the law, are the Supreme Administrative Court, the Chancellor of Justice (appointed by the President of the Republic) and the Parliamentary Ombudsman (elected by Parliament for a period of four years).

The government auditing system has two pillars. The State Audit Office is part of the State administration under the auspices of the Ministry of Finance, and is mandated to ensure that publicly funded government organisations operate in accordance with the law and good management practice. The second pillar comprises the five Auditors nominated by the Parliament. Their annual reports comment on the activities of various administrative authorities and receive wide political and public interest.

The municipalities have their own system for the control of the administration and of the economy. Elected bodies have traditionally played an important role in the municipal auditing system. The new legislation on municipal administration emphasizes the need to strengthen the position of professional auditing. The auditing board and at least one full-time auditor are compulsory bodies in every municipality.

In the Finnish appeal system, the appropriateness of administrative actions is examined within the administration. The Council of State is the highest decision-making body. Legal matters are dealt with by administrative courts headed by the Supreme Administrative Court.

Part of the internal control system is the use of semi-judicial bodies dedicated to legal matters and citizen's interests in specific fields. An example is the Centre for Legal Protection in the Health Services. This body handles complaints by citizens concerning health care personnel. The decisions of the Centre can be subject to further process in the Supreme Administrative Court. There are also special commissioners who assist citizens on questions of social rights. Special commissioners handle issues such as data processing protection, equal rights and consumer rights.

1.2 Powers

Nature of sub-national institutions

The provincial governments operate under the Council of State and more precisely the Ministry of the Interior. They are directed by a Governor who is nominated by the President of the Republic, and are internally organised into departments and other sub-units. The district authorities are headed by a director. They operate as central government agencies and their task is to implement national policies in their respective sectors.

The highest decision-making body at the municipal level is the municipal council elected in a direct proportional system by municipal residents for a period of four years. The size of the council varies from 17 to 85 depending on the population of the municipality. The minimum number of members is 13 in Finland, except in the Åland Islands where it is nine.

The new Municipal Act has changed the compulsory basic organisation in municipalities . In addition to a council, every municipality is now obliged to have a municipal board, municipal manager and auditors. The board, the manager and the auditors are elected by the municipal council. The composition of the municipal board thus reflects the political structure of the council and the number of members varies from 5 to 15. In addition, the municipal administration includes sectoral boards or commissions, the number and functions of which can now be decided by the municipality itself.

The municipal manager is responsible for the executive functions together with municipal officials. The new law stresses the political accountability of the manager by making it possible to decide that a manager with the same term as the council be also elected to the chair of the municipal board. In practice the municipal managers are at the head of the administrative machinery.

If the municipal council so decides, the appointment of the municipal manager can now be for a limited period (previously the period was always unlimited).The municipal manager can also be dismissed by the decision of the council on the basis of lack of confidence. This kind of decision requires the support of two thirds of the members of the municipal council. Since changes of the legislation in 1993 the scope for the municipal council to dismiss a municipal manager is rather wide. There were 12 cases of dismissal of a manager in the period 1993-94.

The highest decision-making body of a joint municipal authority is the council, nominated by the municipalities that are members of the joint venture. The executive body is the board of the joint municipalities. Joint municipal boards have their own budgets which are financed by the member municipalities.

The Regional Councils have the same administrative structure as the other joint municipal boards The councils are elected for a four-year term, which coincides with the period of municipal elections. Most of the council members are also members of the councils of the member municipalities. The executive body is the board elected by the council. The size of the council varies between 20 to 100 representatives, depending on the number and size of member municipalities. The number of board members is between 10 and 20. The permanent staff of the Regional councils averages about 25 to 30 persons.

Type and degree of autonomy

The position of the municipalities has traditionally been strong in Finland. According to the Constitution the municipalities have an autonomous status – they are self-governing. National interests have been taken care of by the regulatory system as well as by the way in which the State allocates financial resources to municipalities. Both have been changed so as to increase the operational freedom of municipalities. The new Municipal Act reinforces the autonomous status of municipalities by giving them more freedom in deciding on their own organisation and functions.

The Constitution states that municipalities have a "general authority" in their territory. This means that they themselves decide on the range of their duties. The Constitution also states that municipalities can only be given new tasks and obligations by a parliamentary law. Accordingly, the municipalities have been given specified tasks through laws including the Planning and Building Act (1958), the Social Welfare Act (1982), the National Health Care Act (1972) and the Comprehensive School Act (1983).

The municipalities are free to decide on their internal affairs and organisation, according to the principles defined in the general law on municipalities, the Municipal Act. A new Municipal Act came into force in July 1995 and gave municipalities more managerial freedom in running their daily duties and setting priorities.

The new Municipal Act also confirms the principle according to which the municipalities are free to contract out services they are obliged to provide and to decide to what extent they apply user charges.

The municipalities have the power to raise income taxes from their residents and landowners. The municipal income tax is proportional to income. The municipalities are free to define the level of taxation, but national legislation defines the types of taxes, and they are collected by the State. The provincial governments do not have the right to collect taxes.

The municipalities can issue some local regulations e.g. concerning safety and order, but they do not have full regulatory powers.

District authorities now enjoy a lot of managerial freedom and are accountable for their results to a varying degree depending on the extent to which they operate under market principles. Net budgeting is used in some fields.

1.3 Responsibilities

Distribution of responsibilities

Most of the activities of the State local authorities are connected with direct service production in their respective fields. By law the provincial government is responsible for the needs of the province, its general development and the well-being of its inhabitants. In the field of educational and cultural policy its tasks include developing the network of schools, assessing educational performance, and developing library and cultural services. The provincial government is also responsible for monitoring and assessing the development of social and health services, promoting housing production and improving housing conditions in the province.

The provincial governments have important tasks in the fields of safety and legal protection including examining complaints against local authorities. They also allocate funds for the police districts and are the electoral authority in their areas.

There has been a trend to transfer sectoral tasks away from provincial governments. This was the case for example in the reform of the environmental administration where the tasks of the district units of the Ministry of the Environment and those of the environmental departments of the provincial governments were merged under the Ministry of the Environment. The establishment of the Regional Councils has resulted in a transfer of power from the State's regional administration to the municipal sector.

The nature and functions of the districts varies: some (e.g. the labour administration districts) are of an administrative nature in that they oversee and direct local authorities. In some sectors the district organisations provide services directly to customers or undertake tasks such as road construction and maintenance. In the autumn of 1997 several existing district offices will be merged into new Employment and Economic Development Centres in accordance with a decision of the Finnish parliament in December 1996.

Municipalities, either individually or jointly, are responsible for most of the social welfare functions (basic education, vocational education, social and health care, child care). In fulfilling duties such as running big hospitals, municipalities operate jointly. Physical planning is another important municipal task. The municipalities are in many respects service production organisations, as well as political-administrative organisations.

The Regional Councils combine the tasks of the former joint municipal boards which were responsible for physical planning and those of the associations of municipalities for the general promotion of development. The new legislation has also made it possible to transfer general regional development functions to them from the provinces.

Thus the Regional Councils have two statutory functions: regional physical planning according to the Building Act, and general regional policy. In the latter role the Regional Councils co-ordinate the preparation of regional development programmes in co-operation with their member municipalities, the provinces, districts and local industries. In addition to these two statutory functions the Regional Councils also have the role of representing the interests of their regions vis-à-vis the member municipalities and the State administration.

Mandatory, optional and shared responsibilities

Although municipalities have a high degree of autonomy in executing the tasks for which they are responsible, the State and municipal levels are closely linked. The main mechanisms by which the State can steer and control the functioning of the municipalities are regulations and subsidies.

Central government is responsible for defining national welfare policy. The municipalities implement national policies and are largely autonomous in doing so. Special legislation or regulations usually cover minimum standards of services and how municipalities should handle their service provision. The number of municipal functions that are mandatory by law has gradually increased.

Municipal functions that are too extensive or expensive to be handled by a single municipality are given to joint municipal authorities (boards). These are formed either voluntarily or by legal obligation.

2. MANAGEMENT FUNCTIONS

2.1 Policy-making and co-ordination

Coherence, consultation and conflict resolution

The main steering mechanisms used by the State government are the budget and financial management system, the regulatory system, and personnel policies. The nature of the steering is different in the State and municipal sectors due to the different status of the organisations in each.

The main tool for the horizontal co-ordination of policies across sectors is the new frame budgeting and the result-oriented financial management system (performance management). In the process of defining budget frames for the next one and three years, the government (Council of State) has an opportunity to both prioritise and co-ordinate policy areas. The Ministry of Finance, which prepares the process and provides the Council of State with the budget calculations, has a key role in this process.

After the budget frames have been given to sectoral ministries, they must then implement the result-budgeting system in their own fields. Each ministry is, in principle, responsible for ensuring the vertical coherence of policies. The ministries, sometimes in co-operation with a State agency, holds "result discussions" with the agencies and sometimes directly with the regional units. These discussions provide another process for promoting policy coherence.

At the regional level the main issues of horizontal coherence are those related to regional policy and overall regional development. The State provincial government had a strong role in co-ordinating regional development initiatives in its area but this has now been largely transferred to the new Regional Councils. As yet there is very little practical experience on how the new co-ordination process between the State and municipal authorities will function and what will be the real role of the Regional Councils in this co-ordination. However, the importance of the co-ordination function of the Regional Councils is increasing with Finland's membership in the European Union (EU) since the regional development programmes now also cover projects funded by the EU.

With the recent administrative reforms, the steering system (both regulations and subsidies) of the municipalities has undergone major change. But a door has also been opened towards accepting the idea of some variation between municipalities in their service production and their selection of priorities.

Formal and informal mechanisms

The government has various permanent committees of ministers co-ordinating the most important policy issues. The guidelines which they produce are of great importance in policy-making and co-ordination between policy sectors and affect activities at all levels of government. Examples include the committee of ministers on economic policy and that on fiscal policy.

Various mechanisms of a more informal nature are also used to ensure the horizontal co-ordination of policy implementation. They vary from *ad hoc* negotiations to the everyday flow of information. Co-ordination bodies such as government commissions or working groups may be set up for this purpose with varying degrees of formality.

Frameworks (Programmes of Objectives) for regional development are defined by the Council of State and give the government an important steering and co-ordination mechanism on national policy and priorities of regional development.

The Ministry of the Interior has a steering role in the co-ordination of the funds used through regional development authorities as it decides on the allocation of those funds to the regions. Line ministries are represented in the process of preparing regional development programmes through their regional units.

The Ministry of the Interior also has a special role in the co-ordination of regional level policies as it is under its mandate that the annual result agreements are negotiated for the State provincial governments. The Ministry of the Interior is responsible at the State level for the co-ordination of municipal affairs.

Joint municipal boards are also powerful co-ordination mechanisms between municipalities. Other types of contract-based mechanisms for co-operation and the sharing of responsibilities between municipalities are also being used to an increasing extent.

2.2 Financial management

The State's regional and local units are financed by the State budget. The new frame budgeting and performance management has significantly increased the financial autonomy of the administration at the regional level which now receives the appropriation on operational expenditure as one lump sum instead of the earlier earmarked funds for various expenditure items. Legal changes have also been made to enable increased use of user charges and net budgeting in State agencies. Administrative units which have adopted net budgeting can charge clients for their services, either externally or from within the State administration and then use the funds to cover directly the costs of the services produced.

Sources of revenue

The municipal sector in Finland covers some two-thirds of the public sector consumption and investment expenditures.

Municipal income tax represents some 36 per cent of the total revenue of the municipal sector. In 1993 a new tax was introduced (replacing and combining some earlier charges) which entitled municipalities to collect a tax on real estate. Both residents and landowners pay this tax which is based on the assessed market price of property and which varies depending on the type of the property. The municipalities have the right to decide on the level of this tax within the limits defined by law.

Another important source of income for municipalities is State subsidies which represent some 30 per cent of municipal income. User charges cover about 18 per cent, selling municipal property accounts for some 7 per cent, and loans cover 6 per cent. This distribution varies considerably however between municipalities.

User charges are levied mainly from services delivered by municipal enterprises such as those in charge of energy distribution and water supply. The share of user charges in the fields of social and health care or education and culture services is, as yet, minor. User charges on services produced by municipal enterprises has, in some cases, offered municipalities a means to cover deficits in their overall budgets. An example is with electricity on which municipalities have been able to overcharge. The current trend of opening up the electricity market to competition will increase transparency in pricing and significantly limit possibilities for this kind of hidden taxation.

Financing of Regional Councils and other joint municipal authorities comes from the member municipalities (as well as from State subsidies for statutory duties). The financial responsibility of each municipality is defined in the agreement made by the member municipalities when the joint board is established.

Expenditure responsibilities

As shown in Table 3 the two largest sectors of municipal expenditure are social welfare services, and education and culture, each accounting for about 25 per cent of total current expenditure. As the table also shows, the largest increase in expenditure between 1985 and 1990 was in social welfare services, which more than doubled.

Table 2. **Main revenue sources of sub-national governments (1985, 1990)**

	1985		1990	
	(Mk million)	%	(Mk million)	%
Total current revenue *of which*	**66 717**	**87.9**	**104 914**	**86.4**
Taxes	30 188	39.8	47 881	39.4
State grants and compensations	15 098	19.9	26 399	21.7
Payments and compensations	11 703	15.4	15 996	13.2
Internal income	4 247	5.6	6 725	5.5
Capital revenue *of which*	**9 167**	**12.1**	**16 562**	**13.6**
State grants and compensations	738	1.0	1 568	1.3
Borrowings	2 828	3.7	5 446	4.9
Depreciations	4 196	5.5	6 632	5.5
TOTAL revenue	**75 883**	**100.0**	**121 476**	**100.0**

Source: Ministry of Finance.

Table 3. **Main expenditure patterns of sub-national governments (1985, 1990)**

	1985		1990	
	(Mk million)	%	(Mk million)	%
General administration	2 681	3.6	4 307	3.5
Public order	1 294	1.7	2 166	1.8
Public health care	10 047	13.4	16 451	13.4
Social welfare services	12 183	16.3	24 648	20.1
Education and culture	16 044	21.4	25 899	21.1
Community planning and public works	3 831	5.1	5 738	4.7
Real estate	3 131	4.2	5 086	4.1
Business and services	11 464	15.3	15 018	12.3
Finance	1 674	2.2	2 686	2.2
Total current expenditure *of which*	**62 349**	**83.3**	**102 001**	**83.2**
Wages and salaries	21 208	28.3	34 848	28.4
Other personnel expenditure	5 114	6.8	9 427	7.7
Imputed interest expenses and depreciations	6 423	8.6	9 921	8.1
Shares	7 117	9.5	11 909	9.7
Grants	2 373	3.2	5 607	4.6
Capital expenditure *of which*	**12 546**	**16.7**	**20 548**	**16.8**
Acquisitions fixed assets	10 441	13.9	16 746	13.7
Repayments on loans	1 596	2.1	2 831	2.3
TOTAL expenditure	**74 884**	**100.0**	**122 549**	**100.0**

Source: Ministry of Finance.

Balance between discretion and control

During the past five years Finland has implemented major budget reforms, the core of which was completed in the 1995 budget. The reform has introduced a system whereby administrative units and their management are given more operational freedom and their accountability for results is emphasised. The State subsidy system was also reformed, as from the beginning of 1993. In contrast to the earlier system where allocations from the State budget were largely earmarked to specific municipal functions and heavily regulated by the State authorities, the new system is based on lump sums. This gives municipalities more room for manoeuvre in deciding on the use of State subsidies. The aim of the reform was to encourage municipalities to improve their economies and their effectiveness.

In May 1995 the Council of State set up a project and appointed a one-man committee charged with drafting a proposal for a Government Bill to overhaul the system of State subsidies to municipalities, to come into effect at the beginning of 1997. This would change the basis for deciding on State subsidies for specific functions. Additional proposals were made aimed at clarifying and rationalising the division of labour and costs between the State and municipalities. In October 1996 the government put a Bill before Parliament which proposed a complete reform of the State subsidy system. From 1st January 1997, function-specific State subsidies would become based on average expenditure per resident, student, age group etc. and on the municipality's own contribution to funding. The grounds for deciding the level of State subsidy would take into account specific cost factors such as low density of settlement, a bilingual population, and if located in the archipelago.

In the State budget there is an appropriation for "funding through regional development authorities". The Regional Councils decide on how to use this funding to support local industries and other economic activities after the Ministry of the Interior has allocated it to the regions. In the 1995 budget this appropriation amounted to some 125 million Mk. Most of the State financial support for the regional development is, however, allocated through the line ministries and their regional representatives from their own funds. When deciding on the use of their regional development funds, the State authorities use the regional development programmes, co-ordinated by the Regional Councils, as a guideline.

2.3 Performance management

Mechanisms

All levels of government have recently been, or are currently being, subject to restructuring as part of the overall public management reform. The major characteristics of this are a move to a result oriented management and increased use of market discipline and market-type mechanisms. Result orientation has meant a new emphasis on performance as well as a continuing process of devolution of decision-making powers both within organisations as well as between levels of government. In accordance with this trend the role of the State Audit Office in performance auditing is being strengthened.

The district units of the State administration now operate under the result-management system. This means that their managerial freedom has been increased together with their accountability for results and requirements on the quality of their services. In the frame budgeting and result management system the district authorities usually negotiate and agree on the performance targets for the local units. The district authorities monitor the result targets and report to the respective ministry or State agency. As part of the State administration, the provincial governments are now result-budgeted units, reporting to the Ministry of the Interior.

No general framework for monitoring local government performance has been developed. There is, in fact, a strong view that this is not necessary, given the high degree of electoral and financial autonomy of local governments.

Quality standards

There is considerable interest in both auditing and service standards projects. A working group with representatives of the Ministry of Finance, the Ministry of the Interior and the Association of Finnish Local Authorities has been set up to investigate the roles of different levels of government in service quality and the possibilities for replacing existing norms regulating the service production with service standards and consumer rights. The three organisations are also jointly examining possible new forms of service production, particularly those which might increase consumer choice and producer competition such as vouchers.

No national service quality standards have been established (with the exception of child care services) and it is unlikely that any will be developed. Similarly, there is no national established charter for services. There are however examples of charters at the municipal level, for example in the city of Hämeenlinna.

2.4 Human resource management

Statutory distinctions

Separate laws define the status of the personnel in the State and municipal administrations. In both administrations the personnel may be either civil servants or operate under individual agreements, as employees. In the State administration the main type of service relationship is as a civil servant – a status which has been made more flexible in recent years. One aim is to transfer all personnel in the new public enterprises to the category of employees. Legal provisions concerning employees both in the State and the municipal administrations are covered by the general labour legislation.

The rights and obligations of municipal officials are defined in the Municipal Act. Their legal status is in principle similar to the status of State civil servants. The new Municipal Act also favours the status of employee in municipal administrations.

The following table shows the distribution of employment by level of government since 1980.

Table 4. **Public sector employment by level of government (1980, 1985, 1991-1994)**

	1980	1985	1991	1992	1993	1994
State administration	122 443	141 300	145 877	145 100	140 000	133 000
Municipalities [1]	337 000	427 000	458 000	448 000	411 000	400 000 [3]
TOTAL GOVERNMENT [1]	**459 443**	**568 300**	**603 877**	**593 100**	**551 000**	**533 000** [3]
State enterprises	76 937 [2]	71 956 [2]	64 958	60 299	53 000	23 000
TOTAL PUBLIC SECTOR	**536 380**	**640 256**	**668 835**	**653 399**	**604 000**	**556 000** [3]

1. Including municipal public enterprises.
2. Not formally State enterprises.
3. Preliminary figures.

Source: *Public Management Developments: Update 1995*, OECD, 1995.

Managerial autonomy

A new State Civil Servant Act came into force in 1994. It has increased the managerial freedom of individual administrative units in the areas of staffing, remuneration and dismissal. At the same time the tasks of the State Employer's Office (the Personnel Department of the Ministry of Finance) are now more directed towards policy questions and general guidelines rather than the detailed steering of personnel management in the agencies. In the public enterprises in particular, State controls have been relaxed to a large extent. In the State sector, staffing levels are decided (until 1997) in the annual budget process.

There has been a centralised collective agreements system for determining salary levels in the public sector since 1970. Before then the State and the municipalities each determined the salaries and other terms of employment of their employees. The 1970 legislation gave the organisations of public employees both negotiation and contract rights similar to those in the private sector. Public employees (including civil servants) have the right to strike.

According to the Collective Agreement for State Civil Servants Act and the similar law for municipal officials, the bargaining system is to a large extent the same as in the private sector, although some issues fall outside the agreements and are defined by law. These include establishing and reorganising public posts, obligations and responsibilities.

Agreements are made at both the State and local levels. Collective agreements for the public sector, fitting into the general framework of central collective agreements, previously determined both minimum and maximum pay and benefits. With the new result-oriented management system the collective agreement no longer has a maximum level as since 1992 the result-budgeted agencies may decide on individual pay which exceed those of the collective agreement. Each authority concludes agreements on personnel employed on a contract basis.

In the municipal sector each municipality has the authority to decide on its staffing level. This authority has also recently been widened since the new State subsidy system no longer allocates State financial support for certain posts and functions.

The salary bargaining system of the municipal sector functions in roughly the same way as in the State sector. The Commission for Local Authority Employers negotiates with the unions representing the municipal employees. Negotiation power has also to a large extent been transferred from the State level to the local level in line with the general trend to devolve authority.

2.5 Regulatory management and reform

The regulatory system comprises acts of Parliament and lower level legislation adopted by the President, the government, a ministry or a central government authority. Although legislative and regulatory power is spread across government bodies, ministries have the key role in the Finnish regulatory system. Authorities under the ministries play a much more restricted role in regulatory management in Finland than, for example, in common law countries. Regulatory power is also very limited at the regional and local levels. Ministries are responsible for drafting government bills to be presented to Parliament and for issuing ministerial resolutions that take the form of administrative regulations. An act is often accompanied by either by a decree or government resolution. Ministries also prepare presidential decrees as the President does not have an agency or staff for that purpose.

Most regulatory reform in Finland started in the 1980s. The Ministry of Finance initiated a project in the mid-80s to reform the delegated legislation issued by ministries and other central government bodies and to decrease the amount of lower level legislation. This "Norm Project" was the first ever aimed at subordinate legislation. It can be considered a success given that the 7 500 norms existing in 1987 were reduced to about 5 500 by 1991 – although some were transformed into recommendations or guidelines.

At the end of the 1980s the government initiated a Licence Reform Project aimed at cutting down the number of administrative permissions, licences and approvals. This initiative has been less successful numerically, with a drop from 1 700 to 1 600 between 1989 to 1993, but procedures have been rationalised and simplified.

Despite these efforts, regulatory inflation accelerated in 1992-94 due to European integration as Finland had to adapt its national legislation to meet the requirements of membership of the Agreement on the European Economic Area (since 1994) and the European Union (since 1995).

Regulatory management reforms by the Ministry of Justice also started in the early 1980s. It aimed at improving the preparation of legislation in ministries, but further reform was needed in the mid 1990's due to widespread concern about the declining quality of legislation. This took the form of a joint initiative by the ministries of justice and finance which led to the approval by the government, in May 1996, of a programme comprising 33 measures to improve law drafting and regulatory management in ministries.

The government does not have any overall deregulation policy, but there has been notable economic deregulation in areas such as telecommunication, financial markets and energy markets, and some deregulation in the road transport sector.

The number of regulations issued by the State government on municipalities was significantly reduced and the quality of regulations was improved at the end of the 1980s. The number and detail of regulations issued by the State government remains an important State government mechanism for guaranteeing coherence in the implementation of policies that are implemented by the municipalities. In addition, reform of the State subsidy system in 1991 made some significant changes to the relationship between the State and the municipalities.

3. TRENDS IN REDISTRIBUTING AUTHORITY ACROSS LEVELS OF GOVERNMENT

3.1 Evolving tendencies

Due to the many recent changes in the Finnish public administration, the whole system of management across levels of government is in a considerable process of change. Decentralising authority from the State administration to local and regional levels has been a trend in Finland for a long time. Major steps were taken in the 1993 reform of the State subsidy system and the simplification of regulations. This trend is likely to continue, although the level of local autonomy is subject to constant debate. These questions will be dealt with in the large new project set up by the government to review State-municipal relations and especially the existing State subsidy system.

The latest developments in the Finnish public administration have also changed the tasks and the functioning of the provincial governments – and reduced their number from 11 to 5. Notably reforms such as that of the State subsidy system which have increased the authority of municipalities, have changed the role of the provincial governments from supervising the functioning of municipalities towards promoting development and improving general conditions in the area.

Major structural changes have taken place at the regional level. As from 1994, with the emergence of Regional Councils, there is a new level of administration. On the other hand the new regional units have been created on basis of the former structures in the sense that they now combine functions such as physical planning, which were previously undertaken by joint municipal authorities. The process of establishing the new Regional Councils is also evolving as the division of powers between them and the State has not yet been completed or generally agreed.

Issues relate to the role of the Regional Councils in the process of financing regional development projects that will get funding from the European Union. It is likely that this will be organised in the same way as the present sectoral development funding, in other words by giving the State authorities the final decision.

In the State regional administration two trends can be recognised: on the one hand there is a trend towards merging regional organisations in some sectors; for example the number of regional offices of the State road administration decreased from 13 to 9 in 1994. On the other hand there are attempts to merge horizontally those organisations with similar fields of expertise, notably in the environmental area. A law has been passed which combines the State district units of the Ministry of the Environment and the departments of environmental affairs that existed within the State provincial governments.

The rationale behind these trends is primarily financial, given the current severe budgetary constraints. This has led, in many instances, to pushing forward attempts to rationalise organisations and to minimise administrative costs.

In the State regional administration the developments mentioned above are closely linked with the major reform of public enterprises. State functions that were earlier organised as traditional administrative agencies are now functioning as public enterprises with much more operational and managerial freedom than before. The public enterprise reform has radically changed the nature and organisation of State regional units and decreased the number of personnel there.

Increasing managerial freedom means that the central organisations of these new public enterprises, as well as corporations, have also been given more freedom in organising their functions internally. To fulfil the requirement of functioning profitably in the markets, there has also been a call to reduce administrative costs by merging or abolishing regional units.

A gradual merging of local units has taken place in the State local administration. In the tax administration, for example, between 1992 and mid 1995 the number of local tax offices was reduced from over 200 to some 110. There is a determined plan to continue this trend so that the target number of local tax offices is close to the number of State local districts, i.e. about 90.

The present government's Programme includes the objective of decreasing the number of administrative units at the regional level and will strengthen the trends that have already started in the

State regional and local administration. The number of provincial governments on the mainland will thus be decreased from 11 to 5.

Before the changes to the general municipal legislation and the reform of the State subsidy system, important steps were made in the Free Municipalities experimentally started in 1989. This gave the pilot municipalities participating in this project exemptions from obligations to submit certain municipal decisions for approval by the State authorities and was less restrictive regarding the ways in which municipalities organised their internal administration. This experiment ended in 1993 and has had an important impact on the reforms that have now given municipalities more operational freedom.

An important project was recently launched to examine the scope for reviewing the relationship between the State and municipal governments. As a first stage, the economic responsibilities and a redefinition of the basis of State subsidies to municipalities will be on the agenda. The second phase of the project will cover other policy questions related to the duties and tasks of each sector.

3.2   The current debate

The new government since April 1995 is a coalition of five parties. The present government programme reflects the need to clarify administrative structures and the roles of various organisations. There is an emphasis on improving the structures and functioning of the regional and local levels of government, in particular the need to clarify the role of the Regional Councils as the general authorities for regional development. The government programme also refers to abolishing overlaps and decreasing the number of organisations at the regional level.

Recent initiatives seek to develop a State local administration on the basis of the present 95 local districts. According to some plans these local administrative units would combine functions of the local police, prosecution, and registrations. One controversial issue of this reform is whether the new local organisations should operate under the auspices of the Ministry of the Interior or the Ministry of Justice. As of 1st December 1996, the local State administration was re-organised on a "local district" basis, the country being divided into 90 districts for policing, public prosecution, and registration purposes. These "local districts" replace the previous rural police districts and population register districts of the Ministry of the Interior, and the city prosecutor and bailiff's departments of the Ministry of Justice.

Finland's recent accession to the European Union (EU) has had a great impact on regional policies. Questions to be resolved include: who will have the right to negotiate with the EU on subsidies from regional funds; how will the decision-making process in Finland be organised; and which organisations, the State provincial governments or the new Regional Councils really represent the Finnish regions vis-à-vis the European Union?

3.3   Driving forces

The present economic situation in Finland has raised new issues for debate. These include in particular the number of administrative units at the regional level. Merging or abolishing regional or local units is often severely opposed by the local community and local authorities as it is seen to weaken local economic prospects as well as to increase unemployment.

Clearly the State's downsizing policies will continue to have effects on municipal economies. The debate on by how much and where municipalities need to cut their expenditure and how cuts affect municipal services are on the current agenda. As municipalities have been given much more operational freedom with the recent reforms, the priorities given to different services is subject to much social and political debate.

The present government's programme guarantees the basic services of the welfare State, but the need to raise productivity in the public services has also provoked arguments about the risk of lowering service quality and equity in the access to publicly provided services

FRANCE

1. INSTITUTIONS AND AUTHORITY

1.1 Structures

Description of levels

It is essential in France to distinguish between sub-national governments (*collectivités territoriales*) and administrative districts (*circonscriptions administratives*).

Sub-national governments are public law legal persons whose autonomy – guaranteed by the principle of administrative freedom for local authorities, which is enshrined in the Constitution – is reflected above all by the fact that they have been administered, either entirely (since the Acts on Decentralisation of 1982 and subsequent years) or in part (prior to 1982 in the case of *départements*), by assemblies elected by their respective constituencies.

In France, since 1982-86, there have been four levels of administration (if the term "level" is reserved for authorities enjoying the autonomy guaranteed by the Constitution under the concept of administrative freedom). Since, from a legal standpoint, there is no hierarchy among sub-national governments, which are all subordinate to the State in the same manner yet independent from each other, "level" must be construed in a geographical sense. The State, which is unitary, covers the entire republic. The total area of France is 1 165 651 square metres and the total population in 1990 was 58 453 000. [These 1990 data include the DOM/TOM (*Départements et Territoires d'Outre-mer*) and regions with a special status; for metropolitan France exclusively, its area is 549 000 square metres and the population in 1994 was 57 960 000.]

Since the French Revolution, the municipality (*la commune*) has been the base-level local authority; at that time, most municipalities corresponded simply to Catholic church parishes. Theoretically, the same regulations apply to all 36 772 municipalities (as at 1/1/1995), regardless of population, although there are exceptions for those located in DOMs and TOMs/CTs, as well as for the two Alsatian *départements* and that of Moselle, which have kept some principles of the law that prevailed prior to, or during, their incorporation into the German empire, from 1870 to 1918 ("Alsace-Lorraine"). While there is absolutely no legal distinction between rural municipalities and urban ones, population differences can alter the make-up of institutions or, more rarely, affect the ability to wield certain powers (e.g. town planning functions). The city of Paris is both a municipality and a *département*, its institutions (the Council of Paris and the mayor) being those of a municipality. The cities of Paris, Lyon and Marseilles, while each constituting a municipality, are further divided into *arrondissements*, which since 1982 have had their own mayors and councils, but whose powers are essentially advisory.

The 100 *départements*, which are intermediate local authorities, were created at the time of the Revolution, in 1789, on a geographical basis, as provinces, cities and other intermediate entities were being abolished. The same regulations theoretically apply to all *départements* (with the same sorts of exceptions as for municipalities). The overseas territories (TOM), as well as the two territorial communities (CT) (Mayotte, and Saint Pierre and Miquelon), fall under a different system, in some cases conferring sweeping internal autonomy.

All 26 regions have the same legal system, although institutions and powers can differ significantly for both Corsica (which, moreover, in 1992 ceased to be called a "region") and overseas regions (Guadeloupe, Guiana, Martinique and Réunion), each of which consists of a single *département* with the same geographical entity possessing both departmental and regional institutions – which is not without its problems as regards the division of responsibility.

The borders of the State's **administrative districts** usually coincide with those of sub-national governments, as in the case of regions and *départements*, as well as municipalities for certain powers (e.g. registry of births, marriages, deaths; elections). Other districts do not correspond to sub-national governments, as is generally the case with *arrondissements* (the domains of sub-prefects) and such special-purpose divisions as *academic districts* ("*académies*" – the geographical entities of the Ministry of Education, which are under the authority of Government-appointed rectors) and Court of Appeal jurisdictions. These administrative districts have neither legal personality nor autonomy – they are run by State officials hierarchically subordinate to ministers and the Prime Minister.

Table 1. **Area and population of sub-national governments (1990)**[1]

	Regions	Départements	Municipalities
Number	26	100	36 862 [2]
Area (km^2)			
Largest	45 348	10 000	
Smallest	1 100	176	14.89 [3]
Population			
Largest	10 660 000	2 532 000	2 188 918
Smallest	114 678	78 800	0

Population size	Number of municipalities
0-1 000	28 183
1 000-5 000	6 629
5 000-10 000	898
10 000-50 000	738
50 000-100 000	67
over 100 000	36

1. Figures include overseas *départements* (DOM), overseas territories (TOM) and special status.
2. There were 36 772 municipalities as at 1 January 1995.
3. Average.
4. Metropolitan France.

Source: *Structure and Operation of Local and Regional Democracy: France*, Council of Europe, 1993.

As of 1 January 1995, there were 36 772 municipalities in France, of which 36 559 were located in Europe, and 213 in overseas *départements* (DOMs), overseas territories and special "territorial communities" (TOMs/CTs). There have been 96 French *départements* in Europe since 1975 (83 at the time of the Revolution, 90 from 1919-68 and 95 from 1968-75) and four overseas *départements* (DOM) since 1946. In all there are 26 regions, of which 22 are in Europe.

The size of French municipalities varies in population from zero (a number of municipalities, in mountainous areas in particular, have lost all their year-round inhabitants) to 2 175 200 (Paris). This territory of a *département* can cover only a single municipality (Paris) up to several hundred, the average being 383 and the maximum 895 (in Pas-de-Calais). Regions vary in size from two *départements* (Corsica, Alsace) to eight (Rhône-Alpes).

Central government at sub-national levels

The State representatives in each of its administrative districts are national career civil servants, appointed and removed at the Government's pleasure to serve in regions (26 regional prefects) and *départements* (100 prefects). A regional prefect is also the prefect of the *département* in which the seat of regional government is located. In municipalities, the State is represented by the elected mayor, who holds administrative policing powers (to maintain order) in the municipality and is also the civil registry and criminal investigation officer. All relations between local authorities and the State are channelled through the prefects, who also have power to review the administrative acts of local government institutions. Until 1982, a prefect's administrative control over the actions of mayors and the elected assemblies of sub-national governments was of the conventional supervisory type still to be found in other Western European countries: in some cases, local decisions required the prefect's prior approval, in others, he could reverse them, and, in a limited number of cases, he could replace local authorities and exercise their powers himself. This control always covered the legality of local decisions and, very frequently, their advisability (especially from a financial or fiscal perspective) as well. Since 1982 (and excepting a few highly specific areas such as the police powers of mayors), prefects have been left with only one means of exercising the State's administrative control over local authorities (provided for by the Constitution), i.e. by referring matters to the independent judicial bodies that are empowered to annul or alter disputed decisions, namely the administrative courts and the new regional courts of audit.

Creation, elimination and restructuring

The Constitution of the Fifth Republic (Article 72) refers to *départements* and municipalities, and gives Parliament power to create other sub-national governments. It would therefore require a constitutional amendment to eliminate municipalities and *départements* as categories, and none is envisaged. The creation of new *départements* (or the merger of several into one, which has never taken place) is possible only through an Act of Parliament. The same holds true for the creation of new municipalities. The merger of municipalities has been possible since 1971, subject to the approval of a majority of the inhabitants and the municipal councils involved (there were just over 800 mergers between 1971 and 1992). It is far easier to create or abolish regions, or to alter their boundaries, not only because their existence is not protected by the Constitution, but also because they are much less deeply rooted in French society. Regions have taken hold as a political reality, however, and their boundaries would seem unlikely to change. Two or more regions can be merged by decree of the Council of State (*Conseil d'État*) with the assent of the respective regional councils and approval by a qualified majority of the general councils.

A number of restructurings have taken place, the main recent development being the establishment of the region. Regions have been sub-national governments only since 1982 (Corsica), 1983 (overseas regions) or 1986 (regions in continental Europe).

Local authorities may join together in public entities created to undertake projects of common interest. Such entities can bring together local authorities of the same level (for example, consortia of municipalities, inter-departmental bodies, and inter-regional institutions) or local authorities of different levels (mixed consortia). All these entities are public organisations, invested with legal status and financial independence. Their acts are subject to control by the prefects.

Most of these entities are freely created by the authorities coming together, and decide their own field of responsibilities – which may be single or multi-purpose. Conurbations, however, are an exception. They are created by an Act and a law lays down a set of compulsory activities. In practice, however, conurbations were instituted as a result of a voluntary procedure. Associations of municipalities and of towns (*communautés de communes et de villes*) are created by agreement of their constituent localities. Conurbations and associations of municipalities and of towns are alike in that their powers are defined by law, although of course there are variations.

Control bodies

Administrative courts may review acts of the State (other than legislation) and of sub-national governments, at the instigation of private citizens as well as the State (the prefect in the case of local decisions) and incorporated public bodies (any sub-national government or public organisation can therefore contest the acts of the State or of other sub-national governments or public organisations). The administrative courts therefore play a vital role in upholding each authority's autonomy and ensuring consistency of public policies by annulling decisions or regulations that are contrary to legislation or to the general principles of law. Rulings by the Council of State, the highest administrative court are therefore particularly important in setting the basic ground rules.

Regional courts of audit play an essential role in budgetary and financial matters. If a prefect detects irregularities, and particularly if an unbalanced budget has been adopted, he may refer the matter to the regional court of audit, which is empowered, if necessary, to take certain decisions in the place of local authorities.

Although administrative courts and regional courts of audit are separate from the ordinary courts [their members are recruited through the National School for Administration (ENA) rather than the National School for Judges and Prosecutors (École Nationale de la Magistrature) and the court of last instance is the Council of State rather than the Court of Appeal (Cour de Cassation)], they are entirely independent.

1.2 Powers

Nature of sub-national institutions

Each sub-national government has a representative assembly elected through direct universal suffrage for a fixed term: for municipalities, it is the municipal council; for *départements*, the general council; and for regions, the regional council. Each of these three types of assemblies has its own electoral system, with an added distinction in the case of municipal councils, between municipalities having a population of more or fewer than 3 500. Elections for a given category of authorities are generally held on the same date throughout the Republic. The number of members of these representative assemblies is set by law and varies according to the population of the entity involved. In the event a representative assembly is unable to function, the Government may dissolve it, in which case new elections are held to choose another one, which simply serves out the unexpired term of the body that has just been dissolved. Such dissolutions are extremely rare: between 1977 and 1993, 137 municipal councils were dissolved, 106 of which in municipalities having a population of under 1 500. The regional council of Corsica was also dissolved in 1983.

Some exceptions to this uniformity deserve mentioning. Corsica, for example, does not have the same common law regional institutions as there is an "Assembly of Corsica". The regions' two departments, Upper Corsica and Southern Corsica, on the other hand, have the same institutions as any other *département*. Overseas territories and territorial communities have neither general councils nor regional councils. French Polynesia has an Assembly; and New Caledonia is divided into three provinces having elected assemblies which together constitute the territorial assembly of New Caledonia.

Prior to 1982, the chief executive of each *département* and region was the prefect, a Government-appointed national career civil servant who was also responsible for representing the Government in the respective *départements* and regions. Accordingly, prefects exercised administrative control over the legality of acts of municipal, general and regional councils, as well as over those of mayors. This meant that regions had no administrative services of their own, and those of the *départements* were scant, with prefects using national administrative services to perform most of their functions. Today, each authority also has a chief executive, elected by the representative assembly from among its members and serving the same term of office: municipalities are headed by a mayor, *départements* and regions by the chairmen of the general and regional councils respectively. It is a system similar to that of the national President: the executive authority cannot be voted out of office in mid-term, and power is concentrated in the hands of a single person, who is assisted by other officers or by deputies, who do not, however, share his responsibility. Should it become impossible for local institutions to function, the Government may suspend or revoke the chief executive, but such cases are extremely rare: between 1977 and 1993 only seven mayors were removed in this way.

In Corsica, an authority which constitutes an exception to the norm, the "Assembly of Corsica" elects a collegiate executive which is answerable to the Assembly during its term of office. The government of French Polynesia is similarly answerable to the Assembly during its term of office. The executive in New Caledonia is the High Commissioner, a national career civil servant appointed by the Government.

Type and degree of autonomy

The Constitution of the Fifth Republic (Articles 34 and 72) reiterates the principle of administrative freedom for sub-national governments, developed by the rulings of the Constitutional Council. What that principle basically means is that each such authority must have a representative assembly elected through direct universal suffrage, and its own powers which, while obviously subject to the law, are exercisable without interference from the State. Since France is a unitary State, sub-national governments have no general regulatory power, let alone any legislative power. Parliament alone may pass laws, whether they be applicable throughout the Republic or in a limited geographical area only. It is the Prime Minister who wields regulatory power, which enables the Government to clarify the detailed provisions of the law or regulate such matters as are not constitutionally reserved to the legislature. Regulations (called decrees or ministerial orders) applicable throughout the country are adopted by the Government; regional and departmental prefects, as well as mayors, may also adopt regulations (known as prefectoral or municipal orders) applicable solely in their respective districts. The sole exception to these principles is the territorial assembly of French Polynesia, which has regulatory powers over its own territory, but still subject to decisions of the national Parliament.

Only Parliament has the authority to establish a tax and fix its rate (see also section 2.2).

The organisational powers of sub-national governments are limited to running their own administrative services. Only the State has the responsibility of defining its own responsibilities and may organise itself and freely determine how its public powers are apportioned. Under the Constitution, all rules as to how institutions are organised (the composition and workings of representative assemblies and their executives) are a matter for Parliament.

Table 2. **Institutions of sub-national authorities**

	Region	Département	Municipality
Assembly	regional council	general council	municipal council
Term of office	6 years	6 years (half of the council being up for renewal every 3 years)	6 years
Electoral system	proportional representation, departmental lists, minimum: 5% of the total vote	two-round vote for a single rep. = "cantonal elections"	two-round vote from list if pop. <3 500; adjusted proportional representation if >3 500
Number of members	minimum: 31 maximum: 209	minimum: 13 maximum: 76 Paris: 163	minimum: 9 maximum: 69 Paris: 163, Lyons: 73 Marseilles: 101
Chief executive	Chairman of the regional council	Chairman of the general council	Mayor
Term of office	6 years	3 years	6 years
Representative of the State	regional prefect	prefect	mayor

1.3 Responsibilities

Although the Act of 7 January 1983 affirms the principle of specific responsibilities for each category of local authority, the issue is made fairly complex by the fact that the current competencies derive not only from pre-1983 devolution by the State and subsequent changes in the division of responsibilities, but also from a responsibility for "local affairs" – a concept developed by the courts – for each level of authority. Theoretically, the division of responsibilities is straightforward, but in practice many responsibilities are found on more than one level (concerning different aspects). The theoretical principle underlying the 1983 Act is that "clusters of responsibility" are assigned to each level of sub-national government.

This principle has, however, its limitations:

- It is particularly difficult to determine such clusters when the responsibilities involved are related.
- The State has not wished to transfer certain responsibilities that in France are traditionally considered as belonging to the national level though they involve local responsibilities (by virtue of the republican principle of equality, teachers, school curricula and where schools are located have remained matters for the State, whereas the construction and maintenance, as well as the operation, of school facilities have been transferred to sub-national government under the principle of decentralisation.
- Sub-national government each have general jurisdiction over matters of local concern; accordingly, in any one area (e.g. a municipality), responsibilities attributed to a particular type of administrative unit are exercised at the same time as the general responsibilities invested in higher authorities (*départements* or regions).

But, aside from the fact that Parliament has not totally respected the logic of clusters of responsibilities, the concept of a cluster may encompass only a portion of overall authority. In education, for example, the cluster for local authorities relates to school buildings, whereas for the State, it relates to all aspects of education.

Distribution of responsibilities

The responsibilities of **municipalities** involve matters of relevance to the immediate vicinity, such as town planning, municipal infrastructure and subsidised housing, local public services (lighting, water, household waste treatment, public transport), health and social services (e.g. optional creation and maintenance of hospitals, aid to the elderly), education (primary school construction and maintenance), cultural affairs (museums, theatres), policing (security, public order, hygiene) and aid to employment and to businesses (particularly indirect assistance such as zoning provisions), subject to compliance with the principle of the freedom of trade and industry and with European Community law. The material extent of most of these responsibilities is significantly greater in medium- and large-sized urban municipalities than in rural areas.

The responsibilities of ***départements*** essentially involve the management of everyday affairs (excluding their responsibilities for departmental roads): welfare benefits, health care benefits (child and maternity care, preventive public health efforts), placement assistance for the unemployed, education [creation and maintenance of *collèges* (which provide the first four years of secondary education), school bussing] and local transport.

The responsibilities of **regions** focus chiefly on land-use planning and economic development: vocational training, education [creation, maintenance and operation of *lycées* (which provide the last three years of secondary education)], rail and waterway transport, and economic support measures. In the latter area, it must be stressed that regions alone may take the initiative of making direct grants to businesses (in which case *départements* and municipalities may make supplementary direct grants) – subject, here again, to competition law.

Mandatory, optional and shared responsibilities

The State has some parallel responsibilities to those of local authorities, and in all sectors the State may have varying degrees of responsibility, as illustrated by the following examples:

- In education, the State determines primary and secondary school curricula, certifies higher education degrees, administers personnel at all levels and makes overall plans for the location of educational establishments. Municipalities build and maintain primary school premises and school cafeterias and pay for non-teaching operating costs; *départements* do the same for *collèges* and regions for *lycées*; the State builds and maintains university premises and student housing, although it is possible for regions to add their financial assistance for universities to that of the State.

- Responsibility for policing is vested in municipalities as well as the State. Prefects may step in for mayors who fail to take the measures necessary to ensure safety, health and hygiene; criminal investigations are conducted by State officials, but mayors also perform some of the same functions (in particular by recording offences); police officers (who are under orders to the prefect as regards administrative matters, and to the State prosecutor for criminal investigations) are State civil servants in municipalities of over 10 000 inhabitants, whereas rural municipalities are policed by (military) *gendarmes*. Nevertheless, in order to exercise their responsibility for administrative policing, mayors may also, within certain limits, constitute police forces having lesser powers than the national police.

In the social sphere, the guaranteed minimum income policy, which was instituted in 1988, is a much more highly developed example of joint administration: the State finances allowances to the indigent, while *départements* must fund and develop measures to find them jobs. Prefects and general council chairmen jointly administer this policy, in which municipalities and social security bodies also play a role. It is therefore not possible, to summarise simply, clearly and precisely how responsibilities are divided among local authorities at the various levels of the State in France.

2. MANAGEMENT FUNCTIONS

2.1 Policy-making and co-ordination

Coherence, consultation and conflict resolution

The State alone has general regulatory powers. The framework for local public policy-making is therefore determined by the State, and freedom of choice within that framework varies extensively from one domain to another. A number of services are incumbent upon local authorities, with respect not only to security, health and hygiene, but also to matters such as social affairs, education and school bussing. Local politicians often complain, moreover, that the State's financial contribution is not enough to enable local authorities to administer these services. In the case of non-mandatory services, the latitude of local authorities, not only to pick and choose but also to manage, is much greater. The State intervenes in these areas by offering incentives, which may take the form of contractual planning (as is particularly the case with State/region plan contracts, which are concluded for five-year periods).

Thus, the institutions of sub-national governments have only non-regulatory powers, i.e. to make investment and administrative decisions as authorised by legislation giving them responsibilities in specific fields. Whenever a mayor exercises a regulatory power within his municipality, he acts not in his capacity of municipal chief executive elected by the municipal council, but as the State's representative in the municipality. (It is also in that capacity that he registers births, marriages and deaths and organises elections).

French law lays down the principle of equality between sub-national governments. This implies, in particular, that there is no hierarchy of municipalities, *départements* and regions. Accordingly, regions, unlike the State, have no formal means of imposing choices or co-operation on *départements* or municipalities within their boundaries, nor do *départements* on municipalities. However, this principle is being relaxed somewhat in the system of direct aid to businesses: municipalities and *départements* can only make such grants to supplement regional assistance, but regions can impose certain choices on municipalities or *départements* by excluding particular firms or areas from their systems of direct aid.

A number of laws require that State services consult with local authorities in formulating public policies. However, there is no general consultation requirement – if one excludes the case of overseas *départements*/regions, which the Government must consult if it proposes not to apply a national regulation or legislation to those territories. In contrast, the principle of equality among sub-national governments means that there are fewer requirements for consultation between different levels.

Formal and informal mechanisms

French law provides for a range of co-operative systems, for municipalities in particular, given that there are so many small ones with scant resources. A distinction can be made between:

- groupings of municipalities for general purposes, exercising a range of powers via a single body: intermunicipal alliances or conferences, multi-purpose municipal boards, districts, conurbations, and associations of municipalities and of towns (see section 1.1);
- specialised groupings: new towns, joint committees, and intermunicipal charters for development and land-use planning (which may be considered more as spatial planning documents than as groupings in the strict sense of the word).

In each *département*, an intermunicipal co-operation committee makes evaluations and formulates proposals on a strictly advisory basis. Its membership breaks down to at least 60 per cent mayors, 20 per cent representatives of public intermunicipal co-operation boards and 15 per cent general council representatives.

Formal co-operation also takes place between sub-national governments at other levels:

- interdepartmental alliances, interdepartmental conferences and interdepartmental institutions;
- inter-regional conferences, joint utility bodies and inter-regional agreements and alliances.

In addition, there are groupings that link local authorities of different levels: joint boards, inter-urban groups, departmental agencies and local-purpose public interest groups.

Prefects, and particularly regional ones, play an essential role in policy co-ordination by exercising a number of powers:

- they co-ordinate the deconcentrated services of the State in their respective *départements* or regions;
- they have resources, especially funding, at their disposal for local development – in this respect, economic and financial directorates in prefectures play a particularly important role;
- they represent the State vis-à-vis sub-national governments and handle most contacts between local authorities and the national government;
- their power to control, noted above, contributes to ensuring better co-ordination.

A number of changes have recently taken place: the elimination of supervisory authorities (*tutelles*) radically changed the State's formal means of co-ordination and considerably increased local autonomy. This is considered one of the main features of decentralisation in France.

In France, two informal co-ordination mechanisms have long operated in relations between the State and local authorities, as well as those among local authorities themselves. Prefects have always kept in close contact with local authorities, at times even speaking on their behalf to central ministries or the Government. Moreover, by holding a number of different offices, local elected officials were essential in co-ordination. Classic examples were mayors who were also members of Parliament, or senators as well as members of their departmental general councils (and regional councils, from 1972). As such, they sat in the decision-making bodies of the State (Parliament), *départements* and regions, for the greater good of their municipalities. This multiple office-holding was far from having advantages only and was therefore considerably curtailed: since 1985, a member of Parliament (National Assembly or Senate) may concurrently hold only one other important office (European MP, regional councillor, general councillor, Paris councillor, mayor of a municipality of 20 000 inhabitants or more, or deputy mayor of a municipality of over 100 000 inhabitants). Most regional and general councillors hold another local office (general or municipal councillor).

A new, informal co-ordination mechanism is gradually taking shape through co-operation between the administrators of various authorities and those of the State, although it has yet to be studied in detail.

An example of this is how the use of European Union structural funds has led to the establishment of "follow-up committees" representing the relevant prefectures and general and regional councils.

Although there are associations of local elected officials, including the Association of French Mayors, there are no national associations of local authorities, unlike in a number of other European countries.

2.2 Financial management

Sources of revenue

Each sub-national government has a number of different revenue sources:

- Local taxes, collected by the State on behalf of municipalities, *départements*, regions and groups of local authorities (land tax on developed and undeveloped property, residence tax, trade tax); on behalf of municipalities or groups of municipalities (garbage collection and street cleaning charges); and on behalf of *départements* (annual motor vehicle tax, registration fees and fees for land and property advertising) and regions (motor vehicle registration fees).
- State subsidies (block operating grant, capital investment and decentralisation grants).
- Subsidies from other authorities (subsidies from regions to *départements* and municipalities, from départements to municipalities and from municipalities to *départements*; subsidies from the European Union to areas eligible for European structural fund grants).
- Borrowing (which accounts for between 10 and 15 per cent of local revenue).
- Payment for services rendered and sales of certain publicly-owned resources (e.g. timber from municipal forests). This type of revenue is important for municipalities, where it exceeds the proceeds from borrowing.

In 1993, aggregate tax revenue accounted for about half the income of regions, *départements* and municipalities, whereas total transfers covered just under a third of the budgets of sub-national governments (see Table 3).

Table 3. **Main revenue sources of sub-national governments (1985, 1990, 1993)**
(millions of French francs)

	Regions			Départements			Municipalities		
	1985	1990	1993	1985	1990	1993	1985	1990	1993
Tax receipts	11 068	25 799	31 374	58 951	93 106	106 765	103 385	147 713	179 112
of which: proceeds 4 taxes	4 750	12 248	17 443	38 766	52 391	69 278	87 228	113 765	138 287
Transfers received	3 781	13 505	18 537	49 153	60 904	65 680	87 841	116 987	133 657
of which: DGF[1]	(2)	(2)	(2)	9 965	13 307	14 846	53 899	69 533	76 975
Borrowings	2 647	4 967	10 327	10 197	10 444	27 444	29 459	40 440	43 686
Miscellaneous	701	3 338	2 851	4 085	7 857	8 438	32 082	50 930	58 423
TOTAL	18 197	47 609	63 089	122 386	172 380	208 327	252 767	356 070	414 878

1. Block operating grants (*dotations globales de fonctionnement*).
2. Not applicable to regions.
Source: Direction de la comptabilité publique, in : *Les Collectivités locales en chiffres*, Édition 1995, Direction générale des collectivités locales.

Expenditure responsibilities

In 1993, two-thirds of regional expenditure was earmarked for capital investment, whereas *départements* and municipalities had to bear proportionally higher operating expenses, which accounted for over half of their expenditure. For municipalities, these operating expenses consist primarily of substantial personnel costs, whereas *départements* make a large volume of transfer payments. Most investment expenditure is for capital equipment at the three sub-national levels, although the burden of repayment falls rather heavily on municipalities and *départements* (see Table 4).

Expenditure trends at the three levels of administration over the past ten years show that regional spending has been growing proportionally faster than that of *départements* or municipalities; in fact, regional expenses have more than tripled, whereas those of *départements* and municipalities barely doubled. This pattern probably stems from the fact that regions are a recent creation. It should be noted, however, that the regions still account for a small share of aggregate sub-national expenditure (less than 10 per cent in 1993).

Table 4. **Main expenditure patterns of sub-national governments (1985, 1990, 1993)**
(millions of French francs)

	Regions			Départements			Municipalities		
	1985	1990	1993	1985	1990	1993	1985	1990	1993
Operations	7 061	16 209	22 378	88 099	110 883	130 878	168 490	227 339	273 330
of which:									
personnel expenses	417	889	1 375	11 982	14 306	18 681	71 241	95 883	116 180
interest	1 278	1 946	3 675	6 786	7 642	9 709	20 359	27 185	30 888
transfers	4 891	11 802	14 965	58 450	74 264	87 648	36 892	50 302	59 853
Capital investment	11 179	31 467	40 070	31 641	63 264	77 044	80 926	127 333	140 565
of which:									
debt repayment	511	2 092	4 493	5 390	11 456	16 335	13 637	26 849	32 009
gross investment[1]	781	9 911	10 724	16 216	30 523	34 389	59 449	88 622	92 044
subsidies	8 338	14 123	18 431	(2)	(2)	(2)	(2)	(2)	(2)
TOTAL	18 240	47 676	62 448	119 740	174 147	207 922	249 516	354 672	413 895

1. For regions only: "reintegrated capital expenditure", funded by advances set aside in previous years, should be added to each year's gross investment figure. This expenditure totalled FF 1.4 billion in 1990 and FF 3.9 billion in 1993.
2. Non-existent for *départements* and municipalities.

Source: Direction de la comptabilité publique, in : *Les Collectivités locales en chiffres*, Édition 1995, Direction générale des collectivités locales.

Balance between discretion and control

Limits to local autonomy with respect to the expenditures of sub-national governments are primarily through budgetary and financial control (see 1.2). There is *ex-post* control by the administrative courts and regional courts of audit (upon referral by the prefect) – to which may be added the accountancy rules which govern expenditures.

Concerning revenues, there are two fundamental limitations on revenue autonomy (apart from the population's financial capacity and the area's taxable activity):

- the principle that budgets must be balanced;

- the requirement that public authorities have their cash managed by the public Treasury (part of the State administration) which, in principle, denies them a share in any interest earned thereon.

The degree of autonomy in spending depends solely on whether services are mandatory or not (see above). On the whole, local authorities enjoy broad autonomy in this area. This is less true for small municipalities, because of their meagre financial base and the relative share of mandatory expenditure in their budgets.

On the revenue side, a whole series of factors combine to give French local authorities considerable autonomy : while Parliament alone is empowered to establish a tax and determine its base, municipal, general and regional councils have some latitude in setting tax rates. This is reflected in the substantial disparities in local taxation from one locality to another.

Since 1979, the State has gradually replaced specific grants by block grants, which are felt to be more conducive to local autonomy.

Since 1990 local authorities have been free to borrow wherever they please (including abroad and in foreign currency) except for foreign currency bond issues which require ministerial approval.

The shift towards greater financial autonomy for sub-national governments predated decentralisation legislation, since State grants were first made in block form in 1979. Since then, the tendency has gradually gathered speed with the transfer to regions and *départements* of certain State taxes and the replacement of the former monopoly on lending to sub-national governments by freedom to tap the market.

2.3 Performance management

Management control takes the form principally of a formal control of legality as noted in section 1.1.

2.4 Human resource management

Statutory distinctions: Administrative law distinguishes between private employees, who are subject to the Labour Code and to applicable collective agreements, and public officials, who are subject to the principles of public law. The courts have held that a public official is anyone who takes part in "the actual execution of public service" – a definition that covers most of the staff of sub-national governments. But that does not make every public official a civil servant, since administrative law also draws a distinction between civil servants (established officials holding permanent posts in an administration) and contract staff. The latter are subject to public law but do not have much of the protection accorded to civil servants, including guaranteed employment, and can be recruited much more freely.

Since 1984, special conditions of service have applied to the sub-national civil service, modelled on those for State civil servants which date from 1946. Sub-national civil servants have the same rights and responsibilities as their State counterparts. These include guaranteed employment (except in the event of serious misconduct or manifest unfitness for a job), a career system, a disciplinary system, and a duty to be impartial. Under the Constitution, most of these service conditions are contained in an Act of Parliament.

The Act of 26 January 1984 laying down general service conditions for sub-national civil servants has been amended several times, giving those concerned greater protection and making it easier for sub-national governments to meet their recruiting needs.

The jobs of each authority or establishment are created by the deliberative body of the sub-national government concerned. Individual decisions regarding the recruitment or careers of sub-national officials are taken by the sub-national government, in accordance with statutory provisions at the national level. Personnel management arrangements which are shared by several sub-national governments have been established. These include career management units (*Centres de gestion* – CDGs) and interdepartmental delegations of the National Centre for the Sub-national Civil Service (*Centre national de la fonction publique territoriale*, CNFPT). The latter is a public organisation with a board of directors made up equally of representatives of the sub-national governments and representatives of sub-national civil servant trade unions, and whose primary role is to organise training and certain "category A" and "category B" competitive examinations. Responsibilities for organising the examinations are shared between the sub-national governments, the CDG and the CNFPT.

Recruitment by sub-national governments of non-established staff is provided for under the Act of 26 January 1984 in specific instances and for limited periods of time, in particular to replace established staff who are absent or to fill posts involving duties that no civil servants would be able to perform.

Civil servants (established staff) are theoretically selected by competitive examination, on an equal opportunity basis and scored by an independent panel. Successful candidates are admitted to an employment pool (equivalent to the national civil service "corps"), governed by special rules. However, in contrast to the State civil service, local authorities are not bound by the ranking order established by the examination panel. A candidate who has passed the examination and been put on the waiting list for the sub-national, as opposed to the State, civil service may therefore not be recruited immediately.

Contract staff are not recruited with a view to making a career in the civil service. The careers of established civil servants are governed by the special rules applicable to each employment pool.

Promotions within a given pool, i.e. changes in grade and thus in remuneration, combine seniority (there are rules setting the minimum length of service for a change in grade) with selection (among officials with the requisite length of service). This is handled by career management units, if the sub-national governments are affiliated to one, otherwise by the authorities themselves. In contrast, employing authorities are free to transfer staff, as long as they fill vacancies with officials from the relevant pool and of the appropriate grade. If a civil servant is relieved of his duties or his post is eliminated, he is protected by the Act of 26 January 1984, under which, *inter alia*, he is paid by the regional delegation of the CNFPT or the management body, depending on his category, until he finds a new job.

The remuneration of sub-national officials is based on a number of factors. Basic salaries are determined first by grade, then by job, which makes it possible to set pay with reference to civil service salary scales. Most officials get bonuses, which may not exceed the ones paid to State civil servants performing equivalent duties and which can vary from one authority to another and, where applicable, reflect an official's particular responsibilities and in some cases his productivity. Very little is known about the exact amount of these bonuses, as is the case with the State civil service. The combination of salary and bonuses, while (generally) not as high as for corresponding private sector jobs, provides enough total remuneration to ensure that the sub-national civil service has no problem finding the staff it needs.

The principle of parity between the levels of civil service implies that sub-national officials may not enjoy a higher level of benefits than their counterparts in the State civil service.

Table 5. **Employment by type of administration (1983, 1989, 1994)**

	1983	1989	1994
State civil service[1]	2 813 800	2 844 800	2 208 000
Sub-national civil service	1 103 000	1 211 100	1 350 000
Public hospital service[2]	750 300	800 800	828 000
TOTAL	4 667 100	4 856 700	4 386 000

1. Excluding *La Poste* (postal service) and France Telecom in 1994 (new status).
2. Estimated figure for 1994.
Source: INSEE (for the State, data supplied by the *Ministère de la Fonction publique*), in : *Les Collectivités locales en chiffres*, Édition 1995, Direction générale des collectivités locales.

Table 6. **Personnel in local administrations (1985, 1991, 1993)**
(31 December)

	1985	1991	1993
Regions	2 900	5 900	6 700
Départements	155 000	154 300	157 200
Municipalities	862 800	935 600	952 400
Intermunicipal bodies	81 200	88 300	93 400
Other bodies [1]	83 300	124 600	136 900
Home child-minders	44 100	56 900	56 600
TOTAL	1 229 300	1 365 600	1 403 200

1. Including various private and semi-public administrative bodies, various "industrial and commercial" public bodies, trade unions, private bodies for local action, public HLM offices (controlled rent housing), municipal credit banks.
Source: For 1985 : *Annales statistiques de la fonction publique*, INSEE-Résultats n°28-29
For 1991 and 1993 : *Les effectifs des collectivités territoriales*, INSEE-Résultats n°95-96.

Statistics on sub-national staff are harder to establish reliably than State figures, because of the greater numbers involved, and because sub-national governments are freer than the State to make use of contract staff. As at 31 December 1990, there were a total of 1 263 927 sub-national civil servants, i.e. 28 per cent of all public officials. The 647 800 officials of the public hospital system (14 per cent of the total), although many aspects of their recruitment and careers are dealt with nationally, work for local public employers, since hospitals are either municipal or departmental. The breakdown by type of employing authority was as follows: municipalities 854 167, *départements* 151 826 and regions 5 103, the remainder working for intermunicipal groupings.

Mobility: Statutory distinctions between national and sub-national civil servants, together with the traditional separation of the French administration into different corps does not encourage mobility across levels of government. That said, movement is more frequent for senior staff than for lower grades.

3. TRENDS IN REDISTRIBUTING AUTHORITY ACROSS LEVELS OF GOVERNMENT

3.1 Evolving tendencies

A significant phase in the administrative history of France was a move towards centralisation and concentration of power that stretched from the 16th century to the early 19th, culminating in the Napoleonic administration. From 1830, the pendulum swung back to a gradual decentralisation marked by three main phenomena. The appointment of local officials was gradually replaced by their election; administrative districts were to some extent replaced by sub-national governments with legal personality and overall jurisdiction over matters of local concern; and powers and appropriations in fields previously administered by the State's deconcentrated services were gradually transferred to sub-national governments. This decentralisation trend is accompanied by a certain movement towards "deconcentration".

The policy initiated by President Mitterrand as soon as he came to power in May 1981 was to some extent a break with the timidity of the decentralisation measures that had been contemplated or undertaken since the early 19th century, but it was also a continuation of the deconcentration trend that had been accelerated by General de Gaulle's governments of the early 1960s.

There are four basic aspects to the decentralisation reforms of 1982 and subsequent years:

- The introduction of the region as a new sub-national government. Preceded by the setting up of regional action districts and, later, of regional public organisations by the State, the Act of 1982 made the regions into new sub-national governments organised on similar lines to municipalities and *départements* but whose responsibilities were more medium-term oriented. Since the Act stipulated that the new regional institutions could only come into being once regional councils had been elected, most regions were not established until 1986, except for Corsica (1982) and the four overseas regions (1983). The voting arrangements for electing regional assemblies and the types of responsibilities with which they were invested made regions less important than *départements* or municipalities in the administration of public policies.

- The transfer of power between the State and sub-national governments. The principle adopted in 1993 was to transfer responsibilities in clusters (the so-called "layer cake" system), although it could not be fully implemented.

- The replacement of the prefect by an elected official as chief executive of the *département* and the region.

- The changing nature of State control over sub-national governments (henceforth *ex-post* jurisdictional control) which gives great freedom to French local authorities.

This institutional change is accompanied by two important phenomena:

- real regional (and especially departmental) administrations have been set up;
- new local political elites have been created.

This decentralisation is accompanied by a continuing move to deconcentration: ten years after the Act that defined the rights and freedoms of municipalities, *départements* and regions, the Act of 6 February 1992 on the sub-national administration of the Republic attempted to supplement, and on certain points rectify, decentralisation reforms. The new Act had four objectives: to improve the functioning of local democracy, spur co-operation between sub-national governments, tighten the State's administrative control over their actions and, above all, to establish deconcentration as the keystone of State administration (subject to some degree to the principle of subsidiarity). The Act was implemented by the "Deconcentration Charter", which was adopted by a governmental decree of 1 July 1992. It strengthened the power of the prefects to co-ordinate all deconcentrated services of the State within their respective districts and established a hierarchy between regional prefects and those of *départements*.

3.2 The current debate

The government that was formed in the wake of the March 1993 elections has carried on the decentralisation and deconcentration reforms of the past decade.

Nevertheless, it has two projects that add new dimensions.

- In November 1993, the Prime Minister set up a commission (*Commission Picq*) to take stock of the functions of the State (broadly defined as all public authorities) and how they are divided among the various levels of administration.

- In addition, the Ministry of the Interior has developed major planning proposals which might ultimately lead to an administrative restructuring of the State, and even a redistribution of powers and boundaries among sub-national governments. The legislation adopted by Parliament in 1994, however, contains no radical changes.

3.3 Driving forces

On the whole, the forces driving the move towards decentralisation seem to emanate much more from political circles than from any other segment of society.

Political forces: The political climate of the 1980s made political parties one of the chief proponents of decentralisation. The reforms were undertaken at the personal initiative of President Mitterrand and his Minister of the Interior, Gaston Defferre. While they squared with the Socialist Party platform, they probably went farther than a significant percentage of the party faithful, steeped in Jacobin tradition, would have wished. In this case the opposition did not slow reform but rather helped to legitimise it, in contrast to its stance towards the nationalisation programme that was under way at the same time.

"Local notables" have traditionally played an important role in French society. As the number of responsible positions increased, generated by the transfer of executive authority from prefects to council chairmen, as well as by transfers of powers, it had a cumulative effect: dynamic personalities ran for such offices and, once elected, demanded more power. As a result, local elected officials gave political parties added leverage.

State civil servants: They were initially reticent about these reforms, which deprived them of some of their power and could even, in some cases, cause them to be re-assigned through staff transfers. Later, however, the growth of sub-national administrations and their staffs had a stimulative effect – so much so that it was not uncommon for State civil servants (including prefects) to arrange to be seconded to sub-national administrations or the private offices of general or regional council chairmen.

Economic forces: In France as elsewhere, economic forces favour less bureaucracy and closer links between the administration and the business world. Nonetheless, it is not clear that those forces play much of a role in decentralisation, since they frequently do better with well managed deconcentrated services of the State than they do with local administrations. However, some businesses undoubtedly push for decentralisation, seeing it as a potential gateway to official support for their investment projects – in a lower key, but more readily accessible.

Social forces: Whether organised (unions, associations, etc.) or not, social forces appear to support decentralisation. They advocate it on the regional level and, to some extent, in the *départements*, but to a much lesser degree at the municipal level.

GERMANY

1. INSTITUTIONS AND AUTHORITY

1.1 Structures

Description of levels

The Federal Republic of Germany is a federal State. Its administrative apparatus has three levels: federal, *Land* (state), and local. The federal and *Land* administrative authorities are considered institutions of "direct" State administration; while the local authorities which, from a legal point of view, form independent bodies of self-government, are considered institutions of "indirect" State administration.

Germany is composed of 16 *Länder*. There are 13 territorial *Länder* and 3 "city-states" (Berlin, Bremen and Hamburg) which are both a *Land* and a local authority.

Local self-government falls into two levels: municipalities (*Gemeinden*) on the one hand, which may be organised as unitary municipalities (*Einheitsgemeinden*) or as a kind of association of municipalities (*Ämter, Verbandsgemeinden, Verwaltungsgemeinschaften*) and, on the other hand, the counties (*Kreise*) consisting of the municipalities within the county territory. Bigger towns may be non-county municipalities (*kreisfreie Städte*) – i.e. independent of a county and thus combining the two levels of local self-government (see).

Federal and Länder government at sub-national levels

As the execution of laws is delegated from the federal government to the *Länder*, there is no need for federal representation at the *Land* level. For those areas in which laws are executed by the federal level, higher, intermediate and lower-level federal authorities have been established. All except the higher-level authorities have regional sub-structures.

Most *Länder* also have a three-level administrative organisation: higher, intermediate and lower level. Higher-level authorities fulfil administrative functions for the entire *Land* from one central location, are immediately subordinate to the *Land* ministries and do not have any administrative substructure. Intermediate-level authorities fulfil functions for an administrative district within the *Land* but do not exist in all *Länder*. Staff working for these administrations are civil servants and employees of the *Länder*. Lower-level authorities may be either *Land* authorities or local authorities acting on behalf of the *Land*.

Creation, elimination and restructuring

The existence of *Länder* and municipalities is guaranteed by the Constitution. This means that the German federal structure i.e. the existence of *Länder*, towns, municipalities and non-county municipalities is guaranteed, even if the existence of an individual *Land* or municipality is not.

New boundaries of federal territory are effected by federal statutes which require confirmation by referendum, as was the case recently in Berlin and Brandenburg. New local boundaries may be effected by *Land* statutes. The *Land* constitutions contain provisions on the procedures for and content of such statutes. The *Land* parliaments are responsible for such processes.

Table 1. **Size and number of sub-national governments**

	Länder	
Number	16 of which 3 (Berlin, Bremen, Hamburg) are "city states"	
	area (km²)	population
Largest	70 000 (Bavaria)	17 700 000 (N. Rhine-Westphalia)
Smallest	2 600 (Saarland)	1 100 000 (Saarland)
"city state"	400 (Bremen)	700 000 (Bremen)

	Number of local authorities		
	Old Länder	New Länder	TOTAL
County (Kreise)	237	92	329
Non-county municipalities (Kreisefreie Städte)	91	24	115
Municipalities (Gemeinden)	8 512	6 403	14 915

Source: Federal Ministry of the Interior.

Between 1965 and 1977, local units at both county and municipal levels were subject to far-reaching administrative and territorial reforms. The individual Länder adopted different approaches. All reforms aimed at creating bigger and more capable local governments able to offer a wide range of modern services. In some Länder, smaller municipalities were merged to form bigger ones (Einheitsgemeinden, unitary municipalities), while in other Länder smaller municipalities remained independent, but were grouped together, to form associations of municipalities with a joint administration (Ämter, Verbandsgemeinden, Verwaltungsgemeinschaften). Thus, in the old Länder, only half of the approximately 8 500 remaining municipalities (compared with approximately 24 000 prior to the reform) has its own administration.

Territorial reform was also conducted at the level of the counties. A great number of smaller counties were merged, bringing down the number of counties and non-county municipalities from 425 and 137 (as at 1 January 1960) to 237 and 91 respectively.

In the new Länder overall territorial reform has not yet been conducted at the level of the municipalities. However, as a lot of smaller municipalities are not able to provide today's modern services, associations of municipalities were formed for many municipalities either as laid down by statute or on a voluntary basis (Ämter in Brandenburg and Mecklenburg-Western Pomerania, Verwaltungsgemeinschaften in Saxony, Saxony-Anhalt and Thuringia).

The reform to create sustainable and capable counties and non-county municipalities has now almost been concluded. Prior to the reform there were 189 counties (Kreise) and 26 non-county municipalities (kreisfreie Städte) in the new Länder, now there are only 92 and 24 respectively.

Control bodies

From a legal and political point of view, the Länder and municipalities perform their tasks within the framework laid down by statutes not requiring Bundesrat consent and by the Constitution independently and on their own responsibility.

From a constitutional point of view, the Länder generally execute federal statutes as matters of their own concern. The Federation merely exercises supervision to ensure that the Länder execute the statutes in accordance with applicable law. In the case of the specific federal statutes referred to in the Basic Law and which the Länder have to perform as agents of the Federation, federal supervision also covers the legality and appropriateness of execution.

Where local authorities perform their designated tasks, legal supervision is exercised by the Land; where they perform other (discretionary) tasks, the Land, within the framework set by statute, also exercises supervision regarding the legality and appropriateness of execution. The office of the head of the county government executes public supervisory functions vis-à-vis the municipalities and towns forming part of a county. In the eight Länder where there are intermediate-level public authorities (Regierungsbezirke) i.e. administrative units covering a number of counties and non-county municipalities, the chief executive (*Regierungspräsidenten*) supervises the counties and non-county municipalities. In the *Länder* which do not have such intermediate-level authorities, the supervision of the counties is incumbent on the Ministry of the Interior of the *Land* – which, in all the *Länder*, are at the same time the supreme local supervisory bodies. The local authorities are subject to direct instructions where they execute Federal or *Land* statutes as agents of the Federation or the *Länder*.

Judicial controls over sub-national government: Local administrative courts and higher administrative courts (*Verwaltungsgerichtshof* or *Oberverwaltungsgericht*) check if the federal or *Land* authorities comply with federal or *Land* law. The higher administrative courts ensure, in particular, that the law is interpreted uniformly. There are also a federal Constitutional Court (see 1.2), social courts and fiscal courts. The Federal Court of Audit and the *Land* Courts of Audit are independent fiscal bodies and are responsible for monitoring budget and performance matters.

1.2 Powers

Nature of sub-national institutions

Legislative bodies: each *Land* has its own constitution, parliament and government. The members of the *Land* parliaments are elected directly by the electorate of the individual *Länder* under *Land*-specific electoral systems (e.g. election by proportional representation, electoral systems in which votes are cast for a candidate rather than a party, with reserve lists being kept to make up for proportions of votes cast which are not reflected in the distribution of seats, personalised election by proportional representation). Their term of office is four or five years, depending on the *Land*.

The Basic Law provides that citizens should also have a representative who is elected directly at the level of the counties and municipalities. The size of the municipal and county councils is laid down by *Land* law and depends on the number of inhabitants. Depending on the *Land* law, the representative bodies are elected for a term of four or five years. The powers of the municipal and county councils vary from one *Land* to another. They also depend on the position of the mayor in the local government. So as to prepare, deliberate and decide on matters within its remit, the representative body may set up committees of members of the local council which, in some cases, are necessary to comply with *Land* law.

Executive bodies: The general policy in each *Land* is determined by its head of government (*Ministerpräsident*) – if this power is not reserved for the *Land* government as a body.

In accordance with the dual nature of the counties as both bodies of local self-government and of the *Land* administration at the local level, the *Landrat* is both the chief executive of the county and the chief executive of the *Land* in the county government. In the *Länder* of Lower Saxony and North-Rhine/Westphalia (where this will soon cease to be the case), local administrative structures have been modelled on the British ones and a separation is made between the *Landrat* as the exclusive representative of the *Land* and the *Kreisdirektor* as head of the administration. As the chief executive official of the *Land*, the *Landrat* or *Kreisdirektor* performs the obligatory public tasks and the supervisory tasks conferred on the counties. As the top public servant at the local level he or she is responsible for all routine administrative procedures, and the meetings of the county council and ensuring that the decisions are put into practice.

There is no nation-wide procedure for the selection or qualification of the *Landrat*. This is regulated in the provisions on the form of local government of the individual *Länder*. The *Landrat* can either be elected directly by the inhabitants, or from among the members of the county council, or, as an external applicant, be elected by the county council. In some *Länder*, the administration is also involved in the election process in various ways. The county council vote may be confirmed by the Ministry of the Interior, the supervisory body may be involved in a pre-selection, or the chief executive may be made a public official on a limited term appointment under the legal provisions of the *Land* concerned.

Similarly, at the level of the municipalities, there is no nation-wide organisation of the executive bodies. Depending on the form of local government, executive functions rest with the local council, the mayor (*Bürgermeister*) or the chief executive (who is not the mayor).

In most *Länder*, the mayor is at the same time the head of the local council and chief executive. In twelve of the thirteen territorial *Länder*, which have an independent level of local government, the mayor is (or will be) elected directly by the electorate. (This is not the case with the three city states.) Only in Lower Saxony is the mayor not elected directly, and the separation between the mayor's function and that of the chief executive upheld, as in the British system of local government. So far, North-Rhine/Westphalia has also applied this practice at the level of the counties and municipalities. For a transitional period up to the local elections in 1999, the *Land* may also uphold this system or decide that the local council may elect a mayor. As of 1999, the North-Rhine/Westphalian electorate, too, will elect the mayor.

Type and degree of autonomy

The *Länder* have important law-making responsibilities, among which are local government law (which differs widely from *Land* to *Land*), the major part of police law, the administration of justice, and legal regulations concerning cultural and educational affairs (e.g. primary and secondary education, and universities).

Through the *Bundesrat* (Higher Chamber) the *Länder* participate in the federal legislative process. It consists of members of the *Land* governments who are appointed and recalled by them. Each *Land* may appoint as many members as it has votes. The *Länder* have between three and six votes depending on their size. The *Bundesrat* may submit its own bills, and some 60 per cent of federal statutes require *Bundesrat* consent. The *Bundesrat* may veto statutes which do not require its consent. Such veto, however, may be rejected by the majority of *Bundestag* members.

The Federal Constitutional Court (*Bundesverfassungsgericht*) has ruled that by-laws are the typical legal form by which local authorities make regulations for implementing their self-government tasks. The right to issue by-laws is at the centre of local self-government. These by-laws may regulate local community matters in so far as statutes do not provide otherwise. Where local self-government bodies perform tasks delegated to them, by-laws may only be issued where statutes so provide. Important local by-laws include standing orders (*Hauptsatzung*), the budget by-laws, by-laws relating to building law (development plans, local building provisions), and by-laws regulating road laws and businesses owned by local government. By-laws are exclusively adopted by the representative body.

Fiscal matters are laid down in detail in the Basic Law. This applies to the distribution of the burden of expenditure on the Federation and the *Länder*; fiscal law-making power and the distribution of tax revenues (see also 2.2).

The *Land* constitutions must conform to the principles of democratic, federal and social government based on the rule of law as provided by the Basic Law. Otherwise, each *Land* is free to shape its constitution as it wishes. The administration of *Land* courts is also independent of federal authorities. Differences in the specific needs of the *Länder*, and in their historical background, result in differences in their organisational and administrative structures. Nonetheless there are similarities, especially among *Länder* of similar size.

The organisational, personnel, fiscal, planning and territorial or administrative sovereignty of the local self-government bodies presents one of the important pillars of local democracy and provides local authorities with considerable scope to regulate their own affairs.

1.3 Responsibilities

Distribution of responsibilities

The primary function of the federal government is to prepare political decisions and legislation, while administrative responsibilities are mainly devolved to the *Länder* which have general competences. Tasks are then undertaken for the most part at the local level or, to a lesser degree, by the *Länder*. Compared to some other federal systems the scope of tasks undertaken by the federal administration is rather limited. The few areas which, according to the Basic Law, *must* be undertaken by federal authorities are the foreign service, federal finance, the armed forces, the federal waterways and the Federal Border Guard. The *Länder* are deeply involved in matters of security, police, civil defence and education (in partnership with semi-public bodies and churches). Some responsibilities are also shared between the federal government and the *Länder* (see below).

Local authorities: The municipalities are responsible for social matters. They provide financial services such as social assistance and housing allowances (paid out by the local authorities but financed by the federal government) and material services such as the provision of day-care centres and publicly funded housing, and counselling for underprivileged persons. These material services are rendered by municipality-owned institutions or through grants paid to independent non profit organisations.

In the education sector, the municipalities provide and maintain school buildings both for young persons and adults. Cultural institutions such as libraries, museums, theatres, orchestras and music schools are provided depending on the number of inhabitants. Sports facilities may be made available to sports clubs, often by putting school sports facilities to a dual use. In the technical field, local authorities draft land use and local development plans, construct buildings and roads, and create and maintain parks. Where the supply of electricity, gas and water has not been contracted-out to private companies, it is undertaken by the municipalities. Municipalities or counties are responsible for waste and sewage disposal as sovereign tasks under *Land* provisions.

Municipalities may choose from a variety of organisation patterns to fulfil these tasks. Services may be provided, for example, by the administration itself, by local-government owned enterprises, by enterprises which are owned by the municipalities but are organised under private law, or by private businesses commissioned to do so. Municipalities may also form joint authorities (*Zweckverbände*) to fulfil given tasks.

Mandatory, optional and shared responsibilities

The exclusive tasks of the *Länder* include the adoption and execution of *Land* law, and the execution of federal law, in so far as responsibility does not rest with federal authorities. The concept of co-operative federalism, promoted by Basic Law amendments in 1967-69, provides for tasks to be undertaken jointly by the Federal government and the *Länder*. Joint activities deal with matters such as regional economic structural policy and universities. Typically, responsibilities shared across all levels of government are found in the health and transport (roads) sectors.

To describe the responsibilities of the municipalities and counties in detail, one would have to address them *Land* by *Land*. Generally, a distinction is made between tasks which the municipalities and counties fulfil within their own remit and delegated tasks. The former include voluntary tasks as well as tasks which the local self-government bodies are under an obligation to fulfil.

Obligatory tasks of local authorities include building and maintaining primary and secondary schools, nurseries, cemeteries, fire brigades, water supply and sewerage systems. Voluntary tasks include the maintenance of libraries, children's homes and young people's clubs, homes for the elderly, sports facilities and parks, promotion of local businesses, cultural institutions, hospitals, swimming pools, and housing.

The counties tend to perform such tasks when they exceed the financial, administrative or technical capacity of the municipalities in the county. In order to fulfil their planning responsibilities, counties are increasingly united in regional associations.

The municipalities and counties perform numerous delegated and mandatory tasks as directed by the federal and *Land* levels or as their agents. These tasks, and the extent to which they are bound by instructions when executing them, vary. However, as opposed to self-government matters, local governments are not only subject to supervision as to the legality of these tasks but are also given detailed instructions on how to execute them. Delegated and mandatory tasks include the registration of births, marriages and deaths, matters relating to passports, responsibilities as the lower building law authority, looking after refugees, trade inspection, preparing elections to the *Bundestag* and the *Landtage* (*Länder* parliaments), health care, food inspection, roads, water supply and sewerage systems.

2. MANAGEMENT FUNCTIONS

2.1 Policy-making and co-ordination

Coherence, consultation and conflict resolution

The principle of *Länder* sovereignty implies that the Federal Parliament cannot object to laws passed by a *Land* parliament (if the constitutionality of a law is under question, only the federal and *Land* constitutional courts can decide).

About three-quarters of all federal statutes are addressed directly to the *Länder* and local governments and must be implemented by them. In this task they act independently and on their own responsibility. Only a few administrative tasks, which are in principle listed in the Basic Law, are carried out by the *Länder* as agents of the Federation.

Formal and informal mechanisms

The co-ordinating bodies for joint activities between the Federation and the *Länder* are planning committees in which representatives of both levels participate.

For the co-ordination of policies between the governmental tiers, high-level councils are set up. The most important one is the Financial Planning Council, which makes non-binding recommendations on the co-ordination of the budgets and financial plans of the federal government, the *Länder* and municipalities. It is chaired by the Federal Minister of Finance and consists of the *Länder* Ministers of Finance, the Federal Minister of Economics, and representatives of the municipalities and the German Federal Bank. It is assisted by a number of high-level experts. Another important committee, made up of representatives from federal and *Land* authorities and municipalities, is the Economic Policy Council chaired by the Federal Minister of Economics. Although such councils do not have any official decision-making power, their recommendations carry much weight in departmental policies. Consultative and advisory bodies assist at all levels of administration.

2.2 Financial management

Sources of revenue

Some 72 per cent of *Land* revenues are made up of *Land* taxes, such as capital tax, inheritance tax, and so-called joint taxes (i.e. taxes the revenue of which is shared by the Federation and the *Länder*, and sometimes also by the municipalities), such as turnover tax, corporation tax and income tax. The *Land* taxes account for approximately 13.5 per cent of *Land* revenue, income and corporation tax for approximately 53 per cent and turnover tax for some 27 per cent. Transfers account for another considerable share of *Land* revenues.

The Basic Law provides that the municipalities must get a share of federal tax revenues. A share of the revenue from income tax accrues directly to the municipalities. They also receive a percentage of the *Land* share of the tax revenues shared by the Federation and the *Länder* (income, corporation and turnover taxes). The municipalities are also entitled to revenues from the so-called taxes on objects, i.e. the land tax and the trade tax as well as from the local excise taxes and taxes on certain non-essential spendings (e.g. beverage tax, dog tax, entertainment tax, hunting and fishing taxes). The municipalities may vary these levels of taxation, and thus they have an instrument for attracting businesses. Tax revenues total approximately 38 per cent of all local revenues, the major tax receipts for local authorities being from the income tax and the trade tax.

Another source of independent local revenue is the fees and contributions for services provided by the local authorities to their citizens, although they only account for about 15 per cent of local revenues. The collection of such fees and contributions is governed by acts on local taxes issued by the *Länder*. The local authorities are free to assess the level of fees for tasks within their own remit. The levels of fees, however, must not exceed the costs. As costs are rising, there is an ongoing public discussion as to how to bring them down and whether tasks should be performed by private companies or contracted out.

Grants from Länder account for approximately 28 per cent of local revenues and thus present the second largest source of income. Most allocations are made within the framework of financial equalisation carried out in each Land and based on the code for allocation of revenue or on financial requirements. There is a complicated procedure for calculating the amount to be given to each municipality, based on its size and financial capacity, i.e. taking into consideration its local tax revenues. Where a municipality fulfils central functions such as maintaining schools, cultural and sports facilities, this increases its financial requirements. The financial equalisation at the local level is designed, above all, to equalise the financial capacities of the municipalities and thus to create equal standards of living. However, it is also aimed at enforcing political objectives at the Land level. In addition to the allocations under the financial equalisation process, the municipalities also receive allocations tied to specific purposes such as investments or running specific local institutions. The Federation also pays its part by allocating to the Länder funds for, e.g. promoting social housing, urban development projects and improving local transport. Thus, local allocations contain some elements of central control. On the other hand it would not be compatible with the right to local self-government if the Federation promoted local projects too purposefully, thus undermining the local scope of action.

The local authorities have other revenues, composing almost 20 per cent of the total, mainly in the form of income from rents, leases, gains transfers of local enterprises, royalties and property sales.

County revenues come mainly from the contributions paid by the municipalities belonging to it, from allocations made by the Federation and the Länder and, to a small extent, from fees.

All the figures mentioned above refer only to the situation in the old (West) German local authorities. Since 1995, the new (East) German local authorities have been fully tied into the federal fiscal and financial equalisation system, so that the structure of revenues will, over time, become similar across the country.

Table 2. **Revenues of sub-national governments (1985, 1990, 1995)**
(millions of DM and percentages)

	1985		1990		1995	
	Länder	Municipalities	Länder	Municipalities	Länder	Municipalities
Net revenue of which (percentages):	218 240.3	144 620.9	266 769.5	181 524.9	417 130.6	224 121.1
Taxes [1]	72.1	39.0	73.8	38.1	71.5	35.0
Federal government "United Germany" funds	14.5	–	14.6	–	15.5	–
General grants from Länder	–	13.4	–	12.9	–	12.8
Investment (capital) grants from Länder	–	6.2	–	6.0	–	4.5
Fees	–	12.2	–	13.1	–	14.8

1. The figures for municipalities include tax-like revenues.
Source: Federal Ministry of Finance.

Balance between discretion and control

The Federation and Länder manage their own budgets independently from each other but are bound by the Basic Law to take into account the requirements for general economic balance. They should also take account of recommendations of the Financial Planning Council (see 2.1).

The Basic Law provides that the Länder must pay for the tasks which they exercise for themselves. Where they act as agents of the Federation, the Federation covers the costs. Within the framework of co-operative federalism, the Federal government funds investments made by the Länder or the local

Table 3. **Expenditure of sub-national governments (1985, 1990, 1995)**
(millions of DM and percentages)

	1985 Länder	1985 Municipalities	1990 Länder	1990 Municipalities	1995 Länder	1995 Municipalities
Net expenditure	235 138.4	143 553.4	286 110.8	185 287.7	463 884.0	236 236.3
of which(percentages):						
Personnel	40.7	16.7	39.7	26.7	37.2	42.6
Interest repayments	7.9	3.3	7.7	4.3	6.8	6.8
Investments	16.6	14.6	15.8	24.6	16.8	32.6
Transfers to municipalities	17.9	–	18.8	–	21.8	–
Current expenditure for goods and services	–	11.6	–	18.4	–	28.6

Source: Federal Ministry of Finance.

authorities. But by doing so, the Federation can exert considerable influence on Länder and municipality policy. In the case of joint tasks, the Federation and the Länder share the financial burden equally.

The Basic Law provides that a reasonable amount of equalisation must take place between financially strong and financially weak Länder, taking into consideration the financial capacities and financial requirements of the municipalities or associations of municipalities. This is ensured by the distribution of tax revenues and by a system of supplementary allocations.

The Länder are responsible for ensuring that their municipalities are adequately funded. To equalise the different financial capacities of their municipalities, the Länder have adopted legal provisions on local financial equalisation. Also, the municipalities may transfer tasks which exceed their financial capacities, to supra-local units such as the counties.

A major factor in negotiations between the Federation and Länder on fiscal equalisation is that the negotiating partners are unequal. On one side is the Federation and on the other, the 16 Länder a majority of which must agree the solution. It is therefore usually easier for the Länder to get their way.

Issues concerning fiscal equalisation and levels of responsibility often count a great deal in policy appraisal, but they are of much less importance to most citizens who consider that essential public services should be carried out by "the government", irrespective of its levels. If urgent action is required, the first demand is that it be taken by the government, which is interpreted in the first instance by German citizens as the "Federal government". Consequently the central government and in particular the Federal Minister of Finance is held to account in many fields for which it is not responsible under the public finance system. This was the case in 1980 for example when a programme to combat AIDS had to be drawn up as quickly as possible. Although this was a task for the Länder, since the Federation's jurisdiction for health care is limited to legislation, it financed amenities and measures on a comprehensive basis for a transitional period.

2.3 Performance management

Mechanisms

Germany has traditionally been governed predominantly by the "rule of law", which means that control does not primarily focus on performance. The Basic Law excludes any federal control over the form or content of the Länder budgets, the preparation and implementation of which are entirely the responsibility of the Länder. The Land parliaments use the Land Courts of Audit (which have quasi-judicial independence) for supervision and control.

The Land Courts of Audit are mandated by the Land parliaments through committees to which they are accountable. They may themselves submit specific or general measures for examination. They are not bound by instructions from the Länder Ministries of Finance, nor by the administering sectoral departments.

In the municipalities, the budget serves as the reference base for the inspection authority in each municipality. The municipalities have internal auditing and, in some Länder, an independent organisation which controls the municipal budgets.

Quality standards

In Germany standards are set to respond to specific objectives, such as:

- environmental protection (e.g. air traffic noise control);
- social policy (e.g. identifying need for social help);
- traffic circulation (e.g. safety standards); and
- land-use planning (e.g. constructions standards).

Most such standards are established by the Länder, and resource allocation to municipalities is often tied to the observance of certain standards. When there is too much regulation, compliance with standards can incur excessive administrative costs, and the monitoring of standards also brings additional administrative burdens. During periods of budgetary constraint there is a tendency to suppress standards – and political objectives become more important (for example the right to a place in a kindergarten).

One of the main concerns behind the territorial reforms that took place between 1965 and 1977 at the local level was to enable the work of civil servants to become more professional so that bigger local authorities should mean better quality outputs for local services. Achieving an "optimum" size of community as a result of territorial reforms has also reduced administrative costs and has, in particular, simplified the monitoring function of the municipal inspection authorities. Nevertheless it remains difficult to draw conclusions on the impact of the restructuring of municipalities in economic terms.

Some efforts have also been made to implement quality standards in the municipalities. This development, which has occurred since the 1960s (rather early compared to many other European countries), is now part of general policy on quality improvement. It includes debureaucratisation efforts, citizen-oriented measures (e.g. citizens' offices), personnel development, and the introduction of internal contract management.

2.4 Human resource management

Statutory distinctions: The duties of the public service are discharged by civil servants (Beamte), employees (Angestellte), and workers (Arbeiter) at all levels of administration. The status of a Beamter is governed by public law; while Angestellte and Arbeiter are employed with private law contracts. The existence of a uniform public service across the country constitutes an important centralising element.

In the Länder and local authorities, the status of civil servants is regulated pursuant to federal framework provisions; and in the Federation their status is regulated by federal statute. The pay and benefits in all levels of the administration are regulated by federal statute. Representatives of all levels of government participate in determining the pay of civil servants, and the opinion of the civil servants themselves is taken into account. The legal status, pay and additional old-age pensions for employees and workers in the public service are mainly based on collective agreements concluded between the trade unions and the public employers of the Federation, Länder and municipalities. For the most senior positions, where conditions go beyond those covered by the collective agreement, "individual" contracts may be concluded with terms above the rates laid down in the collective agreement.

The Federal Ministry of the Interior plays a central role. It is responsible mainly for "exclusive" legislation on the status of persons employed by federal authorities and by federal corporations under public law. It also provides basic legal guidelines on the status of persons employed by the Länder, municipalities and other corporations under public law. Collective bargaining on wages and other benefits (e.g. holidays) takes place between the Federal Ministry of the Interior, together with representatives of the Länder and municipalities on behalf of the federal employer, and the trade unions for the public service employees and workers. Wages of the civil servants are voted by the Bundestag and follow generally the wage agreements for the public employees. The Federal Ministry of the Interior is also responsible for adjusting the pay of civil servants. The number of staff at the federal and sub-national levels is presented in Table 4. It shows that over 40 per cent of current public service employment in Germany is at the Land level and a further 30 per cent is in the municipalities.

Table 4. **Public service employment in Germany (1991, 1992, 1993)**[1]
(30 June, head count, full-time and part-time)

	1991	1992	1993
Direct public service of which:	**6 412 600**	**6 305 000**	**6 114 700**
Federation [2],[3]	652 000	624 700	602 900
Länder [3]	2 572 000	2 531 300	2 511 100
Municipalities	1 995 900	2 015 200	1 883 800
Inter-municipal associations	55 500	58 300	62 400
German Railways	473 800	433 900	417 700
German Post and Telecommunications	663 500	641 500	636 800
Indirect public service	**325 100**	**352 200**	**387 800**
TOTAL	**6 737 800**	**6 657 200**	**6 502 500**

1. Sum of the former Federal Republic, new Länder and East Berlin.
2. Including military conscripts (257 300 in 1991, 245 800 in 1992 and 230 900 in 1993).
3. Including police.

Source: Federal Statistical Office.

Mobility is possible under specific circumstances within the German public service in the form of temporary secondment to another public authority (*Abordnung*); temporary or permanent internal transfer (*Umsetzung*); or permanent transfer to another public authority (*Versetzung*). A Bill on public service law reform is currently in the legislative process and aims to further increase the mobility of civil servants by extending the period of secondment to five years and extending possibilities of transfers.

3. TRENDS IN REDISTRIBUTING AUTHORITY ACROSS LEVELS OF GOVERNMENT

3.1 Evolving tendencies

After the collapse of the highly centralised Nationalist Socialist State, local self-government was re-instituted as the first step to promote a democratic federal political culture. The decentralised political process is reflected in the constitutional provisions of the Länder which were created then and later (1949) in the Basic Law of the Federal Republic of Germany.

The 1969 constitutional reform partly altered the legal base of the relations between the levels of government. The newly introduced joint tasks (*Gemeinschaftsaufgaben*), which include joint planning, decision-making and financing, are geared to achieving national objectives, settling conflicts among the regions, reducing economic imbalances between regions, and rationalising the use of resources. The Länder, however, have retained extensive rights to participate in drafting federal policies. The towns, municipalities and counties, which are grouped together in local authority associations, also have considerable possibilities for influencing federal policies. Co-ordination and consensus were the staple rule of inter-governmental relations. The same applies to the relations between the Länder and the municipalities. Joint decision-making harboured some problems, however, as it was difficult to determine clear priorities when making joint plans; the Länder and municipalities protected their remits against federal interference; and joint decision processes in the co-operative federalism supported the dominant role of the executive power vis-à-vis the elected political decision bodies.

Furthermore, co-operation among the administrative levels turned into barter trade hardly conceivable from outside.

There have been two main trends over the last decades:

- Local government reforms: The local territorial restructuring was aimed at increasing the administrative capability of the local levels so as to improve land use planning and local self-government.

- Improving citizen participation: Apart from territorial reforms, some *Länder* carried out far-reaching reforms of the provisions on the nature of local government. These aimed not only at promoting local self-government and increasing the administrative capability of the local levels, but also at strengthening the influence of citizens and giving them more scope for participation. This has been achieved by introducing the direct election of the mayor or the chief executive official in almost all *Länder*. Additionally, the instruments of the referendum (*Bürgerentscheid*) and provisions for the electorate to request a referendum (*Bürgerbegehren*) have been introduced. These steps have enabled the electorate to influence decisions (between local elections) on individual matters falling within the sphere of local government.

3.2 The current debate

The Federal government presently considers the reform of public administration as a central political task. In this context, specific importance is attached to the reform of public service law. In October 1995, the Federal government presented a bill designed to orientate public service law as a whole more to the principles of merit and performance, and to make its application more flexible and transparent.

In the framework of the public service law reform, public employers will be given more opportunity to be performance-oriented, flexible and geared to the specific requirements of circumstances. For instance, it is intended to facilitate secondments and transfers – (including to other career structures and posts) – in order to make best possible use of the personnel resources of the public service by increased mobility of the staff – both with regard to expertise and place of employment – but against a background of staff reduction and reallocation.

Furthermore, it is planned to assign senior management posts for an initial period of two years. Only if the candidate proves him or herself on that post, will he/she be assigned on a long-term basis. And before any other promotion, civil servants will have to prove their qualification for a higher-rated post in a probation period with the new functions.

The idea of the merit principle is, in particular, strengthened by the introduction of new performance-oriented elements in the pay system. These are accompanied by stronger differentiation in the practice of efficiency rating by preventing assessors from giving too many candidates top marks (for example by fixing general quota for specific marks).

In July 1995 the "Lean State Advisory Council" was created by the Federal Cabinet as an institution independent of the administration and constituted by the Federal Minister of the Interior in September 1995 with 17 members representing all levels of government, industry, the trade unions and academia. Its secretariat is located in the Federal Ministry of the Interior. Within a year of its constitution, a number of recommendations had been made and some were already being implemented. A conference in early 1997 will mark the end of its work. Matters to be addressed in the final report will include ways of easing the burden on the judicial system, reducing the number of legal standards, improving personnel management and possible privatisations.

There has been more discussion recently about reforms in public administration. In the area of local government, it has been above all the Joint Local Government Agency for the Simplification of Administrative Procedures (*Kommunale Gemeinschaftsstelle für Verwaltungsvereinfachung*) which has made reform proposals. These refer especially to organisational change and the budget process. The latter envisaged that the implementation of the budget would be made more flexible and that responsibility for the budget would be decentralised, i.e. responsibilities will be delegated to largely independent divisions. The political management of the local authority would restrict itself to giving guidelines or to setting an objective to be achieved by means of the funds earmarked for it. Business-type elements are to be increased, requiring some amendments to the local budget law. As a first step, such amendments should be tested in a geographically limited area. The objective is to step up the capability of the local authorities, taking into account the principle of cost-effectiveness and to enable them to become service centres closer to the citizens.

3.3 Driving forces

Financial problems: Since the mid 1970s, the consequences of tighter public resources and the rising number of political and administrative deadlocks have come under increasing criticism. Over-regulation and bureaucratisation have been the key words used in the debate. The critics have also called for consolidation measures and for the deregulation and privatisation of public institutions and for turning back to self-help.

Economic and social forces: In the 1950s and 1960s, the gradual emergence of the welfare State started to reduce the importance and autonomy of local authorities. The increasing detail of legal provisions and the financial consequences arising from them restricted the room for manoeuvre and the financial scope of local authorities. The Federation managed to influence decentralised politics only by granting financial incentives to the lower levels.

The post-war boom ended with the recession of 1966/67. In its wake, problems which had previously been obscured by continuous economic growth became apparent. Macro-economic management, the harmonisation of social conflicts, the equalisation of horizontal/vertical and social/regional disparities, ecological dilemmas – all required increased governmental intervention and changes in the relationships between federal, *Länder* and local government (cf. the 1969 constitutional reforms).

Over the last decades, the changes in the Federal Republic's economic and socio-cultural structure have confronted both central and local institutions with the need for significant modifications in their routine tasks. Economic structural change is a national task, even if there are calls for the use of decentralised means. There is a discussion going on about the future of federalism in the unified Germany. Questions have arisen about reducing the number of *Länder*, improving administrative action by simplifying law and administration and by making organisational work processes in the administration more efficient, critically evaluating tasks and contracting-out some of them. As a result of the new socio-economic and cultural context, the political importance of local government, particularly in the metropolitan areas has grown: decentralisation, the "re-discovery" of local self-government and the call for a "grass roots revival of politics" are all being discussed.

GREECE

1. INSTITUTIONS AND AUTHORITY

1.1 Structures

Description of levels

Sub-national administration in Greece is divided into deconcentrated central government agencies and authorities and local self-government, which includes "first tier" and "second tier" authorities as shown in Table 1. The existence of a deconcentrated structure of central government and of first tier self-government (municipalities and communities) is entrenched in the 1975 Constitution. Special arrangements have been developed for the urban agglomerations of Athens and Thessaloniki. The prefectoral system of regional administration was introduced in 1833, soon after the creation of the modern Greek State. The system of local government, which was already in existence under the Ottoman occupation, was confirmed by law in the same year.

Table 1. **Relationship between geographical divisions and sub-national administration levels**

Geographical divisions	Regional or supra-prefectoral	Prefectoral (*nomarchiako*) ("second tier" authorities)	Sub-prefectoral	Local ("first tier" authorities)
Region	Administrative Region [13] (appointed)			
Prefecture (*Nomos*)		Administrative Regional Services under a Secretary-General (appointed) [54] Prefectoral Self-Government (PSG) (elected) [1] [50]		
Local			Area Council (local authority unions, formed by central government)	Local Self-Government Organization (OTA) (elected): Municipality [434] and Community [5 394]

1. The term "self-government" is used to cover two elected tiers of sub-national government. Local self-government organisations, i.e. municipalities and communities are known in Greece as "first tier" authorities; while prefectoral self-governments are "second tier" authorities.

The prefecture (*nomos*), headed in the past by a central government-appointed prefect who has been phased out and replaced by elected prefectoral authorities, is now known as second tier local self-government. Newly elected prefects were installed on 1 January 1995, and since then the country has been going through a transitional period of regional government.

First tier local government units are called "organisations of local self-government" (*organismoi topikis aftodioikisis* or OTA). There are two types of OTA: Municipality (*dimos*) and community (*koinotita*). Municipalities with a population over 150 000 are sub-divided into "municipal departments" (*dimotika diamerismata*). A municipality or community can divide its area into neighbourhoods and set up "neighbourhood councils" (*synoikiaka symvoulia*). Self-contained settlements (*synoikismoi*) of over 150 inhabitants have a delegate in the council of the local authority of which they are part.

Central government at sub-national levels

Deconcentrated State authorities exist at two levels, that of the 13 "administrative regions" and that of the 54 prefectures (*nomos*) under a "Secretary-General". A region includes several prefectures and a regional development fund operates in each region as a legal entity of private law.

Table 2 provides information on the number of prefectures included in each administrative region and its total area and population. There are branches of the central government's administrative regions known as Regional Administration Services, in each prefecture. There are now also 50 prefectoral self-governments (PSGs), including one which covers the area of the Athens and Piraeus prefectures. The number of municipalities and communities tends to change every year either because former communities are given municipal status or because several communities are merged into a single municipality.

Table 2. **Administrative regions and prefectures**

Administrative Region	Number of prefectures	Area (1 000 km^2)	Population 1 000s (1991)
Eastern Macedonia and Thrace	5	14.2	570
Central Macedonia	7	18.8	1 736
Western Macedonia	4	9.5	293
Epirus	4	9.2	339
Thessaly	4	14.0	731
Ionian Islands	4	2.3	191
Western Greece [1]	3	11.4	702
Central (Sterea) Greece	5	15.5	579
Attica	4	3.8	3 523 [2]
Peloponnese [1]	5	15.5	606
North Aegean	3	3.8	198
South Aegean	2	5.3	263
Crete	4	8.3	437
Greece	54	132.0	10 264

1. Part of the geographical division of the Peloponnese belongs to the administrative region of Western Greece.
2. Aggregate figure of the 4 *nomoi* of the region of Attica: Athens (1 157), Western Attica (645), Eastern Attica (765), and Piraeus (956).

Creation, elimination and restructuring

Sub-national administration was restructured in 1994, with two successive acts of parliament, which updated and extended the provisions contained in legislation of 1986. Further amendments were introduced in 1995. The aim of this reform, which took place in two stages, was (a) to establish a level of regional administration, with an important role in development planning, and (b) to replace the traditional, central government-appointed, prefectoral administration by elected, "second tier", self-government. This restructuring was a declared government policy since the early 1980s. The objectives were, in the first case, to modernise public administration in the regions, to strengthen development planning, to ensure better sectoral co-ordination and to improve co-operation with local government. In the second case, the objectives were to involve elected local authorities more effectively in political life and economic development, to provide higher quality services to citizens, and to enhance local cultural identity.

Administrative regions are created by presidential decree, as authorized by law. The institution of prefectoral self-governments (PSGs) was introduced by law in 1994 to replace the existing centrally-appointed prefectoral administrations. New PSGs can be created by presidential decree, authorised by law. Area councils are being created by presidential decree, which is issued once, under the specific authorisation contained in the 1994 legislation. Several have been created already.

New first tier organisations of local self-government (municipalities and communities) are also created by presidential decree, signed by the Minister of the Interior, on the advice of a special committee functioning in each prefecture. Municipal departments and neighbourhood councils are created by the local authority concerned, but in the first case the decision is automatically taken, once the necessary population threshold is exceeded, while in the second case the decision is optional. Since 1994, the general rule for the designation of a municipality is that it must have a population exceeding 5 000 or be the capital of a prefecture or be a spa or historic settlement. Prior to 1994 the population limit was 10 000. The municipality of Athens, with a population of 772 000 is the largest in the country, but it is only part of Greater Athens, which has a population of over 3 000 000. Communities (*Koinatita*) are local authorities which do not qualify for municipal status. The condition for the creation of a new village is that it should have a population exceeding 1 500, that the population remaining in the village from which it is being detached is not less than 2 000, and that the new community should be financially viable. There are incentives for the creation of municipalities out of existing communities. The large majority of communities have a population below 1 000, and many fewer than 200.

Regional development funds were created by law in 1994. The new administrative regions like the old style prefectures, are not separate legal identities, but legally part of the State, in contrast to the elected first and second tier local governments, which are legal bodies under public law. Under the old prefectural system, the execution and management of public works in every prefecture was entrusted to the prefectural fund, a legal identity of public law, chaired by the prefect. Prefectural funds are now being abolished as the new prefectural self-governments take over and assume the functions of the prefectural funds. However, the regional development funds (which are legal bodies of private law) are responsible for managing public investment and European Union funds and for assigning funding to, for example, the prefectural self-governments.

Control bodies

The legality of the actions of a regional administration is controlled by the Minister of the Interior, who appoints the General Secretary of the region. Such control can be exercised on the initiative of the minister, either *ex ante* or *ex post*. It can also be exercised following a formal petition of individual citizens. In contrast to the control of legality, the control of whether a particular action is advisable or expedient (*elenhos skopimotitas*), exists only when specifically instituted. Administrative performance is subject to assessment by the minister in charge.

The actions of elected local authorities are not subject to control of expediency. This type of control was explicitly abolished in 1994. The same law introduced a control procedure based on a special committee, functioning in the seat of every prefectural self-government. The General Secretary of the region concerned can refer any action which he deems to be illegal to this committee. Individual citizens can also appeal to the General Secretary of the region, or, if the committee has already passed judgement, to the appropriate minister, under new legislation. The same committee can pass judgement following a petition by citizens against the actions of municipalities and communities. An appeal can be made to the appropriate minister, as in the previous case. The procedure of referral to the above special committee, and of control exercised by the General Secretary over the legality of actions of prefectural self-governments, applies also in the case of municipalities and communities. Second-tier local government has no control powers over first tier local authorities.

Control in cases of maladministration can be exercised by the "public administration controllers", at the initiative of the Minister to the Prime Minister. Financial control is primarily exercised by public auditors, who are members of the Auditors' Court (*elengtiko synedrio*), which is both a court and an administrative body, and by the branch services of the Ministry of Finance. Decisions of the administration can be challenged before administrative courts and, on appeal or in a number of cases directly, before the Council of State (*Symvoulio Epikrateias*).

1.2 Powers

Nature of sub-national institutions

Under both the old (centrally appointed) and the new (elected) prefectural system, the prefecture administration includes a large number of sectoral directorates (e.g. Town Planning and Engineering Services or Development Planning and Management). The central government has issued guidance to all newly elected prefectural self-governments (PSG) to assist them in drafting their own statute and internal organisation chart. Each PSG had the freedom to introduce its own particular requirements and variations and to approve its own statute and charter, in accordance with the 1994 legislation. The General Secretary of each administrative region merely checked the legality of the procedure. These statutes incorporate existing provisions of delegation of power from central government ministries to prefects, but there is not a comprehensive register of administrative acts delegating powers and responsibilities to prefects.

A typical administrative structure of a PSG has 15 directorates, which with the exception of the Planning and Programming Directorate are grouped in five sectors, each under the control of a prefectoral committee as follows:

- Planning and Programming Directorate;
- Administration \ Finance \ Trade \ Transport and Communication Committee;
- Public Works \ Environment \ Industry and Energy Committee;
- Agriculture \ Stock Breeding \ Fisheries and Forestry Committee;
- Education \ Culture \ Tourism and Sports Committee;
- Health \ Welfare and Employment Committee.

The bodies of the rather complex variety of sub-national administration are summarised below.

Administrative Region:

- Regional Council, composed of the General Secretary of the region as chairman, the elected "*nomarches*" (prefects) of the region, the chairmen of unitary prefectoral self-governments, and representatives of first-tier local self-government, professional organisations, business chambers and agricultural or trade unions;
- General Secretary of the region, appointed by the central government as government representative in the region and administrative head of the regional services of central government ministries.

Regional Development Fund:

- Administrative Board, with members appointed by its chairman, i.e. the General Secretary of the region, from among the members of the regional council;
- Chairman of the Fund's Administrative Board.

Prefectoral Self-Government (elected), introduced on 1 January 1995:

- Prefectoral Council, the main decision-making body in second tier local government, with elected members whose number varies between 21 and 43;
- prefectoral committees, composed of council members and charged either with sectoral responsibilities or to represent the provinces (*eparchies*), which exist in certain prefectures, especially those fragmented into several islands;
- Prefect (*nomarchis*), elected majority leader in the council and head of the prefecture's administration;
- the prefecture's advisory Economic and Social Committee, with members representing first tier local authorities, trade unions, professional chambers, employers' organisations, rural co-operatives etc.

Unitary Prefectoral Self-Government (elected), introduced on 1 January 1995:

- Prefectoral Self-Government Council, composed of all the elected prefectoral council members of the constituent prefectoral departments;

- Chairman of Prefectoral Self-Government (elected), who chairs its council and heads its administration, excluding that of the constituent departments.

Prefectoral Department, introduced on 1 January 1995:

- as in prefectoral self-governments, but within a unitary prefectoral self-government.

Area Council (i.e. association of organisations of local self government):

- Administrative Board (equivalent to the municipal council), composed of elected councillors of the constituent local authorities;
- Executive Committee (equivalent to the mayoral committee of a municipality);
- Chairman (equivalent to the mayor and the municipal council chairman).

Municipality:

- Municipal Council, the main municipal decision-making body with elected members whose number varies between 11 and 41;
- Mayoral Committee, which has 2 to 6 members and is chaired by the mayor or a deputy mayor;
- Mayor, elected majority leader in the council and head of the municipality's administration, assisted by deputy mayors;
- department councils and chairmen, for those municipalities divided into municipal departments because of their size;
- neighbourhood assemblies, councils and chairmen in case a municipality has created neighbourhood councils;

Community:

- Community Council, the main decision-making body with elected members, whose number varies between 7 and 11;
- Community Chairman, elected majority leader in the council and head of the administration;
- neighbourhood assemblies, councils and chairmen in the rare case of a community, which has created neighbourhood councils.

Type and degree of autonomy

Within the framework of existing legislation, a local authority can formulate its own policy and issue administrative acts (*kanonistikes apofaseis*) containing legal rules, in the form of by-laws. The share of certain taxes (income tax or property transaction tax) which is distributed to local self-government is fixed by central government. The latter can fix certain rates (e.g. for advertising, parking, or granting building permits) when they have been given this power, but they are often faced with local resistance. Theoretically, local authorities can impose or increase rates, such as those mentioned above. Freedom to finance local government activity has therefore increased, but is checked by their inability to collect rates or to overcome local resistance to the imposition of new rates or the increase of old ones.

The degree of autonomy and policy freedom of prefectoral self-governments (PSGs) depends on the powers delegated to them by presidential decrees, in accordance with the 1994 legislation. PSGs, like first-tier authorities, can impose rates and have the right to issue administrative acts containing regulations, in those areas for which they are responsible. These authorities have generally inherited the powers of the appointed prefects, although some of them have been delegated to Regional Directors, i.e. to officials of deconcentrated central government. This issue is not yet settled. The administration of hospitals, for example, is now a responsibility of Regional Directors and not of elected prefects, as was the case with the appointed prefects.

Administrative regions have considerable policy making powers, through their participation in development planning, subject however to approval by the Ministry of National Economy. Through the regional development funds created in 1994, which they control, the administrative regions can manage funds allocated to them and impose rates.

Some redistribution of power is now taking place with the gradual implementation of the 1994 legislation on prefectoral self-government. Much depends on the powers to be delegated to the new second-tier local self-government and the powers which will be retained for the central government. Problems arise in the case of conflict with prior sectoral legislation. Health legislation, for example, requires that local health centres be supervised by prefectoral hospitals. In terms of administrative responsibility, the intention to allocate the former to municipalities and the latter to PSGS runs counter to the provision of the legislation on self-government which stipulates that there will be no relationship of control or dependence between its two tiers.

1.3 Responsibilities

Distribution of responsibilities

Local self-governments are charged with the administration of local affairs, the precise definition of which is currently a matter of debate as although local government responsibilities are stated in the Municipal and Community Code, the list is not exhaustive. These responsibilities were extended in 1994 legislation. Further amendments to the Municipal and Community Code were made in 1995. Hospitals, and, indirectly, local health centres, are still supervised by (appointed) regional directors and not by elected prefects or municipalities, while in the field of education, municipalities are now responsible for building maintenance, but staff administration for both primary and secondary education is entrusted to prefectoral self-governments.

Municipalities and communities remain responsible for a broad range of policies and programmes, which they are empowered to implement and execute, subject to the financial means available. These include social and cultural facilities, municipal infrastructure, refuse collection and disposal, urban development programmes, town plan implementation, traffic management, commercial and industrial premises, and manpower development programmes. Municipal companies may be set up either to undertake construction or to engage in economic activities, such as the development of tourism.

Mandatory, optional and shared responsibilities

The crucial distinction between mandatory and optional activities is between activities for which rates are collected in return for delivered services, and activities financed from revenue which is not tied to mandatory municipal services. The latter are in theory very extensive, but in practice restricted by the availability of funds, staffing and political considerations. A local authority is free to request additional responsibilities (such as amending town plans, granting building permits or managing kindergartens) provided that it satisfies certain requirements.

Local authorities now have a considerably extended list of exclusive responsibilities. Until 1994 the Municipal and Community Code referred separately to exclusive and concurrent responsibilities. The latter were responsibilities which were not normally exclusive local government responsibilities, but which could be undertaken if the local council so decided. This distinction was abolished in the 1994 legislation which refers to activities which are "especially the responsibility of municipalities and communities". However, there remain responsibilities which are optional for local authorities, e.g. kindergartens, local bus operations or town planning.

A form of shared responsibility is the formation of an association of local authorities e.g. for a particular service. However, responsibility then rests with the association and not with the authorities which created it. The same is also true of development associations.

Shared responsibilities between central government and its deconcentrated government agencies in the regions depend on the extent of power delegated to prefects or regional secretaries.

2. MANAGEMENT FUNCTIONS

2.1 Policy-making and co-ordination

Coherence, consultation and conflict resolution

The aim of the system of development planning established in 1986 was to ensure vertical and horizontal coherence between national, regional, prefectoral and local development policy through a hierarchy of development plans. It remains to be seen how the system introduced by new legislation in 1994 will work under the new regime of sub-national government. Meanwhile the vertical co-ordination of development policy takes place through the Community Support Framework 1994-99, agreed between the European Union and the Greek government. It has 13 regional operational programmes and a large number of sectoral operational programmes, which bind all levels of government to a strictly controlled investment programme.

There is no formal provision for specialised co-ordination units within either deconcentrated agencies or elected local governments, other than the administrative organs (councils, committees, etc.), already mentioned earlier. However, the model of a group of special advisors acting as policy co-ordinators, already in existence in the office of central government ministers, has now been adopted for the office of mayors and elected prefects.

Apart from the possibility of formal appeals, the Greek administration and political system favours conflict resolution through informal routes and procedures which, although lacking transparency and independence from party politics, are sometimes more effective in defusing conflictual situations. This tends to reinforce political clientelism and to obstruct administrative modernisation and collective decision making.

Formal and informal mechanisms

In the Greek government system, the role of the ministers remains dominant, despite the introduction of local self-government. This is due to the small size of the country, the extensive powers held by ministers and the dependence of sub-national administration on delegated powers and funds. Hence, the lead role in co-ordination is inevitably reserved for central government ministries and the minister remains the final arbiter in all matters.

At the regional level, the General Secretary is the central government's representative with responsibility for implementing government policy, a role reserved in the past for the appointed prefect. This power, and the presence in every prefecture of services of central government which report to the General Secretary, makes it clear that the new regional authorities will have important duties of co-ordination, a function until now rather weak in the Greek administration.

2.2 Financial management

Sources of revenue

At the regional level, the programmes and works executed by the Regional Development Fund (RDF) are financed from the central government's public investment budget, from other public sector organisations or from European Union programmes. The RDF's own main sources of revenue will be a percentage of all funding for the region which it is handling, a share from the region's participation in European Union programmes, rates, dues for the use of services offered, and borrowing.

The revenues of the elected prefectoral and local self-governments are divided into ordinary and extraordinary. At the prefectoral level, ordinary revenues include a share from national taxes and centrally reserved resources, local rates and dues, as instituted by law, an annual central government grant for the discharge of responsibilities delegated from central government, credits from the public investment programme, income from property, and "reciprocal" fees charged "in return" for specific services. Extraordinary revenues include mainly loans and donations, government subventions, European Union grants, revenues from sales of property, and charges for the use of works financed from borrowing.

Ordinary revenues of the municipalities and villages include:

- grants as a share of income tax, vehicle licence fees and property transaction tax;
- income from property;
- dues and "reciprocal" fees for services; and
- various other municipal taxes, fees, dues and specific contributions.

The share of income tax and vehicle licence fees allocated to municipalities and villages is distributed mainly, but not exclusively, on the basis of population. Property transaction taxes are levied but the main municipal tax is levied on properties on the basis of floorspace for which electricity is supplied. All taxes require prior national legislation.

Fees are imposed by the local authorities themselves. Some are "reciprocal", e.g. the municipal fees for cleaning and refuse collection and water rates. Other categories of fees include those for the use of open space, for advertising, parking, obtaining a building permit, and charges on hotel and restaurant bills. Traffic and other fines are also included in ordinary revenues. Dues are also imposed by the local authorities and are collected for the use of municipal facilities and premises such as cemeteries, slaughterhouses and markets, for the use of pastures, for trading bottled mineral water, etc. Contributions (*eisfores*) on the other hand require national legislation, in the form of a presidential decree. Contributions are a special form of revenue, collected when a particular area is covered for the first time with a statutory town plan. When this happens, contributions, proportional to the size of property, are paid by property owners whose land is brought into the town plan, either in cash or in the form of land appropriated for the provision of public facilities. Another type of revenue classified in local government law as a contribution, is the voluntary payment made by individuals for the construction of municipal works, from which the persons concerned expect to benefit. Municipalities and communities also receive extraordinary revenues similar to those of prefectoral self-governments.

Regional Secretary-Generals can delete from the budget of a municipality or community any expenditures and revenues which are not legal, and can enter mandatory expenditures, which have been omitted. He can also order the raising of additional revenue, if the budget is not balanced (power of "substitution").

Table 3. **Main revenue sources of sub-national governments (1982, 1989)**
(percentage)

	1982	1989
Ordinary	57.1	51.5
Property revenue	3.6	3.4
Rates and dues	23.9	18.6
Taxes and other sources	29.6	29.5
Extraordinary	26.9	35.5
Grants and subsidies	12.3	24.4
Other	14.6	11.1
Revenue from previous fiscal years	4.6	3.5
Balances	11.3	9.5
TOTAL	99.9	100.0

This table was calculated from statistical yearbook data and refers to first tier local self-government only (i.e. municipalities and communities). The statistics are collected by the National Statistical Service from Ministry of Finance sources and are not totally compatible with the classification used in the Municipal and Community Code and in this report.

Expenditure responsibilities

Municipal and community expenditures are classified into mandatory and optional. According to the Municipal and Community Code, mandatory expenditures include administration and management expenses, including salaries and rents, repayment of debts, annual contributions to local government associations, and grants to foundations and organisations created by the local authorities themselves. Optional expenditures can be included in the budget at the discretion of the local authorities. Expenditures for the execution of projects and public works must be included in the budget before work starts.

Table 4. **Main expenditure patterns of sub-national governments (1982, 1989)**
(percentage)[1]

	1982	1989
General	10.7	7.8
Special	79.2	75.9
Salaries and wages	34.4	28.3
Investment	30.7	27.8
Other	14.1	9.8
Transfer payments	2.2	7.0
Interest payments	1.9	2.7
Other	6.0	6.6
TOTAL	100.0	100.0

1. See note to previous table.

Balance between discretion and control

With the exception of mandatory expenditures and reciprocal fees, the freedom of local authorities to finance their activities has increased in the last decade. The range of activities in which they can engage has expanded considerably, at least on paper, in the fields of culture, social welfare, town planning and public works. They can also raise additional revenue, borrow in the private market or enter into agreements with other public or private bodies. The main limitations are the general fiscal squeeze in the Greek economy and citizen resistance to an increase in local government rates. At a time of intense central government effort to broaden the tax base and combat tax evasion, conditions are not considered to be appropriate for an increase in local rates.

Budgetary control in the public sector is generally exercised by the central or regional officials of the Ministry of Finance. Control of financial management is exercised by public auditors who are members of the Auditors' Court, which is both a court and an administrative body. Budgets of public corporations are subject to the control of the appropriate ministry, and control over their financial management is the responsibility of chartered accountants.

2.3 Performance management

There is no established procedure for the assessment of performance across levels of government. Quality standards are not used. Effective use of investment funds is a yardstick used to assess efficiency of performance, but in a rather erratic way. No supervisory powers exist between the two tiers of elected local authorities. Control of the latter by centrally appointed regional administrations is limited to legality of action and no longer extends to purpose. The main innovation which is currently being introduced in the field of performance assessment is the use of private project managers and evaluators for programmes and projects financed partly by the European Union (EU). This is already happening in the case of Regional Operational Programmes or major infrastructure projects funded out of the EU Community Support Framework. Such programmes require that performance standards be set in advance for monitoring purposes.

2.4 Human resource management

Statutory distinctions

Public sector personnel, including those in central government and its deconcentrated bodies, and in local self-governments, are classified into categories and grades. Categories are determined according to level of education and professional and specialised skills may require specific qualifications. A separate category of "special posts" covers some senior central government officials. Otherwise, grade A civil servants can serve as heads of general directorates, directorates, and sections, etc. Grades and posts are not automatically linked, such that grade A employees do not necessarily for example hold the post of unit head.

The basic civil service statute is the Presidential Decree, known as the Civil Service Code, and its subsequent amendments, including legislation enacted in 1994. A separate statute deals with local self-government personnel, but all legislation concerning them repeatedly refers to the Civil Service Code. Thus, issues such as personnel grades, appointments and staffing are dealt with in legislation applying equally to all posts of the public sector. The 1994 legislation on local self-government explicitly states that the hiring and appointment of staff is regulated by the same statute as that which applies to central government civil servants and public corporation personnel.

Table 5. **Public sector employment by level of government (1990-94)**
(at 31 December each year)

	1990	1991	1992	1993	1994
Ministries	231 558	234 006	228 509	235 568	230 250
Public establishments	89 230	84 234	85 361	86 712	92 966
Local authorities	39 995	41 078	41 575	42 129	39 693
Public enterprises	137 500	133 565	115 867	113 321	120 507
Public Enterprise Rehabilitation Board	21 899	13 644	4 163	3 932	4 408
TOTAL	520 182	506 527	475 475	481 662	487 824

Source: *Public Management Developments: Update 1995*, OECD, 1995.

Managerial autonomy

All civil servants are placed on a 23-point salary scale. Negotiations between employees and employers are organised nationally, given that salary increases and other claims are settled at the level of central government. In the case of local government, although the employer is the authority concerned, bargaining is conducted with the central government.

Final decisions on levels of staffing are also made by central government. Appointments of permanent staff are made only if vacancies exist in the authority concerned. Exceptions however can be made, in which case a personal post is created. Apart from permanent staff, recruitment of staff employed under private law for an indefinite period, but without civil servant status, is also possible. Recruitment in all cases is based on estimates of need and demands made by the authority concerned, but final decisions are made by the central government. Appointments of university graduates (except when specific degrees are required), technical education graduates and holders of secondary education qualifications are decided on the basis of a public examination, organised by a special national body. A centrally administered system of points is used for the appointment of university graduates with specified degrees or holders of compulsory education qualifications. Different procedures apply in the case of special scientific personnel or temporary employees, at all levels of government.

Managerial autonomy on pay is limited to appointments to posts of heads of units, which carry a special salary allowance, or to granting certain additional benefits. Salary graduations are virtually automatic. A prerequisite for promotion is a minimum number of years spent in a particular grade. Employees considered as worthy of promotion are included in promotion lists, compiled by service councils, which take into account assessment reports. All those included in these tables are automatically promoted. Dismissals are only justified in the case of a serious breach of discipline, or more rarely, in the case of a public sector agency being abolished.

Mobility

Mobility between levels of government is limited, although civil servants can be transferred from central departments to deconcentrated services. A list of employees to be considered for transfer is compiled on the basis of a points system, but in practice, transfers are rare and temporary secondments are preferred. Voluntary moves are currently being encouraged. Transfers between regional authorities and secondments to local authorities are possible, but unusual. A real threat to prefectoral self-governments is the tendency of their staff, who until recently enjoyed the status of central government civil servants, to seek a transfer to services remaining under the authority of central government, for fear that their promotion or retirement prospects will suffer under their new status as local self-government employees.

2.5 Regulatory management and reform

The 1975 Constitution (article 102) stipulates that local affairs are the responsibility of local self-government of which municipalities and villages constitute the first tier, while other tiers will be determined by law. Second and third-tier authorities were created in 1986 and then 1994. Despite the new administrative structures created in the regions and the replacement of appointed prefects by elected ones, rule-making has remained essentially in the hands of central government. Certain powers of approval, licensing and enforcement have, however, been devolved to lower levels of government. Economic development and land use planning are basically the responsibility of central ministries or their regional branches and only the less important investment decisions or plan amendments are independently determined at a lower level. However, this does not exclude instances of local self-governments sometimes exceeding their powers or expenditure targets.

A prefect or municipality may have the power to amend certain types of plan or to make amendments within certain limits beyond which only the minister has decision making authority. The current problem is the uncertainty surrounding the powers of prefects, and in particular of the chairmen of unitary prefectoral self-governments, who remain without a clear role and with few resources.

Local government reforms since the mid-1980s put much emphasis on creating co-operative arrangements between government agencies at all levels and on uniting small local authorities into more viable organisations. New municipalities, municipal associations and, more recently, area councils were created but there is as yet little evidence to suggest that the task of making and enforcing rules has appreciably improved.

Sub-national governments rarely see it as their role to facilitate the operation of private business and to create a favourable climate for entrepreneurship. Hence, it is too early to speak of competition among units of regional or local government in an effort to attract private firms, by reducing the impact of unnecessary regulation. The bulk of the administration (central, regional and local) still largely perceives its role as that of a controller, rather than as that of an enabler. The absence of streamlined and transparent procedures, acts as a further obstacle to the smooth operation of the market. Administrative behaviour requires generally over-bureaucratic and discourages individual initiative and low salaries and poor rewards fuel indifference and are detrimental to business interests.

3. TRENDS IN REDISTRIBUTING AUTHORITY ACROSS LEVELS OF GOVERNMENT

3.1 Evolving tendencies

Reforms in the structures and responsibilities of, especially, regional government, are too recent to identify evolving tendencies. The recent past has however been marked by some conflicting tendencies, first in favour of prefectoral decentralisation and autonomy, as expressed in legislation of June 1994, and then in the form of a restraint on that second tier local government, expressed in a law in

September of the same year, when the (deconcentrated) institution of Regional Directors was legislated. Now a growing interested in elected authorities at the level of the 13 presently appointed administrative regions can be detected.

3.2 The current debate

It is already being realised that the geographic unit of the prefecture (of which there are 50) is demographically, socially and economically too small and weak to support viable self-government administrations. The argument expressed by a number of commentators is that the reform towards prefectoral self-government came too late, at a time when the move should have been towards elected authorities at the level of the administrative region. Another (potential) tension is between the elected prefect and the mayor of the capital city of each prefecture, especially in those with a large population.

3.3 Driving forces

In the context of the European single market, there are clear advantages in strengthening the regions at the expense of the prefectures. The regional level is clearly favoured by current European Union policies. However, competition among traditional prefectures works against this development, as recent experience in the unitary prefectoral self-governments has shown in the form of bitter disputes over the seat of these authorities. In addition, the prefecture level may be a better option than the region in terms of local democracy objectives. It is conceivable that the best strategy is a combination of a substantially strengthened first-tier local government and elected regional authorities. However, the quality of municipal administration and the present economic situation make a move in this direction difficult. Administrative performance at the municipal level is undoubtedly linked with the poor quality of staff that local government is able to attract. The economic situation is exerting pressure for greater efficiency in project planning and implementation. This pressure seems to be strengthening the role for private sector consultants, hired as public project managers, rather than strengthening local and regional governments themselves.

More viable, active and responsible local government is needed. Fragmentation is a negative factor, but the innovation of area councils may help to overcome this. The fear of a misuse of power by parochial municipal administrations could lead to the development of checks and balances able to act as a countervailing force to arbitrary town hall practices. More active local communities and the protection of citizens' rights, for example, can counter municipal malpractices, more than a policy of withholding powers from municipal authorities. There are already promising examples of such local authority activities. In addition to capitalising on this experience, experimentation is needed with new organisational forms able to undertake development projects with the participation of central, regional and local government, as well as the private sector.

The early enthusiasm for local government power has been somewhat blurred by criticism of economic inefficiency, favouritism and irresponsible spending. But unless local self-government is given the chance to prove itself and learn by doing, decentralisation will never be achieved.

ICELAND

1. INSTITUTIONS AND AUTHORITY

1.1 Structures

Description of levels

There are two levels of administration in Iceland; central and local government. The Local Government Act of 1986 states that the country is divided into local authorities which run their own affairs under their own responsibility. Those authorities are legal entities (rural districts or towns) and are autonomous in the sense that they can have rights and responsibilities. Towns have a population exceeding 1 000. Regional committees have a supervisory role over various projects run by several local authorities but they do not constitute separate units of administration.

The number of local authorities as of December 1996 was 165. The number in December 1995 was 170. Around 45 percent of the local districts have less that 200 inhabitants. The total area of Iceland is 103 000 square kilometres and the population in December 1996 was 269 735. As the country is very sparsely populated there is a wide disparity in population in different authorities. Table 1 summarises the distribution of population in the municipalities.

Table 1. **Area and population of sub-national governments (December 1996)**

Number	Municipalities 165	
	Area (km^2)	Population
Largest	6 205	105 487
Smallest	300	28

Number of municipalities and population distribution	
Population size	Number of municipalities
up to 1 000	132
1 000-5 000	25
5 000-10 000	2
10 000-100 000	5
over 100 000	1

Source: Ministry of Finance.

Central government at the sub-national level

There are only two separate levels of authorities in Iceland, central government and local government with no administrative link between the two levels. Central representatives are not directly involved in decision-making at the sub-national level. There are, however, several types of organisations that might be called "deconcentrated State administration" as follows:

- The *Syslumadur* is the institution closest to the prefect. They are appointed directly by the minister (of justice) and enforce many different laws and regulations for many ministries. They are usually also the head of the police and of customs in the region. Although the *Syslumadur* has wide responsibilities, he is not involved in the decision-making of the municipalities, nor is he involved in the management or decision making of other deconcentrated administrations.

- Tax offices are an example of deconcentrated administrations. They are separate organisations which report directly to the minister and not to the central tax administration. Their managers are appointed by the minister.

- Many social services are run by the State with managers usually appointed by the minister. These include hospitals, health centres and secondary schools. The services have local boards which are also appointed by the minister, but the majority of the members are nominated by the municipalities in the region. These organisations, although formally a part of the central government, are more at an arms length from the minister than the other "deconcentrated" organisations.

Creation, elimination and restructuring

The legislation applying to local government in Iceland is based on Clause 76 of the Icelandic Constitution of 1944. This states that the right of communities to be in charge of their own affairs, under central government supervision, shall be guaranteed by law. Legislation concerning local authorities in Iceland is in two categories: general law on local administration and a number of special laws, mainly relating to the activities and responsibilities of local authorities. The Constitution asserts that the autonomy of local authorities exists and cannot be abolished without an amendment to the Constitution – which is one of the reasons why the amalgamation process had to be voluntary.

A Local Government Committee reporting to the Minister responsible for local government affairs in 1992 made recommendations for a more balanced distribution of population in local authorities. The aim was to increase the efficiency of the administration through amalgamation of local authorities and experiments with "pilot" authorities. This plan is based on two objectives. The division of power between central and local government should be clear, and each field of responsibility, as far as possible, should be dealt with by a single actor, so that the design, implementation and financial responsibility (for initial costs and for operation) are united. On the other hand, local authorities are, on the whole, responsible for local matters, and central government for those matters which are more efficiently dealt with on a national basis.

The Committee's report states that the most successful means to achieve these objectives is to strengthen local government, by having fewer, larger local authorities. This was seen to enable them to take over various responsibilities from central government, and to have decision-making power in more fields thus enhancing local democracy, and possibly increasing efficiency by putting the provision of services closer to the citizen. The methods suggested by the Committee included a plan for the merger of local authorities, and an experiment with so-called pilot authorities. Through the latter, municipalities will receive, on the basis of applications, the authority to undertake new projects for a given time; to be exempted from certain legal obligations which limit their decision-making freedom; to experiment with new methods of operation and financing in certain fields; and to develop administrative innovations.

The Local Government Committee recommended that the main method of amalgamation should be through elections on the issue i.e. voluntary unification and not through legislation forcing local authorities to amalgamate. The Committee suggested that a vote should take place on the proposed revised boundaries in autumn 1993. Special boundary councils were formed to make proposals for reorganised local authority areas. The resulting proposals would have reduced numbers from 196 to at most 43 local authorities. The vote, on 20 November 1993, rejected most of the recommendations, stalling the amalgamation process for some time. However there was the biggest reduction ever in local authorities (from 196 to 171) on 11 June 1994, representing a considerable amalgamation compared with the 229 local authorities which existed in 1950.

Control bodies

Professional auditing for local authorities is done by private consultancy. If a disagreement on local government actions arises, the ministry responsible for local government matters can make a ruling. There are three ways to appeal against decisions of local authorities: by the ministry, an appeals committee or the courts. A ruling of the ministry or the appeals committee does not affect the right of parties to pursue the matter further in the courts.

1.2 Powers

Nature of sub-national institutions

Every local authority has a deliberative body, the local council, which consists of an odd number of representatives, ranging from 3-5 to 15-27 representatives according to the population. All voters are eligible to stand for election. Every citizen over the age of 18 legally residing in a district has the right to vote. Local government elections take place every fourth year and are not linked to the political cycle of national government.

The local council usually elects an executive body known as the district or town board which is elected for a term of one year. However in authorities where council members number three or five no executive board is elected. The executive board, together with the local authority's chief executive, is responsible for the management and financial administration of the local authority, in so far as these are not delegated to others. The board supervises the local authority administration in general, and its financial management in particular, prepares budget plans, and ensures that the local authority accounts conform with prescribed procedures. The chief executive makes arrangements for council and executive board meetings, and is responsible for the implementation of the decisions they make.

Type and degree of autonomy

Local authorities have the right to decide on expenditure priorities, and on the execution of projects undertaken by the authority, provided that other provisions are not made by legislation. The sole responsibility for the execution of the duties which are legally assigned to the community, and for ensuring that the council's resolutions, laws and regulations on local government matters are complied with, lies with the authority itself.

The independence of authorities is legally guaranteed. The ministry responsible for local government matters should, however, ensure that local authorities carry out their obligations according to the Local Government Act and other legally-binding texts. The autonomy of local authorities is also confirmed in the European Charter of Local Self-government, drawn up under the auspices of the Council of Europe, signed by Iceland in November 1985 and ratified by the Parliament in 1991. If a local authority neglects its responsibilities, the Ministry shall issue a warning, and require the local authority to make good its failings. Should the local authority not comply with the Ministry's instructions within the stated period, the Ministry may resort to other actions and thus de facto supervise the performance by local authorities of their legally-binding duties, although not on a regular basis.

Local governments have limited taxation powers. On the other hand, they have considerable discretion to charge fees for the services which they provide, and do not require the authorisation of central government to raise loans.

1.3 Responsibilities

Distribution of responsibilities

The State is responsible for security and police, justice, secondary and higher education, and the financing of churches, roads, airports and communications.

Local governments deal with the running of harbours, fire protection, kindergartens and primary education, welfare assistance, home services to the aged, regional and spatial planning, water supply and purification, refuse collection and disposal, cemeteries and crematoria, parks and open spaces, sport and leisure facilities, urban road transport and district heating.

In an experiment with pilot authorities, some central government responsibilities are being transferred to participating local authorities, which are exempted from various obligations that normally apply to local authorities. The authorities concerned are also able to experiment with their financing and managerial arrangements.

The transfer of all responsibility for primary education from central to local government took place in August 1996, accompanied by central government provisions to ensure that sufficient funds will be available for local authorities to run primary schools. Since then primary schools are totally run and financed by local authorities. Similarly services for the disabled are generally the responsibility of local governments, while institutions for the disabled are largely built and run by central government. The government and local governments have agreed upon a plan to transfer all public services for the disabled from the State to local government by 1999.

Mandatory, optional and shared responsibilities

Responsibility for policy implementation between levels of government is rather unclear. The uncertainty is especially acute in the smaller authorities and central government has tended to solve overlapping competences on an ad hoc basis. Joint financing of responsibilities has been common because of the weakness of the local government level.

It may be regarded as natural for central government to undertake more responsibilities in Iceland than in neighbouring countries, because of the small population in local authorities. This has led to many matters being dealt with jointly by central and local government since local authorities have not had the financial means to undertake the tasks typically assigned to them in neighbouring countries. Paradoxically the smallness also means that central government is closer to the public than in other countries.

Some responsibilities are shared between the central and local level. This is the case for new school buildings for secondary education and building new houses for the health service, but the Government and local authorities are planning to change this.

Some other responsibilities are dealt with by both the State at the central level and by the municipalities at the local level. This is the case for civil defence and disaster relief, town planning, theatres and concerts and other activities in the field of culture and tourism.

Municipalities and the State share responsibilities at the local level in the following fields: adult education, hospitals and convalescent homes, personal health, housing and health and environmental protection.

In addition to such collaboration between central government and local government, many local authorities work closely together at a "regional" level. In many cases, two or more communities join forces to deal with particular services. Examples of this are:

- accommodation and services for the elderly;
- refuse collection and pollution prevention;
- culture, sport and youth work;
- the bus system in the Reykjavik metropolitan area;
- joint management of local heating systems and other utilities;
- co-operation in running primary schools and music schools.

Local authorities have some mandatory responsibilities but other activities are optional and can be undertaken without any interference from central government. Any optional activities are, however, constrained by financial considerations, as in recent years local authorities have been experiencing severe financial difficulties stemming from the slump in the economy and growing unemployment. In this context many local authorities have engaged in private enterprises, e.g. fishing and operating fish-meal factories. In most instances the goal has been to prevent local unemployment but some of the enterprises have made profits.

The general policy on the distribution of responsibilities is evolving towards a clearer division of competences between central and local government but the situation has not yet stabilised. Modification in the division of responsibilities has been a continuing issue in the management of relations between the two levels of government in recent years. It is not expected that this process will be totally halted by the negative results of the vote on amalgamation.

2. MANAGEMENT FUNCTIONS

2.1 Policy-making and co-ordination

Coherence, consultation and conflict resolution

Through the years the policy-making capacity of local government has, in many ways, been similar to that of central government. Central government is clearly more powerful but both levels suffer from a limited capacity to make policy because of weak policy-making structures. Decision-making by local authorities is not contingent on the approval or supervision of other public bodies, so long as decisions conform with the law, and do not encroach on territory assigned to other bodies by law. Local authorities manage their own affairs under their own responsibility and central government has no authority to intervene in local government policy.

The Parliament and government can, depending on the issue, make decisions which affect local communities in general, but in such cases the government is legally bound to consult the associations of local authorities. No policy or management decision which affects the interest of a specific local authority can be taken without consulting the authority concerned. Central government is, however, not formally bound by the opinion of local government.

Local democracy and devolution of political power are the main reasons for the existence of local authorities. Public participation on the local level takes various forms including referendums and public meetings. Referendums are not usually binding upon the local authority, unless it has been decided in advance that it shall be so. Public meetings are often held in rural districts although there is no reference to them in the legislation on local government.

Formal and informal mechanisms

Some reforms have sought to improve co-ordination. The review process that has been taking place over recent years, especially through the Local Government Committee, has examined the relationship between the two levels of government. This committee constitutes the first formal organisation guiding co-operation between the two levels. In January 1993 a co-operation agreement between central and local government was entered into. In it the parties agreed to co-ordinate their public management policy to make it possible to attain the economic goals set by the government and Parliament at any given time. At least two consultative meetings are held every year, attended by the Ministers of Social Affairs, Finance, Health, Education and Environment and a representative from the National Economic Institute, and on behalf of the local authorities, the board of the Union of Local Authorities.

Both meetings cover the outlook for the national economy, the finances of local authorities, and the employment situation. At the Spring meeting specific financial proposals made by individual ministries which concern local authorities are discussed. Any proposals which modify the division of responsibilities between central and local government are also discussed together with government policy on new legislation concerning local authorities, their sphere of activity or their tax base.

The autumn meeting covers policies concerning operations, investments and the use of the tax base during the coming year. Any provisions of the State Budget concerning the interests of the local authorities are also discussed, together with any requests presented by the local authorities. It is expected that the Budget Committee of Parliament, or its representatives, attend this meeting during the discussions on the State Budget.

There are also several sectoral co-ordination bodies which relate more to regulation and implementation than to policy-making. Examples are the education authorities which regulate and direct school activities and ensure that all requirements and responsibilities are met.

There is formal co-operation of local authority associations at both the local and regional levels. The Union of Local Authorities is a federation of all local authorities in the country. The union provides a national forum for consultation for local authorities and plays an important role in protecting the interests of local authorities. It provides a national forum for consultation for local authorities, government, and other bodies. Each region has a federation of the local authorities in the region. These federations, which now number eight, aim to protect the interests of the local authorities, to collect information and give information on the authorities, and to provide a forum for discussion for the local authorities in the region.

2.2 Financial management

Sources of revenue

The main sources of revenue for local authorities are: local income tax (paid by all wage earners), property tax, and contributions from the Communal Equalisation Fund. Local authorities also receive revenues from their own institutions, sewer fees, rents for land, bonds, licences and fees for various services. Two forms of revenue on businesses (turnover tax and a national income levy for local government) were abandoned in 1993. Local authorities compensated for this by raising local income and property taxes. Contributions from the Communal Equalisation Fund are by nature central government grants while local income tax and property tax are direct local taxation. The central government grants comprise both block and special grants. Block grants from the Communal Equalisation Fund are distributed to local authorities on a per capita basis usually accounting for 10-14 per cent of the total authority income. Special grants from the Communal Equalisation Fund are directed to low-income authorities to assist in various activities such as primary, secondary and comprehensive schooling. Other types of special grants paid by central government are subsidies to meet expenditure in fields including harbour-building, and main-road construction. The composition of local government revenues is shown in Table 2.

Table 2. **Main revenue sources of sub-national governments (1985, 1990, 1995)**
(millions of *krónur*, current prices)

	1985	1990	1995
Income from property	748	1 954	2 800
From public enterprises	110	592	1 856
Interest income	529	998	517
Dividends and rental income	109	363	428
Tax revenue	7 270	23 289	29 427
Indirect taxes	3 491	9 590	8 258
Direct taxes	3 780	13 699	21 170
Other income	56	1 380	2 696
TOTAL	8 074	26 623	34 924

Source: Ministry of Finance.

Expenditure responsibilities

Local authority expenditure was about 22 per cent of total public expenditure in Iceland in 1994 – which is very low in comparison with neighbouring countries where local authority expenditure accounts for 60-70 per cent of total public expenditure. This is explained by the fact that in Iceland, central government is responsible for various costly undertakings, which tend to be dealt with by local authorities in other countries.

Table 3. **Main expenditure patterns of sub-national governments (1985, 1990, 1995)**
(millions of *krónur*, current prices)

	1985	1990	1995
Administration and law enforcement	533	2 558	2 729
General administration	419	2 170	2 118
Law enforcement and security	114	388	611
Social services	5 248	15 991	24 595
Education	1 147	4 237	6 965
Health	935	525	311
Social security and welfare	1 347	4 798	7 697
Housing, town planning, rubbish removal, sewage	650	1 895	3 195
Cultural affairs	1 169	4 536	6 428
Economic affairs	1 701	4 626	6 015
Energy	9	0	0
Agriculture	33	67	169
Fisheries	56	106	-25
Manufacturing and construction	83	288	541
Communications and transport	1 456	4 021	4 352
Other	64	143	978
Other municipal services	213	1 719	857
Interest expenditures	368	1 533	2 174
Depreciation	184	521	747
TOTAL	8 246	26 948	37 117

Source: Ministry of Finance.

Balance between discretion and control

The level of local income tax, property tax and other public levies must be within the prescribed limits set by central government. These limits give local authorities some latitude within the minimum and maximum levels. Local authorities have the right to determine the level of fees in their own institutions, such as utility companies, but such fees have to be confirmed by central government.

Local authorities do not require authorisation from central government in order to raise loans. There is a special Local Authorities Loan Fund which is an independent institution, jointly owned by all local authorities. The fund has its own board, and operates under central government supervision. The main aim of the fund is to grant loans to local authorities for projects which are so costly that they could only be financed from local authority revenues over a very long period. The fund also grants loans for the conversion of existing loans which have unfavourable terms, if better terms cannot be negotiated with the relevant financial institution. In 1991, 46 per cent of the fund went to conversion loans.

Local authorities do not have the right to impose public levies upon the inhabitants of the community other than fees for their own institutions. This can be seen as limiting the power of local authorities and giving central government sole power over taxation. Funding, except from special grants, is earmarked to the relevant responsibilities and a well run authority can take decisions to increase the level of service if it has sufficient funds.

Central government involvement in the finances of local authorities is minor although various government institutions have a supervisory function over some specific financial arrangements of local authorities. These supervisory functions should however be considered as consultative rather than investigatory of local finances. When a local authority is in severe financial difficulties it can be put under the direct administration of the ministry responsible for local government. This practise is, however, very rare and only called for in cases of extreme financial difficulties.

In recent years, government authorities have placed much emphasis on consistency between local authority actions and central government policy – especially in relation to debt. Though central government has tried to influence local authorities in these matters, it has no authority to intervene regarding local government expenditure. This is confirmed in the co-operation agreement whereby the parties pledge to collaborate in order to attain the economic goals set by the Government and Parliament.

The Equalisation Fund seeks to balance the financial position of local authorities given their large number, varying numbers of inhabitants, and differing potential for raising revenue. Contributions are of various types: fixed contributions, special contributions, initial-cost contributions, contributions for primary schools, contributions for music schools, revenue equalisation contributions, and service contributions. Contributions have also been paid from the Equalisation Fund in order to meet the costs of amalgamating local authorities – a role which has been enhanced in recent years.

The Equalisation Fund received extra funding to fulfil its role in furthering the amalgamation process using positive monetary incentives. In the short term the fund was to pay for the cost of amalgamating i.e. the remuneration for the boundary councils, the execution of the elections, and promoting temporary support and compensating measures. In the long term the fund is for compensating between bigger, more populated authorities and smaller ones – particularly in relation to their debts as bad debt has often stood in the way of amalgamation.

2.3 Performance management

Mechanisms

The National Audit Office audits the State Budget but professional auditing for local authorities is done only by private consultancies. If there is reason to believe that there are serious irregularities of accountancy at the local level, the ministry responsible for local government has powers to intervene. The National Audit Office has grown stronger in recent years since it was put under the authority of the Parliament instead of the Government. This seems to have enhanced its autonomy.

There are no formal broad public management reforms taking place in local government; most initiative being with individual local authorities. The ethos of the public management reform in central government has, however, clearly spilled over to local government. These reforms have aimed to lessen pressures to increase taxation, to finance the budget deficit which currently accounts for about 2.2 per cent of the GDP and to introduce some market-type mechanisms in the provision of public services. The main management reforms in central government thus relate to the use of:

- contracting out in the field of supplies;
- the use of nominal user fees to influence demand for public services;
- a pilot project in contract management (i.e. devolved budgets), and
- privatisation.

Quality standards

The law defining the division of responsibility between central and local government and other more specific legislation include frameworks for local authority services, but no formal quality standards have as yet been developed. Local authorities decide on the quality and quantity of their service within these frameworks, taking into account the wishes and demands of inhabitants, and financing.

A new law on primary schools provides, as from 1995, for formal evaluation of the quality of education but this has not yet been evaluated. However, the fact that evaluation is mentioned in a law is, in itself, an innovation.

2.4 Human resource management

Statutory distinctions

The autonomy of communities in dealing with their own affairs also applies to the appointment of staff, and to the local authority projects to which staff are assigned. All those employed in local administrations have the rights and duties of public employees. Conditions of employment are in accord with general wage agreements between the level of government in question and its employees. There are some regional differences in pay as local authorities have tended to pay higher overall wages to compensate employees for moving from one region to another. This practice of regional pay is, however, on the wane, at least in some authorities, as unemployment in Iceland has increased in the public sector as well as in the private sector.

Distinctions are made between local authority employees according to the nature of their work and consequently they belong to different trade unions, but the majority are members of the Federation of State and Municipal Employees. The unions range from those for unskilled labour to those for specialists (represented by many small unions). Collective bargaining takes place between the different unions and representatives of the relevant level of government. Central government has a committee responsible for all bargaining between central government and its employees. The Union of Local Authorities does not have a formal role in negotiating wage agreements and the local wage agreements are usually on similar terms as the central one.

Decisions on the level of staffing are taken at each level of government and are put forward in the State Budget and local authority budget plans respectively. However in the light of recently rising unemployment both central and local governments have tried to inflate the demand for labour and made some changes to working hours. Table 4 shows the evolving distribution of employment across levels of government.

Mobility: There are no formal rules on how employees move between levels of government but the practice is rather common since conditions of employment are similar. There is no organised mobility of staff – either between the two government levels or internally among local authorities. However, employees may leave a job in one level of government and then be hired by the other level.

Table 4. **Public sector employment by level of government (1985, 1990, 1993)**
(person years)

	1985	1990	1993
Central government	12 500	14 600	15 100
Local government	8 800	9 700	10 600
TOTAL	21 300	24 300	25 700

Source: Ministry of Finance.

2.5 Regulatory management and reform

The only major area of regulation under the responsibility of the municipalities is health and environmental inspection. Each municipality is responsible for health inspection in areas such as restaurants, food distribution and processing (excluding fish handling and processing, slaughtering and milk processing which fall under State health inspection), schools and public establishments. The municipal health inspection system has in recent years received the added responsibility of environmental inspection, including the control of emissions of toxic substances into the environment. This function is performed in accordance with regulations set by the Ministry for the Environment.

There are no major reforms underway in this area, although some minor reorganisation is taking place under the Pilot Scheme for Municipalities. The current regulatory management of municipalities may be expected to change in concert with new regulations stemming from the European Economic Area as well as through regulations pertaining to improved environmental control.

3. TRENDS IN REDISTRIBUTING AUTHORITY ACROSS LEVELS OF GOVERNMENT

3.1 Evolving tendencies

There are no proposals for new levels of government but co-operation between levels and authorities is increasing. There was a political movement, mainly in the north of the country, arguing for a regional tier but the issue now seems to have died. The main arguments against a regional level were based on the limited efficiency of the authorities and the view that a new level would not necessarily make the system more efficient. Instead of proposals for new levels, amalgamation has been proposed in order to increase both efficiency and local democracy. It remains to be seen whether this policy of amalgamation will be implemented further and how.

Some recent proposals recommended a change in the distribution of responsibilities between central and local authorities, mainly concerned with the amalgamation of local authorities and the so-called pilot authorities. These involved a fundamental reappraisal of the division of powers and competences following a reorganisation of local authority boundaries. In March 1992, the Local Government Committee reported to the Minister responsible for local government affairs on a policy of amalgamation following the Government's 1991 White Paper: "Prosperity on a Sustainable Basis". The objective of the Committee's work was to seek means of ensuring a more balanced distribution of the population, increasing local power and enhancing the efficiency of the administration.

3.2 The current debate

Decentralisation through amalgamation of local authorities is on the policy agenda of both levels of government although the amalgamation process has been halted for the time being. The Union of Local Authorities and the Government still see amalgamation as the prerequisite to further modifications in the division of responsibilities between central and local government. A modification in the division of responsibilities is generally a decentralisation issue in the Icelandic context. There are signs that the strategy of voluntary unification of local authorities, as followed by the central government and wholly supported by the Union of Local Authorities, will not further the amalgamation process. There are two other options: to use negative monetary incentives through the Equalisation Fund; or forced unification through legislation from central government.

The amalgamation process is also seen as an opportunity to enhance local democracy by making it possible for local authorities to take over new activities and responsibilities such as primary education. The number of small local authorities in Iceland has led to increased centralisation not decentralisation and the amalgamation process is thus seen as a part of a larger decentralisation process. Nevertheless the referendum in 1993 rejected most of the recommendations and successfully stalled the process.

Most of the small local authorities are not able to perform many of their current responsibilities and it has been argued that regional federations are a less democratic way to solve the problems of small authorities. It can, however, be argued that there is a need for a change in strategy given the vote on the proposed revised boundaries in autumn 1993. Modifications in the division of responsibilities is evolving but they are somewhat contingent upon the amalgamation process.

The small size of local authorities in Iceland clearly weakens the capacity of local government to take over tasks from the centre. It has been argued that this not only inhibits feelings of loyalty at the local level, but is harmful to the process of organised democracy in the smaller authorities. The strategy of voluntary unification of local governments is, however, undermined by the fact that feelings of loyalty are stronger in the smaller local governments than in the larger ones. Thus it was argued that only through national legislation is Iceland likely to create sufficiently large local authorities to be able to systematically transfer tasks to the local level and consequently improve its chances of winning greater loyalty. It has also been argued that both local and central government are in need of increased flexibility in personnel management in order to be better able to react to unexpected opportunities.

3.3 Driving forces

The driving forces of this evolution are a combination of economic, political and democratic influences. The economic case for amalgamation, pilot authorities and changes in the division of responsibilities between central and local government is accepted by all concerned. There has however been a reluctance by all political parties to force authorities to amalgamate and even the use of negative monetary incentives has not been adopted. The democratic argument is also well established given the low population density and difficulties in transportation. Providing more local public services could enhance local democracy, increase the quality of services and might also increase efficiency – objectives which will be difficult to reach as long as local authorities remain small and weak.

IRELAND

1. INSTITUTIONS AND AUTHORITY

1.1 Structures

Description of levels

Sub-national administration in Ireland can be divided into (a) local government bodies, which approximate to the general definition of "sub-national government" and (b) other local or regionally-based bodies, usually with sector-specific executive roles. Some national institutions also have sub-national elements.

There is, strictly speaking, only one level of directly elected local government but local authorities can be categorised as City/County, made up of five county boroughs (cities) and 29 counties, and Sub-County. The term "sub-county" is, strictly speaking, a slight misnomer. These are town authorities which generally operate independently of the county council (although with more limited functions). The relationship is not hierarchical, but mainly geographic in nature. While the State is fully divided into counties, there is not a comprehensive sub-county network, town authorities being "isolated" units within counties. "Sub-county" comprises five boroughs, 49 urban districts and 26 other towns. The sub-county level was the subject of a review by a statutory Commission, published in June, 1996, which is referred to further in section 3.1. There are also regional authorities made up of groupings of counties and county boroughs, but these are not directly elected. The total area of Ireland is 70 300 square kilometres and the population in 1996 was 3 621 035.

Other local or regionally-based bodies operate separately from the local government system although, in some cases, having a degree of linkage with it (e.g. part or all of their membership appointed by the local authorities). Such bodies generally have specific executive or service functions within a particular sector. The main regional bodies, their functional areas, and populations (1996 census preliminary figures) are:

- Fisheries Boards: Seven regions with areas based on sea and river catchment areas.

- Health Boards: Eight regions with areas ranging from 464 064 hectares (Eastern) to 1 380 088 hectares (Western) and populations from 205 525 (Midland) to 1 293 964 (Eastern).

- Regional Tourism Organisations: Six regions (all regions except Mid West) with areas ranging from 92 156 (Dublin) to 1 380 088 (West) hectares and populations from 314 281 (North-West) to 1 056 666 (Dublin).

- Udaras na Gaeltachta (Authority for the Irish-speaking [Gaeltacht] area): A combination of several geographically separate districts which had a total population of approximately 83 000 in 1991.

- Western Development Partnership Board (WDPB): An area of 2 514 014 hectares comprising seven counties with a population of 655 900.

In addition the following local bodies also exist and perform specific functions:

- Vocational Education Committees: Thirty-eight bodies based on the five city areas, twenty seven of the counties and six towns.

Table 1. **Area and population of local authorities (1996)**[1]

Number	City/County authorities 34 (5 county boroughs + 29 counties)		Sub-County/Town authorities 5 boroughs + 49 urban districts + 26 other towns	
	Area (ha.)	Population	Area (ha.)	Population
Largest	742 257 (Cork Co.)	480 996 (Dublin City)	2 443 (Dundalk UDC)	25 774 (Dundalk UDC)
Smallest	1 904 (Limerick City)	25 032 (Leitrim Co.)	24 (Ballybay TC)	474 (Ballybay TC)

Number of local authorities and population distribution	
Population size	Number of local authorities
up to 10 000	68
10 000-20 000	9
20 000-50 000	7
50 000-100 000	15
100 000-500 000	15
over 500 000	0
TOTAL	114

1. Preliminary figures
Source: Census of Population 1996, Preliminary Report (Central Statistics Office)

- Harbour Authorities: Twenty-five bodies responsible for administration of individual harbours.

- County Enterprise Boards: Thirty-five bodies based on city/county areas.

- Leader Groups: Local representative groups under the European Union Community Initiative on local development in 37 areas.

- Area Partnership Companies: Social/economic development groups in 38 disadvantaged areas.

Central government at sub-national levels

In addition to local authorities and other autonomous regional/local bodies, some national institutions have internal regions or divisions for organisational purposes, which, however, do not generally, have autonomous budgetary or decision-making capacity. The areas (and hence populations) involved differ in certain cases, to facilitate the organisation of particular services or other relevant factors. There are two broad categories, as follows:

Central Government Institutions: Certain institutions of central government have regional organisational arrangements which generally form part of a centrally led chain of command. Examples include the Department of Social Welfare, which introduced a regional management structure in 1991 to facilitate development of local services and liaison with other regional agencies; the Revenue Commissioners; the schools inspectorate of the Department of Education; the architectural, engineering and heritage functions of the Office of Public Works; the driver testing and audit services of the Department of the Environment; the Army; the Garda Siochana (police force) and the Courts; and local offices of the Department of Agriculture, Food and Forestry which monitor disease and process applications under various schemes for modernisation and development of farming enterprises. A major programme of relocation of central government offices has also been implemented in recent years.

"Semi-State" Bodies: Various autonomous national bodies established, by or under statute, to carry out particular functions or to provide particular services have internal regional or local structures. For example, the national bus and rail companies have regional management structures with responsibility for day to day matters in their areas but policy decisions are taken centrally. Other examples include national telecommunications and broadcasting services, the industrial development and training/employment authorities, the national electricity supply board, the health and safety authority inspectorate, the agriculture and food development authority and the national forestry board.

Creation, elimination and restructuring

All local and regional authorities are corporate bodies established by or under statute. They derive their powers, functions and duties from, and operate within, that statutory framework. While the statutory framework of local government was mainly defined in late 19th century legislation, aspects of the system are also a product of earlier historical evolution, and subsequent legislation has also made some modifications. City, county and urban district authorities were created directly by statute. Regional authorities were established by ministerial order under a 1991 Act. Town commissioners were established through voluntary adoption of provisions of an 1854 Act. Some urban authorities originated under British royal charters dating as far back as the 12th century but these have been superseded by statute law.

The non local government bodies are also mainly corporate bodies established by or under statute. Regional Tourism Organisations were established by the Irish Tourist Board under statutory powers. County Enterprise Boards were initially created by the government and subsequently accorded a statutory basis. The government provided the impetus for establishment of the Area Partnership Companies and the Western Development Partnership Board but they were established independently.

Restructuring in local government bodies has occurred as part of a reform programme initiated by the government in 1991 following a report by an advisory expert committee. It involved the following steps:

- Regions were formally designated and regional authorities established with effect from 1 January 1994, by order of the Minister for the Environment under statutory powers. The regional authorities have a co-ordinating role among public authorities (including local authorities). It is also government policy that other existing public agencies should, as far as possible, align their operations and areas with the statutory regions. The regional system is at a very early stage of development.

- Local government structures in the Dublin area were re-organised by statute with the establishment, on 1 January 1994, of three new county councils – Fingal, Dun Laoghaire-Rathdown and South Dublin – to replace the former Dublin County Council (1991 population 564 915) and Dun Laoghaire Borough Corporation. The aim is to provide more manageable, efficient and locally-focused structures for the area, which has seen rapid development and population increase in recent decades.

- The future classification and related attributes of town authorities was the subject of a recent review.

Regional Tourism Organisation boundaries were adjusted in 1989 and their internal corporate structures were revised in 1993 to improve effectiveness. County Enterprise Boards, Leader Groups, Area Partnership Companies and the Western Development Partnership Board are of relatively recent origin. Certain harbour authorities are shortly to be replaced by new semi-State companies.

Overview/support bodies

The Department of the Environment is responsible for general overview of the local government system, as are other departments in relation to sub-national bodies under their aegis. Public accountability is ensured through legal requirements of accounts, reports and audit. Local authorities and certain other local bodies are statutorily subject to financial and regularity audit by a corps of local government auditors appointed by the Minister for the Environment. They are professionally independent in the conduct of their audits and have wide ranging (including some quasi-judicial) powers. Other public bodies are subject to audit either by the Comptroller and Auditor General (a Constitutional Office of central government) or by commercial auditors, in accordance with requirements of their governing provisions. Expenditure of European Union funding is also subject to audit by the European Court of Auditors and to individual audit check in the context of the relevant Structural Funds. Many authorities have their own internal audit procedures.

The following national agencies also have overview functions:

- Environmental Protection Agency, which licenses, regulates and controls activities with significant pollution potential, has supervisory functions in relation to local authority monitoring of the environment and of the operation of local authority treatment plants. It also has default powers to take direct action and has a role in advising and assisting local authorities generally on their environment functions.

- National Roads Authority, which has overall responsibility for development of the strategic national road network (with local authorities normally acting on behalf of the authority in, for example, design and supervision of road improvements and the placing of contracts). It also has default powers vis-à-vis local road authorities and power to specify standards, issue directions and allocate funds to specific road projects.

- Local Appointments Commission, which provides recruitment selection services for local authorities, health boards and harbour authorities.

- Arts Council, which uses a network of local arts officers based in county and city councils in its role of promoting the arts.

- Various semi-State bodies which provide support services to local authorities and other sub-national bodies.

1.2 Powers

Nature of sub-national institutions

Local government bodies: The legal character of the local authority comprises two separate elements which share responsibility for performing local authority functions: (i) the elected members who constitute the "council" of the authority, and (ii) a full-time salaried chief executive, the City/County Manager who is also manager for every sub-county local authority in the county.

Local authority members are elected for five-year terms under the single transferable vote system of proportional representation. All residents over 18 years are eligible to vote. The elected members exercise what are termed "reserved functions" defined by law, comprising mainly decisions on important matters of policy and finance. The Manager discharges what are termed "executive functions" – in effect the day to day running of the authority – within the policy parameters determined by the elected council. Any function which is not a "reserved function" is automatically an executive one performable by the manager.

The Manager's power to exercise the executive functions of the local authority is derived directly from statutory provisions (rather than delegation by the council) but the elected members have various powers enabling them to oversee the activities of the Manager and to give directions in certain circumstances. In turn, the Manager has a duty to advise and assist the elected members in the exercise of their functions. A manager has the right to attend and speak at council meetings, but not to vote. While the division of functions between manager and council are clearly defined for legal purposes, in practice policy and executive decisions are not totally divorced and the manager and elected members operate together, with the latter, who act by resolutions adopted at meetings, having the pre-eminent role.

The regional authorities are statutory corporate bodies, consisting of elected members of the county and city councils in each region who are appointed by their local authorities through a procedure specified by law and are not directly elected to the regional authorities.

Non local government bodies: The sub-national bodies in question are generally statutory corporate bodies with legal authority vested in the board members and appropriate functions delegated to a chief officer. Regional Tourism Organisations, County Enterprise Boards and Area Partnership Companies are autonomous companies limited by guarantee.

Membership of these bodies is determined mainly by appointment rather than direct election (U*daras na Gaeltachta* is an exception in that some members are democratically elected by the people of the *Gaeltacht*). Membership usually consists of local authority/ministerial appointees and in some cases, nominees of State bodies in an area or other relevant interests. The more recently established local development bodies also contain representatives of the social partners, business and the local community.

Type and degree of autonomy

Local government bodies: The local authorities are legally autonomous in the exercise of their powers under relevant legislation. Within the general supervisory arrangements (see section 1.1), the policy parameters and administrative procedures (see section 2.1) and certain financial controls as set out in section 2.2, they are not, for the most part, subject to direction in the exercise of their functions. The powers vested in town commissioners are, however, extremely limited, most functions being exercised by the county council. The latter are also legally responsible for certain functions in the areas of the urban district councils and boroughs (e.g. national and regional roads, fire services, and certain housing functions).

Dual membership of local government and national parliament is generally permitted, and it is usual for a significant proportion of members of parliament to hold local authority membership. However, restrictions on this "dual mandate" have been introduced in recent legislation, involving the exclusion of certain public office holders, including Ministers and Ministers of State, from local authority membership. Legislation in 1994 provided for repeal of ministerial power to postpone local elections, further emphasising the autonomous status of local government.

The powers of local authorities involve a combination of regulatory, executive and representational roles. The regulatory role, involves a limited "legislative" element in terms of local authority bye-law making powers, but otherwise it consists mainly of activities such as granting of licences and permissions and various enforcement functions. Essential services (e.g. fire service), important regulatory matters (e.g. planning control) and major infrastructural functions are generally mandatory legal functions of the local authorities concerned, but with appropriate discretion and flexibility in their actual discharge. However, certain powers such as the provision of amenities and making of bye-laws are purely discretionary.

The right of local authorities to "tax" consists of the power to levy "rates" (property tax based on valuation) on commercial/industrial property and to make charges for services (commonly water and refuse collection).

A wide range of central controls on local authorities have been removed. These affect matters such as land disposals, staffing, car parks, local authority procedures, certain personnel matters, and housing construction. Recent local government legislation has also enhanced the position of the elected members within the local government system through measures such as statutory recognition of members' policy-making role, reservation of additional powers to members rather than management, new systems of annual allowances and chairpersons' allowances and various provisions to enhance the civic role and status of members. The role of elected members is to be further enhanced through, for example, involvement in proposed Strategic Policy Committees (for the main service areas) and a Corporate Policy Group.

The removal or relaxation of various requirements for central government approval has also meant an effective redistribution of discretion in favour of local authorities. So, also has the enactment of the general competence provision allowing local authorities a discretionary power to take action in the interests of the community. Previously they were constrained by the "ultra vires" principle of law which required specific legal authority for every action. These changes have given greater emphasis to the developmental and community-related role of local authorities.

The recently-established regional authorities play a region-wide, inter-sectoral role across a wide range of public services but do not have policy implementation competence. The establishment of regional authorities has not involved any loss of power by the county or town authorities, or indeed any other statutory bodies. As in the case of local authorities, they are legally autonomous subject to statutory provisions and broad supervisory arrangements. However, both the nature of their constitution and their co-ordinating role mean that linkage with other public authorities, particularly their constituent local authorities (in the latter case for funding and membership as well as functional purposes), is an essential element of the regional authorities' operations.

Non local government bodies: The functions of the other sub-national bodies are largely of an executive/service nature, exercised within particular sectors with varying degrees of regulatory authority (for example, harbour authorities may make bye-laws governing pilotage while some types of bodies have no regulatory role). They are generally autonomous in the exercise of their functions subject to their governing provisions and the supervisory, policy, funding and other arrangements with the relevant central agencies.

Regional Tourism Organisations have a mainly promotional/support role in the tourism sector, particularly the organisation of the tourism industry at the regional level.

County Enterprise Boards are primarily agencies for facilitating, promoting and supporting local development and economic activity, with emphasis on a "bottom-up approach", complementing the work of other State agencies.

Leader Groups have the role of implementing business plans for their areas under the European Union Community Initiative on rural development. An essential feature of their operations is that decisions on programmes to be funded in the implementation of business plans are made by the groups themselves. *Area Partnership Companies* are cross-functional executive bodies with the role of formulating and implementing plans for integrated social and economic development in their areas, with emphasis on targeting socially and economically marginalised groups.

The *Western Development Partnership Board* is a non-executive body whose role is to formulate an action plan to promote and assist economic development of the western area with the objective of achieving population stability.

The main functions of the non local government bodies tend, by the nature of their specific roles, to be mandatory rather than optional, but with discretionary elements in their discharge, as in the case of local authorities. They do not have power to levy tax. However, the "bottom-up" role of many of the local development agencies is inherently more discretionary in nature.

1.3 Responsibilities

Distribution of responsibilities

Local authorities: Local authorities are multi-purpose bodies responsible for a range of functions, which in the case of county councils, county borough corporations, borough corporations and urban district councils, are classified into eight programme groups, as follows: (1) Housing and Building, (2) Road Transportation and Safety, (3) Water Supply and Sewerage, (4) Development Incentives and Controls, (5) Environmental Protection, (6) Recreation and Amenity, (7) Agriculture, Education and Welfare, (8) Miscellaneous Services.

Local authorities in Ireland are not primarily responsible for such functions as education, health, police and social welfare, which are the responsibility either of separate local or regional bodies or of central government departments, although there are linkages with the local government system in some cases (e.g. nominations and contributions to vocational education committees). On the other hand, local authorities in Ireland have responsibility for some services such as water supply, which are provided by specialist bodies in some countries.

Among the most significant recent changes in local authority powers have been the transfer of certain environmental functions to a national Environmental Protection Agency and the establishment of a National Roads Authority with a supervisory role in relation to national roads functions and special development agencies such as a new Dublin Docklands Development Authority to be established shortly. Technical and economic requirements have also led to particular local authority functions being located primarily at county level. New housing legislation in 1992 was based on the approach of aligning, as far as practicable, the range of functions of different classes of authorities with the financial, organisational and personnel resources representative of each class. Accordingly, county and city councils have the full range of housing functions, but boroughs, urban district councils and town commissioners have successively narrower ranges of functions. However, some larger town authorities have been given housing functions otherwise performable by the county councils by Ministerial order under the 1992 Act. Similarly, following rationalisation of roads functions between county and sub-county authorities in a 1993 Roads Act, some larger town authorities may exercise county council functions in relation to national and regional roads and since 1980, responsibility for fire services has rested with 35 larger (mainly county level) authorities.

Local authorities have acquired additional functions in areas such as urban renewal, housing, the environment, physical planning, road traffic, amenity provision, building control and the general development and promotion of their areas. In addition, a major aim of the local government reform programme has been to increase local authority powers, independence and discretion. Recent Roads, Road Traffic and Local Government legislation made provisions for local authorities to take action in the interests of the local community and extensive modernisation of the general code of local government law. Local authorities have also been given full responsibility for various new social housing schemes and for licensing and control of taxis.

Regional authorities: Within their general role of promoting co-ordination, the main functions of regional authorities include the review of the provision of public services; submission of observations, proposals, recommendations, etc., to public authorities in the region; review of development needs and local authority development plans; review and advice on the implementation of European Union assistance programmes and publication of a five-yearly overall review of the region. There is also provision for inter-regional co-ordination and joint action between regional authorities.

Non local government bodies: Their main areas of responsibility are as follows:

- Health Boards: Provision of health care services, the delivery of which is organised for administrative purposes under three broad programmes: general hospital services, special hospital services (i.e. those catering for the mentally ill) and community care services.

- Fisheries Boards: Development and protection of inland fisheries and development of angling.

- Tourism Organisations: Visitor servicing, including tourist information offices, booking services and information materials; tourism product development, including development and operation of visitor attractions and administration of grant schemes and marketing.

- Vocational Education Committees: Provision of vocational and continuation education, including management of vocational schools.

- Harbour Authorities: Operation and maintenance of individual harbours and administration of pilotage. (Authorities for some commercial harbours are shortly to be replaced by new semi-State companies).

- County Enterprise Boards: Promoting employment opportunities in small business through developing county enterprise plans, local enterprise awareness/enterprise culture; providing local enterprise support services and business information, advice, counselling and mentoring.

- Udaras na Gaeltachta: Encouraging the preservation and extension of the use of the Irish language as the principal medium of communication in the *Gaeltacht* areas. Industries and productive schemes of employment are assisted in order to provide employment in the *Gaeltacht*.

- Area Partnership Boards: Liaison with State agencies to improve effectiveness and targeting of mainstream education, training and enterprise support programmes; funding of services not provided by mainstream bodies; community development and services to the unemployed.

Mandatory, optional and shared responsibilities

Whereas much early local government legislation was adoptive in nature (the local authority could decide whether particular provisions should apply to its functional area), the general tendency in modern legislation is for mandatory provisions, particularly in the case of major services or regulatory functions. European Union legislation has also resulted in certain mandatory requirements on local authorities, particularly in the environmental area.

Each local authority has exclusive legal responsibility within its own functional area for carrying out the functions vested in it. However, the functional jurisdictions of different classes of authorities vary for the purposes of particular functions. In particular, county councils are legally responsible for provision of certain services e.g. some roads, fire and library services, in the urban areas - referred to as "county at large" functions. In practice, county councils also provide certain other services on behalf of urban authorities on an agency basis or assist the latter in the exercise of their statutory functions (e.g. by affording them the use of staff or other resources). These functional interactions are reflected in corresponding financial arrangements between the various authorities. There is not a significant problem of overlapping competencies.

The regional authorities provide further vehicles of co-ordination between local authorities and public authorities generally, without, however, affecting the responsibilities or competencies of the various authorities.

Considerations such as economies of scale, capacity, specialist needs and national and European Union requirements have led to some movement of functions from sub-county to county level and to a certain extent, from the local authority sector to specialist national institutions. Moreover, some area/community-based structures have, in recent years, developed outside the local authority system, particularly in the field of local development and enterprise initiatives e.g. based on integrated strategies to tackle long term unemployment and enterprise support. The approach here tends to be a multi-sectoral one to harness the capabilities of local communities and enable them to play a lead role in creating enterprise and addressing unemployment and social exclusion at local level.

2. MANAGEMENT FUNCTIONS

2.1 Policy-making and co-ordination

Coherence, consultation and conflict resolution

Ad *hoc* directions or guidelines are commonly issued to sub-national bodies by the relevant departments. A major instrument for influencing and directing the implementation of policy through sub-national bodies is the process of financial allocations and associated controls and conditions, both generally and through the monitoring and control of specific projects.

The relevant line departments are responsible for financial control and on-going liaison with the bodies under their aegis, and within these departments, responsibility tends to rest with the relevant functional units rather than central or co-ordinating units. This contact exists at the technical as well as the administrative level.

The "parent" government departments (e.g. the Department of the Environment in the case of local authorities, Department of Health in the case of health boards, etc.) play important roles in the provision of advice, guidance and co-ordination generally in relation to the various sub-national bodies under their aegis. There are also specialist semi-state agencies (national level) which provide services, advice and assistance to local authorities, including: National Building Agency, Housing Finance Agency, Local Government Computer Services Board, Local Government Management Services, Fire Services

Council, National Safety Council, Library Council. A Central Fisheries Board is responsible for the co-ordination of the work of the seven regional fisheries boards. Bord Fáilte (Irish Tourist Board) supports and works in co-operation with the Regional Tourism Organisations. Area Development Management Ltd., an independent company under the aegis of the Department of the Taoiseach (Prime Minister) supports local area-based partnerships in integrated local economic and social development.

Other means for achieving coherence and co-ordination between central and local level include liaison between departments and representative associations of local authority members, and participation at relevant conferences, etc. Other national agencies mentioned in section 1.1 also play an important role in co-ordination of and securing adherence to national policy. Contact at political level e.g. between ministers and delegations from local authorities or their representative associations forms another important means of communication and influence. More structured approaches to co-ordination and liaison with sub-national authorities are being established in the context of a Strategic Management Initiative (see section 2.3).

The regional authorities have the role of promoting co-ordination of the provision of public services in each region, co-ordination between central government and public authorities in the regions and providing a forum for consultation and co-operation between public authorities.

Decisions by public authorities may be subject to judicial review and in certain cases there is specific provision for appeal to the courts (e.g. under planning and environmental legislation in relation to unauthorised development or pollution) or submission to the European Union Commission or petition to the European Parliament.

Formal and informal mechanisms

Sub-national authorities operate within a general framework of legislation, policy and planning developed by central government through the relevant Ministers/Departments and monitored by the relevant Departments. Consistency with national policy is secured through a variety of administrative, financial and political interactions. In recent years, national policy across the various sectors has been integrated and articulated in a series of plans/programmes, co-ordinated by the central Departments of Finance and the Taoiseach (Prime Minister) as follows:

- government programmes – usually published at the start of a government's term of office setting out its main objectives and policies in key areas;

- National Agreements – between government and the main "social partners", setting out broad parameters for social and economic policy and industrial relations on a multi-annual basis;

- a comprehensive National Development Plan – prepared with particular reference to European Union funding programmes and containing details of policies, objectives, programmes, targets and financial implications;

- a series of Operational Programmes related to European Union assistance provide further elaboration and refinement on the National Plan in respect of particular sectors or groups of related sectors.

As well as supporting the implementation of national programmes, local authorities and other sub-national agencies also provide important input to national planning and policy formulation through identification of needs and proposing projects which are incorporated in national programmes.

Voluntary national representative associations of local authority elected members facilitate co-ordination and consultation on local government matters at the political level. The Association of Municipal Authorities of Ireland represents urban authorities. The General Council of County Councils represents county level authorities. In addition a Local Authority Members Association represents elected members in their own right as distinct from their authorities. There are similar members' associations in the education and health sectors.

Practical co-operation and co-ordination between county level authorities is common, for example, in the case of infrastructural projects crossing local authority boundaries. There is specific statutory provision for making agency-type agreements on a formal basis, for the joint discharge of functions (e.g. roads and fire service functions) and for formal structures of co-operation between local authorities by way of joint committees (both for executive and advisory purposes). The initiative in relation to joint committees and inter-authority agreements rests primarily with the local authorities but there is provision for central direction in certain cases (e.g. agreements in connection with roads and fire service functions). The advent of the National Roads Authority has brought an added element of overall statutory co-ordination to the national road development function as has the Environmental Protection Agency. A report by a Reorganisation Commission published in June 1996 entitled *Towards Cohesive Local Government – Town and County* recommended greater cohesiveness and co-operation between, town and county local authorities, including greater staff and organisational integration at operational level, increased linkage between town and county elected members and establishment of joint (town/county) services centres to provide more comprehensive, customer-oriented services. The "Programme for Change" states that there will be greater co-operation between county councils and town authorities with the provision of services in towns on a harmonised basis and co-ordinated plans of action for town improvements.

The role of the regional authorities is to help to promote "horizontal" co-ordination between sub-national bodies. In the local development field, County Strategy Groups on which the County Manager, Area Partnership Companies, County Enterprise Boards, Leader Groups and other relevant bodies are represented will facilitate co-operation and co-ordination. The regional authorities also have a further potentially important role in helping to ensure coherence and compatibility in the implementation of policy by virtue of their responsibility for monitoring and advising on the implementation at regional level of the various Operational Programmes under the European Union Structural and Cohesion Funds. There are also national monitoring committees for the Operational Programmes and Community Support Framework, which include representatives of departments, agencies and the European Commission.

Contact with public authorities and citizens or local groups is mainly on an informal, ad hoc basis. It is common for local authorities to have special (informal) consultative relationships with local voluntary representative groups such as community/residents associations. Meetings with delegations from such bodies commonly occur and also with groups such as chambers of commerce and other representative organisations and interest groups. Communication and consultation with the public is facilitated both formally, through various requirements for public notice of local authority proposals and decisions and informally, through extensive public reportage of local authority business in the local media. The general public are to be given express legal right to attend council meetings; and representation of local interests on the new Strategic Policy Committees of local authorities is proposed. Proposals are also to be developed for pilot "one-stop-shop" centres for a wide range of public services.

Local public representatives frequently provide an informal "mediation" role between their constituents and the authorities. The law also provides for formal public inquiries/consultation in specific areas such as compulsory land purchase, motorway proposals, and integrated environmental licensing. There is provision for arbitration in relation to compulsory purchase terms and for appeal (including by third parties) to a national planning appeals board, An Bord Pleanala, against local authority decisions on physical planning (i.e. land use/development) applications and local authority licensing of water discharges. Persons can lodge formal objections at audit on which the auditor is obliged to adjudicate and there is provision for the public to inspect local authority accounts. There are public rights of access to certain environmental information in accordance with European Union requirements. Citizens can bring complaints to the Ombudsman against sub-national authorities. The current government programme proposes an Administrative Procedures Act, which would be administered by the Office of the Ombudsman, to provide for such matters as minimum response time to citizens' cases, guidance to the public and the form and content of decision communication (including basis of decision and citizens' rights in the matter). The government programme also proposes improved access to environmental information and the development of a customer/client approach to public services generally. It is proposed that a comprehensive list of public rights to information from local authorities will be published.

Many of the formal procedures referred to above are also relevant to relations between local authorities and other public authorities. However, any difficulties in that regard would more usually be submitted for resolution informally in the first instance between the parent national authorities of the respective bodies. Such occurrences are very infrequent.

2.2 Financial management

The information in this section reflects the system applying up to and including 1996 but a new funding system was announced in the "Programme for Change" from 1997 onwards. From then, instead of receiving revenues from charges for domestic water and sewage services and the rate support grant, local authorities will be assigned the proceeds of the motor tax. There are also provisions for discretionary local contributions towards specific development projects or programmes.

Sources of revenues

Local government bodies: The following table indicates the main sources of local authority revenue, distinguishing between current and capital accounts, and their evolution since 1985.

Table 2. **Local authority revenue (1985, 1990, 1996)**

	1985		1990		1996	
	Ir£ m.	%	Ir£ m.	%	Ir£ m.	%
Current						
Government grants	736	64.5	470	43.7	531	41.2
Services	264	23.1	366	34.0	418	32.5
Commercial rates	141	12.4	239	22.3	339	26.3
TOTAL	1 141	100	1 075	100	1 288	100
Capital						
Government	477	79	297	80	612	77
Internal Capital Receipts	32	5	68	18	103	13
Borrowing	92	16	4	2	81	10
TOTAL	601	100	369	100	796	100

Source: Department of Finance.

Local property taxes (rates) are levied by local authorities – other than town commissioners – only on commercial and industrial property. There are no local property taxes on domestic dwellings. Local authority income from services, etc., derives mainly from housing loan repayments (Ir£ 106 m.); local authority housing rents and annuities (Ir£ 84 m.); and service charges in respect of domestic and commercial water supplies, refuse collection etc. (Ir£ 108 m.). Internal capital receipts arise mainly from the sale of local authority rented housing to tenants and capital repayments of local authority housing loans. In addition to a limited degree of long term borrowing, local authorities use temporary overdraft accommodation through the banking system to meet short term funding requirements pending the receipt of rates, state grants and other revenue.

Central government grants to local authorities comprise both general and specific grants. Grants for capital purposes are specific in nature and relate to particular expenditure programmes such as housing, roads, and sanitary services.

The Rate Support Grant is the most significant type of general grant towards current expenditure, accounting for 36 per cent of total revenue account grants and 15 per cent of overall local authority current expenditure. Other current account grants tend to be tied to specific responsibilities or projects, but discretionary (block) grants are also provided, for example, to supplement local authorities' own expenditure on maintenance and improvement of non-national roads. In 1995, a 10-year restoration programme for regional and county roads was initiated, involving payment of grants to county councils which can be categorised as "discretionary" in that the local authorities concerned determine the roads to be improved subject to general guidelines issued by the Department of the Environment. Revenue

Table 3. **Government grants (current) (1996)**[1]

	Ir£ m.	%
Rate Support	193	36.3
Roads	164	30.9
Higher Education	75	14.2
Social Employment	41	7.7
Other	58	10.9
TOTAL	531	100

1. Estimates
Source: Department of Finance.

from local sources such as commercial rates and service charges is mainly available for general use rather than specific projects.

Grants to local authorities for various capital programmes include Roads - Ir£ 316 m.; Housing Ir£ 154 m.; Water & Sanitary Services - Ir£ 122 m.; Environmental Services - Ir£ 7 m.; Fire and Emergency Services - Ir£ 4.5 m.; Miscellaneous - Ir£ 14 m. (1996 figures).

Funding for regional authorities is provided mainly by the constituent local authorities by way of general contributions to their net expenses in proportion to the populations of the constituent areas. Being non-executive bodies at a very early stage of development, the annual expenditure of regional authorities is relatively low.

Non local government bodies: Other non-local government bodies are funded to a significant extent by way of grants from central government. For example, Health Board funding is provided mainly from general taxation (including an ear-marked health contribution) and is allocated to the Health Boards by the Department of Health. Additional funding is provided by hospital charges and through the National Lottery. Allocations to the Health Boards are made annually and are based broadly on demographic factors and the levels of service within each board. At the regional level each Health Board is responsible for allocating its resources to the services it provides. Regional Tourism Organisations derive their income from a variety of sources namely, Tourist Board subvention, local authority subscriptions, other membership contributions and commercial activities. Vocational Education Committees are funded mainly through State grants with some local authority contributions. Other local development/enterprise bodies referred to in this chapter are financed through a combination of European, national and private funding under European Union Operational Programmes.

Expenditure responsibilities

The breakdown and evolution of local authority expenditure in terms of broad areas of responsibility is shown in Table 4.

The areas of responsibility in which local authorities may incur expenditure are determined by law, but, as already stated, they were recently given wide authority to act in the interests of their areas. The legality of local authority expenditure is subject to adjudication at audit. The level of expenditure and its distribution are determined by the elected members in the context of the annual estimates (budget) process, having regard to relevant demands and priorities. Procedures in relation to the estimates are prescribed in law. While responsibility for the adoption of the estimates rests with the elected members of the authority, in practice, formulation of proposals is primarily a function of management. The budgetary decisions of local authorities are significantly influenced and constrained by a number of factors, such as:

- the overall availability of funding as determined in particular by the level of State grants and the local revenue base;
- the requirements and priorities of national and European Union programmes, policies and standards; and
- the need to make adequate provision for certain essential services such as water and fire services.

Table 4. **Main expenditure patterns of local authorities (1985, 1990, 1996)**

	1985 Ir£ m.	1985 %	1990 Ir£ m.	1990 %	1996 Ir£ m.	1996 %
Current (per local authority estimates)						
Housing	361	31.2	226	20.9	235	18.2
Roads	313	27.0	391	36.1	358	27.8
Water services	167	14.4	112	10.4	150	11.6
Environment services	103	8.9	123	11.4	178	13.8
Recreation and amenity	64	5.6	92	8.4	141	10.9
Other	150	12.9	138	12.8	226	17.7
TOTAL	1 158	100	1 082	100	1 288	100
Capital (per public capital programme)						
Housing	361	44	84	23	320	40
Roads	128	30	192	52	316 [1]	40
Water services	98	23	73	20	122	15
Environment services	8	2	16	4	21	3
Recreation and amenity	–	–	4	1	5	1
Other	6	1	–	–	12	1
TOTAL	601	100	369	100	796	100

1. For accounting reasons Ir£ 97 million of this amount is included in local authority current expenditure.
Source: Department of Finance.

As in the case of other public bodies, a substantial part of expenditure arising in any particular period is determined by past decisions. For example, in 1996 employment-related costs accounted for 45 per cent of total local authority current expenditure, while other overheads, debt service, insurance and statutory demands from other public authorities represented a further 25 per cent.

Balance between discretion and control

The main instrument for control of local authority finances at local level is the formal estimates process in which decisions are taken by the authority for each year in relation to local sources of income (principally commercial rates and service charges) and levels of expenditure under the various programmes. There are no legal limits on the revenue-raising capacity of local authorities but practical constraints result from factors such as the extent and valuation of commercial property and the number of persons liable to pay service charges. On the expenditure side, local authorities are, as already indicated, somewhat constrained by the demands of national and European Union requirements and the fact that their discretionary expenditure is, in practice, limited.

The major overall determining factor on local authority spending is the central government budgetary process, given the significance of State grants to local authority funding. However, from 1997 local authorities will have an assigned source of revenue instead of the principal general grant currently paid to them (the Rate Support Grant). The amounts available to local authorities by way of State funding are determined by government in the annual Public Service Estimates and Public Capital Programme. The distribution of funding between particular authorities is determined by way of allocations issued by individual government departments (or other relevant State agencies e.g. the National Roads Authority in relation to national roads) for different programme areas. Expenditure on particular projects is determined by their agreed budgets and scheduling, with transfer of grant funding being commensurate with satisfactory progress.

Borrowing by local authorities must be approved by the appropriate minister (normally the Minister for the Environment) in accordance with statutory provisions.

2.3 Performance Management

Mechanisms

Responsibility for performance and standards of service rests primarily with local management who are accountable to the members of the relevant authority, the latter in turn being, accountable, in the case of the elected local authorities, to the electorate.

The statutory requirements relating to accounts, audit and annual reports of public authorities ensure a high degree of public accountability. For example the local government audit system (see section 1.1) involves a thorough scrutiny by qualified auditors who have wide ranging powers. County level local authorities are legally obliged to publish annual reports and a number of other authorities also do so in practice. Various controls and procedures such as internal audit, inspectorate reports, returns by sub-national bodies to parent departments and overview and monitoring by departments are relevant to performance management. Overview and monitoring apply both in relation to targets in national programmes and in terms of appraisal and control of specific projects so as to maximise effectiveness and value for money. The various national support/advisory bodies referred to in section 1.1 also play a valuable role in promoting standards in their areas, as do the relevant professional institutes/associations. It is proposed that performance standards and financial indicators will be used to measure and compare local authority activities in the delivery of key services.

Quality standards

Recent developments of particular significance to the areas of performance and standards include the establishment of a Value for Money Unit within the Department of the Environment which undertakes reviews, by research and enquiry, of selected local authority operations with a view to improving the economy, efficiency and effectiveness of operations. This complements value for money initiatives by individual local authorities themselves. A major new development is also the introduction, initially at central government level, of a Strategic Management process to establish targets, performance indicators and systems for review and evaluation of progress. This process is now being extended to public bodies generally, including sub-national authorities. For example, in March 1996 the Minister for the Environment asked county and city councils to begin their formal involvement in the Strategic Management Initiative by preparing strategy statements for their own organisations.

County Enterprise Plans formulated by each County Enterprise Board will include annual targets, quantified objectives and performance indicators and the Boards will be subject to ongoing performance assessment by the Department of Enterprise and Employment and by the European Commission. The Leader Programme will be subject to ongoing evaluation by consultants and an external evaluator will also assist in monitoring achievement of objectives by Area Partnership Boards.

2.4 Human resource management

Statutory distinctions

Local authority staffing comprises administrative, clerical, professional and technical staffs (35 per cent) together with craft and general workers (65 per cent). In all there are approximately 30 000 local authority staff (including part-time and full-time workers). The administrative, clerical, professional and technical staff are known as "officers" and a special body of law applies to them concerning the creation of offices, appointments to offices, qualifications, duties, tenure of office, abolition of offices, suspensions, removal from office, etc. All staff, administrative and technical, are subject to the county or city manager. The main administrative personnel are the assistant city/county manager (grade does not apply in all areas), county secretary and finance officer, and the town clerk in the case of the town authorities, while the chief technical official is the county engineer. A new management tier with responsibility for individual programmes and a lead role in new Strategic Policy Committees is proposed.

Table 5. **Public service and public sector employment (1985, 1990-1994)**
(as at 1 January, full-time equivalent)

	1985	1990	1991	1992	1993	1994 [1]
Civil service	31 564	27 845	28 379	29 097	29 715	29 844
Garda Siochana (National Police)	11 387	10 900	11 234	11 303	11 463	11 468
Defence forces	15 880	14 387	14 761	14 564	14 361	14 090
Education	54 100	51 306	51 666	52 910	54 466	55 821
Non-commercial State bodies	9 424	7 110	7 100	7 940	8 010	8 113
Health services	62 503	57 329	58 743	59 504	60 566	61 810
Local authorities *of which*:	32 566	26 468	26 681	26 715	26 793	27 060
Officers	10 082	8 759	8 939	9 098	9 217	9 553
Servants	22 484	17 709	17 742	17 617	17 576	17 507
TOTAL PUBLIC SERVICE	217 424	195 345	198 564	202 033	205 374	208 209
Commercial State bodies	85 711	71 932	71 875	66 655	64 628	63 422
TOTAL PUBLIC SECTOR	303 135	267 277	270 439	268 688	270 002	271 631

1. Estimated figures except for local authorities, which are from the Department of Finance.
Sources: *Public Management Developments: Update 1995*, OECD, 1995.

Regional authority chief officers are seconded from other public authorities. Staff of central and local government can, accordingly, compete for appointment. Other regional authority staff needs are provided mainly on an agency basis by public authorities in the region (regional authorities staff complements are very limited.)

Concerning non-local government bodies, staffing matters are largely the responsibility of the bodies themselves. Terms and conditions of employment for Health Board employees are determined by the Department of Health. Recruitment for senior and professional posts in Health Boards is carried out by the Local Appointments Commission. Other personnel are recruited directly by the boards, subject to the approval of the Department of Health, which controls the overall numbers employed in the health service. Staffing of County Enterprise Boards will be subject to the terms of their Memorandum and Articles of Association and Operating Agreements with the Department of Enterprise & Employment and to expenditure limits approved by the Minister for Enterprise and Employment.

Managerial autonomy

The individual local authority is the employer for bargaining purposes but a central (semi-State) agency, the Local Government Staff Negotiations Board (LGSNB), provided services as required for staff negotiation purposes to local authorities and Health Boards. A separate body was established to provide staff negotiation services for health agencies, including the health boards, with effect from 1 July 1996. A new Local Government Management Services Board was also established with effect from January 1997 to provide a comprehensive support system for the human resources functions of local authorities. This board took over the functions of the former LGSNB which previously had an industrial relations focus.

The staffing requirements of local authorities is a matter for individual local authority managers to determine. In the case of officer grades, the creation of offices requires the consent of the elected council (if an increase in the number of permanent offices is involved) and either the general or specific approval of the Minister for the Environment. In the context of the implementation of the Strategic Management Initiative in the local authority service, the Minister recently dispensed with controls on the creation of offices up to middle-management levels, subject to compliance with overall policies on public sector staffing numbers. Further devolution of decisions on human resources to local authorities is proposed.

Local authority salary levels are determined in accordance with overall public service pay policy and are sanctioned by the Minister for the Environment for implementation by the local authorities.

Apart from specific functions related to the appointment and suspension of managers, all functions related to staffing are executive functions of the manager. The Minister for the Environment declares/approves the qualifications and particulars of office for all officer posts. Access to officer posts is open to all persons who fulfil the qualifications for the office. However, the qualifications for certain middle management administrative grades confine eligibility to certain staff of local authorities, Health Boards and Vocational Education Committees. Vacancies for senior administrative and professional posts are filled by the local authority concerned, following public advertisement and open competition, on the recommendation of a central agency, the Local Appointments Commission. Vacancies for other local authority offices are filled directly by the local authority concerned in accordance with a procedure which is laid down in statutory regulations. Selection is by competitive examination and/or interview in accordance with directions issued by the Minister from time to time.

There is to be a review of recruitment. Greater opportunities for graduate entry; a code of practice for the employment of people with disabilities; and a development programme aimed at increasing the number of women are proposed.

Recruitment of craft and general workers and their qualifications and procedures for appointment are matters for the local authority manager and their level of remuneration is sanctioned by the Minister for the Environment.

Mobility: There is considerable mobility between local authorities. Staff in one local authority can compete for posts in other authorities which are subject to open competition and in practice the career paths of senior personnel tend to show considerable movement between authorities. There is a limited degree of mobility between central and local level and between local authorities and non-local government bodies. Staff at each level can compete for posts which are subject to open competition.

3. TRENDS IN REDISTRIBUTING AUTHORITY ACROSS LEVELS OF GOVERNMENT

3.1 Evolving tendencies

A wide-ranging programme of local government reform has been implemented on a phased basis since 1991. Many changes have already been made to strengthen and modernise the powers of local authorities, give them greater flexibility and independence of action and ensure that local government structures are more relevant and meaningful to local communities and at the same time more effective and efficient. Future legislation affecting local authorities will continue these trends, wherever possible. The document "Better Local Government – A Programme for Change", published in December 1996, now provides the programme for further action on local government reform.

The regional authorities, established in 1994, were the first new authorities to be created within the local government system in almost a century and recent reorganisation in Dublin involved the establishment of new county councils for the first time since the inception of the county council system in 1898.

Other evolving tendencies of significance include the acquisition of additional functions by local authorities in certain areas and movement of others to different levels or agencies, as outlined in section 1.3.

Significant changes have taken place in the system of local government financing. Prior to 1978 the local property tax base included domestic dwellings and agricultural land as well as industrial and commercial properties. Legislation enacted in 1978 abolished the property tax (rates) on domestic dwellings and replaced it by a central government grant – the Rate Support Grant – which, in each year between 1978 and 1982, fully recouped the loss of income to local authorities. With effect from 1983 the property tax on agricultural land was terminated as a result of a Court judgement, with the result that the levying of local property tax was confined to commercial and industrial property. Two further important changes were made by legislation to the system of local government finance at that time. First, the obligation on central government to recoup local authorities fully for the loss of property tax income from domestic dwellings and agricultural land was removed. Second, local authorities were given much greater powers to levy local charges for their services.

Prior to 1988 local authorities borrowed (mainly from State agencies) for various capital purposes such as housing, water and sewerage, libraries, fire service facilities, etc., with State subsidy to assist them in paying the resulting loan charges. In 1988 this system was replaced by direct capital grants from central government for the relevant projects. In addition, local authorities have been relieved of various "statutory demands" from other public authorities for such matters as social welfare supplementary allowances, arterial drainage, agricultural services and compensation for malicious injuries. Central government funding has also been introduced or extended in some new areas such as local roads and urban renewal works.

The foregoing developments have resulted in significant changes in the composition of local authority funding. For example, the termination of the largely circular loan charge and subsidy system for capital projects and its replacement by direct capital grants involved significant reduction in local authority current expenditure and a reduction in the proportion of local authority current expenditure met by government grants and subsidies (e.g. from over 60 per cent in 1987 to 45 per cent in 1988) with significant increase in the capital grants element. In 1996, 41 per cent of local authority current expenditure and 77 per cent of capital expenditure were met from government grants.

3.2 The current debate

The main issues under consideration in local government have included the question of future sub-county local government, devolution of powers from central government to local authorities, local government funding and issues arising from the emergence in recent years of sub-national agencies outside the local government system, strengthening the decision-making powers of elected members, and the delivery of quality cost-effective and accessible local services.

The structures and powers of town local authorities have been the subject of debate for some years, one of the key issues being how best to achieve a modern and effective system of town government, providing a good quality of democratic representation, while at the same time securing the position of the county councils as the primary units of local government.

A report on town local government (i.e. the sub-county level) by an independent statutory Local Government Reorganisation Commission was submitted in April 1996 to the Minister for the Environment on such matters as the future classification, functions, staffing, financial and other organisational arrangements for town authorities, relationships between town and county authorities and criteria and procedures for the possible establishment of new town authorities. Among the principal recommendations in the report are, establishment of a single class of town authorities – "Town Councils"; development of town authorities' role in new directions with emphasis on areas such as town development and social and community-related matters and representational functions; concentration of certain infrastructural and regulatory functions at county level; a more meaningful role for small town authorities; greater flexibility in local arrangements for discharge of functions; emphasis on effective and customer-oriented services (including joint services centres); more structured linkage between local authorities and local communities; updating of town boundaries, subject to improvements in the system of financial relationships between town and county authorities, and greater cohesiveness between town and county authorities. The latter includes organisational integration, linkage between elected members, structures and procedures for consultation, joint arrangements and programmes, and increased input by town authorities in various county functions.

The question of devolution has also been the subject of discussion for some time. While there has been significant enhancement of the scope, flexibility and discretion of local authorities in the exercise of powers, the possibility of additional functions being devolved from central to local level is also a matter for debate in the context of public service organisation generally.

Reform of local government finance has been a recurring theme in recent years in terms of demands for increase in the overall level of funding available to local authorities, greater local discretion in revenue raising and change in the basis of distribution of central funding. The questions of devolution and funding have tended to be viewed through a common perception, particularly on the part of local authority members, of insufficient local authority power and discretion and excessive centralisation in certain matters.

A relatively recent trend has been the emergence of agencies outside of the local government system, including new structures at local level such as the County Enterprise Boards, local groups for implementation of European Union Leader programmes, Area Partnership Companies and other area-based local development groups, designed to respond to the complex and wide-ranging factors giving rise to social and economic exclusion, particularly in disadvantaged areas. The emergence of such local structures has given rise to some concern on the part of local authority members. There are proposals to link the systems of local government and local development more closely. In other sectors such as education, the possibility of reduction in the direct involvement/influence of local authority members has also been a subject of debate e.g. in connection with reduction in representation on certain third level institutes and proposals relating to primary and second level education involving the creation of new regional education boards and restructuring of the Vocational Education Committees. Legislation enacted in 1996 provides for reorganisation of the Harbour Authorities, also with implications for representation of elected members in this sector.

3.3 Driving forces

Government initiatives in the form of policy programmes and government-commissioned reviews, studies, etc., have been significant factors in relation to local government reform. For example, many of the reforms already referred to, such as granting of a general competence to local authorities, relaxation of various central government controls on local authorities, provisions to enhance the position of elected members, reorganisation of local government in the Dublin area and establishment of regional authorities, followed on recommendations in a 1991 report of an advisory expert committee commissioned by the government. The recommendation to establish regional authorities was influenced by a range of factors such as, the fact that various sectoral authorities are organised on a regional basis, the desirability of providing a democratic input to these and bringing them together with the local authorities, the need for a strategic regional approach across different local authorities and sectors and between central and local government, the need for a regional approach in relation to the National Development Plan and European Union assistance programmes and the desirability of promoting greater standardisation of regions for various purposes. The current government programme proposes expanding the role of regional authorities in relation to the preparation of regional strategies. It is proposed that they be assigned new responsibilities for promoting sustainable development and that the Dublin and Mid East regional authorities will draw up land use planning guidelines for the Greater Dublin area.

In addition to such initiatives, local government reform issues have been shaped by various and in some cases conflicting, factors and influences. Local authority elected members and their representative associations are among the main proponents of reform, particularly in relation to local authority powers and funding. The subject of reform has also been raised by various academic commentators both in terms of enhancement of democratic structures and claims of potential economic benefits (results of devolution in other countries often being cited). At the same time, economic factors have also exerted certain countervailing influences. For example, cost, technical complexity and requirements of specialist expertise and other resources, have produced a trend towards increased scale in the organisation of certain functions. Meanwhile, the desire for an area-based or "bottom-up" approach has influenced the development of certain new initiatives outside of the local government system. A variety of factors are also evident in local government finance issues. Moves towards a formula-based method of government grant distribution (which was the subject of a recent study) have not yielded agreement, due particularly to the possibility of some authorities being adversely affected and the apparent volatility of the proposed method.

With regard to democratic influences, local government reform has not featured as significantly as might possibly be expected in public opinion generally, although issues such as service charges and certain local authority responsibilities (e.g. local roads) are frequently the subject of debate. Nonetheless, reform has been a relatively prominent political issue, being a recurring theme in party policy documents and government programmes. The current reform programme was initiated in 1990/1991 and has been pursued with a high degree of continuity by successive governments. Arising from the current government's programme, a Devolution Commission was established in 1995 to oversee a programme of devolution and local government renewal under the aegis of the Department of the *Taoiseach* (Prime Minister). The Commission was required to make recommendations in relation to the following:

- significant additional functions to be devolved to the local government system on the basis of a phased programme;
- local authorities to be meaningfully involved with policy and administration regarding functions which are not devolved directly to them;
- local authorities to become the focus for working through local partnerships involving local community-based groupings, voluntary bodies, the private sector, and public agencies;
- the efforts of local authorities and those of existing groups such as County Enterprise Boards, Leader groups, and Area Partnerships to be co-ordinated.

The Commission submitted an interim report to the government in August 1996. A key recommendation was that the existing local government and local development systems should be brought closer together and simplified. The Commission is to prepare a further report on powers and functions for devolution to the local level.

The government programme also provided for a professional study of the system of local government financing with a view to the publication of government proposals and to developing maximum consensus on this issue. In July 1995 consultants were commissioned to undertake this study to be carried out in two stages. The study focused on the current finances of local authorities and examined relevant issues such as the expenditure needs of local authorities, residential property tax and service charges. A report was published in June 1996 in relation to various options for in-depth examination.

In December 1996 a major programme for the renewal of local government entitled: "Better Local Government – A Programme for Change" was launched by the Minister for the Environment. Reference to some of its specific proposals have already been made in this chapter. The main features of the Programme's proposals, the implementation of which is proceeding as a matter of priority, are:

- a considerable strengthening of the decision-making powers of councillors within the local government system;
- widening the scope of local councils to influence the delivery of all public services provided locally, not just those delivered by local government itself;
- rationalising the existing complexities involving Area Partnerships, County Enterprise Boards, and LEADER groups; and moving the local development system closer to the local government system;
- new emphasis on developing an efficient and responsive local government system wherein services are delivered promptly, to a high standard, and cost-effectively;
- ensuring that demarcations in the delivery of services by different categories of local authorities are broken down in the interests of a comprehensive a service to local citizens;

- local services to be delivered from locations close to the customer, and "one-stop-shops" for all public services to be developed, initially on a pilot basis;
- a new funding system under which:- charges for domestic water and sewerage services will be abolished, local authorities will be assigned the full proceeds of the motor tax and will have discretion to vary rates within fixed parameters, and an equalisation fund will be established;
- further modernisation and consolidation of local government law.

In addition to the question of local government reform, proposals for change and development in the structures and functions of sub-national authorities generally are shaped by the ongoing process of policy formulation, review and discussion, which as already indicated, have a particular focus in the National Development Plan, the government programme and national agreements with the social partners.

ITALY

1. INSTITUTIONS AND AUTHORITY

1.1 Structures

Description of levels

The Italian Constitution approved in 1948 provides for a three-tier system of sub-national government: regions, provinces and municipalities. The total area of Italy is 301 200 square kilometres and the population in 1993 was 57 190 000.

The regions are of two types: ordinary statute regions (of which there are 15) and five special statute regions. The latter are classed as "special" in that they have wider legislative and administrative powers. They were founded between 1946 and 1948, mainly with the aim of containing separatist movements (two, Sicily and Sardinia, are large islands and the others are frontier territories). One of the special statute regions, Trentino-Alto Adige, has delegated almost all its legislative and administrative powers to the two component provinces of Trento and Bolzano which, although called autonomous provinces, can for all intents and purposes be considered to be regions in their own right.

Table 1: **Area and population of sub-national governments (1992)**

	Regions		Provinces		Municipalities	
	Area (km^2)	Population	Area (km^2)	Population	Area (km^2)	Population
Largest	25 708	8 939 429	7 520	3 986 838	1 508	2 791 354
Smallest	3 262	115 995	212	94 146	0.10	30

Number of municipalities and population distribution	
Population size	Number of municipalities
0-1 000	1 935
1 000-5 000	3 964
5 000-10 000	1 166
10 000-50 000	898
50 000-100 000	95[1]
over 100 000	44[1]

(1) figure supplied in 1996
Source: *Structure and Operation of Local and Regional Democracy: Italy*, Council of Europe, 1993.

There are two types of provinces: ordinary statute provinces (of which there are 101) and two autonomous provinces. Both types have rather limited and specific functions.

There are 8 104 municipalities which are the sub-national governments in closest contact with citizens. A number of other sub-national government entities have been created through national legislation. Some of these are multipurpose (like the 344 highland communities operating between the province and municipality) while others are monofunctional, e.g. the approximately 200 local health authorities. Table 1 summarises the distribution of sub-national authorities by size.

Central government at sub-national levels

In each of the 101 provinces there is a "Prefect of the Republic" modelled on the French example, nominated by the Council of Ministers and acting as a general representative of the government in the province. He is responsible to the Minister of the Interior. Up until 1970, the powers of the prefect were considerable. Today, his principal function is to ensure public order. Each municipality has attached to it a "municipal secretary" who is also directly responsible to the Minister of the Interior. He is a State civil servant and ensures the legality of municipal actions.

Creation, elimination and restructuring

This three-tier system of sub-national government is laid down in the Constitution and hence can be modified only by constitutional amendment which is a complicated procedure. Constitutional amendment is also necessary to alter the number of regions or regional boundaries. The regions are empowered to legislate the suppression or creation of municipalities and make boundary changes. The creation of municipalities or the redrawing of their boundaries may be done after consultation with the local inhabitants concerned.

Regional authorities may, in certain cases, create associations of municipalities for the management of activities and services concerning adjacent areas. Consortia of municipalities may be formed between municipalities and provinces for the joint management of one or more services. Each consortia has its own legal personality and autonomy and its status is approved by the councils of directors of the associated authorities. Each consortia has a deliberative body, the Assembly, composed of the political heads of the associated authorities which in turn elects an administrative board.

Unions of municipalities may also be established between two or more municipalities with less than 5 000 inhabitants in the same province, in anticipation of their eventual merger, for the joint execution of a number of various functions or services. They are run on a system similar to that of the municipality. If no merger occurs within ten years, it is dissolved.

Control bodies

Regions: A supervisory commission, chaired by the State commissioner for the region, oversees the administrative actions of the region. Constitutional legitimacy of regional legislation is exercised by the Government (the Council of Ministers). Administrative acts of the regions are subject to ex ante control by the Supervisory commission. The types of act falling under this control were drastically reduced in 1993. A presidential decree may, after consultation with the parliamentary committee on regional affairs, dissolve the regional council if it performs unconstitutional acts or seriously violates the law. The Chairman of the Council of Ministers may suspend by a decree regional officers found guilty of serious crime

Provinces and municipalities: The supervisory committee for the region (a regional body operating according to a national law) exercises control over the legality of administrative acts of provincial and municipal councils. The President of the Republic may dissolve (by decree) a provincial or municipal council if it performs unconstitutional acts or seriously violates the law. For the same reasons, the Minister of the Interior may by decree remove any mayor, provincial chairman or member of a council.

The Court of Audit is the national audit office responsible for auditing the regularity of expenditure by both the central and sub-national public administration (see section 2.2).

1.2 Powers

Nature of sub-national institutions

Regions: Legislative and administrative powers are uniform for the 15 "ordinary statute" regions. Legislative power lies with the Regional Council which is elected for five years by residents in the region using a mixed voting system with a large majority component. The regional council elects from among its members its president, the regional executive council and the president of the executive council.

The deliberative body of the provinces and the municipalities is the council. The executive body of the provinces and the municipalities is the "junta". The electoral system for the municipalities was changed in 1993 such that the mayor and council members are now elected by majority rule, if necessary with a second ballot. The mayor appoints members of the junta – who need not necessarily be councillors.

Type and degree of autonomy

The regions enjoy considerable independence in matters of internal administration and organisation. They also have legislative and regulatory power for the areas of responsibility assigned to them. Article 117 of the Constitution lays down the functions of the ordinary statute regions. Those of the special statute regions are broader and are contained in special legislation with constitutional force. Legislation passed by ordinary statute regions must receive the *null osta* of central government that it is not in conflict with the general principles contained in national legislation, nor with the Constitution. Laws of special statute regions are not, in some matters, subject to the basic principles of State legislation. Conflict between national and regional legislation is very common and in the last instance is resolved by the Constitutional Court. Regional councils propose legislation to the national parliament and issue opinions on territorial changes to regions and provinces; they also approve the regional budget and determine regional taxes.

The statute (constitution) of a region lays down the structure and organisation of its administrative apparatus and the powers of the individual regional government departments. The regions delegate most responsibility for programme implementation to the municipalities, provinces, highland communities, local health authorities, etc. along with the necessary funds. Under Law 142, the municipalities and provinces have their own statutes and decide on their internal organisation and the structure of their administrative apparatus.

1.3 Responsibilities

Distribution of competences

The most important responsibility for the regions is health care. This accounts for well over half of their total expenditure. The regions have also an important role in the implementation of European Union agricultural structure policy, economic development, manpower training, housing and capital programmes for environmental protection. They also cover the operating deficits of regional and local transport systems and finance their capital expenditure. The regional role goes beyond financing lower levels of government and also includes planning, regulation and auditing. The regions also co-ordinate the capital programmes of the municipalities and provinces located in their territory.

The provinces have a limited number of functions – in particular the maintenance of designated provincial roads, school building maintenance and pollution control. The municipalities, on the other hand, perform a wide range of functions, either directly or using contracted suppliers (for example, citizen records, street lighting, garbage collection and disposal, urban transport, local police, nursery schooling, public welfare and public housing). Some of these services – especially urban transport and garbage collection and disposal – may be delivered by communally owned companies. This may mean that they compete with the private sector (for example, in the sale of fresh milk and milk derivatives) or with public companies operating at the national level (in the case, for example, of gas and electricity distribution).

The municipalities, like the regions, have important regulatory functions including land use zoning, environmental control and the issue of trading permits.

The period since 1970 has seen the transfer of numerous functions from the State to the regions: for example in the fields of agriculture, manpower training, health care, transport, environmental protection and economic development. This has been accompanied by a transfer of resources, personnel and facilities. Law 142, passed in 1990, set the stage for a reorganisation of the provinces and municipalities. This should lead to a major reallocation of functions between the different government levels. Law 142 also provides for the creation of nine metropolitan cities and also (in article 3) that the region should establish the functions of the provinces and municipalities, other than those guaranteed by national legislation. However, many of the directives provided by this law have not been implemented, and it is probable that it will be amended.

2. MANAGEMENT FUNCTIONS

2.1 Policy-making and co-ordination

Coherence, consultation and conflict resolution

Although the regions and an intricate network of local governments exist, government in Italy is still highly centralised and the national government possesses a variety of instruments for co-ordinating and controlling the activities of sub-national governments. These are broadly of two types: general instruments and instruments for specific sectors or fields of activity. An important general instrument is the power, noted above, to oversee regional legislation and to supervise the administrative activity of all sub-national governments.

All regional statutes require that the region consults with the labour and industrial organisations and with the provinces and municipalities when preparing its annual and pluri-annual budgets and sectoral plans.

Formal and informal mechanisms

Perhaps the most important specific instrument for co-ordination by the regions is the Permanent Conference on State-Region Relations. This is made up of the presidents of the regional executive councils. Recently, a "State-City Conference" has been created, composed of representatives of the provinces and municipalities and the Ministers of the Interior and of the Regions. Central government must, by law, transmit to the Conference questions of direct and significant pertinence to regions (general Acts such as the State budget and Acts regarding individual fields such as health care, environmental protection and European Union programmes). The opinions expressed by the Conference are not however binding on central government.

The Central Commission for Local Finance is a co-ordinating body which reviews the annual accounts of municipalities and provinces which are officially declared to be in financial crisis and examines the measures which they propose for re-establishing financial health.

The regions, but even more so the municipalities and provinces, have powerful lobbies in the form of their national associations which can exert considerable influence over the national legislative process. These associations also co-operate with government authorities in the drawing up of sectoral policies by representing their members' interests and issuing opinions as sometimes provided for by state law. Such associations exist at the regional level (Centre for Interregional Studies and Documentation), at the provincial level (Union of Italian Provinces) and at the municipal level (National Association of Italian Municipalities and the League of Autonomies).

2.2 Financial management

Sources of revenue

Government in Italy is still highly centralised in the area of finance. The main sources of funding for sub-national governments are specific and global transfers. In 1991, transfers represented 93 per cent of total revenues for the ordinary statute regions, 89 per cent for the special statute regions, 75 per cent for the provinces and 55 per cent for the municipalities. 14.5 per cent of municipal revenues came from local taxes and 17 per cent from service tariffs. Three quarters of the transfer revenue of communes came directly from the State and only 18 per cent from the region. Moreover, the major part of regional transfers to the municipalities is pass-through funding from the State.

Table 2. **Revenues of sub-national governments (1989, 1991)**
(billion lira)

Level of government	Year	Own taxes	Tariffs and other own source income	Global transfers	Specific transfers	Loans	TOTAL
A) Regions, ordinary statute	1989	636	497	6 834	71 897	1 603	81 467
	1991	2 128	405	6 946	88 765	4 416	102 660
B) Regions, other statute	1989	163	528	13 627	19 177	1 327	34 822
	1991	205	767	17 315	19 100	3 714	41 101
C) Provinces	1989	593	439	4 595	2 418	1 560	9 605
	1991	633	627	5 362	2 181	1 170	9 973
D) Municipalities	1989	10 259	10 808	30 019	13 969	15 826	80 881
	1991	12 993	15 235	34 588	14 828	12 196	89 840
			percentages				
A) Regions, ordinary statute	1989	0.8	0.6	8.4	88.3	2.0	100
	1991	2.1	0.4	6.8	86.5	4.3	100
B) Regions, other statute	1989	0.5	1.5	39.1	55.1	3.8	100
	1991	0.5	1.9	42.1	46.5	9.0	100
C) Provinces	1989	6.2	4.6	47.8	25.2	16.2	100
	1991	6.3	6.3	53.8	21.9	11.7	100
D) Municipalities	1989	12.7	13.4	37.1	17.3	19.6	100
	1991	14.5	17.0	38.5	16.5	13.6	100

Source: Based on data from Ministero del Bilancio e del Tesoro *Relazione generale sulla situazione economica del Paese* 1993, Istituto Poligrafico dello Stato, Rome, 1994.

Financial equalisation arrangements between municipalities and provinces are based on criteria taking into account the cost of services weighted by coefficients including the size of the area, the population of the municipality or province, and per capita income.

Other sources of income for regions, provinces and municipalities comprise charges, rents, receipts for public services and revenue from bond issues.

Regional level: The ordinary statute regions rely more on own-tax revenues. These are raised mostly from vehicle taxes and piggy-back taxes (on electricity and gas consumption); the regions can select tax rates to be applied within upper and lower limits set by national laws. The two types of region are however broadly similar in how they spend revenues from specific transfers. By far the most important area is health care which alone accounts for over 60 per cent of regional revenues, followed by regional transport and agriculture. Specific transfers to finance European Union agricultural structures programmes are also important.

Local level: The main municipal taxes are the urban garbage tax, property taxes and a tax on the income of the self-employed. The municipalities rely increasingly on own-tax and tariff revenues. These rose by eight percentage points as a share of total revenues between 1989 and 1991.

Expenditure responsibilities

In 1992 most expenditure by the regions was on social affairs, i.e. healthcare (see Table 3). This accounted for 78.3 percent of total expenditure in the "ordinary statute" regions, but only 46.5 percent in the special statute regions. The latter devote a substantial part of their overall expenditure to economic development (16.8 percent compared with 5.9 percent in the ordinary statute regions). Amounts spent on general administration, education and housing is also relatively more significant in the special statute regions than in the others. Current expenditure, compared with capital expenditure, is more important in the ordinary statute regions. The provinces devote their expenditure primarily to education and culture (27.7 percent) and to transport (26.6 percent). The municipalities, on the other hand, spend most on social affairs (28.4 percent).

Table 3. **Sectoral breakdown of expenditure by regions, provinces and municipalities, 1992** [1]
(Percentage)

Sector	Regions ordinary statute	Regions special statute	Provinces	Municipalities
General administration	4.8	8.1	15.9	15.4
Justice	0.0	0.0	0.0	0.5
Police	0.0	0.4	0.0	3.1
Education and culture	1.4	4.8	27.7	13.6
Housing	1.1	3.5	(3)	2.7
Social affairs [2]	78.3	46.5	5.9	28.4
Transport	6.2	3.7	26.6	13.3
Economic development	5.9	16.8	10.9	4.8
Non attributable	2.0	12.0	6.4	10.3
Repayment loans	0.3	4.2	6.7	8.0
Total current expenditure	86.7	60.3	67.7	63.3
Total capital expenditure	13.3	39.7	32.3	36.7
TOTAL (billion lire)	104 098.0	46 064.6	10 441.3	93 977.3

1. Or nearest year.
2. Mainly health care for the regions, mainly social welfare and public health for the provinces and municipalities.
3. For the provinces, expenditure on housing is included in social action.

Source: Based on data from *Relazione generale sulla situazione economica del paese per il* 1993, Istituto poligrafico dello Stato, Rome, 1994.

Balance between discretion and control

Increasingly, specific transfers are being made conditional on prior presentation by the region of detailed indications of how the funds will be used and on donor ministries monitoring implementation. Moreover, Parliament is now asking for more information on the activities of sub-national governments, requiring central ministries and the Court of Audit to report on the state of implementation of key sectoral laws. The crisis in public finances has created much more interest in performance. The State and the regions are signing agreements for specific policy sectors (for example, environmental protection, public works, depressed areas) which establish priorities, quantify funding levels, set completion times and assign tasks to different levels of government.

The own-source revenue raising capacity of sub-national governments (taxes, charges and borrowing) has been tightly controlled and sub-national governments rely rather heavily on central transfers. Specific transfers are particularly important for the regions where over 70 per cent of revenues come in the form of central specific transfers. Central government grants specific transfers either directly to the provinces and municipalities or through the regions in fields where the region has responsibility. Specific transfers may be made conditional on minimum performance or service delivery levels being guaranteed by the beneficiary governments.

Regional level: Ordinary and special statute regions differ markedly in terms of their command over resources. The latter have 16 per cent of the national population but receive over 29 per cent of the total funding available to the regions as a whole. They are also more independent in how they spend: in 1991, 55 per cent of their revenues were in the form of tied transfers compared with over 88 per cent for ordinary statute regions. Global transfers to special statute regions take the form of revenue sharing. Quotas are set by special legislation having constitutional force and therefore with particular procedures for modification. They relate to individual income tax and value added tax revenues raised within the regional territory and are returned to the region. Levels of global transfers for the ordinary statute regions, amounting in any case to only 7 per cent of their revenues, are decided annually by central government.

Local level: Since the early 1980s, central government policy has been to strengthen the own-source revenue raising capacity of the municipalities. Both they and the provinces have considerable independence on the expenditure side of the budget: untied revenues (own taxes and tariffs plus global transfers) account for 70 per cent of municipal and 66.4 per cent of provincial revenues. As with the regions, the municipalities are free to select tax rates within a centrally set band.

Central government's intent in increasing municipal own-source revenue raising capacity, accompanied by a reduction in central transfers, is to make the municipalities more accountable for how they manage their resources and limit central expenditure obligations. Central government has ceded authority for property taxation to the municipalities. The own-source revenue raising capacity of the regions has also been increased, mainly since 1990. Central transfers, particularly specific ones, remain, however, the principal revenue source for the regions.

2.3 Performance management

Mechanisms

In Italy, external and internal government audit has traditionally been seen in terms of ascertaining if individual acts of the public administration conform with the laws and regulations governing them. This legalistic approach has conditioned the introduction of performance auditing in the public sector. Attempts have been made to "normatise" performance by legislating what constitutes acceptable or unacceptable performance in public agencies with the hope of thereby making it possible to legally sanction deviation from these norms. Not surprisingly, this approach has had little success.

Despite the predominance of the conformity audit, many individual administrations, particularly at the sub-national level, have for some time been active in developing internal auditing systems aimed at improving economy, efficiency and effectiveness. It was not, however, until 1990 that central government addressed the question of performance auditing at the sub-regional level. Law 142 requires municipalities and provinces to adopt accounting systems which allocate expenditure by individual programmes and which relate costs to results. Annual accounts must be certified by external auditors (who may be from private accountancy firms). These auditors are also required to make public reports on the performance of municipalities and provinces.

The civil service reform introduced in 1993 makes managers accountable for the performance levels of their departments or offices. It also requires all government agencies to begin measuring staff work loads using methodologies approved by the Civil Service Department. A law approved in early 1994 reduces the scope of the conformity audit while strengthening the external performance audit of sub-national governments. Additional powers in this respect are given to the Court of Audit.

2.4 Human resource management

Statutory distinctions

Sub-national government employees are civil servants in all respects and, broadly speaking, enjoy employment conditions similar to those of central government staff. Since 1993, these conditions (pay, working hours, career structures, pension rights, etc.) are set out in private law contracts (privatisation of public employment) which are negotiated by the civil service trade unions, representatives of sub-national government associations and the Civil Service Department of central government.

Managerial autonomy

Sub-national governments have only limited independence in human resource management, i.e. in terms of numbers of staff to be hired and specific posts to be filled; payment of overtime and incentive awards (the special statute regions can vary basic pay rates); and, last but certainly not least, day-to-day utilisation of personnel. Hiring freezes have been applied on a number of occasions at all levels of government as part of broader strategies to contain public expenditure. Exemption from these freezes has required central government authorisation.

1993 legislation introduced sweeping reform of the civil service at the national and sub-national levels aimed at improving public performance. This gave managers much greater freedom in how they organise and use human resources. To this end, personnel job descriptions, included in the national labour contracts, have been made much less specific and constraining.

Table 4. **Public sector personnel (1985, 1990, 1993)**

	1985	1990	1993
Ministries [1]	272 188	289 795	278 425
Non-commercial public organisations [2]	80 790	77 739	76 641 [5]
Local authorities [3]	697 768	798 228	728 686 [5]
Autonomous bodies	301 760	298 672	274 261
Local health units	691 954	645 591	657 435 [5]
Research establishments	19 820	17 384	16 854 [5]
Schools	1 040 203	1 061 184	998 833
Universities [4]	90 752	107 708	102 721
Armed forces	273 616	305 493	349 146
Military corps and others	80 936	97 658	130 068
TOTAL	3 549 787	3 699 452	3 613 069

1. Including magistrates, managers, posts to be suppressed, municipal and provincial secretaries.
2. Including managers.
3. Including salaried personnel of regions with special status and of the autonomous provinces of Trento et Balzano.
4. Including university professors, managers, and posts to be suppressed.
5. 1992 figure.

Source: *Public Management Developments: Update* 1995, OECD, 1995.

Table 5. **Staff in sub-national governments 1990 (31 December)**

Sub-national governments	Staff
Regions	
– special statute	26 279
– ordinary statute	56 495
Provinces	
– ordinary statute	69 305
– autonomous	13 088
Municipalities	576 830
TOTAL	741 997

Source: ISTAT (1993), *Le regioni in cifre, edizione* 1993, Rome.

3. TRENDS IN REDISTRIBUTING AUTHORITY ACROSS LEVELS OF GOVERNMENT

3.1 Evolving tendencies

Apart from the creation of a small number of regions, all with particular geographical and/or ethnic characteristics, sub-national government has, until recently, consisted of the provinces and municipalities. The provinces, following the Napoleonic model, were in effect the *longa manu* of the State while the powers, responsibilities and organisational arrangements of the municipalities were identical – as laid down in a 1934 law – irrespective of their population, economic base and any other distinguishing features. The system was, that is, highly centralised. The chief exception was finance where municipalities had a high degree of autonomy. In 1965, for example, 50 per cent of municipal current revenues came from own taxes and another 14 per cent from non-tax own-sources, while only 16 per cent arrived in the form of State transfers. The system of local government finance had, however, for some time been under attack for horizontal and vertical inequities in the distribution of the tax burden and in levels of provision of local services. There was also concern about expenditure control and high administrative costs. In 1972, virtually all responsibility for taxation was shifted to the centre accompanied by a major expansion in the grants system to compensate municipalities for lost revenues.

Probably, the most important institutional event in Italy after the founding of the Republic in 1946 and the approval of the Constitution in 1947 was the creation of the ordinary statute regions in 1970. The constitutional provision for the regions was finally implemented: although provided for in the Constitution, it took well over 20 years for a political consensus to be reached on their realisation. A rather minimalist view of the regional role prevailed in that the regions were granted concurrent or shared legislative powers with the State rather than exclusive powers – a source of endless intergovernmental dispute in the future. The regions were not per se, formally represented in the bicameral national legislature, nor were they assigned any revenue raising capacity.

This imbalance between revenue raising and expenditure decision-making became more marked over the years as more functions were transferred to sub-national governments and has seriously marred intergovernmental relations. A leitmotif of State-municipality relations has been how to cope with the accountability problem created by the centralisation of tax authority. Since the beginning of the 1980s, there has been a gradual restitution of revenue-raising power to the municipalities.

3.2 The current debate

Italy has quite wide interregional economic differentials, expressed in a north/centre-south divide. This has been another leitmotif in public policy: until recently, almost any measure involving concession of central government funding contained special treatment for southern regions, while there was a plethora of programmes specifically dedicated to southern economic development. This created an impression of massive north-south redistribution of resources, but southern development policy has had relatively limited success in reducing the north/centre-south divide.

There has however been a qualitative change in the debate on decentralisation with some regions now demanding a greater voice in the decision-making process for determining levels of, and conditions for, central transfers. Redistributive issues were an element in the emergence of the new political party, the Lombardy League (whose success quickly encouraged the formation of other associated northern leagues). The key feature of the programme of this political configuration is the introduction of a strong version of federalism.

The question of constitutional reform is on the agenda of Parliament, which during the summer of 1996 approved the creation of a bicameral commission to amend that part of the Constitution relating to the regions. However, in order for this commission to start its work its creation must be approved a second time by Parliament, with a two-thirds majority.

3.3 Driving forces

Political: The overall context has been one characterised by very considerable historical, cultural and socio-economic heterogeneity at the sub-national level where the sense of local identity is strong. An important route to national politics has been through municipal and regional politics. National politicians have carefully nurtured their local political machines, carrying home whenever possible public expenditure projects. However, with the exception of Alto-Adige, a German-speaking zone in the northeast with a history of separatist movements, national politicians have used their local power base instrumentally and have been projected to the national scene. At least this was true until the advent of the Northern Leagues in the late 1980s.

Financial: The question of public expenditure control has been a factor behind the centralisation of tax powers. Public finance considerations have been a constant feature in the backcloth to decentralisation trends. The annual general government deficit has been above 10 per cent of GDP for the entire period since 1980 and public debt rose from around 60 per cent of GDP in 1980 to just under 105 per cent in 1991. The problem was not only deficit spending; there was persistent deficit "slippage" or overshooting of planned deficit levels. This was particularly a problem in the first half of the 1980s. The reasons for this slippage are several but the more important are: additional expenditure approved by Parliament during the fiscal year; excessive optimism regarding once-and-for-all measures, in the main to increase revenues; failure to implement restrictive measures announced. Structural factors are also important (for example, in health care, social security and education). These make it particularly difficult to secure significant and immediate results in containing expenditure with macro policy measures.

The issue of public expenditure control has increasingly conditioned public policy. Concern with containing expenditure has been a key feature of health care policy virtually since the creation of the National Health Service in 1978, leading, for example, to the extended use of patient co-payments which has gradually pushed the Service toward a kind of "conditional universality". It was decisive in creating a climate for the drastic reorganisation of the National Health Service which took place in 1992-3 and accelerated the pace of decentralisation in this sector.

The central public administration: Another constant in the context in which decentralisation has evolved is the character of the central public administration – which has not been reformed since the transfer of administrative functions to the regions in 1970 and 1977. In November 1996, a branch of Parliament approved a government-delegated law for the reform of ministries. This should be finally approved in early 1997. Civil servants in the upper career levels are, unlike in some other countries, not drawn from socio-economic or intellectual elites. For decades, a large proportion of staff has come from the southern regions – traditionally, the public administration has been seen as offering job security. Most graduates employed have law degrees which may help to explain the fact that the dominant administrative culture tends not to be managerial or problem solving oriented. For a variety of reasons, senior civil servants tend to have a limited influence on policy-making.

The bureaucracy has been relatively impermeable to attempts at reform; politicians have hesitated to antagonise this lobby, but another obstacle has been the intricate nature of legislation regulating the public administration. Some key ministries, like the Treasury, are an exception to the rule while institutions like Parliament, the Bank of Italy and the Constitutional Court apply extremely rigorous standards in recruiting staff. The generally low technical capacity of the central public administration has probably had an important retarding influence on decentralisation tendencies. Over and above its innate reluctance to cede power, common to all civil services, doubts about its ability to adequately manage a strongly decentralised system and guarantee goals of national interest, such as equity, may have deterred many who might otherwise have been active proponents of decentralisation.

JAPAN

1. INSTITUTIONS AND AUTHORITY

1.1 Structures

Description of levels

The total area of Japan is 377 800 square kilometres and the total population in 1994 was 124 960 000. Japan has a two-tier local government system comprising prefectures and municipalities. Although there are a significant number of sub-national governments, the national bureaucracy commands significant power over the administration of the country's various public policies.

The New Constitution of 1947 included for the first time a chapter on local government. The Local Autonomy Law was enacted at the same time. While the pre-war local government system was modelled on the old German approach, the new one was strongly influenced by the American spirit of self-government. The Local Autonomy Law defined a two-tier structure of prefectures and municipalities. It further defined, in accordance with the principles of the Constitution, the structure, composition and powers of local elected legislative bodies and of chief executives at both levels.

Local Government: Administratively, Japan is divided into a total of 47 prefectures (including the metropolis of Tokyo, and the prefectures of Osaka, Kyoto and Hokkaido). Prefectures are further divided into municipalities which consist of cities, towns, and villages. Cities have a population of 50 000 or more and towns and village have a population of under 50 000.

The boundaries of the prefectures are determined historically and thus populations and areas vary greatly from prefecture to prefecture. Prefectures stand midway between the national government and the municipalities and their functions are divided into two categories: intermediation between national government and municipal governments, and area-wide administration. They are responsible for matters that affect broad geographical areas within their jurisdiction or for which a single standard needs to be maintained throughout the prefecture ; for large-scale jobs that municipalities cannot handle on their own ; and for liaison between the national government and municipalities and providing advice and guidance to municipalities.

Municipalities are classified into cities, towns and villages depending on the size of their populations, the density of buildings, the structure of industry, and the extent of urban facilities. Cities display some differences in organisation and function, but they still share the same basic character as the level of local government closest to the ordinary citizen. However, twelve cities with populations of over 500 000 and designated by government ordinance differ from ordinary municipalities in that they handle some of the services that are normally performed by prefectures.

Prefectures and municipalities are referred to as ordinary local public entities, but there are also bodies known as special local public entities. For example there are special wards. Tokyo has a unique function as the capital of Japan, and its central area is therefore divided into 23 special wards which are similar in character to cities but with several distinguishing features. There are also regional affairs associations, which may be responsible for any of a wide range of services which individual municipalities are unable to deal with fully on their own, or which can be more effectively handled collaboratively.

Table 1: **Area and population of sub-national governments (1995)**

Number	Prefectures 47		Municipalities 3 232	
	Area (km^2)	Population	Area (km^2)	Population
Largest	83 451	11 542 468	1 408	3 281 280
Smallest	1 875	619 238	1.27	197

Number of municipalities and population distribution	
Population size	Number of municipalities
up to 10 000	1 526
10 00L0-20 000	716
20 000-50 000	542
50 000-100 000	231
100 000-500 000	198
over 500 000	19
TOTAL	3 232

Source: Japan Municipalities Handbook, (1996); Residential Register, (1996)

Central government at sub-national levels

Local branch offices are established by law when it is necessary to divide-up the administrative affairs of national bodies such as the Prime Minister's Office, ministries, commissions, or agencies. Fundamental jurisdictional areas are "regional", which divide the nation into 8 to 10 regions, and "prefectural" or "municipal" which roughly correspond to the local governments' jurisdictions. Specially designated areas are also used when appropriate. The national bodies which have both regional and prefectural or municipal offices include the Management and Co-ordination Agency, Ministry of Justice, Ministry of Finance, National Tax Administration Agency, Ministry of Agriculture, Forestry and Fisheries, Ministry of Construction and Ministry of Posts and Telecommunication.

The administrative responsibility and authority of the ministries and agencies which are allocated to these local branch offices, are executed by them in the areas under their jurisdiction. Many other organisations (experimental laboratories, educational facilities, etc.) of ministries and agencies are also established in local areas. These are sometimes called "local administrative bodies".

Creation, elimination and restructuring

After World War II, the role of municipalities as the basic autonomous body grew in importance and they were vested with more responsibility for the administration of public affairs. However, as the smaller towns and villages did not always have enough administrative and financial capabilities, a law was enacted in 1953 to promote the consolidation of towns and villages throughout the country during three years (see Table 2).

This policy of amalgamation aimed at assuring a minimum population of 8 000 in each town or village as a rule, with the hope that each town or village would be able to afford to have at least one junior high school and to hire at least one case-worker in the welfare service.

As a result of the amalgamation of towns and villages, the efficiency of the administration was improved. At the same time various construction projects were begun.

1.2 Powers

Nature of sub-national institutions

Local governments in Japan, that is prefectures and municipalities, have a political system which differs from that of national government. The national level has a parliamentary system, while the sub-national government is run by a presidential system of government. Each local unit has a popularly

Table 2. Evolution of the number of municipalities (1945, 1953, 1956, 1993)

Date	Number of cities	Number of towns and villages	TOTAL	Notes
October 1945	205	10 315	10 520	
October 1953	286	9 582	9 868	– Law to Promote the Amalgamation of Towns and Villages enacted.
September 1956	498	3 477	3 975	– The above law had lost its effects
April 1993	663	2 573	3 236	

Source: *The Management and Reform of Japanese Government*, Second Edition, The Institute of Administrative Management, 1995, Tokyo.

elected chief executive (called the governor in a prefecture, and the mayor, in a municipality); and a unicameral legislative body (Assembly).

Local governments are all legally entitled to create public enterprises and to manage them either singly or jointly. Public enterprises are creatures of the State, established by a government charter emanating usually from a legislative body, and are under the direction and control of the chief executives of local governments.

Local Assemblies: Each local government establishes its own assembly. It is composed of members elected by direct popular vote. The number of assembly members is defined by the Local Autonomy Law according to the population of the local area. This number can be reduced by a by-law. The term of office of an assembly member is four years.

The most important power of local assemblies is local decision-making, particularly the enactment, amendment and repeal of by-laws and adoption of the budget. Their authorisation is also required for the appointment of deputy governors and mayors and members of boards of education and public safety commissions, and for settling accounts. The assembly deliberates on bills, the draft budget and other matters in its regular sessions (held no more than four times a year) and in special sessions convened as required. Local by-laws may not violate prefectural by-laws, and prefectural by-laws may not contravene national laws.

Executive branch: The chief executive, who plays the leading role within the executive branch of local government, is elected directly by the people for a four-year term. He represents the local authority and looks after its general affairs. He submits bills to the assembly, co-ordinates and implements the budget, levies local taxes and users' fees, acquires, manages and disposes of property, and handles all tasks which do not fall under the jurisdiction of any other executive body. The chief executive enjoys broad-ranging powers in order to carry out these functions, including the right to establish regulations, appoint and dismiss personnel, provide supervision and direction and set up any necessary administrative organisation. He is also vested with general co-ordinating authority which extends over other executive bodies.

In addition to the chief executive, there are other executive bodies (Committees) as provided for by the Local Autonomy Law. They are allowed to work independently of the chief executive for the purpose of political neutrality and unbiased functions. These independent executive bodies are as follows:

- In both prefectures and municipalities:
  - Education Committee:
  - Election Administration Committee:
  - Personnel (or Equity) Committee:
  - Inspection Committee;
- Only in prefectures:
  - Public Safety Committee;

- Local Labour Relations Committee;
- Expropriation Committee;
- Maritime District Fishery Adjustment Committee;
- Internal Fishing Grounds Administration Committee;

• Only in municipalities:

- Agricultural Committee;
- Realty Valuation Re-examination Committee.

There is no "non-partisan" tradition in Japan where all local elective offices are "partisan". In the local elections, political parties take an active part in recruiting and electing various candidates. Additionally, Japanese elective posts are not honorary but full-time positions with monthly remunerations and other financial supports. They are, therefore, required to commit their entire time to activities in the local political scene.

There is also often a reverse relationship between the level of election and the rate of voter turnout in Japanese elections. Ordinarily, the lower the level of government, the higher the rate of voter turnout. In the council elections for towns and villages, the voter turnout often reaches 90 per cent. In 1991, it was 87.18 per cent, although the average turnout of the elections for the House of Representatives remained at around 70 per cent. In the 1994 Lower House election, the turnout rate was only 67.26 per cent.

Type and degree of local autonomy

The 1947 Constitution states that "local public entities shall have the right to manage their property, affairs and administration and to enact their own regulations within law." Despite this provision for local autonomy, the basic pattern of managing service delivery in Japan remains generally centralised.

The system which emerged in 1947 is one where the national government lays down a centrally defined uniform structure and ground rules within which local entities function. In general, as compared to the pre-war system, the new model can be characterised as more decentralised in that the new Constitution recognised a principle of local self-government which is reflected in arrangements such as the direct participation of citizens in local administration.

Under the current local autonomy system, it is hard to draw a clear line between the jurisdiction of local governments and that of central government, although it is mostly agreed that the degree of autonomy of local governments is limited and that many policies are formulated and decisions taken at the central level. The type and degree of autonomy which local governments are entitled to have differs greatly across sectors. This is the result of complexity of practices accumulated over a long time, rather than the application of a set of principles.

Local authorities can do anything (except in certain fields – see section 1.3) so long as they do not infringe on the national legal framework. In the Japanese legal system, national laws and Cabinet ordinances (which must be based on national laws) always take precedence over by-laws of prefecture governments; and by-laws of prefecture governments over-rule those of municipalities. The fact is, however, that the central government has established national laws in major policy areas, keeping control over local governments. This situation can partly be attributed to the highly centralised system of administration in the pre-war period.

The Local Tax Law provides the framework for local taxation, including the kinds and rates of taxes allowed. There is little room for local governments to take discretionary decisions. Normally, the tax offices of local governments are in regular contact with the Local Tax Bureau of the Ministry of Home Affairs and follow directions and guidance from it, whether they are legally compulsory or not.

The Local Autonomy Law also has provisions on the maximum number of internal departments allowable in prefecture governments and other details on the internal organisation of local governments. Local governments have, therefore, only limited authority for their own organisational design.

1.3 Responsibilities

Distribution of responsibilities

The Local Autonomy Law stipulates that authority is distributed between local governments and central government according to the premise that local governments do *not* deal with the following:

- juridical affairs;
- criminal punishment;
- transportation and communication at the national level;
- postal services;
- national institutions of education and research;
- national hospitals and sanatoriums;
- facilities for navigation, meteorology, and sea channels;
- national museums and libraries.

The major sectors where local governments have a policy role according to the principle of local autonomy and where their activities are not confined to the implementation of policies decided on elsewhere, include:

- social welfare and health;
- local development including city planning and water supply;
- local business development;
- youth policy and basic education including management of primary, junior high and senior high schools;
- environmental protection including pollution prevention.

These activities of local governments are referred to as the "inherent functions" of local governments.

Mandatory, optional and shared responsibilities

The activities of local governments are divided into two categories: "inherent functions" and "delegated functions". Inherent functions are those which are supposed to be carried out by local governments according to the principle of local autonomy, while delegated functions are the activities of central government which have been delegated to local governments for implementation.

The inherent functions are noted above and also include the management of public hospitals, the local police system, and the fire fighting system. Central government also exerts influence over local governments in these fields through mechanisms such as subsidies and due to the precedence of national laws over local by-laws.

Delegated functions are sub-divided into "mandated functions" and "agency delegated functions". Mandated functions are those entrusted to local government by central government, public corporations and other bodies by statutes and Cabinet ordinances. Local governments have some degree of discretion in carrying them out, e.g. in designing programmes, and local assemblies can deal with these functions in the same way as the inherent functions. Examples of these functions include the construction of primary and secondary schools and the establishment of hospitals for infectious diseases.

The agency delegated functions are different from mandated functions in that local governments have virtually no discretion with respect to the former. They are not entrusted to the local government as a whole, but to the chief executives or other executive bodies of local government. In implementing these functions, the chief executives and other executive bodies are regarded as "agencies" of central government and must comply with the directions and orders received from the relevant minister. In principle, local assemblies do not have the right to discuss and decide on issues relating to the "agency delegated functions". In order to implement such functions in local governments, the "mandamus" system is applied.

There is evidence of a trend towards a decrease in local government autonomy through the growth in the number of both mandated functions and agency delegated functions. Currently the number of agency delegated functions is over five hundred. Some estimate that they account for 70 to 80 per cent of all the activities of prefecture governments.

2. MANAGEMENT FUNCTIONS

2.1 Policy-making and co-ordination

Coherence, consultation and conflict resolution

The issue of policy co-ordination is perhaps less problematic in Japan than in many OECD countries due to the strong and extensive role of the central government. In the major policy fields, the typical relationship between central government and local governments is one where central government, as the senior authority, decides on policies, sets directions and gives guidance which chief executives of local governments follow and implement as agents of individual ministries. In this sense, there is less necessity for mechanisms to secure policy coherence in Japan.

But the Japanese administration is facing a different kind of problem regarding policy co-ordination. Individual ministries tend to set up regulations, directions, and guidance and to impose them on local chief executives that act as their agents without sufficient policy co-ordination internal to the central level. As a result they may be duplicative or even contradictory. Critics claim that the lack of effective policy co-ordination at the central level leads to inefficiency in local governments.

2.2 Financial management

Sources of revenue

Local taxation is the most important source of revenue of local governments and accounts for 35 per cent to 40 per cent of the total, although there has been a major drop in the last six years; from 44.3 per cent in 1988 to 35.2 per cent in 1993. In 1950, the system of local taxes was totally revised and the Local Tax Law was introduced to establish the current local tax system. While taxes added onto national taxes were the core of the former local tax system, local taxes are in principle independent in the current system. The Local Tax Law provides the framework of the local system, including taxable items and their rates. In addition, individual tax systems are managed by local governments in close consultation with the Local Tax Bureau of the Ministry of Home Affairs. There is, therefore, little variety between the individual tax systems of local governments.

Japan has a system of grants from central government to local governments, to fill the gap between the expenditure local governments are supposed to carry out and the revenue that they can actually raise. The central government grants can be divided into two categories: global grants (usage decided by local governments); and grants where the usages are predetermined by central government ("National Treasury Reimbursements" in the Japanese terminology).

There are two kinds of global grants; a "Local Allocation Tax Grant" and a "Local Transfer Tax Grant". In 1993, the former accounted for 88.5 per cent of the total amount of global grants. The Local Allocation Tax Grant is a major system of equalisation between the financial capabilities of local governments. Its main purpose is to enable local governments to provide a "standard level service" solely with this grant and local tax revenues. A certain portion of revenue from national taxes (at present 32 per cent of the total amount of income tax, corporation tax, and liquor tax; plus 24 per cent of consumption tax and 25.5 of tobacco tax) is statutorily reserved for this grant.

Table 3 shows the composition of local government revenues and Table 4, the proportion of income from different local taxes.

Table 3. **Main revenue sources of sub-national governments (1993)**
(per cent)

	Prefectures	Municipalities	All local governments
Local Taxes	31.2	35.6	35.2
Global Grants from Central Government	18.1	18.7	18.3
Specific Grants from Central Government	18.5	8.9	14.4
Grants from Prefectures to Municipalities	–	4.7	–
Bonds	14.5	12.4	14.0
Others	17.7	19.7	18.0
TOTAL	100.0	100.0	100.0

Source: "Chiho Zaisei Hakusho" (White Paper on Local Finance), 1995, Ministry of Home Affairs, Government of Japan.

Table 4. **Composition of local government by resource item (1992)**

	Revenue (billion yen)	(%)
Prefectoral Taxes:		
Enterprise Tax	5 694	38.4
Prefectoral Inhabitants Tax	4 912	33.1
Automobile Tax	1 412	9.5
Light Oil Delivery Tax	901	6.1
Real Estate Acquisition Tax	670	4.5
Others	1 244	8.4
TOTAL	14 833	100.0
Municipal Taxes:		
Municipal Inhabitants Tax	10 179	51.6
Fixed Assets Tax	7 179	36.4
City Planning Tax	1 110	5.6
Tobacco Consumption Tax	648	3.3
Others	619	3.1
TOTAL	19 735	100.0

Source: The Management and Reform of Japanese Government, Second Edition, The Institute of Administrative Management, 1995, Tokyo.

Expenditure responsibilities

The total annual expenditure in the ordinary accounts of all local governments in fiscal year 1992 (1 April 1992-31 March 1993) amounted to 95 533.5 billion yen, of which 47 439.7 billion was spent by prefectural authorities and 48 093.8 billion by municipal authorities including Tokyo's wards. After the adjustment for transfer payments between local governments, the net annual expenditure in the same fiscal year was 89 559.7 billion yen. The evolution of this amount since 1975 is shown in Table 5.

The enormous increase in local government expenditure during the last 30 years has been caused not only by inflation but also a great expansion of local government functions in various fields,

Table 5. **Comparison between central and local government expenditures (1975, 1985, 1990, 1992)**
(gross annual expenditures in selected fiscal years)

	1975	1985	1990	1992
Central government	22 758.4	55 148.3	74 190.7	77 140.7
Local government	25 654.5	56 293.5	78 473.2	89 559.7

Source: Local Public Finance in Japan, 1995, Ministry of Home Affairs.

encouraged by the spread of the concept of the "Welfare State". Major expansion occurred in particular in the following fields:

- education: extension by three years of the term of compulsory education; and a great increase in the number of children and high school students;

- social welfare: enactment of the Livelihood Protection Law, Child Welfare Law, Aged People Welfare Law, and other statutes;

- public health service;

- public works, such as the construction of roads, bridges, and other infrastructure development.

The allocation of public expenditures needed by central and the local governments is stipulated by the Local Finance Law, as follows:

a) In principle the expenditures required by a local government or its bodies to execute its functions must be borne by the local government concerned.

b) Central government bears the entire or partial cost of expenditures mentioned in (i) incurred in the execution of certain categories of work.

c) Local government has no obligation to bear the cost of work it performs exclusively in the national interest and is being carried out by the local government only because local execution is more efficient and convenient for the public (e.g. expenditure concerning election of Diet members, and the national census).

d) Local government pays part of the cost of large-scale public construction or disaster restoration projects by the central government when legally stipulated.

Table 6. **Total annual expenditures of all local governments by purpose (1992)**
("Ordinary Account", fiscal year)

Expenditure (by purpose)	Amount (million Yen)	(%)
Public Works	21 633 239	24.2
Education	18 405 977	20.6
General Administration	10 108 692	11.3
Social Welfare and Security	9 935 321	11.1
Debt Charges	7 114 956	7.9
Agriculture, Forestry and fisheries	5 676 190	6.3
Health and Sanitation	5 614 255	6.3
Commerce and Industry	4 445 366	5.0
Police	2 970 319	3.3
Fire Protection	1 577 309	1.8
Local Assembly	570 957	0.6
Employment and Industrial Relations	538 136	0.6
Disaster Restoration	536 560	0.6
Miscellaneous	426 770	0.5
TOTAL	89 559 705	100.0

Source: Local Government Finance Bureau, Ministry of Home Affairs.

Balance between discretion and control

Distribution among local governments is decided according to a set of formulae established by central government, taking into account factors such as population. There is also a mechanism of control by the central government over bonds issued by local governments. Local governments must obtain permission from the Minister of Home Affairs in order to issue local bonds, and the central government often purchases local bonds by using financial resources from postal savings.

2.3 Human resource management

Statutory distinctions: Public employees are divided into national public employees working in central government organisations and public employees in local government. The local public employees are governed by the Local Public Service Law, administered by the Public Service Personnel Department of the Ministry of Home Affairs. The Local Public Service Law provides a single uniform personnel system for both prefectures and municipalities. It establishes ground rules for key personnel functions such as selection, appointment, position management, working conditions, status, promotion, discipline, training (mostly provided by prefectures and municipalities within their own training institutes), work performance evaluation and the protection of employee benefits and welfare. In addition, it exempts local public service employees from many of the national laws dealing with labour relations and creates a special labour relations environment for the public service which permits employees to organise and to bargain, but does not give the right to strike. Specific categories of local public employees, such as police and teachers, are subject to special laws, in addition to the Local Public Service Law. Special treatment is given in the Local Public Service Law to "Special Service" public employees (e.g. political officers, such as chief executives of local governments, and members of local assemblies and committees).

The Local Public Service Law stipulates that prefecture governments and so-called "designated cities" should have a Personnel Committee and other municipal governments should have either a Personnel or an Equity Committee. These committees have a major role in implementing the ground rules established by the law, in formulating personnel management policy, and in determining pay and other working conditions. They are allowed to work independently of the executive and legislative branches, in order to secure political neutrality in the administration and desirable working conditions for local public employees. They are vested with the authority to submit opinions to the chief executive and to the local assembly on the introduction and revision of by-laws regarding personnel management. Normally, pay revision for local public employees takes place in accordance with the opinions of these committees. Generally speaking, personnel policies initiated by them follow the personnel policy for public employees in central government, in part due to guidance from the Ministry of Home Affairs.

Japan's local governments employ a total of 3.3 million workers, of which Tokyo Metropolitan Government (the largest in terms of the number of public employees) has a total of 204 270 officials including over 64 000 school teachers and some 41 000 police officers; and serving a population of over 12 million.

The number of government employees by level of government is presented in Table 7.

Table 7. **Government employees by level (1980, 1985, 1990, 1993)**
(fiscal years and fixed numbers)

	1980	1985	1990	1993
National	1 199 177	1 187 526	1 171 763	1 163 943
Local (prefectures)	1 705 587	1 744 633	1 741 447	1 742 121 [1]
Local (cities, towns and villages)	1 462 157	1 477 386	1 486 871	1 512 170 [1]
TOTAL	4 366 921	4 409 545	4 400 081	4 418 234

1. 1992 fiscal year.
Source: Public Management Developments: Update 1995, OECD, 1995.

2.4 Regulatory management and reform

Prefectoral governments act as co-ordinating bodies on issues that transcend any one municipality, and as agents for the national ministries with respect to policies carried out by the municipalities. The role of the prefectures is, however, a subject of considerable discussion in Japan. At this time, their status is not very clear as the prefectural government is a regional local government in the present local government system, but it operates virtually as an agent of the central government.

Despite the principle of local autonomy, expansion of mandates and "delegated" functions from national ministries to local governments has created a "highly centralised" regulatory system. This reflects in part the desire of national ministries to have policies implemented nationally in a uniform and standardised manner, and in part a distrust in the national ministries concerning the capacities of local government.

Centralisation has, however, only recently begun to be reversed. The *"Guideline for the Promotion of Reform concerning Relationships between National and Local Governments"* was adopted as Cabinet policy in 1989 in accordance with the Second Report of the Provisional Council for the Promotion of Administrative Reform (PCPAR). In 1991, after several earlier versions had failed, the Diet succeeded in enacting a bill expanding the influence of local assemblies over delegated functions. Another law transferring regulatory authorities from the national to local governments, including decisions on agricultural land usage and municipal planning, and abolishing other regulations was enacted in April 1991.

In 1992, the Third PCPAR recommended that 10-20 pilot local governments be designated "to promote decentralisation of power," and that such pilot governments be given more autonomy in a number of areas, including city planning and development, welfare, public health, and education, each of which currently requires some kind of approval by national ministries or by prefectural governors as agents of central government.

The incremental nature of decentralisation reform, despite its high political priority, indicates that, as officials of the Management and Co-ordination Agency have noted, it has been "the most difficult of reform goals" and local governments, it is fair to say, are not necessarily happy with the progress made.

Local government use of its regulatory authorities has also been a concern. Improvement of the permission/authorisation requirements implemented at local levels has been, for example, a significant part of the deregulatory programme. Since 1985, the Ministry of Home Affairs has supervised a scheme of local administrative reform intended to realise "simple but efficient mechanisms" at the local level.

3. TRENDS IN REDISTRIBUTING AUTHORITY ACROSS LEVELS OF GOVERNMENT

3.1 Evolving tendencies

Japanese experience indicates that decentralisation is extremely difficult to achieve due to many political and administrative impediments which often work against the dispersion of powers. However, ongoing experience seems to suggest that decentralisation is inextricable from the democratisation of the country. From the late 1960s to the early 1970s, Japan witnessed the rise of progressive local governments in different urban communities. As often as not, these governments initiated various innovative policies long before the national government adopted them as nation-wide programmes. These local policies contributed much to the alleviation of pollution and the improvement of various health and welfare programmes of the country.

In December 1991, Japan's Third Provisional Council for the Promotion of Administrative Reform (PCPAR) submitted a report to the Prime Minister. It proposed to designate a number of cities or coalitions of municipalities with a population of more than 200 000 as "pilot local governments".

This scheme has the purposes of devising special measures concerning national permissions and authorisations, subsidies, etc., the issuance of local government bonds and commissioned affairs, so that cities, towns and villages (separately or jointly) will be able to display more independence and responsibility in dealing with regional development; making the transition to a system based on an evaluation of results; and planning more promotion of decentralisation.

The idea was approved by the national government and put into effect in April 1993. Initially, the national government planned to designate approximately 20 local authorities as pilots, and 33 communities had been designated by 1995.

A certain lack of enthusiasm for this initiative may be accounted for by several factors. One is that as in many other countries, Japanese officials in the national administration tend to form "fiefs" to protect their own jurisdictions and to fend off encroachment by other officials. This recalcitrant tradition can impede the transfer of power from national to local levels. This is particularly true where licensing and approval is involved.

3.2 The current debate

After the split of the Liberal Democratic Party (LDP), the first non-LDP government in the last thirty-nine years was formed under the leadership of Prime Minister Hosokawa in July, 1993. The Hosokawa Cabinet put administrative reform high on the policy agenda and showed a strong determination to promote decentralisation. Accordingly, ministries were required to take further steps towards decentralisation.

Mr. Hosokawa stepped down in April 1994. The party composition of the ruling coalition changed, with the LDP coming back to power, and the Murayama Cabinet was inaugurated in June 1994. There has, however, been no major change in decentralisation policy and decentralisation has remained a top policy issue. In December 1994, the Murayama Cabinet adopted and announced the "General Guideline for Decentralisation". This spelled out basic policy on the devolution of national powers and called for a bill, "Decentralisation Promotion Law", to be submitted to the Diet with a view to establishing a legal basis for promoting decentralisation. The bill became a law in May 1995.

The Decentralisation Promotion Law provides a time schedule and legal and administrative procedures which central government should follow in the promotion of decentralisation, but does not stipulate which components of decentralisation should be carried out by central government. The planning of items to be devolved is left to the "Decentralisation Promotion Commission", which the law newly established in the Prime Minister's Office. It consists of seven commissioners from the private sector and a Secretariat composed of government officials. The Commission is scheduled to make a recommendation to the Prime Minister on decentralisation and other relevant issues by the end of 1996.

It remains far from clear, however, to what extent devolution of authority from central government to local governments will be successful, because of strong opposition to decentralisation in the central bureaucracy. For example, 33 of the 47 governors regard the central bureaucracy as a major obstacle to decentralisation. The Decentralisation Promotion Commission can expect to face many impediments in planning a decentralisation package.

3.3 Driving forces

The argument in favour of central control may have been tenable in the 1950s or 1960s, when Japan was less affluent. Since then the Japanese society has become more diverse and complex. Needs in one locality do not always correspond to those in other areas. In Tokyo, for instance, the demand for public day-care nursing facilities stays strong especially among young working families, while in rural areas there has been an out-migration of young people causing the median age of the population to increase substantially. In these areas, local governments must prepare programmes to cope with the ageing of the population.

In these more pluralistic circumstances, centralisation can appear inappropriate or even obsolete, and decentralisation holds appeal as a new guiding principle, particularly among Japanese academics. The idea of decentralisation has, as a result, become one of the major rallying points for both conservative and progressive political parties.

LUXEMBURG

1. INSTITUTIONS AND AUTHORITY

1.1 Structures

The Grand Duchy of Luxemburg is a sovereign independent State with a hereditary constitutional monarchy. It has a population of approximately 400 000 its territory covers an area of 2 587 km Council of Ministers. Legislative power is exercised by the members of the Chamber of Deputies who are elected for a term of five years. Bills must be submitted for the opinion of the Council of State whose members are appointed by the Grand Duke.

The only levels of local government in the Grand Duchy are the municipalities (*communes*) and there is no intermediate tier of government between these local authorities and central government. Limited powers of government are vested in the municipalities under Article 107 of the Constitution.

Description of levels

As a small country, Luxemburg has no regional or departmental authorities: the decentralisation principle operates solely at municipal level. These are autonomous units, delimited by geographical boundaries and each has legal personality.

Table 1. **Area and population of municipalities**

	Area (km^2)	Population
Maximum	50 approx.	75 000
Minimum	10 approx.	180

Number of habitants	Number of municipalities
fewer than 500	10
501-1 000	50
1 001-3 000	41
3 001-5 000	8
5 001-10 000	6
over 10 000	3

Source: Structure and Operation of Local and Regional Democracy: *Luxemburg*, Council of Europe, 1993

In 1995, Luxemburg had 118 municipalities grouped into districts. In 1950 there were 126 municipalities.

Central government at the sub-national level

The Grand Duchy is divided into three administrative districts. In each of these, a civil servant, the District Commissioner, is appointed by the Grand Duke. The District Commissioners operate under the supervision of the Minister of the Interior, except in emergencies and where otherwise provided by special laws or regulations.

The jurisdiction of the District Commissioners extends to all municipalities in their district, except for the city of Luxemburg which is under the direct control of the Minister of the Interior. The duties of the District Commissioners, defined in section 114 of the Municipalities Act of 13 December 1988, include, among others;

- ensuring the implementation of national and local laws and regulations and the proper administration of the assets and income of the municipalities; auditing the budgets and accounts of the municipalities and those of the public bodies under their supervision or the supervision of municipal associations;
- the direct supervision of local government and local government officers.

District Commissioners are required to report any problems with the financial or administrative management of municipalities to the Minister of the Interior.

Creation, elimination and restructuring

Legislation is required to create new municipalities, either by merging parts of one or more existing municipalities or by merging two or more municipalities, and to change the boundaries of a municipality. Apart from the mergers of some municipalities in 1920, 1977 and 1978, there have been hardly any boundary changes since the early 19th century. Such mergers are subject to the agreement of the municipalities concerned.

There are also municipal associations, set up with a specific purpose in view and solely on the initiative of municipalities that wish to pool their resources so that they can provide better quality services at lower cost to the population they serve. The formation of such associations is governed by law and is always on a voluntary basis at the initiative of the local councils concerned. Some associations are single-purpose, some are multi-purpose. From 15 or so such associations in the 1960s, there were around 50 in 1995.

Associations of municipalities are governed by the Grand Ducal Order on their institution and by the statutes it incorporates, as published in Luxemburg's Official Journal. Municipal associations (like municipalities themselves) are responsible to the Minister of the Interior and are subject to the provisions of the Municipalities Act. They have their own management structure.

Control bodies

The Constitution provides for a system of local government control exercised by the Grand Duke, the Minister of the Interior and central government through the District Commissioners. The Grand Duke can annul any general or specific act of local government that is contrary to the law or the public interest and can declare void both regulatory acts and specific decisions of the council, board or mayor. The Minister of the Interior can suspend any act of general or specific application by a commune that is contrary to the law or the public interest. Lastly, a number of decisions by municipal councils are subject to the assent of the Grand Duke or the Minister of the Interior: only the Grand Duke has power to levy, alter or abolish local taxes and associated regulations.

Any intervention by the body responsible for administrative control on the grounds of the advisability of decisions taken by municipal councils is deemed to be *ultra vires*. Municipal authorities have the right to appeal to the Litigation Committee of the Council of State against any decision by a control body.

Municipal accounts are scrutinised by the District Commissioners and audited by the municipal accounts audit division of the Ministry of the Interior.

1.2 Powers

Nature of sub-national institutions

Although they derive from the Constitution, the powers of municipalities are subordinate powers in that they are both prescribed and circumscribed by the law. The Municipalities Act of 1988 defines the powers and functions of the municipal authorities. They are required to comply with the general laws and regulations from which local by-laws may not derogate. By municipal authorities is meant the municipal council, the mayor and aldermen's boards, the mayor, the tax collector and the bodies of the Municipal Associations and public corporations for which the municipalities are responsible.

The most recent legislation on purely municipal affairs dates back to the 1868 Constitution. One has to go back as far as the decree of 14 December 1789 relating to the Constitution of municipalities, still in force in the Grand Duchy, for a definition of independent powers at municipal level. Under this decree: "The functions of municipal government are to manage the collective assets and revenues of towns, villages, parishes and communities; to settle and acquit those local expenditures that must be paid from the common purse; to ensure that the populace enjoys the benefit of good rule, particularly as regards cleanliness, health, safety and order in its streets, public places and buildings."

Municipal powers extend only to the boundaries of the municipal area and are exercised by two bodies: a decision-making assembly and an executive body. The assembly is the municipal council, directly elected every six years by constituents who are eligible to vote. The number of councillors varies with the size of the population (from 7 to 27 councillors). Each municipality forms one electoral constituency. Elections are normally by straight majority voting, but where municipalities have a population of at least 3 500, or one electoral division of at least 3 000 inhabitants, elections are by proportional representation, as for national elections.

As the main organ of municipal power, the council decides on all matters of purely municipal interest. Councils are empowered by law to issue by-laws, and impose sanctions for breaches thereof. Jurisdiction is unlimited with regard to anything concerning the internal administration of the municipality. The council decides on all matters relating to municipal assets, revenue, expenditure, building work, its public agencies, etc. With the assent of the Minister of the Interior, it appoints, dismisses and accepts the resignation of the municipality's public servants and staff, and appoints the members of the boards of community homes and welfare services. The council decides on the municipality's annual budget and balances the accounts. With the assent of the Grand Duke it may levy municipal taxes, and it oversees the board of aldermen which is the municipality's executive body.

Executive power is exercised by the mayor and aldermen's board, which consists in each municipality of the mayor and usually two aldermen. The number of aldermen can range from three (in municipalities with a population of 10 000 to 25 000) to six (in municipalities with a population of over 50 000).

In towns, mayors and aldermen are appointed for a term of six years by the Grand Duke; aldermen in other municipalities are appointed by the Minister of the Interior. They are chosen from among the members of the council. The powers of the aldermen's boards are both general and local. As the executive arm of central government, it is the duty of the board of aldermen to implement within its territory Grand Ducal and Ministerial Acts and Orders, except those relating to the police.

As the executive arm of local government, it is the duty of the mayor and aldermen's board to publish and execute Resolutions of the municipal council and to supervise the proper operation of local services. The board also represents the municipality in judicial proceedings and keeps records, certificates and registers of births, marriages and deaths.

As an executive officer of the municipality, the mayor is the chairman of the municipal council and of the board of aldermen. As an executive officer of central government, the mayor is charged with implementing Grand Ducal and Ministerial Acts and Orders relating to the police (Act of 29 July 1930 as amended regarding State control of local police). The Mayor is an officer of the law and also carries out the duties of registrar.

Although each council is free to make its own internal rules of procedure, standard rules for municipal councils have been drafted by the Ministry of the Interior.

Type and degree of autonomy

In principle, municipalities are free to set local rates and to institute new types of local tax, always providing that they are not contrary to the public interest. There are no additional (local) charges on national taxes. By virtue of the principle of their autonomy, municipalities can, for example, introduce taxes and charges in order to finance the provision of discretionary services. Their role in public health, family policy, culture, leisure and transport services comes under this category. In all of these areas the ministries concerned operate a subsidisation policy in order to raise the awareness of the municipalities and to prompt them to provide good local infrastructure coverage.

1.3 Responsibilities

Distribution of responsibilities

Municipalities are directly responsible for all regulations relating to their own internal administration and for by-laws in their own area (except as regards hunting and fishing which are exclusively the prerogative of central government) for roads, water supply and sports facilities.

Central government and the municipalities share responsibility for refuse disposal, environmental protection (municipalities can draft "green plans" which are partly subsidised by central government), road building and maintenance, the provision of crèches, nurseries, and nursing homes. Gas, urban heating and electricity are functions of central government.

Every municipality is required to provide pre-school and primary education for children in its area for nine consecutive years. The construction and maintenance of school buildings for primary education and the purchase of educational materials are the responsibility of the municipalities. Primary school teachers are appointed by the municipal councils on the advice of the inspector and with the approval of central government. Teachers' salaries are paid initially by central government, with one third of the cost being refunded subsequently by the municipality. The provision of secondary, vocational and higher education are not the responsibility of the municipalities.

As regards health matters, municipalities are required to make by-laws determining the measures necessary to protect public health and improve sanitation. The building and management of hospitals and old people's homes is a function that is shared by central and local government. Every municipality in the country has to provide welfare support to the needy (in the form of money or by finding them employment).

The Act of 20 March 1974 enables the government to implement national, regional and sectoral development plans. Plans drafted at national level can be imposed on municipalities by the State Council (*Conseil de gouvernement*). Moreover, every municipality in Luxemburg is now required to draft or have drafted a local development plan under the Act of 12 June 1937 on the development of towns and other built-up areas.

Mandatory, optional and shared responsibilities

Although there has never been any formal distinction, the actions of municipalities can be divided into two categories; mandatory and discretionary functions.

The "mandatory" duties usually include those which derive from two decrees dating from 1789 and 1792 which define the particular functions to be carried out by the municipality. As a general rule, the following duties are the responsibility of the municipalities alone:

- the organisation and operation of the municipality as an autonomous administrative unit; public safety; hygiene and sanitation; local roads; aid for the needy; pre-school, primary and complementary education (though two-thirds of teachers' salaries are paid by central government).

Among the "discretionary" services are those which are not considered indispensable at the municipal level but which are necessary at the national level;

- activities in the public health sector (such as hospitals and dispensaries); initiatives in the welfare area (e.g. crèches, homes) cultural activities and sports facilities; the provision of public transport; the supply of electricity and gas, and the creation of industrial and leisure complexes.

The areas of responsibility of municipal associations generally include water supply, hospitals, old people's homes, refuse collection and disposal, public hygiene, the construction and maintenance of schools, sports centres, swimming pools, crematoria, parks, sewerage plants, municipal information management, and regional industrial areas.

2. MANAGEMENT FUNCTIONS

2.1 Policy-making and co-ordination

Coherence, consultation and conflict resolution

The principle of the autonomy of the municipalities is deeply entrenched in public life in Luxemburg. Central government has implemented an incentive policy in order to maintain or secure a uniform level of service provision country-wide. A number of standards and benchmarks have been established and municipalities are encouraged in various ways – principally through government subsidies – to adopt them. The incentive principle is applied at all levels including partnerships with private sector institutions and associations.

Referenda and public consultations at the local level are purely consultative in nature. Referenda, instituted under the 1988 Act, are called by the municipal councils and are limited to registered voters. Less formal public consultation, provides all residents, not just registered voters, with an opportunity to air their views on a specific problem.

Formal and informal mechanisms

The country's 118 municipalities are all members of Luxemburg's Towns and Municipalities Association, which was set up in 1951. The Association operates as a non-profit making body.

1986 saw the formation of another umbrella association for towns and municipalities, SYVICOL, with a similar legal structure. SYVICOL is run by a committee of 15 members who must be local elected representatives. Its main objectives are in two areas:

- Protecting the joint interests of the member municipalities. The association examines municipal grievances and forwards them to the appropriate body for settlement;

- Taking part in the legislative and regulatory process. The Government recognises SYVICOL as the representative of the municipalities. The association is consulted on legislative and regulatory texts that concern the municipalities. In important matters, the municipalities may be consulted individually.

In addition SYVICOL members sit on many commissions and working parties set up by the government, such as the Central Commission (which deals with all matters relating to public service at municipal level), the National Environmental Protection Committee and the Higher Regional Development Council.

2.2 Financial management

Sources of revenue

Each municipality has two different budgets: a current (or operating) account and a contingency (or capital) account. Revenues to the current account include the following.

a) Approximately two-thirds are non-appropriated or are block subsidies, essentially from fiscal sources:

- municipal commercial taxes (CI) based on profits and operating capital. This tax is collected from businesses by central government on behalf of the municipalities.

- property tax (IF), levied directly by the municipalities on properties within their area.

- municipal transfer funds (FCDF), which represent the municipalities' contributions to State taxes (income tax, value-added tax, vehicle taxes, plus a lump-sum appropriation).

b) One-third consists essentially of taxes and charges or specific subsidies for the provision of mandatory or discretionary services and facilities. The taxes and charges are calculated on the basis of usage of the various services by residents in the municipal area. These are generally services that are part of the statutory duties of the local services (see section on Responsibilities).

Although, generally, the main sources of revenue can be broken down into three roughly equal shares, the shares of the three current types of revenue in the total revenue of a municipality can vary a great deal from one authority to the next, chiefly with the size of the resident population and area.

Capital resources (contingency account) are from two sources:

a) The municipality's own resources (for example a surplus of revenues over expenditure on the current account, contingency taxes and charges, revenue from the realisation of assets or the repayment of loans which constitute a sort of compulsory savings on the current account and hence a kind of obligatory, systematic self-financing).

b) Capital transfers from the State in the form of subsidies from the Ministry of the Interior (to re-establish the investment capacity of one municipality relative to the others in the event of investment in basic facilities and infrastructure); specific subsidies from the various government departments (promoting the necessary public facilities at national level, the rates of which vary according to national priorities and regional coverage).

Table 2. **Trends in municipalities' current account revenues (1980, 1985, 1990, 1993)**
(in millions of Luxemburg Francs)

	1980	1985	1990	1993 [3]
Local tax revenues	4 084	7 088	7 935	11 391
Other local receipts (in accordance with the interim account) [1]	4 555	7 993	9 606	11 300
Transfers of unallocated revenues from the State to the municipalities. Effective income [2]	3 516	5 113	8 557	10 495
TOTAL current account receipts (in accordance with the interim account) [4]	12 154	20 194	27 098	33 096

1. Other local receipts comprise all receipts from income tax and charges as well as income from utilities such as gas and electricity, etc. Spending on both the current and contingency accounts of the municipalities must be set against these revenues.
2. Transfers of unallocated revenue from the State to the municipalities include:
   a) the municipal fund, up to and including 1987;
   b) municipal contributions to certain State taxes;
   c) municipal financial compensation fund (in 1987 only).
   From 1988 onwards, transfers under a), b) and c) are grouped under the municipal transfer fund (FCDF).
3. Adjusted accounts.
4. The figures are rounded and totals may not be exact.

Source: *Rapport d'activité* 1994, Ministry of the Interior, Grand Duchy of Luxemburg (February 1995).

Operating and investment expenditure by municipal associations is financed solely by the contributions of the member municipalities, contributions which must be entered in municipal contingency and current accounts. Each association has its own account, which it manages itself. Associations receive subsidies for the purpose for which they were formed. Apart from these specific funds they have no powers to raise taxes. This procedure maintains the independence of the municipality, while enabling it to fulfil its role as a platform for democracy at local level. In this way, local people are closely involved in the running of their local authority even if some of its functions are delegated to an inter-authority entity.

Loans of more than LF 300 000 are subject to the approval of the Minister of the Interior. Such loans are authorised if an examination of the financial position of the municipality shows its ability to repay the loan from the budget for future years. Repayments are entered into the current account each year. If the municipality's budget does not balance, it is required to rectify the situation by its own means in which case it is the municipality's discretionary functions that are usually cut first.

As a general rule, municipalities take out loans with commercial banks, since borrowing on the capital market has always been, and still is, virtually non-existent. No legal or regulatory provision prohibits borrowing from public or quasi-public bodies abroad or from obtaining loans on foreign capital markets.

Expenditure responsibilities

When obligatory spending concerns several municipalities, they each contribute a share proportional to their expected gain from the investment. Where there is refusal or disagreement on the share to be contributed, the matter is referred to the Minister of the Interior for resolution. The Minister's decision can be appealed through the Litigation Committee of the Council of State, which judges the merits of the case and is the final court of appeal.

Table 3. **Trends in municipal accounts (1980, 1985, 1990, 1993, 1994)**
(data from interim accounts in millions of Luxemburg Francs)

	1980	1985	1990	1993 [1]	1994 [2]
Current receipts	12 154	20 194	27 098	33 096	32 308
Current expenditure	10 153	16 400	22 263	28 547	30 000
Extraordinary receipts	1 863	1 354	2 600	6 509	11 218
Extraordinary expenditure	4 157	3 648	7 460	14 353	16 143

1. Adjusted accounts
2. Accounts

Source: *Rapport d'activité* 1994, Ministry of the Interior, Grand Duchy of Luxemburg (February 1995).

Balance between discretion and control

Municipalities are responsible to the Ministry of the Interior, which co-ordinates and supervises financial matters at local level. Municipal accounts and some special subsidies are allocated by the Ministry.

2.3 Performance management

Efficiency is not monitored in Luxemburg. The only checks made are for compliance with standards (which determine whether or not subsidies will be paid out) and budgetary and financial supervision. Municipalities have an obligation to balance their budgets and verify that they have been used properly.

2.4 Human resource management

The status of municipal civil servants was defined by the Act of 24 December 1985. The terms for entry into the civil service, promotion, resignation and salaries as well as the rights and duties of civil servants and municipal employees are prescribed by law and, within the limits of the law, by resolutions of the municipal council duly approved by the Minister of the Interior. Their status is similar to that of central government civil servants. Wages are negotiated by central government and the civil service trade unions. The wages of local government staff and workers are determined by collective agreements between the municipalities and the employees and workers.

Legal provisions govern conferral of the status of "civil servant". It is conferred on those who, on a permanent basis, have been appointed by the municipal council to the staff of a municipality (by secret ballot of the council under absolute majority voting rules) subject to approval by the Minister of the Interior, to exercise a function pursuant to a legal or regulatory provision, or a function created by a special resolution of the council. Municipal staff are also appointed by the council: workers are appointed by the Board. All of these staff members are under the authority of the board of aldermen.

The mix of civil servants, other staff and workers employed in the different parts of the municipality varies. In 1991, for instance, 38 per cent were civil servants and 52 per cent were workers; as opposed to 22 per cent and 31 per cent respectively in municipal associations and five per cent and 43 per cent respectively in public corporations.

Table 4. **Salaried staff in local government (1981, 1989, 1994)**
(Data as at 312 December)

	1981 (1)	1981 (2)	1989 (1)	1989 (2)	1994 (1)	1994 (2)
Municipalities	5 610	5 139	6 542	5 931	7 054	6 442
Municipal associations	539	500	720	653	850	760
Public corporations	705	679	1 011	957	1 428	1 313
TOTAL	6 854	6 318	8 273	7 541	9 332	8 515

1. Number of posts.
2. Full-time equivalent.

Source: Ministry of the Interior

3. TRENDS IN REDISTRIBUTING AUTHORITY ACROSS LEVELS OF GOVERNMENT

3.1 Evolving tendencies

In the 1960s a plan to merge municipalities along the same lines as in Belgium aimed at reducing the number of municipalities to about 30. This plan met with some resistance on the political front and despite a series of Acts (1970, 1977 and 1978) only a few of the mergers went ahead, all on a voluntary basis. There are now 118 municipalities instead of 126 as in the 1950s. The Government therefore decided to encourage the formation of municipal associations, offering them larger subsidies for capital investment. These associations have been quite successful, as there are now over fifty, as opposed to fifteen or so 30 years ago, and the numbers are still rising.

In 1988 a new Municipalities Act was drafted, superseding the old 1843 Act. This did not make any fundamental changes nor did it affect political structures. What it did do was to make provision for ensuring greater democracy in the running of local councils. At the same time, administrative controls were relaxed – and the number of legal requirements were reduced (except in fiscal matters, which are covered in the Constitution). The municipalities were also given the right to appeal administrative decisions.

3.2 The current debate

In 1995, the Government began a process of discussion on a wide-ranging reform of the administration. The respective functions and roles of central and local government are among the issues being addressed as are ways and means of reducing the over-accumulation of current regulations. Since Luxemburg is a small country, the introduction of an intermediate tier is not being considered.

MEXICO

1. INSTITUTIONS AND AUTHORITY

1.1 Structures

Description of levels

The United Mexican States is a representative, democratic federal republic composed of 31 states and a Federal District (*Distrito Federal*), the seat of the federal government. It is divided into three branches: executive, legislative (bicameral) and judiciary.

The Constitution was adopted in 1917 at a convention during the final phase of the Revolution. One of its goals was the reaffirmation of the federal system which would guarantee sovereignty and freedom to its member states. Since then there has been a gradual strengthening of state governments.

The Constitution lays down the structure of the State and decrees that all states must adopt a representative, republican and popularly elected government. It establishes the powers and obligations of sub-national governments, stating that functions not expressly attributed to the federation are reserved to the states. The local constitutions and state and municipal laws must respect and adopt the general principles and basic rights provided by the federal Constitution.

Article 115 of the Constitution defines the "free municipality" as the fundamental unit of sub-national government. Municipalities are legal entities with specific attributions. Article 115 has been modified several times in order to consolidate the power of municipalities, to enlarge their competencies and reinforce their autonomy.

The total area of Mexico is 1 953 162 square kilometres and the population in 1995 was 91 458 290. There are currently 2 412 municipalities, most of which have less than 1 000 inhabitants. The Federal District is the biggest and most populated urban area in the country with a population of over eight million. In 1993 important legal reforms modified its political structures. The government of the Federal District – which was previously an administrative agency of the federal government – then became a local government divided into three branches. These are the legislative (Assembly of Representatives whose members are elected by direct vote), judiciary (whose magistrates are appointed by the Mayor of Mexico City with the Assembly's approval) and executive (which will be directly elected for the first time in 1997). Some legislative powers were reserved for the federal Congress, among them, to legislate its Statute of Government. The Federal District is currently divided into 16 areas (*Delegaciones*) and at the head of the government of each is a *delegado*, appointed by the Mayor of Mexico City.

Table 1. **Number and population of sub-national government (1995)**

	Number	Population
States	31	
Largest (Mexico)		11 707 964
Smallest (Baja California Sur)		375 494
Federal District	1	8 489 007
Municipalities	2 412	

Source: *Anuario Estadístico de los Estados Unidos Mexicanos*, 1995.

Central government at sub-national levels

Federal Secretariats (ministries) and decentralised (semi-public) bodies have offices (delegations) in the states. Functions originally belonging to the Federal Government have been transferred to the states, particularly in the health and education sectors. The responsibilities of the state offices of the deconcentrated federal social security bodies have been enlarged to give them technical and administrative autonomy. These changes have helped to strengthen the federal system and gave an impetus to the decentralisation efforts which took place in the 1990s.

Creation, elimination and restructuring

Due to the large number of municipalities, co-ordination procedures and regulations were established in the main metropolitan areas in the early 1990s in order to provide public services and other functions more efficiently. There remains much scope for amalgamating small municipalities into larger, more cost-effective units better able to provide a wide range of services.

Control bodies

The Federal Secretariat of Interior (*Secretaría de Gobernación*), among other functions, is responsible for the relations between the federal executive, state governments and municipal authorities, as well as relations between the federal executive, legislative and judicial powers. The Federal Attorney General's Office (*Procuraduría General de la República*) is responsible for the prosecution of federal offences and is appointed by the President with the approval of the Senate.

1.2 Powers

State Government

State governments are structured according to their own constitution and local administrative laws. The structure of state governments generally parallels that of the federal level, the exception being that all state legislatures are unicameral. The Federal Constitution requires that state government be divided into three separate branches: executive, vested in the Governor; legislative, vested in the state congress; and judicial power, vested in the local Superior Tribunal. The head of the state government is a Governor elected by direct vote for a six-year term but who cannot be re-elected. Governors must be Mexican-born and natives of the state or have lived in the state for a five-year period before voting.

The Governor nominates his most important staff. The main appointee is the State Government Secretary General (*Secretario General de Gobierno*) who:

- co-ordinates the work and activities of other offices as well as the relations between the state executive and the local legislative and judicial authorities;
- represents the Governor, if deemed convenient, before federal or municipal authorities;
- countersigns covenants and other decrees by the Governor;
- executes and monitors the implementation of decrees, by-laws, and regulations passed by the state government.

The Governor also nominates the Chief Executive Officer (*Official Mayor*) whose main task is to oversee the civil servant staff: their appointment, conditions, responsibilities and other functions set by law. He also nominates the Secretary of Finance and Budget (*Secretario de Finanzas*). The main responsibilities of the Secretariat of Finance and Budget are to collect taxes; evaluate, monitor and control the budget; and pay civil servants' wages. The number and competences of other offices or "secretariats" (*secretarías*) depends on local requirements.

Legislative power is vested in the state Congress (Chamber of Representatives). Representatives are elected by direct vote for a three-year term. The number of representatives in state congresses is fixed by the federal Constitution. A state with up to 400 000 inhabitants must have at least 7 representatives, those with up to 800 000 inhabitants must have at least 9 representatives, and those with over 800 000 inhabitants must have 11 representatives. Representatives are not eligible for immediate re-election. Local electoral laws regulate proportional representation.

The main functions executed by state congresses are to:

- examine and approve the state's public accounts of the previous year;
- approve the state budget and determine taxes;
- approve the Municipal Councils' Income Law and control their public accounts;
- legislate in areas relating to state government;
- introduce regulatory decrees and by-laws;
- approve or reject the nomination of magistrates of the local Superior Tribunal;
- resolve conflicts between municipalities;
- if necessary suspend the municipal council or remove members, according to state law;
- declare the validity of state governor elections;
- reform the state Constitution when approved by at least half the municipalities of the state;
- create new municipalities.

Judicial power is vested in the Superior Tribunal established by state constitutions. Local laws establish formalities for nominating magistrates and their training (*Ley Orgánica del Poder Judicial*). Requirements to become a state magistrate are the same as those to become a Superior Court magistrate, for instance: they must be Mexican-born and have at least ten years of experience as practising lawyers.

Since 1934 and until very recently, state Governors, who are elected by direct vote, belonged to the majority party i.e. the Institutional Revolutionary Party (PRI) since 1946. This is due to the fact that all political disputes amongst the revolutionary factions took place within the bounds of this party. In 1989, for the first time, an opposition party candidate was elected as Governor in the State of Baja California; in 1991, the Guanajuato State Congress appointed a National Action Party (PAN) member as acting Governor; and in 1992, the PAN won the state election in Chihuahua. Since President Zedillo took office at the beginning of 1995 three governors belonging to the PAN have been elected – in the states of Jalisco, Guanajuato and, once again, Baja California. However, it is at the municipal level that opposition parties have been most successful.

Municipalities

Municipalities are the basic administrative units of state governments as provided in the Constitution. Article 115 defines them as legal entities with limited regulatory powers. The municipal president and municipal council (*ayuntamiento*) are elected by direct vote for a three-year period and they are not eligible for immediate re-election. The municipal council is composed of the municipal president; a "public trustee" (*síndico*); and councillors (*regidores*).

In municipal elections citizens vote for a municipal president of a particular party and a "slate" (*planilla*) of councillors who make up the town council (*cabildo*). In all cases, seats on the council are proportionally allocated in accordance with the votes each party received, thus ensuring that main opposition parties are represented.

The municipal council's main functions are to:

- organise the structure and functions of the municipal administration;
- present its public accounts to its state congress;
- make agreements with state or federal agencies for the construction of infrastructure or public works and for the supply of public services;

- approve urban development plans and programmes and make agreements with other municipalities in order to implement co-ordinated metropolitan policies;
- implement laws and decrees by the state congress concerning municipal matters;
- analyse and approve the budget and the municipality's draft "Incomes Law".

The municipal president's main functions are to:

- publish an annual review of the municipal administration's accounts;
- remove and appoint those employees and civil servants appointed exclusively by the council;
- supervise the implementation of municipal and state development plans and programmes.

The public trustees (*síndicos*) defend the municipal interests and legally represent the council in any lawsuits in which it is involved. They are also responsible for supervising the municipal treasury administration. The main functions of the public trustees are to:

- monitor municipal finances;
- keep an up-to-date inventory of all goods belonging to the municipality;
- review and sign the municipal treasury's bank statements and send them to the audit office of the state congress;
- ensure that the public account is presented in time for its annual review by the state congress as well as the monthly financial and accounting statements;
- supervise the implementation of the municipal budget.

The councillors' (*regidores*) main functions are to:

- supervise the committees of the municipal administration;
- present draft municipal regulations for organising and administering the municipality and the functioning of its services;
- propose "agreements" for improving the administration's various sectors and services;
- substitute for the municipal president in his temporary absences.

The *Cabildo* (town council) brings together the members of the city council in order to exercise its responsibilities. Ordinary sessions are held each month to inform members of the city council of work in progress. Extraordinary sessions are held when requested by the municipal president or a majority of councillors to deal with urgent issues.

The committees distribute responsibility for the functioning of the municipal administration amongst the councillors. The main committees are:

- Municipal Treasury;
- Ruling and government;
- Public safety and transport;
- Public health and social security;
- Public services and public works;
- Education and recreation;
- Commerce, markets and slaughterhouses;
- Urban development and environment.

Federal District (Mexico City)

As a result of important political reforms to the Federal District's structure in 1993, the local legislative body is now the Assembly of Representatives composed of 66 members, of which 40 are elected by direct vote for a three-year term. The others are selected on the basis of proportional representation through party lists. In August 1996 the Federal Government and the main political parties reached an agreement to amend the Constitution to the effect that the Mayor of Mexico City will be directly elected in the 1997 elections.

The Federal District Assembly of Representatives has similar functions to those described above for state congresses; but it has limited legislative powers.

Advisory Citizens' Councils are bodies made up of non-partisan citizens elected by direct vote for a three-year term. Their main functions are to supervise the administration and to advise, evaluate and, sometimes, approve programmes concerning each of the 16 areas (*Delegaciones*) of the Federal District. As from the year 2000, the heads of the *Delegaciones* will also be elected by direct vote.

1.3 Responsibilities

The Federal Constitution prohibits certain activities by state governments in order to preserve the federal system, and for some specific issues, subjects them to Congressional approval. These activities include, entering into agreements with foreign countries; printing money; setting local taxes on merchandise or on people travelling through the state; and obtaining loans from foreign states or foreign private corporations. The Constitution also determines that only the Federal Congress has the power to legislate matters concerning certain strategic economic areas, such as petroleum; mines; commerce, banking and financial services; nuclear and electric power; and cinemas.

According to the Constitution (article 124) all competences which are not explicitly attributed to the Federation or the municipalities are the responsibility of the states. Other articles define several important areas of joint responsibility. These include health and education (shared between the federal and state levels). The states have no exclusive responsibilities, but are involved in providing infrastructure which goes beyond municipal boundaries. Much of the problem in the division of responsibilities between levels of government, however, lies in the limited capacity of lower levels to carry out the functions in terms of the necessary financial and/or human resources.

In 1992, through the National Covenant for the Modernisation of Basic Education, the federal government transferred to the states the operation of educational services. The Secretariat of Public Education transferred responsibility for teaching establishments, budgets, human resources, moveable property and equipment to the states. The main role of the Secretariat became to promote the harmonious development of education across the country.

Article 115 of the Constitution was significantly modified in 1983 to give new competences to the municipalities. These reforms included:

- reinforcing their legal authority by conferring some regulatory powers without prior agreement from the state congress;
- fixing minimum fiscal responsibilities; granting exclusive authority for real estate tax; and granting the right to partake of public revenue;
- setting minimum public service fees.

During the 1989-1994 administration the National Development Plan established as one of its priorities the strengthening of the "free municipality". As a result, steps to consolidate the free municipalities were taken, including:

- redistributing decision-making in social, economic and cultural areas;
- finding solutions to municipal problems using own resources;

- decentralisation programme;
- training of local civil servants.

Municipal functions were enlarged after the 1989-94 reforms, especially concerning:

- approval and administration of urban development plans and metropolitan co-ordination programmes;
- legalisation of land holding;
- granting of construction permits and administration of ecological reserves;
- passing decrees, by-laws and other administrative regulations in their jurisdiction;
- providing public services such as water, electricity, sewer and police;
- administering their incomes;
- approving the budget.

The 1995-2000 National Development Plan put forward strategies for the "plural integration" of municipal councils; and for promoting citizens' participation in public affairs – particularly in the definition and prioritisation of municipal social programmes. New formulae will be sought to strengthen the role of municipalities, as a basis for sound state government, especially through the preparation of sectoral and regional development plans. It is also intended to strengthen the representation and participation of indigenous peoples and communities by mechanisms which respect their forms of organisation and decision-making procedures.

The distribution of responsibilities is currently evolving very rapidly (see also 3.). A process for strengthening the federal system – New Federalism – aims at more decentralisation and an enlargement of state and municipal responsibilities and powers. It has been promoted by the central government through sweeping economic liberalisation measures and the democratic process itself since the end of 1994.

2. MANAGEMENT FUNCTIONS

2.1 Policy-making and co-ordination

Federal level

The National Development Plan and the co-ordination agreements between federal and state governments are important instruments for implementing federal programmes in the three tiers of government. The Executive is responsible for the preparation and implementation of the Plan, through which objectives are fixed, resources assigned, responsibilities and time frames defined and an evaluation system set up.

State and municipal participation in the preparation of this plan is important especially as its objectives include to promote regional development and to strengthen municipalities.

The Planning Law provides that the Secretariat of Finance and Public Credit (*Secretaría de Hacienda y Crédito Público*) co-ordinates regional planning with the states and municipalities and develops special programmes designed by the Federal Executive. Agreements between the Federal Executive and state governments are used to co-ordinate participation of local governments in the preparation and implementation of the National Development Plan, and ensure its consistency with regional plans.

One of the most important strategies for strengthening the municipalities between 1988-94 was the National Programme of Solidarity (PRONASOL). This aimed to fight poverty through co-ordination of the three government levels with municipalities considered as the nucleus, acting as co-ordinators of institutional efforts. During the first years of PRONASOL the state governments and municipalities designed joint welfare programmes which were then included in Single Development Agreements (*Convenio Unico de Desarrollo*, CUD).

The Secretariat of Social Development (SEDESOL) was created in 1992 and took over PRONASOL activities. Among its main functions are the shaping and co-ordination of federal executive action with state and municipal authorities. The Single Development Agreements were replaced by Social Development Agreements (CDS) which are now considered one of the main instruments for promoting decentralisation in social development. Through this instrument the Federation, states and municipalities define priorities and programmes of common interest. However it is the states and municipalities which play the most important role in choosing priority objectives and in formulating new demands.

In June 1995, the PRONASOL programme was replaced by the National Welfare Alliance (*Alianza Nacional para el Bienestar*). This new programme aims at transferring to local governments the administration of the budget assigned to PRONASOL.

In order to promote regional development and decentralisation, SEDESOL has created a new agency, the General Co-ordination for Decentralisation. Through it, financial resources will be transferred to states around the end of 1997. A follow-up commission will then be set up in SEDESOL to control this transfer and its implementation. This will make states and municipalities responsible for the execution of social development policy (see also 2.2).

State level

The State Planning Law (*Ley de Planeación*) establishes the statesõ planning principles. It defines the state executiveõs functions; his power to fix the nature of democratic consultation in preparing the State Development Plan; and the criteria to formulate, implement, control and evaluate the plan and its development programmes. This law also determines the bodies responsible for the planning process and the basis on which the state executive can co-ordinate actions, through agreements with the municipalities, and work together with the social and private sectors to prepare and execute the plan.

Another important instrument for co-ordinating federal, state and municipal activities is the Planning Committee for State Development (*Comite de Planeación para el Desarrollo Estatal*, COPLADE). This is a decentralised body of each state government with legal personality and its own budget. Its main functions are to:

- co-ordinate planning measures between the federal, state and municipal governments;
- prepare and keep up to date the State Development Plan;
- propose to federal and state governments an annual investment programme for the state and the municipalities;
- evaluate the programmes and actions agreed upon by the Federation and the states.

COPLADE is made up of:

- a president, who is the State Governor;
- a co-ordinator who is a state civil servant nominated by the Governor, and generally head of the unit in charge of the planning and finances of the state;
- a Technical Secretariat;
- an Assembly;
- a Permanent Commission made up of civil servants at the head of state departments and the heads of the representations of the federal administration, as well as municipal presidents and representatives of the social and private sectors;
- regional and special sub-committees.

The Social Development Agreements are another important mechanism for co-ordination. They contain different programmes through which the Federation transfers to states and municipalities the resources needed to achieve goals fixed in plans and programmes. Some of the most important programmes are the Programme of State Investment; the Programme for Co-ordination and Execution of Regional Policies; and the Programme for Rural Development.

Municipal level

The legal bases for municipal development are the:

- Federal Constitution;
- Federal Planning Law;
- State Constitution;
- State Planning Law;
- Municipal Organic Law.

The Municipal Organic Law determines the ability of the municipalities to participate in the approval and execution of plans and programmes concerning health, education, urban development and housing.

The Planning Committee for Municipal Development (*Comite de Planeación para el Desarrollo Municipal*, COPLADEM) is a decentralised body with legal personality and its own budget. It is created by decree by the state Governor or by the state congress. Its task is to promote and co-ordinate the formulation, implementation and evaluation of the Municipal Development Plan in co-ordination with actions taken at the municipal level by the state and federal governments.

Municipal Development Agreements (*Convenio de Desarrollo Municipal*, CUDEM) are agreements through which state governments transfer resources to the municipalities and encourage joint municipal and state development. The Municipal President and the Treasury Committee are members of the Validation and Follow-up Committee which inform inhabitants about the implementation of Development Agreements. Special Solidarity Committees have also been created recently to co-ordinate projects and community needs.

2.2 Financial management

Sources of revenue

In the period up to 1980, fiscal relations among the three tiers of government were rather complex. State and municipal governments were heavily dependant on subsidies from the federal administration as most tax revenues were generated by the federal government.

During the 1982-88 administration a new fiscal co-ordination system was established in order to strengthen state revenues. Arrangements for the states improved but the Federal Districtōs incomes were reduced.

From 1988 to 1994 significant reforms to the Law of Fiscal Co-ordination (*Ley de Coordinación Fiscal*) introduced new fiscal policy between federal and sub-national governments. Three important objectives were achieved: increase the bases of federal contributions, change the distribution formula of VAT and provide a new and better equalisation system based on the levels of development and population size in each state. The Municipal Promotion Fund was created in order to help those local bodies with lowest levels of development, by providing them with an income directly from the federal government. Similarly the Municipal Solidarity Fund currently constitutes the central plank of federal social welfare programmes implemented at the state and municipal levels.

Municipalities administer their own incomes, which comprise revenues from property values, real estate taxes, and revenues coming from the public services they provide. The Municipal Council approves its own budget but state legislatures determine annually the amount of federal income to be distributed to the municipalities.

In 1990 the federal level received 96.1 per cent of the National Fiscal Income, which reduced to 83.6 per cent after transfers to the state and municipal levels. The municipalities, on the other hand, initially obtained 1.8 per cent of the National Fiscal Income which increased to 4.1 per cent after receiving their share of transfers.

State congresses approve their own budgets, determine taxes and examine and approve their public accounts of the previous year. They also approve the Municipal Council's Law and control their public accounts.

In fact municipalities in general generate little revenue due to the deficiencies of administrative systems, old cadastral registers, insignificant incomes from real estate taxes (most of the small-sized municipalities are rural) and under-qualified staff. The financial survival of states and municipalities largely depends on federal transfers, which constitute the most important variable for the regional policy of the country. One form of financial control exercised over municipalities is the practice of withholding funds that have already been allocated by slowing down their delivery.

Fiscal reform took place in June 1995 with a view to decentralising some areas of taxation. Measures were also taken to reduce delays in transferring revenues to the states (see section 3).

Table 2. **Gross revenues by sub-national levels of government (1980, 1985, 1993)**

	TOTAL (thousands of new pesos)	Taxes	Grants	Public Debt	Others
States					
1980	170 739	9.05	43.28	8.81	38.86
1985	2 021 206	1.71	49.09	7.94	41.26
1993	68 140 995	2.66	43.83	10.63	42.88
Municipalities					
1980	27 532	12.24	26.31	2.40	59.04
1985	423 325	12.12	57.08	4.50	26.30
1993	15 671 486	19.66	44.37	8.04	27.93
Federal District					
1980	68 238	10.74	36.90	41.37	10.99
1985	592 416	6.46	46.89	40.46	6.19
1993	13 914 493	25.32	45.02	2.85	26.82

Source: Anuario Estadistico de los Estados Unidos Mexicanos, 1995, INEGI

Table 3. **Expenditure by sub-national levels of government (1980, 1985, 1993)**

	1980	1985	1993
States	170 739 (64.1%)	2 021 206 (65.4%)	68 140 995 (69.8%)
Municipalities	27 532 (10.3%)	423 325 (13.7%)	15 671 485 (16.0%)
Federal District	68 238 (25.6%)	646 352 (20.9%)	13 914 494 (14.2%)
TOTAL	266 509 (100.0%)	3 090 883 (100.0%)	97 726 974 (100.0%)

Source: Anuario Estadistico de los Estados Unidos Mexicanos, 1995, INEGI

Balance between discretion and control

The Fiscal Co-ordination Law which came into effect on 1 January 1980 introduced a National System of Fiscal Co-ordination (*Sistema Nacional de Coordinación Fiscal*, SNCF). It is based upon two agreements, the National System of Fiscal Co-ordination and the Administrative Collaboration for Fiscal Federal Issues. The system exclusively reserves the following taxes to the federal government: income tax (on individuals and corporations), assets tax, value-added tax, special production and service tax, new automobile tax, general taxes on imports and exports and tax on vehicle ownership or use. The sources of income available to state governments vary from one state to another.

To obtain their due shares, the states have to agree to adhere to the SNCF. This agreement is reached through the Secretariat of Finance and Public Credit and must be approved by the state legislature. If there are disagreements with the declaration made by the Secretariat of Finance and Public Credit, it is possible to appeal to the Supreme Court. An important incentive to persuade states to forego their constitutional right to tax certain sources was that the state governments were guaranteed more income from the new system.

Initially state governments initially administered the new federal VAT and benefited from this arrangement in that they could keep the income from interest on short-term deposits which amounted to considerable sums. In 1989, the administration of the VAT was recentralised and the revenue-sharing formula was modified in order to strengthen population size compared with economic production.

The most important part of the SNCF is the participation system. The states depend highly on this revenue-sharing system because they have abandoned their independent tax sources in exchange for shares as determined by a formula. The states in turn are required to pass to their municipalities, through the General Participation Fund, a minimum of 20 per cent of the funds received through revenue sharing (the state that passes on most is Nuevo Leon with 35 per cent, the states that redistribute least are Mexico, Hidalgo and Sonora, each with 20 per cent).

In 1994 an amendment was made to the fiscal co-ordination system concerning the co-ordination of fees paid for public services (*derechos*). This covers licences, public authorisations, registrations, etc. Only two states have not yet signed the agreement.

Article 115 of the Federal Constitution guarantees the autonomy of municipalities. Nevertheless, each month municipalities have to send to the state congress all documents concerning their incomes and expenses. Congress then verifies that expenses are executed according to the Income Law (*Ley de Ingresos*) and in case of violation sends recommendations (*pliego de observaciones*) that have to be implemented. There have been regular efforts to strengthen municipal autonomy through the redistribution of functions and financial resources. Municipal taxes and the Municipal Income Law (*Ley de Hacienda Municipal*) are, however, decreed by each state's congress. In some cases the state congress enacts the same Income Law for all its municipalities or for groups of municipalities without taking into consideration the different needs and structures of each municipality.

Table 4. **Transfers to states and municipalities from the federal government (1982, 1987, 1992)**
(1 000 million new pesos)

	Total federal receipts	Transfers to states and municipalities (including the Federal District)	Transfers (percentages)
1982	969.1	259.3	27.1
1987	21 359.6	4 958.2	23.2
1992	132 031.3	31 828.5	24.1

Source: *Quinto Informe de Gobierno*, 1993, Mexico.

Table 5. **Distribution of federal grants to the federal district and to the states and municipalities (1985, 1992)**

	1985	1992
TOTAL amount (1 000 million new pesos)	1 355.2	32 134.6 [1]
of which:		
Federal District (%)	20.2	17.9
States and municipalities (%)	79.8	82.1

1. Including reserves for contingencies and compensation.
Source: Secretariat of Finance and Public Credit.

2.3 Performance management

Some gradual changes have taken place in the organisational culture through the Management Modernisation Programme by aiming for results in the context of an incentive-sanction scheme. There has also been some work focusing on measuring activities and performance rather than depending purely on budgetary allocations. Performance standards will continue to be developed in 1997 as a means of evaluating efficiency in public expenditure. Pilot projects will be launched in specific programmes in the areas of health, nutrition, education and labour – each using 15-30 performance standards to measure efficiency, efficacy, quality and results.

2.4 Human resource management

The 1917 Constitution established that labour legislation was reserved to the states. In 1931 the Constitution was modified, labour law came under federal jurisdiction, and the Federal Labour Law was adopted.

Article 123 of the Constitution establishes the principal rights of workers. It is divided into two parts. Part A concerns any labour relationship and mainly private sector workers; and Part B deals with federal public workers, including industries falling within federal competence i.e. the textile, energy, cinema, mining and petroleum industries. States and municipalities have their own laws regulating public servants according to principles set forth by the Federal Constitution. State workers are affiliated to the Institute of Security and Social Services of State Workers (ISSSTE) and to the Institute of the National Fund for Housing for State Workers (FOVISSSTE).

The Federal Law of Public Workers (*Ley Federal de los Trabajadores al Servicio del Estado*) was adopted in the late 1940s. It deals with relations between federal workers and the federal government. However, not all workers in semi-public bodies are ruled by this law, some such as Pemex and the Federal Electricity Commission fall under Part A of Article 123 of the Constitution (i.e. are treated as private sector workers). The Law also regulates relations between the state governments and state workers "*de base*" who cannot be removed because they are necessary to ensure the smooth running of the body. Their posts (*plazas*) are listed in a catalogue authorised in the Expenses Budget (*Catalogo general de Puestos del gobierno Federal*).

The labour relationships between the state governments and state public workers, and between municipalities and municipal public workers are ruled by Local Congress Laws. An aim of the laws ruling labour relationships between a public authority and its workers is permanent employment security; and there are provisions to that effect. There have been improvements in labour conditions in areas such as length of workday, social security and fringe benefits. The head of each unit fixes the general conditions of work in his area – but they must be authorised by the Secretariat of Finance and Public Credit. A "promotion system" (*sistema de escalafón*) operates. This is a points-based system through which the hierarchical superior makes evaluations and gives points which may lead to a higher and better-paid post if the worker complies with other conditions such as length of service, discipline, etc. An employee can contest the evaluation and bring it before the Commission of Promotion (*Comisión Mixta de Escalafón*).

The Law defines senior officials (*de confianza*) who have management, monitoring, financial or audit responsibilities, and have decision-making authority or represent the federal government, but explicitly excludes them from its provisions. These officials therefore benefit from wage protection and social security benefits only – there are no provisions regarding permanent employment security and such officials are not allowed to belong to unions. In fact, the Law allows the existence of only one union and strikes are allowed – if organised according to the law.

There is a large training network and there have been several initiatives in this field. These include a document on "Training in the Public Service" by the General Civil Service Direction which contains numerous proposals. As shown in , in 1993 80 per cent of all workers in the public sector were employed at the federal level (taken to include the Federal District and semi-public bodies). However, deconcentration and decentralisation programmes initiated in 1992 in the education sector and in 1996 in the health services area, have reduced these numbers significantly by transferring their contracts to the state governments.

Table 6. **Size and composition of the public sector, 1993**
(number of effective workers)

Sector	Number of workers	percentages
Federal government	3 071 000	81.9
Central	1 480 000	39.5
Federal District	182 000	4.9
Semi-public bodies	1 409 000	37.5
State governments	454 000	12.1
Central	394 000	10.5
Semi-public bodies	60 000	1.6
Municipal governments	226 000	6.0
TOTAL	3 751 000	100.0

Source: *Size and composition of the Mexican Public Administration*, Ministry of Audit and Administrative Development.

Regional negotiations take place to take into account the different conditions and costs of living for federal employees throughout the country. To this end the Inter-secretarial Commission of the Civil Service has defined petroleum, border, coast, tourist and development zones.

Each state congress enacts the law governing the relations between the state, the municipalities and their workers according to principles set by article 123 of the Federal Constitution. Municipalities may however enact administrative decrees and rules (such as the regulation of working conditions in each municipality).

2.5 Regulatory management and reform

During the 1988-94 administration emphasis was placed on the transfer to states and municipalities of functions that have gone through the General Programme for Simplification of Federal Public Administrations.

Other important reforms which took place include the deconcentration to state capitals of some federal bodies and the transfer to the state and municipal offices of several ministries of decision making and review functions. For example, field offices of the Secretariat of the Environment, Natural Resources and Fisheries now have the authority to deliver fishing and hunting permits, and the right to enter into agreements with state governments in matters concerning environmental policies, and field offices of the Secretariat of Commerce and Industrial Promotion may now grant export and import permits.

On 23 November 1995, President Zedillo issued a decree to cut unnecessary red tape and other bureaucratic obstacles that slow or inhibit business growth. The new measure – the *Acuerdo para la Desregulación de la Actividad Empresarial* – is the most comprehensive federal deregulation initiative in Mexico's history.

The President has also signed a Co-operative Agreement (*Acuerdos de Cooperación*) with each state in order to implement and promote similar deregulation procedures at the state and municipal level throughout the country. As at February 1996, 15 states had organised state Deregulation Councils, in association with the business community, to supervise the review process.

3. TRENDS IN REDISTRIBUTING AUTHORITY ACROSS LEVELS OF GOVERNMENT

3.1 Evolving tendencies

During the 80s, centralisation was seen as an enormous obstacle to achieving development in Mexico. It was then that the National Democratic Planning System was incorporated into the

Constitution in order to encourage economic growth and to promote public participation in the design of the Plan and its subsidiary development programmes. The National Development Plan is mandatorily followed by all bodies of the Federal public administration.

Through this planning process, goals are fixed, responsibilities and time frames are defined, and an evaluation system is set up. The President is constitutionally authorised to enter into agreement with state governments to co-ordinate efforts for the implementation of the Plan. Furthermore, the Plan provides that the Federation and the states can draw up agreements whereby the states execute functions previously carried out by federal institutions. The states were also given the authority to make agreements with municipalities in order to decentralise functions and delegate some of their powers to municipalities, thereby reinforcing their authority.

A first step towards decentralisation took place in the 1990s with the creation of semi-public bodies in order to co-ordinate federal and state competences specially in the health and education areas.

Since taking office at the beginning of 1995, one of President Zedilloōs key objectives has been the implementation of a "New Federalism". This fundamental agreement aims at the redistribution of State power, the reinforcement of the autonomy of the different political communities and respect for the spheres of competence of each tier of government. A key instrument is the National Development Plan.

The National Development Plan for 1994-2000 fixes objectives for a new federalism through redistribution of responsibilities, decentralisation of functions, fiscal co-ordination, new formulae for municipal participation in development planning, representation and participation of Indian communities, reform and modernisation of the public administration and promotion of administrative decentralisation.

Since 1995, the administration of President Zedillo has promoted legal reforms and the signing of agreements with state governors that transfer resources, authority and powers to each state. The decentralisation process started in the education sector in 1992 and has extended to health, agriculture, social development, transport and communications.

In 1996 the federal government signed a national agreement with local governments in the health area, based on a redistribution formula that takes into account the demand by states for health services, the risk of regional epidemics, and costs. In 1997, this agreement will double the amount of transfers in 1996, to reach over 10 000 million new pesos.

The Secretariat of Social Development will continue to transfer to local authorities 65 per cent of the budget for combating poverty, through the Fund for Municipal Social Development. The aim of this fund is to support the development of social infra-structure in the municipalities. These resources are also distributed using a formula based on poverty indicators.

The Secretariat of Agriculture, Cattle Raising and Rural Development (*Secretaría de Agricultura, Ganadería y Desarrollo Rural*) has started the process of decentralisation by signing agreements with state governments and by creating a special fund to promote investment and productivity in the sector. The fund is financed by resources from the federal government, states and producers.

The Secretariat of Transport and Communications has signed agreements with eleven states, transferring resources, authority and power to local authorities. The process of decentralisation is just starting, but in 1997 the amount of resources transferred to states will be three times that in 1996 to total 272 million new pesos.

The Committee for Municipal Strengthening of the federal Chamber of Representatives is currently examining projects of reforms aimed at strengthening the autonomy of municipalities; reducing administrative difficulties of obtaining low interest-rate loans; achieving administrative simplification; enlarging the powers of municipal councils and lengthening the constitutional term of municipal councillors.

3.2 The current debate

The "Political Reform of the State", which took place in 1996, deals with electoral reform, the reform of political powers, federalism, social communication and citizen participation. Reforms concerning the Indian communities have still to be implemented. The section on federalism deals with relations between the federal government, states and municipalities; political reform of the Federal District; fiscal federalism; and municipal "renovation" – i.e. their diversity, sphere of competence, and political representation.

Another current debate focuses on the implementation of new measures which will grant to states and municipalities the collection and administration of some taxes which are now with the federal administration. The Secretariat of Finance and Public Credit will present proposals to modify the Fiscal Co-ordination System. Among the federal taxes which might be granted to states and municipalities is that on the acquisition of real estate properties.

It is likely that in the short term the structures of sub-national government bodies will be modified as institutional change is needed to strengthen the capacity of state and municipal authorities to obtain further income.

As part of the 1995 State of the Nation Report, President Zedillo set forth the basis for the development of a "New Federalism". In this context he proposed to the Federal Congress the creation of a Federal Higher Audit Committee (*Auditoría Superior de la Federación*) within the sphere of competence of the Federal Chamber of Representatives, in order to enhance control over public finance.

In his statement to Congress in September 1995 the President emphasised the need to deeply restructure the tax system to obtain clear accounts, fight corruption, reinforce democracy and improve the balance between the three constitutional powers. A law will be drafted in order to ensure and strengthen the legislative controlling authority.

3.3 Driving forces

Two important driving forces are reshaping the functions and structures of the states. One factor is that the democratic process initiated in the early 1990's is already changing political forces. Public opinion has become aware of the importance of democratic changes and is very active in demanding this change.

Another important force has been the financial crisis and devaluation of the Mexican currency which had a very negative impact on state finances. To try to curb these negative effects, which include high interest rates, the federal government introduced a Credit Reinforcement Programme for States and Municipalities in May 1995.

This Programme was necessary due to the public and private debt of the states and municipalities and the spectacular rise of interest rates. It contains an agreement with commercial banks through which they accept debt restructuring with lower interest rates and an extension of deadlines for paying back loans. Two parallel mechanisms were established: the application of additional revenues coming from a rise in the price of petrol and VAT to cover 10 per cent and 30 per cent of private debt and fixed interest rates of 7.5 per cent and 9.5 per cent.

In mid-1995 states and municipalities owed 17 370 million new pesos to private banks and 9 600 million to state banks. This represents 48 per cent of the total contribution which they will receive in 1995. At the same time states may now enter into agreements with a state bank to help them to recover their financial capacity for social welfare services and help them restructure their debt.

The crisis has provoked new demands from states to alleviate their indebtedness, to obtain new resources and to be granted more fiscal revenues. For example, a covenant concerning resources from highways and border bridge crossings was increased in 1996 in favour of municipalities along the country's northern border.

It is important in this context to consider the imbalance that exists in regional development across the country – something which is also taken into account in the latest National Development Plan. The south of the country is made up of regions of peasant cultivators and large Indian communities. In contrast, the Northern Region borders the United States and has developed important cities along the frontier that are strategic points for border-crossings, tourism and light-assembly plants. The economy of these cities is linked very closely to the American economy so that devaluation had particularly negative effects on many of their activities. (It is in these northern cities that the PAN opposition party has acquired its major support.)

Other special programmes have been developed to help fight the economic crisis. These include the Programme of Industrial Policy and Economic Simplification, the Special Employment Programme (which seeks to create 28 000 new jobs in rural marginal areas) and the Emerging Plan (which aims to reinvigorate production and employment by helping especially small and medium-sized enterprises.

The current economic crisis is paralleled by a crisis concerning the power of the central government and of the Executive. President Zedilloõs attitude of not wanting to dominate the internal affairs of the Revolutionary Institutional Party (PRI) has reinforced regional powers and is changing the PRI's internal cohesion. Prior to President Zedilloõs administration all Presidents were heads of the PRI and participated actively in party life. The comeback of *"caciquismo"* (local chiefs) in some regions, the changes which the central power is experiencing and the financial crisis are some of the principal challenges which the "New Federalism" will have to face.

NETHERLANDS

1. INSTITUTIONS AND AUTHORITY

1.1 Structures

"Managing across levels of government" in the Netherlands involves the concept of the "decentralised unitary State", with its emphasis on the compound nature of the Dutch State. A certain balance is suggested between centralisation and decentralisation, i.e. between unity and local autonomy.

Description of levels

The structure of the Dutch administrative system has both a territorial and a functional dimension. In political administrative thinking the notion of territorial decentralisation is preferred, but the functional mode of service delivery has gained weight in recent years. The system of territorial decentralisation consists of three levels of government (*bestuurslagen*):

- central government;
- provinces; and
- municipalities.

The concept of *bestuurslagen* has a specific meaning in the Netherlands. First, it involves entities directly elected by the citizens. Second, a general purpose government is implied. Finally these bodies are considered to be in charge of their own affairs in that they are basically independent in deciding the scope and size of the tasks deemed necessary for performing their role and function. There are certain limitations to the degree of autonomy local governments enjoy. The definition as given is applicable only to territorial decentralised governments.

Municipalities: Municipalities constitute the most important type of sub-national government. They by far outweigh the provinces in terms of tasks, the level of expenditure and the number of personnel. In practical terms the range of the municipal tasks, the volume of expenditure, and the number and the quality of civil servants vary considerably. The variation can be explained by differences in the population size and related to the political administrative potential of the communities. The smallest Dutch municipality in 1994 (Schiermonnikoog) had 981 inhabitants while Amsterdam had 724 096 inhabitants.

Provinces: At present there are twelve provinces. Whereas municipalities and sometimes central government are in direct communication with the citizen, the province is more a "government for governments". For the average citizen the province has slipped out of sight, although some provinces, mainly in rural parts of the country, have more visibility.

Central government at sub-national levels

There is a widespread misunderstanding among the general public that municipal and provincial governments have a monopoly on sub-national (territorial) administration. In reality central government plays a major part in policy implementation at the local level. First, central government policy is often directly aimed at the community; and a wide range of field agencies have been created in order to implement national policy or secure the vital interests of central government. The system of field administration is not considered to be a form of territorial decentralisation. It is, rather, deconcentration with ministries keeping direct responsibility and being organised along functional lines. Field agencies are created on policy areas related to specific government departments. Of late there has been a tendency to convert some field agencies into independent public boards (*zelfstandige bestuursorganen*).

Some concerns have been expressed about possible negative effects of the functional organisation of field administration, reinforced by the diverging demarcation of administrative districts of the agencies involved. However, the creation of a system of field administration of a general purpose character, as is the case for instance in France, goes against the fundamental principles of Dutch administrative thinking. Many regional entities formed by inter-municipal co-operation were established either top-down by legal prescription, or bottom-up voluntarily, for reasons of efficiency. These regions, often different in size and structure for each function, are considered to be competing with, and as such eroding, provincial and municipal government.

Two separate categories of field agencies can be distinguished. Public Works (*Rijkswaterstaat*) and the Inland Revenue are examples of agencies that have been created for administering national interests at a regional level. The specific and technical nature of their tasks calls for a regional approach in the implementation of national policy. A second variety of field agencies have a specific responsibility in monitoring and advising provinces and municipalities. In the past complaints have been made about undue interference of these agencies in municipal and provincial affairs.

In addition to the field agencies and functional regions a wide range of independent functional authorities exists on the national level. "Statutory industrial organisations" (*publiekrechtelijke bedrijfsorganisatie*) are active in many (but not all) areas of trade and industry. Their legal foundation is in the Constitution and the Industrial Organisation Act (*Wet op de bedrijfsorganisatie*, 1950). Compulsory social security insurances are also administered by independent authorities by branch of industry and/or trade, whereas the compulsory health-insurance system is organised in functional bodies.

A second variety of functional decentralisation takes the form of "independent public boards" which are created by Act of Parliament. Although independent in their functioning, the powers and the composition of the boards are outlined by central government. These independent public boards have become more popular since the early 1980s as a means of reducing the size of government departments and the ministerial responsibility for policy administration.

Of late, all of these independent authorities and boards have attracted criticism for their lack of financial and democratic accountability. A general review was initiated in 1995 and in some sectors political conclusions have been reached to either privatise or to introduce stricter control by ministers and stricter parliamentary scrutiny.

A very special form of special purpose governments is the "waterboards" (*waterschappen*). In 1995 there were around 90 waterboards responsible (in co-operation with the provinces) mainly for the maintenance and quality control on surface water in their respective areas. The representational structure of the waterboards is quite complicated as it differs according to the task area and involves a combination of direct and indirect elections. In the last decades their number has been reduced from over 3 000.

Table 1. **Area and population of sub-national governments (1992)**

	Provinces		Municipalities	
Number	12		647	
	area (km²)	population (1991)	area (km²)	population (1991)
Largest	5 015.27	3 245 447	465.71	702 444
Smallest	1 358.66	221 505	1.71	933

Source: *Structure and Operation of Local and Regional Democracy: The Netherlands*, Council of Europe, 1993.

Creation, elimination and restructuring

With the creation of the province of Flevoland in 1982 the first new province was introduced since the middle of the nineteenth century. The provincial position in the Dutch system of government has remained somewhat ambiguous since the fall of the Dutch Republic at the end of the eighteenth century. The old Dutch Republic was really a confederation of semi-sovereign and powerful provinces. Abolished in the French era, they were reintroduced in 1815 after the creation of the modern Dutch decentralised unitary state. Nevertheless they lost their (much criticised) pre-eminent position of earlier times. A too powerful province was feared to endanger national unity. The balance of power shifted therefore from the provinces to central government and the municipalities.

Due to the ongoing decentralisation process and concerns over minimum standards of performance, central government is pursuing an active policy of amalgamation. The number of municipalities has gradually been reduced from 1 050 in 1950 to 636 in 1994. For the creation or abolition of a province or a municipality an act of parliament has to be drawn up. Although provinces and municipalities are involved in the process, final responsibility remains with parliament.

Table 2 shows the rapid decline in the numbers of small municipalities.

Table 2. **Number of municipalities distributed by population size (1950, 1970, 1994)**

Population size	1950	1970	1994
up to 5 000	624	406	64
5 000-20 000	314	389	381
20 000-50 000	53	78	135
50 000-100 000	13	26	36
over 100 000	11	14	20
TOTAL	1 015	913	636

Source: *Statistical Yearbook of the Netherlands*, Central Bureau of Statistics.

At present intermunicipal (although not exclusively) co-operation is the official government solution to regional problems. A number of areas have been designated in legislation on which municipalities have to combine forces on a voluntary basis, but there are some doubts about this approach. First, while a "blue-print" for co-operation is easy to make, it does not address the problem of incompatibilities between different catchment-areas. Secondly, the voluntary character of the co-operation is causing problems in urban areas. Voluntary regional co-operation is far easier to accomplish in rural areas than in urban (especially metropolitan) areas. In rural areas municipalities need each other in order to be able to perform tasks. In metropolitan areas there is more conflict and competition between municipalities, but at the same time there is an urgent need for comprehensive policy making – especially in the areas of economic development and spatial planning. New initiatives have been taken which move away from intermunicipal co-operation and in the direction of forming new style "provinces" in these areas. The tasks of these "regional" provinces are much wider than the "standard" provinces. In seven urban areas regional public bodies have been established on the basis of the so-called *Kaderwet*. The creation of these new style provinces is envisaged in the urban areas of Rotterdam, Amsterdam and The Hague. These "urban provinces" would have the traditional provincial competences and some of the responsibilities of municipalities, as well as more instruments to deal more effectively and efficiently with metropolitan problems.

Referenda held in Rotterdam and Amsterdam rejected these plans. The citizens of both cities did not oppose the plans for the creation of an urban province, but they overwhelmingly rejected the plan to partition their cities. A new plan in which the government proposed less partition of the city of Rotterdam was rejected by the second chamber of Parliament. The government has therefore withdrawn its proposal.

In April 1996 central government outlined a new initiative in this field. The idea is that in the area of Rotterdam, with its large port, the competences of the authorities will be extended. For the other six major urban areas decisions are expected to be taken before 1997 to pave the way to a more effective and modernised structure.

In the other areas a redistribution of responsibilities between provinces and municipalities is planned. This re-allocation will have effects on the existing co-operation between municipalities. Therefore it may be necessary to adapt the Inter-Municipality Co-operation Act in the sense that obligatory co-operation in certain areas will be either limited or extended.

A second continuous (but fiercely argued) component of sub-national government reform has been the policy on merging municipalities. The basic thought behind this policy was and still is efficiency and consolidation of municipal service delivery. There is a close link between this policy of municipal mergers and both the regional and the decentralisation policies. The basic idea is that the scale of sub-national government has to be adapted to the new larger scale of social and economic developments. Each municipality must have a minimum population size in order to be able to perform a certain minimum number of functions in an effective and efficient way. This policy is reinforced by the decentralisation initiatives as only "viable and strong" municipalities are thought able to perform the tasks that are under consideration for transfer to sub-national government.

Control bodies

Supervision of sub-national affairs can take two forms: preventive and repressive supervision. Under a regime of preventive supervision, certain sub-national government decisions only take legal force when they are approved by a higher level of government. The instrument of preventive supervision is used, for instance, in the approval of the annual budget (and changes in the budget during the year) by a province in the case of municipalities with structural budget deficit. The same is the case with participation of municipalities and provinces in private law enterprises and companies. Changes in, or the establishment of, new sub-national government taxes have to be approved by central government. Supervision does not entail telling a sub-national government what to do. It can only be told what *not* to do. When applied it constitutes only a negative sanction.

Repressive supervision is the case when a decision or regulation is nullified although this decision or regulation has taken legal force. Repressive supervision is used in situations where sub-national government action is in conflict with the (higher) law or the "general interest". This is associated with the negative limitation of the autonomous (domain and the co-operation formula under the co-administration. This kind of supervision is rarely used. It should be noted that from a formal perspective repressive supervision is rarely used. When conflicts arise between municipalities and provinces or between a sub-national government and central government parties normally will use informal consultation to solve the disagreements. The same applies to the instrument of preventive supervision. But there is, nevertheless, a marked preference for replacing preventive with repressive forms of supervision. Asking permission before being able to take action is considered to diminish the independent status of sub-national government.

A traditionally important provincial responsibility has been the supervision of municipalities and waterboards. The importance of this task has been reduced as supervision is used less. Finally the province has a responsibility in supervising and stimulating regional co-operation between (mainly) municipalities on basis of the Act on Joint Provisions. The province has to demarcate regions for intermunicipal co-operation and stimulate co-operation in an integrated way.

1.2 Powers

Nature of sub-national institutions

The general framework of the municipal government system has a remarkable degree of uniformity. This framework is provided by the Municipal Act, which was revised in 1994. The same degree of uniformity applies to the provinces under the Provincial Act, although there is some variation in the number of representatives on the council and the executive (daily) board. Only the new Municipal

Act allows for some degree of formal (functional) differentiation between municipalities. This differentiation mainly relates to the decentralisation of central government tasks.

The political structure of both the province and municipality consists of a council and an executive body. Municipal and provincial councils are (formally) the highest authority in their respective municipality or province. Elections for these councils take place at four year intervals on the basis of a system of proportional representation.

The number of councillors depends on the population size of the provinces and the municipalities. Day to day work is done by executive boards (the daily boards) of the provinces and the municipalities. These are composed of aldermen and the burgomaster in the municipality or provincial deputies and the commissioner of the Queen at the provincial level. These aldermen and provincial executives are elected for a four year term immediately after the municipal or provincial elections out of the councils. They remain councillors after their election to the daily board. A proposal has been submitted to widen the recruitment base of aldermen and to allow for the selection of candidates from outside the council.

The chairman of the daily board and of the council, the burgomaster and the Queen's commissioner are appointed by the national government. These central government appointments have been called the "aristocratic twist in a democratic drink". The Queen's commissioner was in earlier times primarily a central government official and had a special duty in supervising sub-national affairs. The burgomaster, however, has always been an integral part of the municipality and his salary was, and is, paid by the municipality. Nowadays both the burgomaster and the Queen's commissioner are considered to be functionaries of respectively the municipality and the province and not of the central government. Proponents of the present system argue that by appointing these officials local governments have a more direct access to central government. Opponents have stated that these appointments are an example of central government interference in local affairs. Political initiatives to change this system have been in vain. The only change that has taken place is that the municipal and provincial councils are consulted on the desired qualities of the burgomaster and Queen's commissioner. Central government is not obliged to follow the advice of the councils.

Although sub-national councils are technically the highest authority and the supreme legislative bodies, most political power resides with the executive (daily) boards. Councillors are officially only occupied part-time with local affairs whereas members of the executive board (primarily in the larger) municipalities and provinces are full-time (professional) politicians. In addition to this particular advantage the executive board is assisted by a large and specialised bureaucracy. Attempts are being made to improve the position of the council by enhancing the flow of information to councillors and a more extensive use of commissions in the earlier stages of drafting legislation.

Both the municipal and provincial executives in the daily boards have a collective responsibility. In many larger municipalities and provinces each alderman and provincial executive has a special responsibility for a specific policy area. Particularly in the larger municipalities, power has gradually shifted from the burgomaster to the aldermen. Nevertheless even in these municipalities the burgomaster still has important duties to perform particularly on the area of public order and safety.

Type and degree of autonomy

As noted earlier regulation concerning the political structure of municipal and provincial government is quite uniform. Although in practice some variation exists, the acts provide detailed guidelines for the (political) organisation of provincial and municipal government. The new Municipal Act has opened the way to some additional differentiation. Nevertheless some feel that this measure does not go far enough. The municipalities and provinces are considered independent political units in the context of the Dutch State. These local governments should, therefore, be able to regulate their own internal political organisation. To guarantee the accountability of these self-regulating local governments to citizens, adequate democratic and legal measures are needed.

Both provinces and municipalities operate according to two principles of legal authority: autonomy; and co-administration. These principles have, traditionally, played an important part in defining the position of sub-national governments and determining the nature of inter-governmental relations. This division is based on the Dutch Constitution and the Provincial and Municipal Government Acts.

Autonomy refers to the (legal) autonomous domain of sub-national governments. This notion is described as the "open household". Sub-national governments in the Netherlands are free to develop any policy initiative they deem necessary without having to ask prior consent to a "higher level government". However, changing municipal taxes requires approval by central government. The basic idea behind the autonomous domain is that sub-national government powers are not derived from central government but that entitlement to these powers is an independent right. Article 124 of the Constitution states: *"The powers to decide on and administer their own household is left to the provinces and the municipalities"*. The open formulation of the autonomous sub-national domain prohibits a general enumeration of the autonomous tasks. Thus there are no particular limits on sub-national government autonomy. The restriction is that an act made by central government overrides a (prior) local initiative.

1.3 Responsibilities

Distribution of responsibilities

Central government is generally responsible for tasks concerning Dutch society as a whole. This implies a responsibility for the system of justice (courts and public prosecution), defence, foreign affairs, tax collection, and infrastructure (in a wide sense). Central government also provides general guidelines for future development. The main function of the province is to translate central government plans to their territory. Municipal government is seen as the main provider of public services to the citizens.

Provincial governments overall play a mediating role between central government and the municipalities. These intermediary tasks primarily relate to co-ordinating and planning activities in areas such as welfare, culture, spatial planning, public housing and environmental affairs. (The guidelines given in these provincial plans are not always compulsory for municipalities.) There is a limited number of executive tasks in areas such as (provincial) public works (including water management) and the environment.

Municipal governments are active in a vast array of policy areas including public order, education, housing, public health care, social security, and welfare. Direct public service delivery is concentrated in these local governments. However, this does not imply that all powers in these fields are in the hands of local governments. In education, for example, municipalities have direct executive tasks in public schools, where they form the boards. However, most schools have their own private boards, often inspired denominationally. Subsidies are funded directly by the State – except for school buildings (since 1996) and transport facilities, which are financed by the municipalities. Other municipal involvement in education tends to reflect local conditions, especially concerning problems such as ethnic relations and inadequate sports facilities. Similar relationships exist in housing where large private housing associations administer most social premises on a co-operative basis. Most municipal housing corporations were privatised in the 1980's. Subsidies are becoming less important for financing housing, even in urban renewal areas. On the other hand, many local subsidies are being invested in neighbourhood social and physical infrastructure.

The planning and programming duties of local government are, however, becoming more comprehensive. And local government is increasingly the focal point from which others in the community are empowered to contribute to public facilities. The police is an example of executive powers being laid down outside the municipality, but the function in local public life is very important and demands good communication. Public health care is also partially a local duty (e.g. care for drug addicts) but hospitals and doctors are organised privately, within a State-regulated insurance system.

Thus each field has its own arrangements and balances between the private sector and the three tiers of government.

Mandatory, optional and shared responsibilities

The (legal) autonomous domain of sub-national government has been reduced over the years. Most provincial and municipal tasks nowadays come under the heading of co-administration. What was forgone from a perspective of autonomy to central government, returned to local administration under the title of co-administration. Autonomy implied that only the more active local governments took up certain (vital) new tasks. The reason for centralising local tasks was very often to offer an equal standard of public service delivery to the whole country. Examples can be found in sectors such as education, social security, welfare and spatial planning.

The situation, after three decades of the centralising influence of State regulations and the decentralisation of executive and financial responsibilities, is the predominance of inter-active government. Many key problems associated with matters such as income policy and unemployment, care of the elderly, or environmental pollution can only be dealt with effectively by a mix of national and local government – the latter primarily in an executive or complementary role. The national government generally sets a framework, sometimes by simply assigning a specific duty to municipalities and providing facilities for performance monitoring and improvement (e.g. childcare and crime prevention). Sometimes more elaborate regulations and financial arrangements are provided by the State – particularly for relatively new tasks such as environmental protection – until local policy-making has become more routine and regulations can be moderated.

2. MANAGEMENT FUNCTIONS

2.1 Policy-making and co-ordination

Coherence, consultation and conflict resolution

The principle of co-administration or co-governance is specified in the Provincial and Municipal Government Acts. This concept refers to the duty of sub-national governments to implement general regulations issued at a higher level of government.

Although in some policy-areas (for instance education and social security) strict guide-lines are attached to the local implementation of co-administration tasks, the overall picture is somewhat more balanced. The implementation or execution of many (though not all) co-administration tasks is not a neutral nor technical operation. There is often ample discretionary power for local governments to adjust the execution of these tasks to their local needs. Co-administration also implies that municipalities and provinces have a responsibility for making regulations on certain topics without having detailed guidelines by central government on how to do so.

There are, however, some serious draw backs attached to these new style inter-governmental relations. It is easier to adopt a new line of inter-governmental relations in theory than in practice. As emphasis is put on negotiation, inter-governmental decision-making can take some time. Although extra time is spent on the formulation of policy, and conflicts in the implementation of the particular policy can be avoided, this nevertheless can test the patience of the officials involved. At the same time the extent to which the policy agreements between central government, provinces and municipalities are legally binding is somewhat uncertain. It primarily depends on the good faith of the participants.

Formal and informal mechanisms

With respect to tasks and finance, sub-national government depends on central government but central government also depends on sub-national government. Although central government can create new field agencies, using municipalities or provinces is considered more efficient, effective and democratic (i.e. decentralisation is preferred to deconcentration). Central and sub-national government are very much interdependent. Especially in recent years, less emphasis has been put on hierarchical relations and more attention paid to closer co-operation between the different levels of government on the basis of a partnerships. This partnership is apparent in the increasing number of policy agreements (*convenanten*) that have been concluded between sub-national governments and their representatives on the one hand [for instance the Dutch Union of Municipalities (VNG) or the IPO for the provinces] and central government (with the Ministry of Home Affairs in a facilitating role) on the other.

2.2 Financial management

Sources of revenue

The sources of Dutch sub-national government finance are divided into three main categories: taxes/fees, general grants and specific grants from central government.

For the municipalities the most important tax is the property tax. Other sources of own income are constituted by fees and local government enterprises. The amount of the property tax is related to the size of the general grant. A second source of income take the form of general grants from the central government. These general grants are paid out of a Municipal and a Provincial fund which is administered and fed by central government and funded by a certain percentage of the national tax revenue.

Specific purpose grants are a third source of sub-national income. These are associated with tasks which are co-administered and have the advantage of being a better way of providing for diversification in service delivery. Their number has reduced from 532 in 1980 to 161 in 1994.

Sub-national taxes and other sources constitute only a small fraction of the total municipal income. The same applies to the division of provincial resources. The evolution of the various sources of municipal revenue since 1950 is shown in Table 3.

Table 3. **Sources of municipal revenue (1950, 1960, 1970, 1980, 1990, 1994)**
(percentage)

	1950	1960	1970	1980	1990	1994
Municipal taxes/own sources	14	11	7	6	10	11
General grants	56	41	39	31	26	29
Specific grants	30	48	55	63	64	59
TOTAL	100	100	101 [1]	100	100	99 [1]

1. Rounding-off.
Source: 1950-1985: Th. A.J. Toonen (1991), "Change in continuity: Sub-national and urban affairs in the Netherlands" in J.J. Hesse (ed.), *Sub-national government and urban affairs in international perspective* (Baden-Baden).

Prior to 1980 the sub-national tax percentage was continuously decreasing. The relative size of the general grant has, until recently, also significantly been reduced over the last thirty years. The specific grants have gradually become increasingly the most important source of sub-national government income.

A major current problem is that with central government cutbacks, sub-national government is "sharing" a part of the financial burden because of imposed reduction of both the general and the specific grants. In trying to decrease the dependency of sub-national government on central financing, initiatives have been taken to increase sub-national taxes. The effect can be seen from the rise of this area from 6 per cent in 1980 to 11 per cent in 1994. This increase can partially be explained by a rise in the amount received from levies and other forms of income.

Expenditure responsibilities

The volume of municipal expenditure (56 642 million guilders in 1993) is almost ten times as large than that of the provinces (6 344 million guilders in 1993).

Table 4. **Municipal gross expenditure by functions: 1980 and 1992 (estimates)** [1]
(Dfl per capita)

	1980	1992
Social security and welfare	606	1 248
Physical planning and housing	341	699
Education	472	422
Culture and recreation	200	340
Transport, roads and dykes	369	318
General administration	259	200
Public health	62	266
Public order and safety	194	198
Economic affair	63	30

1. Functional categories have slightly changed over this period.
Source: Ministry of Home Affairs

Balance between discretion and control

Each year, central government decides on the percentage of national tax revenue to go into the Municipal and Provincial Funds. Before deciding on this, in the case of the municipalities, advice is asked from the Municipal Finance Council. The actual size of the general grant to individual municipalities and provinces is determined in accordance with specified criteria mentioned in the (Municipal) Financial Relations Act and the Provincial Act. These criteria are currently being altered in order to support larger municipalities with a regional function and relatively higher proportions of poorer people and low-cost housing. Criteria concerning income level and social structure are given more weight and from 1997, the municipal tax capacity (value of real estate) is being taken into account before calculating the general grant for each municipality.

Some conditions with respect to proper use are attached to payments of specific purpose grants. Until recently, this was seen as encouraging central government intervention in the affairs of sub-national governments. Many specific grants, however, have been introduced at the explicit request of sub-national government for satisfying the needs of their citizens.

The importance of specific grants is associated with the growth of co-administration tasks. The changes in the composition of municipal income gave rise to concerns about increasing centralism in inter-governmental relations. Sub-national governments are free to use the income from their own resources (including taxes) and the general grant for the expenditure they consider necessary for their community. As stated earlier, the use of specific grants is preconditioned. This might – though not always – limit the freedom of sub-national government. This problem can be intensified as some specific grants are not sufficient to deal with actual expenditure needs. When having a deficit, a local authority has to cover it from its own taxes and general grants. In response to these problems a policy has been devised that aims at the reduction of specific grants and the curtailment of the special conditions attached to these grants. The number of these grants has been reduced by combining smaller ones in broader special (block) grants and transferring a number of these grants to the municipal and provincial funds.

2.3 Performance management

Mechanisms

Performance measurement is relatively well developed at the sub-national level; and performance management questions at the national level almost invariably involve sub-national government issues. Dutch local government has developed a positive attitude to performance measurement and a number operate performance budgeting systems. The Government Accounts Act (1976) which focused on costs and volumes of outputs at the central level was followed by a similar budget renewal process implemented in 1985. The competence of the Court of Audit is limited to national government.

There is no systematic monitoring by central government of the performance and efficiency of local government. This is generally considered to be the domain of the municipalities and provinces themselves, and many cities now compare their costs and service levels with other cities (including the use of league tables that provide comparisons of cities' performance in a variety of areas). When specific grants are provided, specific information is required in the interests of accountability. In the recent covenants between the State and the largest Dutch cities concerning a comprehensive "city challenge" action programme, monitoring with respect to fixed performance targets plays an important role.

The Public Services Quality Monitoring System (see below) surveys the quality and efficiency of services provided by local government bodies which have frequent client contact. However, it is not compulsory and the role of national government in developing this system is purely that of a facilitator.

The "BBI" process is a system of output budgeting used by some 200 municipalities. The key objective of the system is to establish strong links between policy objectives, budget allocations and results and thus enhance democratic accountability. The system includes political objectives, specifies how they will be reached, and develops performance indicators to monitor progress.

Quality standards

The Public Services Quality Monitoring System provides information on the quality and efficiency of service provision by local governments. The purpose is to help local governments set their own priorities for service quality. The information is used in devising, elaborating, implementing and assessing policy on service standards. The system has two components:

- standards of customer contact, which involve keeping a record of the way in which individuals are dealt with in the service system, using interviews with customers; and

- efficiency, by assessing the time and number of steps it takes to supply a given product.

The system develops standards for comparing past and present performance and the performance of different organisations. It uses a "case-history" approach, tracking clients and their perceptions of the services received. So far 20 out of about 600 municipalities have adopted the system. Some national agencies (social welfare and the police) are developing similar approaches and others may follow.

2.4 Human resource management

Each sub-national government has the power and responsibility to adopt its own regulation with respect to the legal position of government officials within the framework of the Civil Servants Act 1929 (Ambtenarenwet 1929). Most government personnel is appointed under this act, although some are hired on a private law basis. There is no legal distinction made between white and blue collar workers.

Matters of staffing, career decisions, labour relations, training and management development programmes are the domain of the different sub-national governments. There is a tendency for each level of government to decentralise practical personnel issues to each administrative unit. Thus the importance of central personnel units has diminished in recent years while at the same time the position of line agencies (and managers) has been reinforced.

Over the last few years some important changes have also taken place with respect to the system of wage negotiations. Until 1993 there was a more or less uniform system of conditions of employment across levels of government. This was particularly centralised with regard to pay levels. These conditions of employment were the results of negotiations between the national government and the major trade unions of national civil servants, although in fact, the government was able to fix the terms of employment almost unilaterally. When the results of negotiations at the sub-national level differed from the central government standards, the pay settlement could be nullified on the basis of a special provision in the 1929 Act which stipulates that the national government has the power to revoke pay settlements which go against the law or the general interest.

Since the early 1990s the importance of pay differentiation between sectors of government and a more equal position between government employers and trade unions have been acknowledged to be essential. This stems from the desire to modernise labour relations in the public sector and to bring it more in line with the private sector. A more balanced relationship between government employers was established in 1984 by the creation of a board of arbitration charged with settling disputes in the event of a breakdown in negotiations. In order to implement the decentralisation of this new system nine different government sectors have been defined and are shown in the following table.

In each sector (unions of) government employers negotiate with trade unions on pay settlements and terms of employment. The only exception are pensions and social security issues which are still dealt with at the central level. For example in central government each of the ministries are considered as employers and the Ministry of Home Affairs serves as a co-ordinating body; in the provinces the IPO (an inter-provincial co-operative body) is involved; and in the case of the municipalities it is the Dutch Union of Municipalities (VNG) which acts as the employers' representatives. The cities of Amsterdam, Rotterdam, The Hague and Utrecht negotiate directly with the labour unions.

Table 5. **Government employment by sector (1985, 91, 93)**
(number of persons full-time and part-time)

Government sector	1985	1991	1993
Central government[1]	154 400	113 744	116 894
Judiciary	1 277	1 583	2 020
Provinces	18 357	13 951	13 433
Waterboards	7 275	7 815	7 888
Municipalities	214 806	196 017	186 387
Inter-governmental corporations	–	21 222	21 750
Police	30 714	35 689	36 029
Defence (including conscripts)	103 160	121 064	108 910
Education (public)	304 782	302 929	370 915
TOTAL	784 949	814 014	864 226

1. Excluding civilian military personnel since 1991.
Source: Public Management Developments: Update 1995, OECD, 1995.

Research has shown that there is not much mobility between different levels of government. The same applies to inter-departmental mobility, although these are measures in central government to increase mobility in higher ranks by introducing a general "civil service" (*algemene bestuursdienst*). The exchange of personnel between municipalities is higher. Generally, however, the different governments are fairly compartmentalised with respect to employment.

3. TRENDS IN REDISTRIBUTING AUTHORITY ACROSS LEVELS OF GOVERNMENT

3.1 Evolving tendencies

During the latter part of the 18th century many abortive attempts were made to alter the political administrative system of the day – and experience with the (very centralistic) unitary state during the French Era was not very satisfactory either. The present Dutch administrative and local (municipal and provincial) government design is, however, indisputably associated with the initiatives of the nineteenth century liberal statesman Thorbecke in response to dissatisfaction with the inept federative structure of the Dutch Republic. His legislative labour encompasses the introduction of the first modern democratic Constitution (1848), the Provincial Government Act (1850), and the Municipal Government Act (1851). With some minor revisions this legal structure still determines the present day administrative system. (In 1994 a new Municipal Government Act came into force, although it only differs marginally from the original one.)

The basic legal framework relating to local government in the Netherlands is, therefore, characterised by a high degree of continuity. Although at the outset it was general enough to allow for administrative development and new initiatives at the sub-national level, the "Thorbeckian" system nowadays appears to have been elevated to an almost sacrosanct status. Nevertheless societal changes have had a profound influence on sub-national governments.

Reform of the system of sub-national government has had a high position on the political agenda for over thirty years. These reforms have mainly focused on the inter-related issues of the regions; municipal mergers; and decentralisation.

Regions

Since the end of the First World War there has been discussion about the existence and nature of regions in the Netherlands. The growth of the economy and of the population blurred the demarcation between cities and the surrounding country-side and often between cities themselves. In policy-areas including social affairs, industrial activity, housing and spatial planning, collective interests emerged which cannot be dealt with at the same scale as the present, territorial-based, three-tier system of government. The so-called "regional question" thus consists of an administrative gap between the provincial and the municipal levels of government.

At first this problem was especially apparent in the western, most populated and industrialised part of the Netherlands. In this area, conurbations came into existence around the larger cities of Amsterdam, Rotterdam and The Hague. At a later stage it spread to other (the eastern and southern) parts of the country. Administrative solutions have ranged from inter-governmental (mainly intermunicipal) co-operation to the establishment of a regional level of government.

The demand for regional public service provision has increased especially since the World War II. The demand for regional service delivery pertains particularly to the area between the provinces and the municipalities of government. Although in the past several efforts have been made to introduce a directly elected regional government, present government policy is opposed to a regional addition to the three tier system. The opposition is inspired by the perception that a regional government could erode local government and complicate the system of sub-national government. Intergovernmental and primarily intermunicipal co-operation has therefore been the favoured solution to regional problems. Although working in "rural" and "semi-urbanised" surroundings, experience with inter-municipal co-operation in urbanised areas has not been very successful. New initiatives are under way to create "new style provinces" with more powers and responsibilities in the areas around Rotterdam, The Hague and Amsterdam. This approach can be seen as a departure from the intermediatory provinces described earlier.

Although inter-municipal regional co-operation is preferred, many so-called functional regions (targeted on specific policy areas) have been created. The most important functional region is that of policing.

Municipal mergers

There is also a problem associated with the policy on merging smaller municipalities into larger ones – partly as a way of dealing with regional problems. As the size of (particularly rural) municipalities grows, the regional gap is closed, but at the same time a local gap emerges as the distance to the citizen increases.

One of the most debated topics is the minimum population size of a municipality considered necessary. The relation between population size and the quality of municipal service delivery has been contested but without much avail. The Dutch Union of Municipalities (VNG) has also subscribed to a large scale municipal merger policy in order to avert the introduction of a separate regional level and has suggested a minimum population size of 18 000.

Decentralisation

Decentralisation has been an important element in central government policy from the beginning of this century. Consecutive governments have made proposals to decentralise government tasks and means. Most emphasis nowadays is put on territorial rather than functional decentralisation.

The arguments for decentralisation policy mainly relate to strengthening citizen participation (the democracy argument) as sub-national government is seen as the ideal level for citizen participation. Although many decentralisation proposals have been introduced, the results of these efforts were, until the middle of the 1980s, rather limited. The attitude of sub-national government towards decentralisation was quite cynical. The history of decentralisation has been considered by many of them to be a tale of "grand" and "broken" promises.

Since the middle of the 1980s an important change has taken place in central government policy on the role and function of the public sector and of central government in particular. The reduction of the size of (central) government was seen as imperative to solving budgetary problems on the one hand and on the other to improving the steering capacity of government. One of the instruments for reducing the size of central government is to decentralise its tasks. Decentralisation policy has gained momentum and at the same time the driving force has shifted from democratic arguments to ones of efficiency and effectiveness. Tasks are mainly decentralised to municipalities, either individually or on the basis of the Act on Joint Provisions. Sometimes a task is given to a larger municipality and, in the case of smaller towns, inter-municipal co-operation is used.

A problem is that although the task load of municipalities has increased considerably, financial resources have not risen at the same rate. Over recent years local governments have shared in the cutback policy of central government. For example, a reduction has been made in central government's contribution to the municipal and provincial fund. This has had some serious consequences for the financial situation of municipalities and provinces. Solving these difficulties is considered to be one of the main challenges for local government authorities in the 1990's. Generally this has implied raising taxes (mainly the property tax in the case of the municipality) and fees (for instance on garbage collection) and, more importantly, making cutbacks.

3.2 The current debate

The Netherlands is often characterised as a "decentralised unitary State" in terms of its government organisation. What this apparent contradiction signifies in terms of a balance between centralisation and decentralisation or for inter-governmental relations has been a topic of much debate. Two important questions in this respect are "to what extent is the framework of Dutch public administration characterised by centralist and decentralised elements and what should the balance be?"

Inter-governmental relations in the Netherlands have both unitary and decentralised elements. The legal framework has emphasized the hierarchical elements and hence the unitary components of policy-making and co-ordination across the levels of government. This perspective focused attention on the ongoing process of centralisation, and has to be seen in the context of an assertive central government role in societal development from the end of the World War II to the beginning of the 1980s. Local government was involved but primarily used to implement the schemes. This conception of inter-governmental relations tended to overlook the fact that central government was dependent on local government for implementing many tasks. The alternative, of setting up expensive field agencies, was considered not to be attractive. It was also held that local government had no freedom to manoeuvre beyond the guidelines given by central government. But implementation is not neutral – it often involves a reformulation of policy. Ideas have to be put into practice. At the same time insufficient attention was paid to the fact that central government legislation was very often only a framework for making regulations or taking measures. The detailed content has to be decided by local government itself.

A new perspective of inter-governmental relations was then developed. This stressed the interdependency between the different actors in the local government system. Instead of looking at inter-governmental policy co-ordination as intrinsically hierarchical; equality between governments each having their own role was emphasized. The municipalities are considered as the main provider of services to the citizens. The role of the province is seen as intermediary between central government and the municipalities. Central government has to provide the national framework for development. Each level of government is, therefore, dependent on co-operation with the other. This implies close collaboration and negotiations between different levels. Instead of hierarchical command, more use is made of policy agreements (covenants). This new approach is being adopted more and more in official policy documents. For example, in the reorganisation of local government in the urbanised areas, the views of the municipalities were solicited before central government made its proposals.

3.3 Driving forces

The driving force behind the efforts to reform the Dutch system of government can be grouped into two separate developments. First are the financial and economic aspects. The reorganisation of local government and changes in their functions reflect a desire to increase the efficiency and effectiveness of local government. This stems from the need to cope with reduced finances. This in turn impacts on the internal organisation of governments as well as on the division of tasks and relations between levels of government.

A second motivation is to improve the relationship between government and the citizen. By transferring tasks to local governments, the aim is to improve both citizen involvement and government performance. As the municipality has, at least in theory, a closer relationship to the citizen than central government, the municipality can be more responsive to the needs of citizens.

NEW ZEALAND

1. INSTITUTIONS AND AUTHORITY

1.1 Structures

This description of sub-national administration maintains the OECD distinction between local and regional governments and those parts of the central administration which have been deconcentrated. In the latter category is the sub-national administration of health and education which, in New Zealand, have a formal primary responsibility to a central government agency including financial and management accountability.

Description of levels

"Local government" in New Zealand is an inclusive term containing regional councils and district and city councils. The latter two are collectively termed "territorial authorities". Although there are some minor exceptions, in general a group of territorial authorities is defined within the boundary of a regional council. In some cases a territorial authority may have the statutory functions of a regional council. These bodies are known as "unitary authorities".

The number of bodies in each category is as follows:

- regional councils: 12
- territorial authorities: 74 (including 4 unitary authorities).

Since the unitary authorities are territorial authorities which have been made responsible for regional council functions, they are also included in the 74 territorial authorities. This means there is a total of 86 local authorities in New Zealand. Local communities may initiate action to form unitary authorities in their region so that number may increase or decrease. Local community action could also result in the constitution of new regions and districts, or their amalgamation. The resulting area and population distributions are as follows:.

Table 1: **Area and population of sub-national governments**

Number	Regional Councils 12		Territorial Authorities [1] 74	
	Area (km^2)	Population	Area (km^2)	Population
Largest	42 200	1 002 700	31 000	327 800
Smallest	4 518	33 800	21.7	5 057[2]

1. Includes four Unitary Authorities.
2. Excluding Chatham Islands Territory with 756 inhabitants.
Source: New Zealand Official Yearbook, 1994.

Central government at sub-national levels

The changes within national and sub-national administration since 1984 have included changes in the ways that central government functions are administered at regional and local levels. Some government departments operate regional offices (e.g. Ministry for the Environment). Health and education are functions of central government in New Zealand.

Prior to 1993 there were 14 Area Health Boards. Since 1993 a sub-national structure of four Regional Health Authorities (RHAs) has operated with the responsibility for purchasing health and disability services from public and private health providers. The public hospital system now consists of 12 Crown Health Enterprises (CHEs) and funding allocated by the Ministry of Health. These public service providers contract with their respective RHAs to provide health care and disability services for specified geographical areas containing a 24-hour acute care hospital. CHEs can also tender for specialist services (e.g. heart transplant surgery) in other parts of the country. Private hospital and specialist medical areas (e.g. radiology) also compete for service contracts from RHAs. General medical practitioners and physicians also operate as part of this sub-national system.

In addition to the Crown Health Enterprises, there is provision for a local community to run its public hospital through a community trust. This option is usually taken up when a small local hospital is to be closed by the relevant CHE.

A programme of education reform was initiated under the 1984-90 Labour Government. This included changes at the sub-national level where the ten regional education boards were abolished and replaced by a system of local area Boards of Trustees for the management of all state primary and secondary schools. The Boards consist of elected representatives of parents, staff and students (secondary schools only). The Principal is also a member of the Board. Co-option is also possible to ensure gender balance and to reflect the ethnic and socio-economic character of the school population. Funding for each Board is provided through Vote: Education in the national Budget and distributed by the Ministry of Education.

National level institutions control the legality and efficiency of actions of the Boards of Trustees. Each Board establishes a Charter which is approved by the Minister of Education. This Charter is then monitored by the Education Review Office (ERO) as part of its function to prepare quality assurance reports, effectiveness review reports and evaluation reports on management systems, curricula content, and delivery of education services. Boards of Trustees are subject as Crown entities to the Public Finance Act 1989.

Creation, elimination and restructuring

The 1989 amendments to the Local Government Act 1974 resulted in a reduction from 22 to 14 regions. In 13 of them regional councils were to be elected, while one (Gisborne) had a district council which was a unitary authority. Territorial authorities fell in number from 205 to 74. Special purpose or ad hoc authorities (e.g. drainage boards, harbour boards, rabbit boards etc.) whose members were often directly elected, had their numbers reduced from over 400 to just seven. Health and education authorities and electric power boards were also restructured in separate exercises.

The local government boundaries on which the present pattern is based occurred through a process led by the Local Government Commission. For regional councils, in addition to economic factors, a major consideration has been the underlying topographical structure of the region, with particular emphasis on river catchments. At the territorial authority level a range of demographic, social, cultural, administrative and efficiency criteria apply.

Since 1992 a change to the boundary of a particular local authority or a transfer of functions may be proposed and dealt with by one of the local authorities involved, without the involvement of the Local Government Commission, unless there is an appeal. There is no formal role provided for the Minister of Local Government in the process of developing the recommendation, although the 1974 Act does enable the Secretary for Local Government to make submissions on a proposal.

Proposals for new regions or districts are separately provided for in the Act. Groups of electors, a local authority affected or the Minister may initiate proposals -- which are assessed by the Local Government Commission against criteria set out in the Local Government Act. Proposals must gain approval from a poll of electors before they may be implemented. In any of these proposals electors may not include any reorganisation of functions unless they relate to boundary changes.

The imposition of the present boundaries of local government by the Commission in 1989 means that a number of communities have maintained campaigns to regain their own councils. One proposal is still in train.

Control bodies

Since local government is a creature of central government, with only the powers granted to it by statute, there are provisions to control the legality and/or efficiency of its actions. At the same time local authorities are elected bodies, with councillors accountable to their electors and with a need for appropriate monitoring internal to the local body itself. This latter requirement also enables the elected councillors to exercise control over the chief executive officer and his or her staff. The respective control provisions are summarised in Table 2.

Table 2. **Control provision by level**

Level of control	Agency	Function	Sanctions
Central Government	Audit Department	Financial and performance audit	Tagging audits
Council	Elected members	Decision-making	
Community	All residents, ratepayers and community bodies	Public consultation through the Annual Plan process; annual review through the requirement to prepare an Annual Report	Triennial elections or legal action.

Other review agencies include the Ombudsman, the Courts, the Parliamentary Commissioner for the Environment, the Planning Tribunal and Ministerial review.

1.2 Powers

Nature of sub-national institutions

Local government bodies are directly elected for three-year terms. Elections are conducted by postal vote using the First Past the Post method. Territorial authorities are headed by a mayor who is directly elected by the voters, whereas regional councils are headed by a chairperson who is elected by the councillors from among their number.

Type and degree of autonomy

The powers of local government and of a local authority to carry out works and engage in functions are provided in the Local Government Act and in other legislation where central government chooses to devolve responsibility. Local authorities do not have a power of general competence. The *ultra vires* doctrine is applicable. In the field of territorial planning and environmental management, for example, power is devolved through the Resource Management Act 1991 to regional councils and territorial authorities for sub-national level policy, development approvals, monitoring and enforcement. Specific aspects of public health are also devolved through the Health Act 1956 (Part II) to local authorities.

The right to tax property (real estate) is determined through the Rating Powers Act 1988. Under this Act a local authority can levy a charge on the legal owner of land holdings in order to raise revenue. This is the principal source of local revenue (see section 2.2). The levy may be applied differentially across properties, through a council exercising a discretion to determine the most appropriate spread of the rating burden through out the community, subject to only certain parameters.

There is also authority to borrow money for special purposes (Local Authority Loans Act 1956), subject to the principle that a council "... shall provide for its ordinary obligations and engagements in any year out of its revenue for that year...". Ministerial controls apply to long-term capital borrowing although there has been some general freeing-up of control over borrowing powers.

1.3 Responsibilities

Distribution of responsibilities

The responsibilities of local government and the sub-national administration of health and education are specified through the statutes governing those administrations, which are all creatures of statute. During the 1987-89 Local Government Reform process consideration was given to providing local authorities with the power of general competence, but this was not included in the amendments to the Local Government Act. Local government continues, therefore, to operate within a system where central government sets functional and operational limits, with councils constrained by these while responding to the expectations of their local communities.

In addition to the limits set by central government, local community attitudes to the appropriate responsibilities of their councils are important. The conventional New Zealand view is that councils collect rates (property taxes) in order to deliver a simple range of services: often referred to as rubbish, roads, and regulations. The last of these came about through the need for control over public nuisances, such as dogs, and local public health, buildings and town and country planning. The ability of councils to broaden their responsibilities to include social programmes such as housing and employment, and local economic development schemes, has been constrained by these traditional attitudes, although the legislation providing for such activities allows a considerable degree of discretion.

In the redistribution of functions which occurred through the 1988-89 reforms this traditional view of local government responsibilities was maintained. The responsibilities of ad hoc bodies (e.g. drainage boards and pest boards) were given to local government but other responsibilities such as education were not. Thus, when the policy decision was made to remove Education Boards and replace them with a community-based management body for each primary school, Boards of Trustees were introduced. The government sees the bulk funding of schools, including staff salaries, as an important part of its devolution of responsibilities to Boards of Trustees.

2. MANAGEMENT FUNCTIONS

2.1 Policy-making and co-ordination

Coherence, consultation and conflict resolution

The degree to which sub-national bodies can set the agenda depends on the willingness of central government to permit it. For example, in the area of road safety implementation, plans are developed at national, regional and local levels. The process followed includes procedures to ensure these plans are integrated. The same applies to civil defence responsibilities.

Consultation, collaboration, and liaison generally relies on ad hoc arrangements. The process depends on the approach adopted by central government departments. For example, the police have encouraged local authority liaison over crime prevention programmes. Other examples include the funding of co-ordinators for Safer Cities and Healthy Cities programmes within local councils.

Formal and informal mechanisms

With local government operating principally through statute, mechanisms for policy making vary across sectors. Increasingly local authorities are adopting strategic planning as a means of achieving policy coherence and co-ordination. This has not been a statutory requirement, but is seen rather as a practical way to meet corporate planning requirements. However, recently enacted legislation [the Local Government Amendment Act (No.6) 1996] will require long term financial planning from July 1998. The other sub-national administrations for health and education are also following these processes.

For planning and resource management, for example, the Resource Management Act includes provisions which spell out its purpose and principles; local government performs its policy making and other functions under the Act subject to those provisions. This ensures a degree of central government influence on policy coherence which is augmented by a further provision for National Policy Statements. Regional councils and territorial authorities are required to amend their policy and regulatory documents to ensure they are consistent with the direction set by the national policy set out in such a Statement. (To date no such National Policy Statements have been promulgated, other than a New Zealand Coastal Policy Statement.) Similarly, territorial authorities are required to ensure that their policies and regulations are consistent with those of the appropriate regional council.

The Resource Management Act requires, among other things, that councils check that any policy and rule has a defined objective, is necessary to achieve the purpose of the Act, and is the best method or means to achieve its objective. The achievement of an objective through another Act or other means available to the council (e.g. public information, education, or the carrying out of a public work), creates an opportunity for seeking policy coherence and co-ordination.

Parliament also requires a separation within local government between regulatory and non-regulatory functions. This brings a need for additional procedures for co-ordination and monitoring. There is also a further separation of operations which compete directly with the private sector. For the latter, in the case of roading and passenger transport, councils are required to establish stand alone business units (SABUs) or local authority trading enterprises (LATEs) with council-appointed management boards. This central government requirement is enforced through restrictions on government funding to local authorities for functions and responsibilities which should be by way of a SABU or LATE. For example, government subsidies for public transport are only paid to local authorities where their transport operation is a separate company. It follows that subsidies are also paid on the same basis to private transport operators. Public transport policy and subsidy disbursement responsibilities rest with regional councils within an overall national strategic framework for land transport currently under development. Subsidies are paid to operators following a competitive tendering process administered by the Regional Councils.

Land transport is also an example where a hierarchy of programmes and plans provides the basis for co-ordination and central government funding. Through a process which builds on proposals developed from local level needs, national priorities and annual expenditure plans are constructed on the following hierarchy:

- National Land Transport Programme (Transit New Zealand Authority);
- Regional Land Transport Programmes (Regional Councils);
- District Land Transport Programmes (Territorial Authoritie.s)

The district programme contains recommendations on local roading, construction and maintenance, state highways, research, and administration. Within each regional council, a Regional Land Transport Committee prepares the public transport component of the Regional Land Transport Programme and comments on the roading priorities in the District Land Transport Programmes which are provided to the Transit New Zealand Authority. This central government authority submits the national programme to government for the funds, which are subsequently distributed back through the hierarchy. The Authority's operational body, Transit New Zealand, administers this system. It has no construction or direct programme implementation responsibilities, consistent with the separation of function principle being applied by central government to local authorities.

2.2 Financial management

Sources of revenue

Sources of revenue vary across the range of sub-national administrations. However, there is a common principle applying; since all administrations operate by central government fiat, the amount of revenue coming from central government, and any conditions attached to it, are determined through the annual national Budget. Information on financial needs is supplied to the government during the preparation of the Budget but the outcome is not negotiable. The bodies concerned are advised of the revenue decisions and then budget accordingly. For the sub-national administrations for health and education the principal revenue source is determined through the annual national budget.

For local government the allocation of revenue by central government is limited to direct programme grants (e.g. for land transport programmes), and payments in lieu of property taxation where land is owned by central government. For example, the national housing body (Housing New Zealand) makes payments to territorial authorities for its public housing properties. Total government grants, subsidies and levies amounted to NZ$ 310.4 million, or 10 per cent total income for local authorities in 1994-95. There is a mixture of both tied and general grants where central government funding is concerned. In land transport, for instance, the funding is tied to the specifics established in the national and regional programmes.

Other sources of revenue for territorial local authorities are principally through property taxation, as well as special taxation (e.g. petroleum tax), fines, receipts from operations (service charges and fees) and rental income from properties. The petroleum tax produced revenue of NZ$ 21 million in the 1991/92 year. A separate petroleum tax to fund passenger transport applies in certain regions.

Capital expenditure may be financed through borrowing. Long-term debt amounted to NZ$ 1.7 billion (June 1993) with a further NZ$ 0.5 billion as short term debt. The total debt for local authorities at that time was equivalent to NZ$ 650 per head of population or 134 per cent of Annual Rates.

Regional councils obtain their revenue principally through property taxation. In most (but not all) regions, this is collected by the territorial authorities on behalf of the regional councils.

Table 3. **Main revenue sources of local authorities (1994-95)** [1]
(percentage)

Source	%
Rates	57
Sales and other income	19
Grants, subsidies and levies	10
Investment income	8
Fees and Fines	4
Petroleum Tax	1

1. Figures are rounded and do not add up to 100 per cent.
Source: Statistics New Zealand.

Balance between discretion and control

The management model being applied by central government generally has meant some changes in the balance between local autonomy, discretion, and direction, and control from the centre. As already noted, the principle of having centrally determined policies and programmes while enabling the sub-national administrations to then decide on the most efficient and effective means to achieve the prescribed outputs and outcomes, has resulted in more regional or local autonomy on day to day operations. For local government the change *vis-à-vis* central government is not as apparent since its locus of accountability has been primarily to the local community.

Responsibility for internal financial management is set out in the statutes. A process of developing corporate plans applies, with responsibility resting with the controlling "board". In the case of local government the elected councillors comprise the "board" while for the health sector this is the controlling body appointed by the Minister of Health. For education, the role is played by the Board of Trustees for each school.

The senior officer for each body functions as a Chief Executive Officer (CEO). While the ultimate responsibility for expenditure rests with each "board", the day to day authorisations are by the CEO. The CEO is accountable to the "board" for performance against stated policies, programmes and plans.

For local government the Local Government Act prescribes a process for preparing an annual statement of objectives and outcomes and their associated expenditures and receipts. This is presented in the form of an Annual Plan. The draft of the Annual Plan is subjected to a public consultation process. Auditing of performance against the Plan is also a public process with a statutory requirement under the Act for each council to prepare, at the end of each financial year, an Annual Report of actual achievements and expenditure compared with those in the Plan. The extent to which funding is tied to responsibilities varies across sectors.

Tools used to control spending and revenue-raising capacities within the sub-national administrations reflect those laid down for central government by the Public Finance Act 1989 and the Fiscal Responsibility Act 1994. The essence of the latter Act is:

- the specification of desirable financial criteria for government;
- a requirement to nominate each year objectives for total spending, taxation and borrowing for a period of years;
- a requirement to account explicitly for deviations from these targets.

Currently this latter Act does not apply to local government. However, the Local Government Amendment Act (No. 6) 1996, which will come into force in July 1998 will reduce government's control over borrowing by local government and apply the principles of the Fiscal Responsibility Act 1994 to its financial management.

The Act introduces a set of principles aimed at ensuring the prudent handling of the funds and revenues of local authorities. It makes it mandatory for local authorities to adopt every three years a long term financial strategy. This covers a 10-year period, and includes consideration of:

- estimated expenses;
- means of funding them;
- estimated cash-flow projections;
- the creation and realisation of reserves, investments and assets;
- estimated changes in net worth, and estimated long-term borrowing requirements.

The Act also provides for procedures to deal with situations involving variations between long-term financial strategy and funding, investment, or borrowing management policies. Similar provisions are made for annual reporting to the public on financial matters. Additional weight is given to user-pays charging regimes by linking direct benefits to direct costs.

There are several elements of the financial management system already in place:

- statements of objectives and service performance in financial statements;
- accrual accounting as the basis of financial statements.

The annual budgeting system links the processes of strategic and corporate planning with budgetary implications of decisions. As noted above, for local government this annual process is a public one, and the financial statement requirements play a significant role in making local government accounts more transparent. There is no statutory rate capping to limit revenue from that source, but historically there has been significant public pressure against annual rate increases. The use of loan moneys and non-use of rate moneys to pay for specified items is also controlled.

Local government has been constrained in terms of increases in its indebtedness through ratepayers' polls and oversight by the Local Authority Loans Board. This body was abolished by the Local Government Amendment Act (No. 6) 1996.

2.3 Performance management

Performance standards at the local government level are specified as targets in Annual Plans, and are used as benchmarks for Annual Reports produced at the end of the financial year.

The city of Christchurch provides an example of the reform of local government in New Zealand and the significance of local initiatives. Organisationally, Christchurch City Council is divided into "business units", whose functions vary depending on whether they are Enabling/Client Units, Service Providers or Support Services. These organisational units are largely independent and have all the financial, personnel and organisational control they need. "Provider Units" deal with buildings and equipment, vehicles, computer systems, etc. The notion behind this distinction is that the business units should be responsible only for their own performance and should be free to choose the best provider of services, whether this be an internal Provider Unit or the private sector. Christchurch has succeeded in ensuring that this new way of thinking has been accepted and implemented by all managerial staff. In three area its performance has been particularly impressive: in co-operation between citizens, politicians and the administration in the planning and controlling cycle; in client orientation; and in motivating its employees to embrace the new philosophy and the idea of "total quality management" on the basis of customer satisfaction.

2.4 Human resource management

Statutory distinctions: As with financial management, the systems for the employment of central and local government staff are based on private sector models. This is in contrast to the situation prior to State sector reforms in 1986 when the Public Service was seen as having a liberal influence on private sector employment practices. For example, maternity leave and other Equal Employment Opportunity (EEO) provisions were introduced first into the Public Service. The Public Service reforms culminated in the State Sector Act 1988. They were also applied to local government in the Local Government Amendment Act 1989.

By 1991 the Employment Contracts Act had replaced the traditional award system under previous statutes. This removed the system of national awards established for industrial groups. It also removed any right under law to require a worker to be a member of a trade union as a condition of employment in that industry. The central role of a trade union to negotiate employment conditions was replaced by a provision for individual or collective bargaining where any person could represent the employee in negotiations. A trade union could still perform that representation role if invited to do so by the employee or group of employees.

As a consequence of these changes since 1989 employers in central and local government apply systems which are common to public and private sectors. They also apply private sector human resource management principles. For example, each organisation carries out reviews of positions within the organisation involving comparisons of job descriptions, and a search for comparability in work done and level of position, with commensurate pay levels. A points based approach is often used in these exercises. In short, there has been a greater attempt for rationality in the levels and task descriptions within the organisations and private sector equivalents.

There is a statutory responsibility for government bodies (national, regional and local) to be a "good employer". For local government this is expressed in the Local Government Act. The principle of a "good employer" calls for "fair and proper treatment of employees in all respects of their employment". Expressly included is the need for an Equal Employment Opportunities (EEO) programme which is also prescribed in the Act. The same requirements apply to the health and education sectors (as Crown entities) through the State Sector Act, and are over seen by the State Services Commission.

Managerial autonomy: The principle that managers perform most effectively if made fully accountable for the efficient running of their organisations has been taken into local government human resource management. The Chief Executive Officer is appointed by the elected council and is the sole employer of all staff. The CEO assumes the accountability obligations for the performance of his or her staff. The Local Government Act prescribes the responsibilities of an executive officer, including being "...responsible to the local authority for employing, on behalf of the local authority within his or her area of responsibility, staff of the local authority and negotiating their terms of employment."

The real change made here was that the Chief Executive is accountable to the Council and all other staff are accountable to the Chief Executive. The elected members cannot circumvent the Chief Executive and become involved in day to day management. This means that decisions on the level of staffing are made by the by CEO. The number of staff are determined by the CEO taking into account the resources required to implement the council's policy. CEO delegation is possible to Human Resources sections or line managers or Heads of Business Units/LATEs.

Table 4. **General government and public sector employment (1989-94)**
(filled jobs, February figures) [1], [2]

	1989	1990	1991	1992	1993	1994
General government [3]:	238 700	242 600	248 200	236 500	241 800	244 700
Central government non-trading	215 700	214 500	219 000	212 800	218 800	221 200
Local government non-trading	23 000	28 100	29 200	23 700	23 000	23 400
Central government trading	81 100	61 800	40 800	37 600	28 700	22 300
Local government trading	18 900	14 800	14 500	17 200	15 600	14 400
TOTAL PUBLIC SECTOR [3]	338 700	319 300	303 600	219 200	286 100	281 400

1. Includes the armed forces (civilian and military employment).
2. Includes only activity units with more than two full-time equivalent employees.
3. Figures may not add due to rounding.
Source: *Public Management Developments: Update* 1995, OECD, 1995.

2.5 Regulatory management and reform

The post 1984 context for government was based on the principle of reducing regulatory "interference"; that is, the concept of the minimal state which precludes excessive intervention in economic and social systems. This is illustrated within the Resource Management Act by the test on the need for regulation alongside other means or methods to achieve a policy. There are also provisions for the non-notification of resource consent applications; for regional and district plans to provide for permitted activity categories; and minimum time lines for completing regulatory processes. One effect of these changes in regulatory management is to reduce the level of public intervention in the process.

3. TRENDS IN REDISTRIBUTING AUTHORITY ACROSS LEVELS OF GOVERNMENT

3.1 Evolving tendencies

The Labour government (1984-90) introduced major public sector reform measures including ones that altered substantially the structure of local government through devolution and decentralisation. Local government reform was initiated after economic deregulation and the restructuring of the central government sector. These were a response to a deteriorating economic situation, a large public debt, and a fall in New Zealand's economic performance vis-à-vis its partners.

The election of a National Party Government in 1990 saw further changes introduced. In local government the powers of regional councils were focused on resource management and related functions, and regional council service delivery functions were dropped. The major service delivery activities of the Auckland Regional Council were handed over to a new body, the Auckland Regional Services Trust, which had a legal requirement to privatise many of them as soon as was prudently practicable. The Nelson-Marlborough Regional Council was abolished and its functions transferred to three existing territorial authorities which combined the functions of territorial authorities and regional councils.

Features of the Reforms

The essential features of the local government reforms were:

- A smaller number of large territorial local authorities were established through a process of major amalgamations.

- Community boards were set up within their boundaries to provide a vehicle for local expression and influence and to help overcome the remoteness of the larger units.

- Directly elected regional councils were established although their powers were reduced later in the reform process.

- Ad *hoc* or special purpose authorities were virtually abolished.

- Regulatory and service delivery functions were separated.

- Provision was made for local authority trading activities to be corporatised through Local Authority Trading Enterprises (LATEs). This was optional except where the efficiency of the national economy was affected: for airports, seaports, electricity and gas and public passenger transport, the establishment of arms-length companies was required.

- Contracting-out and privatisation were also encouraged.

- New approaches to accountability were introduced. Accrual accounting was made mandatory. Corporate planning processes based on objectives, annual plans involving public consultation, and annual reports to the public were made compulsory.

- Chief executives were appointed on contracts for up to five years. They, in turn, became the employer of all other staff.

- Local authorities were required to be good employers.

The comprehensive nature of the reforms reflected a strong belief in the desirability of the minimal state i.e. that its role in economic and social life should be marginal rather than central. At the same time personal freedom was advocated and free markets viewed, therefore, as the most efficient and effective mechanism for allocating social and economic resources.

3.2 The current debate

The public face of debate around the devolution or decentralisation of sub-national administration is rather veiled. The underlying features of the reform process have focused on fiscal discipline rather than on opening further windows of opportunity. Rather than providing access to further sources of revenue, central government has given priority to ensuring improved efficiency in the local government sector. This means that immediate moves to increase revenue sharing, for example, are unlikely. The reform process has built on traditional views of the nature and purpose of local government, i.e. a limited role for local government and a lack of trust in it.

A few communities are still disputing the amalgamation principle. They are not convinced that larger units of territorial authorities have brought the promised efficiencies. Part of their argument is the remoteness of councillors from communities; the contributing value of community boards has not answered this problem because of a perceived lack of effectiveness. Similarly, the specification of management as the responsibility of the CEO, not elected officers, has not reduced concerns about technocrats making decisions which should be made by locally elected representatives.

Related to this is the tension between the authority of councillors and the CEO over officer actions; the shift of power from elected councillors to the CEO and officers through the division of responsibilities. Councillors are restricted to policy areas, with implementation being assigned to officers who are not seen as being as politically accountable.

3.3 Driving forces

A mix of economic, political, and democratic factors have influenced the changes to sub-national administrations. There was an economic need for decentralisation and devolution, but the political and democratic influences which drove the reform process were ideologically and value determined.

A decade later the pace of change has slowed. Political interest in further reform or development has lessened as other issues have come to the fore. The move from a "first past the post" national electoral system, based on the Westminster model, to proportional representation in October 1996 is creating new checks and balances that broaden the base and modify some of the decision making processes. Parties with 5 per cent of the national list vote, or one electorate seat may now enter Parliament, thus reducing the dominance of the two traditional parties and direct Maori representation has been increased.

NORWAY

1. INSTITUTIONS AND AUTHORITY

1.1 Structures

Description of levels

Norway has a two-tier system of central and local government. There are two separate branches of sub-national government: counties (officially known as county municipalities) and municipalities – but there is no hierarchical relationship between them. There are presently 19 counties and 435 municipalities. Oslo is classified as being both a county and a municipality.

There has been a tradition of regional government in Norway for centuries, but the present system of directly elected county councils with the right to tax directly did not exist until 1976. Unlike many other countries, local self-government is not established in the Constitution – counties and municipalities are guided by law or regulation, but not by instruction.

The total area of Norway is 324 200 square kilometres and the total population in 1994 was 4 337 000. The municipalities differ considerably in size and population – there is no such thing as a "typical" Norwegian municipality. Over half of them have less than 5 000 inhabitants, and only eight of them have more than 50 000 inhabitants. The range is summarised in Table 1.

Table 1. **Area and population of sub-national governments (1995)**

	Surface area (km^2)		Population	
	Counties	Municipalities	Counties	Municipalities
Largest	48 637	9 704	483 401 (Oslo)	483 401 (Oslo)
Smallest	454 (Oslo)	6	76 629	336
Average	20 366	890	228 864	9 996

Source: Population Statistics of Norway, Norwegian Office of Statistics, 1995.

Central government at sub-national levels

In each county a Governor represents central government and ensures that the activities of local authorities are carried out in accordance with the legislation, regulations and budgetary provisions of central government. The County Governors are an old institution. They represent central government in each county, are appointed for life, and are often former politicians. Their role was reduced when the directly elected counties were set up in 1975, but more recently their function has increased in importance again. In particular their advisory and co-ordination functions concerning the counties and municipalities in fields such as environment, social welfare and justice have been strengthened.

Creation, elimination and restructuring

A special Act (1956) dealt with changes in municipal boundaries. This was driven in part by additional tasks (particularly in education) being given to municipalities and the need for larger units to carry them out. There was a wave of amalgamations from the late 1950s, significantly reducing the number of municipalities by some 40 per cent (there were 744 municipalities in 1958), and most of the mergers were completed by 1965.

Small changes of municipal boundaries can be decided by the county governor if the municipalities involved agree. Otherwise the decision is taken by the Ministry of Local Government and Labour, or Parliament if amalgamations or more substantial changes are involved. Local referendums are usually held when there is a suggestion to amalgamate municipalities, but they are only consultative. The municipalities themselves decide whether to carry out local referendums or not.

Co-operation between municipalities is a feature in sectors such as waste disposal and in water supply schemes; and through the joint ownership of entities such as power companies .

Control bodies

There is not a hierarchical relationship between the counties and the municipalities. The county governors, on the other hand, have many control functions over the municipalities, one of them being to control the legality of local government budgets. According to the 1992 Local Government Act, a group of three or more council members can ask the county governor to review the legality of a decision made by a county or municipality. This may be seen as a way of counter-balancing the trend to decentralise more responsibilities and give more spending discretion to the municipalities.

The new Local Government Act introduced a mandatory "control committee" in every municipality and county to monitor the administration on behalf of the local council. All municipalities and counties are required to employ an auditor or to participate in an inter-municipal auditing body. There is no national audit body in Norway.

1.2 Powers

Nature of sub-national institutions

Each county and municipality is governed by a council elected for a four-year period. The electoral system is based on the principles of direct election and proportional representation in multi-member constituencies. This is known as the "Board of Aldermen" model. In it, representation in the executive council (or executive committee/board) is drawn from the municipal council on a proportional basis. Thus, in this model, a party that gets 50 per cent of the votes has the right to that proportion of seats in both the municipal council and the executive committee. The 1992 Local Government Act also permits an alternative form of government: the "Parliamentary" model. In it the majority party alone assumes the executive role.

The number of county council members depends on the number of inhabitants, a minimum of 19 for the smallest, and a minimum of 43 for the largest. The county council elects approximately one-quarter of its members (but not more than 15), to form a county board of aldermen. The council elects a chairman (mayor) to be the political head and preside over both the council and the board of aldermen. The council also appoints a chief executive officer as the head of the entire county administration and a chief treasurer. The main tasks of the executive officer are to prepare and execute decisions, and he/she may be authorised to create or abolish positions and to make decisions concerning employees.

Municipal councils have not fewer than 11 members but, as for the county council, the minimum depends on the number of inhabitants. Each municipal council elects one-quarter of its members to form a board of aldermen and a chairman to preside over both the council and the board of aldermen. It also elects standing committees for school administration, social administration, and building control – although according to the 1992 Local Government Act, this is not strictly necessary and considerable freedom of committee structure is allowed for.

Type and degree of autonomy

The right of counties and municipalities to levy taxes is limited to maximum and minimum rates determined by the Parliament (Storting) each year. In 1995 the maximum rate of local government personal income tax was 12.25 per cent for municipalities and 7.0 per cent for counties. The maximum rate for companies is lower. In practice, all local authorities levy the maximum rates and this lack of differential may be seen to dilute local financial accountability. Municipalities are also entitled to levy a property tax on commercial property and on housing in urban areas. Each municipality decides whether or not a property tax will be levied (in 1992, slightly fewer than half of all municipalities had revenues from property tax). A major change introduced in the 1992 Act permits each county to choose its own organisational structure.

1.3 Responsibilities

Local government services represent two-thirds of Norway's public service production making municipalities and counties important actors in the national economy.

Distribution of responsibilities

There is no stipulation in the Constitution nor in any general legislation about how government functions are to be divided among the State, counties and municipalities. The division of functions between the various levels of government is decided by the *Storting*, but counties and municipalities may voluntarily assume tasks or functions not assigned to other authorities by law. The distribution which results is a mix of Parliamentary decisions and local government initiatives, and is a recurrent theme of debate. In recent years, for example, there has been discussion about whether or not central government should be made responsible for the entire hospital sector.

The counties provide the services not handled by central government and which require a larger population base than that found in the municipalities. Most of the tasks performed by counties are established compulsorily in the legislation. Counties are, however, free to perform functions and provide services of their own choosing, if they are within the framework of existing legislation and have not been allocated to another authority.

The main compulsory functions of counties are:

- hospital and other specialised health services;
- secondary education and vocational training;
- child welfare institutions;
- institutions for the care of drug and alcohol abusers;
- construction and maintenance of county roads;
- co-ordination and provision of local public transport;
- regional planning.

In recent years local government has taken over more tasks from central government, some being carried out on an inter-municipal basis. At present municipal government is responsible for the following services and functions:

- primary and lower secondary education;
- nursery schools;
- services for elderly and disabled persons in their own homes;
- institutions for elderly and disabled persons;
- economic support for needy people;
- primary health care;
- public libraries;

- maintenance of local roads and parks;
- water supplies;
- fire services;
- sewerage and removal of garbage;
- physical planning and building control;
- urban renewal.

As with the counties, municipalities – in addition to the tasks determined by legislation – may undertake any local functions which are not vested by law in other authorities.

Until 1975, the county councils were elected by the municipalities and financed by taxes paid by the municipalities. After 1975, the autonomy of the counties has steadily increased. Over the past 15 years, however, the largest change in financial terms has been a transfer of authority and functions from counties to municipalities. This has included the transfer of responsibilities for nursing homes in 1988 and, especially, for the mentally disabled in 1991 from the county to the municipal level.

Mandatory, optional and shared responsibilities

In addition to the distribution of functions noted above, two levels of government may be involved in providing some services in some sectors (e.g. transport) and it is not always clear who pays for what. Another aspect of shared responsibility is the role of the county governor as the representative of central government in decision-making. His office handles complaints and has the authority to overturn decisions made at the municipal level, even on matters concerning payments made by municipalities to individuals.

2. MANAGEMENT FUNCTIONS

2.1 Policy-making and co-ordination

Coherence, consultation and conflict resolution

Local governments, being largely service providers, have strong links with sectoral ministries such as health and education. The Ministry of Local Government and Labour has amongst its responsibilities, the co-ordination of government measures concerning municipalities and counties. It evaluates whether such measures are in accordance with general guidelines concerning the distribution of activities between different levels of administration. It monitors the relationship between the Local Government Act and sector legislation; and is also responsible for drafting municipal legislation.

The Ministry oversees the distribution of funding between municipalities and counties and is responsible for the development and implementation of the revenue system by which government grants are distributed to counties and municipalities. It is also in charge of drawing up the total local government budgetary framework in connection with the national budget. The County Governor has general advisory and co-ordination functions concerning the municipalities and counties. This function is changing as the nature and content of the dialogue between levels of government evolves: the role in inter-governmental relations is becoming more important.

Formal and informal mechanisms

In Norway, in large part due to its small size, informal dialogue is an important co-ordinating mechanism. Nevertheless, it has been recognised that there has been insufficient coherence between central policy-making and local implementation capacities. Since the beginning of 1995, therefore, there has been a new set of control procedures in the form of instructions requiring the main ministries concerned with sub-national affairs to consult with local bodies on the implementation of new measures. Thus the Ministry of Finance is now required to consult on costs; the Ministry of Government

Administration on the administrative effects; and the Ministry of Local Government and Labour on local impacts. A report has been prepared which includes a section on the economic and administrative consequences of proposals. This has become an important, if "soft", new tool in co-ordinating central government actions concerning sub-national bodies.

The Norwegian Association of Local and Regional Authorities (KS) is a service and interest organisation that represents all the municipalities and counties in the country. It is a consultative body acting on behalf of local government vis-à-vis the State, and as such receives for comment those government draft policy documents that are considered of special relevance for local governments. After the various bodies consulted have sent their comments on the government draft, the central government considers the reactions to the policy document before preparing the final bill. The KS also promotes co-operation and exchanges of experience between members, and serves as the central collective bargaining agent with regard to unions for those employed in local government. Other functions include training and information dissemination.

2.2 Financial management

Sources of revenue

There are great variations between individual municipalities and counties in the proportion of their total income which comes from taxation. The range is from about 15 to 85 per cent in municipalities, and from about 20 to 70 per cent in counties. County tax revenues come entirely from income tax; while municipal tax revenues come mainly from income tax and taxes levied on property. illustrates the main sources of local government incomes.

Table 2. **Main revenue sources of sub-national governments (1993)**

	Counties	Municipalities
Block grants from central government	36	22
Earmarked grants from central government	18	14
Net tax revenues	41	48
Fees and charges, etc.	5	16
TOTAL	100	100

Source: Report on the calculation, Committee for Local Government Finance, June 1994 as cited in Local Government Financing in Norway, Royal Ministry of Local Government and Labour, 1995.

The proportion of total local government revenues from taxation has been decreasing since 1945. The most important reason for this is that central government has imposed new and costly responsibilities on counties and municipalities (see section on "Responsibilities"). The goal of providing municipal services of a more or less equal scope and quality across the country has also made it necessary to increase central government transfers.

In the 1980s, general purpose (block) grants from central government replaced conditional (earmarked) grants. The block grant scheme for hospitals was introduced in 1980 and similar financing arrangements were introduced for municipal health and social services in 1984. These reforms were in many ways the precursors of the new General Purpose Grants Scheme (GPGS) for counties and municipalities introduced in 1986. It is based on a system of block grant which replaced some 50 earmarked grants. From 1986 to 1994 counties received a general income support grant and three sectoral grants: for secondary schools, transport, and health. In 1994, the three sectoral grants were amalgamated into a single expenditure equalisation grant. A parallel system operates for the municipalities with sectoral grants for primary schools, health and social service, and culture. These have now also been amalgamated.

Presently, nearly 70 per cent of central government transfers to counties and municipalities are distributed through the GPGS in the form of a lump sum (not earmarked for special purposes). At the same time there are about 100 specific grants from central to local governments – in most cases with conditions requiring the local authority to contribute a proportion of the costs itself.

Local government also earns revenue from fees and charges paid for local services including water, sewage and waste disposal. Municipalities have a large degree of freedom to determine the size of fees and charges. Where an activity is considered as a natural local government responsibility, or where the municipality has a monopoly, the cost price principle applies.

Expenditure responsibilities

By far the largest amount of local government operating expenditure (in both counties and municipalities) – as shown in Table 3 – is for health and social services, and about one-quarter of their total operating expenditure is devoted to education.

The GPGS is central government's main instrument for distributing income. It equalises differences in both municipal tax revenues (by evening out differences in levels of tax revenue per inhabitant) and expenditures (by ensuring equal standards of municipal services). Differences in expenditure can have two causes: differences in demand for a service (e.g. due to variations in age structure) and/or differences in the cost of providing the same service (e.g. due to variations in population density). Expenditure equalisation has two components: the cost key (consisting of a number of weighted criteria such as age structure) and the proportion of own financing. The latter varies according to the number of inhabitants as all municipalities must contribute the same amount of money per inhabitant for the services provided.

Table 3. **Main operating expenses in counties and municipalities (1993)**
(percentage)

	Counties	Municipalities
Health and social services	58	42
Education	24	28
Central administration	3	7
Communication services	10	3
Housing, environment, other economic affairs	3	5
Church and cultural purposes	2	6
Technical purposes	0	9
TOTAL	100	100

Source: *Statistical Yearbook*, 1995.

Balance between discretion and control

The Ministry of Finance, responsible for overall control of public expenditure, establishes the amount of growth, the amount to local authorities, and how much revenue will be raised through taxes (both the tax base and associated tax rates). There is then close co-operation with the Ministry of Local Government and Labour to fix transfers – earmarked grants are decided by each line ministry and summed; general grants make up the rest.

The 1992 Local Government Act was drawn up to balance regard for effective local democracy with regard for national control. It had as its paramount objective, to strengthen and further develop county and municipal autonomy, while establishing conditions to enable counties and municipalities to become efficient suppliers of services to their inhabitants. This is realised mainly by giving them more freedom to organise their activities according to local needs and circumstances; and by toning down the central government's supervision and control of the local government sector. In fact, since 1986 it has been central government policy to have fewer specific grants in favour of more general grants, but in practice many specific grants for a fixed term remain. (In the 1992 State Budget there were 110 earmarked grants to the local government sector. They may not be used for any purpose other than that specified).

The new Act also, for the first time, requires every municipality and county to have a "finance plan" – a long term budget, the contents of which are stipulated in regulations issued by the Ministry of Local Government and Labour. Other conditions, such as need to have approval by the Ministry to raise loans, remain unchanged.

There is a degree of municipal dissatisfaction with the fact that although they have considerable discretion over the allocation of funds within the total amount transferred from the centre, they have no control over what that total amount is. Also, the number of specific grants has been reduced but the volume involved has increased. There is, however, a trend towards an increasing amount of municipal independence over how money is spent locally.

2.3   Performance management

Mechanisms

Audit is not institutionalised in Norway in the way it is in Sweden, for example. It is more based on financial monitoring than on performance. Experience has shown the need to pay closer attention to internal supervision and control in each local authority. The mandatory "control committee" introduced in every municipality and county by the new Local Government Act (see section on "Control bodies") emphasises the importance of an extensive and efficient auditing system. The requirement for all municipalities and counties to employ an auditor or participate in an inter-municipal auditing body reflects a perceived need at the centre for larger auditing units and most inter-municipal audit bodies are not voluntary but the result of central government requirements.

The new Act entails rather sweeping changes in central government supervision and control of local government by abolishing the need for government approval of the budget and replacing it by a control of legality by the Ministry or the County Governor. This represents a shift from checking if a budget is "good" to checking if it is "legal".

The Act also requires that the best possible provision be made for public insight into the local administration, including active measures to provide the public with information. A specific innovation is that generally meetings of popularly elected bodies be open to the public.

Quality standards

Counties and municipalities are obliged to supply considerable amounts of information to many different central ministries, but at the moment there is little systematic collection and analysis of data designed for comparison of performance or productivity either across time or across local authorities. Service standard objectives are, however, seen as an integral part of performance management reforms. A project in the Directorate of Public Management of *Statskonsult* is seeking to improve information resource management. A pilot experiment with 30 reference and four pilot municipalities will report on possibilities of developing result indicators and service profiles in 1997 after a year of monitoring.

There has also been a recent tendency, particularly in sectors such as health and education, towards the use of "charters" and "guarantees" clarifying the legal rights of individuals to specific services (for example, a maximum of six months on a hospital waiting list before getting treatment). This has, sometimes, been without sufficient consultation between central and local governments to ensure the feasibility of the proposals. As a result a new committee was set up in 1994 to calculate, neutrally, the cost implications of Parliamentary reform initiatives which have to be implemented by local government. It brings together representatives of both central and municipal authorities with the aim of testing feasibility and improving consultation (see also "Formal and informal mechanisms").

2.4   Human resource management

The new Local Government Act contains provisions concerning the municipality and county as an employer and provides for the involvement of employees. This is done by, for example, requiring all local governments to establish at least one "jointly constituted committee" to deal with matters on relations between employees and employers, and having representatives of both.

Local government presently accounts for about one-fifth of the total working population in Norway and 75 per cent of all employment in the public sector. The share of local government has steadily increased since 1980 (see Table 4).

Statutory distinctions

Staff in central and local administrations are governed by two different pieces of legislation and by different rules and regulations. Both central and local levels have a scale comprising 75 steps but the two systems are separate for the purposes of salary negotiations – that for the centre being done by the Ministry of Government Administration, and that for local governments by the Association of Local and Regional Authorities. Teachers (of whom there are about 100 000) are employed by the counties and municipalities, but wage bargaining is done by an informal central government committee of the Ministry of Government Administration. Pension rights are the same for central and sub-national staff.

Mobility: mobility across levels of government is possible. There is some movement from local to central government but not a lot; and some chief executives at the local level have previously worked in central government.

Table 4. **Personnel in central and local government (1980, 1985, 1990, 1994)**

	1980	1985	1990	1994[1]
Central government services	133 600	141 500	150 800	152 600
Local government services	326 900	376 300	429 200	491 000
TOTAL general government	460 500	517 800	580 000	643 600
TOTAL employment	1 942 500	2 031 400	2 054 200	2 066 100

1. Break in homogeneity due to revision of national accounts according to EU standards.
Source: Statistics Norway, 1995.

2.5 Regulatory management and reform

The 1992 Local Government Act is based on a "Proposition" by the government which assumes that the current legislation entails too much detailed regulation of local government and that central government control should, to a greater extent, be exercised through management by objectives.

In the same year a general law on "Experiments in Public Management" was passed with the aim of providing more freedom to adapt to local needs by developing county and municipal management structures and promoting a more effective distribution of tasks between levels of government beyond the existing legislative framework.

Education tends to be heavily regulated from the centre, with requirements about class sizes, the allocation of teachers, and curriculum content. There is some pressure to deregulate here. Social services are also rather regulated with requirements on income support entitlements (although the level of support can be decided by municipalities); and on the rights of disabled people to live at home.

A Business Legislation Committee was appointed by the government in February 1990. The terms of reference of the committee are to examine legislation that affects businesses and to table proposals for simplification and other changes that can stimulate business activities. The objective of the work is to achieve smoothly functioning regulations which can create conditions for enhanced efficiency and productivity in the business sector and thereby improve competitiveness. The needs of small and medium-sized enterprises have been focused on particularly in the terms of reference of the committee. The committee has tabled 19 proposals since it was appointed. Some of these proposals involve both national and local legislation, but in general the committee works primarily with national legislation.

3. TRENDS IN REDISTRIBUTING AUTHORITY ACROSS LEVELS OF GOVERNMENT

3.1 Evolving tendencies

Norway is increasingly being governed by means of objectives and framework management. There has been a shift by central government to give more local discretion by providing more general rather than specific grants. The General Purpose Grants Scheme (which replaced some 50 separate earmarked grants) distributes central government grants to individual counties and municipalities according to criteria. This results in the local government sector having little influence over the total amount of funding it receives from the centre. There are no limitations to the proportion of funds going to specific sectors, making these grants an important element in the trend to greater local self-government. On the other hand, this approach provides central government with better control over total local expenditures, in particular allowing the Ministry of Finance to send signals on spending levels to local governments. What it does not provide is a mechanism for reconciling the strong signals from sectoral ministries for increasing their expenditure.

3.2 The current debate

Central government cannot instruct local government. In this context there are signs of a reaction against decentralisation in terms of a need for greater transparency in the system of governance. There is, for example, some dissatisfaction and tension concerning the distribution criteria for the general grants scheme – particularly among the poorer local authorities and in the health sector. Some say that this is the price of greater transparency. The process was simplified in 1994 by merging three grants into a single large general grant. But hospitals are still financed by a mix of general and specific grants which makes it difficult to determine exactly how much financing they receive – and there are pressures to give more general grants to counties for health services.

An expert committee was set up in 1995 to look at the General Purpose Grants Scheme and the financing of the local government sector in general. Its first report was presented to Parliament in 1996. The result was some minor modifications of the system. The second and last report from the expert committee, dealing with the financing of the sector and in particular taxes and user charges, is currently (Spring 1997) submitted to official hearing.

There is, at the same time, a degree of satisfaction with the present decentralised system. This is largely because it has its feet firmly planted in two domains where its advantages are much appreciated: (*i*) the degree of local autonomy and the implications for local democracy; and (*ii*) the quality of service provision and the associated nature and extent of the welfare state.

There is also some discussion of local government amalgamation in the context of municipalities now having a wider range of responsibilities, the need for efficiencies of scale, major changes in communications and the pattern of settlement. The Ministry of Local Government and Labour initiated some reform proposals in a White Paper of May 1995. Parliament decided that, for the time being, the question of amalgamation should be handled by local authorities themselves.

There is trend away from the detailed specification of standards, but another debate is on whether there is a need for national legislation to introduce minimum standards. The Ministry of Local Government and Labour is trying to develop better data on standards of service provision from different ministries; and some key economic indicators are being developed in sectors such as education. This in part is a reflection of the lack of a national audit body.

An underlying issue is that central government sees the local level mostly as a service delivery system, and sees its task therefore to be to make such delivery as efficient as possible. The alternate view is that while service provision is an important function, local government is legitimate in its own right as an essential component of the democratic system.

3.3 Driving forces

The demand for decentralisation has been driven to some extent by the search for more cost-effective delivery systems, but a counter-force is the limits in the capacity of counties and municipalities to service the demands. This is in part a factor of the small size of some units and a concern with efficiencies of scale. This seems to reflect a long-standing tension between the traditional independent status of municipalities and the need to satisfy central goals. The new focus on individual rights is one approach, but for which there is as yet no well established process.

The trend to information-technology-based systems is also a factor in changing inter-governmental relations in terms of the facility with which information can be shared. This is occurring between ministries (e.g. new collaboration between the Ministries of Finance and Local Government on statistical data aimed at exploring the optimum size of units for selected types of services); between central and local government; and between local authorities.

Norway is depicted as a small, consensus-oriented country in which informal rather than formal channels tend to be used. More use is being made of negotiation; and the centre is less able to impose directives. The balance between the service delivery and democratic functions of sub-national government is being adjusted. This implies a readjustment also, in the relationships between local and central government and between local governments and local citizens.

PORTUGAL

1. INSTITUTIONS AND AUTHORITY

1.1 Structures

Description of levels

Portugal is a republic and a unitary State which retains some traditional features of a centralised country. There are presently two levels of local government: municipalities and parishes (*freguesias*). Insular Portugal (the Madeira and Azores archipelagos) consists of two autonomous regions which have their own political and administrative systems and governing bodies.

The total area of Portugal is 92 400 square kilometres and the total population in 1994 was 9 900 000. There are currently 305 municipalities in the country compared with 303 in 1950. summarises the distribution of population between them. There are also 4 220 parishes (3 853 in 1950) but their role in local government is very minor and most have a population in the range of 1 500 to 7 500.

Table 1. **Area and population of sub-national governments (1995)**

	Municipalities		Parishes	
	Area (km^2)	Population	Area (km^2)	Population
Largest	1 721 (Odemira)	659 649 (Lisbon)	373 (Penamacor)	79 999
Smallest	7 (S. Joao da Madeira)	393 (Corvo)	0.054 (de Castelo)	47

Municipalities according to size of population	
Population range	Number of municipalities
less than 1 000	1
1 000-5 000	25
5 000-10 000	76
10 000-50 000	157
50 000-100 000	23
over 100 000	23

Source: Structure and Operation of Local and Regional Democracy: Portugal, Council of Europe, 1993.

In 1991, a decision of the Assembly of the Republic created two metropolitan areas, in Lisbon and Porto. This reflects the particular problems of managing large and expanding urban areas. The Lisbon metropolitan area has 2.7 million inhabitants covering 18 municipalities and 203 parishes while that of Porto has a total population of some 1.2 million in 9 municipalities and 130 parishes.

The Constitution provides for the establishment on the continent of administrative regions which would have a Regional Assembly and a Regional Committee. Their functions would be to help to draft and implement regional plans; provide support for the management of municipalities; and run regional public services. A framework law to this effect has been enacted but has yet to be implemented, although the new (October 1995) government is clearly putting regionalisation back onto the political agenda (refer also section 3.2).

Central government at sub-national levels

Continental Portugal has 18 administrative districts, each headed by a central government representative, the Civil Governor.

There are also five Regional Co-ordination Commissions (CCRs) at the regional level which are directly subordinate to the Minister of Infrastructure, Planning and Territorial Administration. They were created in December 1979 as a temporary response to the concept of regional government as provided for in the Constitution. Geographically they correspond to the five present regions (North, Centre, Lisbon, Alentejo and Algarve). They provide assistance to local authorities with their management needs (staff, computer technology and local finances); help them to prepare local and regional development plans; and manage funds coming from the European Union for regional development (FEDER) for municipal projects. They also monitor the implementation of regional development plans and co-ordinate, at the regional level, the activities of ministries in fields such as land use planning, regional development and the environment (refer also section 2.1).

Deconcentration has also started as some of the larger ministries have begun to create their own regional structures. At the beginning of the 1980's ministries started establishing their own administrative units in the regions and to delegate authority to them. A wider deconcentration took place in 1992 when, for example, the Ministries of Health, Social Security, Environment, Education and Industry established regional bodies in the five regions. In 1993, other ministries were significantly re-organised and the Directorate General for Local Administration examined the implications of this restructuring in a report entitled "Deconcentrated Services at the Regional Level".

In the two autonomous regions, the Minister of the Republic co-ordinates the activities of central government departments where these affect the region's interests. He also co-ordinates the activities of government offices with those of the region.

Creation, elimination and restructuring

The Constitution provides that the creation, dissolution or territorial modification of local governments is a matter reserved exclusively to the Assembly. No reorganisation of municipal boundaries was deemed necessary during the constitutional reforms of 1976 and the pre-1974 division was retained. The present municipal boundaries are, therefore, essentially the result of reforms introduced during the last century. The two main reasons taken into account for maintaining them were the established historical and traditional attachment of citizens to the existing units and the fact that their average size was already large – on average over 300 sq. km., making them amongst the largest in Europe.

The average size of the parishes, on the other hand, is less than 22 sq. km. About 200 new ones were created recently by sub-dividing others.

There is a growing interest in inter-municipal co-operation. Municipalities may form associations with other municipalities for the joint management of certain facilities and resources. This has proved to be a valuable and effective means of providing low-cost services, particularly in small and isolated communities (refer also section 2.1).

Control bodies

Administrative supervision of local governments by central government takes the form of checking the legality of all local government acts in accordance with the Constitution. This is done by the Inspectorate-General of Territorial Administration (IGAT) which is headed by a judge and has some independence but is directly attached to the Minister for Infrastructure, Planning and Territorial Development. The Directorate-General of Local Authorities in the same ministry is more concerned with matters of efficiency, but it can only suggest and not impose proposals for improvement, including the criteria used for the financial equalisation fund. It also co-ordinates some of the contract programmes between sectoral ministries and municipalities. The Inspectorate-General of Finance and the Court of

Audit monitor the legality of the use made of municipal financial resources. The Court of Audit examines all requests for contracts exceeding a specified sum and performs an annual ex-poste control over all local authority accounts.

1.2 Powers

The basic feature of the local government system in Portugal is the separation of the executive and deliberative functions between two bodies, both with the same political legitimacy.

Nature of sub-national institutions

Municipalities have two governing bodies as follows:

- The Municipal Assembly, which is unicameral and approves all major municipal policies including voting the budget and land use plans. It consists of the presidents of the executive boards of all the parishes and an equal number, plus one, of directly elected representatives.

- The Municipal Chamber, which is the municipality's executive collegiate body and is elected directly by the municipality's electorate. It has between five and eleven members including a chairman (mayor) who is at the top of the list which obtained the most votes. Lisbon's, because of its size, has 17 members.

The deliberative body of the parish is the directly elected Parish Assembly. It has similar functions as the Municipal Assembly at the neighbourhood level. Its main purpose, however, is to elect the executive body, the Parish Committee (junta), which has from three to seven members including a president. The president is the main representative of the parish, a position taken by the leader of the list which obtains the most votes in the Assembly election. The parishes generally act both as units of self-government and as delegated units of service delivery on behalf of the municipality.

Citizens vote simultaneously but separately for the Municipal Assembly, the Municipal Chamber, and the Parish Assembly – all for a four-year mandate. Elections are by direct universal suffrage under a list system of proportional representation with seats allocated according to the Hondt highest average method.

The organic structure of the two new Metropolitan Areas is similar to that of the municipalities. It comprises a deliberative body – the Metropolitan Assembly – the members of which are elected by the Municipal Assemblies; and a Metropolitan Committee (Junta) which is the executive body and composed of the mayors of all the municipalities. Thus in Lisbon, the Metropolitan Assembly and Junta have 50 and 18 members respectively; and in Porto the equivalent figures are 27 and 9 members. There is in addition a consultative advisory body, the Metropolitan Council which should play a key role in co-ordinating services across the various administrative levels. The Metropolitan Council is made up of members of the Junta together with the President of the Regional Co-ordination Commission and the heads of the other main bodies providing public services in the area.

The Autonomous Regions of the Azores and Madeira have political and administrative autonomy with legislative powers and are not considered to be local authorities like municipalities, parishes and the administrative regions planned for the continent. The governing bodies of the two autonomous regions are the Regional Assembly and the Regional Government. The Regional Assembly is elected by proportional representation by direct universal suffrage. The Regional Government is politically answerable to the Regional Assembly – its president is appointed by the minister for the region and its other members are appointed or dismissed by the minister for the region on the proposal of the president of the Regional Government.

Type and degree of autonomy

Local democracy is clearly provided for in the Constitution according to four important principles:- the autonomy of local units of administration; the existence of local government within the democratic organisation of the State; the financial and patrimonial autonomy of local authorities; and local government's regulatory capacity. A Statute-Law of 1984 stipulates that municipalities may define their own staff structures according to local requirements.

Local authorities have access to the capital market and may issue bearer-bonds. There are, however, strict limits on the extent to which municipalities may borrow money and incur debts, although a number of municipalities are currently experiencing deficit problems.

Despite the Constitution's provisions for local autonomy, there are limits to the financial resources directly available to local governments. Municipalities depend on grants from the centre to the extent that their authority to impose local taxes is limited, and because Parliament fixes limits on tax rates. In fact, only one of the six local taxes (the *derrama*, a supplement to the tax on corporate incomes) is determined and collected locally. Each municipality decides whether or not to apply it and at what rate (up to 10 per cent). Portugal may, nevertheless, be described as having a neutral policy towards financial transfers from central to local government in that the latter may act freely within a legally pre-determined framework which gives them a degree of autonomy over most of their receipts (refer also section 2.2).

1.3 Responsibilities

Distribution of competences

Local authorities are responsible for matters specifically concerning them and the interests of their inhabitants, for which they have general authority. These include the administration of their assets, local development and service infrastructure, public health, education, care of children and the elderly, cultural and sporting facilities, environmental protection and quality of life, and public safety. The role of the parishes is essentially one of neighbourhood administration. In practice their range of functions is very narrow; the financial resources at their disposal are generally insignificant; and (except in the main urban areas) their technical and administrative capacity is very limited.

Mandatory, optional and shared responsibilities

Since 1976, following constitutional and local reforms, there has been no differentiation between compulsory and optional responsibilities. Equally there are no differences between municipalities concerning how tasks are carried out. In accordance with present legislation the State may take part jointly in investments, within the framework of regional and local development, through contract-programmes carried out between the central administration and municipalities, their associations or concessionary companies. The specified ares in which these contracts may be drawn up include the following: basic sanitation, environment and natural resources, transport and communications infrastructure, culture and sport, education and vocational training, public safety, social housing, promotion of economic development, health, and social security.

2. MANAGEMENT FUNCTIONS

2.1 Policy-making and co-ordination

Coherence, consultation and conflict resolution

At the national level, the weekly meetings of the Secretaries of State plays an important horizontal co-ordinating role. It screens proposals for bills or decrees and drafts decisions before they are submitted to the Council of Ministers. It sorts out possible problems of overlap, duplication or misunderstanding – including matters concerning sub-national government.

The Constitution gives a high priority to the notion of citizen participation and the implication of this political choice is greater in local authorities than in the central administration. Local authorities may consult their electorates on matters related to their mandate and the result of such a referendum becomes the final political decision.

Formal and informal mechanisms

In the mid 1970s the 275 mainland municipalities were grouped into about 50 blocks, each having a technical support offices (known locally as a GAT). These employ professional staff who have the status of civil servants. Their costs are shared by central and local governments and priorities are defined annually by the mayors of the municipalities in each block who also monitor progress. The Head of each GAT is appointed by the minister concerned after names have been put forward by the municipalities in the block. This has helped develop a sense of supra-municipal consciousness. Co-ordination is ensured by the five Regional Co-ordination Commissions (CCRs), to whom the GATs report, but as the CCRs broadened their responsibilities and some GATs had slow response times to local needs, their relevance reduced.

The CCRs are an extension of central government with an essentially co-ordinating function. They ensure cohesion in administrative, financial and technical support provided to local authorities, their most important programmes being those which encourage inter-municipal co-operation (refer also section 1.1). The PROSIURB programme, directed at multi-sectoral development in medium-sized towns, notably in the social and agricultural fields, is one central government tool for both horizontal and vertical co-ordination.

Management of funds from the European Union has also provided a strong stimulus for co-ordination, especially at the regional level. In the context of the European Support Framework (CCA), the Regional Development Fund (FEDER) accounts for over 50 per cent of the structural funds from the European Union to Portugal and requires monitoring and co-ordination at the regional level through the CCRs.

The National Association of Municipalities is an active and well organised lobbying body which must be formally consulted in most government decisions about local authorities and which will certainly be involved in the upcoming debate on transfers of responsibilities. As, however, its leaders are mayors, the extent to which it can fulfil its consultative role is limited by the technical and professional capacities of those holding office. A National Association of Parishes has also recently been created.

Portugal, like other countries, has some shortcomings in both formal and informal co-ordination across its administration. There is considerable informality in inter-institutional relations – particularly at the local level between neighbouring local authorities (but less so between administrations at different levels and of a different nature).

2.2 Financial management

Sources of revenue

The financial resources of municipalities come largely from the central budget in the form of grants. In 1993, these accounted for ten per cent of the central government budget, or four per cent of GNP. The main annual lump-sum grant from the State to municipalities is the Financial Equalisation Fund (FEF).

The total amount of the central government general grant to be transferred each year is linked to the anticipated trend in Value Added Tax. It is distributed to municipalities according to a formula defined by law which aims at a fair sharing of public resources and balancing social and economic differences. The calculation of shares is made in three main steps. The first step divides the total amount into three parts: the mainland and the two autonomous regions according to criteria of population, number of municipalities and area. The second divides the amount amongst the component municipalities, and the third distinguishes between capital and current expenditure by reserving 40 per cent of the available funds for investment projects.

Portuguese municipalities also receive grants from the European Union through the Structural Funds and, in particular, from the European Regional Development Fund (FEDER). Grants from the

European Union currently total about 10 per cent of total municipal revenues. In some cases municipalities have a problem of absorbing the funds and of contributing their own participation.

Table 2 shows the evolving distribution of municipal receipts. It demonstrates the four-fold increase in the total over the seven year period and the reduced importance of general grants in favour of European Union funds and taxes over the same time.

Local taxation, loans and user fees for certain local services are the other sources of local finance. Local taxes are mainly based on property values. In 1993, property tax revenues accounted for about 8 per cent of all local revenues.

The resources of the parishes does not usually exceed five per cent of total local government income and expenditure. Municipalities are required to distribute 10 per cent of the current transfers they receive from central government to the parishes, according to criteria of population and area.

Table 2. **Main sources of local revenues (1986, 1990, 1993)**
(percentage)

	1986	1990	1993
General grants (FEF)	55.6	36.9	34.1
Specific grants	5.6	5.7	4.3
European Union funds	1.1	5.4	10.2
Charges, Properties	11.9	12.1	13.9
Taxes	15.8	27.1	23.3
of which:			
property tax	8.6	7.7	7.8
vehicle tax	1.5	1.3	1.6
transfer duties		11.2	8.7
suppl. to corporate tax	3.3	4.8	4.1
other	0.6	0.6	0.1
VAT/tourism (shared)	1.8	1.6	0.9
Loans	3.5	5.3	6.8
Other	6.6	7.6	7.5
TOTAL	100.0	100.0	100.0
TOTAL (million contos) [1]	140.9	348.3	570.7

1. 1 *conto* = one thousand escudos.
Source: General Directorate for Local Authorities (DGAA).

Expenditure responsibilities

Municipalities have very limited involvement in the areas of education, health, social housing or public security. They are responsible for pre-primary and primary schools; school transport; providing local infrastructure; cultural, sports and recreational facilities; promoting tourism; urban public transport; town planning and environmental protection. indicates the recent evolution of expenditure patterns in the municipalities.

Balance between discretion and control

The present financial management system does not provide municipalities with any real financial decision-making power. Their only flexibility is a little discretion over the rate of the urban property tax and the corporate income tax – but in both of these cases, Parliament determines the maximum permissible rates. Specific grants allocated through the contract-programmes system or from the European Union also imply a framework of regional or sectoral targets according to criteria set nationally. Recourse to these specific grants does, however, also depend on agreement between central and local authorities on aims and strategy.

Table 3. **Main expenditure and investment patterns of municipalities (1986, 1990, 1993)**
(percentage)

	1986	1990	1993
Personnel	31.7	30.1	26.8
Goods and services	14.2	14.9	15.3
Debt interest payment	4.2	2.6	2.8
Investment	38.0	37.7	40.6
of which:			
Land		0.9	1.1
Housing		4.0	3.7
Municipal buildings		8.4	8.5
Sport, culture, education		4.0	4.2
Social equipment		0.2	0.1
Transport/streets		6.4	7.8
Sewerage		2.5	2.7
Water supply		2.4	2.4
Rural roads		4.8	6.2
Waste disposal		0.1	0.4
Transport/equipment		3.6	2.9
Other		0.5	0.5
Capital repayments	1.7	2.3	2.0
Other	10.2	12.3	12.5
TOTAL	100.0	100.0	100.0
TOTAL (million contos) [1]	138.0	349.2	583.4

1. 1 *conto* = one thousand escudos.
Source: General Directorate for Local Authorities (DGAA).

Nevertheless, all limiting rules are explicitly spelt out in the 1987 Local Finances Act which defines the financial autonomy of local government. This limits interference from the current central government and reduces its margins for manoeuvre. It provides the financial framework for the municipalities in terms of sources of funding (both own revenues and central grants); budgetary principles; local fiscal policy; scope for municipal borrowing; and the financial relationship between municipalities and parishes. More specifically it sets the relationship between current and capital expenditures; fixes a borrowing ceiling; and defines minimum transfers to parishes.

On the other hand, receipts from the Financial Equalisation Fund may be spent at the discretion of municipalities so that they determine their own spending priorities within the level determined centrally – except that the annual State Budget Act specifies the percentage to be assigned to current and capital expenditure.

2.3 Performance management

Mechanisms

Guidelines on how to prepare "Quality Charters" have been prepared by the Secretariat for Administrative Modernisation (SMA) which also provides technical assistance and is involved in quality training programmes for municipalities. Several local authorities now have their own quality charters.

Quality standards

A pilot exercise was launched with nine municipalities under the Enterprise-Administration Commission (CEA) of the SMA led by the Debureaucratisation Project Team. Activities gave priority to rationalising the operation of units and personalising contact with the public. Guidelines for preparing quality standards have been developed by the SMA and quality pilot projects are being adopted by local authorities across the country. Since 1994 the State, through the Ministry which supervises local authorities, has made agreements on administrative modernisation between municipalities and their associations. These local entities may put forward proposals annually to obtain financial support within the framework of global modernisation programmes in order to raise the standards of services provided. A qualitatively different administration at the service of the community, and development and based on values of public service and the permanent search for better operational-levels, is envisaged. Supervision in Portugal is of an inspection nature and aims to check conformity with legal provisions. Administrative supervision is a strict counterpoint to the principle of autonomy for local authorities and the concept of administrative decentralisation. It does not use performance management although the inspection reports which are made include suggestions for overcoming shortcomings as well as a verification of the facts.

2.4 Human resource management

Statutory distinctions: Entry into the public service is through compulsory entrance exams and the Directorate-General of Public Administration (DGAP) of the Ministry of Finance plays an important role in recruitment and selection. Local authority employees are part of the same system, under the same regime, and subject to the same regulations as those for central government officials. Portuguese local authorities have autonomous powers as regards their staff. These powers reflect the principle of autonomy laid down in the Constitution and stipulated in the European Charter on Local Autonomy of which Portugal is a signatory. 1984 legislation states that municipalities must have their own staff complements which must be structured in accordance with the permanent needs of municipalities. Permanent tenure is ensured through legal appointment which confers the status of a public servant. Non permanent tenure is established by contract. Under the terms of the Constitution, the recruitment of local authority staff is always by public competition. The rules governing officials and personnel of the State apply equally to officials and personnel in local administration.

Table 4. **Employment structure of administrative public sector in 1994**

	1994 Number	%
Central administration	536 552	86.1
Local administration, of which:	86 985	13.9
Management	2 524	2.9
Senior technicians	2 942	3.4
Technicians	723	0.8
Professional technicians	6 192	7.1
Administration	9 727	11.2
Auxiliaries	34 166	39.3
Labourers	25 307	29.7
Firemen	2 126	2.4
Other	2 778	3.2
TOTAL	623 537	100.0

Source: The Structure and Operation of the Local and Regional Democracy, Director General of the Local Administration, 1996

Managerial autonomy: Local governments have the authority to independently manage their staff. One weakness of local governments, in common with many other countries, however, is the low level of administrative and managerial training for local authority staff. Insufficiently qualified staff is a reflection of the fact that municipal responsibilities are becoming increasingly technical and of the trend towards contracting out of tasks to the private sector. In the central administration, less than three per cent of employees are manual workers and less than 20 per cent are auxiliaries; while comparable figures in local government are over 40 per cent and 35 per cent respectively. Another weakness is the limited political experience of many newly elected local representatives.

Mobility: While an official from the central administration can apply for a job in a local administration, the reverse is not possible since, in accordance with the Constitution, local administrations are not subject to regulations freezing public employment and local administrators do not go through a selection process comparable to that of the central level. Some ten years ago there was considerable movement from the central to local level as the municipalities (which do their own recruitment) had problems attracting staff. This situation has changed as medium-sized towns, where universities and hospitals have recently been built, are now perceived as attractive places to live and work.

3. TRENDS IN REDISTRIBUTING AUTHORITY ACROSS LEVELS OF GOVERNMENT

3.1 Evolving tendencies

In the late 1970s some regulatory measures were taken in order to implement the autonomy granted to local authorities by the new Constitution.

The year 1976, with the new regime and new Constitution, was a major turning point in the democratisation and decentralisation of Portugal. It established the power of local authorities; granted politico-administrative autonomy to the two island archipelagoes; and defined "administrative regions" on the mainland as an intermediate tier of government.

1986, when Portugal joined the European Union, was another benchmark in the country's regional evolution. This culminated in 1991 with the publication of the Administrative Regions Law which set out the principles to be taken into account in the process of regionalisation, and defined the competences and bodies of such regions without actually creating them or fixing their geographic boundaries. At the same time another law made possible the creation of metropolitan governments, and this led to the creation of metropolitan areas in Lisbon and Porto.

There has been some devolution of responsibilities from the Directorate-General of Territorial Planning and Urban Development to the Regional Co-ordination Commissions – for example in approving requests for providing sports facilities. This has been achieved through the joint development of criteria for analysing such requests, which are now applied by the CCRs. The extent and nature of CCR involvement is, however, a factor of the sector concerned.

There is also a growing use of municipal co-operation through associations set up for specific sectors and services such as water supply and data processing.

3.2 The current debate

Regional government has been a matter of political discussion for many years. Some see it as a constitutional obligation and claim that it would bring decision-making and service provision closer to the public. Others consider the creation of a middle layer of government as an unwise use of resources in a country as small as Portugal.

Local finance is another issue permanently being debated – especially in terms of the distribution of general grants from the centre to municipalities, and the associated notions of transferring new responsibilities to local governments and resolving their debt problems. There is also some discussion of allowing all municipalities to collect taxes locally, to replace the present system whereby they are collected by central government then paid back to the municipalities less a collection fee of 1.5 per cent. The feasibility of extending the powers and resources of the parishes for some functions as a way of bringing public matters closer to the citizens is also being discussed.

One view is that the concern now is more with ways of fine-tuning the system: improving relations between levels of government by enlarging the scope for local action and perfecting legal forms of control and tutelage so as to give coherence and unity to local actions. However, given that most of the basic infrastructure and road network is now in place, increasingly the main concern in medium sized towns is to provide jobs and reduce migration towards the larger urban areas.

The programme of the new (October 1995) government refers to the intention to apply the principle of subsidiarity through decentralisation, deconcentration and deregulation and in the context of reforming the public administration, to simplify the rules governing administrative procedures. It places the transfer of responsibilities to local government clearly on the political agenda for the coming period and will require new legislation. Areas being considered for transfer to local government include pre-school care, social housing, public security, tax collection and environmental matters.

The new programme sets, as a top priority for the government, new legislation to create administrative regions. Regionalisation is seen as part of a strategy for balanced development designed to eliminate differences, promote equal opportunities, economic and social cohesion, national solidarity and competetiveness. The strategy is based on principles of subsidiarity (through decentralisation) and partnership (through contracting). Regionalisation is not expected to build upon existing local government responsibilities, but rather to define specific new tasks to be taken over from central government. A new commission is examining the problems and possibilities in this politically sensitive area. The debate includes how many regions there should be, where boundary lines should be drawn, and if the constitution should be changed to allow a referendum on the subject.

3.3 Driving forces

The desire to bring public services closer to the citizens is strong in Portugal and this is seen as a natural partner of the drive towards more efficiency and better accountability. There is also an acceptance of the relevance of local government to governance as a whole. This is shown, for example, by the interest of national politicians in running for local election.

SPAIN

1. INSTITUTIONS AND AUTHORITY

1.1 Structures

Description of levels

The structures, powers and responsibilities of sub-national governments have experienced a radical transformation in the last 20 years. From a highly centralised system in which there were only two levels of government (central and local) Spain has moved to a three-tier system, with central, regional and local governments. The structure of the levels that can be compared (central and local), while remaining very similar in appearance, have experienced drastic and important change as they have evolved from an authoritarian regime into full fledged democratic bodies.

From a constitutional point of view Spain may be characterised, together with Italy, as a "regional state", in order to differentiate it from centralised systems and federal structures. In the Spanish case the system tends to operate more like a federation than a centralised state. Article 2 of the Constitution proclaims the unity of the Spanish Nation and "recognises and guarantees the right to self-government of the nationalities and regions of which it is composed". In devising the distribution of powers between central and sub-national governments the constitutional drafters had to reach numerous political compromises. This has resulted in a complex system of territorial organisation which has become progressively clearer in recent times.

The total area of Spain is 505 989 square kilometres and the total population in 1994 was 38 143 400.

Spain can be described now as a politically decentralised country in which the distribution of functions and the system of governance in general are very close to those of a federal state. The Spanish State is divided into 17 "self-governing communities" (*Comunidades Autónomas*"), or regions, 50 provinces and about 8 000 municipalities.

Regional level: The regional level is made up of 17 "self-governing" (autonomous) communities established between 1978 and 1983. Although the structure of all regions is very similar, the powers that have been devolved to each are not the same. However, this is a temporary situation.

Under the Constitution, the cities of Ceuta and Melilla have their own statutes, giving them similar organisational structure, competences and powers to Autonomous Communities, whilst retaining the status of municipalities.

Local level: The local level of government in Spain is sub-divided into two tiers: provinces and municipalities. Although all territorial units are supposed to be "autonomous" or self-governing, in practice provinces are often little more than administrative machines for the delivery of certain functions, and many municipalities lack the resources necessary to bring their self-rule to full fruition. In the island territories, the island, as a local entity, plays a role similar to that of the provinces.

Spain is divided into 50 Provinces following an administrative division established in 1833 using both political and objective criteria. Today many people still consider the provincial division as artificial and in some regions there have been attempts to do away with provinces as local government entities.

They were created following the example of the French *départements*, as both local units and circumscriptions of central government, and to this day the provincial division serves this dual purpose. Any modification to the boundaries of provinces has to be agreed within the framework of State organic law and approved by the Parliament.

The basic unit is the municipality, of which there are 8 097, ranging in size from a few inhabitants to over three million, as indicated in Table 1. The vast majority of municipalities are very small, 92 per cent having fewer than 10 000 inhabitants, and 60 per cent fewer than 1 000.

Table 1. **Area and population of sub-national governments (31 December 1995)**

	Self-governing Communities (Regions)	Provinces	Municipalities
Number	17	50	8 097
Area (km^2)			
Largest	94 193	21 766.31	1 750.33
Smallest	5 014	1 980.33	0.36
Population			
Largest	7 314 644	5 181 659	3 029 734
Smallest	268 206	94 396	4

Number of municipalities and population distribution	
Population	Number of municipalities
0-999	4 885
1 000-4 999	2 066
5 000-9 999	524
10 000-49 999	506
50 000-99 999	61
100 000 and over	55

Source: Ministry of Public Administration, Directorate-General for Territorial Co-operation, 1996.

Central government at sub-national levels

At the regional level, a government-appointed Delegate General is the permanent representative of central government in the region and has responsibility for directing the State administration in the Autonomous Community and co-ordinating it where necessary with the regional offices of the Community's own administration. At provincial level, the Civil Governor (equivalent to the French Prefect) carries out these duties. A draft Bill submitted to Parliament by the government in June 1996 proposes the abolition of the Civil Governors and their replacement in the provinces by "Deputy-Delegates" who will be professional rather than political.

The State still has a presence sub-nationally, notably in the following areas:

- labour (unemployment and social security benefits);
- security (police and armed forces);
- infrastructure (national roads, and waterways, ports and coasts);
- fiscal matters;
- health and education (in those Autonomous Communities where these responsibilities have not been transferred).

In order to operate, these services depend upon the respective ministries and, at the regional level their respective Delegate General or, at the provincial level, the Civil Governor (sub-Delegates in the proposed reform).

It is important to recognise that despite the political and administrative transformation resulting from the division of the country into self-governing communities and the transfer of important powers to them, the structure of central government has remained largely unchanged. Some departments have reduced the number of their employees, and there are fewer departments, but there has been no systematic effort to restructure the government according to the new situation. However, the Government presented a Bill to Parliament in 1996 which should become law in early 1997 and which seeks to adapt central and territorial structures to the new situation.

Creation, elimination and restructuring

In accordance with the provisions of their respective statutes, Autonomous Communities may establish on their territory supra-municipal or district authorities (*Comarcas*) or other entities grouping several municipalities having common interests requiring separate management or calling for the provision of services covering an entire area. The legislation of the Autonomous Communities defines the territorial boundaries of the *Comarcas*, the composition and operation of their executive bodies, as well as the powers, authority and economic resources assigned to them.

Competence to modify boundaries of municipalities resides with the Autonomous Communities by right or at the initiative of the municipal councils, after consultation with the municipalities concerned. Incorporation, merger and separation are the responsibility of Autonomous Communities concerned and, in all cases, respect the general principles set by basic State legislation concerning the establishment of local authorities.

Control bodies

Central control is exercised over Autonomous Communities by the Constitutional Court for regulatory matters; by the Court of Audit with regard to financial and budgetary matters; and by the Government in consultation with the Council of State. Most Autonomous Communities have, in turn, provided for the creation of their own Court of Audit exercising authority over their own territories.

1.2 Powers

Nature of sub-national institutions

All regions have a similar institutional structure with separate executive and legislative branches. Regional Parliaments are all unicameral and directly elected by the residents of the region. Parliament elects "from among its members" the head of the regional executive, who then appoints the members of his or her government.

The governing body of the province is the provincial assembly (*Diputación Provincial*) made up of local councillors who are elected by their peers from among the councillors of municipalities. They in turn choose a president from among themselves.

Municipalities are governed by a municipal council (assembly) of directly elected representatives, who elect among themselves a Mayor. Mayors appoint their deputies from among the councillors. On the other hand, in municipalities with the open council system (notably those with fewer than 100 inhabitants), residents elect a mayor directly and function as a council.

There is no such thing as a professional city manager, although in larger cities the different departments of the municipal administration are generally headed by a professional without prejudice to the decision-making functions reserved for the elected members of the local authority.

In municipalities with over 5 000 inhabitants there should be a governing board (composed of the mayor and the councillors he appoints). There may also be information committees which report on the responsibilities of the full committee, and which, in fact, exist in all the largest municipalities. Decisions are adopted by the full committee and by the mayor, according to their respective responsibilities, although many of them may be adopted by delegation by the governing board or delegated councillors.

Type and degree of autonomy

Regional level: The system is based on two separate sets of functions: one, contained in article 148 of the Constitution, enumerates the powers that *may* be adopted by the Regions, the other, in article 149, lists the powers which are the *exclusive* competence of the State. In matters not enumerated in these two articles the residual power is left with the central level as long as the regions have not claimed the competence in their regional basic law, known as "Statute of Autonomy" (E*statuto*). According to article 149, in case of conflict central legislation will prevail over regional norms unless the region has claimed the matter as of its "exclusive" competence. This distribution of powers has been interpreted and clarified by the case law of the Constitutional Court.

The Constitution also establishes a system under which regional powers can have several degrees of intensity, depending on whether the region assumes full legislative and executive powers, limited legislative powers or only executive functions. The Constitution also provides that Central Government functions can be passed on to the regions by Act of Parliament, and that central authorities can delegate their functions to the regions. One group of regions (the Basque country, Catalonia, Galicia, Andalucia, and to some extent, Valencia, the Canaries and Navarra) has been able to claim from the outset the fullest degree of self-government possible under the Constitution. The remaining regions have been obliged to wait before being able to demand the same level of autonomy. This process began in 1992 and in 1996 is now almost completed.

This means that the number and intensity of functions performed by the regions is not always the same and is subject to variations that are often difficult to explain. The trend is towards gradual homogenisation of the powers for all regions, and some legislation was adopted to that effect in 1993-94.

Regional Parliaments have the power to pass legislation in matters not reserved to the State. In many cases regional legislation is bound by national mandates or by directives of the European Union, but there are other instances in which only the Constitution determines the limit on the ability to legislate. As a result there is an increasing number of topics that are subject to different legislation in different parts of the country. While this provides opportunities for diversity and competition, it may create some confusion and complicate the operations of firms active in more than one region.

The Constitution recognises the financial autonomy of the Autonomous Communities in order to guarantee them an appropriate degree of autonomy in exercising their functions. The law on the financing of the Autonomous Communities defines the framework of the financial system, using the principles established in the Constitution. It gives the Fiscal and Financial Policy Council (a body composed of representatives of the State administrations in the Autonomous Communities) the role of co-ordinating and deciding on how the model should be put into practice. According to the system operating until 1996, the Autonomous Communities had the right to set their own tax rates, within strict legal limits, or to put a surcharge on existing taxes. The new system approved for the period 1997-2001 gives the Autonomous Communities a degree of decision-making autonomy over the taxes transferred by the State as well as over part of the personal income tax. Municipalities also have a certain amount of autonomy to set (within the legally defined limits) the rate to be applied to their main tax bases and to establish taxes of a local nature.

With regard to borrowing, the Autonomous Communities and the municipalities are subject to restrictions: for example, all borrowing must be used for capital investment and, in addition, co-ordination and control systems have been introduced.

1.3 Responsibilities

Distribution of competences

The introduction of the regional level in 1978 completely altered the Spanish panorama and forced existing governments, and most notably central government, to reconsider their purpose and scope. The process of devolution is not over yet, and may never be, but the trend is clear enough to describe in general terms. The competences listed in the 1978 Constitution can be found in the annex.

The system that emerged from the new constitution tends towards a division of powers in which central government retains policy making and implementation in a few areas, such as foreign policy, defence, fiscal and monetary policy (under European Union guidance) and criminal law.

In many other areas central government remains as a general policy-maker, setting the basis for the action of other administrations and ensuring that certain minimum standards are met and some degree of co-ordination is attained. Implementation is then left to the regions and, as the case may be, to municipalities. In a large number of matters central institutions issue basic legislation which is then developed by the regions into their own set of laws and regulations, going far beyond mere implementation of national mandates. This is the case in areas such as environmental policy, land use and physical planning, forestry, transportation, cultural heritage and economic development.

Provinces bring together all the municipalities within their boundaries, but their action concentrates on smaller municipalities, since their role is basically to assist and complement local communities. In addition to providing general assistance to municipalities in their area (especially the smaller ones) by integrating activities into provincial plans, the provincial administration concentrates on a limited number of services such as hospitals and provincial roads.

Local level: The powers of municipalities were broadly defined in the Local Government Act of 1985, but are subject to further specification by legislation both from central and regional governments. On paper local governments have many powers, but in practice their activities are limited to a few sectors such as local police, fire-fighting, refuse collection, street cleaning, land use control, urban transportation, etc. Only the larger municipalities participate in the delivery of services such as education or health, although all of them may provide the land for the establishment of service facilities. Local governments may not impose a surcharge on State taxes.

Mandatory, optional and shared responsibilities

Municipalities have only limited implementation capabilities, being subject to national and regional legislation. While central and regional governments are subject to legal obligations in a general sense, local governments are bound by law to provide certain minimum services, according to the size of their population. The number of mandates and their intensity can be modified by law, and although in theory new mandates should be accompanied by new resources, this has not always been the case.

There are very few instances of competencies that are exclusive to one level, and there are many cases of "grey areas". For instance, it seems constitutionally very clear that foreign relations are the exclusive competence of central government. However, some self-governing communities have decided that it is in their best interest to have their own offices in Brussels and maintain direct contacts with the European Union. Such initiatives have been contested by central government, but the Constitutional Court has ruled that this can not be considered as "foreign relations" and, therefore, the regions are entitled to having their own representative offices in Brussels for information services and relations with European institutions which do not affect those international relations reserved for the State.

It is difficult to describe in detail the activities shared by different levels of government in Spain as that would almost require an examination at the level of each sector.

2. MANAGEMENT FUNCTIONS

2.1 Policy-making and co-ordination

Coherence, consultation and conflict resolution

Policy-making authority is vested in a minority of cases in central government but in most instances is shared between central and regional levels. In practice this means that central institutions set the broad policy and regional ones make it more specific and adapt it at the regional level. It is also customary for major State bills to be presented to the Autonomous Communities before being submitted to the legislature, even in cases where these bills are clearly within the State's jurisdiction. Obviously, it falls to central government to decide whether this consultation is necessary or advisable.

The legalistic approach which has until now guided inter-governmental relations without considering functional or other objective parameters has proved detrimental to the smooth operation of the system. One result has been that the Constitutional Court is over-worked and cases may take between 3 and 5 years to be tried. Despite the volume of cases submitted to the Constitutional Court, their number has decreased apace with consolidation of the State's attitude to autonomy.

In domains such as housing and agriculture, in which central government contributes important financial resources but lacks specific implementation powers, there has been considerable success in establishing co-operative agreements, with some 330 being signed every year. Whilst agreements of this type are extremely diverse, they may, however, be divided into two kinds:

a) agreements whereby different administrations agree to finance certain activities jointly, that is, to pool their financial resources for greater viability;

b) agreements whereby the signatory administrations undertake to co-operate in other ways, for example:

- management of a service which is within the competence of one administration is entrusted to another;
- different administrations co-operate in providing a service;
- a system of procedural co-operation is set up, so that more than one administration participates in a given procedure;
- real estate or other property which is no longer needed by one administration after reorganisation is transferred to another administration, or the two carry out an exchange.

Formal and informal mechanisms

There are some formal mechanisms aimed at preventing conflicts, mainly through resort to intergovernment boards or "sectoral conferences". There are 27 sectoral conferences, which are co-operative bodies in which central government and the governments of 17 Autonomous Communities participate under the chairmanship of the minister concerned. The meetings cover the main subjects of interest to both parties. As far as local government is concerned, there is a National Commission for Co-operation with Local Authorities, which is the highest level consultative body for co-operation between the State and local governments. There is no uniform pattern of co-operation between local authorities and the Autonomous Communities, since it is for each Autonomous Community to establish these relationships as and when required.

2.2 Financial management

Sources of revenue

The sources of revenue for self-governing communities are threefold:

- revenues obtained through regional taxation;
- income transferred by the State;
- resources from the Inter-territorial Compensation Fund.

The main sources of income for municipalities are taxation on businesses and property; charges for the costs of individual services; State grants (mostly of a general nature) and loans. Municipalities are now demanding greater resources and more autonomy. The main sources of income for the Provinces are similar to those of the municipalities: internal taxation on private goods and services; a tax on property; state grants (general and specific); and loans.

Table 2 shows that the State provides a very substantial proportion of revenue, accounting for 68.5 per cent of the Autonomous Communities' total financial resources in 1986 before dropping to around 56.5 per cent in 1990 and then rising again to 65.3 per cent in 1994. As far as the municipalities are concerned, the revenue contributed by the State is falling gradually but continuously (31.5 per cent in 1986; 29.5 per cent in 1990; 29 per cent in 1994).

Table 2. **Main income of territorial administrations (1986, 1990, 1994)**
(millions of pesetas)

	1986		1990		1994	
	Regions [1]	Local government [2]	Regions [1]	Local government [2]	Regions [1]	Local government [2]
Income from the State, namely:	1 408 782	543 461	2 770 620	1 007 079	4 303 595	1 135 904
-- share of State revenues & individual income tax [3]	524 018	496 112	1 177 109	864 225 [5]	1 842 473	1 035 820 [5]
-- health care and social security transfers	394 578	207	1 018 298	54 702	1 717 421	39 269
-- Inter-territorial Compensation Fund	194 842	--	120 044	--	128 844	--
-- Other specific transfers	295 344	47 142	455 169	88 152	614 857	60 815
Regional taxation, namely:	419 068	858 771	1 501 044	1 489 224	1 513 730	2 317 440
-- transferred taxation [4]	378 547	--	1 407 934	--	1 369 413	--
-- own taxation, surcharges and levies	40 521	858 771 [5]	93 110	1 489 224 [5]	144 317	2 317 440
Other income,	230 726	306 923	629 156	919 504	772 038	443 554
-- borrowing and financial assets	230 726	306 923 [5]	629 156	919 504	772 038	443 554
TOTAL	2 058 576	1 709 155	4 900 820	3 415 807	6 589 363	3 896 898

1. Autonomous Communities.
2. Provinces and Municipalities.
3. For 1994, each territory's share of individual income tax has been taken into account.
4. Including taxation aligned on regional tax regimes.
5. Figures produced on the basis of budgets out-turns, consolidated with those of autonomous bodies and social security management agencies.

Source: Ministry of Public Administration.

Expenditure responsibilities

As shown in Table 3, the State's share of expenditure has fallen (71.6 per cent in 1985, 60.5 per cent in 1994). The Autonomous Communities have gained most from this trend (15.2 per cent of expenditure in 1985, 25.3 per cent in 1994).

Both the State and the Autonomous Communities are convinced that it is essential to go ahead with reforms to the financing system which balances the expenditure discretion of the Autonomous Communities with that which they enjoy for fixing revenues. This process of "fiscal balance" started with the agreements between the State and the Autonomous Communities on 23rd September 1996.

Table 3. **Trend of consolidated public expenditure by level of administration (1985, 1990, 1994)**
(millions of pesetas)

	1985	%	1990	%	1994	%
State [1]	7 416 923	71.6	11 507 174	61.1	16 780 694	60.5
Autonomous Communities (Regions)	1 571 899	15.2	4 263 583	22.6	6 998 210	25.3
Local Government	1 375 375	13.3	3 077 677	16.3	3 944 580	14.2
TOTAL	10 364 197	100.0	18 848 434	100.0	27 723 484	100.0

1. Excluding social security and other pensions.

Source: Ministry of Economic and Financial Affairs, Directorate-General for the Co-ordination of Territorial Finances.

Balance between discretion and control

In spite of the growing importance of regional taxation, the bulk of regional finances originate from resources appropriated by central government. Only about 20 per cent of the regional income comes from sources administered by most self-governing communities. Of the remaining about 80 per cent, half is in the form of unconditional appropriations or grants, the remainder is linked to specific programmes or agreements.

From a financial perspective, the Autonomous Communities divide into two categories. First, those known as *"foral"* -- the Basque country and Navarra -- are characterised by the fact that they themselves collect and manage their own taxes and those levied in their area by the State; and then transfer part of those revenues to the State as a contribution to general charges. Second, in the other Autonomous Communities, for which the State's contribution, as noted above, accounted for about 80 per cent of their total revenues up to 1996. Within this second group a special fiscal regime applies to the Canary Islands and the cities of Ceuta and Melilla.

Although local governments have a much lower participation in total public expenditures than regional authorities, they have better control over their income, since between 50 per cent and 60 per cent comes out of their own sources and 30 per cent originates in a block grant that is distributed according to objective criteria. This means that although municipalities have a much lower level of financing than regions, they enjoy comparatively greater autonomy.

2.3 Performance management

Mechanisms

There has been little activity in the domain of performance management. Audit and accountability mechanisms are still basically of a strict accounting nature, and the budget process is still largely unchanged although it is now presented as a "Programme Budget".

Control over public expenditure takes place first within each administration by specialised bodies of civil servants. There may also be outside control by the "Court of Accounts", which has national jurisdiction; and by the Court of Accounts of the Autonomous Communities within their respective areas. The controls performed are of a legalistic and formal nature, and there is little control over the effectiveness or efficiency of government units. This is in part because there are no data collected for this purpose, and budgets are not organised in a way conducive to performance analysis.

Quality standards

The office in charge of government accounting has been experimenting in recent years with approaches more geared towards "operative auditing", but these are yet to be widely used. The exception is in the field of health care, where, efforts are under way to introduce real performance measures and new accounting and auditing systems.

2.4 Human resource management

Total public sector personnel in Spain (2 121 100) in 1995 is still at moderate levels compared with other OECD countries, around 56 per cent belong to central government (if social security and public corporations are included), 25 per cent to the self-governing communities and 19 per cent to local governments. The total number of employees in the payroll of Autonomous Communities has, however, been rising steadily since they were established. This growth is to be expected since these are totally new institutions. Personnel numbers are likely to grow considerably as most of the regions still have to receive effective powers concerning two of the most labour intensive functions: health care and education.

The establishment of these new administrations has, in most cases, resulted in a reproduction of the bureaucratic institutions already found at the central level.

Statutory distinctions: The majority of public employees have civil servant status and are not subject to ordinary labour legislation but to their own special statute. The principles applying to civil service in general are set at the central level, although the regions can adopt their own legislation for the implementation of such principles, and have done so.

There is no central control over the personnel policies of the self-governing communities, and they are free to decide the level of staffing and salaries they can afford. In the past few years the number of regional employees has been rising steadily as the communities have organised their administrations and received their functions. Regional personnel policies are closely patterned after the central government model and suffer from rigidities that make it difficult to vary the number of employees over a short period of time.

Municipalities, due to their very low level of resources, have traditionally been understaffed, except in the largest cities. Local authorities are also entirely free in deciding the levels of staffing and retribution within their administrations although they are bound by the general principles set forth by national legislation as to the statute of civil servants. One peculiarity is that the city clerk and controller must be appointed from persons belonging to two national bodies of specialised civil servants.

Recruitment at all levels of government is regulated by the basic statute established at national level and is based on public competition. Promotion is also regulated by national statute although regional and local authorities have more leeway in establishing their own detailed rules.

Table 4. **Public sector salaried employees by type of administration (1987-1995)**
(at fourth quarter of each year, except for 1995 [second quarter])

Year	Central administration	Autonomous Communities (Regions)	Local administration	Social security	Public enterprises and institutions	Other (non classified)	Total public sector
1987	550 800	363 900	309 700	232 900	353 900	4 000	1 815 100
1988	529 000	383 200	359 700	257 100	375 500	6 000	1 910 700
1989	576 400	416 400	372 000	290 800	410 100	3 600	2 069 300
1990	555 200	448 500	389 200	307 200	417 400	4 200	2 121 700
1991	562 700	480 700	416 700	313 300	394 300	9 100	2 176 900
1992	571 700	464 300	401 200	321 000	382 500	2 100	2 142 700
1993	552 900	503 100	395 600	311 600	338 600	5 900	2 107 800
1994	537 400	510 900	393 500	291 600	310 500	4 600	2 048 500
1995	576 400	521 900	396 800	295 000	327 300	3 700	2 121 100

Sources: For 1987 to 1993: *Survey of the labour force*. National Institute of Statistics.
For 1994 and 1995: Ministry of Public Administration.

Mobility: There is not, however a single body of civil servants, but rather three different ones, as central government, regional governments and local authorities have each a different statute. In practice it is possible to move between the three groups, however, the transfer of civil servants from the Autonomous administrations to that of the State can only be considered as an exception and requires a special authorisation.

2.5 Regulatory management and reform

Unfortunately there have been no efforts to modify the regulatory responsibility of each level of government, other than the changes derived from the transfer of powers to the regions.

The fact that detailed regulations are now passed and implemented at regional level does not mean that there has been a simplification or a better accommodation to local peculiarities. In many cases it has meant a multiplication of regulation and a superposition of norms that makes it difficult at times to decide what regulation is to apply in a given case.

3. TRENDS IN REDISTRIBUTING AUTHORITY ACROSS LEVELS OF GOVERNMENT

3.1 Evolving tendencies

Creation of Autonomous Communities: In spite of the reduced role of local government, Spain can be considered to be a rather decentralised country. This has not, however, always been the situation as it has emerged very late in the twentieth century. There have nevertheless been recurrent attempts to establish some sort of federal or regional system for the past two hundred years.

The last bid for decentralisation took place under the Spanish Republic (1931-1939) with the approval of the Catalan, Galician and Basque Statutes of 1932 and 1936. These efforts were short-lived and completely suppressed by the regime of General Franco.

The transformation of Spain into a democratic nation after 1975 brought with it renewed claims for self-government in some parts of the country, notably the Basque Country and Catalonia. By 1977 it was clear that these two regions would have to enjoy some form of self-rule if Spain was to see the peacefully installation of a democratic regime. By the time the Spanish Constitution was adopted in 1978 these two regions had already a limited degree of self-government patterned after the system of 1932-1936.

The 1978 Constitution integrated the demands of the regions with historic claims to self-rule and devised a system which allowed for a generalisation of political decentralisation to the entire country. The wording of the Constitution allowed different interpretations and modes of implementation, and it was not until 1981 that it was decided that autonomy would be extended to all regions in Spain and not only to those claiming their historic national rights.

By 1983 the entire country had been divided into 17 "Autonomous Communities" enjoying a considerable degree of self-government (the cities of Ceuta and Melilla have had autonomous status since 1995). The process is still evolving, since a new "package" of functions was devolved in 1992-93.

Thus, decentralisation in Spain is clearly and firmly rooted in political origins, as opposed to other systems in which the redistribution of powers stems largely from administrative considerations. At the time when the Constitution was drafted "decentralisation" was to many people synonymous with "democratisation". It was clear to many that if Spain was to exist as a democratic country it would be a decentralised one. Decentralisation in Spain was not brought about by a quest for greater efficiency, but by the need for greater democracy. Everything else took a secondary role.

Financial management is also evolving but has yet to achieve a stable configuration. The evolution of the system can be divided into three clearly defined periods. In the initial period (up to 1987) the emerging regions were receiving their devolved powers. During the years 1987-91 there was a set method of transferring to the regions the resources necessary to continue the functions that they were being allocated. Since 1992 funds have been complemented by resources from a "Territorial Compensation Fund", aimed at reducing inter-regional disparities.

Evolution at the municipal level: Municipalities have traditionally been greatly underfunded, and in recent years there has been a move towards obtaining more resources and more effective autonomy. There is a view that in the decentralisation process that came with the advent of democracy, municipalities were left out in favour of the newly created self-governing communities. A comparison of the functions performed by municipalities 20-30 years ago and today shows little difference. What has changed is the *form* of government -- the content of local governance has remained fairly stable over time. The larger municipalities have now united in a concerted campaign to reform this situation and continue the decentralisation drive by extending effective self-government down to the lowest level.

3.2 The current debate

In spite of its flaws, the Spanish decentralisation effort has to be considered as largely successful. In fact it can be rated as a clear success in achieving its major goal: transforming an autocratic state into a democracy while maintaining national unity. At the same time it must be said that democracy has been brought closer to the citizen by the establishment of democratically elected governments at the regional and local levels, and responsiveness to the citizen has been favoured by the increased proximity to the people.

Of course this has not come without costs, and the most apparent has been the increased size of the Spanish Administration. In the second quarter of 1995, central government employed 576 400 civil servants, regional bodies 521 900, and local governments 396 800. This means that the number of people employed in the civil service rose from 1 115 366 in 1982 to 1 589 053 in 1993, a 42.5 per cent increase in 10 years. (The total number of public employees is much higher, since in 1992 the total figure was 2 134 500, of which 1 195 900 were in central government.) This rise in the number of public servants cannot be considered, nevertheless as an entirely negative matter, since it would have to be compared to the variation in the level and quality of public services that has taken place during this period.

This has indeed been one of the main criticisms that has been directed at the decentralisation process in Spain. To most analysts the nation has lost a historic opportunity to restructure central government and its bureaucracy, and instead has chosen to replicate, and sometimes duplicate, central structures at the regional level.

On the positive side is the considerable accomplishment of a political nature, making democracy possible and establishing a system which has been able to maintain Spain's unity while providing room for diversity.

On the negative side a series of shortcomings should be noted by those tempted to adopt a similar course:

- lack of clarity in the distribution of functions;
- lack of uniformity of regional functions; however, between 1992 and 1995, a programme to standardise the powers of the Autonomous Communities was implemented and is now virtually completed;
- imitation when establishing regional governments, leading to a continuation of the same bureaucratic and centralist habits, reproduction and duplication of bureaucratic machineries;
- local government was left aside, which makes the deepening of democracy much more difficult and prevents a more rational distribution of delivery functions;
- maintaining the structure and model of central government as it was before the democratisation and decentralisation process began;
- relations between tiers of government first appeared to lead to confrontation rather than co-operation; however, conflicts have become less frequent over the years;
- lack of sufficient financial resources for regional and local governments, and establishment of financial mechanisms that tend to perpetuate certain forms of administration.

In the final analysis the performance of public functions in general and service delivery in particular have not been greatly affected by the decentralisation process.

Reform of the Senate is now planned in order to make the Autonomous Communities into constituencies for the election of senators (instead of the provinces as is the case at present). The Senate's function of territorial representation should not change. A number of measures have already been implemented to facilitate this reform, including the establishment in the Senate of a General Commission of the Autonomous Communities.

3.3 Driving forces

In federal systems there is often a clear division of functions which puts policy-making in the hands of the central level and leaves implementation to sub-national levels, even if it implies further legislation. In the Spanish case some functions are divided along these lines and some are attributed exclusively to the regions, but there are few set rules as to how far both levels of government can go.

This constitutional division of powers has been complemented by the different Regional "Statutes" in a way that has given rise to numerous conflicts. Due to the fact that the Constitution was the subject of political consensus among several parties, some of them representing regional interests, the wording of many articles was left deliberately ambiguous on some points, one of them being the distribution of powers among the central and regional levels of government. The lack of constitutional definition of terms like "exclusive powers", or "basic legislation", have led to numerous conflicts and will give rise to more.

If the division of powers between central and regional authorities is less than clear in the Constitution, the role of the other sub-national levels is still less well defined. Regarding the functions of provinces and municipalities the Constitution has remained entirely silent, leaving the matter fully in the hands of ordinary legislation.

As a result it could be said that local governments received less attention than they deserved in the design of the new decentralised system as all efforts focused on the regions. This serious flaw is now having an impact on the way functions are being performed and services are delivered to the citizen, and is putting serious strain in the relations between municipal governments on the one hand and central and regional authorities on the other.

ANNEX:

CONSTITUTIONAL DIVISION OF POWERS

The lists of powers contained in the 1978 Constitution are as follows.

Article 148: functions that can be assumed by the Regions.

1. Organisation of their institutions of self-government.

2. Changes in municipal boundaries.

3. Regional/spatial planning; land use planning and; housing.

4. Public works of regional interest.

5. Railways and roads running entirely within the region, and associated transportation activities.

6. Ports of refuge; recreational ports and airports; and, in general, ports and airports not performing commercial activities.

7. Agriculture and livestock raising in accordance with general economic policy.

8. Woodlands and forestry.

9. Implementation of environmental protection in matters.

10. Building and operating hydraulic infrastructures and resources of regional interest (e.g. channels, and irrigation projects).

11. Fishing in inland waters and rivers; and hunting.

12. Domestic trade fairs.

13. Promotion of regional development within the framework of national economic policy.

14. Handicrafts.

15. Museums, libraries and music conservatories of regional interest.

16. Historical heritage of regional interest.

17. The promotion of culture and research, and, when appropriate, the teaching of the regional language.

18. Promotion and planning of tourism within their boundaries.

19. The promotion of sports and of the use of leisure time.

20. Social assistance.

21. Health and hygiene.

22. Surveillance of their own buildings. Co-ordination and other powers regarding local police under the terms of an organic law.

As a counterpart to this, **Article 149** lists the functions that are considered to be of the exclusive competence of Central Government:

1. Regulation of the basic conditions that guarantee the equality of all Spaniards in the exercise of their constitutional rights and duties.
2. Nationality, immigration, emigration, alienage and right of asylum.
3. International relations.
4. Defence and Armed Forces.
5. Administration of justice.
6. Commercial, penal and penitentiary legislation; procedural legislation.
7. Labour legislation.
8. Civil law, except in those matters regulated by traditional regional legislation; contract law.
9. Industrial and intellectual property law.
10. Customs and import duties; foreign trade.
11. Monetary system; foreign exchange; basic regulation of credit, banking and insurance activities.
12. Legislation on weighs and measures, determination of the official time.
13. Setting the basis for and co-ordinating the general planning of economic activity.
14. General Treasury and State debt.
15. Promotion and co-ordination of scientific and technical research.
16. Basic regulation and co-ordination of health care; legislation on pharmaceutical products.
17. Basic legislation on social security, to be implemented by the regions.
18. Basic legislation on public administration, as well as the regulation of administrative procedure and expropriation.
19. Sea fishing.
20. Merchant shipping; ... ports and airports of general interest; air traffic control; air transportation.....
21. Railways and inland transportation when it takes place over the territory of more than one region.
22. Legislation and regulation of water resources when they flow over more than one region; ... electrical power when it affects more than one region.
23. Basic legislation on environmental protection; and on woodlands and forestry.
24. Public works of general interest or involving more than one region.
25. Basic legislation on mining and energy.
26. Production, sale, possession and use of arms and explosives.
27. Basic legislation regulating the press, radio and television ....
28. Preservation of the Spanish cultural, artistic and monumental heritage.
29. Public safety, without prejudice to the possibility of establishing a regional police force ....
30. Academic degrees and professional qualifications ....
31. Statistics for State purposes.
32. Authorisation to consult public opinion by means of a referendum.

SWEDEN

1. INSTITUTIONS AND AUTHORITY

1.1 Structures

Sweden is a parliamentary democracy. The Parliament has until recently been elected for a three-year term. From 1994 the term is four years. The Parliament is elected directly and representation is strictly proportional. This promotes a multi-party system. Direct and proportional elections are also held for county councils, municipalities and parishes.

Sweden has four constitutional laws, and one of these, the Instrument of Government provides constitutional protection for regional and local authorities. Chapter 1, section 7 reads: "There are in Sweden primary units of local government (municipalities) and county councils. The right of decision in municipalities and county councils is exercised by elected assemblies. The municipalities and county councils may levy tax for the performance of their duties."

Description of levels

The ministries in Sweden are relatively small. State agencies and boards (around 300) handle most of the State responsibilities and administration. Some State agencies only work at the national level. Others can have regional and local branches. At the regional level, the central administration is represented by 24 counties. Around 250 000 persons are employed by the State including defence, and some State companies (railroads, post, airports).

Sweden is divided into county councils (23), municipalities (288) and parishes (2 500). The counties are primarily a central government administrative division at the regional level. The parishes are local units of the State church administration.

Approximately 734 000 persons are employed by municipalities, 303 000 persons are employed by county councils and 25 000 persons are employed by the church.

The total area of Sweden is 450 000 square kilometres. Its population of 8.8 million is spread over an area almost 30 per cent larger than Germany. There is a need, therefore, for an extensive regional and local government even if the number of inhabitants in each constituency may be quite small.

Central government at sub-national levels

Within the central government there is also a deconcentrated regional and sometimes local administration. County Administrative Boards act on behalf of central government at the regional level. These boards are responsible for both planning and administration. The heads of the boards are the County Governors, appointed by the government. The 14 members of each board are appointed by the government on the proposal of the county councils concerned. The County Administrative Boards exercise supervision over the municipalities in their respective counties and are the reviewing authorities for appeals against decisions by the local authorities that are covered by special laws. In recent years they have concentrated to an increasing extent on regional policy and physical planning, as well as government sectoral planning.

Table 1: **Area and population of sub-national governments (1992)**

Number	Counties 24[1]		Municipalities 288[1]	
	Area (km²)	Population	Area (km²)	Population
Largest	98 911	1 641 669[2]	19 447	672 452[2]
Smallest	2 941	57 108	9	2 959

Number of municipalities and population distribution	
Population size	Number of municipalities[1]
0-1 000	0
1 000-5 000	10
5 000-10 000	56
10 000-50 000	181
50 000-100 000	30
over 100 000	11

1. Figures from 1996.
2. Stockholm, which is both a county council and a municipality.

Source: *Structure and Operation of Local and Regional Democracy: Sweden*, Council of Europe, 1993.
Ministry of Finance for 1996 figures.

Regional organisations established by central government agencies are called county boards. They are responsible to their parent agency but have lay advisory boards. Where agencies have no regional organisation, the County Administrative Boards perform the functions of the agencies. Central government bodies at the local level are the local tax offices and social insurance offices.

Creation, elimination and restructuring

The boundaries of regional and local authorities are defined by the Act Amending the Division of Sweden into Municipalities and County Councils. Municipal boundaries can be altered by the amalgamation or division of two or more municipalities or by the incorporation of part of a municipality into another. Such decisions are made by the government. Cases of minor importance may be decided by the County Administrative Boards. Municipalities have no veto in such cases, but under the Act, local opinion has to be taken into account.

The present number of municipalities has come about through a radical reduction in several steps in the period 1950-1974, starting with 2 500 municipalities and ending with about 280. This process was initiated and controlled by the central government and caused considerable opposition. In later years some municipalities have, at their own request after a local referendum, been divided, so that the number has increased slightly to 288 (1996).

The motivation for increasing the size of the municipalities was to strengthen their capacity to handle public sector responsibilities. A large number of tasks have been decentralised, to the new structure of enlarged municipalities.

Swedish local and regional authorities are free to set up associations subject to public law for co-operation on matters or common interest. Provisions relating to such associations are contained in the Local Authority Associations Act. The formation of such associations is voluntary, but in a few cases it may be a compulsory requirement for certain purposes (housing, regional planning and public transport).

Control bodies

There is no authority with responsibility for exercising general administrative supervision over the legality or expediency of the acts of local authorities. The government is collectively responsible for public administration. Municipalities are supervised by the County Administrative Boards, other State agencies with supervisory functions, and, in turn, by the government.

Municipal activities are also subject to supervision of courts if – and only then – a member of the municipality makes a formal appeal against decisions taken by the municipality or the county council. There is no central authority with the task to monitor the legality of all decisions taken by municipalities or county councils or the spending of tax income. Local/regional authorities appoint their own auditors.

The Swedish Government has an overall responsibility for the whole public administration but no direct powers within the "self-government area". Changes must by executed through the Parliament and laws.

Government's supervision is divided among a large number of agencies. The County Administrative Boards are directly responsible to, and supervised by, the government. The County Administrative Boards in their turn supervise the municipalities in some specific areas.

Local governments are to some extent supervised by the central government. Supervision has become less and less intensive over a long period of time. Formerly many decisions by municipalities had to be submitted to a central government agency to be confirmed. Today there is but one such provision left, regarding local government decisions on foreign aid.

In fields that have been decentralised to local governments by special laws, dissatisfied individuals may appeal to central government agencies and courts and in some instances ultimately to the Cabinet.

1.2 Powers

Nature of the sub-national institutions

Government has four levels: central, regional (county), local (municipal) and parochial. There are directly and proportionally elected councils (parliaments) at the central, regional, and local levels. 23 county councils are elected at the regional level and 288 municipal councils at the local level. Parishes within the state church are the smallest local entity at which elections are held. Elections to all levels take place at the same time (parishes four weeks later). Increasingly voters vote for different parties in the three elections. Majorities therefore differ.

Municipal councils and county council assemblies themselves decide on the number of their members (not less than 31 when the number of people entitled to vote is less than 1 200 and not less than 101 when the number of people entitled to vote exceeds 300 000). Local elections are held in conjunction with the Parliamentary elections.

The municipal and county council executive boards have a management and co-ordinating functions within their unit of government and are responsible for the administration and supervision of the various committees (but cannot intervene in their activities). They are also responsible for policy on certain important economic matters and submit any proposals they consider appropriate to the elected councils or other authorities.

The head of the municipality is the chairman of the municipal executive board and is appointed by the municipal council. The county council appoints the chairman of the county council executive board. The chairmen of these boards have only limited decision-making powers. Most decisions are taken collectively by the boards.

Type and degree of autonomy

The principle of local self-government is stated in the Instrument of Government. Even the right of taxation is explicitly stated there. All four levels of government have the right to tax their citizens. Local taxes are income taxes, which since a couple of years are restricted to personal income. Only the national parliament has legislative authority. Municipalities have the power to issue local statutes of order.

Municipal council and county council assemblies have the right to set the tax rate in the form of a percentage of personal income. All other tax related administration and decisions are handled by the State. Taxes are collected by government agencies. Neither municipalities nor county councils may introduce any new types of local tax without legislative authorisation by the national parliament.

In 1991 a new Local Government Act suspended several restrictions on the internal organisation of municipalities and county councils. Formerly, a set of committees, with specified authority, were prescribed. Now, only an executive committee is required. Municipalities and county councils therefore have almost complete freedom to organise themselves as they like. In a very short time after the new act, the organisational pattern has become very varied.

Central government can use several means to exercise influence over local government, in particular through legislation which can be used to prescribe tasks, prohibit activities or shape the process of decision-making. For instance the central government has imposed legislation in two important areas aiming at uniform service standards, that eliminate the local freedom of variation. One area is welfare payments, the other is support of handicapped. Welfare payments and support of a handicapped person are stated as citizens' rights. A dissatisfied individual may appeal to an administrative court to have the decision changed. Viewed in a long-term perspective, court decisions on the municipal provision of public services is something quite new in Sweden.

1.3 Responsibilities

Distribution of responsibilities

Swedish municipalities and county councils have, in the Local Government Act, the right to undertake "a matter of general concern which are connected with the area of the municipality or county council or with their members." Exceptions are activities relying only on the State or other organisations. The Local Government Act is supplemented by a number of laws defining the powers, and the restriction of powers, in various fields. In these laws the Parliament can express the general goals for local services. These laws can also regulate various aspects of production, provision and financing. As much as 70-80 per cent of the services provided by municipalities are in some way or other regulated by national laws. The Government/Parliament has the overall responsibility for the whole public administration and can – through laws and finance powers – regulate matters of national concern.

Broadly, the central government provides for defence, police, courts, and university education; and operates the fundamental social benefit schemes – pensions, children's allowances, health and unemployment insurance and housing subsidies. Local governments on the other hand provide individual services – health care, primary, secondary and high school education, social welfare services – and to a lesser extent handle social benefits. Both the central government and municipalities engage in infrastructure provision.

Areas which are in principle the prerogative of the central government include macroeconomic planning, business cycle policies, regional development, redistribution, public law, business promotion and regulation, labour market policies, environmental policies and foreign policy.

Municipalities and counties are free to engage in all kinds of activities that lie within the general frame of authority stated in the Local Government Act. The authority is quite wide, but it prohibits for-profit business activities and activities that go beyond the territory of the municipality. In addition, municipalities and counties must engage in activities that are explicitly decentralised to them by law. Many tasks have been decentralised and are mandatory for the municipalities, such as primary and secondary school, old-age and child care, social welfare payments and fire-fighting. Other tasks such as the provision of housing, local transport, and adult education are optional. Municipalities and county councils also engage in cultural and leisure activities and the promotion of local business. Health care is, with some exceptions, decentralised to county councils. County councils also deal with other matters, i.e. regional co-operation in the fields of regional planning and promotion, public transportation, social welfare, education and culture. A long time ago parishes were the cradle of local democracy. Today they deal exclusively with the operations of the state church at the local level. A separation of the Protestant church from the State has been discussed for many decades. It now seems likely that it will come about in the year 2000 when parishes will cease to exist as general democratic institutions.

Municipalities have a very strong role in district planning. In 1987 a new law on building regulation was adopted which strengthened the role of the municipality. At the same time the Natural Resources Act was adopted making explicit the right of the central government to intervene in the planning process only when stated national interests in the law is at stake.

Mandatory, optional and shared responsibilities

A recent law states that local government is responsible for supplying adequate child-care services. From a local government perspective the consequence of such legislation is that they lose control. Services that must be provided regardless of their cost can, and are, directed towards local governments.

Not all activities of local governments are mandatory in a formal sense and that obligations sometimes are not very specific. In 1977 mandatory activities were estimated to occupy only 40 per cent of municipal expenditures. Since then, however, obligations have been extended in the fields of social welfare, health and education. In the beginning of the 1990s two investigations estimated that mandatory tasks constituted as much as 75-90 per cent of local government expenditures. Mandatory tasks have expanded and been extended. Day-care for all children and secondary school have both become mandatory tasks and have expanded. A large part of the shift between 1977 and the 1990s, however, reflects a change of definitions. In the broad framework laws of 1980 on social welfare and of 1983 on health care, municipalities and county councils respectively, finally were given the ultimate responsibility for these broad areas. The responsibility is, however, to a large extent a matter of judgement and resources. Within those responsibilities local governments exercise considerable freedom.

2. MANAGEMENT FUNCTIONS

2.1 Policy-making and co-ordination

Coherence, consultation and conflict resolution

Local governments have a co-ordinating function. One of their important tasks, perhaps the *"raison d'être"* of municipal governments, is the geographic co-ordination of community planning. County councils to some extent also perform this kind of co-ordination on the regional level – a task also sometimes performed by unions of municipalities (*kommunalförbund*).

The central government uses several means to exercise influence over local government. Legislation may be used to prescribe tasks, prohibit activities, or shape the process of decision-making. This is the fundamental means of control, in order to achieve co-ordination between local governments and between policy areas. Nowadays, legislative regulation is seldom very detailed.

Concerned individuals may appeal to the county administration and to administrative courts and sometimes to the agency concerned and have local government decisions repealed. The agency has the right of inspection and to some extent the possibility of prescribing. In areas of general authority citizens may appeal to courts if the local community decision is considered to go beyond its general authority.

Formal and informal mechanisms

As already noted, the county administration serves as regional offices for those central agencies that do not have them. This places the burden on the county administration to co-ordinate central government policies in fields such as communications, environment and education at the regional level.

The Swedish Association of Local Authorities and the Federation of County Councils are governed by private law. All the municipalities are members of the Swedish Association of Local Authorities. The association has an advisory role on economic, legal and technical matters. It also speaks on behalf of the municipalities in relation to central government and other authorities and organisations. The Association can only make recommendations. It has a governing body consisting of elected representatives from all municipalities on the basis of the distribution of the political parties. The Federation of County Councils consists of all the county councils and has the same duties and organisation as the Swedish Association of Local Authorities.

2.2 Financial management

Sweden has a very large public sector. At present public expenditures amount to approximately 70 per cent of GNP. Public consumption amounts to roughly 30 per cent of GNP. Sweden also has a very decentralised system for delivering government services. Almost 80 per cent of public consumption is accounted for by local governments.

Sources of revenue

Financially local governments are quite independent. Less than 20 per cent of local governments' revenues stem from central government grants, the balance coming from local taxes and user fees. County councils and municipalities are financed by local taxes, fees for services and government grants. Their most important source of income is the income tax paid by all wage earners. Local taxes are now based on a flat rate representing a certain proportion of income.

Grants from central government are still used to stimulate some activities of local governments. But since 1992 the number of specific grants has been heavily reduced. Specific grants have been replaced by one general block grant, with the sole aim of equalising financial prerequisites on the different municipalities and county councils. Formerly specific grants were often created when local governments were to take over a specific task from the central government. Changes in the general grant will now have to be undertaken.

In 1996 a new equalisation system for municipalities and county councils was introduced. The main components of the new equalisation system are income equalisation, equalisation of structurally related cost differences, a general block grant and certain transitional rules.

The income equalisation system implies a far-reaching equalisation of both municipal and county council taxation revenue. After equalisation, all municipalities and county councils are to have revenues corresponding to the national average. Municipalities and county councils with a taxable income per capita falling short of the national average will receive equalisation grants. Municipalities and county councils with a per capita taxable income exceeding the national average are to pay an equalisation charge to the State.

The cost equalisation system implies an equalisation of structurally related cost differences between municipalities and county councils respectively for mandatory and certain optional activities and for certain non-operational expenditure. Municipalities and county councils with relatively disadvantageous structural conditions will receive an equalisation grant from the State, whereas those whose structural conditions are relatively favourable will pay an equalisation charge to the State.

The general block grant gives the State an opportunity to control the financial scope of the local government sector. The total volume of State grants to the municipalities will be decided annually by the Parliament, with reference to an assessment of the economic scope available for local government activities. The general grant can also be used for regulating financial relations between the State and municipalities/county councils, e.g. when changes are made to the allocation of responsibilities.

For many municipalities and county councils, the new system of grants and equalisation will have substantial financial effects. For this reason, the new system is being progressively introduced over a period of eight years.

Table 2. **Main revenue sources of sub-national governments (1990, 1993)**
(per cent)

	Municipalities		County councils	
	1990	1993	1990	1993
Local income tax	48	55	69	71
Central special-purpose grants	22	8	3	3
Central block grants	4	14	6	6
Fees and co-payments	16	15	16	14
Other sources	10	8	6	6
TOTAL	100	100	100	100

Source: Ministry of Finance.

Expenditure responsibilities

Local governments operate almost 70 per cent of the service production (their share of public consumption). Local governments and national government invest almost the same sums. The national government is responsible for almost 90 per cent of transfer payments to households. Transfer payments to others, except to local governments, are also mainly a national government affair. The national government is responsible for the major social security schemes such as pensions, children's allowances, housing subsidies, subsidies to agriculture, etc. Local governments are responsible for social welfare payments, which fill in when other social benefits are not enough. Until recently local governments have also handled some housing subsidies. Local governments also subsidise local non-profit organisations for various purposes, such as education, culture, and youth affairs.

The total expenditures of Swedish municipalities and county councils in 1991 amounted to 25 per cent of the GDP. This represented a decrease of 2.6 percentage points over the preceding 10 years. Education is by far the largest component of total municipal spending, followed by childcare (12 per cent) and care for the elderly (10 per cent). Effective from 1992, the municipalities assumed greater responsibility for care for the elderly, and over 20 billion SKr has been transferred from the county councils to the municipalities for this purpose.

Table 3. **Municipal and county council operating expenditures by field (1992)**
(per cent)

Municipalities		Counties	
Social services	35	Health care	75
Education	23	Services for the mentally retarded	9
Energy, water and waste management	7	Educational and cultural programmes	5
Joint municipal administration	9	Central administration	3
Recreation and cultural affairs	6	Social welfare programmes	1
Land and housing	8	Miscellaneous programmes	7
Environmental, health and protective services	5		
Transportation and communications	4		
Labour market and business sector	3		
TOTAL	100	TOTAL	100

Source: Ministry of Finance.

Balance between discretion and control

Central government exercises only general supervision over local authorities' finances. Every year, Parliament specifies a frame for local authority expenditure in terms of desirable volumes. Both the municipalities and county councils have the right to determine local tax rates, but the Parliament can freeze taxes for a certain period. In recent years, the government has controlled local authority expenditure by means of a local tax freeze through manipulation of the tax base and by putting a temporary cap on local government tax rates. The replacement of many matching grants by one block grant per municipality was another mean of controlling the expansion of the local government sector. Apart from this, the government has no means of controlling expenditure by individual municipalities or county councils. The Local Government Act contains general provisions concerning responsible financial management by local and regional authorities.

During the 1980s, the central government changed the right of local governments to levy taxes. Formerly, local government taxes included taxes on corporate profits. This is no longer the case.

2.3 Performance management

Mechanisms

Performance management in a stricter sense is not used by the central government to govern the county councils and the municipalities. The central government governs by setting national objectives in the laws that regulate education, health, social welfare, etc. The central government is implementing new methods to monitor the county councils and the municipalities, especially regarding education, health and social welfare services. For instance, agencies which used to deal with these matters, now decentralised to local government, play a role in policy framing based upon evaluation and inspection. They also have a role of inspection and approval of privately owned centres for care and schools. New ways are also being developed to communicate, on a yearly basis, the overall performance and results of local governments to Parliament. The State conducts inspections of municipalities and county councils in different ways. The National Agency for Education, for example, has a regional body especially for this purpose, and there is a similar body attached to the National Board for Health and Welfare.

Many – but not all – local governments have implemented performance management. New financial management systems have more generally been introduced and at the same time financial responsibility have been delegated to schools, day-care centres, hospitals, etc. It is in principle the task of the local government auditors to audit the yearly performance reports. The county councils and the municipalities appoint their own auditors.

Quality standards

A lot is happening at the local level in areas such as health, schools and aged care. Considerable work has been done at the local level on service standards issues, in particular by the Local Authorities Association on the benchmarking of individual authorities in terms of levels of services and costs. This aims to assist individual authorities to decide where to place themselves in terms of level of service and to evaluate their relative performance in terms of cost and efficiency. A lot of efforts have been put into the development of performance indicators for more complex services. Following are some reported examples of quality indicators for schools:

- test results;
- percentage of examinations and drop-outs;
- average number of pupils per class;
- educational level of the teachers;
- special services for the disabled, etc.;
- access to computers;
- pupils' and parents' satisfaction level.

Many local governments are working with "Quality Management" programmes. These represent a shift from a more traditional management culture based on rules and procedures to a more client-oriented culture are often aiming at developing clear targets and performance measurements.

One good example of a more advanced application of performance measurement in management is Nacka municipality outside Stockholm. They publish a budget and activity plan document which contains measurable goals for activities. For each goal a measurement technique has been approved and a desired result has been set – in figures or other controllable facts.

2.4 Human resource management

Statutory distinctions

Local governments are free to hire and fire personnel at their own will, restricted of course by the general laws of the labour market.

Municipalities and county councils are completely independent of central government in making decisions with regard to the administrative and financial status and the recruitment of their staff. The conditions of service are not linked to those of the national civil service.

Table 4. **Public sector employment by level of government and sector (1990, 1994)**
(full-time equivalents)

	1990	1994
Municipal personnel	600 500	616 900
County council personnel	322 500	236 200[1]
TOTAL	923 000	853 100
Public sector employees by sector:		
Education	230 700	203 300
Health care [1]	298 000	205 900
TOTAL	529 300	409 200

1. The responsibility for long-term care of the elderly was transferred from the county councils to the municipalities in 1992. The county council personnel was transferred to the municipalities and registered as "social welfare personnel".
Source: Statistics Sweden.

Table 5. **Personnel in the government sector by level (1980, 1985, 1991, 1993)**
(number of persons full-time and part-time)

	1980	1985	1991	1993
Central government [1]	427 300	423 100	387 400	309 500
Local and county council government	867 200	951 900	1 134 100	1 062 560
TOTAL GOVERNMENT SECTOR	1 294 500	1 375 000	1 521 500	1 372 060

1. Excluding conscripts.
Source: Public Management Developments: Update 1995, OECD, 1995.

2.5 Regulatory management and reform

There are different kinds of legislation in relation to local governments. One kind states the general authority of local governments, another states specific authority. Taking all kinds of regulation that is specific for local government services, as much as 80 per cent of the services provided are in some way or another regulated. The laws regulating specific authority may either prescribe mandatory tasks or may authorise optional tasks. Central government control is different for these different kinds of laws. In areas of specific authority there is always a central agency in charge of that area.

There are two important areas in which the central government has introduced regulation causing local governments to loose some of their control. Both aim at creating competition. Firstly, since 1993 there is a voucher system in primary and secondary school. Such that parents may choose a private school for their children. A child has the right to transfer 75 per cent of the average cost of the municipal school to any school approved by the National School Board which the parents choose. Secondly, from 1995 physicians have the right to establish themselves as practitioners, with the same degree of subsidies from the county councils as publicly provided primary health care. Both reforms have been the subject of political controversy and it is quite possible that these decisions may be changed.

In areas such as social welfare (welfare payments, old age homes, day-care centres for children), health, schools and district planning detailed regulation has been replaced by frame-work legislation, in which general goals and aims play the major role and rules stand back.

3. TRENDS IN REDISTRIBUTING AUTHORITY ACROSS LEVELS OF GOVERNMENT

3.1 Evolving tendencies

The growth of the local government sector and the accompanying decentralisation of public services should be viewed in relation to the deconcentration that has taken place within the central government sector as the two are often considered as alternatives. A centralisation movement could be observed at the same time.

Centralisation

Examples here are transfer payments and taxes, i.e. areas in which local variations are not desirable. The social security administration has over the decades become more and more unified. Recently the regional agencies for the administration of student aid and grants were abolished and merged under the central agency. The central government tax administration has been centralised in three steps, first by creating a central agency in 1971, then by removing the regional tax administration from the county administration in 1987, and thirdly by abolishing local tax offices as separate agencies.

Several tasks have also been moved from local governments to the central government: the employment of disabled and handicapped persons; the administration of a housing subsidy, transferred in 1994 from municipalities to the central government. In 1995 the only remaining municipal housing subsidy was transferred to the central government.

Deconcentration

Some minor modifications to the county administration were undertaken in the 1970s. A major change took place in 1991 when a series of regional offices of State agencies were discarded and some of their responsibilities were transferred to the State county administration. Another important case of decentralisation within the central government is the freeing of the universities from central control. The first step was to increase regional influence by appointing representatives of local government and other regional interests on the regional boards of the universities. This arrangement was discarded in the early 1980s. But in 1992 the National Board of Universities was abolished with the aim of increasing local autonomy.

A "free municipality" experiment was carried out between 1984 and 1991. The purpose of the experiment was to see what happened when a municipality did not have to follow certain State regulations. Exemptions were made by the government on request for participation from municipalities.

Thirty-eight municipalities and four county councils took part in the project. Around 300 applications were made to the government for exception from State regulations. About three-quarters of the applications received a positive response from the government. In many cases existing rules did not have to be changed – other actions were taken.

The experimental scheme presented problems on two main levels: the constitutionality of not treating all municipalities alike and what the experiment was to include. It soon became clear that the experiment was constitutionally possible. The overall purpose was defined as that of "exploring the possibility of substantially increasing local autonomy". Liberty for the municipality to alter its internal structure was an important part of the experiment. Exemptions from State regulations which impede the efficient conduct of municipal activities also was an important part. Development of procedures for better co-operation between municipalities and between municipal and central government agencies was important. The limits of the experiment were fundamental principles concerning the fair distribution of social services, protection of citizens' life and health, protection of vulnerable groups, security under the law and national economy.

In the education sector the experimental activities were aimed at more flexible State grants and greater liberty in the organisation of school work. In the planning and building sector the municipalities looked for simplification of existing rules toward the citizens. Other experimental activities in the health sector led to uniform charges to patients and medicine prescriptive rights for district nurses. Many other activities were performed in other sectors.

The final political evaluation of the experiment came in the autumn 1991. The government stated that the "free municipality" experiment had played an important part in the development and the renewal of local government activities. The government also stated that the experiment had stimulated a climate of change which had done a great deal to make it possible to introduce reforms in the school sector, in planning and building, etc.

The most important result of the project was the new Local Government Act (1992) which extended to all municipalities the right of the "free municipalities" to choose their own organisational structures.

Some old, powerful central agencies have been reduced heavily in size and their powers sharply curbed. This is the case of the National Board of Education and the National Board of Health and Welfare. Both deal with matters that have been decentralised to local governments. They used to have the role of authorisations, approving grants, prescriptions etc. They have now been deprived of most of their powers and their mission is best described as policy framing, based upon inspection and evaluation. These agencies have, however, acquired a completely new domain of powers. It has to do with inspections and approvals of privately owned centres for care and schools, which is a consequence of the spread of contracting-out and the use of vouchers.

Decentralisation

Over a period of time, the local government provision of services has grown tremendously. Growth has taken place in the traditional areas for local government service provision: schools, health care, old-age and child care. Responsibilities in these areas were transferred from central government to county councils and municipalities over a period starting in the 1960s. For instance, in the education sector the transfer of the high school system to municipalities and county councils was the first step of a process which ended in 1991 with the decentralisation of the primary, secondary and high school systems to municipalities. Wage negotiations for teachers (who are employed by municipalities) were also transferred from central government to the municipalities. Changes of responsibility in the health care sector followed a similar pattern : in the beginning of the 1980s county councils had complete responsibility for health care in Sweden until 1992 when municipalities were given increasing responsibility for long-term medical care of elderly and of handicapped, county councils retaining responsibilities for specialist medical care of these patients. During that same period, public transportation on a regional level was transferred from the central government to the county councils.

These changes follow the logic of an established division of responsibilities between national, regional and local governments. This logic is less evident in some other instances of changed responsibility. For example, municipalities have been given considerable responsibility for the inspection of local environmental problems, although the environment policy is in all other respects regarded as an (inter)national issue. The area of schools for juvenile delinquents has been transferred forth and back.

During the era of rapid expansion of the public sector as a whole (1960 and onwards) decentralisation was promoted by political ambitions to take government closer to the people in order to become more democratic. During that period few problems were recognised in connection with the decentralisation of service delivery. Equal treatment of citizens has for long been a competing value but could be said to have been taken care of through a far-reaching scheme of equalising the tax bases of different local communities.

Beginning in the 1980s and reinforced by the deep recession in the beginning of the 1990s a different view emerged. It is the view that government should operate more business-like. Stress is put on efficiency, service quality, client choice, contracting out and other market-like arrangements.

There are two other important views that help to explain the change of policy *vis-à-vis* local governments that evolved during the 1980s. The first is the need to slow down local government expansion in general. The second is the view that there ought to exist some contractual relationship between the tax-paying citizen and the service providing government. The contractual view on the public sector obviously has been inspired by similar views that called for more business-like operations.

The situation at the beginning of the 1990s is a situation representing different tendencies. One tendency is of decentralising more and more tasks of local governments – especially to the municipal level. Generally, the change of responsibilities have strengthened the traditional division of responsibilities between the national, regional and local governments and made it more logical in relation to the nature of the tasks. The decentralising tendency has been reinforced by liberating local governments from detailed regulation and matching grants. However, the combination of financial constraints and the widening and the growth of mandatory tasks have limited the area of local government discretion.

The other tendency is to make it possible for local governments to use different market mechanisms. Connected with this tendency is the new emphasis on citizens' rights.

3.2   The current debate

The system of local government may be viewed in two different perspectives. One is that local self-government is the foundation of political democracy and that as such it may not be questioned. The other is that local self-government is merely a practical way to supply public services. According to this perspective the central government decentralises whatever tasks and powers seem practical to municipalities or counties. Decentralisation is not forever, but may be suspended at any time. The latter view is supported by the proposition that 80 per cent of municipalities' and counties' activities (prior to the abolition of the many matching grants in 1993) could be said to be regulated, in some way or another, by the central government. The former view gains support from the fact that not all activities of local governments are mandatory in a formal sense and that obligations sometimes are not very specific.

It is interesting to note that up to now reduction of legislative controls and block grants go hand in hand. There is a case for interpreting legislative regulation and matching grants as substituting means of control. But they seem instead to be complementary. When one has been used, so has the other. When one has been discarded, so has the other. It is, however, too early to preclude the possibility of renewed regulation when the central government for some reason wishes to increase its control.

Today, local governments are at a cross-road. Reduction of control has taken great leaps forward and at the same time a new kind of regulation has been introduced. Deregulation is in line with a long-standing tradition. It rests not only upon the arguments of democracy and participation, but also on the arguments of efficient choice of inputs and adaptation to local needs.

There is at least one instance in which reducing central government control has aimed at creating competition. Formerly profit-based day-care centres were not eligible for central government grants. This is not so any longer. Otherwise, competition for the provision of local government services and citizens' freedom of choice has produced regulation of a new kind. Also, the framing of citizens' rights is a new way of regulating the activities of local governments. From the central government point of view reduction of controls has created an increased demand for following-up and assessment of local government activities. What will come out of this demand is not yet obvious, but may include new regulation in the future. There is a discussion on the grant system in favour of several block grants instead of only one. These block grants would be general grants per capita for different purposes, calculated on a per pupil, per child, per old-age person etc. basis. The present block grant is calculated in this way but amalgamated into one lump sum for each local government.

A debate is under way as to how activities at regional level should be organised in Sweden. Should the numbers of counties and county councils be reduced? How can the power of the regions be strengthened? Which decisions should be taken at national, regional and local level respectively? Should development issues, for example, be the responsibility of the State's regional bodies, or should they be dealt with by new popularly elected regional bodies? Certain changes are probably forthcoming, but they will not take place until there is agreement between the central government and the county councils on how the relevant bodies in each region should organise their activities. To this end a new distribution of regional political power will be tested in the counties of Kalmar, Gotland, Skåne and Jämtland between June 1997 and the end of the year 2002.

There is a growing need for collaboration between central and local government. Various forms for this collaboration are currently being developed. There are "Citizens' Service Centres" where the public can receive services from the State administration and municipalities, and also other services. The State administration and municipalities are also concluding reciprocal agreements on joint efforts to help unemployed young people. Moreover, there are pilot projects in which the State administration, municipalities and county councils are jointly financing such activities as rehabilitation of occupational-injury victims.

At local government level, disparities in services and charges are increasing. This is due to the greater freedom secured by the municipalities and county councils when detailed control has been removed, and also reflects local political priorities. But there is a limit to what is considered reasonable. Hitherto, the centre has noted disparities of this kind but taken no action to offset them. The measure now being adopted is aimed at improving central government monitoring of how service quality develops in different policy areas.

In some cases, the State has given the public statutory rights for which the municipality is obliged to be responsible. A citizen may, for example, bring a court action to claim a particular minimum allowance if he lacks a means of livelihood. This type of legislation is criticised by representatives of municipalities, on the grounds that courts of law should not take decisions that are fundamentally political. But there are strong arguments for, and a long tradition of, rights that can be upheld in court.

The early 1990s saw major changes in terms of using competition as a way of enhancing efficiency in public administration. In the sphere of local government, for example, ten per cent of child care is now provided by municipally contracted companies. Independent schools can be opened that are eligible for municipal grants. In such areas as communications and property management, large portions of activities are being run on a contracting basis with public financing. A debate is now in progress about matters such as enhancing public access to information about activities conducted on a contracting basis, evaluating whether democratic control is affected, and ascertaining whether there have been financial benefits.

A stronger emphasis is also being laid on the public's scope for choosing which municipal units are to provide services. People are free to select their own doctors, day nurseries, schools, etc., and this freedom is encouraging competition in municipal administration. In the public debate, the desire to give more power to the individual is expressed. Both democracy and efficiency are cited as reasons for such a development.

The public is also formulating demands for greater influence over activities. Swedish schools will, under the current Government education Bill, be permitted to set up governing boards on which parents and users form a majority. Several other measures aimed at the same purpose have been implemented previously. A hospital may, for example, be managed by a group of experts if the politicians are willing to waive their administrative decision-making right.

Substantial savings have been made in the public sector, and more savings are called for. Today, however, it is hardly feasible to find cost-cutting measures that have no external impact on activities.

How savings are to be achieved has, accordingly, become a political issue. The central government has opted primarily to save on direct transfers to individuals. Service activities like education and health care have not needed to save as much. The public debate is about the future financing of the public sector. One relevant issue in this connection is whether charges should be used more extensively.

Municipalities and county councils have secured considerable freedom to choose how they organise their own activities. This great freedom necessitates improved monitoring of activities, but there are shortcomings at present. Nation-wide statistics are lacking, and in many cases those that exist are subject to time lags. The quality and comparability of information inputs leave much to be desired. Nor can existing information on activities always be related to established national objectives. There is therefore no overall picture of how the savings implemented have affected activities and users.

If the division of functions between the central and local government is modified, there must be financial control to prevent costs being passed on to any party. However, this principle prompts many discussions on when such financial controls should be carried out, and on the size of the sums involved. Nevertheless, the formal situation is that the final decisions are taken by the government.

3.3 Driving forces

Decentralisation within the central government has mostly been justified with efficiency: savings of over-head staff, fewer levels of authority and speedier handling of cases, increased flexibility and adjustments to local demands and circumstances, exploitation of local knowledge of production, etc. Freeing the central level of tedious handling of cases would open up the possibility for long-term strategic thinking, development of management and management systems.

But there has also been an argument for increased citizens' influence and for increased democratic control. In some case of decentralisation various forms of citizens boards were created. A motive that is sometimes seen in this connection is the hope that decentralisation will bring about a renewal of service and the process of production. The most pronounced motive is, of course, that of democratic control. Local self-government is seen as a value in itself, one of the pinnacle of popular rule.

Other motives have been less explicitly stated, for example that the central government may rid itself of responsibilities without having to pay local governments or that the central government hands over the difficult task of down-sizing and activity to local governments instead of doing it itself.

The prerequisite for handing over new tasks to local governments has been that they should be capable of handling them. Before the reorganisation of the many small municipal governments to larger ones got started in the 1950s, it was deemed impossible to levy any new tasks upon them.

The merging of municipalities – from about 2 800 to 288 – and the growth of the number of municipal civil servants successively widened the platform for not only taking over new responsibilities but also for abandoning detailed control and supervision by central government. This has turned into a dynamic process. Those fields in which local governments from the outset have been active have experienced a tremendous increase in demand and have therefore grown. This has made local governments more competent to take on more responsibilities.

SWITZERLAND

1. INSTITUTIONS AND AUTHORITY

1.1 Structures

Description of levels

The Swiss Confederation is a federal State – with a total surface area of 41 300 km government:

- federal level;
- canton level (23 cantons, three of which are divided into demi-cantons, bringing the total to 26);
- municipal level (just under 3 000 municipalities in 1996).

The official name of the country, the Swiss Confederation, can lead to some confusion since it is in fact a federal State. In 1848, its constituent member States decided to avoid the disruption of changing the country's name, particularly since the German title *"Eidgenossenschaft"* has no exact equivalent in French.

The present system of government in Switzerland developed from the bottom up. The cantons were originally sovereign States and they first set up the Confederation on the crest of a revolutionary wave. When discussing administrative management in Switzerland it is important to bear in mind that unlike most States which have decentralised their governments from the top down, Switzerland developed its structures from the bottom up. Central government has never derived its legitimacy from a monarch, and the cantons derive theirs from the people and the democratic process. The country has no head of State as such, instead, it has a government council, although in the early days this was composed of no more than about ten secretaries. The cantons are sovereign States within the Confederation as defined in Article 3 of the Swiss Constitution "The cantons are sovereign so far as their sovereignty is not limited by the Federal Constitution...".

Cantons. In terms of population size, the cantons vary widely. For instance, Appenzell Inner Rhodes has a population of 14 000, whereas Zurich has a population of over one million. They vary in area as well: for example Bagnes, the largest municipality in Switzerland (in the Valais canton), covers an area larger than the entire canton of Zug.

Municipalities. In 1995 there was a total of 2 973 municipalities in Switzerland. Like the cantons, they vary enormously in size, population and resources (see table 1). But where they differ most is in their statutes. They are subject only to the law of the cantons, which are the intermediate level between the federal government and the municipalities. The statutes of the municipalities vary widely, depending on the history and influence of the cantons to which they belong. Those belonging to cantons which operate along the lines of the Germanic corporation model are larger, richer and more powerful; those belonging to cantons which have followed the French system are more numerous, smaller and less powerful.

Switzerland is unusual in that several types of "municipality" exist alongside each other within the same geographical boundaries in many of the cantons. First, there is the municipality proper – the political and geographical unit – and often (in twenty or so cantons), there is still a "Burgesses' municipality" consisting of local townspeople, as well. Then there are parish "municipalities" set up by residents of the same religious denomination (in twenty or so cantons). There are school "municipalities" in six or so cantons. The result is that some cantons in German-speaking Switzerland (Saint Gall, for example) have up to five types of "municipality", while in two cantons of French-speaking Switzerland (Geneva and Neuchâtel) there is only one type of municipality – the political unit. These "special-purpose" municipalities are often attached to a particular area. The executive officers of these bodies and the officers of the municipality proper are elected by local residents in separate elections.

Table 1. **Area and population of sub-national governments (1993)**

Number	Cantons and demi-cantons 26		Municipalities 2 912[1]	
	Area (km^2)	Population	Area (km^2)	Population
Maximum	7 105	1 179 044	87.97	365 043
Minimum	37	13 870		23

	Municipalities ranked by size of population[2]	
	Population	Number of municipalities
	under 100	204
	100-199	299
	200-499	717
	500-999	578
	1 000-1 999	502
	2 000-4 999	452
	5 000-9 999	159
	10 000 and over	110

1. Political unit only
2. 1990 figures for a total of 3 021 municipalities

Source: Banque de données sur les structures des administrations cantonales (BADAC), Institut des hautes études en administration publique (IDHEAP), 1995.

Some cantons have established "arrondissements" or "districts" (such as B*ezirke* and K*reise* in German-speaking Switzerland) forming an intermediate level between the canton and the municipalities. There are more than 200 districts throughout the country. Each is headed by a "Prefect" who is either elected by universal suffrage or appointed by the government.

Central government at sub-national levels

Switzerland has no official central government representation at canton or municipality level in the way that France's "Prefects" represent central government. This can be explained by the way in which government structures in Switzerland developed – from the bottom up – as previously mentioned. Since the cantons bear the main responsibility for the proper functioning of government, central government representation is considered unnecessary and largely irrelevant.

Central government is nonetheless a force through a number of laws which apply at canton level. The Federal Council is the federal organ responsible for supervising such legislation. However, the cantons may each incorporate federal legislation in different ways. Most federal laws that have to be implemented by the cantons require the introduction of enabling legislation, which must incorporate the administrative mechanisms provided for in federal laws into local administrative structures. Sometimes problems can arise, as there are important factors which have to be taken into consideration, such as: the degree of (de)centralisation between cantons and municipalities, which can vary a great deal; whether the laws are to be implemented by central government itself, by the municipalities, or even partly by the cantons and partly by the municipalities. Then, too, other criteria such as administrative procedures, appeals systems, and civil liability must be taken into account.

In addition Switzerland also has some decentralised federal authorities employing civil servants who, despite working outside the capital, are subject to federal statutes. This is the case mainly for its

Postal and Telecommunications services (PTT), the Swiss Federal Railways (CFF) and the Customs and Excise service. For administrative purposes these decentralised services are divided into different "circles" or districts usually run by a district office.

Creation, elimination and restructuring

The Swiss Confederation was formed by an alliance of sovereign cantons, in accordance with Articles 1 and 3 of the Federal Constitution of 1874. Although the sovereignty of the cantons is in fact limited, this provision sheds light on one fundamental aspect of Swiss federalism: the confederation originated with the cantons, not the other way around. Furthermore, under Article 5 of the Constitution, the Confederation guarantees the territory and sovereignty of the cantons.

The federal government therefore has no powers to create, abolish or restructure the cantons, quite the reverse – its role is to guarantee their sovereignty. The Jura crisis provides a good example of this. When the canton of Berne took constitutional steps to create a new canton (December 1969 amendment to the Constitution), the Confederation acted as referee and observer as well as guarantor of the legality of the process. The need to amend Article 1 of the Constitution and therefore to obtain the assent of the majority of the electorate and of the cantons, confirmed the Confederation's special role as *observer*. However, as the Jura case is still unresolved, many observers wish to see the Confederation more closely involved in the process.

The cantons also have sovereign powers over the statutes of the municipalities. They are concerned about the size of the municipalities, which are so small as to be barely self-sufficient. To remedy the situation they are encouraging municipalities to merge. In Thurgau, for instance, the government wishes to halve the number of municipalities. In Fribourg there is roughly one merger per year. In Switzerland as a whole, the number of municipalities fell from 3 205 in 1850 to 2 973 in 1995 (a reduction of only 7 per cent over a period of 150 years). However, unlike many other countries, neither the cantons nor the Confederation have been able to restructure the municipalities and turn them into larger, stronger administrative units. Switzerland remains, together with France, the country with the smallest municipalities in all of Europe.

To offset the small size of some municipalities, municipal associations have been set up. The need for co-operation has led to the establishment of various types of inter-municipal organisation. In the future, in some cantons, such organisations could form an intermediate level of government between the cantons and the municipalities. Fribourg's latest law on urban areas (entering into force on 1 January 1997) is one example of this trend.

Control bodies

Federal government exercises control over the actions of cantons through a system of prior approval. The constitutions of the cantons must have the assent of the Federal Assembly. Some laws passed by the cantons or certain of their provisions are subject to the approval of the federal government. To ensure that federal legislation is transposed into the law of the cantons, the latter are required to submit progress reports to the Federal Council and to its administration. Some laws even allow for inspectors to be sent to conduct inspections in the cantons. However, spot-checks of this type are very rare and are only ever used as a last resort.

As regards penalties in the event of failure to implement federal laws, there are many loopholes in the Constitution. In fact, no disciplinary action can be taken against the government of a canton or its staff; the threat of cuts in federal grants is never used and military intervention is the only measure that is provided for in extreme cases. The most effective sanction is still a Federal Council circular reminding cantons of their obligations and, on occasion, making public the state of progress on incorporating federal law into canton law. This suggests that the Swiss Confederation is coming closer towards the European Union's approach on implementing legislation than are some other European federal States.

We should add that the Federal Tribunal does, nonetheless, have powers to ensure the implementation of federal laws. However, these are limited to issuing administrative decisions, since court injunctions and orders of "mandamus" such as exist under Common Law systems do not exist in the Swiss Confederation.

The cantons supervise the actions of the municipalities through various authorities, including the Prefects (in a minority of cantons), the federal department responsible for the municipalities (generally the Home Affairs Department) and, ultimately, the cantonal government. Their supervisory powers are subject to judicial review by the Federal Tribunal. Unlike France, such controls are not confined to questions of law and *ultra vires*. Cantonal law may also provide for discretionary controls. Some cantons have made it possible to take disciplinary action against civil servants and even the chairmen of municipalities.

On budgetary matters, cantons have the power to conduct financial audits. In extreme circumstances, municipalities may be placed under administrative supervision, but this depends on the regulations applicable in the individual canton.

1.2 Powers

Nature of sub-national institutions

Cantons: Each canton has its own constitution, parliament, government, administration, courts and regulations, chiefly applicable to citizenship. Nevertheless, the sub-national institutions all have many features in common.

The cantons, like the Confederation itself, combine elements of direct democracy and representative democracy. On financial matters, for instance, some municipalities hold referenda on their budget and finances. These give the local population a say in important issues such as road and school building, or whether to set up a cantonal university.

In most of the cantons, the supreme legislature is the canton parliament, which is always a single-chamber assembly. It is generally known as the Grand Council (*Grand Conseil*, *Grosser Rat*, or *Gran Consiglio* in Ticino), sometimes as the *Kantonsrat* or the *Landrat* in some of the German-speaking cantons and as the *Parlement* in Jura. Usually it is elected for a four-year term by a form of proportional representation, except in Apenzell Inner and Outer Rhodes and Grisons, which have a majority voting system.

The canton parliaments are responsible for a number of functions in all fields of government. They pass cantonal laws and legislation to implement federal laws, approve the government budget and accounts, grant pardons, authorise naturalisation, and sometimes appoint magistrates. They can also form parliamentary commissions of enquiry (the PUK – *Parlamentarische Untersuchungs-kommissionen*). Nevertheless, they have to "share" these powers with the electorate of the canton to some extent, since there are many more institutions of direct democracy at cantonal than at federal level (legislative initiatives, referenda on finances or on administrative decisions).

Ticino and Zug have instituted proportional representation. Decisions by the canton government are only valid if voted by a majority of members, all with an equal vote. Each member heads a government department. The political accountability of the executive to parliament is limited, and it cannot be dismissed by a vote of censure. Some cantons have made provision in their constitutions for the dismissal of the government if a prescribed number of citizens call for a referendum. This ensures the independence of the cantons. There are no provisions for sanctions by the Confederation against a member of the canton government.

Executive and administrative powers in the cantons are vested in the State Council (*Conseil d'Etat*, *Conseil-executif*, *Gouvernement*, *Regierungsrat*, *Staatsrat*, *Standeskommission*, *Consiglio di Stato*) which is elected by the people by various majority voting systems for different periods of office, depending on the canton, but usually for a four-year term.

The State Council is organised along the same lines as the federal executive: its president changes every year (rotating presidency) and collegiality is the rule. The system is reminiscent of the Directory under the Second Republic in France. It is a non-hierarchical body and the ministries generally take it in turns to head the executive (except in Inner and Outer Rhodes). State Councils are composed of five to nine members (seven in over half of the cantons), each of whom heads one (or more) departments of the canton government. In 14 cantons, there are the same number of departments as "ministers"; in 12 there are more departments than ministers. In the vast majority of cantons, State Councillors are now full-time politicians unlike the case some decades ago, when many of them worked only part-time as Councillors. The president of the State Council, who changes each year as we have said, is nominated by the canton parliaments or the *Landsgemeinde*, a public assembly of all the electorate of the canton. As at federal level, most public functions are exercised by agencies directly responsible to the departments or by public corporations such as the cantonal banks.

The instruments of direct (or rather semi-direct) democracy vary from one canton to the next. In fact there are only limited federal requirements in this area, as the only rights accorded under Article 6 of the Federal Constitution are the right to a referendum on the constitution and the right to initiate amendments to the constitution if 50 per cent of the people so wish. In practice, the cantons are much more generous in the political rights they accord their populations. The constitutions of all of the cantons allow for referenda to be held to oppose laws, and for referenda on the canton's finances and budget as well as for citizens' initiatives to amend the constitution and to propose legislation (the latter does not apply at federal level), if enough signatures are collected – the percentage is much lower than 50 per cent, around 1 to 3 per cent. Some cantons even provide for the right to convene or dismiss an authority (cantonal parliament or government) although these provisions are of limited effect in practical terms.

The administration of justice, rules of procedure, rights and duties of lawyers and notaries, enforcement provisions, prisons, etc. also come within the jurisdiction of the cantons. This means that there are major disparities between them, although there are some common denominators: there are generally three levels of jurisdiction, for example. With the globalisation of trade, such disparities have prompted the cantons to sign a number of co-operation agreements (called *concordats*) on mutual assistance on legal matters and enforcement.

Today, almost all of the cantons have instituted administrative tribunals, with which the public can file appeals. But these tribunals are regulated by the constitution of the canton, not by federal law. This said, the administrative structures of the cantons were standardised recently thanks to the increasingly stringent federal legislation, which has now been implemented by the cantons, on the procedures and establishment of administrative tribunals. Furthermore, Article 6 of the European Convention on Human Rights has also had a pronounced effect on the cantonal appeals system.

The most well-known of all of the institutions at canton level are the *Landsgemeinde*. These still exist in the two Appenzell demi-cantons (Inner Rhodes and Outer Rhodes), the two Unterwalden demi-cantons (Obwalden and Nidwalden) and in Glarus canton. Contrary to a popular misconception, this people's assembly does not replace the canton parliament, it supplements it. Combining as it does constitutional and legislative powers, the *Landsgemeinde* gives the electorate a direct means of expression since it assembles all voters once a year to vote on the issues laid before it by the canton parliament. The role it plays varies with the size of the five cantons. In Obwalden and Nidwalden (only very recently in the latter) it simply provides a forum for debate, as voting by a show of hands is considered a violation of the secrecy of the ballot. However, despite the fact that some people are opposed to them and that the *Landsgemeinde* have long since been abandoned by three cantons in Central Switzerland (Zug in 1840, Schwytz in 1848 and Uri in 1928) it is an institution that enjoys wide popular support in the five cantons where it still exists.

Municipalities: Although, here again, there are differences between the cantons, municipalities generally comprise two main bodies: a legislature and an executive. Some also have a local judicial authority and some have intermediate bodies such as the Municipal Commission (*Gemeindekommission*) in Rural Basel and Saint Gall, for example, or an extended executive body (*Gemeinderatskommission*) as in Solothurn and Grisons.

In four out of five municipalities, the legislature, in accordance with the tradition of direct democracy, is composed of an assembly of the people known as the municipal assembly. This is the supreme authority of the municipality and it meets regularly. In larger municipalities – towns in particular – this body may be an elected assembly, called the General Council. Its members are elected by either proportional representation or majority voting systems.

The executive is generally a collegial body, called the *Gemeinderat* or *Stadtrat* in German-speaking Switzerland; *municipalité, conseil municipal, conseil communal* or *conseil administratif* in French-speaking Switzerland and the *municipio* in Ticino. The council consists of three to nine members elected by universal suffrage, usually for a term of four years. The mayor (*Syndic, Gemeindepräsident, Stadtpräsident, Stadtammann* or *Sindaco* depending on the canton) is, in theory, merely the *first among equals* and is designated by his or her peers, by the electorate, or by the legislature. The mayor does, however, play a more important role than the heads of the federal and cantonal executives in that he has special administrative and decision-making powers. Even in small municipalities this is often a full-time job.

Type and degree of autonomy

The different levels of government are independent in the exercise of their constitutional powers.

As sovereign States, the cantons exercise all those rights and powers which have not been delegated to the federal power (Article 3 of the Federal Constitution). They have powers to promulgate their own constitutions and legislation and over the administration of justice. As sovereign bodies, every canton has its own constitution which lays down the fundamental principles of government. They are all also free to set up an administrative tribunal or even an "ombudsman" (although only the Zurich Canton has an ombudsman at present).

In addition to deciding on the structure, procedures and responsibilities of the canton government, the cantons also organise their own internal structures. They decide on the structures of the municipalities, on the division of responsibilities between the cantons and the municipalities, and on regional powers, such as those of the Prefect in a few cantons.

The cantons have full jurisdiction over the main aspects of the structure and funding of the cantonal government, over procedural aspects and the terms of employment, pay and disciplinary sanctions that apply to civil servants and the administration. In other words, they are free to decide how far they will go with the introduction of new principles of administrative management. It should also be pointed out that the cantons are also completely free to opt for the privatisation of some areas of administrative management.

The restrictions on the cantons' organisational autonomy are limited and aim to guarantee the democratic exercise of power. The cantons must "ensure the exercise of political rights according to republican (representative or democratic) forms" (Article 6.2b of the Federal Constitution), and consequently are free to chose between the different forms of representative and direct democracy. The constitutions of the cantons must also be approved by the people and it must be possible to amend them when a majority of the people so requests. The purpose is to guarantee a certain degree of direct democracy, but in reality the cantons have been much more generous in the rights of initiative that they have accorded to citizens, which require far fewer votes than an outright majority.

While it is true that the legislative powers of the cantons have been circumscribed by federal legislation, even in the increasing number of spheres in which federal laws have been passed the cantons have retained powers to draft the relevant enabling legislation. This situation, true for 90 per cent of all federal laws, means that federal and cantonal legislation are closely interlinked.

The cantons also have extensive constitutional powers over financial matters. Their parliaments set taxes, pass the budget, approve the accounts, decide on borrowing and, subject to financial referenda, vote on expenditure. As a general rule one can say that expenditure and income are split between the Confederation, the cantons and the municipalities on a one-third-each basis.

The cantons determine what types of institutions the municipalities will have and their degree of autonomy. The Confederation's powers are now increasing at the expense of those of the cantons – a development that may well affect the municipalities. However, the Federal Tribunal guarantees all local powers (constitutional or other) provided that the municipalities enjoy considerable autonomy in the relevant sphere. This last provision is becoming very important as legislation is increasingly based on general rules and provisions, broad programmes or loose concepts, which leave the executive authorities quite a lot of discretion.

This said, the autonomy of the municipalities is purely formal. Its scope is not guaranteed at federal level, as it is in Germany's constitution, for example. It is the cantons that determine the extent of the autonomy enjoyed by their municipalities. This means that the cantons can also curtail that autonomy substantially or withdraw it altogether. The cantonal authorities are, however, required to obey the law and the Federal Tribunal is now assuming the role of the defender of municipal autonomy which is regarded as a fundamental, if unwritten, right.

The executive does not have the right to interfere with the autonomy of the municipalities unless there is constitutional or legal authority for so doing. The same safeguards apply to the implementation of federal and cantonal laws by the municipalities, inasmuch as some leeway is left to the latter. So, control mechanisms become necessary solely in cases where only limited autonomy has been left to the lower authority.

The degree of "centralisation" varies substantially from canton to canton. Briefly, one can say that municipalities in the German-speaking cantons and Grisons have more autonomy than those in the French-speaking cantons. In Bern, for instance, municipality staff account for 60 per cent of all public sector employees, as opposed to only 30 per cent in Vaud. As regards elections to municipal councils, some cantons have instituted standard ballot procedures while others allow more local variation.

However, municipal assemblies, in rural areas in particular, have extensive decision-making powers in budgetary and fiscal spheres and in matters including building and town-planning regulations, primary schools, and social assistance.

Nevertheless the cantons can restrict the actions of the municipalities. The methods used are: information gathering, withholding approval and direct intervention. Information is gathered mainly through reports drafted following inspections of municipal activities or in response to requests. Some decisions by the municipalities are subject to the approval of the relevant authority at canton level, principally regulations, accounts, loans and property transactions. Intervention can range from simply issuing a recommendation to carrying out a task in the name of the municipal authority when it fails to do so (direct administration).

The municipalities also have real fiscal powers which allow them to set taxes within a scale established at canton level as a percentage or by specific amounts. The borrowing capacity of the municipalities is subject to review by a federal commission.

Given the foregoing, it is clear that Switzerland's cantonal systems differ greatly in terms of the powers and responsibilities of the municipalities, inter-cantonal structures, geographical area and finances.

Where taxes are concerned, the Swiss system allows a great deal of importance to the political rights of its citizens. At federal level, taxes and maximum rates applicable are specified in the Constitution. Since a referendum is compulsory before any amendments can be made to the Constitution, amendments relating to types and rates of taxes are only adopted if they are voted by both a majority of cantons **and** a majority of voters. At canton level, referenda are also held on expenditures (financial referenda).

1.3 Responsibilities

The division of responsibilities among the municipalities, the cantons and the Confederation is guided by the subsidiarity principle. In fact, the cantons have ceded functions to federal authorities only as far as necessary to ensure their own survival and in order to ensure recognition as a sovereign State at the international level.

In the 150 years of its existence, the process of centralisation has been very slow in the Confederation. The electorate has put a brake on the transfer of functions. The governments of the cantons have often been ready to hand over some onerous and complex tasks to the Confederation, but the electorate has fiercely opposed such moves, for fear that democratic control would slip out of its hands.

Distribution of responsibilities

The division of responsibilities between the cantons and their municipalities varies considerably from canton to canton. Most public duties, however, are carried out by all three levels jointly. Institutional practice, as established by the 1874 Constitution, particularly in Article 3, has gradually resulted in an extremely complex division of responsibilities. The cantons have retained their sovereignty in the areas of police, culture, education, public health, roads and social services.

The division of responsibilities between the levels of government has its basis in the Federal Constitution. Article 3 in particular stipulates that every responsibility of the federal government must be stipulated in the constitution (as is the case with the constitutions of Germany and the United States, but not those of Canada and Belgium). This has major consequences since the Constitution has to be amended every time a new function is added. In other words the assent of the majority of the electorate and of the cantons has to be obtained. As a result, more than 100 amendments have been made to the Federal Constitution, almost all of which relate to the assignment of new responsibilities to federal government.

These amendments often run counter to citizens' initiatives. They contain concrete directives for the legislature and the Federal Council, directives which have usually been part of parliamentary party programmes. The logical conclusion is that the federal and democratic systems have gradually changed the very function of the Swiss Federal Constitution.

Furthermore, it should be pointed out that free trade is protected under the Federal Constitution. This is rarely the case in the constitutions of other States. The Swiss Constitution stipulates the extent to which the legislature can intervene in the market, i.e. the cyclical and protective measures that it may have to take when necessary. Any exceptions to the principle of free trade of course require an amendment to the Federal Constitution.

Although this is one of the most difficult areas of Swiss constitutional law, we must confine ourselves here to a brief outline of five broad functions that are either totally the responsibility of the cantons or totally the responsibility of federal government.

- First, areas in which the federal government has no powers whatsoever. These include public order, Church/State relations, public education, arts and culture, building legislation, civil engineering, public health, the police and fire services. Here, the cantons have the sole legislative power.

- Second, areas in which federal government functions mirror those of the cantons: for example, taxes, civil and criminal proceedings, and the organisation of the State. In these cases both the federal government and the cantons have the power to legislate.

- Third, areas in which federal government has concurrent legislative powers but which are limited to general provisions in some areas. For example, the federal government has the power to pass framework legislation on forestry, hunting and fishing, and regional development. The cantons still have the power to legislate in these areas but only on the detailed provisions.

- Fourth, areas in which the federal government has concurrent powers which are not limited to framework legislation: i.e. civil law, copyright, suits for debt and bankruptcy, criminal law, and labour law. The cantons' individual powers to legislate cease where the federal government has passed "comprehensive" legislation covering an issue. In the absence of such comprehensive legislation, the cantons retain limited powers to legislate where an issue has not been fully covered.

- Fifth, areas in which the federal government has exclusive legislative powers. These include national defence; customs and excise; railways; post, telegraph and telephone services; the minting of coins and issuing of banknotes; and foreign affairs. In all of these areas, the cantons have no powers.

With the current budget constraints, many Bills relating to the division of responsibilities between the public authorities, particularly where the responsibilities of the municipalities are concerned, are in the pipeline, although this is an area that is proving extremely difficult to manage. Hopes that had been raised by a federal Bill proposing a new division of functions between the federal and canton levels, have now been dashed.

Swiss federalism has three levels of government, but the separation of functions between the cantons and municipalities is not based on the optimisation principle. It has evolved as a result of historical, political, socio-cultural, ethnic and geographical factors. Consequently any proposals to modify the status quo are resisted, often regardless of the merits of the case. This makes it exceedingly difficult to decide what political level should be responsible for a new duty and, perhaps even more so, to transfer a duty normally carried out at one level to another.

After lengthy studies, which took over a hundred laws into account, a first draft Bill was presented in the form of framework legislation stipulating three lists of basic responsibilities to be attributed to municipalities and cantons. While the basis was technically sound, the cantons ultimately decided not to adopt the overall framework legislation, opting instead for sectoral changes. A first draft relating to ten or so cantonal laws was submitted in August 1995.

The federal government's main spheres of intervention are the traditional public services such as national defence, foreign affairs and social security. However, it should be noted that the cantons retain some very limited powers in all of these areas either through international treaties or in the implementation of legislation. The federal government also has substantial powers in agricultural and national transport matters.

The cantons have the main say in education and health matters. There is no federal minister for these areas, only federal offices at sub-ministerial level. The cantons are also responsible for the operation of the judiciary. Federal and cantonal laws are separate. The fundamental provisions of civil and criminal law are the same, while the administration of justice and associated rules of procedure are the responsibility of the cantons.

Important functions of the municipalities include environmental protection and water and energy supply, maintaining public order in the widest sense (municipal property, health and sanitation, construction, civil defence) and public transport. The duties delegated to the municipalities are determined by the cantons, except for those duties that have been delegated to them by federal government: registry duties, for example.

Mandatory, optional and shared responsibilities

Of the 160 areas of responsibility that have been identified in Switzerland, two-thirds are shared by the federal government. In accordance with the "executive federalism" principle, the federal authorities issue general regulations which are then implemented by the cantons. The result is a complex intermixing of the activities assigned to the different levels of government. The more extensive the services to be provided, the more complex the mix. In some essential areas, the federal government can take direct action. This applies, for example, to education. Although the cantons are chiefly responsible for education and the country's eight universities are therefore run by the cantons, the federal government has set up two federal polytechnics, more or less equivalent to universities, for technical studies.

The cantons are sometimes called upon to share their responsibilities with semi-public bodies. For example, although the cantons are theoretically the main authority for public health matters, the country's AIDS policy has been spear-headed by the semi-public sector on a purely national basis.

Among the services provided jointly by the cantons and the municipalities, in accordance with the executive federalism principle (this time at canton/municipal level), are the police, regional development and social services.

Some duties that have to be carried out by the municipalities, but on a scale that is beyond the means of the average municipality (for example the provision of schools for primary and secondary education, old people's homes, water and sewerage) have prompted the establishment of numerous municipal associations.

2. MANAGEMENT FUNCTIONS

2.1 Policy-making and co-ordination

Coherence, consultation and conflict resolution

Under the principle of executive federalism, federal laws are generally implemented by the cantons, except, of course, in the areas of responsibility reserved for the federal level. Consequently, federal legislation only has an indirect impact on the lives of citizens, although it plays a fundamental role. Moreover, some canton provisions for implementing federal laws must be approved by the federal government.

The cantons participate in the preparation of federal laws. The federal legislative procedure provides for a consultative phase, during which the cantons, as well as other partners, may express their views. Constitutional amendments, moreover, must be approved by the majority of cantons in addition to a majority of the popular vote. Nevertheless, the role played by cantons in the federal legislative decision-making process should not be overestimated. Before the cantons are consulted, committees of experts made up of numerous federal officials and representatives of major associations and interest groups have already done much to set priorities and determine the content of Bills.

The Council of States, the upper chamber of the federal parliament, is the body through which the cantons participate directly in the decisions of the Confederation. Each canton is equally represented within this Council, a system similar to that of the United States.

However, in the National Council, which is the lower chamber of the federal parliament, the cantons are only represented indirectly. The deputies of the National Council, who are nominated by political parties for popular election, reflect the political preferences of the moment and, above all, the differing interests of cantons.

There is also considerable co-operation at the administrative level. For example, there is close co-operation between chemists working in canton administrations, and between the heads of public education boards. However, there are no centralised institutions responsible for the general and continuing training of civil service staff as in France, nor is there an inter-cantonal training body. Each canton takes responsibility for training its own staff.

The federal government and the cantons co-operate actively in order to ensure the consensus without which the Swiss State could not survive. This co-operation has become even closer in recent years. When conflicts arise between the federal government and the cantons, there are no institutional means for settling such matters. Instead, close personal or official ties make it possible to settle conflicts through negotiation rather than through coercive measures.

What is more, the system of direct democracy gives such legitimacy to the decisions of the federal government and the cantons that they are normally accepted by all concerned. Popular initiatives at the national or canton level, or the referral of conflicts to popular vote, are also important means of solving conflicts through democratic decision-making.

By law, any contact between the federal government and municipalities must be preceded by consultations with the cantons.

Formal and informal mechanisms

In many cantons, the establishing of co-operation mechanisms between various levels of government is hindered by the very strong attachment to the principle of local autonomy. The lack of such mechanisms is all too evident in sectors in which there is a strong need for co-ordination, such as environmental protection or public transport.

The Federal Constitution lays down the procedures for co-operation between cantons in cases in which they need legal or military assistance, or if they must request the help of the police forces of other cantons to maintain law and order. Although the Constitution does not require them to do so, the cantons also co-operate in many other fields, such as transport, physical planning, energy, education, and finances. The main mechanisms for this co-operation are the Regional Conferences of Canton Governments; the National Conferences of the Directors of Canton Departments; and, since 1993, the Conference of Canton Governments, which brings together cantons at the highest level and whose secretariat is provided by the CH Foundation for Confederal Co-operation. However, the number of high-level inter-cantonal conferences is limited, as there are only five governmental conferences and 17 ministerial conferences. Conferences of officials below the ministerial level, though, are far more numerous.

The recently created Conference of Canton Directors is a new instrument for horizontal relations between cantons. There are also conferences of the directors of various canton departments in fields including education, public health, welfare, justice and police, and construction. All canton governments are collegial, like the Federal Council, and are therefore divided into a number of departments (types of "ministries" such as education, heath care, justice, and agriculture), each of which is headed by a councillor of State, who is a member of the canton government. These individuals meet in conferences that bring together all the heads of the same departments, such as the conferences of canton directors of health care, public education, justice and police, and finances. There are ten or so such conferences, which make it possible for cantons to harmonise their positions *vis-à-vis* the federal government.

Within canton governments, the scope of co-ordination mechanisms varies, primarily depending on the size of cantons. The cantons with the largest population and the strongest economy (Zurich, Bern or Vaud, for example) have large administrative staffs responsible in particular for questions of information and co-ordination.

As regards co-operation between municipalities, in addition to associations of municipalities, which have institutional status and legal personality, there are also agreements between municipalities and inter-municipal associations aimed at implementing common policies in specific fields, such as water supply, physical planning, environmental protection or sewerage. However, co-operation with other municipalities varies enormously from one canton to the next. If the canton of Bern is compared with the canton of Vaud, each of which has a similar number of municipalities (401 municipalities in the canton of Bern and 385 in the canton of Vaud), the former has 315 associations of municipalities as compared with 54 in the latter.

In addition to co-operating through associations governed by public law, municipalities also co-operate by establishing associations or companies governed by private law. For example, public limited liability companies have been created to manage waste disposal and electricity. However, it must not be forgotten that this co-operation among municipalities is the responsibility of the cantons and that legislation may therefore vary significantly from one canton to another.

2.2 Financial management

Sources of revenues

Each level of government (federal, canton, municipality) finances the expenditures necessary to carry out its respective responsibilities through tax revenues and through complementary sources of financing such as various other levies and transfers from one level to another. In theory, indirect taxation was originally the responsibility of the federal government, while income and wealth tax were reserved for sub-national levels, but in reality the federal government also levies direct taxes (advance taxes, direct federal tax), a portion of which is transferred to cantons. The municipalities also receive a portion of some canton tax receipts.

The financial transfers from the federal government to the cantons and from the cantons to the municipalities are a major source of revenue for sub-national levels of government. There has been no move to consolidate appropriations, and these transfers are still divided into a large number of specific appropriations. This type of contribution accounted for slightly less than half of the overall revenues of cantons and municipalities in 1995 (see Table 2).

The resources of municipalities vary from one canton to another. Their revenues derive mainly from taxes that are also levied at the canton level (with different levels and rates), such as income tax and wealth and inheritance tax. Municipalities also receive interest, annuities and dividends from State-owned enterprises, electricity companies and commercial or savings banks. All these revenues account for slightly less than two-thirds of their current receipts (see Table 3).

Table 2. **Main sources of revenue of cantons (1985, 1990, 1995)**
(in million of Swiss francs)

	1985 [1]	1990	1995
Taxes:			
income and wealth taxes	15 187	19 907	23 251
property and sales taxes	1 050	1 213	1 485
Patents and concessions	–	459	550
Income from property	–	1 268	1 914
Current account:			
contributions	–	5 400	7 482
shares, non-earmarked contributions	1 633	2 492	3 164
grants and indemnities	–	6 357	9 304
Capital account:			
grants	–	2 353	2 733
other capital receipts	–	112	739
TOTAL [2]	29 420	39 264	50 147

– Not available.
1. A new statistical definition was introduced in 1990.
2. Double counting between cantons not included in the total.
Source : Federal Administration of Finances.

Expenditure responsibilities

The federal government, the cantons and the municipalities each finance virtually equal shares of consolidated general government spending. As Table 4 shows, in 1993 the expenditures of cantons were greatest in the field of education, which accounted for between one-fourth and one-third of the total. Other expenditures that accounted for more than 10 per cent of the total were, in decreasing order, spending on health care, social services and transport.

Table 3. **Main sources of revenue of municipalities (1985, 1990, 1992)**
(in million of Swiss francs)

	1985 [1]	1990	1992
Current receipts:			
Taxes	8 538	14 763	15 912
Patents and concessions	–	70	122
Income from property	–	1 884	2 324
Shares and non-earmarked contributions	465	1 086	1 116
Contributions	–	6 571	8 104
Subventions	–	4 084	4 967
Capital receipts:			
Grants	–	1 331	1 174
Other capital receipts	–	392	529
TOTAL [2]	22 230	29 423	33 339

– Not available.
1. A new statistical definition was introduced in 1990.
2. Double counting between municipalities not included in the total.
Source: Federal Administration of Finances.

Table 4. **Expenditure of cantons (1985, 1990, 1993)**
(in million of Swiss francs)

	1985 [1]	1990	1993
General administration	1 463	2 211	2 670
Justice, police	2 421	3 368	4 113
National defence	478	540	487
Education	7 980	11 023	13 477
Culture, recreation	712	966	1 068
Health care	4 988	7 241	8 436
Social services	3 471	4 829	8 567
Transport	3 465	4 604	5 104
Environmental protection and physical planning	790	1 199	1 511
State-owned enterprises	1 546	2 567	3 437
Finances and taxes	1 846	2 569	3 524
TOTAL [2]	29 158	41 116	52 392

1. Figures adjusted in line with the new statistical definition of 1990.
2. Since 1990, without double counting between cantons.
Source: Federal Administration of Finances.

Municipal spending in the field of education was also the largest budget item, although it was proportionately smaller (approximately one-fourth of total spending), followed by health care and social services expenditures. Municipalities also differ from cantons in the relatively large amounts they spend on environmental protection and physical planning (see Table 5).

Balance between discretion and control

The autonomy of cantons can be seen clearly in the field of finances. Some two-thirds of Swiss general government expenditures and revenues are the responsibility of cantons and municipalities. However, these resources are distributed very unequally among cantons; for example, the expenditures of the canton of Zurich are nearly a hundred times greater than those of the canton of Appenzell Inner Rhodes. A federal system of equalisation is aimed at ensuring that cantons have the necessary resources to carry out their functions without imposing an excessive tax burden on their citizens. The first aspect of this equalisation of financing consists of providing cantons with a portion of federal revenues based on their financing capacity, which is reassessed every two years. The second aspect is the proportional adjustment of federal aid to the investments and current expenditures of canton authorities, again based on their financing capacity. Most cantons have their own internal systems of

Table 5. **Expenditure of municipalities (1985, 1990, 1992)**
(in millions of Swiss francs)

	1985	1990	1992
General administration	2 060	2 873	3 249
Justice, police	990	1 360	1 610
National defence	417	560	490
Education	4 962	6 673	8 213
Culture, recreation	1 427	1 988	2 141
Health care	3 217	4 826	5 958
Social services	2 110	3 365	4 209
Transport	2 056	2 642	2 952
Environmental protection and physical planning	2 377	2 782	3 234
State-owned enterprises	589	1 022	1 105
Finances and taxes	1 887	2 154	2 808
TOTAL [1]	22 089	30 245	35 968

1. Double counting between municipalities not included in the total.
Source: Federal Administration of Finances.

financing equalisation, which compensate for imbalances between municipalities. However, this practice is not found in French-speaking Switzerland, since there is no internal equalisation system in the cantons of Vaud or Geneva.

The level of transfers received by municipalities depends on their financing capacity and the interest shown by the federal government or the cantons in developing a specific service. It also varies depending on the overall number of programmes each municipality has. As a result, the largest transfers are mainly in fields such as education, health care or social services. Except for certain areas in which specific transfers are made, municipal financial decisions are generally not subject to supervision by other levels of government, other than the basic review of their legality and the auditing of accounts.

It should be emphasized that the powers of the federal government to levy direct taxes and capital gains taxes are limited in both time and amount since the Constitution imposes time limits as well as ceilings on the percentage rate of taxes. Thus, at the end of each decade the federal government is required to ask the people and the cantons to agree to new taxes. Swiss tradition requires that the federal government's proposal must lay down, firstly, that a portion of its revenues will be allocated to cantons; secondly, that there will be a balance between indirect taxes (which is in the interest of parties on the right) and direct taxes (in the interest of parties on the left); and, thirdly, that its power will be limited in time. In practice, this has the result of giving a right of veto to small cantons, which can use this to block the entire funding system to the detriment of large cantons.

The people's funding powers have a direct impact on the financing of Swiss government. The democratic control of the spending of cantons and municipalities prevents certain abuses sometimes found in countries with parliamentary systems. For example, a party in power will not be able to undertake ill-advised expenditures in order to try to remain in power at upcoming elections.

2.3 Performance management

Mechanisms

At the beginning of the 1980s (in 1982 in the canton of Ticino), reforms were implemented at different levels of government with a view to rationalising public spending and responding to requests from citizens for improved public services. In a number of cities and cantons, reforms are aimed at making the heads of the largest administrative units more accountable for their management. The goals set only concerned provision of services. A consolidated budget was also implemented on a trial basis in 1995. The following are some examples in this field:

- In the canton of Valais, a general process of reform of the public sector was launched in 1994, leading to a reduction in government jobs (the "Government 2000" project).

- In the canton of Bern, steps were taken to introduce practices in line with "new public management" (separation of administrative and policy functions, delegation of decision-making, greater accountability and monitoring, subcontracting of some services to the private sector).

- The canton of Zurich is trying to reform its social welfare and health care policy by setting up a system of agencies and of consolidated budgets.

- In 1995, the canton of Solothurn also undertook reforms; primarily aimed at reducing the size of the public sector (*Schlanker Staat* project).

- The city of Bern has also introduced pilot projects with a view to reorganising public services based on principles of new public management. These projects include taking into account user satisfaction in each service.

A number of other cities, such as Lucerne, Zurich or Winterthur, are preparing similar reforms. Moreover, it must be emphasized that since the beginning of the crisis in the early 1990s virtually all cantons have had to take steps to rationalise their administrations. The common features of these measures are the desire to develop agencies, to renew financial management practices by consolidating budgets and to modernise personnel management.

Quality standards

Improvement of quality is at the heart of the efforts being made to implement a new style of public management. Given the experimental nature of these projects, no quality standards have yet been issued, and this matter is still at the discussion phase.

2.4 Human resources management

Statutory distinctions: Compared to the other Member countries of the OECD, regulations governing civil servants are kept to a minimum in Switzerland. At the three levels of government, the public sector and private sector are in principle governed by separate legislation. The main differences concern the right to go on strike (see later), methods of recruitment, remuneration and methods of terminating contracts. The latter point is especially important, since the government cannot terminate a civil servant's contract under Swiss civil law governing work contracts; the terms of termination are laid down by public law and are highly favourable to civil servants. Currently, there is a trend towards eliminating the special status of civil servants in order to meet the needs of new public management.

Although the statutory rules governing the civil service vary from one canton to another, all legislation shares certain common features. The personnel employed in the civil service includes civil servants and other staff categories (permanent and temporary employees). Civil servants are generally appointed for four years, but in practice they are usually reappointed until they retire. The elimination of this four-year rule is being considered with a view to making personnel management even more flexible. As explained above, Switzerland has become concerned – albeit only recently – with keeping special regulations for civil servants to a strict minimum.

Civil servants do not have the right to go on strike, except in the canton of Jura. In some cantons teaching staff and some categories of government employees are selected by popular vote.

Despite the differences from one canton to another, there is generally very considerable autonomy in the field of human resource management. Even in the most centralised cantons, such as the canton of Geneva, municipalities are free to recruit and pay personnel as they see fit. For example, they are free to implement systems of merit pay (this option is currently being discussed in many cantons).

Table 6. **Structure of government employment by level of government (1985, 1991, 1995)**

	1985	1991	1995
Federal government [1]	133 009	138 918	131 810
Canton governments	148 806	162 198	158 137
Local governments	102 589	131 496	115 202
Other	46 472 [2]	14 518 [3]	22 094
TOTAL	430 876	447 130	427 243

1. Includes the Postal and Telecommunications Services and the National Railways.
2. Includes public corporations, public foundations, State-owned co-operatives and the Foreign Service.
3. Includes public corporations and official churches.

Source: Federal Office of Statistics, Bern.

Mobility: In Switzerland, civil servants are highly mobile, especially the most highly qualified among them. No level of government is considered to be significantly more prestigious than another, and as a result wage competition is the dominant means of attracting skilled staff. This is all the more true given that for many years economic prosperity let to a relative shortage of civil servants in Switzerland. Highly qualified civil servants have often held jobs in the various levels of government.

2.5 Management and regulatory reform

Some cantons have launched initiatives aimed at limiting the proliferation of regulations. This is an area in which it is difficult to draw general conclusions. In the canton of Vaud, for example, a "Deregulation Committee" was established, but was later renamed the "Re-regulation Committee". Its aim is first to reduce the number of regulations and then to improve their quality. This same canton is also endeavouring to rationalise the internal instructions of its administration.

3. TRENDS IN REDISTRIBUTING AUTHORITY ACROSS LEVELS OF GOVERNMENT

3.1 Evolving tendencies

Switzerland has been a federal State since 1848, and its fundamental principles have remained unchanged though, as in most federations, there has been a general trend towards centralisation. For example, the federal government has become involved in an increasingly broad range of fields, so that it is now nearly impossible for cantons to pass legislation without taking into account the provisions enacted at the national level. In addition, the social changes due to technological progress and the population's rising living standards and greater mobility have contributed to this centralising trend. In many fields, however, the federal government has only limited influence. For example, the relative share of sub-national levels of government in public spending has risen steadily over the past 40 years, while the federal government's share has declined. However, concerning the financial contributions of the federal government to cantons, it can be said that the federal government is increasingly interfering in canton matters through tied transfers (grants and refunds), which have admittedly increased. Finally, the share of federal government employees in general government employment is diminishing (it is slightly more than a quarter today, as compared with half at the beginning of the century).

This is due, among other reasons, to the general increase in the number of tasks performed by government, combined with the system of executive federalism. Since all levels of government have more tasks to perform, these are "theorised" (i.e. defined and legislated) at the federal level, but are still implemented at the canton level. This explains the relative increase in the number of civil servants at the canton level.

In addition, the system has become increasingly interdependent as shared responsibilities (concurrent or parallel) have increased. The overlapping of laws, funding and institutions is one of the major trends of Swiss federalism. Since the 19th century the federal government has progressively emerged as a powerful actor, but this has not prevented the cantons from continuing to exercise their government prerogatives.

There were attempts to renew Swiss federalism during the 1980s, and projects aimed at establishing a new distribution of responsibilities had already been proposed in the 1960s. The main goals of this movement were to improve co-operation between the federal government and the cantons, to achieve a better distribution of responsibilities and a more effective distribution of financing. But although many goals and proposals were set out, they ultimately came to nothing since the federal government and the cantons were unable to agree on a clear direction for reform. Despite the many proposals made, there was no substantial change in the distribution of responsibilities between the federal government and the cantons, which continue to operate as in the past.

This attempt at reform has been described as a "storm in a teacup". Nevertheless, the idea of eliminating overlapping functions is more timely than ever, especially since a new system of equalising financing is being introduced.

3.2   The current debate

Nevertheless, a comprehensive approach aimed at simplifying the Swiss system remains a timely subject, given the overlapping of responsibilities described above. A motion proposing a "renewal of federalism" has been tabled in the Federal Assembly (the Engler/Cottier motion). The overlapping of responsibilities could be eliminated as part of the complete revision of the Federal Constitution, which is currently under way, but this revision must remain formal in scope. Bearing in mind the interminable and ultimately fruitless discussions to which the 1977 project of constitutional revision gave rise, it is likely to be extremely difficult, if not impossible, to redesign the system. The fact of the matter is that the federal government and the cantons sometimes have very different interests. Most often, significant reforms can only be achieved if there is a consensus, given the constraints of the specific rules of Swiss democracy. The "double majority" system is a case in point, since a proposed referendum can only be passed if a majority of both voters *and* cantons vote in favour of it. This means that a minority is able to defeat a referendum. Voters representing a majority in the 12 least populated cantons amount to roughly 15 per cent of the total population, but this minority is sufficient to "block" a referendum.

The Swiss system is also characterised by its high level of decentralisation, which means that there must be effective co-ordination to achieve reforms. Moreover, it functions based on the principles of *executive federalism*, which means that the federal government is dependant on canton governments to implement federal measures and that canton authorities have considerable discretion in interpreting these measures.

The federal system can play an important role in government reform. The high level of decentralisation of government in Switzerland makes it possible to motivate judges, civil servants and even private individuals, who may be entrusted with important responsibilities. For example, individuals may participate in municipal commissions and contribute the personal knowledge and experience they have gained in the private sector. Civil servants at the municipal level are also in closer touch with citizens, making it possible to avoid to a great extent the risks of growing State supervision, which is seen by some as synonymous with the bureaucratisation of government. The driving force of this type of highly decentralised government is often, above all, the motivation of civil servants. Another asset of this federal system is that it permits stringent control of finances. It is normally easier to ensure the transparency of public finances at the municipality level than at the federal level. It may be argued that it is easier to undertake administrative reforms by beginning at the most local (i.e. municipal) level, since it can be more flexible than the federal level.

Within cantons, better co-operation among urban municipalities on the one hand, and between municipalities and cantons on the other, is sometimes presented as a way of dealing better with the problems shared now by all conurbations (drug addiction, and the environment, for example). However, the municipalities remain torn between their desire to solve these problems and the fear of losing their autonomy.

The idea of more mandatory horizontal co-operation between municipalities or cantons is also discussed as a way of requiring the financial participation of those cantons and municipalities that are "free-riders", i.e. that benefit from the policies implemented by their neighbours without having to bear the costs.

A major project is currently under consideration, although it is too early to say if it will produce results. It is aimed at completely redesigning the system of equalisation of financing between the federal government and the cantons, since the present system is far from clear and leads to unnecessary costs. In mid-1994, the Federal Council decided to undertake a process of reform. A working group composed of representatives of the federal government and the cantons was established jointly by the Federal Department of Finances and the Conference of Canton Directors of Finance. The following five "strategic" objectives were set by the Federal Council, aimed at guaranteeing the principle of subsidiarity and strengthening the financing capacity of cantons:

- Canton functions must in principle be financed by cantons, and federal functions by the federal government.

- When the services of one canton benefit a number of cantons (spillovers), these cantons must contribute to more appropriate (i.e. fair and balanced) joint financing by compensating other cantons for the costs incurred.

- In cases in which co-operation between the federal government and cantons is indispensable, each level must play the role it has been assigned so that tasks are carried out effectively. Such tasks should be performed using as few resources as possible by establishing appropriate financing mechanisms between the federal government and cantons.

- Federal grants based on financing capacity should be replaced by non-earmarked resources, some of which would be non-productive.

- Lastly, it is necessary to implement a politically manageable system of equalising resources among cantons, which is more effective and makes it possible to monitor disparities in the financing capacity of cantons.

In February 1996, the Working Group submitted a proposal for reform. It suggested that the overlapping of certain functions be eliminated to the greatest possible extent by assigning them either to the federal government or to the cantons alone. It anticipated that this would lead to the disappearance of numerous earmarked financial flows, which would be replaced by discretionary resources. In the fields in which a complete elimination of overlapping is impossible, the Working Group suggested a new and clear definition of the roles of each partner. This revised distribution of responsibilities should enable cantons to use their financial resources more freely, to make equalisation more effective as regards the fair redistribution of resources to the poorest cantons and to realise substantial savings.

A reform of the way in which the executive levels of governments operate also seems to be mooted with increasing frequency. This aims at making them less collegial by introducing some hierarchy to promote a more effective decision-making process.

3.3 Driving forces

Since Switzerland is governed in a collegial and decentralised manner, it is rather difficult to identify an overall policy impetus underlying different sectoral trends. Similarly, it is difficult to measure the impact of budgetary issues on the relationships between levels of government. Admittedly, there is a wish to control public spending in Switzerland (for example, it is estimated that better management of the federal taxation system would make it possible to realise annual savings of some 3 billion Swiss Francs), but the country's budgetary situation remains relatively enviable in comparison with many other countries.

In the future, reconciling the specificities of Swiss federalism with the emerging practices of "new public management" – if it was decided to implement them – might lead to significant administrative reforms both at the federal and sub-national levels.

TURKEY

1. INSTITUTIONS AND AUTHORITY

1.1 Structures

Description of levels

The total area of Turkey is 780 000 square kilometres and the total population in 1994 was 60 573 000. Central government is administered through a series of national departments and agencies; while at the sub-national level the Turkish Constitution envisages a dual system of government. One functions according to the principles of deconcentration (provinces), while local government comprises a decentralised system of municipalities and villages. There are thus three forms of local government in Turkey: Special Provincial Administrations; municipalities; and villages.

The country is divided into 79 provinces, each subdivided into a total of 847 districts. In addition to the provincial offices of central government departments, bodies known as Special Provincial Administrations (SPAs) function as a sort of local unit of government, carrying out local services beyond municipal boundaries as well as some special local services within the municipal boundaries. The creation of SPAs can be traced back to the late Ottoman period. They were established under the General Administration of Provinces Act in 1913, and defined as bodies assigned responsibility for diverse functions, particularly in the areas of health, education, public works and social security. Creation of a province is a necessary and sufficient condition for the creation of an SPA for that province.

The basic urban administrative units in Turkey are the 2 801 municipalities whose jurisdiction is limited to urban areas and to settlements of more than 2 000 inhabitants and all the districts irrespective of their population. Metropolitan municipalities have been set up in 15 largest cities in the country (Istanbul, Ankara, Izmir, Adana, Bursa, Gaziantep, Konya, Kayseri, Eskisehir, Erzurum, Mersin, Kocaeli, Diyarbakir, Samsun, Antalya), which account for nearly 43 per cent of the total urban population. In addition, 77 other urban centres have been included in the category of metropolitan government. As a result, three kinds of municipalities with widely varying powers, responsibilities and resources have been created in Turkey: "metropolitan municipalities", "district municipalities" (within metropolitan areas) and "municipalities" in other urban localities. Only about 83 municipalities have populations greater than 100 000, but their total population accounts for over two-thirds of all urban dwellers in Turkey. The local government system is therefore characterised by a large number of medium-sized and small urban centres and a relatively small number of larger settlements which have a disproportionate weight in Turkey's socio-political and economic life. In addition there are 35 324 villages in Turkey.

Central government at sub-national levels

Central authorities directly provide many essential urban services in Turkey either through field offices of relevant Ministries or via semi-autonomous central government bodies. Among the most important of these services are security and police (Ministry of the Interior); planning, curricula and staffing for educational institutions at all levels (Ministry of Education for primary and secondary levels, the Board of Higher Education for universities; various health services (Ministry of Health); museums and cultural facilities (Ministry of Culture and Tourism); major intercity expressways (Ministry of Public Works and Housing); major urban water supply and treatment projects (DSI, the State Hydraulic Works);

Table 1: **Area and population of sub-national governments (1995)**

Number	Provinces 79		Municipalities 2 801	
	Area (km^2)	Population	Area (km^2)	Population
Largest	38 257 (Konya)	7 309 109 (Istanbul)	n.a.	724 419 (Konak)
Smallest	100 (Yalova)	107 330 (Bayburt)	n.a.	683 (Dodurga)

Number of municipalities and population distribution	
Population size	Number of municipalities
up to 10 000	2 278
10 000-20 000	209
20 000-50 000	145
50 000-100 000	69
100 000-500 000	80
over 500 000	5
Metropolitan City	15

n.a.: not available.
Source: Ministry of the Interior.

all postal services (General Directorate of Posts), all telecommunications services (Türk Telecomunication A.S.); and, with a few exceptions, all electricity supply and distribution (TEAS: Turkish Electricity Production and Transmission Company and TEDAS: Turkish Electricity Distribution Company).

At the provincial level a Governor represents the State, the government and the ministries. He is appointed by the Council of Ministers and is responsible for maintaining order and public security in the province as head of the provincial security forces. The Governor is also responsible for maintaining and co-ordinating other services. He therefore oversees the operation of the provincial offices of national governmental bodies.

At the district level a sub-governor is appointed by a decree to be signed by the Minister of the Interior, the Prime Minister and the President of the Republic and has powers and responsibilities at district level corresponding to those of the Governor at provincial level.

Creation, elimination and restructuring

Creation and abolition of the provincial offices of any ministry is under the jurisdiction of the ministry concerned. The local government system is based on the 1982 Constitution which defines local authorities as public corporate bodies established to meet the common local needs of citizens of provinces, municipalities and villages.

The main mechanism of the voluntary form of inter-municipal co-operation and co-ordination in Turkey is municipal unions organised at different levels. As public bodies governed by by-laws, unions of municipalities enjoy the authority, powers and rights of municipalities.

Over the period 1970-1980 the municipalities started joining hands to establish associations and unions among themselves for the purpose of tackling problems which went beyond the boundaries of a single municipality and/or were beyond their capacity to solve. The rising demand of civil institutions for a say in decisions affecting urban structure and facilities prompted debate on a concept of local government extending beyond the efficient provision of services alone.

Control bodies

Central control and tutelage over local government in Turkey is exercised by the Ministry of the Interior through its General Directorate of Local Government. The directorate monitors local authority budgets and ensures that their expenditure is in conformity with current laws and procedures, and approves the overall staffing of local authorities. The administrative tutelage at the local level is vested in the provincial governors who report directly to the ministries. The Minister of the Interior has the power to suspend the councils and to dismiss the elected mayors temporarily, pending a judgement by the court, in cases where an investigation or prosecution has been initiated against them on the grounds of offences related to their duties. This is an exceptional power given to the Minister of the Interior.

Administrative courts consist of the Council of State and the Regional Administrative Courts. The Council of State has an important role to play as a consultative body within the framework of the law-making process. By reviewing "acts and proceedings" of the central and local authorities (at the instigation of private citizens as well as of public bodies), the administrative courts help to ensure the consistency and legality of public policies, decisions and regulations.

The Under-Secretariat of the Treasury and Foreign Trade is authorised to manage State domestic and foreign loans of relevance to local government and to approve or reject them, if they are subject to the guaranty of the Treasury.

1.2 Powers

Nature of sub-national institutions

The decision-making bodies of SPAs are Provincial General Assemblies, composed of representatives popularly elected every five years. SPAs are subject to the *de facto* control of the provincial governors who are heads of the assembly and whose ratification is required for all decisions and the budget. The budget must be sent to the Ministry of the Interior for ratification within 30 days.

The principal municipal bodies are common to district municipalities and ordinary municipalities, but metropolitan municipalities have a different structure designed to meet the requirements of metropolitan areas.

Non-metropolitan municipalities have three principal bodies:

- Mayor's Office;
- Municipal Council;
- Municipal Executive Committee.

According to the Constitution, the decision-making bodies of local authorities are to be elected by public ballot. Mayors are elected by public ballot every five years. Their offices constitute the municipal executive body and represents the municipal corporation. Though mayors stand for election as candidates of political parties, once elected they are obliged to resign from any administrative role in their parties. Mayors may also stand for election as independent candidates.

The members of the Municipal Council, the main decision-making body of the municipality, are also elected every five years. The number of municipal councillors varies from nine in the smallest areas to more than 55 in the largest, and the number can be even greater for metropolitan councils.

The Municipal Executive Committee, headed by the mayor, is both a decision-making and executive body, consisting of both elected and appointed members. The number of elected Council members may not exceed half of the number of appointed members and may not be less than two.

The metropolitan government structure consists of three main bodies:

- Metropolitan Mayor;
- Metropolitan Council;
- Metropolitan Executive Committee.

The Metropolitan Mayor is popularly elected every five years. He is chief executive and co-ordinator for the metropolitan area and represents the metropolitan government. He has power of veto over all decisions taken by the metropolitan and district municipal councils, which may, however, override this veto with a two-thirds majority vote.

The Metropolitan Council, the main decision-making body of a metropolitan area, is composed of the Metropolitan Mayor, district mayors, and one fifth of district municipal councillors. The council is elected for a five-year period. The Metropolitan Executive Committee, headed by the metropolitan mayor or a designated deputy, is both an executive and decision making body. Its members are the secretary-general of the metropolitan government, and the heads of the departments of urban planning and development, public works, finance, legal affairs, personnel and administration.

Turkey's 35 324 villages are governed by a popularly elected elder known as the *muhtar* and a council whose members are also popularly elected by all adult village residents. The *muhtar*, as chief village executive, not only represents his village and takes responsibility for carrying out local services, but also acts as the representative of central government for the locality.

A corresponding structure also exists in urban neighbourhoods, each of which elect their own *muhtar*, but he lacks the executive power of his rural equivalent and operates within a very limited framework. The main responsibilities of the author is to keep records of local inhabitants, and convey information about problems in his area to the relevant local or central administration.

In view of the potential capacity of the neighbourhood administrative system, various organisations are in the process of drawing up proposals designed to strengthen and empower neighbourhoods as a means of lessening the burden on local government and enhancing citizen participation in the local decision-making process.

Type and degree of autonomy

All municipalities in Turkey with the exception of the metropolitan municipalities have the same status under the law regardless of size. The 1930 Municipalities Act and various other related laws and regulations provide the legal and regulatory framework for municipal activities.

The Municipalities Act empowers municipalities with a broad competence for taking any and all necessary measures for the health, well-being and welfare of their inhabitants. In addition, the Act assigns 76 specific powers which can be divided into two major categories: service provision and regulatory powers. As corporate public legal entities, municipalities may carry out their responsibilities and establish enterprises and other bodies for such purposes within the limits of the law.

While the 1930 Act provides a broad power base to municipalities, local government has always been a secondary partner to central government. Not only can its structure and operation be changed, at whim, by parliament or cabinet decrees, but many areas of its powers overlap with those of the central authorities.

There has been a trend (at least at policy level) over the past ten years towards the empowerment of municipalities. The 1984 restructuring programme of the municipal system in Turkey, for example, has given municipalities the authority to collect certain taxes such as the property tax and to introduce a tax for solid waste collection. This process is far from complete, however, and in many areas the central government maintains significant powers of control and tutelage. For example municipalities can borrow money from both internal and external sources, but borrowing from internal sources over a certain percentage of their budget, and all external borrowings, are subject to central government approval.

Special Provincial Administrations and villages have very limited financial sources and small power base compared to municipalities. The SPAs are authorised to borrow, subject to a number of conditions. They are only allowed to borrow money to pay for projects in the fields of construction, health and educational services. If the loan does not amount to more than one-third of ordinary revenue, the authority may go ahead with the ratification of the Provincial General Assembly of a loan proposal put forward by the Governor. Loans in excess of this amount and not more than the authority's annual ordinary revenue require approval by the Council of Ministers and the Office of the President. Loans of any greater amount require the promulgation of special legislation by parliament.

1.3 Responsibilities

Distribution of responsibilities

The functional framework of municipalities was set by the Municipalities Act of 1930 which assigns a rather wide range of responsibilities to these local authorities. The major services for which municipalities are responsible according to the law are: roads and drainage, public transport, construction of social housing, fire protection, water supply and sanitation, solid waste collection and disposal, parks and other recreational facilities, clinics and welfare facilities, veterinary services, wholesale markets, slaughterhouses and cold storage. Among the major regulatory functions are the following: land use planning and development control, environmental health and pollution, conservation of areas of natural, cultural and historical value, price regulation and consumer protection.

There have been significant changes in local-level public needs and expectations and in the structure of urban settlements since the 1930s as a result of major socio-economic and technological developments. Certain municipal functions have become obsolete as a result. There has, therefore, been a significant re-evaluation and expansion of the scope of municipal activity to meet the rapidly changing needs of urban life. The most fundamental changes took place when the rapidly accelerating pace of urbanisation of the 1950s began to be reflected in an expansion of municipal functions. A law passed in 1950, for example, added the construction and provision of public housing, and another passed in the mid-1950s added urban planning and development to the list of required municipal functions. In the 1960s the scope of authority of the municipalities in regulating urban economic activities was expanded. In the 1970s, certain duties in the area of environmental protection were added.

From the mid-1970s onwards municipalities were no longer so willing to let the central government dictate their powers and responsibilities. They began to voice their wishes to expand into new areas of public service. For instance, the first major social housing projects were launched by municipalities at this time

Mandatory, optional and shared responsibilities

The 1984 Metropolitan Municipalities Act established the responsibilities and areas of action for metropolitan and district municipalities. According to the Act, metropolitan government's responsibilities can be summarised as follows:

- preparation of investment plans and programmes;
- preparation and implementation of master plans;
- construction and maintenance of major roads;
- traffic management (generally the responsibility of central government, but metropolitan governments have some duties specified by laws);
- building and operation of passenger and freight terminals;
- protection of environmental health;
- providing social, cultural and recreational services;
- establishment and operation of consumer product testing laboratories;
- location, construction and operation of cemeteries;
- selection of solid waste disposal sites and construction of treatment plants;
- naming and numbering of all public thoroughfares;
- construction and operation of wholesale markets and slaughterhouses;
- operation and co-ordination of municipal police and fire services;

- co-ordination of district municipal services in case of conflict among municipalities;
- implementation and co-ordination of city-scale joint ventures.

The 1984 Metropolitan Municipalities Act requires that all intra-city services be carried out in accordance with plans and programmes prepared by the metropolitan municipalities within the framework of the objectives of the National Development Plans prepared by the State Planning Organisation.

The district municipalities are responsible for all "basic" municipal services not specifically allocated to the metropolitan municipalities. As a result they share certain functions with the metropolitan municipalities. For example, whereas the production of master plans are the prerogative of the metropolitan municipalities, development plans, detailed plans and plan revisions are undertaken by both the metropolitan and district authorities. The metropolitan municipalities have responsibility for major roads and thoroughfares and the districts for local roads. Both are responsible for urban renewal. Sewerage and water systems are the function of the metropolitan authorities. The metropolitan municipality manages public transportation, whereas both authorities have responsibility for traffic control. Garbage collection is the responsibility of the districts as is the management of local parks, and cemeteries, whereas street cleaning is in the jurisdiction of the metropolitan municipality. Districts may engage in the construction and operation of wholesale markets and slaughterhouses and provide social, cultural and recreational services – as does the metropolitan municipality.

Village administrations are responsible for carrying out both obligatory and optional functions. Of the obligatory functions, services such as public health, housing, and education have become obsolete in practice, both on account of inadequate funding by central government and due to the fact that these services are provided by the relevant ministries, even if sporadically.

Optional services are defined as those which "assist in raising the quality of life in the village in line with modern standards". Examples include the construction of public laundries, public baths, market places and business premises, and providing recreational parkland.

The SPAs have been subject to many changes in their powers and responsibilities since their foundation. Apart from minor amendments (and a change of name in 1987), the original act of 1913 is still in force today. However, far more sweeping changes have come about indirectly. A high proportion of the powers and responsibilities of the SPAs have subsequently been transferred to various ministries or local authorities, and according to the principle by which more recent legislation overrides previous legislation in the event of contradiction, the scope of SPA powers and responsibilities has shrunk significantly, in practice.

2. MANAGEMENT FUNCTIONS

2.1 Policy-making and co-ordination

Coherence, consultation and conflict resolution

The State alone has general regulatory powers in Turkey. Policy-making, co-ordination and general regulatory arrangements for the various central government bodies with respect to the main issues concerning local government are the formal responsibility of the Council of Ministers. However a number of other governmental bodies play an important role at the central government level with respect to concrete issues of relevance to local government.

There are certain laws and regulations (especially those on environment and crisis management) which require that central government and its associated bodies consult with local governments in formulating and co-ordinating public policies. However, it is difficult to say that this requirement is always followed in practice.

The Ministry of the Interior is formally responsible for the legal framework of local government and for the exercise of central control and tutelage functions. Taxes and finances are handled by the Ministry of Finance; general policies on urbanisation as well as local main investments fall under the responsibility of the State Planning Organisation; financing and physical implementation of municipal infrastructure indirectly fall under the Ministry of Public Works and Settlement through the Iller Bank ("Bank of Local Authorities"), the State Hydraulic Works and Directorate of Highways. The Ministry of Tourism plays a leading role in areas of tourism in developing water and sanitation projects among others. The Ministry of Environment is also playing an increasing role in general anti-pollution efforts and in water and sanitation services.

Though no official comprehensive regional level of administration exists within the Turkish administrative system, a number of provinces are integrated for the purposes of co-ordination and the implementation of certain services administered by various State bodies. The State Hydraulic Works, the Highway Directorate, the National Electricity Generation and Transmission Company, the National Electricity Distribution Company, and the Iller Bank are among bodies which are organised on a regional basis and which may have a direct or indirect impact on local government.

The provincial governors have powers of control and co-ordination on behalf of the central government. They do so via a number of institutions, among the most prominent of which are the Provincial Co-ordination Commission, the Provincial Local Environmental Commission, the Provincial Administrative Commission and the Provincial Assembly.

Formal and informal mechanisms

A range of formal mechanisms and informal modes of co-operation and co-ordination exist within the Local government framework. The relatively large municipalities generally provide support to smaller municipalities or to villages in the form of technical personnel, and the periodic lending of machinery and equipment, etc. The metropolitan government structure initiated in 1984 introduced more formal means of inter-action and co-ordination between municipalities within a defined legal and administrative framework.

At the national level, municipalities are represented by the Turkish Municipal Association, which has a different and less structured organisation than that of the unions. There are also several unions of municipalities which also function at the regional level such as the Union of Municipalities in the Marmara Region, and the Union of Aegean Municipalities.

A number of "informal" policy-making and co-ordination mechanisms also operate between central and local government and among local authorities themselves. These include the activities of political parties, associations and unions, ad hoc committees or panels, training and development programmes, conferences and meetings.

2.2 Financial management

Budgets are drawn up on the basis of estimated income and expenditure on planned services and activities for the year. The funding provided by local government is not in the form of allocations, but can be spent as the local authorities see fit according to the principles outlined above. Donations and borrowing, however, are earmarked for specific projects.

Sources of revenue

In the past the revenues of local authorities have been inadequate to meet their needs. Municipal budget deficits were largely financed by the non-payment of social security taxes on the incomes of local employees, and through moratoria on municipal debts.

Several measures have, however, been taken since the early 1980s to improve the resource base of local authorities. The measures taken in 1984 in particular have led to a significant increase in the revenues of municipalities in absolute terms and as a share of the national budget. These changes emerged from a series of tax laws and government decisions that were passed in the early 1980s. As a result of these measures, municipal shares of national tax revenues were increased, municipalities were granted new forms of local revenue such as real estate tax and the taxation and fees systems of municipalities were rationalised. In addition, significant extra-budgetary funds were created to support local initiatives.

Revenue sources of the municipalities in Turkey can be grouped under the following headings:

- Allocations by central government, including:
  - shares of national tax revenues;
  - financial assistance by central government and other public agencies;
  - loans;
  - grants.
- Locally generated revenues, including:
  - local taxes;
  - fees and user charges;
  - contributions to infrastructural investments;
  - income from municipal assets;
  - revenues from entrepreneurial activities;
  - other income.

A more broadly based grouping of municipal revenues can be made on the basis of "tax revenues" and "non-tax revenues". Tax revenues have three main components: shares of national tax revenues; revenues under the general framework of the national and local taxation system [including taxes on Property (Real Estate), Petroleum Consumption, Advertisement, Electricity and Natural Gas Consumption, Fire Insurance and Environmental Cleaning]; and municipal fees derived from licenses and permits. Non-tax revenues on the other hand, pertain to specific municipal services and activities. These encompass user charges, revenues of institutions and enterprises managed by the municipality, profits of enterprises, revenues from municipal properties, wages, fines and other incomes.

In the case of metropolitan government, the situation differs in that metropolitan municipalities' revenues consist of:

- A share of the national tax revenues allocated to metropolitan and district municipalities on a per capita basis. This share was set by the Council of Ministers as 35 per cent for metropolitan governments and 65 per cent for district municipalities for 1986.
- A minimum of 3 per cent of the national taxes collected within the metropolitan areas. The Council of Ministers is empowered by the same law to increase this rate to 6 per cent. At present the rate is set at 5 per cent.
- Fifty per cent of the tax on energy and gas consumption.
- Twenty per cent of property taxes collected by the district municipalities within their boundaries.
- Loans, aid grants.
- User charges, contributions for infrastructural services.
- Real estate revenues, betterment taxes.

- Various local taxes, fees and charges levied on entertainment, games, sports, recreational, social and cultural facilities.
- Environmental cleaning taxes.
- Taxes on advertising.
- Other revenues.

Metropolitan Istanbul has, in addition, other potential revenue sources, such as those of the Istanbul Water and Sewerage Authority (ISKI), the Istanbul Transportation Authority (IETT), and the Bosphorus Authority. The other municipalities have similar organisations and authorities.

The revenues of Special Provincial Authorities consist mainly of a share allocated from national tax revenues. This share is set by Act 2380, and after various amendments currently stands at 1.7 per cent of total general budget tax revenues. This share is deposited at the Iller Bank, which transfers shares calculated on the basis of population to the SPA of each province.

Apart from this share of national tax revenues, the SPAs have their own tax revenues (port tax, rice tax, quarry taxes and dues, etc.). However, these constitute a very small share (around 1.5 per cent) of overall SPA revenues. SPAs also receive appropriation from the central budget in order to construct local school buildings, rural roads and other infrastructural investments such as village sewerage systems.

Revenues of village authorities derive from five sources laid down in the Villages Act. These are a "level" tax, community service tax, aid to servicemen's families, charges, and dues.

The "level" tax (*salma*) is a specific tax which is collected from villagers in order to provide local services which cannot be financed by the central government. The amount of the tax depends on the cost of the service involved. It was introduced as an exceptional source of funding at times when ordinary village revenue proved insufficient to pay for obligatory services and the monthly wages and annual remuneration for the *muhtar*, watchmen and others engaged in performing village services. However, since the central government has often failed to provide any or only inadequate assistance, the tax has become widely applied. The tax is means-adjusted, has a maximum level, and is payable either in cash, kind or community service (*imece*). Revenues raised from sources other than capitalisation and community service tax are negligible in practice.

The Iller Bank assists local government with financing major investments and with technical assistance in planning, implementation, and other technical aspects of their projects, and provides long-term loans within the framework of annual programmes.

Table 2. **Main revenue sources of sub-national governments (1985, 1990, 1992)**
(million TL)[1]

	1985 SPA [2]	1985 Municipalities	1990 SPA [2]	1990 Municipalities	1992 SPA [2]	1992 Municipalities
Tax revenues	34 469	359 944	456 089	4 394 133	1 170 408	13 066 805
Other revenues	72 639	187 483	1 439 593	2 077 385	5 081 076	8 487 602
TOTAL [3]	107 108	547 427	1 865 682	6 471 518	6 251 484	21 554 407

1. In 1985 $US1 = 517 TL; in 1990, 2 619 TL; and in 1992, 6 860 TL.
2. Special Provincial Administrations.
3. Total of rounded figures.

Source: Ministry of the Interior.

Expenditure responsibilities

As shown in table 3 there has been a substantial increase of expenditure since 1985 at both the provincial and municipal levels.

The Government has embarked upon a programme to set up a modern fiscal management system aimed at improving the management of its financial and budgetary operations.

Table 3. **Main expenditure patterns of sub-national governments (1985, 1990, 1992)**
(million TL)[1]

	1985 SPAs[2]	1985 Municipalities	1990 SPAs[2]	1990 Municipalities	1992 SPAs[2]	1992 Municipalities
Current expenditures	18 099	261 448	287 124	4 562 251	793 965	14 576 037
Investment expenditures	53 538	153 550	1 015 925	1 190 632	3 710 861	5 987 814
Transfer expenditures	17 216	83 979	239 736	1 220 418	741 626	5 810 828
TOTAL [3]	88 853	498 977	1 533 785	6 973 301	5 246 452	26 374 679

1. See Note 1, Table 2.
2. Special Provincial Administrations.
3. Total of rounded figures.

Source: Ministry of the Interior.

The objective of the Public Financial Management Project, financed by the World Bank, is to improve the efficiency and effectiveness of tax administration, expenditure and personnel management, and customs operations. The Public Expenditure and Personnel Management component of the project is aimed at strengthening public financial management by establishing a financial ledger system to be located in the Ministry of Finance.

As part of the fiscal reform process an integrated suite of modern computer-based information systems will be implemented to support the core expenditure management processes. It is expected that the implementation of these systems will improve the efficiency of public resource allocation and use.

Other reform initiatives such as modernising budgetary and accounting control procedures, include actions to strengthen budgetary discipline, increase delegation of budget execution responsibility to the spending agencies, delegate audit authority from the central to the provincial level of government and improve performance audit.

In the Tax Administration, central, regional and local tax agencies will be restructured, and an automated system and third party financial information system will be developed and implemented.

2.3 Performance Management

Performance management is still a very new concept for public sector bodies in Turkey, and examples of its application are rare. Both budgeting and control activities are based on "by the book" calculations where the only criterion is compliance with set forms and the law, ignoring any evaluation of real benefit in terms of performance when determining promotion and wage rises. Instead these are entirely automatic, based on periods dictated by legislation.

2.4 Human Resource Management

Statutory distinctions: The State Personnel Directorate is responsible for defining the principles governing the legal and financial status of public officers and for processing their applications. Both central and local government can employ three categories of personnel: civil servants, workers (permanent workers and temporary workers) and contract staff. Rights and responsibilities vary for each of the three categories, but they remain fixed for those in the same category whether employed by local or central government bodies.

Civil servants do not have the right to strike nor to engage in collective bargaining, and their promotion and pay rises are subject to the relevant articles of the Civil Servants Act. They are employed on the basis of results obtained in examinations. Those employed as workers have union rights, and collective bargaining is conducted at regular intervals between the unions and mayors in the case of local government, and between unions and the authorised central body in the case of central government. Hiring of workers takes place through the Employment Office, where candidates must be registered. Vacancies are filled by means of examinations held by the administration concerned. Even though all of the important positions such as experts, auditors, inspectors, etc. are filled after a series of examinations, it cannot be said that evaluation of the examination results of a few central government authorities and the local governments is based on sufficiently keen and objective criteria. Patronage counts in the hiring of personnel of every type at the local government level, especially during the election periods. The fact that salaries and wages fail to keep up with the high rate of inflation by a wide margin, the lack of job security, and the failure to introduce sufficient incentives for performance in the workplace are other significant factors which reduce efficiency and productivity.

One of the foremost obstacles to administrative development is the fact that central government approval is required for hiring civil servants in local government, and that civil servants at both local and central government level have identical rights and responsibilities. This means that local government structures lack the flexibility to respond to local conditions due to over-dependence on central authorities – leading to setbacks in performing many services.

Table 4 shows the distribution of personnel by level of government and underlines the high proportion employed in the central administration compared with the municipalities.

Table 4. **Public sector employment by level of government (1990, 1993, 1994)**

	1990	1993	1994
Central administration [1]	1 622 396	1 641 544	1 600 866
State economic enterprises [2]	688 594	577 835	519 598
Special Provincial Administrations	199 100	8 251	5 719
Municipalities [3]	n.a.	256 550	244 739
TOTAL	–	2 484 180	2 370 922

1. Personnel of establishments with general budgets, annexed budgets, autonomous budgets and budgetary funds are included. Personnel of the General Secretariat of the Presidency, the Grand National Assembly, the General Commandership of the Gendarmerie and military personnel are excluded.
2. Enterprises covered by the privatisation programme are excluded.
3. Including the personnel of metropolitan municipalities, but not of village administrations.
n.a. = not available
Source: State Personnel Presidency.

Mobility: The mobility of civil servants across levels of government is governed by the regulations in the State Personnel Law. There are no regulations that allow the transfer of other categories of personnel. The State Personnel Law (657) provides that personnel can be transferred to other public organisations, depending on their educational background, and specifies the minimum years of service for appointment to higher grades and to specific managerial posts. These provisions also apply to civil servants working in the State Economic Enterprises (SEEs). However, there are no statutory arrangements for the transfer of contracted personnel from one SEE to another SEE or a public organisation, or vice versa, except in cases of privatisation.

Transfer of personnel between organisations is generally in order to meet a need for experienced personnel (especially for managerial posts) or on individual request, so as to obtain better working (economic or social) conditions. Both organisations involved must give their consent. The transfer is realised only if there are any suitable positions and personnel transfer is not a widespread phenomenon in the public sector in Turkey.

3. TRENDS IN REDISTRIBUTING AUTHORITY ACROSS LEVELS OF GOVERNMENT

3.1 Evolving tendencies

In the 1850s, the first municipal institutions along western lines – modelled on the municipal structure of Paris at the time – were set up, starting with the largely non-Muslim district of Beyoglu in Istanbul. Most municipal institutions established during the latter half of the nineteenth century remained intact until the 1920s. With the establishment of the Turkish Republic in 1923 initiatives in the field of local government and municipal development in the modern "western" sense, whose early examples dated from the Ottoman period, gained momentum. In this context, the Villages Act concerning village administration was passed in 1924, and the Municipalities Act, one of the most successful pieces of legislation of the post-World War I era and one which is still in force, in 1930. This legislation, essentially a transfer of the French local government system to Turkey, opened up new vistas for Turkish municipalities, particularly in such fields as health, transportation, environmental control, consumer protection, and personnel training.

The 1930-50 period was marked by limited urbanisation and social change, and by a hierarchical-bureaucratic approach to local government. From the mid-1950s onwards, urban migration became a significant phenomenon, picking up speed in the 1960s and causing serious problems for local authorities. Despite the democratic and autonomous financial and administrative framework introduced by the 1961 Constitution, the failure to follow suit at the legislative and institutional level meant that municipalities found themselves without the authority, funding or institutions necessary for coping with rapidly increasing urban problems.

Until the 1970s local government in Turkey, both in theory and practice, was characterised by centralism; a structure based on a primarily administrative function; introversion; and passivity. Resourcefulness and innovation were virtually non-existent. Efforts to establish a comprehensive and modern link between local government and democracy emerged to a significant degree in 1973, when a new concept of municipal administration became a widely discussed issue on the social agenda for the first time. The military intervention of September 1980 brought this process to a temporary halt, since the military regime's centralist, bureaucratic, hierarchical, and authoritarian "restoration" attitude was opposed to every kind of autonomy.

After the restitution of an elected parliament in 1984 new legislation was introduced in the area of local government and tackled urban problems, focusing mainly on boosting municipal revenues and improving efficiency. Among the measures taken were the establishment of metropolitan municipalities; relative decentralisation of powers relating to urban development and planning; increases in local (particularly municipal) income; and growth in local investment.

These measures soon lost their impetus, however, and the problems which have faced local government for many years and which derive from both the authority vested in central government and the structure of local government itself, have not only continued but worsened.

3.2 The current debate

The devolution of development planning to municipalities after 1984 was presented as a step in the direction of decentralisation. It is not clear, however, to what extent the long years of debate and discussion in the fields of local government and city planning affected this decision. In view of the way in which the central government has used its powers over land reserved for recreation or of historic interest in the city (most of these areas now boast high-rise hotels today), it appears, however, that local and central government saw this change as an appropriate way of sharing out patronage of the city's economic potential. The transfer of such powers to local governments without the preconditions laid down in western countries (direct public control of development plans and the establishment of mechanisms to provide members of the public with the relevant technical information in the course of exercising this control) has meant that development plans have become open to extensive interference by property and land developers, (who are strongly represented on municipal councils). As a result urban green areas have been made available for development.

There is now a body of sentiment within central government circles which would like to partially reverse some of the process of decentralisation which has taken place and to increase central government powers.

An overview of the Republic since its establishment suggests that centralist and interventionist policies continue to hold sway at the national government level; that sporadic endeavours aimed at decentralisation have been limited to the administrative and functional level, without extending the necessary decision-making powers to give true freedom of action; and that the key steps required to empower local authorities, establish their autonomy and democratise them have not yet been taken. The specific plans and policies of the present government are presented in Annex 1 to this chapter.

3.3 Driving forces

The principal needs being faced today may be described as requiring more of the following:

- strategic approach and planning with a more decentralised and less interventionist policy and a more responsive attitude to divergent local circumstances;

- efficiency, and in particular the development of human and financial resource management, based on mechanisms aimed at transparency, accountability and control (political, administrative, legal and financial);

- institutional reforms including co-operation, co-ordination and joint ventures to deal with the large scale needs of major cities;

- participation by local citizens in government, a sense of "belonging" to the locality, and urban consciousness among local citizens;

- clear division of responsibilities for service provision in cities with both metropolitan and district municipalities;

- attention to the relationship between elected council members and permanent employees.

ANNEX 1:

PLANS AND POLICIES OF THE PRESENT GOVERNMENT

Legal arrangements concerning the sharing of tasks, authority, responsibility and resources between central and local administrations should be restructured and total revenues and the share of own revenues within total revenues should be increased with the aim of reorganising local administrations by placing emphasis on decentralisation.

Arrangements should be made for municipalities to produce a Master Plan which will determine investment priorities as well as increase service demand in municipalities and help to finance investment projects.

Mechanisms to provide co-ordination and co-operation between central administration and municipalities are required in terms of technology, standards and finance for implementation and of important municipal projects such as urban transport, solid waste, natural gas, geothermal energy, drinking water, and sewerage treatment.

Designing and implementing urban transportation plans is required in order to analyse the transportation requirements of metropolitan municipalities and to make them consistent with urban development plans.

An additional share of the general central budget tax revenue of the provinces is given to metropolitan municipalities. This will increase the demand from other municipalities to become metropolitan municipality, emphasize decentralisation and produce pseudo-metropolitan cities.

Objectives, principles and policies

It is estimated that by the year 2000 the municipal population will reach almost 85 per cent of the total population and the ratio of the population of metropolitan municipalities to the total population of municipalities will be 42 per cent.

Comprehensive restructuring of local administrations shall be undertaken in parallel with public administration reform.

Both central and local administrations will be re-structured based on the division of tasks and on co-ordination needs consistent with the principle of administrative "wholeness" and unity of structure.

With a view to increasing efficiency in service production, the rational use of resources, and performing public services in a decentralised framework, local administrations shall be strengthened by reorganising their structures and working methods.

In this context, studies shall be launched to encourage authority, responsibility and resource sharing between central and local administrations.

Those public services which become more effective and efficient when carried out by local administrations and meet common local needs shall be carried out by local administrations.

For this purpose, certain services provided by the central administration such as tourism, environment, culture, sports, rural and social services shall be made the responsibility of the local administration – starting from the Special Provincial Authorities and extending to others. This shall be applied to other sectors during the Plan period.

Local administrations, after performing the duties which are conferred upon them by law, shall be given authority to perform public duties of a local nature which are not prohibited nor given to other administrations by law.

Services required to be performed by the central administration in the interests of service integrity, service areas and for technological reasons shall be carried out by provincial authorities on a deconcentrated basis.

The dependency of local administrations on the central administration shall be reduced by providing regular and continuous income sources for them to provide public services and to do the necessary financial planning.

Resource planning, consistent with the sector and service planning, and involving both central and local administrations, shall be undertaken. Resources of a local nature shall be shifted to local authorities which shall perform their duties with their own resources.

In pricing local services, balance shall be established between costs and prices and those who benefit from the service shall pay the real cost of it.

In order to increase the own resources of local administrations, local councils shall be given authority to determine the rates and amounts of the taxes and charges to be collected, on the condition that minimum and maximum rates shall be determined by the central administration.

Budgeting and accounting systems of local administrations shall be developed; studies shall be undertaken to provide effective resource utilisation; and new models shall be constructed to meet service needs.

Units shall be created within local administrations charged with learning techniques, and making plans, programmes, budgets and financial analysis. Studies shall be started, aimed at adjusting budgeting and accounting systems so as to enable them to measure the services, determine alternative costs and conduct feasibility studies.

Unions of local administration shall be supported with a view to providing services concerning more than one local administration.

Studies shall be conducted in local administrations so as to ensure that staffing is appropriate to their need.

Arrangements shall be made to appoint professional officials in senior posts in the executive bodies of municipalities.

A Provincial Local Management Model and a District Local Management Model shall be designed and implemented. The Provincial Local Management Model (which shall involve local administration units within the province) shall plan the service needs and resources of the province; provide for co-operation and co-ordination between these units; and regularly perform public services. The District Local Management Model shall provide these same duties at the district level.

For the purpose of measuring effectiveness and efficiency and facilitating the supervision of local administrations, an information bank collecting data on local administrations shall be constituted based on regular, reliable and specific standards.

Sources: Government Programme; Seventh Five-year Development Plan (1996-2000).

UNITED KINGDOM

1. INSTITUTIONS AND AUTHORITY

1.1 Structures

The total area of the United Kingdom is 244 800 square kilometres and the total population in 1994 was 58 375 000. The United Kingdom is made up of England, Wales, Scotland and Northern Ireland.

The United Kingdom has a long tradition of democratic local self-government. Local authorities are statutory bodies created by Act of Parliament. This arises from the unitary nature of the British State and the sovereignty of Parliament. As creatures of statute local authorities are subject to the doctrine of *ultra vires* and must be able to adduce specific authority for their actions. There is no regional tier of government imposed between central government and local authorities although there are some differences in the arrangements for local government between the four parts of the United Kingdom.

The present system has its roots in the late nineteenth century, although local administration in one form or other goes back many centuries. The main provisions for the structure of local government in England are set out in the Local Government Act 1963 and the Local Government Act 1972, both as modified by the local Government Act 1992. For Wales the main provisions are contained in the 1972 Act and the Local Government (Wales) Act 1994. For Scotland the main provisions are contained in the Local Government (Scotland) Acts of 1973, 1975 and 1994. The position of Northern Ireland is different again and subject to change whilst important steps are being taken by government to reconcile deep divisions in that society.

In 1950 there were well over 1 600 local authorities of various types in England (outside of London). Today there are about 450. Similarly in Wales over the same period, the number has reduced from 180 to 22 and in Scotland from 430 to 32.

Description of levels

England: In London and the six main conurbations, there is a single tier of local government. In London it is provided by London boroughs and by the Corporation of the City of London (an historic body responsible for the administration of an area representing the ancient city of London). In the other six conurbations, it is provided by metropolitan district councils. Prior to the Local Government Review conducted under the Local Government Act of 1992, throughout the rest of England, local government was provided by two-tier system of local authorities, each being independent of the other: county councils and district councils. The functions of local government were divided between these two types of local authority. As a result of the Review, in certain areas the two-tier system is being replaced by a single-tier system of the kind found in the main conurbations. However, the two-tier system will continue in many areas. Outside of London and mostly in smaller towns and rural areas, parish councils and town councils provide minor local services.

Wales: Local government was until recently provided by a two-tier system of county and district councils. However, from 1 April 1996 a system of single-tier authorities was introduced throughout Wales. In addition there are a large number of community councils (which correspond to the parish councils in England).

Scotland: Local government on the mainland (as opposed to the Scottish Isles) was also provided at two levels by regional and district councils. However, from 1 April 1996 a system of single-tier authorities was also introduced throughout Scotland. In addition, there are community councils but these have no statutory functions.

Northern Ireland: All local government functions are provided at a single level by district councils.

Table 1: **Area and population of local governments (April 1996)**

	Number of units	Area (hectares) Smallest	Area (hectares) Largest	Population Smallest	Population Largest
England		38 100	831 297		
London boroughs including City of London	33			132 996 [1]	313 510
New single-tier authorities	14			90 409	374 300
County councils	35			304 694	1 541 547
Metropolitan district councils	36			152 091	961 041
District councils	274			24 068	270 493
Parish councils	8 200				
Wales					
New single-tier authorities	22			60 000	306 500
Community councils	733				
Scotland					
New single-tier authorities	32	6 515	2 578 379	48 000	625 000
Northern Ireland					
District councils	26			15 100	296 000

(1) excluding City of London
Source: Department of the Environment.

Central government at sub-national levels

Government is administered through a series of central departments and subsidiary organisations. One of the important strands of the reforms introduced by Margaret Thatcher in the 1980s has been the creation of Executive Agencies which in March 1996 totalled 112. These separate out the service delivery/implementation functions of these departments from the core responsibilities of policy-making and strategic direction.

An important exception to this pattern is the National Health Service which has been subject to major reforms, not least to deal with pressures on public spending, but it has not been given separate Agency status. Geographical decentralisation of government was not among the objectives of this reform.

Scotland, Wales and Northern Ireland are exceptions to this pattern of central departments. Each has a "national" department, bringing together most, but not all, domestic policy responsibilities, with its own Secretary of State in the Cabinet. Informal networks and a shared political agenda ensure a high degree of policy uniformity alongside some interesting variations in practice.

In England for many years several government departments have maintained offices in regional locations. However, in 1994 the Government Offices for the Regions (GOs) were formed by bringing together the former regional offices of four central departments: Environment, Trade and Industry, Employment and Transport. The GOs enable the policy and programmes of the central departments to be provided more effectively and efficiently by joint administration at the regional level of central departments' programmes. They provide a comprehensive and responsive service to local authorities, businesses and other bodies – via a single point of reference – fostering effective partnerships between central and local government, without increasing the power or cost of central government. The GOs remain part of the central government machinery but in a deconcentrated form.

Creation, elimination and restructuring

As described above, much restructuring has recently taken place as a result of local government reorganisation, producing a mix of single-tier and two-tier systems in England and the introduction of single-tier authorities in Scotland and Wales.

Local authorities in England and Wales set up various types of joint arrangements under Section 101 of the Local Government Act 1972. These include joint committees and lead authorities (where one authority provides the service for the other). They may also tender to provide services to each under the Local Authorities (Goods and Services) Act 1970. These provisions are often used, for example, for the joint purchase of supplies. A similar provision applies to Scotland.

Statutory joint authorities or joint boards (which consist of nominated representatives of the constituent local authorities and are financed by levying) are also responsible for some functions –e.g. waste disposal in London and some parts of the metropolitan counties. In some cases they may be established by the Secretary of State if voluntary joint arrangements are not satisfactory. The Local Government (Scotland) Act 1973 provides for joint committees.

The number of special purpose agencies (quangos) has also significantly increased (see Mandatory, optional and shared responsibilities).

Control bodies

Local authorities are not subject to general administrative supervision by an external body. They are accountable to their electorate and their actions are subject to challenge on the grounds of unlawfulness in the civil courts like those of any corporate body. But each local authority in England and Wales has an auditor appointed to it by the Audit Commission for Local Authorities and the National Health Service in England and Wales (the Audit Commission), which is independent of government. Auditors have responsibility both on matters of regularity and legality, and in relation to value for money. They have particular powers where there are issues concerning the legality of a local authority's expenditure, and they must be satisfied that a local authority's systems secure value for money. The auditor acts in his individual personal and professional capacity, independent of the Audit Commission – even when on its staff (see also section 2.3).

In Scotland, the responsibility for local authority audit functions rests with the Accounts Commission for Scotland. The functions of the Commission parallel those of the Audit Commission in England and Wales. From 1 April 1995, they are also responsible for the audit of National Health Service bodies.

Local authorities are required to prepare their accounts in a form and to a timetable set down in statutory regulations and a code of accounting practice. They are also required to publish performance information based on a standard set of measures. The auditor is required to comply with the code of audit practice which covers both regularity and value for money.

The Department of the Environment is the main central government department in England dealing with general matters affecting local government.

There are Ombudsmen to deal with complaints about central government and the National Health Service, and about local authorities. The Local Government Ombudsmen of England, Scotland and Wales are responsible for investigating complaints from members of the public who claim to have suffered injustice as a result of maladministration in local government. In Northern Ireland there is an Ombudsman who has powers to deal with complaints form people who have suffered injustice as a result of maladministration by local authorities or other public bodies.

1.2 Powers

Nature of sub-national institutions

In the United Kingdom Parliament is sovereign. The government of the day must secure the approval of Parliament to its legislative measures, including those affecting local government. There is a single Parliament for all four countries of the United Kingdom; debate continues about the possibilities of a measure of devolution to elected assemblies in Scotland and Wales. There used to be a separate elected body in Northern Ireland but that was dispensed with in the 1970s. The only other democratically elected bodies are local authorities. There is no written constitution.

The local authorities are the only locally elected executive bodies. There are no separately elected deliberative bodies. In addition to exercising functions, local authorities have arrangements for consulting their communities (e.g. public meetings) and they may appoint advisory committee with outside representation in respect of their service areas.

The United Kingdom does not have a tradition of directly elected mayors. The mayor or civic head, a ceremonial officer with no executive authority, is elected annually by councillors. Council leaders are indirectly elected. Typically, they are leaders of the majority party of the council, though coalition administrations are far from uncommon. Local authority elections almost never coincide with general elections and elections are held on a first past the post system (in multi-member districts in some cases), except in Northern Ireland where proportional representation is used. Most candidates run for election on a party ticket, and most councils are run on party lines. Voting is by secret-ballot.

County, district and parish councils consist of varying numbers of directly elected councillors. In general a county has between 60-100 members, a district, 50-80 and a parish 5-25 members. County councils and London boroughs hold elections of the whole council every 4 years. Metropolitan district council elections are held in three years out of every four (i.e. in each year without a county council election) with a third of the seats being subject to election. In Scotland each local authority is sub-divided into a number of smaller areas which is subject to periodic reviews by the Local Government Boundary Commission for Scotland. Elections to the new single-tier authorities are held every three years. Scottish community councils are representative bodies which have no statutory functions or powers. There is a parish meeting open to all electors in every parish.

A formal system exists within local authorities for delegating council functions to committees and sub-committees for the various service areas – e.g. education – where an authority has power to act. Arrangements can also be made to delegate functions to individual officers, although are exercised on behalf of the council as a whole. The delegation of council functions to committees- sub-committees and officers is governed by legislation. Certain committees are prerequisite e.g. social services, although others may be chosen. The committee system, used by all types of local authority, enables councillors to play a full part in the work of the authority. Councils have powers to make standing orders regulating the conduct of business on the council and its committees. Where members of a council are divided into political groups the councils are required to ensure the representation of the political groups on committees reflects the political make-up of the council (this is not a statutory requirement in Scotland, but most councils adhere to the principle). Service on local councils is voluntary and unsalaried although members can claim certain allowances. A councillor who has a financial interest in any matter coming before the council must normally disclose this interest.

Type and degree of autonomy

Parliament has the authority to alter local authority structure and operations. Local authorities must be able to adduce specific statutory authority for their actions and have only a limited power of general competence. They can be challenged for acting *ultra vires*.

Local authorities collect two local taxes. The council tax – introduced in 1993 – is set by the local authority and is levied on dwellings according to the value. There are discounts depending on the occupancy of the dwelling and there is also a rebate system for those on low incomes. The non-domestic rate is set by the government and is levied on industrial and commercial property according to value. The income from non-domestic rates is pooled nationally and then distributed to local authorities pro-rata to population as part of central government's grant equalisation system. Different arrangements apply in Northern Ireland.

1.3 Responsibilities

Distribution of responsibilities

Through the decades of growth of the welfare state, local government was given greater responsibilities for managing much public provision of services. It thus grew rapidly between the end of the Second World War and the fiscal crises of the 1970s. It now has become subject to scrutiny with the primary aim of reducing public expenditure. The way in which local authorities exercise their responsibilities is changing. In recent years local authorities' roles have been focusing on those of enabler, regulator, and community leader. The move towards the enabling role has been stimulated by the current framework in which local authorities now operate, i.e. the requirement to consider the use of competition in the delivery of services. The impact of Citizen's Charter principles, the publication of performance indicators, and the increasing need to obtain the best value from resources, encourages voluntary competitive tendering; and compulsory competitive tendering requires tendering for certain services before they can be carried out by the authorities' own internal staff. It is likely that local authorities will increasingly look to others to provide services, while themselves focusing on the levels of service which such providers should achieve and the strategic development of services.

The main areas of expenditure are education, personal social services, police, fire, road maintenance, recreational and cultural facilities, libraries and environmental services (refuse collection, street cleaning, etc.). The allocation of the main functions of local government between county councils and district councils is shown in the following chart. County councils in the main are responsible for functions which benefit from economies of scale or require strategic planning. District councils manage functions which have a more immediate impact on local people. Responsibility for some functions is shared, others (such as the promotion of economic development, museums, parks and licensing) are carried out by both tiers. Single-tier authorities – such as in Scotland and Wales, and in London and the main conurbations – carry out all the functions of local government. In such areas a few functions – such as the fire service and waste disposal – are exercised by joint authorities covering several borough or district areas. Parish and town councils have minor powers (such as the maintenance of village greens or the provision of community centres). They are also consulted by other authorities about the exercise of certain powers.

Distribution of principal functions of local authorities between county councils and district councils

County councils	District councils
Education and libraries	Housing
Fire and civil defence	Planning control and implementation
Highways and traffic	Recreation
Personal social services	Collection of local taxes
Strategic planning	Car parking – where delegated by county council
Consumer protection	Refuse collection
Waste disposal and recycling	Environmental health

The Northern Ireland Office has responsibility for planning, roads, water and sewerage. The district councils deal with environmental and a few other services. Area boards of the Northern Ireland Office administer education, libraries and personal social services.

In recent years, local authorities have lost responsibility for some functions. The Education Act 1993, for example, introduced important changes in local authority responsibilities for education. It provides further opting out of local authority control by schools and changes the role of local education authorities (polytechnic schools, for example, are now centrally funded). In other fields local authorities have gained more responsibility, (e.g. the co-ordination of services to the elderly and infirm and those at risk in the community). They are also community leaders within their areas, being well placed to bring together effective partnerships across a range of local activities, and have a role, for example, in relation to the quality of the built environment in their cities, towns and villages. They equally have such a role in the regeneration of local areas, leading broad partnerships with the private sector and voluntary organisations to compete for government funds.

Mandatory, optional and shared responsibilities

Local authorities in England and Wales may agree for any of their functions to be carried out on their behalf by another local authority; with the exception of education, the police, personal social services and national parks.

At the same time as altering the operations of local government, the Conservative governments have increased the number of special purpose agencies (quangos), that often operate at the local level and are usually subject to an appointed board nominated directly or indirectly by government ministers. These organisations are not subject to local democratic control and are dependent on government grants and central policy direction. As a measure of their scale it has been estimated that in 1992-93 they spent £46.65 billion of public money.

2. MANAGEMENT FUNCTIONS

2.1 Policy-making and co-ordination

Coherence, consultation and conflict resolution

In the United Kingdom successive governments have regarded a system of democratic local government as one of the essential features of the country's democratic society. Democratically elected local authorities are a focus of leadership in local communities, and can be an institution for undertaking regulatory work and securing the provision of services, particularly in those cases best administered at the local level in response to local needs and choices as expressed by local citizens through the democratic process. The specific responsibilities allocated to local authorities have changed from time to time, for example in response to changes in the nature of the services provided or the availability of other service providers.

Local government in the United Kingdom provides a very broad range of functions. It accounts for over 25 per cent of all public spending or about 10 per cent of GDP. As the nature of government and the activities of the State change, so do the nature and activities of local authorities. It may be appropriate for existing services to be provided in a new way, or new services may be developed to meet changes in society. So, for example, in the nineteenth century local government developed its role in public health services, and gas and electricity undertakings. Responsibility for health passed to the National Health Service in 1948. Gas and electricity undertakings were transferred to nationalised industries after the Second World War, and subsequently they have been transferred to the private sector.

In the case of certain services, decisions about their provisions have been brought closer to those affected by them by adopting mechanisms outside the traditional system of electing local councillors. For example, the introduction of locally managed budgets in local authority schools has given school governing bodies, on which parents are represented, control over many of the spending decisions affecting those schools. The option of grant-maintained status provides yet a further degree of self-government for schools. Self-governing status enables decisions to be taken which more closely respond to local needs. The options of tenants on local authority housing estates taking responsibility for the management of their homes from the local authority is another example of moving decision taking closer to the people affected by those decisions.

It can equally be the case that services once provided outside local governments might be more effectively delivered by local authorities alongside their other functions. An example is "care in the community", responsibility for which was transferred to local authorities in 1993. Changes in the functions of local authorities and other local bodies are likely to continue as society changes; these changes will also, rightly continue to attract debate about the features of different forms of control. Local government itself has a voice in this debate. In general, however, the Government has made it clear that local authorities will continue to have responsibility for a very broad range of services affecting the life and well-being of their communities.

At the same time there have been reforms to strengthen the position of users of local authority services. Citizens are entitled to attend local authority committee meetings at which decisions are taken and they are allowed to see the background documents on which those decisions are based. Under the Citizen's Charter citizens are entitled to know the level of services to which they are entitled and to know how to complain when things go wrong. Local authorities are also required to publish performance indicators for a range of activities so that their citizens are in a position to make judgements about the quality of services they are provided with in comparison to the price paid and make their voice heard if they are dissatisfied.

The framework within which local government operates ensures that it plays its part in meeting national aims and priorities. It provides the means for government to influence local authority expenditure, the allocation of resources to local authorities, the level of local taxation, and local authority management practices – thereby facilitating the achievement of national economic and competitiveness goals. It also provides for the government to specify national standards for certain services delivered locally, while at the same time giving local authorities discretion as to how those standards should be achieved in the light of local circumstances. Successive governments have had specific nation-wide objectives in relation to certain services for which local authorities are responsible. For example, the government has national aims and objectives in the fields of business deregulation and education, the achievement of which relies on local government playing its part.

Formal and informal mechanisms

Local people can exert influence on issues of concern to them, for example planning policies, through representation to their local councillor, through membership of parish or community councils or by making representations through relevant voluntary organisations, such as the Civic Trust. Members of the public may also express their view on planning issues. Local authorities are obliged to publicise the content of their plans and representations and objections may be made and must be considered.

Local authorities may co-operate freely with their counterparts overseas and many take advantage of this privilege. They may also belong to the International Association of Local Authorities.

Associations of local authorities are voluntary groupings covering all or most local authorities of a particular statutory category (e.g. the Association of District Councils) and are not controlled by legislation. In 1997 the existing national local authorities will combine to form a single Local Government Association.

2.2 Financial management

Sources of revenue

Income from charges is not an important part of most public service provision in the United Kingdom. For the most part funding comes from the Treasury. There is a principal of working within cash limited budgets which restricts freedom of manoeuvre and a variety of mechanisms, including market disciplines, have been introduced to work within this context. The exception to the complete dependence on Treasury funding from national taxation (without hypothecation) has traditionally been local government.

As already mentioned the system of local authority finance in England and Wales has recently been extensively reformed. As shown in Table 2, central government grants (earmarked and specific in roughly similar amounts) account for 60 per cent of total local authority revenues. The only tax levied by local authorities on its own behalf is the council tax. A local authority is required to set its council tax each year at a level which, taking account of all other sources of revenue income, will be sufficient to meet its estimated revenue expenditure for that year, including any capital expenditure to be charged to revenue. Theoretically an authority could set a zero tax. The council tax is levied on dwellings. The tax base is determined by the number of dwellings entered in the valuation list for the local authority's area and the number of discounts and exemptions awarded.

Government grant takes two forms; a grant for specific services which are earmarked for certain spending initiatives, or a more general revenue support grant distributed on the basis of standard spending assessment (SSA). This calculates for each authority the level of expenditure to provide a standard level of service taking into account the area's demographic, geographic and special characteristics and government public expenditure plans.

The non-domestic rates is essentially a property tax paid on the value of business premises by the owner or occupier. The amount of non-domestic rates payable in respect of a property each year is the product of a rate poundage (expressed as pence per pound) and the rateable value of the property calculated to reflect an annual rental value on the open market. The rate poundage is a uniform amount set each year by government and approved by the House of Commons, and the rateable values of properties are assessed by the Valuation Office, the last revaluation being in 1995. A local authority has limited discretion to grant relief from non-domestic rates to charities, non profit-making bodies promoting the general good through philanthropic and other activities, and businesses which would otherwise suffer hardship. Non-domestic rates are collected by local authorities and paid into a central pool run by central government, from which they are redistributed to local authorities. The amount of non-domestic rates which a local authority receives each year is its share from the national pool of all non-domestic rates collected – that share being *pro rata* to population.

Table 2. **Sources of local authority funding (1994)**[1]
(billions of pounds sterling)

	£	%
Exclusively local taxes	8.6	11.5
Fees and charges	4.7	6.3
Financial transfers:		
of which		
shared taxes (non-domestic rates)	13.0	17.4
earmarked grants	21.4	28.6
block grants	24.2	32.3
Other revenue	2.9	3.9
TOTAL	74.8	100.0

1. The data covers all local authorities, most of which are in the population range 100 000 to 500 000.
Source: Department of the Environment.

Expenditure responsibilities

Local authorities are responsible for about 25 per cent of total public spending. Local authority expenditure (current and capital) in 1994 was £76.5 billion. This represents 11 per cent of gross domestic product and 27 per cent of general government expenditure.

A continuing theme of the period has been the need to reduce, or at least contain, public expenditure. The Treasury has been in the driving seat. The way in which public spending seemed to be out of control in the 1970s has left its mark on the culture and approach of the Treasury. The Treasury maintains strategic controls which are necessary, for instance, for the conduct of macroeconomic policy.

During the 1980s the government introduced a series of measures in an attempt to make the activities of local government more efficient. Compulsory competitive tendering and changes in the administration of a series of key services were among the major reforms changing the way it operated. At the same time, financial controls, increased the dominion of central government. In the mid-1980s, central government grant aid provided less than 45 per cent of local government income. Local revenue is now reduced to around 15 per cent.

The main cause of the change in the ratio between local and centrally funded revenue have been increases in the level of central government grant and the introduction of a "national" non-domestic rating system where the rate of tax is set by central government rather than by local authorities. However, over recent years the proportion of local authority spending met by the locally determined council tax has increased slightly and central government intends that this trend should continue.

Within the council tax regime there is a system of council tax "capping". Where the government considers that a local authority's budget for a year is excessive, or represents an excessive increase over the previous year, this regime enables the Secretary of State to propose a maximum or "cap" to be set for that budget and requires the local authority to reduce its budget in conformity with that maximum and to make commensurate reductions in its council tax. Under the regime a maximum must either be agreed by the authority concerned or approved by the House of Commons.

A key part of the government's economic policy is concerned with the reduction of public expenditure and it is for this reason that the Government is determined that local authorities should play their part in restraining public expenditure to control inflation, to maintain economic progress, and to limit the burden of national and local taxation. The Government influences programmes by providing advice, paying specific grants or subsidies, approving programmes under certain legislation and controlling capital investment.

A report by the Audit Commission published in 1993 provides the results of a major study of standard spending assessments (SSAs). The report was undertaken at the request of the local authority associations using powers under Section 27 of the Local Government Finance Act 1982, which requires the Commission to prepare reports on the impact of legislation or directions or guidance given by ministers on economy, efficiency and effectiveness of local government services. Whereas in 1989/90 central government controlled less than half of local governments total income, in 1993/94 it distributed some 80 per cent of it, over $40 billion, through SSAs. The report concluded that the SSA system works quite well, but that the system is being used to set a "spending ceiling cap" for all local authorities. It was found that the complexity of the formulae tends to obscure decisions and who is responsible for making them. This in turn threatens clear lines of accountability which are essential as a basis for improving economy, efficiency and effectiveness.

2.3 Performance management

Mechanisms

Organisational performance has become more significant in terms of control and influence. Central government is increasingly requiring its component parts, as well as other public bodies and local government, to declare targets and publish performance measures.

Performance management is only one part of an increased emphasis which has been placed on management in general. Running through the various reforms have been a series of initiatives and incentives to steward scarce resources better and to develop sharper, leaner organisations.

The **Audit Commission** was established in 1983 to appoint and regulate external auditors of local authorities in England and Wales. In 1990 its responsibilities were extended to include the National Health Service. It aims to be a driving force in the improvement of public services. It promotes proper stewardship of public finances and helps those responsible for public services to achieve economy, efficiency and effectiveness. A small central staff carry out national value-for-money studies and provide support for auditors. About 40 per cent of the Commission's work, including 30 per cent of the audits, is carried out by external contractors. District Audit, the Commission's own auditing service, has offices across England and Wales. The Commission is financed through audit fees and operates independently of the government. It is a Non-Departmental Public Body sponsored by the Department of the

Environment and the Welsh Office. It has up to 20 members drawn from – but not representing – a range of backgrounds including industry, health services, local government, trade unions and accountancy.

The Audit Commission can and does provide advice for auditors; though it cannot instruct it can replace auditors who fail to follow the Code of Audit Practice. The Commission and its auditors can and do suggest ways in which value for money can be improved. They cannot determine local policy, nor force audited bodies to save money - local authorities are responsible to their local electors and health bodies to the Secretary of State for Health for how money is spent and assessing local needs and priorities.

In its audit of local authority accounts, the Audit Commission begins with an overview to identify strengths and weaknesses. If this suggests that arrangements are satisfactory, then the audit will be concluded. If any potential weaknesses are identified then, more detailed work is carried out.

Under one of the first initiatives inspired by the Citizen's Charter, the Audit Commission was given a legal duty to draw up each year a list of indicators measuring the performance of local government services. Councils are obliged to measure and report their own performance against these indicators. These results must be published in a local newspaper within nine months and the Commission then publishes comparable results nationally. This was done for the first time in March 1995, when comparisons for the year 1993/94 were published.

The Audit Commission produces a national publication of local authority indicators which compares authorities' performance with each other and with previous years. These indicators, which are refined annually, are proving to be an invaluable tool in improving council services. Year-on-year comparisons, in particular, help local people to see whether their council's performance has deteriorated.

Performance indicators have been drawn up for each main council service, consulting widely each summer on proposed changes to the indicators. The indicators cover different aspects of performance:

- the level of service provided – e.g. the proportion of three-and four-year-olds with a school place;
- efficiency – e.g. the average time taken to re-let a council home;
- effectiveness – e.g. the proportion of council tax that has been collected;
- cost – e.g. the amount spent per head of population on the libraries service;
- quality – e.g. the comprehensives of the rubbish collection service measured against a checklist; and
- performance against the council's own targets – e.g. performance against locally set targets for answering letters and telephone calls.

Although each council is developing its own style of reports, effective performance reports will include the following features:

- A presentation of the indicators, distinguishing those which are prescribed by the Audit Commission from those which are the council's own indicators. Reports should also highlight which, if any, of the council's own indicators are intended for publication.
- Names of the officers responsible for the achievement of the reported performance levels.
- Year-on-year comparisons between different periods of the year.
- Comparisons with a group of similar councils for the Audit Commission indicators and for the council's own indicators (where these are collected on a like-for-like basis by other councils)/
- Officers' analysis of the reasons for differences in performance between similar authorities.

- Targets for performance indicators committing the council to achieving a specified future level of performance.

Quality standards

Central government is committed to the Citizen's Charter to define clear standards of service for users of public services and a clearer definition of output targets for public sector organisations. There are currently now 40 main charters, covering all the key public services, which set out the standards of service people can expect to receive. In addition, there are now many thousands of local charters covering local service providers, such as doctors, police forces and fire services. In the early days of the Charter, standards tended to be set by service providers themselves. Increasingly, however, as national charters are drawn up, the public are invited to help set standards, by determining the priorities and targets that are important to them.

2.4 Human resource management

Statutory distinctions: In the United Kingdom, there is in no sense a single public service. A clear division exists between the political and administrative regimes of national and sub-national governments. There is a national civil service which is about servicing national government and its central institutions; and sub-national organisations, local government and the National Health Service which have their own administrative cadres and career structures.

The creation of Executive Agencies has increased the potential for differentiation within the Civil Service, as first the larger agencies and departments and subsequently all of them are being given the freedom – within the overall Civil Service framework – to set their own human resource strategies and policies. Issues about retaining a "corporate identity" were recognised by the government in its Continuity and Change measures, such as the setting up of a wider Senior Civil Service and the promulgation of the Civil Service Code.

Table 3. **Public sector employment (1980, 1985, 1992, 1995)**
(full-time equivalents, mid-year figures)

	1980	1985	1992	1995
Central government:	2 199 000	2 147 000	1 779 000	1 020 000
Civil service	703 000	599 000	573 000	512 000
National Health Service	1 001 000	1 030 000	700 000	80 000
Armed forces	323 000	326 000	290 000	230 000
Other	172 000	192 000	216 000	198 000
Local government:	2 343 000	2 325 000	2 257 000	2 040 000
Education	1 087 000	1 021 000	970 000	807 000
Social service	235 000	256 000	285 000	295 000
Construction	146 000	125 000	97 000	82 000
Police	176 000	182 000	199 000	202 000
Other	699 000	741 000	706 000	654 000
TOTAL general government	4 542 000	4 472 000	4 036 000	3 060 000
Public corporations:	2 007 000	1 236 000	808 000	1 302 000
Nationalised industries	1 785 000	1 118 000	452 000	352 000
NHS Trusts	-	-	252 000	876 000
Other	222 000	118 000	104 000	74 000
TOTAL public sector	6 549 000	5 708 000	4 844 000	4 362 000

Source: *Economic Trends No. 508, February 1996.*

Managerial autonomy: One of the characteristics of human resource management during the last decade has been the new emphasis on performance management. Within the core civil service, for instance, pay increases are dependent upon individuals' performance. Paying more attention to the effective utilisation of people and monitoring/reviewing their contribution has become part of public service management. Individual performance management is however a matter for individual organisations and not a tool of central control.

Recently there has been an increasing trend to delegate personnel management responsibilities to departments and line management in the core Civil Service, as well as to the Executive Agencies. For example, from 1 April 1996 there is no longer any centrally determined basis for civil service pay and grading, except for the 3 000 or so members of the Senior Civil Service. The Office of Public Service retains an interest in strategic issues of Civil Service employment, including the number of civil servants.

In the plethora of other public bodies, including the National Health Service, there is a broad spectrum of practice. Given the proportion of expenditure tied up in staffing budgets, there is constant downward pressure on staff numbers and an interest in pay levels. In general there has been a move away from tight national pay arrangements.

In local government, each council is the employer of its staff and thus free to determine its own pattern of human resource management. Most, but not all, local authorities across the United Kingdom, however, continue to maintain a voluntary national collective bargaining system. This both negotiates national pay scales and defines a grading structure. There is flexibility within this to adjust to local labour markets. Despite some signs of willingness to determine or negotiate pay locally, more than 90 per cent of local authorities stand by the collective arrangements.

Mobility: The public service in the United Kingdom does not experience a large amount of movement between sectors and levels. Convention, and a variety of inhibitions to inter-organisational career patterns, tend to reinforce rigid boundaries. Low levels of movement weaken opportunities to assist policy coherence and co-ordination and reduce a convenient means of enmeshing the different parts of the governmental system. However, both central government and local government take steps to encourage exchanges and secondments between sectors.

Similarly, although many politicians start their political career in local government (the only other part of the governmental system with representative democracy) there is no convention of dual mandates. Election to the national Parliament leads to expected resignation from the local council.

2.5 Regulatory management and reform

National policies about "rolling back the State" have marched hand-in-hand with new regulatory regimes in the United Kingdom, particularly in the utility sector, where independent regulators have been appointed to provide safeguards where suppliers still retain market dominance. These regulators have also been given certain monitoring powers.

The United Kingdom has a strong tradition of local government through which substantial regulatory authority is wielded. Local authorities regulate directly and enforce many regulations established in national departments. They employ, for example, 6 000 environmental health inspectors. They also influence business expansion and development through extensive planning and licensing authorities. Due to the key regulatory role of local governments, a number of the reform activities carried out under the deregulation initiative have targeted local governments.

A major reform of local legislation occurred in the 1970s, when the Local Government Act of 1972 set in process a gradual repeal of outdated laws. By 1986, the number of local acts had been reduced from over 1 000 to 50.

Under the Deregulation Initiative, a review of local regulations, particularly licensing and certification requirements and systems, was begun in the 1980s. Working with local government associations, the Enterprise and Deregulation Unit (EDU), the Home Office, and other departments encouraged local governments to simplify procedures and reduce delays. An experiment with local "one-stop-shops" began in 1988.

Attention to local government regulation has increased since 1991. According to the Department of Trade and Industry, "local authorities carry out a wide range of regulatory functions which are likely to increase in the 1990s as a result of major new regulatory requirements and as public expectations about the standards of business behaviour and the quality of life continue to rise".

In 1991, work began on a code of good regulatory practices to improve co-ordination, communication, consultation, and understanding of regulatory impacts at the local level. In 1992, experimental Local Partnership Agreements were begun, in which local authorities and local businesses agreed on lines of communication, consultation, complaint/appeal procedures, and monitoring of standards by businesses. In 1996 the local authority associations published a good practice guide to the enforcement of regulations.

Since 1992 the number of Local Business Partnerships has increased to 60 with many more being developed. These have proved to be an effective mechanism for promoting dialogue between local enforcement organisations and business with the objective of assisting compliance with regulations.

With the increasing need for local businesses to be competitive in a global market, local authorities keep under review the impact which their regulatory role has on local business and enterprise. Regulation must be consistent with the law and with the proper safeguards to protect residents, but regulation can be unduly heavy-handed. In 1994 a scrutiny carried out by government departments, with the assistance of local authority associations, considered ways in which regulation could be achieved without unnecessary burdens on business. Following the scrutiny, the associations disseminated good practice on enforcement to local authorities. Local authorities are likely to continue this "light touch" with regard to regulatory matters.

In 1994, the majority of national enforcement agencies adopted and applied an "Enforcer's Code", based on principles of openness, transparency and fairness. In the same year, under the Deregulation and Contracting Out Act, powers were introduced to provide business with new rights when subjected to enforcement action. They provide for an explanation of the enforcement action, and the ability to query it before formal action is taken, in order to improve the fairness, transparency and consistency of enforcement. A model mechanism for independent appeals against enforcement actions was put to public consultation in early 1996.

Local authority organisations have combined to produce their own guide to good enforcement practices, and this was published in 1996.

3. TRENDS IN REDISTRIBUTING AUTHORITY ACROSS LEVELS OF GOVERNMENT

3.1 Evolving tendencies

Important as developments in the last fifteen years have been in the United Kingdom, a longer perspective is instructive as centralisation has been a feature of British government for a long time. The last ten or fifteen years have seen new trends and pressures. It has not, however, been a uniform movement and there have been some movements in both directions.

Through the post-war period there was a steady increase in public spending on the welfare state and public services. New activities and developments were coped with through additional spending. By the 1970's a faltering and, in global terms, shrinking economy increasingly raised questions about the ability to finance this. At the same time, in common with other countries, there was growing recognition that the organisational framework of the welfare state had become somewhat bureaucratic and unresponsive, often serving to act more in the interests of the producers of a service than the users. A whole range of administrative, political and professional imperatives seemed to insulate service delivery organisations from their public.

It was against this background that Margaret Thatcher became Prime Minister in 1979. She and her close political allies espoused the latest stages in the evolution of conservative thinking and philosophy. According to this the State had become overbearing; individuals and markets were no longer able to function effectively and efficiently; radical steps needed to be taken to repair the situation and restore a proper balance. A key part of this would be the curtailing of intermediary institutions standing between the individual and markets. Deregulation, competition and privatisation were the means by which the boundaries of the State could be driven back. Intermediary institutions had their powers and importance reassessed or modified to ensure that they did not interfere with individual and market freedoms.

Looked at slightly differently, the United Kingdom's problem was a declining economy. A way of managing this and the need to reduce public expenditure was to shift responsibility to the individual and to the private sector. Some centralisation of power was necessary to make sure this happened along with management reforms designed to increase efficiency and economy.

At this stage a number of generalities can capture the changes which have been instituted by central government but which affect both central and local governments:

- Increased central controls by government have been used to set national direction, standards and policy frameworks for a range of services.

- These powers have paralleled moves to introduce some choice for service users and some significant user control over the local distribution of resources in some services to improve responsiveness.

- Increased emphasis has been placed, through the Citizens Charter initiative, on the rights of the service users to quality services at specific standards and with the rights of redress.

- Mixed economies of service provision have been developed through contracting out, competitive tendering and the introduction of other market-type mechanisms.

- More efficient management of public resources has been encouraged through the new public management.

- A series of moves to deconcentrate activity within central government (e.g. the creation of Executive Agencies) separating out implementation activities from policy-making and advisory functions. These have been within clear policy frameworks set at the centre but have not usually involved geographical decentralisation.

- The temptation for government to "do" (despite the desire to diminish intermediary institutions) has led to the creation of a range of special purpose agencies and organisations, publicly funded, subject to national ministerial policy direction and presided over by boards of ministerial appointees. Some of these act at a national level, some regionally and some locally.

- Major public initiatives and trading enterprises have been privatised. With few exceptions these operate as national rather than sub-national enterprises.

3.2 The current debate

One of the most recent developments affecting the structure of government has been to rationalise part of the government presence at regional level. Integrated offices have been created in London and nine English regional centres, bringing together the outposts of four government departments (Environment, Transport, Education and Employment, and Trade and Industry). The focus of these new offices is on activities concerned with urban re-generation and the consolidation of a disparate set of regeneration initiatives/programmes into a single budget. The main aim is to provide a single, co-ordinated point of contact for the private sector, local authorities and other partners. One major area of domestic social policy, health, is not, however, included in the Government Offices' remit. The importance of this reform is its potential, both as a platform to influence central government's policy-making and as a focus for regional interests to be fed into the government machine.

People have a right to expect that the duties and powers of local authorities will be exercised fairly and competently. The central government are considering the best ways to ensure that the public sector improves its performance and is answerable to the public for any inadequate performance.

Central government wishes to see the development of solutions appropriate to particular local circumstances.

The current debate in the United Kingdom focuses on the relationship between central government and local government. In July 1996 the House of Lords Select Committee on Relations Between Central and Local Government published a report which considered the current state of relations and the factors which have led to the present position. It made recommendations for improving these relations. Whilst the report did not consider local government structure, or the best way of providing particular services, it did consider whether, over a long period of time, local authorities have lost powers and responsibility – either to local authorities or quangos – in a way which has incrementally weakened local democracy, blurred accountability, and produced a strained and less fruitful relationship. The report contained recommendations aimed at improving the relationship between central and local government.

The government responded to the Committee's report in a White Paper published in November 1996. This sets out a programme of action to strengthen local democracy, to promote local authorities' local leadership role, and to improve further the relations between central and local government. Specific measures set out in the White Paper are to:

- legislate in the next Parliament to enable local authorities to undertake experiments with their internal decision-taking arrangements;
- agree with the new Local Government Association and the Welsh Local Government Association a Statement of the role and status of local government;
- develop further with the Association the guidelines for the conduct of business between central and local government;
- review the scope for local authorities to fulfil their local community leadership role in the context of the 1972 Local Government Act, and to assess whether a more general power of local competence is practicable and advisable;
- undertake with the Associations, research on public participation in local government; and
- examine the arrangements in place in central government which are designed to ensure that cross-departmental matters concerning local government are carried forward effectively.

The government rejected a number of the report's recommendations, in particular those aimed at reducing the extent of the influence which central government can exercise on the overall level of local authority expenditure.

3.3 Driving forces

A main objective of recent local government reorganisations has been to offer the taxpayer better value for money but political influence may be considered the key force behind these reforms. Thus there has been a discernible movement of power upwards to central government or downwards to local institutions or service users themselves. The latter, has been characterised, in particular, by the creation of markets or quasi-markets and a series of moves (the Citizen's Charter) enhancing service responsiveness or giving the user better information and access.

The governmental system reflects broader tendencies in British society. While there are distinct national identities in Scotland, Wales and Northern Ireland and a variety of regional loyalties and identities in England, the United Kingdom is dominated by London and the metropolitan south-east. England, in particular, is heavily dependent on national media (press, television and broadcasting) and a metropolitan interpretation of life and events. London is the hub of the national transport system, dominates the financial, commercial and industrial life of the country and is the location of the headquarters or major corporate offices of innumerable private, voluntary and public organisations. It is the home of the legal system, professional institutions, representative organisations, lobbyists and so on. Important as other cities are, they remain relatively insignificant.

UNITED STATES

1. INSTITUTIONS AND AUTHORITY

1.1 Structures

Description of levels

The United States is governed by a federal government, fifty states, 39 000 general purpose local governments (counties, municipalities and townships), and 44 000 special purpose local governments, of which a third are school districts. The United States also includes several islands in the Pacific Ocean and the Caribbean Sea, which are governed as territories or commonwealths, and the District of Columbia, which is the city of Washington, the nation's capital. Washington D.C. and the island territories and commonwealths have non-voting representatives in Congress. The focus this chapter is on the fifty states and on local governments within those states. It does not cover the District nor the island territories and commonwealths.

The total area of the United States is 9 372 600 square kilometres and the total population in 1994 was 260 651 000. States, municipalities and counties vary enormously in population and in their budgets. California, for example, comprises about 15 per cent of the nation's population and has over 60 times as many people as the State of Wyoming. Municipalities and counties are also of widely different sizes, from over 7 million (the City of New York and Los Angeles County) to small hamlets.

Creation, elimination and restructuring

The United States Constitution recognises only the federal government and the states. The existence of the states is guaranteed by the federal Constitution, and no state can be divided without its consent. State constitutions recognise local governments and provide for a variety of ways that state legislatures can regulate local governments.

Congress cannot divide or change the borders of states without their consent, but it can create new states from territories or other dependencies. Hawaii and Alaska took the step to statehood only a few decades ago, and in Puerto Rico and the District of Columbia there are strong but minority political parties favouring statehood.

No large metropolitan region is covered by a single local general purpose government, and most include scores of municipalities and special districts. Several regions include areas in more than one state. Regions have no standing under state or federal constitutions. A few metropolitan areas consolidated local governments in the 1970s, and proposals for further consolidation are still made from time to time. Since these proposals must be approved by each local government and often by the state legislature as well, few succeed.

As seen in Table 1, the total number of local general purpose governments has remained rather stable. The internal breakdown among these governments, however, has changed dramatically. The number of school districts has dropped to 40 per cent of the 1962 total as rural schools have consolidated, usually under pressure from state departments of public education which have been concerned about the capacity of small districts to provide high-quality education. Meanwhile, the number of other special districts and public authorities has grown dramatically, almost doubling since 1962. Districts comprised

20 per cent of all local units in 1962 compared to 35 per cent in 1987. The proliferation of special districts has been a concern of many experts in public administration. Some argue that special districts allow citizens more choice in the array of public services which they receive, but others argue that the result is fragmentation, inefficiency, and inequitable taxation and service delivery.

Table 1. **Division of local government units (1962, 1987)**

	1962	1987
County	3 043	3 042
Municipal	18 000	19 200
Township	17 142	16 691
School District	34 678	14 721
Special District [1]	18 323	29 532
TOTAL	91 186	83 186

Water supply, sewerage, utilities/power, natural conservation, etc., of which bodies there has been a tremendous increase over the past 25 years.
Source: *Public Management*: OECD *Country Profiles*, OECD, 1993.

1.2 Powers

Nature of sub-national institutions

Powers not exercised by the Congress are reserved to the states, but local governments enjoy no such protection – they exist at the pleasure of the states.

States: The distribution of constitutional and political power among the three branches (executive/legislative/judicial) and among key office-holders varies widely from state to state. A few state governors appoint virtually all other top state officials, but other governors must share power with other elected leaders and with strong state legislatures.

Legislative bodies of states are usually organised in the same way as the federal government, with a bicameral legislature. States also have a judicial branch.

The executive branch consists of many agencies headed by a single executive (as with the national government). Altogether, the 50 states elect more than 500 officials to executive office, including 43 attorneys general, 43 lieutenant governors, 38 treasurers, 36 secretaries of state, and an assortment of other officers ranging from the Texas railroad commissioner to the commissioner of public land in New Mexico. There are 7 461 elected state legislators. State bureaucracies are generally staffed by professional administrators.

Local government: Local governments vary widely in their organisation, although virtually all have a council or legislative branch. In many counties and some municipalities, the council appoints the chief executive or wields both legislative and executive power. In others, a mayor or chief county executive is elected directly and manages government agencies. Districts are usually governed by elected boards.

Type and degree of autonomy

The United States is a relatively decentralised federal system. States finance about three quarters of their spending from their own sources. States also borrow on the open market and have direct access to bond markets. There is a standard private system for rating the credit status of states which encourages fiscal discipline on them.

Their budgets are not reviewed nor approved by the federal government. The federal government and states can levy taxes and spend money. State constitutions also allow local general purpose governments to levy taxes, but constitutions and state statutes may classify several types of local governments with different ranges of power and taxing authority.

The federal government and states can directly enforce their laws on individuals through their own courts. State constitutions also allow local general purpose governments to enforce ordinances, but constitutions and state statutes may assign several types of local governments with different ranges of power.

The distribution of power among the federal and state levels has shifted over the decades. The 10th amendment to the federal constitution provides that any powers not expressly granted to the federal government are reserved to the states or the citizens. Until the 1930s, the US Supreme Court periodically ruled that federal social legislation was invalid as an intrusion into state authority. But the Court's willingness to make such rulings has declined sharply and in 1985, the Court ruled (Garcia v. San Antonio Metropolitan Transit Authority) that it will no longer play the role of umpire of the federal system, leaving determination of the scope of national authority to Congress.

A similar story has been played out in many local governments, but without the constitutional dimension except that state legislatures mandate requirements affecting local governments but may not provide compensatory funding. When state revenues were increasing, many local officials welcomed new state programmes of assistance to local government. But when states cut back on local assistance or attempt to hand responsibilities to local governments without providing funds, tensions between states and local officials rise sharply as the cumulative administrative burden and cost resulting from unfunded or inadequately compensated federal and state mandates is significant.

Legally a city is a *municipal corporation* that has been chartered by the state to exercise certain defined powers and provide certain specific services. There are two kinds of such charters: special-act charters and general-act charters. A *special-act charter* applies to a certain named city (for example, New York City) and lists what that city can and cannot do. A *general-act charter* applies to a number of cities that fall within a certain classification, usually based on city population. Thus in some states all cities over 100 000 population will be governed on the basis of one charter. In accordance with the legal principle known as Dillon's rule, the terms of these charters are to be interpreted very narrowly. Under this rule, a municipal corporation can only exercise the powers expressly given it or those powers necessarily implied by, or essential to the accomplishment of, the powers which the state legislature has specifically given the city by law or charter. City officials, needless to say, intensively dislike these restrictions and so argue in favour of a different kind of authorising law, called a *home-rule charter*. Such a charter, now in effect in many cities, especially larger ones, reverses Dillon's rule and allows the city government to do anything that is not prohibited by the charter or by state law. In practice however many home-rule charters have not been so flexible since city laws (ordinances) cannot be in conflict with state laws.

1.3 Responsibilities

Distribution of responsibilities

The federal government provides few direct domestic services, but these include farm price supports, the Postal Service, medical care for veterans, electrical energy production in some parts of the country, and management of parks and wildlife refuges and of federally-owned forests and grazing lands in the West. The federal government also supports scientific and medical research, through government-operated laboratories, laboratories operated under contract, and grants to individual researchers. Aside from these examples, the federal role in delivery of public services is typically indirect, that of financier and regulator, and thus of setting a framework for policy. The financial role involves giving money to individuals, primarily the elderly and the poor, and giving money to state and local governments (see section 2.2). The regulatory role influences the environment, facilities for the handicapped, prison overcrowding, and many other areas.

State governments play a major role in service delivery, including the direct provision of some services. These include highway construction, prisons, institutions for handicapped people, universities and other institutions for post-secondary education, parks, some policing functions, as well as a number of training programmes. Some states deliver social services directly, while others provide funding to counties or other local governmental entities for social and mental health services. States also regulate many professions.

Local governments are heavily involved in service delivery. For the most part, local governments operate virtually all elementary and secondary schools; build and maintain most local roads and most public transportation systems including airports and public transit; provide drinking water, waste-water and solid waste management; provide law enforcement services; and operate local parks, recreation, and senior citizen centres and, in many states, social service programmes. However, since states provide some of the funding for these services, either from their own tax revenues or by passing along federal funds, the design and operation of local services is highly regulated by state and federal requirements.

Mandatory, optional and shared responsibilities

In the early years of the republic, it was relatively easy, both in law and in practice, to distinguish between the respective roles of the federal government on one hand and states and localities on the other hand. "Dual federalism" held that the state and the federal governments functioned separately in their own spheres of authority. As federal regulation and programmes of financial grants to states and localities expanded, mixed responsibilities became pre-eminent, and interest groups, professional groups, and agency personnel working in the same issue area tended to band together across the levels of government, resistant to the authority of elected officials or of government-wide supervisory agencies. The rather complex pattern of funding that resulted from these issue networks is shown in Table 2. The most dominant trend between 1955 and 1980 is the decline in the percent of total spending allocated to primarily federally-funded programmes and the shift of government expenditures towards state and locally-funded education and jointly-funded programmes. Since 1980, expenditures have stabilised with almost a quarter of all government expenditures allocated to programmes which require joint funding from federal, state, and local governments.

Table 2. **Expenditures by function as a share of total (1955, 1980, 1991)**

Function	Total government expenditures (US$ billions)			As a percentage of total spending		
	1955	1980	1991	1955	1980	1991
Primarily federal funding (85 per cent or more federal funding)	57.8	376.3	809.7	60	44	42
of which:						
National defence	38.9	142.4	323.4	40	17	17
Social insurance	7.5	187.5	440.0	8	21	23
Primarily state and local funding (85 per cent or more state and local funding)	14.6	169.2	391.3	15	20	20
of which:						
Education	12.0	140.4	307.9	12	16	16
Shared funding (15-85 per cent federal funding)	15.0	209.8	426.1	15	24	22
of which:						
Welfare and social services	3.1	49.9	105.8	3	6	5
Medical care (Medicaid)	0.2	24.9	102.1	(1)	3	5
Health and hospitals	2.2	23.5	40.6	2	3	2
Transportation	6.8	46.0	83.5	7	5	4
Central expenditures, retirement, and net interest:	9.6	105.7	313.0	10	12	16
TOTAL	97.1	861.0	1 940.1	100	100	100

1. Indicates less than $50 million or less than 0.5 per cent.
Source: Hush, "Federal and State and Local Roles in Government Expenditure", *Public Budgeting & Finance*, vol. 13, No. 2 (Summer 1993).

2. MANAGEMENT FUNCTIONS

2.1 Policy-making and co-ordination

Coherence, consultation and conflict resolution

All legislative powers of the federal government are vested in the United States Congress, but once a law has been passed, full executive authority lies with the President. The United States Supreme Court also plays a role, although in recent decisions the Court has indicated that it will defer to

Congress. The role of the President as Chief of State and Head of the Executive Branch is therefore paramount in policy-making and co-ordination at the national level.

Local officials lobby state legislatures and agencies, just as state and local officials lobby Congress and federal agencies. But in addition, states have cabinet-level departments of local affairs or of community development, which oversee matters such as local taxation. The responsibilities and authority of these departments varies among states, depending on how each state's constitution, statutes, and political traditions deal with state-local issues.

What is often missing in this complex system is a voice for broad, multi-disciplinary approaches to public policy issues. The National Governors' Association, the National Conference of State Legislatures, and similar organisations became important voices for broad policy initiatives in the 1980s, when states and localities were being particularly innovative. The National Governors' Association for example, lobbied for welfare reform, education reform, federal tax reform, and reduction of the federal budget deficit. However, many of the expert staff of these associations are supported by grants from specialised federal agencies, which may limit the energy devoted to broad multi-agency issues.

The reality concerning most aspects of service delivery is fragmentation. There are numerous, separate and often narrowly defined programmes and policies emanating from federal departments with little possibility of co-ordination amongst them. In addition lines of authority may be blurred and goals may be overlapping if not contradictory.

Formal and informal mechanisms

Aside from Congress, there are few other formal mechanisms of co-ordination or consultation bodies and most are weak. Federal law established an Advisory Commission on Intergovernmental Relations (ACIR) in 1959, and 25 states have established their own ACIRs to address state-local issues. In the 1970s, the federal ACIR was well-staffed and conducted many highly-regarded studies. However, as federal grants for state and local programmes have been cut back and intergovernmental tensions have increased, ACIR lost both support from state officials and then most of its funding from Congress. It will cease to exist after 1996.

One method of formally responding to problems confronting several states, but not requiring national uniformity or intervention other than congressional approval, is the interstate compact. And, within states, there are somewhat stronger mechanisms for vertical intergovernmental co-ordination as states have clearer constitutional authority to shape the structure and activities of local governments. Horizontal co-ordination of state-wide matters, however, is generally less well developed.

Lacking strong formal administrative mechanisms for inter-governmental co-ordination, state and local officials are often active lobbyists at the federal level. Lobbying higher levels of government is one of the major responsibilities of many state and local elected officials. In addition to acting individually, state and local officials work through associations of state and local officials. Virtually every kind of state official, elected and career, from governors to directors of drug treatment programmes, has an association with an office in Washington, D.C. These Washington representatives work closely with professional groups, Congressional staff, and federal agencies which operate programmes of interest to their members.

In many metropolitan regions there are active efforts to organise informal regional collaborative activities, often joining business leaders, local elected officials, university leaders, top agency managers and others to promote economic development and sometimes to seek ways to improve conditions in poor inner-city neighbourhoods.

2.2 Financial management

Sources of revenue

Different levels of government rely on different sources of funds. Table 3 gives a sample of some of the various sources of revenue for both state and local governments. Both the federal government and most states rely heavily on individual and corporate income taxes, and the table shows that the average state gets slightly less than one-fifth of its revenue from the federal government. Many states and localities also levy sales taxes and jealously guard against any suggestions that the federal government might levy a sales or value-added tax. Local governments rely heavily on taxes on the value of real and personal property. In 1960, 15 per cent of all state and local expenditures came from federal grants. This figure rose to 28 per cent in 1980 and stood at 23 per cent in 1995.

The federal government also provides some financial assistance directly to local governments. However, such aid declined sharply in the 1980s, as the Reagan Administration sought to reduce all grants and in particular those going to local governments. As a result, local governments now rely much more heavily on state than federal grants. At the same time, state and local governments were mandated new responsibilities by the federal government without equivalent financial support. Complaints of excessive burdens grew until, early in 1995, the Unfunded Mandates Reform Act was passed. This requires the Congressional Budget Office to analyse the costs of any proposed mandates on state and local governments in an attempt to restore equilibrium to the relationships between federal, state and local governments.

Table 3, which follows, shows the pattern of state and local revenue sources in 1992. It demonstrates the importance of tax revenues to sub-national levels of government – particularly sales and income taxes at the state level and property tax at the local level.

Table 3. **Sources of state and local government revenues (fiscal year 1992)**

		$US million	percentage
STATE GOVERNMENT			
Taxes		329 296	44.3
of which: sales	162 989		
income	126 799		
property	6 689		
others	32 820		
Revenue from federal government		159 068	21.4
Insurance trust revenue		129 663	17.5
Charges and miscellaneous general revenue		107 552	14.5
Revenue from local government		10 861	1.5
Utility and liquor store revenue		6 579	0.8
Total:		743 018	100.0
LOCAL GOVERNMENT			
Taxes		227 099	35.1
of which: property	171 723		
sales	33 429		
income	12 591		
others	9 357		
Revenue from federal government		20 141	3.1
Revenue from state government		195 845	30.2
Charges and miscellaneous general revenue		130 169	20.1
Utility and liquor store revenue		55.962	8.6
Insurance trust revenue		18 296	2.8
Total:		647 514	100.1

Source: US Bureau of the Census, *Government Finances*, 1991-1992.

Expenditure responsibilities

Total government expenditures grew from about one fourth of GDP in 1955 to one third in 1975. They have remained stable at that level since then. The federal share of total government spending has also remained stable, at about 70 per cent, since 1955 – despite major demographic changes and programme development.

The federal budget is far larger than state and local budgets, totalling about 30 per cent more than all states and localities taken together. However, federal spending is heavily dominated by defence, transfer payments to the elderly and other individuals, and financing of the national debt. Setting these amounts aside, states and localities account for roughly 88 per cent of all government purchases of goods and services. States and localities spent over $925 billion in 1987, of which federal financial grants-in-aid accounted for about $115 billion. Other federal financial aid, including tax subsidies, loans and loan guarantees totalled nearly $50 billion at that time. Main expenditure patterns in 1993 are summarised in Table 4.

Table 4. **Composition of government spending, by level and function, 1993**
(Percentage of non-interest expenditures)

FEDERAL GOVERNMENT	
National defence	26.6
Social security	23.4
Medicare	13.2
Veterans benefits and services, welfare and social services, and housing subsidies	9.0
Civilian and military retirement	4.9
Other	22.9
Total:	100.0
STATE AND LOCAL GOVERNMENT	
Education	37.5
Medicaid	15.9
Welfare and social services	8.0
Highways	7.5
Police and fire protection	6.2
Corrections	3.7
Water, sewerage, and sanitation	1.5
Other	19.6
Total	99.9

Notes: Data are on a national income and product accounts (NIPA) basis, and are as published in the Survey of Current Business, September 1994. Federal grants-in-aid to state and local governments are not included in federal government expenditures.
Source: Department of Commerce.

Balance between discretion and control

In addition to providing financial assistance to local governments, states have the constitutional authority to place a variety of limits on local government finance, such as controls on local government spending; limits on property taxes (which are an important local government revenue source); limits on expenditures; debt limits; referendum requirements; maximum duration of bonds; interest ceilings; and caps on revenues from all sources. These state-imposed constraints are often more important to local governments than state financial aid.

Equalisation schemes: Richer communities can raise more revenue and afford better public schools and other services than poorer communities, and most states have adopted school finance equalisation measures as part of their subsidies to public schools. However, federal courts have found many state equalisation schemes to be unfair and unconstitutional.

Balance between global and specific federal transfers: A declining percentage of transfers are "project grants", with which federal officials can decide which state or locality submits the most attractive proposal and which give federal officials a great degree of discretion in shaping state and local activities. A much larger volume of funds flows as "formula grants", where the amount provided to each state is established by a statutory formula. With formula grants, federal agencies can require states and localities to submit plans for the use of these funds, but there is little discretion in the amount of the grant. This should reduce federal leverage over states and localities but almost 90 per cent of total federal formula grants are for narrow "categorical" purposes, the remainder being "block" grants which allow more discretion to states and localities. There is active negotiation between levels of government about the terms of grants, but the leverage of states and localities is limited by the narrow purposes of categorical grants. There is much current debate on how the policy-making role for programmes receiving federal financing should be shared between the federal, state and local governments (see section 3.2).

Federal aid: Total federal aid to states declined slightly during the first years of the Reagan Administration but more recently has reached historically high levels. Federal aid to state and local governments comprises grants, loans and tax subsidies. Table 5 shows the breakdown of federal grants by function from 1960 to 1995. In 1995, federal grant outlays totalled $225 billion, those for loans and guarantees totalled $0.2 billion and tax provisions for state and local governments are estimated to be $75.2 billion in 1996. The most noticeable increases since 1960 have come in the areas of transportation; education, training, employment, and social services; health; and income security. Recent increases have come primarily in grants which are passed on to individuals, especially for medical care for the poor. Medicaid is the largest grant programme – its estimated outlays in 1997 will be $105.6 billion. It, and some welfare programmes, are jointly financed by the federal and state governments but administered by the states. In 1980, aid to individuals comprised about 40 per cent of federal grants; this figure rose to over 60 per cent in 1995. About a quarter of federal grants to states and localities are for capital projects (e.g., construction of highways and sewage treatment plants). Social service programmes, including education, and job training, account for most of the remaining 30 per cent. The effect of the shift from programme grants to aid to individuals is that state and local governments have less discretion in how federal funds are spent. However, states have sought waivers from federal agencies to allow greater flexibility in the design of social service programmes, and the Clinton Administration has sharply increased the number of approved waivers.

Table 5. **Trends in federal grants to state and local governments by function (1960, 1970, 1980, 1990, 1995)**
(Outlays; US$ billions)

	1960	1970	1980	1990	1995
Natural resources and environment	0.1	0.4	5.4	3.7	4.1
Agriculture	0.2	0.6	0.6	1.3	0.8
Transportation	3.0	4.6	13.0	19.2	25.8
Community and regional development	0.1	1.8	6.5	5.0	7.2
Education, training, employment, and social services	0.5	6.4	21.9	23.4	34.1
Health	0.2	3.8	15.8	43.9	93.6
Income security	2.6	5.8	18.5	35.2	55.1
General government	0.2	0.5	8.6	2.3	2.2
Other	(1)	0.1	1.2	1.4	2.0
TOTAL	7.0	24.1	91.4	135.3	225.0

1. $50 million or less.
Source: Analytical perspectives.

State aid: The largest form of state grants is for aid to local schools. The methods of distributing assistance among local units may involve returning revenues to jurisdictions in proportion to the amount raised in each, or they may be allocated according to complex equalising formulae similar to those used in federal grants. In many instances, states have elected to assume full responsibility for financing and providing certain services rather than sharing costs or providing grants for local governments. Some municipalities have also been able to shift some functions to the state level. Examples include public health, public welfare, municipal courts, pollution abatement, property tax assessment standards, building codes and land use regulations.

2.3 Performance management

Mechanisms

In the 1980s, several reforms at the federal level required increased oversight and tighter control of public spending, at all levels of government. States and local governments were the first to experiment with performance "benchmarks" and other indicators of whether public programmes were achieving their intended impact on incomes, employment, or the quality of life (see "Quality standards").

Although a few federal agencies experimented with performance management on their own initiative, it was the 1990 Chief Financial Officers Act, the Clinton Administration's National Performance Review, and the Government Performance and Results Act of 1993 which put this issue on the agenda for all federal agencies.

For federal agencies which are direct providers of service, such as veterans' hospitals and customs, implementing performance management systems will be relatively straightforward. A much larger number of federal agencies operate through grants to states and localities or through a complex system of shared regulatory responsibilities. For these agencies, performance management will be much more difficult to design and operate. Programme "re-inventions" which devolve responsibilities from the federal level to states and localities have often left open the question of which level of government has responsibilities for matters such as audits.

The Government Performance and Results Act, 1993, was in part inspired by the comprehensive system of performance management and budgeting used by the city of Sunnyvale, California. Sunnyvale's performance management and budget system evolved out of a more rudimentary effort to link budget with performance in the early 1970's. That initial attempt used the traditional line-item budget, shown under a set of programme performance goals. In 1977 the city began a serious effort to recast the system into a new format, with its hierarchy of goals, objectives and tasks. The general plan which is a long term policy document (20 years) covering each of the 24 areas of city services and forming the blueprint for what type of community the city would like to become over the next two decades, was made meaningful. The long-term performance system was also extended and made more sophisticated through a Ten-Year Resource Allocation Plan, a Two-Year Performance Budget, and Management Achievement Plans. The pay-for-performance system was developed, and these were all linked into a comprehensive Planning and Management system. The system works and in recent years a citizen satisfaction survey has shown that 93 per cent of Sunnyvale residents rated overall city services as "good" or "excellent".

Quality standards

In December 1994, a ground-breaking agreement was made between federal and state and local officials from Oregon. They signed a memorandum of understanding to undertake the "Oregon Option" – a framework for a long-range demonstration project in which Oregon officials and the federal government will identify the benchmarks and strategies for improved delivery of services involving federal, state, and local agencies. The agreement commits the signatories to test an outcomes-based approach and create a new federal-state-local partnership that could serve as a model for improvements nation-wide. Benchmarks are now being used in Oregon as critical indicators about the economy, the quality of life, and the welfare of citizens. They track where the State (or county) stands and how it measures up to its target goals over a specified number of years (e.g. 1995, 2000, 2010) and oblige Oregon and its localities to measure what they do by agreed-upon standards.

2.4 Human resource management

Statutory distinctions

Most full-time federal employees are career civil servants, protected by merit protection systems. However, at topmost levels of most United States agencies there are more political appointees than in most other OECD countries.

States and most larger localities have merit protection systems which are broadly similar to the federal system but which vary somewhat in quality. They are required to establish such systems for a large part of their workforce, and most have developed systems that encompass virtually all employees.

Table 6 shows the evolution of civilian employment by level of government. It demonstrates firstly that in 1992 some 60 per cent of civilian employees were in local governments and a quarter in state governments; and secondly that, since 1980, the numbers of civilian employees in federal, state and local governments have grown by 5, 18 and 14 per cent respectively. Most of the federal growth was in defence and the Postal Service. The growth trend has been reversed since 1993, with a federal work force reduction of almost 10 per cent between then and the end of 1995.

Table 6. **Civilian employment by level of government (1980, 1985, 1990-1992)**
(number of persons, full-time and part-time)

	1980	1985	1990	1991	1992
Federal government	2 898 000	3 021 000	3 105 000	3 103 000	3 047 000
State governments	3 753 000	3 984 000	4 503 000	4 521 000	4 595 000
Local governments:	9 562 000	9 685 000	10 762 000	10 930 000	11 103 000
Counties	1 853 000	1 891 000	2 167 000	2 196 000	2 253 000
Cities	2 561 000	2 467 000	2 642 000	2 662 000	2 665 000
Townships	394 000	392 000	418 000	415 000	424 000
School districts	4 270 000	4 416 000	4 950 000	5 045 000	5 134 000
Special districts	484 000	519 000	585 000	612 000	627 000
TOTAL	16 213 000	16 690 000	18 370 000	18 554 000	18 745 000

Source: *Public Management Developments: Update 1995*, OECD, 1995.

Managerial autonomy

Personnel management at all levels of government is divided among legislatures, central personnel agencies, and personnel offices within operating agencies. Staffing levels are generally set by legislatures, whilst other aspects of personnel management are controlled by central personnel offices. However, in two-thirds of the states, more employees perform personnel duties in line agencies than in the primary jurisdiction. Texas vests personnel management with line agencies, and California has two centralised personnel offices.

Wide variations within and among states and localities, makes generalisation about salary levels, structures, and responsibilities rather difficult. In general, federal salaries are higher than comparable state and local salaries. State and local elected officials usually earn considerably less than the career federal programme managers whom they meet in the course of negotiations over grants and mandates.

At all levels of government, there is increasing dissatisfaction with centrally administered human resources programmes which are perceived as too inflexible and unresponsive to diverse agency cultures. The Clinton Administration's National Performance Review (NPR), calls for significant changes in the management of human resources within the Executive Branch of the federal government. The major thrust is to deregulate human resources management, decentralise authority to line managers at the operating level, and streamline processes to reduce the cost of administration of the human resources system. NPR also proposed increased investments in employee skills and information technology.

In the 1980s, virtually every state has reformed its civil service system in some way, and recently 33 of the 50 were simultaneously working on reform proposals similar to those of the NPR.

Many state and local governments are heavily unionised, and more than 40 per cent of the American public sector work force is covered by collective bargaining contracts that stipulate employment terms. Some states restrict the right of public employees to strike. Unions are important political forces in many localities, and associations of public school teachers are powerful in many states.

In the 1990s, many states and localities, as well as private employers, are contracting out a larger portion of their work. This is often strongly opposed by unions but favoured by governmental managers as a way of down-sizing the workforce and creating greater efficiency by freeing managers from civil service rules.

2.5 Regulatory management and reform

The states have constitutional authority to issue laws and regulations in areas not pre-empted by federal law. The federal government also delegates authority to the states to implement many federal regulatory programs, often on a cost-sharing basis. Municipalities and local governments, such as counties, are creations of the states, and typically have regulatory and legal authorities of their own.

The federal government has adopted policies of reducing federal regulation on the states, and of devolving regulatory authority to state and local governments whenever possible. As in other federal governments, however, the United States has experienced dramatic and increasing centralisation of regulatory power, despite this power sharing between the states and the federal government.

In the 1960s and 1970s, for the first time in the nation's history, federal mandates and regulations began to rival grants and subsidies in importance as federal tools for influencing the behaviour of state and local governments. Complaints grew of cumulative burdens, excessive costs, confusion, and delays caused by federal regulations. Efforts to reform the regulatory process to grant relief to state and local governments began in the late 1970s, in part because the courts had begun to rule against the application of some federal regulations to state governments, and in part because the president and the Congress began to pay more attention to the issue. Several laws were enacted to improve federal regulatory discipline, including the Paperwork Reduction Act of 1980; the Regulatory Flexibility Act of 1980, which required regulatory agencies to minimise regulatory burdens on small governments; and the state and Local Government Cost Estimate Act of 1981, which required the Congress to estimate, prior to enactment, costs of significant legislation on state and local governments.

Despite numerous attempts to reduce regulatory burdens on state and local governments, however, the weight of new intergovernmental regulatory legislation increased in the 1980s. Federalism was explicitly affirmed as a regulatory principle in 1987, when President Reagan ordered that regulations should pre-empt state authority only if pre-emption was required by Congress or necessary to address a problem of national scope. The order required agencies to perform federalism assessments on rules that would have a substantial effect on sub-national governments, and to submit these assessments to OMB through the regulatory review process. Nevertheless, the number of new federal laws imposing significant new burdens on state governments or pre-empting state authority increased in the 1980s relative to the 1970s.

In addition, the federal government has regulated the activities of states themselves, mandating large new burdens and costs that state and local governments are hard-pressed to finance. In this context, the Unfunded Mandates Reform Act was enacted in early 1995 with the intent of restricting the ability of the Congress to impose costly mandates on states, localities and tribal governments (see also section 2.2). The legislation also requires federal agencies to assess the qualitative and quantitative costs and benefits of any proposed regulatory action that would result in annual expenditure of $100 million or more by sub-national governments or the private sector. Agencies must identify and consider a reasonable number of regulatory alternatives and from these alternatives select the least costly, most cost-effective or least burdensome alternative that achieves the objectives of the proposed rule – or explain their decisions if a different action is adopted.

Of separate concern is the substantial volume of regulations issued by the states themselves. Like the federal government, state governments are regulating more. It was observed in 1990 (Bowers) that "this increased rule-making activity threatens to rival, or even replace, state legislatures as the principal source of new laws emanating from state government".

Federal regulatory reform does not affect state regulations, and little has been done to co-ordinate federal regulations with those of the states. Many of the states, however, have employed some form of executive review to oversee their own regulatory agencies. The California Office of Administrative Law, for example, reviews all proposed rules. If it rejects a rule, the rule cannot become effective unless the state regulatory agency persuades the governor (the elected head of the state) to reverse the decision. In three other states, rules cannot become effective unless a governor approves them. Over 40 states provide for advance clearance of proposed rules by the state attorney general.

The federal government is also an important financial and economic regulator. Most federal programmes for social regulation, e.g., environmental quality and industrial health and safety, are implemented and augmented by states. Local governments also are regulators, being for example the primary source of land use regulation in most states.

3. TRENDS IN REDISTRIBUTING AUTHORITY ACROSS LEVELS OF GOVERNMENT

3.1 Evolving tendencies

Since its founding, the history of the United States has been one of quickening, almost relentless extension of the scope of the activity of federal agencies and courts. However, the expansion of the scope of federal activity has not resulted in a coherent system of service delivery. At each level of government, responsibilities are further divided. The roles and responsibilities for providing public services are, therefore, exceedingly complex and diverse. Authority is widely dispersed. As a result, service delivery is more than decentralised – it is fragmented.

The roots of fragmentation can be traced back to the first years of the republic, in the late 18th century. The United States first emerged as a confederation of separate colonies, which had been settled by different religious and ethnic groups and had somewhat different political and cultural traditions. When they joined to form a nation, they insisted on preserving state traditions and responsibilities. As other states were formed, they brought their own distinctive political cultures and patterns of state-local relations.

By the late 1970s, the relationships between levels of government had become so complex and fragmented that the Advisory Commission on Inter-governmental Relations proclaimed a "crisis of competence and confidence" in the American federal system. At the same time the decentralisation of authority which fosters complexity was seen by some as an important source of strength, flexibility and diversity. The fact that since the mid-1950s the share of total government spending by state and local governments has remained at around 30 per cent is seen as testimony to the stability of the system through a period of unprecedented change.

In 1980, President Reagan proclaimed in his first inaugural address that he would redress the balance between the federal government on one hand and states and localities on the other. This rhetoric echoed the views of the Advisory Commission on Intergovernmental Relations. But most observers interpreted the call for a "new federalism" as an excuse to advance Reagan's substantive objectives of deregulation and reduced governmental interventionism. It was also viewed as a means of reducing federal domestic spending. Reagan and the National Governors' Association tried to negotiate a "sorting out" of governmental activities through a process of "swap/turnback". This involved the federal government taking on the costs of Medicaid and food stamps (social programmes and medical care for the poor) while states took over the AFDC federal programme (Aid to Families with Dependent Children) over a 10-year period; and localities gradually assuming community and economic development, and some other transportation and other "local" programmes. Congress prevented most of these cuts from being made. Republican presidents proposed cuts and few new interventionist programmes, while the Democrat-controlled Congress managed to fend off the cuts but could not push through many new large-scale spending programmes.

Instead of a clarification of roles among the levels of government, two other shifts took place over the past fifteen years. The first shift was that states and local governments seized the leadership in many policy areas as well as on management issues. The second shift was the rapid increase of federal mandates on state and local governments, which resulted in the 1995 legislation on unfunded mandates.

3.2 The current debate

In the 1990s, an economic slowdown and the increasing weight of federal mandates squeezed both state and local budgets. State experimentation continued, often in the form of asking for waivers of federal requirements to permit experimentation with prevention and cost-cutting initiatives. In recent years, therefore, many states and local governments have been well ahead of the federal government in experimenting with administrative and organisational reforms, such as privatisation, administrative simplification, and public-private partnerships. The waiver process (requests by state, local or tribal governments to tailor federal programmes to meet local needs) can, however, be costly, complex and time-consuming.

President Clinton came to national office after a career both as a governor and as an advocate for new federal initiatives in welfare reform, education, and technology development. His administration has sought to work in partnership with state and local governments, and has granted waivers for state and local policy experimentation. The Clinton Administration's National Performance Review endorsed the concept of "empowerment" of states and localities as a way of unravelling complex programme requirements and allowing programme managers, front-line workers, and community leaders to redesign programmes around performance objectives, such as changes in income, employment, or quality of life.

These efforts to allow greater flexibility to states and localities have not, however, resulted in greater harmony between levels of government. Instead, the parallel explosion of federal mandates has led to increased inter-governmental tension. In sum, the mid-1990s find the United States with an array of public services that remains very fragmented and complex, with blurred lines of authority and goals which overlap. The reasons for federal leadership in the past may have lost some of their force, but states and localities are both resisting federal leadership and displaying significant leadership themselves. On the other hand, such a decentralised federal system encourages the diversity which can be seen as a strength of the system, despite the enormous complexity which it also brings.

The current debate centres largely on whether to convert existing programmes into block grants and on how much discretion to allow states in determining how those grants should be used. The Clinton Administration strongly supports enhancing the role of states and localities in policy making. In many areas-job training, community development, and welfare, for example – enhanced flexibility for states and local communities is considered likely to yield better results. But this enhanced flexibility must be provided in a way that protects the national interest. The federal government view is that as it has a significant role in financing programmes, it also should have some role in policy in order to ensure accountability. On the one hand, the federal government can influence the pattern of state spending more easily. It is precisely the federal government's desire to influence patterns of state spending that justifies a federal role at all. On the other hand, if the substitution of federal for local funding leads to less diligent monitoring by taxpayers, the money may not be well spent. Federal actions can impose costs on the states, and the federal government may spend state money more readily than funds raised through federal taxes.

The Clinton Administration has put forward a new approach to federal grants:

- The federal government would provide states and local governments with greatly enhanced flexibility: funds from numerous programmes would be consolidated, and regulations would be pared back.

- Accountability would be ensured not by restrictions on the use of funds but by performance measures. Programmes that live up to their stated goals could receive more funding.

- Individuals benefiting from government programmes would also be given as much discretion as possible to choose how those funds should be spent, reducing the possibility that they would be spent unwisely.

In mid-1996, after much debate, Congress passed a welfare reform bill that converts current federal spending into block grants, ends the federal entitlement to welfare benefits, and shifts many responsibilities to the states.

3.3 Driving forces

Political factors: The evolution to a more complex and fragmented situation did not lead to a major national debate about the roles of different levels of government in the delivery of public services. Federalism has not been a high-profile political issue since the 19th century Civil War. The attitudes of voters and politicians towards the respective roles of various levels of government have been shaped by their substantive policy goals, rather than their views of the appropriate scope of federal, state, or local authority. It is not uncommon for politicians to use the rhetoric of decentralisation, state's rights, or local self-determination to argue against a federal initiative in a policy area where they oppose a government action, and then for the same politicians to speak of overriding national concerns which require federal action on another issue.

Financial issues: In 1993, state and local officials protested against "unfunded federal mandates". This state-local uprising is not seamless. States have used their constitutional authority over local policy and local taxes to transfer fiscal burdens to local governments. Furthermore, local governments, reluctant to take on new responsibilities, have often ceded authority over costly programmes to special districts which have been created to provide specific services, such as wastewater treatment, local transportation, or solid waste disposal.

It is difficult to predict where this movement will go. The federal budget deficit has recently been reduced and currently (FY 1996) stands at $118 billion, but this still puts limits on the ability of any federal administration to reduce the budget pressures on states and localities. The current intention of both the Congress and the President, however, is to bring the federal budget into balance by the year 2002.

Economic and social forces: Beyond the immediate issues of budgets and mandates, there are deeper questions about the future federal role in American policy. The scope of federal activity has usually expanded as federal officials mobilise to fight a war, deal with national economic issues, or promote social equity. With the end of the Cold War, the first reason for federal interventionism is substantially changed. It is now difficult to make the case that federal spending on science, transportation or education is necessary to protect against a foreign military threat. The landscape has also changed with respect to the federal role in economic issues as the American economy becomes more integrated into the global economy. This poses new challenges to federal policy-makers. Nations can prosper by upgrading the skills of their workforces, but in the United States, it is states and localities, not the federal government, which have traditionally financed and provided the policy direction for most education and workforce policy.

MAIN SALES OUTLETS OF OECD PUBLICATIONS
PRINCIPAUX POINTS DE VENTE DES PUBLICATIONS DE L'OCDE

AUSTRALIA – AUSTRALIE
D.A. Information Services
648 Whitehorse Road, P.O.B 163
Mitcham, Victoria 3132   Tel. (03) 9210.7777
                             Fax: (03) 9210.7788

AUSTRIA – AUTRICHE
Gerold & Co.
Graben 31
Wien I   Tel. (0222) 533.50.14
                             Fax: (0222) 512.47.31.29

BELGIUM – BELGIQUE
Jean De Lannoy
Avenue du Roi, Koningslaan 202
B-1060 Bruxelles   Tel. (02) 538.51.69/538.08.41
                             Fax: (02) 538.08.41

CANADA
Renouf Publishing Company Ltd.
5369 Canotek Road
Unit 1
Ottawa, Ont. K1J 9J3   Tel. (613) 745.2665
                             Fax: (613) 745.7660

Stores:
71 1/2 Sparks Street
Ottawa, Ont. K1P 5R1   Tel. (613) 238.8985
                             Fax: (613) 238.6041

12 Adelaide Street West
Toronto, QN M5H 1L6   Tel. (416) 363.3171
                             Fax: (416) 363.5963

Les Éditions La Liberté Inc.
3020 Chemin Sainte-Foy
Sainte-Foy, PQ G1X 3V6   Tel. (418) 658.3763
                             Fax: (418) 658.3763

Federal Publications Inc.
165 University Avenue, Suite 701
Toronto, ON M5H 3B8   Tel. (416) 860.1611
                             Fax: (416) 860.1608

Les Publications Fédérales
1185 Université
Montréal, QC H3B 3A7   Tel. (514) 954.1633
                             Fax: (514) 954.1635

CHINA – CHINE
Book Dept., China National Publications
Import and Export Corporation (CNPIEC)
16 Gongti E. Road, Chaoyang District
Beijing 100020   Tel. (10) 6506-6688 Ext. 8402
                             (10) 6506-3101

CHINESE TAIPEI – TAIPEI CHINOIS
Good Faith Worldwide Int'l. Co. Ltd.
9th Floor, No. 118, Sec. 2
Chung Hsiao E. Road
Taipei   Tel. (02) 391.7396/391.7397
                             Fax: (02) 394.9176

**CZECH REPUBLIC –
RÉPUBLIQUE TCHÈQUE**
National Information Centre
NIS – prodejna
Konviktská 5
Praha 1 – 113 57   Tel. (02) 24.23.09.07
                             Fax: (02) 24.22.94.33
E-mail: nkposp@dec.niz.cz
Internet: http://www.nis.cz

DENMARK – DANEMARK
Munksgaard Book and Subscription Service
35, Nørre Søgade, P.O. Box 2148
DK-1016 København K   Tel. (33) 12.85.70
                             Fax: (33) 12.93.87

J. H. Schultz Information A/S,
Herstedvang 12,
DK – 2620 Albertslung   Tel. 43 63 23 00
                             Fax: 43 63 19 69
Internet: s-info@inet.uni-c.dk

EGYPT – ÉGYPTE
The Middle East Observer
41 Sherif Street
Cairo   Tel. (2) 392.6919
                             Fax: (2) 360.6804

FINLAND – FINLANDE
Akateeminen Kirjakauppa
Keskuskatu 1, P.O. Box 128
00100 Helsinki

Subscription Services/Agence d'abonnements :
P.O. Box 23
00100 Helsinki   Tel. (358) 9.121.4403
                             Fax: (358) 9.121.4450

*****FRANCE**
OECD/OCDE
Mail Orders/Commandes par correspondance :
2, rue André-Pascal
75775 Paris Cedex 16   Tel. 33 (0)1.45.24.82.00
                        Fax: 33 (0)1.49.10.42.76
                             Telex: 640048 OCDE
Internet: Compte.PUBSINQ@oecd.org

Orders via Minitel, France only/
Commandes par Minitel, France exclusivement :
36 15 OCDE

OECD Bookshop/Librairie de l'OCDE :
33, rue Octave-Feuillet
75016 Paris   Tel. 33 (0)1.45.24.81.81
                             33 (0)1.45.24.81.67

Dawson
B.P. 40
91121 Palaiseau Cedex   Tel. 01.89.10.47.00
                             Fax: 01.64.54.83.26

Documentation Française
29, quai Voltaire
75007 Paris   Tel. 01.40.15.70.00

Economica
49, rue Héricart
75015 Paris   Tel. 01.45.78.12.92
                             Fax: 01.45.75.05.67

Gibert Jeune (Droit-Économie)
6, place Saint-Michel
75006 Paris   Tel. 01.43.25.91.19

Librairie du Commerce International
10, avenue d'Iéna
75016 Paris   Tel. 01.40.73.34.60

Librairie Dunod
Université Paris-Dauphine
Place du Maréchal-de-Lattre-de-Tassigny
75016 Paris   Tel. 01.44.05.40.13

Librairie Lavoisier
11, rue Lavoisier
75008 Paris   Tel. 01.42.65.39.95

Librairie des Sciences Politiques
30, rue Saint-Guillaume
75007 Paris   Tel. 01.45.48.36.02

P.U.F.
49, boulevard Saint-Michel
75005 Paris   Tel. 01.43.25.83.40

Librairie de l'Université
12a, rue Nazareth
13100 Aix-en-Provence   Tel. 04.42.26.18.08

Documentation Française
165, rue Garibaldi
69003 Lyon   Tel. 04.78.63.32.23

Librairie Decitre
29, place Bellecour
69002 Lyon   Tel. 04.72.40.54.54

Librairie Sauramps
Le Triangle
34967 Montpellier Cedex 2   Tel. 04.67.58.85.15
                             Fax: 04.67.58.27.36

A la Sorbonne Actual
23, rue de l'Hôtel-des-Postes
06000 Nice   Tel. 04.93.13.77.75
                             Fax: 04.93.80.75.69

GERMANY – ALLEMAGNE
OECD Bonn Centre
August-Bebel-Allee 6
D-53175 Bonn   Tel. (0228) 959.120
                             Fax: (0228) 959.12.17

GREECE – GRÈCE
Librairie Kauffmann
Stadiou 28
10564 Athens   Tel. (01) 32.55.321
                             Fax: (01) 32.30.320

HONG-KONG
Swindon Book Co. Ltd.
Astoria Bldg. 3F
34 Ashley Road, Tsimshatsui
Kowloon, Hong Kong   Tel. 2376.2062
                             Fax: 2376.0685

HUNGARY – HONGRIE
Euro Info Service
Margitsziget, Európa Ház
1138 Budapest   Tel. (1) 111.60.61
                             Fax: (1) 302.50.35
E-mail: euroinfo@mail.matav.hu
Internet: http://www.euroinfo.hu//index.html

ICELAND – ISLANDE
Mál og Menning
Laugavegi 18, Pósthólf 392
121 Reykjavik   Tel. (1) 552.4240
                             Fax: (1) 562.3523

INDIA – INDE
Oxford Book and Stationery Co.
Scindia House
New Delhi 110001   Tel. (11) 331.5896/5308
                             Fax: (11) 332.2639
E-mail: oxford.publ@axcess.net.in

17 Park Street
Calcutta 700016   Tel. 240832

INDONESIA – INDONÉSIE
Pdii-Lipi
P.O. Box 4298
Jakarta 12042   Tel. (21) 573.34.67
                             Fax: (21) 573.34.67

IRELAND – IRLANDE
Government Supplies Agency
Publications Section
4/5 Harcourt Road
Dublin 2   Tel. 661.31.11
                             Fax: 475.27.60

ISRAEL – ISRAËL
Praedicta
5 Shatner Street
P.O. Box 34030
Jerusalem 91430   Tel. (2) 652.84.90/1/2
                             Fax: (2) 652.84.93

R.O.Y. International
P.O. Box 13056
Tel Aviv 61130   Tel. (3) 546 1423
                             Fax: (3) 546 1442
E-mail: royil@netvision.net.il

Palestinian Authority/Middle East:
INDEX Information Services
P.O.B. 19502
Jerusalem   Tel. (2) 627.16.34
                             Fax: (2) 627.12.19

ITALY – ITALIE
Libreria Commissionaria Sansoni
Via Duca di Calabria, 1/1
50125 Firenze   Tel. (055) 64.54.15
                             Fax: (055) 64.12.57
E-mail: licosa@ftbcc.it

Via Bartolini 29
20155 Milano   Tel. (02) 36.50.83

Editrice e Libreria Herder
Piazza Montecitorio 120
00186 Roma   Tel. 679.46.28
                             Fax: 678.47.51

Libreria Hoepli
Via Hoepli 5
20121 Milano   Tel. (02) 86.54.46
                             Fax: (02) 805.28.86

Libreria Scientifica
Dott. Lucio de Biasio 'Aeiou'
Via Coronelli, 6
20146 Milano   Tel. (02) 48.95.45.52
   Fax: (02) 48.95.45.48

JAPAN – JAPON
OECD Tokyo Centre
Landic Akasaka Building
2-3-4 Akasaka, Minato-ku
Tokyo 107   Tel. (81.3) 3586.2016
   Fax: (81.3) 3584.7929

KOREA – CORÉE
Kyobo Book Centre Co. Ltd.
P.O. Box 1658, Kwang Hwa Moon
Seoul   Tel. 730.78.91
   Fax: 735.00.30

MALAYSIA – MALAISIE
University of Malaya Bookshop
University of Malaya
P.O. Box 1127, Jalan Pantai Baru
59700 Kuala Lumpur
Malaysia   Tel. 756.5000/756.5425
   Fax: 756.3246

MEXICO – MEXIQUE
OECD Mexico Centre
Edificio INFOTEC
Av. San Fernando no. 37
Col. Toriello Guerra
Tlalpan C.P. 14050
Mexico D.F.   Tel. (525) 528.10.38
   Fax: (525) 606.13.07
E-mail: ocde@rtn.net.mx

NETHERLANDS – PAYS-BAS
SDU Uitgeverij Plantijnstraat
Externe Fondsen
Postbus 20014
2500 EA's-Gravenhage   Tel. (070) 37.89.880
Voor bestellingen: Fax: (070) 34.75.778

Subscription Agency/   Agence d'abonnements :
SWETS & ZEITLINGER BV
Heereweg 347B
P.O. Box 830
2160 SZ Lisse   Tel. 252.435.111
   Fax: 252.415.888

**NEW ZEALAND –
NOUVELLE-ZÉLANDE**
GPLegislation Services
P.O. Box 12418
Thorndon, Wellington   Tel. (04) 496.5655
   Fax: (04) 496.5698

NORWAY – NORVÈGE
NIC INFO A/S
Ostensjoveien 18
P.O. Box 6512 Etterstad
0606 Oslo   Tel. (22) 97.45.00
   Fax: (22) 97.45.45

PAKISTAN
Mirza Book Agency
65 Shahrah Quaid-E-Azam
Lahore 54000   Tel. (42) 735.36.01
   Fax: (42) 576.37.14

PHILIPPINE – PHILIPPINES
International Booksource Center Inc.
Rm 179/920 Cityland 10 Condo Tower 2
HV dela Costa Ext cor Valero St.
Makati Metro Manila   Tel. (632) 817 9676
   Fax: (632) 817 1741

POLAND – POLOGNE
Ars Polona
00-950 Warszawa
Krakowskie Prezdmiescie 7   Tel. (22) 264760
   Fax: (22) 265334

PORTUGAL
Livraria Portugal
Rua do Carmo 70-74
Apart. 2681
1200 Lisboa   Tel. (01) 347.49.82/5
   Fax: (01) 347.02.64

SINGAPORE – SINGAPOUR
Ashgate Publishing
Asia Pacific Pte. Ltd
Golden Wheel Building, 04-03
41, Kallang Pudding Road
Singapore 349316   Tel. 741.5166
   Fax: 742.9356

SPAIN – ESPAGNE
Mundi-Prensa Libros S.A.
Castelló 37, Apartado 1223
Madrid 28001   Tel. (91) 431.33.99
   Fax: (91) 575.39.98
E-mail: mundiprensa@tsai.es
Internet: http://www.mundiprensa.es

Mundi-Prensa Barcelona
Consell de Cent No. 391
08009 – Barcelona   Tel. (93) 488.34.92
   Fax: (93) 487.76.59

Libreria de la Generalitat
Palau Moja
Rambla dels Estudis, 118
08002 – Barcelona
   (Suscripciones) Tel. (93) 318.80.12
   (Publicaciones) Tel. (93) 302.67.23
   Fax: (93) 412.18.54

SRI LANKA
Centre for Policy Research
c/o Colombo Agencies Ltd.
No. 300-304, Galle Road
Colombo 3   Tel. (1) 574240, 573551-2
   Fax: (1) 575394, 510711

SWEDEN – SUÈDE
CE Fritzes AB
S–106 47 Stockholm   Tel. (08) 690.90.90
   Fax: (08) 20.50.21

For electronic publications only/
Publications électroniques seulement
STATISTICS SWEDEN
Informationsservice
S-115 81 Stockholm   Tel. 8 783 5066
   Fax: 8 783 4045

Subscription Agency/Agence d'abonnements :
Wennergren-Williams Info AB
P.O. Box 1305
171 25 Solna   Tel. (08) 705.97.50
   Fax: (08) 27.00.71

Liber distribution
Internatinal organizations
Fagerstagatan 21
S-163 52 Spanga

SWITZERLAND – SUISSE
Maditec S.A. (Books and Periodicals/Livres
et périodiques)
Chemin des Palettes 4
Case postale 266
1020 Renens VD 1   Tel. (021) 635.08.65
   Fax: (021) 635.07.80

Librairie Payot S.A.
4, place Pépinet
CP 3212
1002 Lausanne   Tel. (021) 320.25.11
   Fax: (021) 320.25.14

Librairie Unilivres
6, rue de Candolle
1205 Genève   Tel. (022) 320.26.23
   Fax: (022) 329.73.18

Subscription Agency/Agence d'abonnements :
Dynapresse Marketing S.A.
38, avenue Vibert
1227 Carouge   Tel. (022) 308.08.70
   Fax: (022) 308.07.99

See also – Voir aussi :
OECD Bonn Centre
August-Bebel-Allee 6
D-53175 Bonn (Germany)   Tel. (0228) 959.120
   Fax: (0228) 959.12.17

THAILAND – THAÏLANDE
Suksit Siam Co. Ltd.
113, 115 Fuang Nakhon Rd.
Opp. Wat Rajbopith
Bangkok 10200   Tel. (662) 225.9531/2
   Fax: (662) 222.5188

**TRINIDAD & TOBAGO, CARIBBEAN
TRINITÉ-ET-TOBAGO, CARAÏBES**
Systematics Studies Limited
9 Watts Street
Curepe
Trinidad & Tobago, W.I.   Tel. (1809) 645.3475
   Fax: (1809) 662.5654
E-mail: tobe@trinidad.net

TUNISIA – TUNISIE
Grande Librairie Spécialisée
Fendri Ali
Avenue Haffouz Imm El-Intilaka
Bloc B 1 Sfax 3000   Tel. (216-4) 296 855
   Fax: (216-4) 298.270

TURKEY – TURQUIE
Kültür Yayinlari Is-Türk Ltd.
Atatürk Bulvari No. 191/Kat 13
06684 Kavaklidere/Ankara
   Tel. (312) 428.11.40 Ext. 2458
   Fax : (312) 417.24.90
Dolmabahce Cad. No. 29
Besiktas/Istanbul   Tel. (212) 260 7188

UNITED KINGDOM – ROYAUME-UNI
The Stationery Office Ltd.
Postal orders only:
P.O. Box 276, London SW8 5DT
Gen. enquiries   Tel. (171) 873 0011
   Fax: (171) 873 8463

The Stationery Office Ltd.
Postal orders only:
49 High Holborn, London WC1V 6HB
Branches at: Belfast, Birmingham, Bristol,
Edinburgh, Manchester

UNITED STATES – ÉTATS-UNIS
OECD Washington Center
2001 L Street N.W., Suite 650
Washington, D.C. 20036-4922 Tel. (202) 785.6323
   Fax: (202) 785.0350
Internet: washcont@oecd.org

Subscriptions to OECD periodicals may also be placed through main subscription agencies.

Les abonnements aux publications périodiques de l'OCDE peuvent être souscrits auprès des principales agences d'abonnement.

Orders and inquiries from countries where Distributors have not yet been appointed should be sent to: OECD Publications, 2, rue André-Pascal, 75775 Paris Cedex 16, France.

Les commandes provenant de pays où l'OCDE n'a pas encore désigné de distributeur peuvent être adressées aux Éditions de l'OCDE, 2, rue André-Pascal, 75775 Paris Cedex 16, France.

12-1996

OECD PUBLICATIONS, 2, rue André-Pascal, 75775 PARIS CEDEX 16
PRINTED IN FRANCE
(42 97 03 1 P) ISBN 92-64-15575-9 – No. 49527 1997